Brief Contents

GUIDE TO FIREWALLS AND NETWORK SECURITY: INTRUSION DETECTION AND VPNS

Second Edition

Michael E. Whitman
Herbert J. Mattord
Richard D. Austin
Greg Holden

COURSE TECHNOLOGY
CENGAGE Learning

Australia • Brazil • Japan • Korea • Mexico • Singapore • Spain • United Kingdom • United States

COURSE TECHNOLOGY
CENGAGE Learning™

**Guide to Firewalls and Network Security:
Intrusion Detection and VPNs,
Second Edition**
Michael E. Whitman, Herbert J. Mattord,
Richard D. Austin, and Greg Holden

Executive Editor: Stephen Helba

Senior Product Manager: Alyssa Pratt

Development Editor: Lynne Raughley

Editorial Assistant: Claire Jeffers

Marketing Manager: Erin Coffin

Marketing Coordinator: Shanna Gibbs

Content Project Manager: Matt Hutchinson

Art Director: Kun-Tee Chang

For product information and technology assistance, contact us at
Cengage Learning Customer & Sales Support, 1-800-354-9706

For permission to use material from this text or product, submit all requests online at **cengage.com/permissions**
Further permissions questions can be emailed to
permissionrequest@cengage.com

ISBN-13: 978-1-4354-2016-8
ISBN-10: 1-4354-2016-0

Course Technology
25 Thomson Place
Boston, Massachusetts 02210
USA

Cengage Learning is a leading provider of customized learning solutions with office locations around the globe, including Singapore, the United Kingdom, Australia, Mexico, Brazil, and Japan. Locate your local office at: **international.cengage.com/region**

Cengage Learning products are represented in Canada by Nelson Education, Ltd.

For your lifelong learning solutions, visit **course.cengage.com**

Visit our corporate website at **cengage.com**.

Purchase any of our products at your local college store or at our preferred online store **www.ichapters.com**

Some of the product names and company names used in this book have been used for identification purposes only and may be trademarks or registered trademarks of their respective manufacturers and sellers.

Any fictional data related to persons or companies or URLs used throughout this book is intended for instructional purposes only. At the time this book was printed, any such data was fictional and not belonging to any real persons or companies.

Course Technology, a part of Cengage Learning, reserves the right to revise this publication and make changes from time to time in its content without notice.

The programs in this book are for instructional purposes only.
They have been tested with care, but are not guaranteed for any particular intent beyond educational purposes. The author and the publisher do not offer any warranties or representations, nor do they accept any liabilities with respect to the programs.

Printed in the United States
3 4 5 6 7 15 14 13 12 11 10

Table of Contents

Chapter 2
An Introduction to Networking 37

Chapter 7
Working with Proxy Servers and Application-Level Firewalls. 209

Chapter 8
Firewall Configuration and Administration 233

Chapter 11
Setting Up a Virtual Private Network. 307

Chapter 12
Contingency Planning 337

Chapter 13

Chapter 14

Introduction

THIS BOOK IS INTENDED TO provide an introduction to firewalls and other network security components that can work together to create an in-depth defensive perimeter around a local area network (LAN). Firewalls are among the best-known security tools in use today, and they are growing in popularity with the general public as well as information technology professionals. However, firewalls work most effectively when they are backed by effective security planning and a well-designed security policy, and when they work in concert with anti-virus software, intrusion detection systems, and other tools.

Accordingly, this book examines firewalls in conjunction with the other elements needed for effective perimeter security as well as security within a network. These include packet filtering, authentication, proxy servers, encryption, bastion hosts, virtual private networks (VPNs), log file maintenance, and intrusion detection systems.

Approach

Guide to Firewalls and Network Security: Intrusion Detection and VPNs, Second Edition, provides faculty and students with a single resource that combines the managerial background required for successful network security administration with the technical content required to design, select, and implement many common networking defenses. The book covers the policy, procedures, and managerial approaches needed to build a network defense program as well as the essential technical background in networking, and then progresses through the technical controls needed for network defense such as firewalls, VPNs, and intrusion detection systems.

Some features of the book's approach to the topic of information security are:

Certified Information Systems Security Professionals Common Body of Knowledge— Because several of the authors hold the Certified Information Systems Security Professional (CISSP) credential, the CISSP knowledge domains have had an influence in the design of the text. Although care has been taken to avoid producing another CISSP study guide, the authors' backgrounds have ensured that the book's treatment of information security integrates, to some degree, much of the CISSP Common Body of Knowledge (CBK).

Chapter Scenarios—Each chapter opens with a short vignette that features a fictional company and a cast of characters in and around that company that encounter information security issues commonly found in real-life organizations. At the end of each chapter, there is a brief follow-up to the opening story and a set of discussion questions that gives the student and the instructor an opportunity to discuss the issues that underlie the story's content.

Offline and Technical Details Boxes—Interspersed throughout the textbook, these sections highlight interesting topics and detailed technical issues, giving the student the option of delving into various information security topics in greater detail.

Hands-On Learning—At the end of each chapter, students find a Chapter Summary and Review Questions as well as Exercises, which give them the opportunity to examine the information security arena outside the classroom. In the Exercises, the students are asked to research, analyze, and write responses to questions that are intended to reinforce learning objectives and deepen the students' understanding of the text.

New to this Edition

The second edition provides an overall update the content, including new innovations in technology and methodologies. Specifically:

- **Enhanced sections on information and network security.** The previous edition delved into firewall operations without any foundation in information security or network security. Students without previous information security coursework found themselves at a disadvantage. Instructors using this text in isolation, or in a first course in security, had to supplement the material to bring students up to speed.
- **Reorganized section on security policy and standards.** This edition improves the coverage of policy as a guide for the deployment of security technologies. It also introduces students to major security standards organization, which they can use to guide their enterprise security efforts.
- **Improved and streamlined section on firewalls.** This edition condenses and improves the flow of the firewall material, appropriately integrating VPN and encryption discussions without losing any relevant content.
- **Added section on intrusion detection in the context of incident response.** This edition adds substantial material on intrusion detection technologies in the context of incident response. This edition also presents interesting and relevant material on incident response with digital forensics, a useful skill set needed by most organizations.
- **General Updates.** Examples and references have been updated to maintain currency and relevance.

Author Team

Michael Whitman, Herbert Mattord, Richard Austin, and Greg Holden have jointly developed this text to merge knowledge from the world of academic study with practical experience from the business world.

- Michael Whitman, Ph.D., CISM, CISSP is a Professor of Information Systems and Security in the Computer Science and Information Systems Department at Kennesaw State University, Kennesaw, Georgia, where he is also Director of the KSU Center for Information Security Education (infosec.kennesaw.edu) and the coordinator for the

Bachelor of Science in Information Security and Assurance. Dr. Whitman is an active researcher in Information Security, Fair and Responsible Use Policies, and Ethical Computing. He currently teaches graduate and undergraduate courses in Information Security, Local Area Networking, and Data Communications. He has published articles in the top journals in his field, including *Information Systems Research, Communications of the ACM, Information and Management, Journal of International Business Studies*, and *Journal of Computer Information Systems.* He is a member of the Information Systems Security Association, the Association for Computing Machinery, ISC2, ISACA, and the Association for Information Systems. Dr. Whitman is also the co-author of *Principles of Information Security, Management of Information Security, Principles of Incident Response and Disaster Recovery, Readings and Cases in the Management of Information Security*, and *The Hands-On Information Security Lab Manual*, all published by Course Technology. Prior to his career in academia, Dr. Whitman was an armored cavalry officer in the United States Army.

■ Herbert Mattord, M.B.A., CISM, CISSP completed 24 years of IT industry experience as an application developer, database administrator, project manager, and information security practitioner before joining the faculty at Kennesaw State University in 2002. Professor Mattord is the Operations Manager of the KSU Center for Information Security Education and Awareness (infosec.kennesaw.edu), as well as the coordinator for the KSU department of Computer Science and Information System's Certificate in Information Security and Assurance. During his career as an IT practitioner, he has been an adjunct professor at Kennesaw State University; Southern Polytechnic State University in Marietta, Georgia; Austin Community College in Austin, Texas; and Texas State University: San Marcos. He currently teaches undergraduate courses in Information Security, Data Communications, Local Area Networks, Database Technology, Project Management, Systems Analysis & Design, and Information Resources Management and Policy. He was formerly the Manager of Corporate Information Technology Security at Georgia-Pacific Corporation, where much of the practical knowledge found in this textbook was acquired. Professor Mattord is also the co-author of *Principles of Information Security, Management of Information Security, Principles of Incident Response and Disaster Recovery, Readings and Cases in the Management of Information Security*, and *The Hands-On Information Security Lab Manual*, all published by Course Technology.

■ Richard Austin, MS, CISSP, MCSE is a 30+ year veteran of the IT industry in positions ranging from software developer to security architect. Before pursuing a career as an independent consultant, he was focused on technology and processes for successfully protecting the 14PB storage area network infrastructure within the global IT organization of a Fortune 25 company. He earned an MS degree with a concentration in information security from Kennesaw State University, a DHS/NSA recognized National Center of Academic Excellence in Information Assurance Education, and serves as a part-time faculty in their CSIS department, where he teaches in the Information Security and Assurance program. He holds the CISSP and MCSE certifications and is an active member of SNIA's Security Technical Working Group. He is a Senior Member of the IEEE and also belongs to the IEEE Computer Society, ACM, CSI, HTCIA, ISACA, and ISSA (where he also serves on the International Ethics committee). He is also a frequent writer and presenter on storage networking security and digital forensics.

Structure

Guide to Firewalls and Network Security with Intrusion Detection and VPNs addresses three subject areas. First, it presents an introduction and over view of information security and network security, with an emphasis on the role of data communications in network security. Second, it presents firewalls and VPNs, with a primer on encryption to further the students' understanding of VPNs. Third, it addresses intrusion detection under the umbrella of incident response, with a descriptive section on using digital forensics to support incident investigations. To serve this end, this textbook is organized into three sections and fourteen chapters.

Part I: Network Security

Chapter 1   Introduction to Information Security

This chapter lays the foundation for network security by providing a primer in information security and an explanation of the terms and terminology used throughout the text and in the discipline. The text also presents the threats and attacks the student can expect to encounter while dealing with network security and firewalls.

Chapter 2   Foundations of Network Security

This chapter explains the data communications foundations for network security and introduces modern networking fundamentals, as well as the security issues associated with modern data communications technologies. Using a layer-by-layer approach, the student moves through the structure of the OSI reference model, examining the security components of each stage.

Chapter 3   Network Security Policies and Standards

This chapter explains the need for a policy-driven approach to security, and also describes modern security standards organizations like ISO, NIST, and the IETF. Security programs, including security education, training and awareness, and planning for contingencies, are also presented.

Chapter 4   Vulnerability Scanning and Penetration Testing

This chapter describes the tools and techniques employed by network security professional to evaluate the security of network security equipment, data servers, and other modern information systems. An overview of the common methods used with an emphasis on their use in remediating problems found completes the student's introduction to network security in general.

Part II: Firewalls and VPNs

Chapter 5   Introduction to Firewalls and VPNs

This chapter provides an introduction to firewalls and VPNs, giving the student a foundation in this specific technology. The chapter introduces the generations and categories of firewalls, their deployment in the enterprise, and an introduction to other security technologies, specifically, VPNs and other remote connection protection.

Chapter 6 Packet Filtering

This chapter provides a detailed explanation of how most modern firewalls work. It covers both the traditional static packet-filtering firewalls and the more modern stateful packet inspection firewalls and their assorted rule sets.

Chapter 7 Working with Proxy Servers and Application-Level Firewalls

This chapter describes the function of proxy- and application- appliances, which are used to support high-level functional operations in the enterprise. The chapter examines the use and deployment of these devices and special considerations in their selection.

Chapter 8 Firewall Configuration and Administration

This chapter revisits the rule sets used to configure firewalls, with an expansion of the study of firewall configuration. Here the student also looks at the requirements for ongoing administration of firewall appliances, with specific attention to remote management, log management, and advanced firewall functions.

Chapter 9 Encryption and Firewalls

This chapter completes the review of firewalls by examining the use of encryption to support firewall functions, and the incorporation of VPN technologies. The chapter serves both as a primer on encryption and as a transition to more detailed examination of VPN operations in subsequent chapters.

Chapter 10 Authenticating Users

This chapter describes the access controls used in most servers and network security appliances. The chapter covers modern access control approaches and methodologies, security tools and techniques, and security issues associated with administering access controls.

Chapter 11 Setting Up A Virtual Private Network

This chapter describes in detail the implementation, configuration, and use of virtual private network technologies. The chapter examines how VPNs use tunneling to support their functions and security issues in deploying VPNs.

Part III: Incident Response with Intrusion Detection and Prevention Systems

Chapter 12 Incident Response

This chapter provides an overview of the incident response methodology of prevention, detection, reaction, and recovery. The chapter then explains how to set up an incident response program, as the precursor to intrusion detection. Incident detection and classification are discussed, along with response and recovery strategies.

Chapter 13 Intrusion Detection and Prevention Systems

This chapter covers intrusion detection and prevention systems (IDPS), focusing on their classifications, use, and deployment. The chapter addresses specific issues associated with IDPS, including log functions, automated response, and legal concerns.

Chapter 14 Digital Forensics

The text concludes with a discussion of the use of digital forensics as part of the intrusion response function. This chapter provides a primer on digital forensics and describes the forensic methodologies deployed in the enterprise to examine the root cause of an incident.

Endmatter

- **Glossary:** A complete compendium of all of the acronyms and technical terms used in this book, with definitions.
- **Index:** An alphabetical list of key concepts that tells the reader where they are covered in the text.

Instructor's Materials

The following supplemental materials are available when this book is used in a classroom setting. All of the supplements available with this book are provided to the instructor on a single CD-ROM.

Electronic Instructor's Manual. The Instructor's Manual that accompanies this textbook includes additional instructional material to assist in class preparation, including suggestions for classroom activities, discussion topics, and additional projects.

Solution Files. The Solution Files include answers to all end-of-chapter materials, including the Review Questions, and when applicable, Hands-on Projects, and Case Projects.

ExamView®. This textbook is accompanied by ExamView, a powerful testing software package that allows instructors to create and administer printed, computer (LAN-based), and Internet exams. ExamView includes hundreds of questions that correspond to the topics covered in this text, enabling students to generate detailed study guides that include page references for further review. The computer-based and Internet testing components allow students to take exams at their computers, and also save the instructor time by grading each exam automatically.

PowerPoint presentations. This book comes with Microsoft PowerPoint slides for each chapter. These are included as a teaching aid for classroom presentation, to make available to students on the network for chapter review, or to be printed for classroom distribution. Instructors, please feel at liberty to add your own slides for additional topics you introduce to the class.

Coping with Change on the Web

Sooner or later, all the specific Web-based resources mentioned throughout this book will go stale or be replaced by newer information. In some cases, the URLs you find here may lead you to their replacements; in other cases, the URLs will lead nowhere, leaving you with the dreaded 404 error message, "File not found."

When that happens, please don't give up! There's always a way to find what you want on the Web, if you're willing to invest some time and energy. Most large or complex Web sites offer a search engine. As long as you can get to the site itself, you can use this tool to help you find what you need.

Don't be afraid to use general search tools like *www.google.com*, *www.hotbot.com*, or *www.excite.com* to find related information. Although certain standards bodies may offer the most precise and specific information about their standards online, there are plenty of third-party sources of information, training, and assistance. The bottom line is: if you can't find something where the book says it lives, start looking around.

Visit our World Wide Web Site

Additional materials designed especially for you might be available for your course on the World Wide Web. Go to *www.course.com* and search for this book title periodically for more details.

Acknowledgments

The authors would like to thank their families for their support and understanding for the many hours dedicated to this project, hours taken away, in many cases, from family activities. Special thanks to Carola Mattord, doctoral candidate of English at Georgia State University. Her reviews of early drafts and suggestions for keeping the writing focused on the students resulted in a more readable manuscript.

Contributors

Several people and organizations have also contributed materials that were used in the preparation of this textbook, and we thank them for their contributions:

- The National Institute of Standards and Technology is the source of many references, tables, figures, and other content used in many places in the textbook

Reviewers

We are indebted to the following individuals for their respective contributions of perceptive feedback on the initial proposal, the project outline, and the chapter-by-chapter reviews of the text:

- Richard Baxter, Piedmont Community College
- Larry Choate, Jackson Community College
- Michael Goldner, ITT Technical Institute
- Dean Farwood, Heald College
- Mehmet Kilinc, Gwinnett Technical College
- Dan Guilmette, Cochise College,

Special Thanks

The authors wish to thank the Editorial and Production teams at Course Technology. Their diligent and professional efforts greatly enhanced the final product:

- Alyssa Pratt, Senior Product Manager
- Lynne Raughley, Development Editor
- Steve Helba, Executive Editor
- Matt Hutchinson, Content Project Manager

In addition, several professional and commercial organizations and individuals have aided the development of the textbook by providing information and inspiration, and the authors wish to acknowledge their contribution:

- Tenable Network Security, Inc.
- Our colleagues in the Department of Computer Science and Information Systems, Kennesaw State University
- Dr. Don Amoroso, Chair of the Department of Computer Science and Information Systems, Kennesaw State University
- Dr. Larry Peterson, Dean of the College of Science and Mathematics, Kennesaw State University
- The storage networking and security professionals who participate in the Storage Networking Industry Association (SNIA), Storage Security Industry Forum, and Security Technical Working Group for their insightful thoughts, discussions, and ideas that shape security for the "other" enterprise network.

Our Commitment

The authors are committed to serving the needs of the adopters and readers of this book. We would be pleased and honored to receive feedback on the textbook and its supporting materials. You can contact us via e-mail at gfwns.ct@gmail.com.

Introduction to Information Security

MATTHIAS PAUL LOOKED UP FROM HIS MONITOR TO glance at the clock hanging on the wall. It was 4:15 AM and he had almost four hours to go before his shift was over. From the start of his shift Matthias had been processing new account setup requests for one of the companies serviced by his employer, Advanced Topologies, Inc. Every hour he took a short break to check the logs from the client's network.

Matthias was not exactly sure he knew what he was looking for, but he thought it was a good idea to stay aware of what was happening on the client's network. Matthias had only been on the job at ATI for a few weeks and did not consider himself a critical member of the watch team for this client. Mostly he did semi-clerical tasks, like setting up new users and verifying the deactivation of the client's former employees.

"Matt."

Matthias looked up to see his supervisor, Alfonso Agostino.

"Yes Al, what's up?"

Al looked at Matthias over his glasses and said, "I just got the word that your training plan was approved by Human Resources. You start your classes next week. Your first class will be three days on the basics of information security at the corporate training center."

"Great!" said Matthias. "But why do I need information security training? Wasn't I hired to be a network administrator?"

Al responded, "Sure, but how can you do your job as a netadmin if you don't know the company security policies and practices? The class spends two days covering basic concepts of security, and one day reviewing our company polices. Everyone in an IT-related position takes this class. You'll get more advanced networking training over the next few months—eventually we plan to send you out for some advanced network security training, to fill in any gaps in your college classes on these subjects."

Matthias nodded. "OK. I'll be there."

LEARNING OBJECTIVES:
Upon completion of this material, you should be able to do the following:

- Explain the relationship among the component parts of information security, especially network security
- Define the key terms and critical concepts of information and network security
- Describe the organizational roles of information and network security professionals
- Understand the business need for information and network security
- Identify the threats posed to information and network security, as well as the common attacks associated with those threats
- Differentiate *threats* to information within systems from *attacks* against information within systems

Introduction

Firewalls and network security have become critical components in securing the day-to-day operations of nearly every organization in business today. Security threats like viruses and worms and the software needed to cope with them, such as Symantec's Norton Antivirus, have become familiar to business employees, as well as students and grandmothers. Popular culture does not provide the whole story, however. Before learning how to plan, design, and implement firewalls and network security, it is important to understand the larger topic of information security and how these two components of security, firewalls and network security, fit into this topic. Learning about the overall framework of information security helps you become aware of the factors that affect firewalls and network security, and vice versa. The field of information security has matured rapidly in the past twenty years, and has become so large that those who don't understand these concepts risk being unable to make the best business decisions regarding firewalls and network security.

This chapter offers an overview of the entire field of information security and its effects on firewalls and network security, but it is hoped that the student will find it interesting enough to pursue further study in this area as it relates to and influences the development and implementation of firewalls and network security.

What Is Information Security?

Information security (InfoSec), as defined by the standards published by the Committee on National Security Systems (CNSS), formerly the National Security Telecommunications and Information Systems Security Committee (NSTISSC),[1] is the protection of information and its critical elements, including the systems and hardware that use, store, and transmit that information. Figure 1-1 shows that information security includes the broad areas of information security management, computer and data security, and network security (the primary topic of this book). To protect information and its related systems, organizations must implement such tools as policy, awareness training and education, and technology. The CNSS information security model evolved from a concept developed by the computer security industry known as the C.I.A. triangle. The **C.I.A. triangle** has been the industry standard for computer security since the development of the mainframe. It is based on the three characteristics of information that make it valuable to organizations: confidentiality, integrity, and availability. The security of these three characteristics of information is as important today as it has always been, but the C.I.A. triangle model no longer adequately addresses the constantly changing environment of the computer industry. The current environment of many constantly evolving threats—accidental or intentional damage or destruction, theft, unintended or unauthorized modification, and other misapplication— has prompted the development of a more robust intellectual model that addresses the complexities of the current information security environment. This expanded C.I.A. triangle (sometimes called the Parkerian Hexad[2]) consists of a list of critical characteristics of information, which are described in the next section. C.I.A. terminology is used in this chapter because of the breadth of material that is based on it.

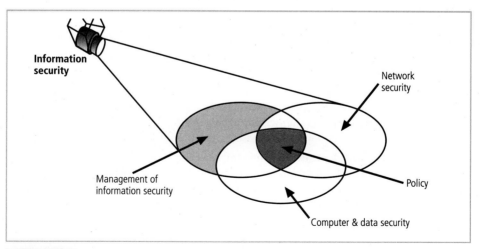

**Information
security**

Network
security

Management of
information security

Policy

Computer & data security

FIGURE 1-1   Components of Information Security

A successful organization should have in place the following multiple layers of security:

- **Network security**, which requires the protection of networking components, connections, and contents, and which is the primary theme of this textbook

- **Physical security**, which requires the protection of the physical items, objects, or areas of an organization from unauthorized access and misuse
- **Personal security**, which requires the protection of the people who are authorized to access the organization and its operations
- **Operations security**, which requires the protection of the details of a particular operation or series of activities
- **Communications security**, which requires the protection of an organization's communications media, technology, and content

Critical Characteristics of Information

The value of information comes from the characteristics it possesses. When a characteristic of information changes, the value of that information either increases or, more commonly, decreases. Some characteristics affect information's value to users more than others do. For example, the timeliness of information can be a critical factor, because information often loses all value when it is delivered too late. Though information security professionals and end users share the same understanding of the characteristics of information, tensions can arise when the need to secure the integrity of information from threats conflicts with the end users' need for unhindered access to the information. For example, end users may perceive a tenth-of-a-second delay in the computation of data to be an unnecessary annoyance. Information security professionals, however, may perceive that tenth of a second as a minor delay that was necessary for the accomplishment of an important task, like the encryption of data. The following are important terms you should know when discussing the security and integrity of information:

- **Availability** enables authorized users—persons or computer systems—to access information without interference or obstruction, and to receive it in the required format.
- **Accuracy** means that information is free from mistakes or errors and it has the value that the end user expects.
- **Authenticity** of information is the quality or state of being genuine or original, rather than a reproduction or fabrication. Information is authentic when it is the information that was originally created, placed, stored, or transferred. Consider for a moment some of the assumptions made about e-mail.
- **Confidentiality** is when information is protected from disclosure or exposure to unauthorized individuals or systems. This means that *only* those with the rights and privileges to access information are able to do so. To protect any breach in the confidentiality of information, a number of measures can be used:
  - Information classification
  - Secure document storage
  - Application of general security policies
  - Education of information custodians and end users
- **Integrity** is when information remains whole, complete, and uncorrupted. The integrity of information is threatened when the information is exposed to corruption, damage, destruction, or other disruption of its authentic state.

- **Utility** of information is the quality or state of having value for some purpose or end. To have utility, information must be in a format meaningful to the end user. For example, U.S. Census data can be overwhelming and difficult to understand; however, the data when properly interpreted reveals information about the voters in a district, to what political parties these voters belong, their race, gender, age, and so on. This information can help form a politician's next campaign strategy.

- **Possession** of information is the ownership or control of some object or item. Information is said to be in one's possession if one obtains it, independent of format or other characteristics.

CNSS Security Model

The definition of information security presented earlier is based in part on the CNSS document called the National Training Standard for Information Security Professionals NSTISSI No. 4011 (*www.cnss.gov/Assets/pdf/nstissi_4011.pdf*). This document presents a comprehensive model for information security and is becoming the evaluation standard for the security of information systems. The model, known as the **McCumber Cube**, was created by John McCumber in 1991; it provides a graphical description of the architectural approach widely used in computer and information security.[3] The McCumber Cube as shown in Figure 1-2 uses a representation in three dimensions of a 3 × 3 × 3 cube with 27 cells representing areas that must be addressed to secure today's information systems. For example, the intersection between the technology, integrity, and storage areas requires a control or safeguard that addresses the need to use *technology* to protect the *integrity* of information while in *storage*. One such control is a system for detecting host intrusion that protects the integrity of information by alerting the security administrators to the potential modification of a critical file. What is commonly left out of such a model is the need for guidelines and policies that provide direction for the practices and implementations of technologies. The need for policy is a critical element for all organizations, and you will find that it is mentioned frequently throughout this textbook.

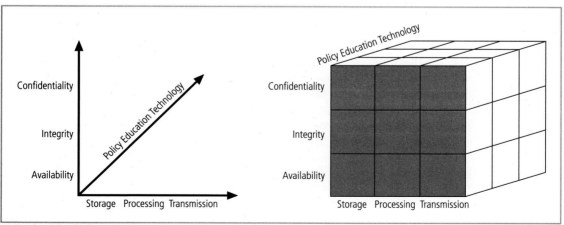

McCumber, John. "*Information Systems Security: A Comprehensive Model.*" *Proceedings 14th National Computer Security Conference.* *National Institute of Standards and Technology.* Baltimore, MD. (October 1991.)

FIGURE 1-2   The McCumber Cube

Securing Components

The security of information and its systems entails securing all components and protecting them from potential misuse and abuse by unauthorized users. When considering the security of information systems components, it is important to understand that a computer can be the subject of an attack, or the object of an attack. When a computer is the **subject of an attack**, it is used as an active tool to conduct the attack. When a computer is the **object of an attack**, it is the entity being attacked. Figure 1-3 illustrates computers as subject and object. There are also two types of attacks: **direct attacks** and **indirect attacks**. A direct attack is when a hacker uses a personal computer to break into a system. An indirect attack is when a system is compromised and used to attack other systems, such as in a botnet or other distributed denial-of-service attack. Direct attacks originate from the threat itself. Indirect attacks originate from a system or resource that itself has been attacked, and is malfunctioning or working under the control of a threat. A computer can, therefore, be both the subject and object of an attack when, for example, it is first the object of an attack and then compromised and used to attack other systems, at which point it becomes the subject of an attack.

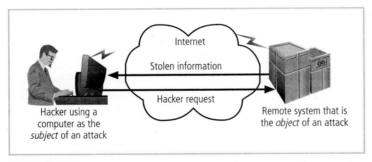

Hacker using a
computer as the
subject of an attack

Remote system that is
the *object* of an attack

FIGURE 1-3   Computer as the Subject and Object of an Attack

Balancing Information Security and Access

Even with the best planning and implementation, it is impossible to obtain perfect information security. Information security cannot be an absolute: it is a process, not a goal. Information security should balance protection and availability. It is possible to permit unrestricted access to a system, so that it is available to anyone, anywhere, anytime, through any means. However, this poses a danger to the integrity of the information. On the other hand, a completely secure information system would not allow anyone access, ever.

To achieve balance—that is, to operate an information system to the satisfaction of the user and the security professional—the level of security must allow reasonable access, yet protect against threats. Figure 1-4 shows some of the competing voices that must be reconciled in the information security versus access balancing act.

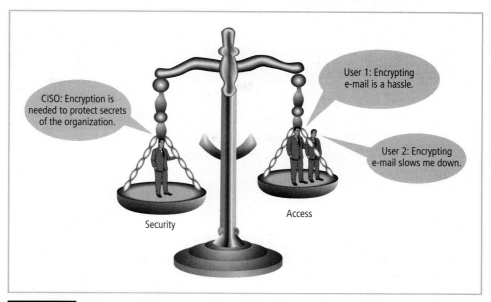

FIGURE 1-4   Balancing Information Security and Access

An imbalance between access and security can occur when the needs of the end user are undermined by too heavy a focus on protecting and administering the information systems. Both information security technologists and end users must exercise patience and cooperation when interacting with each other, as both groups share the same overall goals of the organization—to ensure the data is available when, where, and how it is needed, with minimal delays or obstacles. In an ideal world, this level of availability is met even after concerns about loss, damage, interception, or destruction have been addressed.

Business Needs First

Information security performs four important organizational functions:

1. Protects the organization's ability to function
2. Enables the safe operation of applications implemented on the organization's IT systems
3. Protects the data the organization collects and uses
4. Safeguards the technology assets in use at the organization

Protecting the Functionality of an Organization

Both general management and IT management are responsible for implementing information security that protects the organization's ability to function. Although many business and government managers shy away from addressing information security because they perceive it to be a technically complex task, in fact implementing information security has more to do with *management* than with *technology*. Just as managing payroll has more to do with management than with mathematical wage computations, managing information security has more to do with policy and enforcement than with the technology of its implementation.

Enabling the Safe Operation of Applications

Today's organizations are under immense pressure to acquire and operate integrated, efficient, and capable applications. The modern organization needs to safeguard applications, particularly those that serve as important elements of the infrastructure of the organization— operating system platforms, electronic mail (e-mail), and instant messaging (IM) applications.

Protecting Data That Organizations Collect and Use

Any business, educational institution, or government agency that functions within the modern context of connected and responsive services relies on information systems to support its transactions. Even if the transaction is not online, information systems and the data they process enable the creation and movement of goods and services. Therefore, protecting both *data in motion* and *data at rest* is a critical aspect of information security. The value of data motivates attackers to steal, sabotage, or corrupt it. An effective information security program directed by management is essential to the protection of the integrity and value of the organization's data.

Safeguarding Technology Assets in Organizations

To perform effectively, organizations must add secure infrastructure services matching the size and scope of the enterprise. In general, as the organization's network grows to accommodate changing needs, it may need more robust technology solutions. An example of a robust solution is a firewall, which is a device that keeps certain kinds of network traffic out of the internal network. Another example is caching network appliances, which are devices that store local copies of Internet content, such as Web pages that are frequently referred to by employees. The appliance displays the cached pages to users, rather than accessing the pages on the remote server each time.

Security Professionals and the Organization

It takes a wide range of professionals to support a diverse information security program. Senior management is the key component and the vital force for a successful implementation of an information security program. But administrative support is also needed, to develop and execute specific security policies and procedures, and technical expertise is necessary to implement the details of the information security program. The following job titles describe the information security roles of various professionals in a typical organization.

The **chief information officer (CIO)** is often the senior technology officer. Other titles such as vice president (VP) of information, VP of information technology, and VP of systems may be used. The CIO is primarily responsible for advising the chief executive officer, president, or company owner on the strategic planning that affects the management of information in the organization.

The **chief information security officer (CISO)** is the individual primarily responsible for the assessment, management, and implementation of information security in the organization. The CISO may also be referred to as the manager for IT security, the security administrator, or a similar title. The CISO usually reports directly to the CIO, although in larger organizations it is not uncommon for one or more layers of management to exist between the two.

The information security **project team** should consist of a number of individuals who are experienced in one or multiple facets of the vast array of required technical and nontechnical areas. Many of the same skills needed to manage and implement security are also needed to design it. Members of the security project team fill the following roles:

- **Champion**—A senior executive who promotes the project and ensures that it is supported, both financially and administratively, at the highest levels of the organization.
- **Team leader**—A project manager, who may be a departmental line manager or staff unit manager, who understands project management, personnel management, and information security technical requirements.
- **Security policy developers**—Individuals who understand the organizational culture, existing policies, and requirements for developing and implementing successful policies.
- **Risk assessment specialists**—Individuals who understand financial risk assessment techniques, the value of organizational assets, and the security methods to be used.
- **Security professionals**—Dedicated, trained, and well-educated specialists in all aspects of information security, both technical and nontechnical.
- **Systems, networks, and storage administrators**—Individuals with the primary responsibility for administering the systems, storage, and networks that house and provide access to the organization's information.
- **End users**—Those who will be most directly affected by new implementations and changes to existing systems. Ideally, a selection of users from various departments, levels, and degrees of technical knowledge assist the team in focusing on the application of realistic controls applied in ways that do not disrupt the essential business activities they seek to safeguard.

Data Ownership

Three types of data ownership and their respective responsibilities are outlined below:

- **Data owners**—Those responsible for the security and use of a particular set of information. They are usually members of senior management and could be CIOs. The **data owners** usually determine the level of data classification associated with the data. The data owners work with subordinate managers to oversee the day-to-day administration of the data.

- Data custodians—Working directly with data owners, **data custodians** are responsible for the storage, maintenance, and protection of the information. Depending on the size of the organization, the custodian should be a dedicated position, such as the CISO, or it may be an additional responsibility of a systems administrator or other technology manager. The duties of a data custodian often include overseeing data storage and backups, implementing the specific procedures and policies laid out in the security policies and plans, and reporting to the data owner.

- Data users—End users who work with the information to perform their daily jobs supporting the mission of the organization, and therefore share the responsibility for data security.

Threats

Around 500 B.C., the Chinese general Sun Tzu Wu wrote a treatise on warfare. His *Art of War* contains military strategies still studied by military leaders and students today. In one of his most famous passages, he writes, "If you know the enemy and know yourself, you need not fear the result of a hundred battles. If you know yourself but not the enemy, for every victory gained you will also suffer a defeat. If you know neither the enemy nor yourself, you will succumb in every battle."[4] In the battle to protect information, you must (1) know yourself; that is, be familiar with the information to be protected, and the systems that store, transport, and process it. You must also (2) know the enemy. To make sound decisions about information security, management must be informed about the various threats facing the organization, its people, applications, data, and information systems—that is, the enemy. In the context of information security, a **threat** is an object, person, or other entity that represents a constant danger to an asset.

To understand the wide range of threats that pervade the interconnected world, researchers have interviewed practicing information security personnel and examined information security literature on threats. While the categorizations may vary, threats are relatively well researched and, consequently, fairly well understood.

The 2006 Computer Security Institute/Federal Bureau of Investigation (CSI/FBI) Computer Crime and Security Survey is a representative study. The CSI/FBI study found that 52 percent of the organizations responding (primarily large corporations and government agencies) acknowledged unauthorized use of their computer systems within the last 12 months with an average financial loss of $167,713.[5, 6]

The categorization scheme shown in Table 1-1 consists of 12 general categories that represent a clear and present danger to an organization's people, information, and systems.[7] Each organization must prioritize the dangers it faces, based on the particular security situation in which it operates, its organizational strategy regarding risk, and the exposure levels in which its assets operate. Upon reviewing the right-hand column of Table 1-1, you may observe that many of the examples of threats could be listed in more than one category. For example, an act of theft performed by a hacker falls into the category of *Theft*, but is also often accompanied by defacement actions to delay discovery, and thus may also be placed within the category of *Sabotage or vandalism*.

TABLE 1-1 Threats to Information Security[8]

Categories of Threat	Examples
1. Human error or failure	Accidents, employee mistakes
2. Compromises to intellectual property	Piracy, copyright infringement
3. Espionage or trespass	Unauthorized access and/or data collection
4. Information extortion	Blackmail or information disclosure
5. Sabotage or vandalism	Destruction of systems or information
6. Theft	Illegal confiscation of equipment or information
7. Software attacks	Viruses, worms, macros, denial-of-service
8. Forces of nature	Fire, flood, earthquake, lightning
9. Deviations in quality of service	ISP, power, or WAN service issues from service providers
10. Hardware failures or errors	Equipment failure
11. Software failures or errors	Bugs, code problems, unknown loopholes
12. Obsolescence	Antiquated or outdated technologies

Human Error or Failure

This category includes acts performed without intent or malicious purpose. When people use information systems, sometimes mistakes happen as a result of inexperience, improper training, the making of incorrect assumptions, and other circumstances. Regardless of the cause, even innocuous mistakes can produce extensive damage with catastrophic results. For example, a simple keyboarding error can, as described below, cause worldwide Internet outages.

In April 1997, the core of the Internet suffered a disaster. Internet service providers lost connectivity with other ISPs due to an error in a routine Internet router-table update process. The resulting outage effectively shut down a major portion of the Internet for at least twenty minutes. It has been estimated that about 45 percent of Internet users were affected. In July 1997, the Internet went through yet another more critical global shutdown for millions of users. An accidental upload of a corrupt database to the Internet's root domain servers occurred. Since this provides the ability to address hosts on the net by name (i.e., eds.com), it was impossible to send e-mail or access Web sites within the .com and .net domains for several hours. The .com domain comprises a majority of the commercial enterprise users of the Internet.[9]

Employees constitute one of the greatest threats to an organization's information security. Employees are the individuals closest to the organizational data. They use it in everyday activities to conduct the organization's business. Employee mistakes represent a serious threat to the confidentiality, integrity, and availability of data—even, as Figure 1-5 suggests, relative to threats from outsiders. This is because employee mistakes can easily lead to the following: disclosure of classified data, entry of erroneous data, accidental deletion or modification of data, storage of data in unprotected areas, and failure to protect information. Leaving classified information in unprotected areas, such as a desktop, Web site, or even the trash can, is as much a threat to the protection of the information as is the individual who seeks to exploit the information, because one person's carelessness can create a vulnerability and thus an opportunity that another person may not be able to pass up.

Much human error or failure can be prevented with controls, ranging from simple procedures, such as requiring the user to type a critical command twice, to more complex procedures, such as the verification of commands by a second party. An example of the latter is the performance of key recovery actions in PKI systems. Many enterprise and military applications have robust, dual-approval controls built in. Some systems that have a high potential for data loss or system outages use expert systems to monitor human actions and request confirmation for critical inputs.

Who is the biggest threat to your organization?

Tom Twostory
convicted burglar

Dick Davis a.k.a.
"wannabe amateur hacker"

Harriet Allthumbs
employee who
accidentally
deleted the one copy
of a critical report

FIGURE 1-5   Acts of Human Error or Failure

Compromises to Intellectual Property

Many organizations create or support the development of intellectual property (IP) as part of their business operations. Intellectual property is defined as "the ownership of ideas and control over the tangible or virtual representation of those ideas. Use of another person's intellectual property may or may not involve royalty payments or permission, but should always include proper credit to the source."[10] Intellectual property includes trade secrets, copyrights, trademarks, and patents. Once intellectual property has been properly identified, breaches to IP constitute a threat to the security of this information.

Organizations that purchase or lease the IP of other organizations must abide by a purchase or licensing agreement for its fair and responsible use. The most common IP breach is the unlawful use or duplication of software-based intellectual property, more commonly known as **software piracy**. Many individuals and organizations seldom purchase their software. Since most software is licensed to a particular purchaser, its use is restricted to a single user or to a designated user in an organization. The user who copies the program to another computer without securing another license or transferring the license, has violated the copyright. (See the Offline section on violating software licenses for more details.) Software licenses are strictly enforced by a number of regulatory and private organizations, and software publishers use various control mechanisms to prevent copyright infringement. In addition to the laws surrounding software piracy, two watchdog organizations investigate allegations of software abuse: Software & Information Industry Association (SIIA) at *www.siia.net*, formerly known as the Software Publishers Association, and the Business Software Alliance (BSA) at *www.bsa.org*.

Enforcement of copyright laws has been attempted through a number of technical security mechanisms, such as the using of digital watermarks and embedded code, the requiring of copyright codes, and even the intentional adding of bad sectors on software media. The most common reminder of the individual's obligation to fair and responsible use is the license agreement window that usually pops up during the installation of new software. This screen serves as the legal proof that the user has read and agrees to the license agreement. For a time, these license agreements were referred to as blow-by screens, as users found that if they hit the Enter key repeatedly during installation, these bothersome installation screens quickly vanished. Now, it is more common to see a different type of acceptance screen, one that requires clicking a specific button, or pressing a key other than Enter.

Another effort to combat piracy is the online registration process. Individuals who install software are often asked or even required to register their software to obtain technical support, or full use. Some believe that this process compromises personal privacy, since individuals never really know exactly what information is obtained from their computer and sent to the software manufacturer.

Espionage or Trespass

Acts of espionage or trespass are a well-known and broad category of electronic and human activities that can breach the confidentiality of information. When an unauthorized individual gains access to the information an organization is trying to protect, that act is categorized as *espionage* or *trespass*. Attackers can use many different methods to access the information stored in an information system. Some information-gathering techniques are quite legal, for example, using a Web browser to perform market research. These legal techniques are called, collectively, **competitive intelligence**. When information gatherers employ techniques that cross the threshold of what is legal or ethical, they are conducting **industrial espionage**. Many countries considered allies of the United States engage in industrial espionage against American organizations. When foreign governments are involved, these activities are actually considered espionage and a threat to national security. Some forms of espionage are relatively low-tech. One example, called **shoulder surfing**, is pictured in Figure 1-6. This technique is used in public or semipublic settings when individuals gather information they are not authorized to have by looking over another individual's shoulder or viewing the information from a distance. Instances of shoulder surfing occur at computer terminals, desks, ATM machines, public phones, or other places where a person is accessing confidential information. There is unwritten etiquette among professionals who address information security in the workplace. When someone can see another person entering personal or private information into a system, the first person should look away politely as the information is entered. Failure to do so not only constitutes a breach of etiquette, but is considered an affront to privacy as well as a threat to the security of the confidential information.

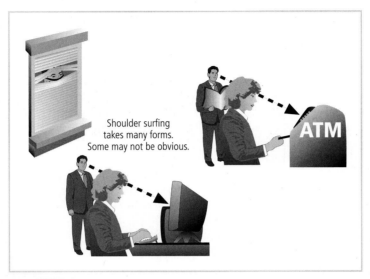

Shoulder surfing takes many forms. Some may not be obvious.

FIGURE 1-6 Shoulder Surfing

Acts of **trespass** can lead to unauthorized real or virtual actions that enable information gatherers to enter premises or systems without authorization. Controls are sometimes implemented to mark the boundaries of an organization's virtual territory. These boundaries give notice to trespassers that they are encroaching on the organization's cyberspace. Sound principles of authentication and authorization can help organizations protect valuable information and systems. These control methods and technologies employ multiple layers or factors to protect against unauthorized access.

The classic perpetrator of *espionage* or *trespass* is the hacker. **Hackers** are "people who use and create computer software [to] gain access to information illegally."[11] Hackers are frequently glamorized in fictional accounts as people who stealthily manipulate a maze of computer networks, systems, and data to find the information that solves the mystery or saves the day. Television and motion pictures are inundated with images of hackers as heroes or heroines. However, the true life of the hacker is far more mundane (see Figure 1-7). In reality, a hacker frequently spends long hours examining the types and structures of the targeted systems and uses skill, guile, or fraud to attempt to bypass the controls placed around information that is the property of someone else.

There are generally two skill levels among hackers. The first is the **expert hacker**, sometimes called **elite** (written in e-mail, text messages, and chat boards as "l33t") **hacker**, who develops software scripts and program exploits used by those in the second category, the novice or **unskilled hacker**. The expert hacker is usually a master of several programming languages, networking protocols, and operating systems, and also exhibits a mastery of the technical environment of the chosen targeted system. As described in the Offline section titled "Hack PCWeek," expert hackers are extremely talented individuals who usually have lots of time and energy to devote to attempting to break into other people's information systems.

Once an expert hacker chooses a target, the likelihood that he or she will successfully enter the system is high. Fortunately for the many poorly protected organizations in the world, there are substantially fewer expert hackers than novice hackers.

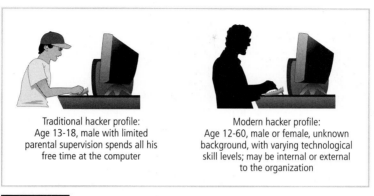

Traditional hacker profile:
Age 13-18, male with limited parental supervision spends all his free time at the computer

Modern hacker profile:
Age 12-60, male or female, unknown background, with varying technological skill levels; may be internal or external to the organization

FIGURE 1-7 Hacker Profiles

Expert hackers are reported to be bored with directly attacking systems, and have turned their attention to writing software that implements exploits. These automated exploits allow novice hackers to act as **script kiddies**—hackers of limited skill who use expertly written software to attack a system—or **packet monkeys**—script kiddies who use automated exploits to engage in distributed denial-of-service attacks (described later in this chapter). The good news is that if an expert hacker can post a script tool where a script kiddie or packet monkey can find it, then systems and security administrators can find it too. The developers of protection software and hardware and the service providers who keep defensive systems up to date also keep themselves informed of the latest in exploit scripts. As a result of preparation and continued vigilance, attacks conducted by scripts are usually predictable, and can be adequately defended against.

There are other terms for system rule breakers that may be less familiar. The term **cracker** is now commonly associated with an individual who "cracks" or removes software protection that is designed to prevent unauthorized duplication. With the removal of the copyright protection, the software can be easily distributed and installed. The terms hacker and cracker denote criminal intent.

A **phreaker** hacks the public telephone network to make free calls or disrupt services. Phreakers grew in fame in the 1970s, when they developed devices called blue boxes that enabled free calls from pay phones. Later, red boxes were developed to simulate the tones of coins falling in a pay phone, and finally black boxes emulated the line voltage. With the advent of digital communications, these boxes became practically obsolete. Even with the loss of the colored box technologies, phreakers continue to cause problems for all telephone systems.

Information Extortion

Information extortion occurs when an attacker or trusted insider steals information from a computer system and demands compensation for its return or for an agreement not to disclose the information. Extortion is common in credit card number theft. For example, Web-based retailer CD Universe was the victim of a theft of data files containing customer credit card information. The culprit was a Russian hacker named Maxus, who hacked the online vendor and stole several hundred thousand credit card numbers. When the company refused to pay the $100,000 blackmail, he posted the card numbers to a Web site, offering them to the criminal community. His Web site became so popular he had to restrict access.[12]

Another example of extortion occurred in June of 2000, when a student discovered how to download books from an online digital book company without paying. He threatened to release this information unless he was provided with "a sum equal to the retail value of the content on the company's Web site, a 2001 Volvo wagon, two digital audio players, and unlimited free downloads of the company's content."[13] Since a single conviction for using the Internet to send blackmail threats could result in two years in prison and fines up to $100,000, this student, who was charged with online blackmail, faced a maximum total of 36 years and fines up to $800,000 if convicted on all counts.

Sabotage or Vandalism

This category of threat involves the deliberate sabotage of a computer system or business, or acts of vandalism to either destroy an asset or damage the image of an organization. These acts can range from petty vandalism by employees to organized sabotage against an organization.

Although not necessarily financially devastating, attacks on the image of an organization are serious. Organizations frequently rely on image to support the generation of revenue, and vandalism to a Web site can erode consumer confidence, thus reducing the organization's sales and net worth. For example, in the early hours of July 13, 2001, a group known as Fluffi Bunni left its mark on the front page of the SANS Institute, a cooperative research and education organization. This event was particularly embarrassing to SANS Institute management, since it provides security instruction and certification. The defacement read, "Would you really trust these guys to teach you security?"[14]

There are innumerable reports of hackers accessing systems, and damaging or destroying critical data. Hacked Web sites once made front-page news, as the perpetrators intended. The impact of these acts has lessened as the volume has increased. The Web site that acts as the clearinghouse for many hacking reports, *Attrition.org*, has stopped cataloging all Web site defacements, because the sheer volume of the acts has outstripped the ability of the volunteers to keep the site up to date.[15]

Today, security experts are noticing a rise in another form of online vandalism, **hacktivist** or **cyberactivist** operations, which interfere with or disrupt systems to protest the operations, policies, or actions of an organization or government agency. A much more sinister form of hacking is **cyberterrorism**. Cyberterrorists hack systems to conduct terrorist activities through network or Internet pathways. The United States and other governments are developing security measures intended to protect the critical computing and communications networks as well as the physical and power utility infrastructures.

Theft

The threat of **theft**—the illegal taking of another's property—is constant. Within an organization, property can be physical, electronic, or intellectual. The value of information suffers when it is copied and taken away without the owner's knowledge.

Physical theft can be controlled quite easily. A wide variety of measures can be used, from locked doors to trained security personnel and the installation of alarm systems. Electronic theft, however, is a more complex problem to manage and control. When someone steals a physical item, the loss is easily detected; the item is gone. With the theft of electronic information, the crime is not readily apparent. If thieves are clever and cover their tracks carefully, no one may ever know of the crime until it is far too late. An example of this type of theft is the data stolen from TJX Companies' Framingham MA headquarters.[16] In that case, the data was stolen in July of 2005, but the theft was not discovered until December of 2006.

Software Attacks

Perhaps the most familiar threat is that from software attacks. Deliberate software attacks occur when an individual or group designs software to attack a system, or a program malfunctions causing unintended results. Most of this software is referred to as **malicious code** or **malicious software**, or sometimes **malware**. These software components or programs are designed to damage, destroy, or deny service to the target systems. Some of the more common instances of malicious code are viruses and worms, Trojan horses, logic bombs, and back doors.

Equally prominent among the incidents of malicious code are the denial-of-service attacks conducted by Mafiaboy on Amazon.com, CNN.com, E*TRADE.com, ebay.com, Yahoo.com, Excite.com, and Dell.com. These software-based attacks lasted approximately four hours, and are reported to have caused millions of dollars in lost revenue.[17] The British Internet service provider Cloudnine is believed to be the first business "hacked out of existence" in a denial-of-service attack in January 2002. This attack was similar to denial-of-service attacks launched by Mafiaboy in February 2000.[18] The following sections describe common malware threats.

Virus

Computer viruses are segments of code that perform malicious actions. This code behaves very much like a viral pathogen that attacks animals and plants, using the cell's own replication machinery to propagate. The code attaches itself to the existing program and takes control of that program's access to the targeted computer. The virus-controlled target program then carries out the virus's plan, by replicating itself on additional targeted systems. Many times users help virus code get into a system. Opening an infected e-mail or some other seemingly trivial action can cause anything from random messages popping up on a user's screen to the complete destruction of entire hard drives of data. Just as their namesakes are passed among living bodies, computer viruses are passed from machine to machine via physical media, e-mail, or other forms of computer data transmission. When these viruses infect a machine, they may immediately scan the local machine for e-mail applications, or even send themselves to every user in the e-mail address book.

One of the most common methods of virus transmission is via e-mail attachment files. Most organizations block e-mail attachments of certain types and also filter all e-mail for known virus strains. The current software marketplace has several established vendors, such as Symantec Norton AntiVirus and McAfee VirusScan, that provide applications to assist in the control of computer viruses.

There are several types of viruses. One is the **macro virus**, which is embedded in the automatically executing macro code common in word processors, spreadsheets, and database applications. Another type, the **boot virus**, infects the key operating system files located in a computer's boot sector.

Worms

Named for the Tapeworm in John Brunner's novel *The Shockwave Rider*, worms are malicious programs that replicate themselves constantly, without requiring another program to provide a safe environment for replication. Worms can continue replicating themselves until they completely fill available resources, such as memory, hard drive space, and network bandwidth. Read the Offline on Robert Morris and the worm he created to learn about the damage a worm can cause. Newer worm variants contain multiple exploits that can use any of the many predefined distribution vectors to programmatically distribute the worm (see the section on polymorphism later in this chapter for more details). Worms can be initiated with or without the user downloading or executing the file. Once the worm has infected a computer, it can redistribute itself to all e-mail addresses found on the infected system. Furthermore, a worm can deposit copies of itself onto all Web servers that the infected system can reach, so that users who subsequently visit those sites become infected. Worms also take advantage of open shares found on the network in which an infected system is located, placing working copies of the worm code onto the server so that users of those shares are likely to become infected.

Trojan horses

Trojan horses are software programs that reveal their designed behavior only when activated. Trojan horses are frequently disguised as helpful, interesting, or necessary pieces of software, such as readme.exe files, which are often included with shareware or freeware packages. Unfortunately, like their namesake in Greek legend, once Trojan horses are brought into a system, they can wreak havoc on the unsuspecting user. Figure 1-8 outlines a typical Trojan horse attack. Around January 20, 1999, Internet e-mail users began receiving e-mail with an attachment of a Trojan horse program named Happy99.exe. When the e-mail attachment was opened, a brief multimedia program displayed fireworks and the message "Happy 1999." While the fireworks display was running, the Trojan horse program was installing itself into the user's system. The program continued to propagate itself by following up every e-mail the user sent with a second e-mail to the same recipient that contained the Happy99 Trojan horse program.

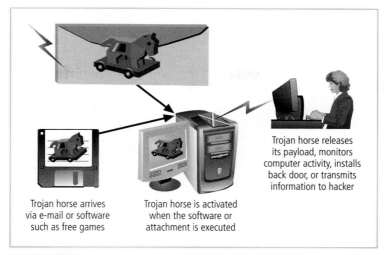

Trojan horse releases its payload, monitors computer activity, installs back door, or transmits information to hacker

Trojan horse arrives via e-mail or software such as free games

Trojan horse is activated when the software or attachment is executed

FIGURE 1-8 Trojan Horse Attack

Back Door or Trap Door

A virus or worm can have a payload that installs a **back door** or **trap door** component in a system, which allows the attacker to access the system at will with special privileges. Examples of these kinds of payloads include Subseven and Back Orifice. On Linux and UNIX computer systems the highest level of access is called *root,* and a **rootkit** is a collection of software tools and a recipe used to gain control of a system by bypassing its legitimate security controls.[19] The most dangerous rootkit program can compromise a system, conceal itself so that the attacker remains in control of the system, and in some cases defend itself against attempts to gain control of the system by other attackers or the system owner.

Polymorphic Threats

A **polymorphic threat** is one that changes over time, making it undetectable by techniques that look for preconfigured signatures. These viruses and worms actually evolve, changing their size and appearance to elude detection by antivirus software programs.

Virus and Worm Hoaxes

As frustrating as viruses and worms are, perhaps more time and money is spent on resolving **virus hoaxes**. Well-meaning people can disrupt the harmony and flow of an organization when they send e-mails warning of dangerous viruses that are fictitious. When individuals fail to follow virus-reporting procedures, the network becomes overloaded, and much time and energy is wasted as users forward the warning message to everyone they know, post the message on bulletin boards, and try to update their antivirus protection software.

There are a number of Internet resources that allow individuals to research viruses to determine if they are fact or fiction. For the latest information on real threatening viruses and hoaxes, along with other relevant and current security information, visit the CERT Coordination Center at *www.cert.org*. For a more entertaining approach to the latest virus, worm, and hoax information, visit the Urban Legend Reference Pages at *www.snopes.com/inboxer/hoaxes/hoaxes.asp* or the Hoaxbusters Web page at *hoaxbusters.ciac.org*.

Forces of Nature

Forces of nature, *force majeure*, or acts of God pose some of the most dangerous threats, because they are unexpected and can occur with very little warning. These threats, which include events such as fire, flood, earthquake, and lightning as well as volcanic eruption and insect infestation, can disrupt not only the lives of individuals, but also the storage, transmission, and use of information. Some of the more common threats in this group are:

- Fire—In this context, a structural fire that damages the building housing the computing equipment that comprises all or part of the information system. Also encompasses smoke damage from a fire and/or water damage from sprinkler systems or firefighters.

- Flood—An overflowing of water onto land that is normally dry, causing direct damage to all or part of the information system or to the building that houses all or part of the information system. May also disrupt operations through interruptions in access to the buildings that house all or part of the information system.

- Earthquake—A sudden movement of the earth's crust caused by the release of stress accumulated along geologic faults, or by volcanic activity. Earthquakes can cause direct damage to all or part of the information system or, more often, to the building that houses it. May also disrupt operations through interruptions in access to the buildings that house all or part of the information system.

- Lightning—An abrupt, discontinuous natural electric discharge in the atmosphere. Lightning usually directly damages all or part of the information system and/or its power distribution components. It can also cause fires or other damage to the building that houses all or part of the information system, and disrupt operations by interrupting access to the buildings that house all or part of the information system.

- Landslide or mudslide—The downward sliding of a mass of earth and rock directly damaging all or part of the information system or, more likely, the building that houses it. May also disrupt operations by interrupting access to the buildings that house all or part of the information system.

- Tornado or severe windstorm—A rotating column of air ranging in width from a few yards to more than a mile and whirling at destructively high speeds, usually accompanied by a funnel-shaped downward extension of a cumulonimbus cloud. Storms can directly damage all or part of the information system or, more likely, the building that houses it, and may disrupt operations by interrupting access to the buildings that house all or part of the information system.

- Hurricane or typhoon—A severe tropical cyclone originating in the equatorial regions of the Atlantic Ocean or Caribbean Sea or eastern regions of the Pacific Ocean (typhoon), traveling north, northwest, or northeast from its point of origin, and usually involving heavy rains. These storms can directly damage all or part of the information system or, more likely, the building that houses it. Organizations located in coastal or low-lying areas may experience flooding (see above). These storms may also disrupt operations through interruptions in access to the buildings that house all or part of the information system. Can sometimes be mitigated with casualty insurance and/or business interruption insurance.

- Tsunami—A very large ocean wave caused by an underwater earthquake or volcanic eruption. These events can directly damage all or part of the information system or, more likely, the building that houses it. Organizations located in coastal areas may experience tsunamis. Tsunamis may also disrupt operations by interrupting access or electrical power to the buildings that house all or part of the information system.

- Electrostatic discharge (ESD)—Usually static electricity and ESD are little more than a nuisance. However, the mild static shock we receive when walking across a carpet can be costly or dangerous when it ignites flammable mixtures and damages costly electronic components. Static electricity can draw dust into clean-room environments or cause products to stick together. The cost of ESD-damaged electronic devices and interruptions to service can range from only a few cents to several millions of dollars for critical systems. Loss of production time in information processing due to ESD impact is significant. While not usually viewed as a threat, ESD can disrupt information systems, but it is not usually an insurable loss unless covered by business interruption insurance.

- Dust contamination—Some environments are not friendly to the hardware components of information systems. Because dust contamination can shorten the life of information systems or cause unplanned downtime, this threat can disrupt normal operations.

Since it is not possible to avoid force of nature threats, organizations must implement controls to limit damage, and they must also prepare contingency plans for continued operations, such as disaster recovery plans, business continuity plans, and incident response plans to limit losses in the face of these threats.

Deviations in Quality of Service

Sometimes a product or service is not delivered to the organization as expected. The organization's information system depends on the successful operation of many interdependent support systems, including power grids, telecom networks, parts suppliers, service vendors, and even the janitorial staff and garbage haulers. Any one of these support systems can be interrupted by storms, employee illnesses, or other unforeseen events. Threats in this category are manifest in attacks such as a backhoe taking out a fiber-optic link for an ISP. The backup provider may be online and in service, but may be able to supply only a fraction of the bandwidth the organization needs for full service. This degradation of service is a form of **availability disruption**. Internet service, communications, and power irregularities can dramatically affect the availability of information and systems.

Internet Service Issues

For organizations that rely heavily on the Internet and the World Wide Web to support continued operations, Internet service provider failures can considerably undermine the availability of information. Many organizations have sales staff and telecommuters working at remote locations. When these offsite employees cannot contact the host systems, manual procedures must be used to continue operations.

A Web hosting provider assumes responsibility for all Internet services as well as for the hardware and operating system software used to operate the Web site. These Web hosting services are usually arranged with an agreement providing minimum service levels known as a **Service Level Agreement (SLA)**. When a service provider fails to meet the SLA, the provider may accrue fines to cover losses incurred by the client, but these payments seldom cover the losses generated by the outage.

Communications and other Service Provider Issues

Other utility services can affect organizations as well. Among these are telephone, water, wastewater, trash pickup, cable television, natural or propane gas, and custodial services. The loss of these services can impair the ability of an organization to function. For instance, most facilities require water service to operate an air-conditioning system. Even in Minnesota in February, air-conditioning systems are needed to keep a modern facility operating. Alternatively, if the wastewater system fails, an organization might be prevented from allowing employees into the building.

Power Irregularities

Irregularities from power utilities are common and can lead to fluctuations such as power excesses, power shortages, and power losses. This can pose problems for organizations that provide inadequately conditioned power for their information systems equipment. In the U.S., we are "fed" 120-volt, 60-cycle power usually through 15- and 20-amp circuits. When voltage levels **spike** (experience a momentary increase) or **surge** (experience a prolonged increase), the extra voltage can severely damage or destroy equipment. Equally disruptive are power shortages from a lack of available power. A momentary low voltage, or **sag**, or a more prolonged drop in voltage, known as a **brownout**, can cause systems to shut down or reset, or otherwise disrupt availability. Complete loss of power for a moment is known as a **fault**, and a more lengthy loss as a **blackout**. Because sensitive electronic equipment—especially networking equipment, computers, and computer-based systems—is susceptible to fluctuations, controls can be applied to the equipment to manage power quality. With small computers and network systems, quality power-conditioning options such as surge suppressors can smooth out spikes. The more expensive uninterruptible power supply (UPS) can protect against spikes and surges as well as against sags and even blackouts of limited duration.

Hardware Failures or Errors

Hardware failures or errors occur when a manufacturer distributes equipment containing a known or unknown flaw. These defects can cause the system to perform outside of expected parameters, resulting in unreliable service or lack of availability. Some errors are terminal, in that they result in the unrecoverable loss of the equipment. Some errors are intermittent, in that they only periodically manifest themselves, resulting in faults that are not easily repeated, and thus, equipment can sometimes stop working, or work in unexpected ways. Murphy's Law (and yes, there really was a Murphy) says that if something can possibly go wrong, it will.[20] In other words, it's not *if* something will fail, but when.

One of the best-known hardware failures is that of the Intel Pentium II chip. The microchip had a defect that caused it to calculate erroneously in certain circumstances. Intel initially expressed little concern about the defect, stating that it would take an inordinate amount of time to identify a calculation that would interfere with the reliability of the results. Yet within days, popular computing journals were publishing a simple calculation (the division of 4195835 by 3145727 by a spreadsheet) that determined whether an individual's machine contained the defective chip and thus the floating-point operation bug. The Pentium floating-point division bug (FDIV) led to a public relations disaster for Intel that resulted in its first-ever chip recall, and a loss of over $475 million. A few months later, disclosure of another bug known as the Dan-0411 flag erratum further eroded the chip manufacturer's public image.[21] In 1998, when Intel released its Xeon chip, it, too, had hardware errors. Intel said, "All new chips have bugs, and the process of debugging and improving performance inevitably continues even after a product is in the market."[22]

Software Failures or Errors

This category involves threats that come from software with unknown, hidden faults. Large quantities of computer code are written, debugged, published, and sold before all their bugs are detected and resolved. Sometimes, combinations of certain software and hardware reveal new bugs. These failures range from bugs to untested failure conditions. Sometimes these bugs are not errors, but rather purposeful shortcuts left by programmers for benign or malign reasons. Collectively, shortcut access routes into programs that bypass security checks are called trap doors and can cause serious security breaches.

In general, software bugs are so commonplace that entire Web sites are dedicated to documenting them. Among the most often used is Bugtraq, found at *www.securityfocus.com*, which provides both up-to-the-minute information on the latest security vulnerabilities as well as a very thorough archive of past bugs.

Obsolescence

Antiquated or outdated infrastructure leads to unreliable and untrustworthy systems. Management must recognize that when technology becomes outdated, there is a risk of loss of data integrity from attacks. Management's strategic planning should always include an analysis of the technology currently in use. Ideally, proper planning by management should prevent technology from becoming obsolete, but when obsolescence is identified, management must take immediate action. IT professionals play a large role in the identification of probable obsolescence.

Recently, the software vendor Symantec retired support for a legacy version of its popular antivirus software, and organizations interested in continued product support were obliged to upgrade immediately to a different antivirus control software. In organizations where IT personnel had kept management informed of the coming retirement, these replacements were made more promptly and at lower cost than at organizations where the software was allowed to become obsolete.

Attacks

An **attack** is an act or action that takes advantage of a vulnerability to compromise a controlled system. It is accomplished by a **threat agent,** that damages or steals an organization's information or physical asset. A **vulnerability** is an identified weakness in a controlled system, where controls are not present or are no longer effective. Unlike threats, which are ever present, attacks occur when a specific act or action may cause a potential loss. For example, the *threat* of damage from a thunderstorm is present during most of the summer in many places, but an *attack* and its associated risk of loss only exist for the duration of an actual thunderstorm. The following sections discuss each of the major types of attack used against controlled systems.

Malicious Code

The **malicious code** attack includes the execution of viruses, worms, Trojan horses, and active Web scripts with the intent to destroy or steal information. The state-of-the-art malicious code attack is the polymorphic, or multivector, worm. These attack programs use several known attack vectors to exploit a variety of vulnerabilities in commonly used software. Perhaps the best illustration of such an attack remains the outbreak of Nimda in September 2001, which used five of the six vectors to spread itself with startling speed. TruSecure Corporation, an industry source for information security statistics and solutions, reported that Nimda spread to span the Internet address space of 14 countries in less than 25 minutes.[23] Table 1-2 outlines the six categories of known attack vectors.

TABLE 1-2 Attack Replication Vectors

Vector	Description
IP scan and attack	The infected system scans a random or local range of IP addresses and targets any of several vulnerabilities known to hackers or left over from previous exploits such as Code Red, Back Orifice, or PoizonBox.
Web browsing	If the infected system has write access to any Web pages, it makes all Web content files (.html, .asp, .cgi, and others) infectious, so that users who browse to those pages become infected.
Virus	Each infected machine infects certain common executable or script files on all computers to which it can write with virus code that can cause infection.
Unprotected shares	Using vulnerabilities in file systems and the way many organizations configure them, the infected machine copies the viral component to all locations it can reach.
Mass mail	By sending e-mail infections to recipients in the address book, the infected machine infects many users, whose mail-reading programs also automatically run the program and infect other systems.
Simple Network Management Protocol (SNMP)	By using the common passwords that were employed in early versions of this protocol, widely used for remote management of network and computer devices, the attacker program can gain control of a device.

"Hoaxes"

A more devious approach to attacking computer systems is the transmission of a false virus report *with a real virus attached*. Even though these users are trying to do the right thing to avoid infection, they end up sending the attack on to their coworkers and friends and infecting many users along the way.

Back Doors

Using a known or previously unknown and newly discovered access mechanism, an attacker can gain access to a system or network resource through a back door. Sometimes these entries are left behind by system designers or maintenance staff, and thus referred to as trap doors.[24] A trap door is hard to detect, because very often the programmer who puts it in place also makes the access exempt from the usual audit logging features of the system.

Password Crack

Attempting to reverse-calculate a password is often called **cracking**. A cracking attack is a component of many dictionary attacks (to be covered shortly). It is used when a copy of the hash of the user's password is obtained and is used in search of a match. When a match is found, the password has been cracked.

Brute Force

The application of computing and network resources to try every possible combination of options of a password is called a **brute force attack**. Since this often involves repeatedly guessing passwords to commonly used accounts, it is sometimes called a **password attack**. If attackers can narrow the field of target accounts, they can devote more time and resources to attacking fewer accounts. That is one reason to change account names for common accounts from the manufacturer's default.

While often effective against low-security systems, password attacks are often not useful against systems that have adopted the usual security practices recommended by manufacturers. Controls that limit the number of attempts allowed per unit of elapsed time are very effective at combating brute force attacks. Defenses against brute force attacks are usually adopted early on in any security effort and are thoroughly covered in the SANS/FBI list of the top twenty most critical Internet security vulnerabilities.[25]

Dictionary

The **dictionary attack**, which is a variation on the brute force attack, narrows the field by selecting specific target accounts and using a list of commonly used passwords (the dictionary) instead of random combinations. Organizations can use similar dictionaries to disallow passwords during the reset process and thus guard against easy-to-guess passwords. In addition, rules requiring additional numbers and/or special characters make the dictionary attack less effective. Another variant, called a rainbow attack, a pre-computed hash attack or a time-memory tradeoff attack, uses a database of pre-computed hashes from sequentially calculated passwords to look up the hashed password and read out the text version, no brute force required.

Denial-of-Service (DoS) and Distributed Denial-of-Service (DDoS)

In a **denial-of-service (DoS)** attack, the attacker sends a large number of connection or information requests to a target (see Figure 1-9). So many requests are made that the target system cannot handle them along with other, legitimate requests for service. The system may crash, or may simply be unable to perform ordinary functions. A **distributed denial-of-service (DDoS)** launches a coordinated stream of requests against a target from many locations at the same time. Most DDoS attacks are preceded by a preparation phase in which many systems, perhaps thousands, are compromised. The compromised machines are turned into **zombies** (or **bots)**, machines that are directed remotely (usually by a transmitted command) by the attacker to participate in the attack. DDoS attacks are the most difficult to defend against, and there are presently no controls that any single organization can apply. There are, however, some cooperative efforts to enable DDoS defenses among groups of service providers; among them is the Consensus Roadmap for Defeating Distributed Denial of Service Attacks.[26] To use a popular metaphor, DDoS is considered a weapon of mass destruction on the Internet.[27] The MyDoom worm attack of early 2004 was intended to be a distributed denial-of-service (DDoS) attack against *www.sco.com* (the Web site of a vendor of a UNIX operating system), and it lasted from February 1, 2004 until February 12, 2004. Allegedly, the attack was payback for the SCO Group's perceived hostility toward the open-source Linux community.[28]

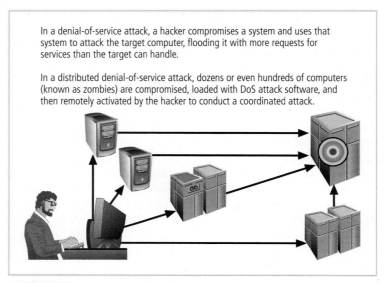

In a denial-of-service attack, a hacker compromises a system and uses that system to attack the target computer, flooding it with more requests for services than the target can handle.

In a distributed denial-of-service attack, dozens or even hundreds of computers (known as zombies) are compromised, loaded with DoS attack software, and then remotely activated by the hacker to conduct a coordinated attack.

FIGURE 1-9 Denial-of-Service Attacks

Any system connected to the Internet and providing TCP-based network services (such as a Web server, FTP server, or mail server) is a potential target for denial-of-service attacks. Note that in addition to attacks launched at specific hosts, these attacks can also be launched against routers or other network server systems if these hosts enable (or turn on) other TCP services (e.g., echo). Even though such attacks make use of a fundamental element of the TCP protocol used by all systems, the consequences of the attacks may vary, depending on the system.[29]

Spoofing

Spoofing is a technique used to gain unauthorized access to computers, wherein the intruder sends messages whose IP address indicates to the recipient that the messages are coming from a trusted host. To engage in IP spoofing, a hacker must first use a variety of techniques to find an IP address of a trusted host and then modify the packet headers (see Figure 1-10) so that it appears that the packets are coming from that host.[30] Newer routers and firewall arrangements can offer protection against IP spoofing.

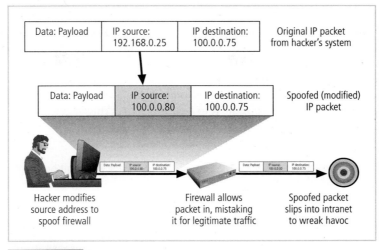

FIGURE 1-10   IP Spoofing

Man-in-the-Middle

In the well-known **man-in-the-middle** attack, an attacker monitors (or sniffs) packets from the network, modifies them using IP spoofing techniques, and inserts them back into the network allowing the attacker to eavesdrop as well as to change, delete, reroute, add, forge, or divert data.[31] In a variant attack, the spoofing involves the interception of an encryption key exchange, which enables the hacker to act as an invisible man-in-the-middle—that is, eavesdropper—in encrypted exchanges. Figure 1-11 illustrates these attacks by showing how a hacker uses public and private encryption keys to intercept messages. For more information on encrypted keys, see Chapter 9, "Encryption and Firewalls."

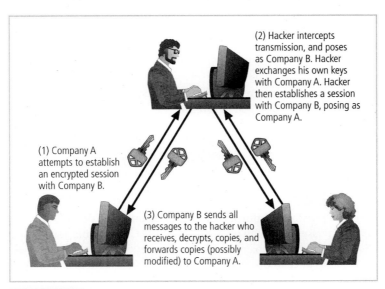

FIGURE 1-11   Man-in-the-Middle Attack

Spam

Spam, or unsolicited commercial e-mail, has been used as means to make malicious code attacks more effective. In some cases, malicious code is embedded in MP3 files that are included as attachments to spam.[32] The most significant impact of spam, however, is the waste of both computer and human resources. Many organizations attempt to cope with the flood of spam by using filtering technologies to stem the flow. Other organizations simply tell users of the mail system to delete unwanted messages.

Mail Bombing

Another form of e-mail attack that is also a DoS attack is a **mail bomb**, which occurs when an attacker routes large quantities of e-mail to the target system. This can be accomplished through social engineering (to be discussed shortly) or by exploiting various technical flaws in the Simple Mail Transport Protocol. The target of the attack receives unmanageably large volumes of unsolicited e-mail. By sending large e-mails with forged header information, attackers can take advantage of poorly configured e-mail systems and trick them into sending many e-mails to an address chosen by the attacker. If many such systems are tricked into participating in the event, the target e-mail address is buried under thousands or even millions of unwanted e-mails.

Sniffers

A **sniffer** is a program or device that can monitor data traveling over a network. Sniffers can be used both for legitimate network management functions and for stealing information from a network. Unauthorized sniffers can be extremely dangerous to a network's security, because they are virtually impossible to detect and can be inserted almost anywhere. This makes them a favorite weapon in the hacker's arsenal. Sniffers often work on TCP/IP networks, where they're sometimes referred to as **packet sniffers**.[33] Sniffers add risk to the network, because many systems and users send information on local networks in clear text. A sniffer program shows all the data going by, including passwords, the data inside files—such as word-processing documents—and screens full of sensitive data.

Social Engineering

Within the context of information security, **social engineering** is the process of using social skills to convince people to reveal access credentials or other valuable information to the attacker. This can be done in several ways, and usually involves the perpetrator posing as a person higher in the organizational hierarchy than the victim. To prepare for this false representation, the perpetrator may have used social engineering against others in the organization to collect seemingly unrelated information that, when used together, makes the false representation more credible. For instance, anyone can call the main switchboard of a company and get the name of the CIO, but an attacker may find it just as easy to get even more information by calling others in the company and asserting his or her (albeit false) authority by mentioning the CIO's name. Social engineering attacks may involve individuals posing as new employees or as current employees pathetically requesting assistance to prevent getting fired. Sometimes attackers threaten, cajole, or beg to sway the target.

An example of a social engineering attack called the Advance Fee Fraud (AFF), and internationally known as the "4-1-9" fraud, is named after a section of the Nigerian penal code. The perpetrators of 4-1-9 schemes often involve fictitious companies, such as the Nigerian National Petroleum Company. Alternatively, they may invent other entities, such as a bank, government agency, or a nongovernmental organization. See Figure 1-12 for a sample letter from this type of scheme. This scam is notorious for stealing funds from gullible individuals, first by requiring those people who wish to participate in the proposed money-making venture to send money upfront, and then by soliciting an endless series of fees. These 4-1-9 schemes are even suspected to involve kidnapping, extortion, and murder, and they have, according to the Secret Service, bilked over $100 million from unsuspecting Americans lured into disclosing personal banking information. For more information, go to *www.secretservice.gov*.

NIGERIA NATIONAL PETROLEUM CORPORATION
PETROLEUM AND PROJECT DIVISION
TEL: +234-80-33084057, 234-1-4805653, FAX: +234-1-2882183,234-1-7591061
P.M.B 2071, LAGOS – NIGERIA.

29TH JANUARY, 2002

DEAR SIR
This letter is not intended to cause any embarrassment in whatever form, rather is compelled to contact your esteemed self, following the knowledge of your high repute and trustworthiness. Firstly, I must solicit your confidentiality, this is by the virtue of its' nature as being utterly confidential and top secret though I know that a transaction of this magnitude will make anyone apprehensive and worried, but I am assuring you that all will be well at the end of the day. A bold step taken shall not be regretted I assure you.

I am Mr. Tony Okeke and I head a seven man tender board in charge of contract awards and payment approvals, I came to know of you in search of a reliable and reputable person to handle a very confidential business transaction which involves the transfer of a huge sum of money to foreign account requiring maximum confidence. My colleagues and I are top officials of the NIGERIA NATIONAL PETROLEUM CORPORATION {NNPC}. OUR DUTIES INCLUDE VETTING, EVALUATION AND FORESEEING THE MAINTENANCE OF THE REFINERIES IN ALL THE DESIGNATED OIL PIPELINES. We are therefore soliciting for your assistance to enable us transfer into your account the said funds. Our country losses a lot of money everyday that is why the international community is very careful and warning their citizens to be careful but I tell you "A TRIAL WILL CONVINCE YOU".

The source of the fund is as follows; during the last military regime here in Nigeria this committee awarded a contract of US$400million to a group of five construction companies on behalf of the NIGERIA NATIONAL PETROLEUM CORPORATION for the construction of the oil pipelines in Kaduna, Port-Harcourt, Warri refineries. During this process my colleagues and I deliberately inflated the total contract sum to the tune US$428million with the intention of sharing the inflated sum of US$28. The government has since approved the sum of US$428 for us as the contract sum, but since the contract is only worth US$400million, the remaining US$28million is what we intend to transfer to reliable and safe offshore account, we are prohibited to operate foreign account in our names since we are still in government. Thus, making it impossible for us to acquire the money in our name right now, I have therefore been delegated as a matter of trust by my colleagues to look for an oversea partner into whose account we can transfer the sum of US$28million.

My colleagues and I have decided that if you/your company can be the beneficiary of this funds on our behalf, you or your company will retain 20% of the total sum US$28million while 75% will be for us the officials and remaining 5% will be used for offsetting all debts/expenses incurred during this transaction.

We have decided that this transaction can only proceed under the following conditions:
1. That you treat this transaction with utmost secrecy and confidentiality and conviction of your transparent honesty.
2. That upon the receipt of the funds you will release the funds as instructed by us after you have removed your share of 20%. Please acknowledge the receipt of this letter using the above telephone and fax numbers. I will bring you into the nomenclature of this transaction when I have heard from you.

Your urgent response will be highly appreciated as we catching on the next payment schedule for the financial quarter. Please be assured that this transaction is 100% legal/risk free, only trust can make the reality of this transaction.

Best Regards,

Tony Okeke
MR. TONY OKEKE

FIGURE 1-12   Example of a Nigerian 4-1-9 Fraud

The infamous hacker Kevin Mitnick once stated:

> "People are the weakest link. You can have the best technology; firewalls, intrusion-detection systems, biometric devices...and somebody can call an unsuspecting employee. That's all she wrote, baby. They got everything."[34]

Buffer Overflow

A **buffer overflow** is an application error that occurs when more data is sent to a buffer than it can handle. During a buffer overflow, the attacker can make the target system execute instructions, or the attacker can take advantage of some other unintended consequence of the failure. Sometimes this is limited to a denial-of-service attack, when the attacked system crashes and is (until it's restarted) unavailable to users. In either case, data on the attacked system loses integrity.[35] In 1998, Microsoft encountered the following buffer overflow problem:

> Microsoft acknowledged that if you type a res:// URL (a Microsoft-devised type of URL) which is longer than 256 characters in Internet Explorer 4.0, the browser will crash. No big deal, except that anything after the 256th character can be executed on the computer. This maneuver, known as a buffer overrun, is just about the oldest hacker trick in the book. Tack some malicious code (say, an executable version of the Pentium-crashing FooF code) onto the end of the URL, and you have the makings of a disaster.[36]

Timing Attack

The **timing attack** works by measuring the time required to access a Web page and deducing that the user has visited the site before by the presence of the page in the browser's cache. Another attack by the same name is a side channel attack on cryptographic algorithms using measurements of the time required to perform cryptographic functions.[37]

Chapter Summary

- Firewalls and network security have become essential components for securing the systems businesses use to run their day-to-day operations. Before learning how to plan, design, and implement firewalls and network security, it is important to understand the larger issue of information security. Learning about the overall picture of information security helps you become aware of these areas that affect firewalls and network security.

- Information security is the protection of information and its critical elements, including the systems and hardware that use, store, and transmit that information. The C.I.A. triangle is based on the confidentiality, integrity, and availability of information and the systems that process it.

- The value of information comes from the characteristics it possesses. When a characteristic of information changes, the value of that information either increases or, more commonly, decreases.
- The CNSS Security model is known as the McCumber Cube and was created by John McCumber in 1991. It provides a graphical description of the architectural approach widely used in computer and information security.
- Securing information and its systems entails securing all components and protecting them from potential misuse and abuse by unauthorized users. When considering the security of information systems components, it is important to understand that a computer can be the subject of an attack, or the object of an attack. There are also two types of attacks: direct attacks and indirect attacks.
- Information security cannot be an absolute: it is a process, not a goal. Information security should balance protection and availability. To achieve balance—that is, to operate an information system to the satisfaction of the user and the security professional—the level of security must allow reasonable access, yet protect against threats.
- Information security performs four important organizational functions: Protects the organization's ability to function, enables the safe operation of applications implemented on the organization's IT systems, protects the data the organization collects and uses, and safeguards the technology assets in use at the organization.
- It takes a wide range of professionals and skills to support the information security program: Senior management, administrative support and technical expertise. The following job titles describe the information security roles: chief information officer (CIO), chief information security officer (CISO), members of the information security project team including team leader, security policy developers, risk assessment specialists, security professionals, systems, network, and storage administrators, and end users, data owners, data custodians, and data users.
- A threat is an object, person, or other entity that represents a constant danger to an asset. Twelve categories have been developed to represent the dangers posed to an organization's people, information, and systems. They are: (1) human error or failure, (2) compromises to intellectual property, (3) espionage or trespass, (4) information extortion, (5) sabotage or vandalism, (6) theft, (7) software attacks, (8) forces of nature, (9) deviations in quality of service, (10) hardware failures or errors, (11) software failures or errors, and (12) obsolescence.
- An attack is an act or action that takes advantage of a vulnerability to compromise a controlled system. A vulnerability is an identified weakness in a controlled system. Attacks occur as a specific act or action that may cause a potential loss. There are major types of attacks including: malicious code, "hoaxes" of malicious code, back doors, password cracking, denial-of-service (DoS) and distributed denial-of-service (DDoS), spoofing, man-in-the-middle, spam, mail bombing, sniffers, social engineering, buffer overflow, and timing attacks.

Review Questions

1. What is the difference between a threat agent and a threat?
2. What is the difference between vulnerability and exposure?
3. How has the definition of "hack" evolved over the last 30 years?
4. What are the three components of the C.I.A. triangle? What are they used for?
5. If the C.I.A. triangle is incomplete, why is it so commonly used in security?
6. Who is ultimately responsible for the security of information in the organization?

7. What does it mean to discover an exploit? How does an exploit differ from a vulnerability?

8. Why is data the most important asset an organization possesses? What other assets in the organization require protection?

9. It is important to protect data in motion (transmission) and data at rest (storage). In what other state must data be protected? In which of the three states is data most difficult to protect?

10. How does a threat to information security differ from an attack? How can the two overlap?

11. List the vectors that malicious code uses to infect or compromise other systems. Which one of these do you think is most commonly encountered in a typical organization?

12. Why do employees constitute one of the greatest threats to information security?

13. What measures can individuals take to protect against shoulder surfing?

14. What is the difference between a skilled hacker and an unskilled hacker (other than the lack of skill)? How does the protection against each differ?

15. What are the various types of malware? How do worms differ from viruses? Do Trojan horses carry viruses or worms?

16. Why does polymorphism cause greater concern than traditional malware? How does it affect detection?

17. What is the most common form of violation of intellectual property? How does an organization protect against it? What agencies fight it?

18. What are the various types of *force majeure*? Which type might be of greatest concern to an organization in Las Vegas? Oklahoma City? Miami? Los Angeles?

19. How does obsolescence constitute a threat to information security? How can an organization protect against it?

20. What is the difference between an exploit and a vulnerability?

21. What are the types of password attacks? What can a systems administrator do to protect against them?

22. What is the difference between a denial-of-service attack and a distributed denial-of-service attack? Which is potentially more dangerous and devastating? Why?

23. For a sniffer attack to succeed, what must the attacker do? How can an attacker gain access to a network to use the sniffer system?

24. What are some ways a social engineering hacker can attempt to gain information about a user's login and password? How would this type of attack differ if it were targeted towards an administrator's assistant versus a data-entry clerk?

25. What is a buffer overflow, and how is it used against a Web server?

Exercises

1. Look up "the paper that started the study of computer security." Prepare a summary of the key points. What in this paper specifically addresses security in areas previously unexamined?

2. Assume that a security model is needed for the protection of information in your class. Using the NSTISSC model, examine each of the cells and write a brief statement on how you would address the three components represented in that cell.

3. Consider the information stored on your personal computer. For each of the terms listed, find an example and document it: threat, threat agent, vulnerability, exposure, risk, attack, and exploit.

4. Using the Web, identify the chief information officer, chief information security officer, and systems administrator for your school. Which of these individuals represents the data owner? Data custodian?

5. Using the Web, find out who Kevin Mitnick was. What did he do? Who caught him? Write a short summary of his activities and why he is infamous.

6. Consider the statement: an individual threat agent, like a hacker, can be represented in more than one threat category. If a hacker hacks into a network, copies a few files, defaces the Web page, and steals credit card numbers, how many different threat categories does this attack cover?

7. Using the Web, research Mafiaboy's exploits. When and how did he compromise sites? How was he caught?

8. Search the Web for "The Official Phreaker's Manual." What information contained in this manual might help a security administrator to protect a communications system?

9. The chapter discussed many threats to information security. Using the Web, find at least two other sources of information on threats. Begin with *www.securitystats.com*.

10. Using the categories of threats mentioned in this chapter, as well as the various attacks described, review several newspapers and locate examples of each.

Case Exercises

Matthias was back on the job Friday night at midnight. He had been out of the data center during his three days at the training center. He was a little sleepy, since he had attended the training during the day shift and now he was back for third shift.

Al walked up and said, "Hi Matt, how was the class?"

Matthias replied, "Pretty good, I guess. I really liked the stuff about the ways that systems get attacked, but I thought the threat stuff was kind of boring."

Al said, "I suppose it can seem that way, but you have to try to figure out how the information about threats can affect our work and how we do our jobs."

Questions:

1. Which of the twelve threat categories listed in Table 1-1 would be most likely to impact Matthias and Al in their jobs as network administrators at ATI?

2. List at least two threat categories not mentioned in this chapter that might be encountered by a network administrator.

3. For each of the three threat categories you listed, list and describe two attacks that could come from these threats.

Endnotes

1. National Security Telecommunications and Information Systems Security, *National Training Standard for Information Systems Security (Infosec) Professionals*, 20 June 1994, file, 4011, Accessed 8 Feb 2004 from *www.nstissc.gov/Assets/pdf/4011.pdf*.

2. Parker, D. Fighting Computer Crime: A New Framework for Protecting Information. New York: Wiley. (1998).

3. McCumber, John. *"Information Systems Security: A Comprehensive Model."* Proceedings *14th National Computer Security Conference. National Institute of Standards and Technology*. Baltimore, MD. (October 1991.)

4. Sun-Tzu. "The Principles of Warfare - The Art of War," Chapter Three: Planning Attacks. Accessed 16 February 2004 from *www.sonshi.com/sun3.html*.

5. The numbers of organizations willing to report the dollar values of their losses on the survey continues to decrease with only 313 (down from 639 in the 2005 survey) providing this information in 2006.

6. Lawrence A. Gordon, Martin P. Loeb, William Lucyshyn, and Robert Richardson (2004) 2004 CSI/FBI Computer Crime and Security Survey. Accessed 21 June 2004 from *www.gocsi.com*.

7. Michael Whitman, "Enemy at the Gates: Threats to Information Security," *Communications of the ACM*, 46(8) August 2003, pp. 91-96.

8. Michael Whitman, "Enemy at the Gates: Threats to Information Security," *Communications of the ACM*, 46(8) August 2003, pp. 91-96.

9. James T. Kennedy, "Internet Intricacies: Don't Get Caught in the Net," *Contingency Planning & Management* 3, no. 1, p. 12.

10. FOLDOC, "Intellectual Property," *FOLDOC Online* (27 March 1997) Accessed 15 February 2004 from *foldoc.doc.ic.ac.uk/foldoc/foldoc.cgi?query=intellectual+property*.

11. Merriam-Webster, "hackers," *Merriam-Webster Online*. Accessed 15 February 2004 from *www.m-w.com*.

12. "Rebuffed Internet extortionist posts stolen credit card data," *CNN Online* (10 January 2000). Accessed 16 February 2004 from *www.cnn.com/2000/TECH/computing/01/10/credit.card.crack.2/*.

13. Brian McWilliams "PhD Student Arrested in Blackmail Attempt," *Internet News Online* (25 May 2000). Accessed 15 February 2004 from *www.internetnews.com/bus-news/article.php/380531*.

14. Lawrence M. Walsh and Anne Saita, "Hacked Off: Black Hat and DefCon Served their Purpose, but Failed to Live up to Expectations," *Information Security Magazine Online* (August 2001). Accessed 15 February 2004 from *www.infosecuritymag.com/articles/august01/departments_news.shtml*.

15. Sam Costello, "Attrition.org stops mirroring Web site defacements," *ComputerWorld Online* (22 May 2001). Accessed 15 February 2004 from *www.computerworld.com/securitytopics/security/story/0,10801,60769,00.html*.

16. Jenn Abelson, "Breach of data at TJX is called the biggest ever: Stolen numbers put at 45.7 million." *The Boston Globe Online*. (March 29, 2007). Accessed 19 October 2007 from *www.boston.com/business/globe/articles/2007/03/29/breach_of_data_at_tjx_is_called_the_biggest_ever*.

17. D. Ian Hopper, "'Mafiaboy' Faces up to 3 Years in Prison," *CNN.com Online* (19 April 2000). Accessed 15 February 2004 from *www.cnn.com/2000/TECH/computing/04/19/dos.charges/index.html*.

18. Bernhard Warner, "Internet Firm Hacked Out of Business," *Tech Update Online*. Accessed 15 February 2004 from *www.techupdate.zdnet.com/techupdate/stories/main/0,14179,2844881,00.html*.

19. Rootkit. *SearchSecurity Online*. Accessed 17 October 2007 from *searchsecurity.techtarget.com/sDefinition/0,,sid14_gci547279,00.html*.

20. "Murphy's Laws Site." Accessed 15 February 2004 from *www.murphys-laws.com/*.

21. Alexander Wolfe, "Intel Preps Plan to Bust Bugs in Pentium MPUs," *Electronic Engineering Times* no. 960 (June 1997): 1.

22. Roger Taylor, "Intel to Launch New Chip Despite Bug Reports," *Financial Times* (London), 25 June 1998, 52.

23. Trusecure, "Trusecure Successfully Defends Customers Against Goner Virus," *Trusecure Online* (18 December 2001). Accessed 15 February 2004 from *www.trusecure.com/company/press/release755.shtml*.

24. SANS Institute, "NSA Glossary of Terms Used in Security and Intrusion Detection," *SANS Institute Online*. Accessed 15 February 2004 from *www.sans.org/newlook/resources/glossary.html*.

25. SANS Institute, "The Twenty Most Critical Internet Security Vulnerabilities (Updated): The Experts' Consensus," *SANS Institute Online* (2 May 2002). Accessed 15 February 2004 from *www.sans.org/top20.html*.

26. SANS Institute, "Consensus Roadmap for Defeating Distributed Denial of Service Attacks: A Project of the Partnership for Critical Infrastructure Security," *SANS Institute Online*, (23 February 2000). Accessed 15 February 2004 from *www.sans.org/dosstep/roadmap.php*.

27. Paul Brooke, "DDoS: Internet Weapons of Mass Destruction," *Network Computing* 12, no. 1 (January 2001): 67.

28. Trend Micro. "WORM_MYDOOM.A." Accessed February 14, 2004 from *www.trendmicro.com/vinfo/virusencyclo/default5.asp?VName=WORM_MYDOOM.A*.

29. CERT® Advisory CA-1996-21 TCP SYN Flooding and IP Spoofing Attacks, CERT, "TCP SYN Flooding and IP Spoofing Attacks," advisory CA-1996-21.

30. Webopedia, "IP spoofing," *Webopedia Online* (4 June 2002). Accessed 15 February 2004 from *www.webopedia.com/TERM/I/IP_spoofing.html*.

31. Bhavin Bharat Bhansali, "Man-In-The-Middle Attack: A Brief." *SANS Institute Online*, 16 February 2001. Accessed 15 February 2004 from *www.giac.org/practical/gsec/Bhavin_Bhansali_GSEC.pdf*.

32. James Pearce, "Security Expert Warns of MP3 Danger," *ZDNet News Online* (18 March 2002). Accessed 15 February 2004 from *zdnet.com.com/2100-1105-861995.html*.

33. Webopedia, "sniffer," *Webopedia Online* (5 February 2002). Accessed 15 February 2004 from *www.webopedia.com/TERM/s/sniffer.html*.

34. Elinor Abreu, "Kevin Mitnick Bares All," *NetworkWorldFusion News Online* (28 September 2000). Accessed 15 February 2004 from *www.nwfusion.com/news/2000/0928mitnick.html*.

35. Webopedia, "buffer overflow," *Webopedia Online* (29 July 2003). Accessed 15 February 2004 from *www.webopedia.com/TERM/b/buffer_overflow.html*.

36. Scott Spanbauer, "Pentium Bug, Meet the IE 4.0 Flaw," *PC World* 16, no. 2 (February 1998): 55.

37. Gaël Hachez, François Koeune, and Jean-Jacques Quisquater, "Timing attack: what can be achieved by a powerful adversary?" (Proceedings of the 20th symposium on Information Theory in the Benelux, May 1999), 63-70.

An Introduction to Networking

2

> There are three kinds of death in this world. There's heart death, there's brain death, and there's being off the network.
>
> **GUY ALMES**

ELIANA WAS VISITING HER ALMA MATER, recruiting network administrators for her company, Advanced Topologies, Inc. The career services group at the school had contacted the Human Resources group at ATI about a month ago, and invited them to participate in this information technology job fair. Now Eliana stood in front of the ATI company information board, ready to screen applicants.

She greeted the first student. "Hello, I'm Eliana. I'm the supervisor of network operations at ATI. Are you interested in our company?"

The student said, "Yes, what kinds of jobs do you have?"

Eliana replied, "We're looking for graduates who are interested in network operations and, eventually, network design."

"Oh, too bad," said the young woman. "Database management and design is my area of interest."

Eliana agreed to take her résumé to the HR department, though she didn't think ATI was hiring in that area.

The next student who approached held out his hand for a business card. "Are you interested?" she asked.

"Sure," he replied. "What are you willing to pay?"

Eliana hid her surprise. Maybe things were different in college recruiting than they used to be. She said, "That depends; how much experience do you have with computer networks?"

LEARNING OBJECTIVES:

Upon completion of this material, you should be able to do the following:

- Describe the basic elements of computer-based data communication
- Know the key entities and organizations behind current networking standards, as well as the purpose of and intent behind the more widely used standards
- Explain the nature and intent of the OSI reference model, and list and describe each of the model's seven layers
- Describe the nature of the Internet and the relationship between the TCP/IP protocol and the Internet

Introduction

Before learning about firewalls and how they are deployed to help secure a network, you must know the basics of how computer networks function. This chapter serves as a brief but complete survey of the essentials of computer networking.

Networking Fundamentals

In a fundamental exchange of information between two parties, one party—the sender—communicates a message to a second party—the receiver—over some medium, as illustrated in Figure 2-1.

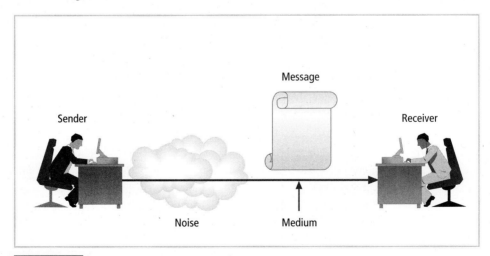

FIGURE 2-1   Basic Communications Model

Communication can only occur when the recipient is able to receive, process, and comprehend the message. This one-way flow of information is referred to as a **channel**. When the recipient becomes a sender, for example by responding to the original sender's message, this two-way flow is called a **circuit**.

Any communications medium may be subject to various types of interference, which is commonly called **noise**. Noise occurs in a variety of forms[1]:

- **Attenuation** is the loss of signal strength as the signal moves across media. Both wired and wireless communications suffer from attenuation. The higher the quality of the media, the less the degree of attenuation. Counteracting attenuation involves either repeating or amplifying the signal, or using a higher grade or type of medium, such as fiber-optic rather than copper cable.
- **Crosstalk** is the effect of one communications channel upon another. Crosstalk occurs when one transmission "bleeds" over to another (for example, from one channel to another). Cable shielding can help minimize the probability of crosstalk, as can changing from electrical or electromagnetic communications to photonic (fiber-optic).
- **Distortion** is the unintentional variation of the communication over the media. Many items can affect the electrical or electromagnetic signal, including solar flares, magnetic interference from fluorescent lighting, and even electrical cables. The same techniques that mitigate crosstalk will counter the effects of distortion.
- **Echo** is the reflection of a signal due to equipment malfunction or poor design. The failure to terminate early coaxial cable based networks caused signal reflection—the echoing of signals as they bounce back from the ends of the network. If you've ever heard your own voice repeated in a telephone conversation, you've experienced echo. Repairing or replacing poorly designed or malfunctioning equipment usually resolves echo.
- **Impulse noise** is a sudden, short-lived increase in signal frequency or amplitude, also known as a spike. Like distortion, impulse noise causes a temporary loss in signal clarity. Some of the same sources of distortion can also cause impulse noise. A solar flare, an overloaded electrical circuit, or a short in a data communications channel can cause impulse noise. Since these problems cannot be predicted or easily diagnosed, countering their effects is usually difficult.
- **Jitter** is signal modification caused by malfunctioning equipment, such as a faulty Network Interface Card or hub. Jitter usually involves extra signal components in, or unwanted modification of, the amplitude, frequency, or phase of the signal. If you've listened to a CD skipping or playing at the wrong speed with odd sounds like tiny clicks, you've heard jitter.
- **White noise** is unwanted noise due to a signal coming across the medium at multiple frequencies; also referred to as static noise. It can be the result of the heat of the electrons moving across electrical communications, or poor-quality communications circuits. The background hiss heard in telephone communications is white noise. Moving from electrical to photonic communications can resolve this issue.

Reasons to Network

Data communications and networking go hand in hand. Data communications is the exchange of messages across a medium, and networking is the interconnection of groups or systems with the purpose of exchanging information. There are a number of reasons to build a network:

1. To exchange information. First and foremost we create networks to exchange information among entities, both human and electronic. This information could be stored in databases, created in processing, or obtained from external inputs. The modern extensions of information exchange include e-mail, instant messaging, videoconferencing, and online seminar broadcasting.
2. To share scarce or expensive resources. A typical organization may not be able to afford expensive equipment for every member. For example, a standard laser printer may cost between $300 and $500. For an organization with 1000 members, the costs to provide one to each member would be $300,000–$500,000. Instead, workgroups could share more expensive, more reliable, and more full-featured equipment, and still save the organization money.
3. To allow distributed organizations to act as if centrally located. With the almost instant communications capabilities of the modern Internet, interaction between members of an organization can be even faster and more productive than face-to-face meetings. Instead of the travel and scheduling complications of face-to-face meetings for dispersed groups, videoconferencing can provide instant exchange of ideas. Communications have evolved to the point where individuals really do not need to care about *where* their peers are, but only if they are able to get responses in a timely manner.

Types of Networks

Networks can be categorized by components, size, layout or topology, or media.

Networks by Components

Networks categorized by components include peer-to-peer (P2P) networks, server-based networks, and distributed multi-server networks. In peer-to-peer networks, the individual users or clients directly interact and share resources, without benefit of a central repository or server. This level of connection is common in small office or home networks. Sharing hard drives or directories on a computer, or sharing a printer, is a common example of this type of networking. An extension of the peer-to-peer network is the **Servant model**, where a client shares part of its resources, serving as a pseudo-server—a device that provides services to others. The Servant model became very popular in the late 1990s when music-sharing services like Napster were quickly adopted by end users. Even after legal issues associated with the unauthorized reproduction and distribution of copyrighted music caused Napster to be shut down, other variants like Kazaa, LimeWire, iMesh, Morpheus, and BearShare adopted the model.

Server-based networks use a dedicated system to provide specific services to their clients. These services may be hosted on a single general-service system, or individual services may be provided by multiple servers. These types of networks are discussed in the sections on local and wide area networks. Distributed multi-server networks add distance and additional services to this model by separating the services outside the organization to other organizations with other systems and servers.

Networks by Size

One of the most common methods of categorizing networks is by size. Originally, network sizes were described as either local area or wide area. The Institute of Electrical and Electronics Engineers (IEEE) first specifications for a **local area network (LAN)** was a link distance of 185 meters and a limit of 30 computers. The current definition of a LAN is a network containing a dedicated server (unlike a P2P network) that connects systems within or between a few buildings, over a small geographic space. LANs are typically owned by a single organization and used to support its internal communications.

The next size up in networks is the **metropolitan area network (MAN)**. A MAN is a network that typically covers a region the size of a municipality, county, or district. The informal definition is a network that is larger than a LAN but smaller than a WAN.

A **wide area network (WAN)** is a very large network that covers a vast geographic region like a state, a country, or even the planet. There are two dominant WANs—the public telephone network and the Internet. (Note that *the* Internet is identified with a capital I, while *an* internet—an internetwork or network of networks—begins with a lowercase i.) A WAN can actually comprise a collection of LANs and MANs.

Networks by Topology

A **topology** is the geometric association of components of a network in relation to each other. The topology can be physical or logical. Physical topology describes how the network is cabled, while logical topology describes how the network functions. The dominant physical topologies are ring, bus, star, hierarchy, mesh, and hybrid. Figure 2-2 illustrates the physical topologies.

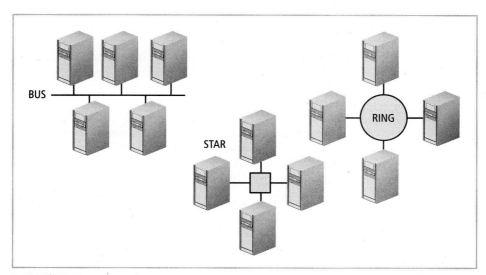

FIGURE 2-2 Physical Network Topologies

The dominant logical topologies are bus and star. A bus is simply a linear communication channel (for example a single long cable) with all associated nodes, while the star connects a central node to other nodes. A bus transmits messages from a single station or node at a time, with each node taking turns; messages can travel in both directions (in the case of a physical bus) or in one direction (in the case of a physical ring). In a star logical topology, each station or node transmits to the central node, which then retransmits the message to all attached nodes.

Networks by Media

Networks are also categorized by media type. Media typically fall into two categories—guided and unguided, also known as wired and wireless. Wired media networks typically use electricity or light waves over cables to transmit messages, while wireless media networks use radio or infrared electromagnetic energy to transmit messages. Media is covered in additional detail later in this chapter.

Network Standards

A number of organizations promote standardized components of data communications. Some seek to standardize the use of communications, while others work on standardizing the design of data communications technologies and protocols—that is, the rules for communications. Protocols that are widely accepted become standards. Some standards are formal, or de jure; these formal standards have been reviewed by a group of experts, and endorsed by a standards body. Other standards are informal, or de facto, and have simply been widely adopted without having been formally reviewed. The Internet standards such as TCP/IP are de facto standards, while Ethernet standards (IEEE 802.3) are de jure standards.

Among the agencies that work on data communications standards are the Internet Society (ISOC), the American National Standards Institute (ANSI), The International Telecommunication Union (ITU), the Institute of Electrical and Electronics Engineers (IEEE), the Telecommunications Industry Association, and the ISO is actually the International Organization for Standardization, despite the acronym.

Internet Society (ISOC)

The Internet Society seeks to formalize many of the standards used to facilitate the development of compatible technologies. ISOC was formed in 1992 with the mission "to assure the open development, evolution and use of the Internet for the benefit of all people throughout the world."[2] ISOC is the parent of a number of other organizations:

- Internet Engineering Task Force (IETF)
- Internet Research Task Force (IRTF)
- Internet Engineering Steering Group (IESG)
- Internet Architecture Board (IAB)

Internet Assigned Numbers Authority (IANA)

Originally part of the ISOC, the IANA is responsible for the coordination of domain names, IP addresses and protocols, and port assignments. In recent years, the IANA was transferred to the Internet Corporation for Assigned Names and Numbers (ICANN), an international nonprofit organization set up by the ISOC. It is closely monitored by the U.S. government and ICANN to ensure no inappropriate activities occur.

American National Standards Institute (ANSI)

The **American National Standards Institute (ANSI)** serves to reinforce the position of the U.S. government and industry while helping to ensure the safety and the health of consumers and ensuring environmental protection. The institute supervises the creation and use of thousands of standards and directives, which directly affect companies and government agencies in almost every sector of the economy. ANSI is also actively committed in the accrediting programs, which evaluate conformity to the standards. The mission of ANSI is to increase the total competitiveness of the businesses in the U.S. and the quality of life for its residents while supporting and facilitating standards and voluntary systems of evaluation.[3]

International Telecommunication Union (ITU)

The ITU is the principal agency of the United Nations for communication and information technologies. Acting as a focus for government interests and the private sector, ITU serves to help the world communicate in three critical sectors: radio communication, calibration, and development. ITU is based in Geneva, Switzerland, and its membership includes 191 Member States and more than 700 member organizations and associations.[4] Additional information on ITU can be found from their Web site at *www.itu.int.*

Institute of Electrical and Electronics Engineers (IEEE)

A nonprofit organization, IEEE is the world's principal trade association for the advancement of technology. IEEE is active in many industrial sectors including computers and telecommunications, electric power, and electronics. The members count on IEEE as an impartial source of information, resources, and engineering for both organizations and individual professionals. To stimulate an interest in the field of technology, IEEE is also active among students at universities around the world. IEEE has:

- More than 370,000 members, including more than 80,000 students, in more than 160 countries
- 319 sections in ten geographical areas of the world
- 1676 chapters which link local members with similar technical interests
- More than 1526 student organizations at universities in 80 countries
- 39 technically oriented companies and 5 councils representing a broad range of technical interests
- 132 publications
- More than 450 IEEE-related conferences every year
- More than 900 active standards with more than 400 being studied[5]

Telecommunications Industry Association (TIA)

TIA is a partnership among information, communications, and entertainment companies. TIA is active in the development of standards, and has a role in the development of both domestic and international policy.[6]

International Organization for Standardization (ISO)

ISO is the global leader in developing and publishing international standards. It is a network of the national standards bodies from among 157 countries with one member per country. The ISO is organized around a Central Secretariat in Geneva, Switzerland, used to coordinate activities across the system. The ISO is a nongovernmental organization that bridges the gap between the public and private sectors. Many of its member institutes are governmental structures within their own countries, while others have their roots in the private economy. Therefore, ISO often represents a consensus for solutions that meet the requirements of business and the broader needs of society.[7]

OSI Reference Model and Security

In 1982 the ISO and the International Telecommunication Union Standardization Sector (ITU-T) began working to develop a vendor-neutral, nonproprietary set of network standards, in an effort to establish a method of creating networking components that used common protocols. This effort was based on an Open Systems Interconnection basic reference model developed in 1977, which rapidly became the dominant method of teaching the functions of a network protocol. The OSI reference model allocates the functions of network communications into seven distinct layers, each layer with its own specific functions and protocols. Figure 2-3 provides an overview of the OSI reference model layers and functions.

OSI Model			
	Data Unit	**Layer**	**Function**
Host layers	Data	7. Application	Network process to application
		6. Presentation	Data representation and encryption
		5. Session	Interhost communication
	Segments	4. Transport	End-to-end connections and reliability (TCP)
Media layers	Packets	3. Network	Path determination and logical addressing (IP)
	Frames	2. Data Link	Physical addressing (MAC & LLC)
	Bits	1. Physical	Media, signal, and binary transmission

FIGURE 2-3 OSI Reference Model

As shown in Figure 2-4, the fundamental premise of the model is that information sent from one host is translated and encoded through the various layers, from the Application layer to the Physical layer. The Physical layer then initiates the transmission across the network to a receiver. The receiver then translates and decodes the message in the reverse order. The receiver interprets the information by processing each layer, thus providing a header with specific information on the function of that layer, and passes the data and header to the next level in turn.

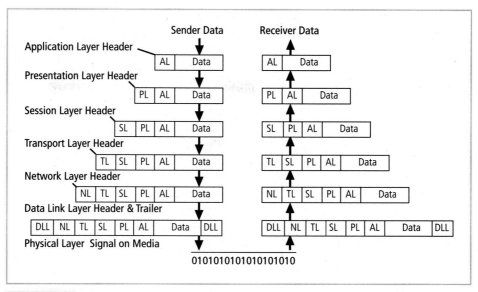

FIGURE 2-4 OSI Reference Model in Action

The Physical Layer

The primary function of the Physical layer is to <u>place the transmission signal carrying the message onto the communications media</u>—that is, to put <u>"bits on a wire."</u> The functions of the Physical layer are:

- Establish and terminate the physical and logical connection to the media
- Manage the flow and communication on the media
- Embed the message onto the signal carried across the physical media

Network Media

Network media can be guided—that is, wire and cables—or unguided—that is, wireless, microwave, and infrared. The dominant media types and standards are discussed in Table 2-1.

TABLE 2-1 Network Media

Type	Description	Comments
Coaxial Cable	One of the first LAN media. It consists of a solid core of copper surrounded by an insulating material, which is surrounded by a mesh of conducting copper fibers whose purpose is to absorb external noise that could interfere with the signal carried on the inner copper core (see Figure 2-5). The entire cable has a protective cover surrounding it.	Coaxial cable is a channel medium—it can only carry one message in one direction. It is widely used for cable television infrastructure to support residential cable modem-based high-speed Internet access.

TABLE 2-1   Network Media (continued)

Type	Description	Comments
Fiber-Optic Cable[8]	Essentially a tube with an ultra-pure glass or plastic core that carries light waves. As shown in Figure 2-6, there are a number of variants of fiber-optic cable. The simplest is single-mode, in which a single beam of light is transmitted down the length of cable. This provides data transmission rates of approximately 10 gigabits per second over distances of up to approximately 35 miles.	To send multiple simultaneous signals, networks use a multimode variant. Multimode transmission speeds are up to 100 Mbps for up to 2 miles, up to 1 Gbps for approximately 500 yards, and up to 10 Gbps for up to approximately 1/5 mile (300 yards).
Twisted Pair Wire	One of the most dominant cabling types in use today; consists of a number of colored wires twisted together to minimize the effect of external noise on the carried signal. There are two types of twisted pair wire—shielded twisted pair (STP), which today is rarely used, and unshielded twisted pair (UTP), which is inexpensive, easy to work with, and physically small compared to other options. UTP has no supplemental shielding, and because the twisting only provides minimal protection, the cable has a maximum effective limit of approximately 100 yards. Note that this distance is between end nodes—that is, the computer and the switch—and not between the computer and the wall outlet.	When installing networks in buildings under construction, it is most beneficial to install networks using physical cable like UTP. UTP is easy to work with, reliable, less subject to interception or eavesdropping, and relatively inexpensive.
Wireless LAN	The most common alternative when installing physical cable in existing buildings becomes too difficult and expensive. Wireless LANs (also called WLANs, or the brand name Wi-Fi) are thought by many in the IT industry to be inherently insecure. The radio transmissions used for the wireless network interface between computing devices and access points (APs) can be intercepted by any receiver within range. To prevent this, these networks must use some form of cryptographic security control.	The standard for wireless networks falls under IEEE 802.11—Wireless Local Area Networks (WLAN). There are three modern standards and a host of legacy systems operating: 802.11a, 802.11b, and 802.11g. While 802.11a was the first formal standard, it was hampered in development by regulation, and 802.11b became the first widely accepted standard. Most modern equipment is downwardly compatible, meaning a device designed to work in the 802.11g range will work on a lower-level network.

TABLE 2-1 Network Media (continued)

Type	Description	Comments
Wireless LAN (continued)	Wireless networks connect to an AP using wireless network interface cards (NICs). The AP provides the connection between the wireless network and the physical network. WLANs use one of three architectures—peer-to-peer (P2P), basic service set, or extended service set. As shown in Figure 2-7, a P2P WLAN works like its wired counterpart, with one client serving as the coordinating point for wireless access. All other clients connect via this coordinating client. The basic service set (BSS) works like a true LAN with a central AP serving as the hub or switch, with all clients connecting through it. An extended service set is a collection of connected APs that allow the client to roam between BSSs, much as a cellular phone customer roams throughout a geographic region without being disconnected.	
Bluetooth	A wireless technology not covered under the 802.11 standard. Bluetooth is a de facto industry standard for short-range wireless communications between devices—between wireless telephones and headsets, between PDAs and desktop computers, and between laptops. Established by Ericsson scientists, it was soon adopted by Intel, Nokia, and, Toshiba. Microsoft, Lucent Technologies, and 3Com joined the industry group shortly after its inception. Bluetooth wireless communications links can be exploited by anyone within the approximately 30-foot range, unless security controls are implemented. It is estimated that there will be almost a billion Bluetooth-enabled devices by 2010. In discoverable mode—which allows Bluetooth systems to detect and connect to one another—devices can easily be accessed, much as a folder is shared on a networked computer. In non-discoverable mode, a device is susceptible to access by other devices that have connected with it in the past.[9]	To secure Bluetooth-enabled devices you must: (1) turn off Bluetooth when you do not intend to use it and (2) refuse incoming communications pairing requests unless you know who the requestor is.

TABLE 2-1 Network Media (continued)

Type	Description	Comments
Infrared	A wireless technique for data connections between personal devices, like personal digital assistants (PDAs) and laptops. The Infrared Data Association (IrDA) defined several standards for short-range (typically less than 1 meter) infrared connections. This worked well for synchronizing personal computing equipment but is ineffective for networking due to its data rate (2.4 kbps to 16 Mbps) and its line of sight requirement.	Older IR LANs mounted central APs in the ceiling, but these were quickly replaced with 802.11 alternatives.

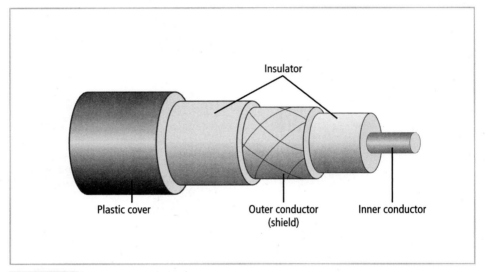

FIGURE 2-5 Coaxial Cable Structure

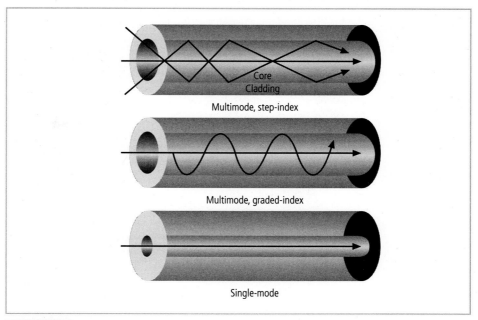

Core
Cladding

Multimode, step-index

Multimode, graded-index

Single-mode

FIGURE 2-6   Fiber-Optic Cable Modes

TABLE 2-2   WLAN Overview

Protocol	Release Date	Operational Frequency	Throughput (Type)	Data Rate (Max)	Range (Radius Indoor) Depends, # and type of walls	Range (Radius Outdoor) Loss includes one wall
Legacy	1997	2.4 GHz	0.9 Mbit/s	2 Mbit/s	~20 Meters	~100 Meters
802.11a	1999	5 GHz	23 Mbit/s	54 Mbit/s	~35 Meters	~120 Meters
802.11b	1999	2.4 GHz	4.3 Mbit/s	11 Mbit/s	~38 Meters	~140 Meters
802.11g	2003	2.4 GHz	19 Mbit/s	54 Mbit/s	~38 Meters	~140 Meters
802.11n	Sept. 2008 (est.)	2.4 GHz 5 GHz	74 Mbit/s	248 Mbit/s	~70 Meters	~250 Meters
802.11y	March 2008 (est.)	3.7 GHz	23 Mbit/s	54 Mbit/s	~50 Meters	~5000 Meters

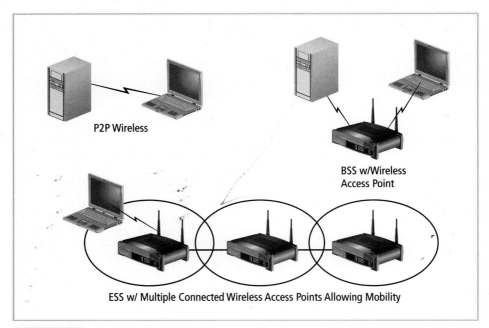

P2P Wireless

BSS w/Wireless Access Point

ESS w/ Multiple Connected Wireless Access Points Allowing Mobility

FIGURE 2-7 WLAN Architectures

Embedding the Message

The method used to embed the message on the signal depends on the type of message and type of signal. As shown in Figure 2-8, there are two types of message (or information). Analog information, such as voice communications, is a continuously varying source, while digital information, such as computer communications, is discrete, between a few values—in this case between 1s and 0s. Analog signals, such as those carried on the public phone network, use continuously varying waveforms, while discrete signals, such as those carried on computer networks, use discrete values in defined voltage levels.

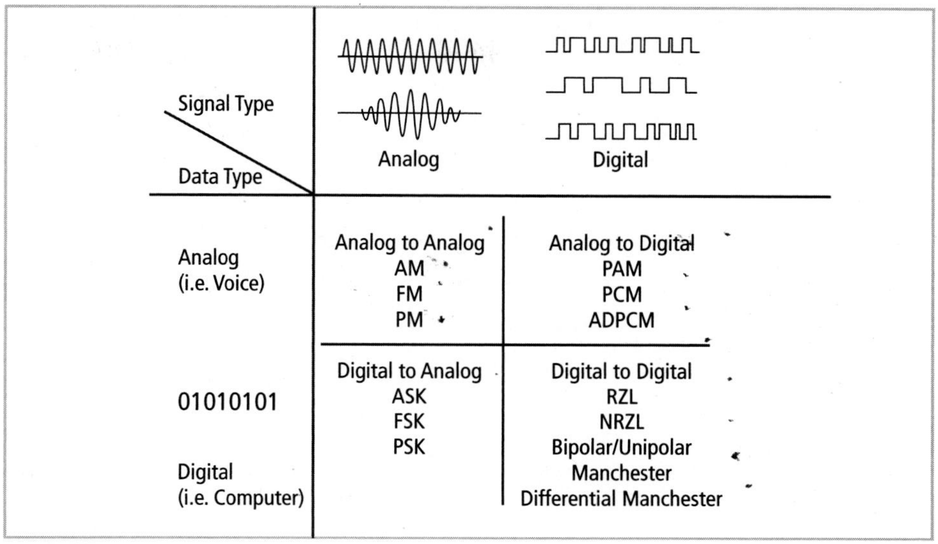

Signal Type → Data Type ↓	Analog	Digital
Analog (i.e. Voice)	Analog to Analog AM FM PM	Analog to Digital PAM PCM ADPCM
01010101 Digital (i.e. Computer)	Digital to Analog ASK FSK PSK	Digital to Digital RZL NRZL Bipolar/Unipolar Manchester Differential Manchester

FIGURE 2-8 Data and Signals

Multiplexing combines several circuits for a high-bandwidth stream to carry multiple signals long distances. The three dominant multiplexing methods are frequency division multiplexing (FDM), time division multiplexing (TDM), and wave division multiplexing (WDM). FDM is used in analog communications to combine voice channels, and works by temporarily shifting channels to higher frequencies, and then moving them back on the far end of the high-capacity connection, as illustrated in Figure 2-9. TDM, which is used in digital communications, assigns a time block to each client, and then polls each in turn to transmit a unit of information. Each station sends its information, which is recompiled into a cohesive data stream on the receiving end of the communication channel. If a station has no data to send, that time slot goes empty. A variant of TDM—statistical TDM—eliminates the dedicated time slots by adding header information to each packet, allowing any station with traffic to transmit on an as-needed basis. This is illustrated in Figure 2-9.

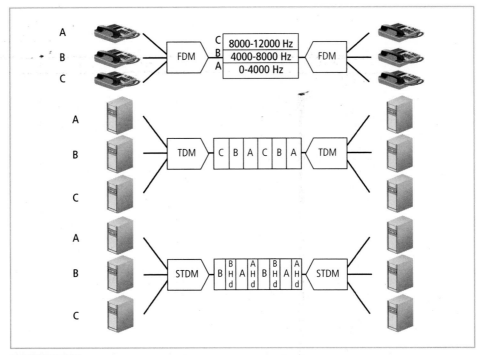

FIGURE 2-9   Multiplexing

WDM, used exclusively in fiber-optic communications, uses different frequencies (colors) of laser light to allow multiple signals to travel on the same fiber-optic cable. This is a derivative of FDM, but only applies to fiber-optic networks.

Managing Communication

Bit (or signal) flow down the media can be conducted in a number of ways. Simplex transmissions flow one way through a medium—this is how broadcast television and radio work. Half-duplex transmissions can flow either way, but in only one direction at a time, similar to a walkie-talkie radio. Full-duplex transmissions can flow both ways at the same time, like the telephone. Serial transmissions flow one bit at a time down a single communications channel, while parallel transmissions flow multiple bits at a time down multiple channels.

Protocols that support asynchronous (or timing-independent) data transmission formulate the data flow so that each byte or character has its own start and stop bit. This method was used in older modem-based data transfers and terminal emulation software to send individual characters between two systems.

Synchronous (or timing-dependent) data transmissions use computer clocking to transmit data in a continuous stream between the two systems. Computer clock synchronization makes it possible for end nodes to identify the start and end of the data flow. If the clocks become unsynchronized, errors can occur; however, this protocol is much more efficient in terms of the ratio of overhead bits to data bits.

Data Link Layer

The Data Link layer (DLL) is the primary networking support layer. It is sometimes referred to as the first "subnet" layer because it provides addressing, packetizing, media access control, error control, and some flow control for the local network. In LANs, it handles client-to-client and client-to-server communications. The DLL is further divided into two sublayers—the Logical Link Control (LLC) sublayer and the Media Access Control (MAC) sublayer. The LLC sublayer is primarily designed to support multiplexing and demultiplexing protocols transmitted over the MAC layer. It also provides flow control and error detection and retransmission. The MAC sublayer is designed to manage access to the communications media—in other words, to regulate which clients are allowed to transmit and when.

DLL Protocols

The dominant protocol for local area networking is Ethernet for wired networks and Wi-Fi for wireless networks. Other DLL LAN protocols include token ring, FDDI, PPP, PPTP, and L2TP. WANs typically use ATM and frame relay.

Ethernet.   Original versions of IEEE standard 802.3 Ethernet worked at 10Mbps, over coaxial cable and UTP. The subsequent iterations of Ethernet are shown in Table 2-3.

TABLE 2-3 Ethernet Variants

Ethernet Variant	Description
10Base2	10 Mbps baseband (not multiplex) Ethernet over thin coaxial cable (RG-58 or similar)
10Base5	10 Mbps Ethernet over thick coaxial cable (RG-8 or similar)
10BaseT	10 Mbps Ethernet over unshielded twisted pair (Cat5 or similar)
10BaseF	10 Mbps Ethernet over fiber-optic cable
100BaseTX	100 Mbps Ethernet over UTP (a.k.a. Fast Ethernet)
100BaseFX	100 Mbps Ethernet over fiber-optic cable
100BaseT4	100 Mbps Ethernet over low-grade UTP
1000BaseX	Generic Term for 1000 Mbps Ethernet (a.k.a. Gigabit Ethernet)
1000BaseSX	1000 Mbps Ethernet over multimode fiber-optic cable
1000BaseLX	1000 Mbps Ethernet over single-mode fiber-optic cable
1000BaseCX	1000 Mbps Ethernet over balanced copper cable (obsolete)
1000BaseT	1000 Mbps Ethernet over UTP

Most UTP installations have limits of 100 meters for the cables from the client to a powered repeater or switch.

For its MAC sublayer, Ethernet uses Carrier Sense Multiple Access with Collision Detection for its wired protocols, and Carrier Sense Multiple Access with Collision Avoidance for its wireless protocols; both are described later in this chapter.

Wireless Ethernet.   Standardized as IEEE 802.11, wireless communications use basically the same Ethernet functions as their wired counterparts. The primary difference between the two lies in the data rates obtainable, and the MAC methods employed. Note that the range estimates assume the use of standard receivers and antennas, and do not set a maximum range beyond which the signal cannot be intercepted by specialized receivers or antennas.

Token Ring.   Ratified as IEEE Standard 802.5, token ring networks use a logical ring topology and require stations to possess a token—essentially a data frame with no data—prior to being allowed to transmit data. In the logical ring, which could be implemented in a physical star with a standard hub (referred to as a MAU or multistation access unit) connected to clients with UTP, the token travels to and from each workstation in turn. Token ring lost the market battle to Ethernet, which is much cheaper, and today it is rarely used.

Fiber Distributed Data Interface (FDDI).   FDDI uses two counterdirectional fiber-optic loops to provide network connections over large areas—up to about 120 miles. The development of Fast Ethernet and Gigabit Ethernet, and their relatively inexpensive implementations, have made FDDI virtually obsolete.

Asynchronous Transfer Mode (ATM).   ATM is a wide area network packet-switching DLL protocol that uses fixed cell (frame) sizes of 53 bytes (48 bytes of data and 5 bytes of header information). Also known as cell relay, ATM is different from other protocols in that it is a connection-oriented DLL protocol, whereas some others, such as Ethernet, are connectionless. ATM provides support for virtual channels and virtual paths to expedite packet transmission. A virtual channel indicates that each cell has a similar identifier (VCI) guiding the cell through the network. The virtual channels may also share a common identifier indicating a virtual path (VPI). A virtual path is a grouping of virtual channels with common endpoints. A virtual path can be established between two systems, with the channels representing communications between systems.

ATM can be implemented in a LAN by means of LAN emulation (LANE). There are still many extant implementations of ATM, as its original 155-Mbps data rate has been upgraded to multi-gigabit speed. However, the development of Multi-Gigabit Ethernet and the low costs associated with Ethernet networks threaten ATM's future.

Frame Relay.   Frame relay is another wide area network protocol that is used to encapsulate voice and data between LANs. Unlike ATM, frame relay uses flexible-length frames and leaves error checking to the endpoints. Like ATM, frame relay uses static allocated virtual circuits for long-term point-to-point data delivery. Developments in Gigabit Ethernet also threaten the future of frame relay.

Point-to-Point Protocol (PPP), Point-to-Point Tunneling Protocol (PPTP) and Layer Two Tunneling Protocol (L2TP).   This set of DLL protocols are used most commonly for computer communications over dial-up telephone networks. DSL still uses PPP in its communication process to multiplex the data signal with the home voice channel. PPP replaced older protocols like the Serial Line Internet Protocol (SLIP), which had poor error-handling procedures. PPP over Ethernet (PPPOE) is the most common implementation today, although PPP over ATM is also used.

Forming Packets

The first responsibility of the DLL is converting the Network layer packet into a DLL frame. Unlike higher levels, the DLL adds not only a header component but also a trailer. When necessary the packet is fragmented into one or more frames, with corresponding information embedded into the frame header. As shown in Figure 2-10, the Ethernet II frame includes a preamble—the series 010101010 to indicate the start of a frame—

followed by a Start Frame Delimiter (SFD), the destination MAC address, the source MAC address, a specification of the type of Ethernet being used, the data payload, and the frame check sequence, which is a 32-bit cyclic redundancy check used in detecting errors in the frame.

| Preamble | SFD | DestinationMACAddress | SourceMACAddress | Eather Type | Payload | FCS |

FIGURE 2-10 Ethernet II Header

Addressing

Addressing at the Data Link layer is accomplished with a number embedded in the network interface card (NIC) by the manufacturer. This number, known as the MAC address, Ethernet hardware address, or simply hardware address, allows packets to be delivered to an endpoint. This 48-bit number is typically denoted in hexadecimal format (e.g., 00-00-A3-6A-B2-1A). The first three octets (or hex sets) are assigned by IEEE as part of their Organizationally Unique Identifier, or Company_id. The database of these addresses can be viewed at *http://standards.ieee.org*.

Media Access Control

One of the primary functions of the DLL is the control of the flow of traffic—that is, determining which station is allowed to transmit when. There are two general approaches to this task, control (or deterministic) and contention (stochastic).

There are a number of ways to implement the control approach. The first is a controlled network, wherein the client must request permission to transmit. In roll call polling, the central control unit, usually a server, polls a client to determine if it has traffic to transmit. If it does, it is then permitted to send that data. If not, the next client on the list is polled. In go-ahead polling, the first client on the list transmits data if it needs to, but if not, it notifies the next client that it may transmit data. Token passing rings and busses work on this principle, using the token as the control mechanism. Control approaches maintain a well-regulated network where traffic is transmitted in an orderly fashion, maintaining an optimal data rate. They also facilitate a priority system, in that key clients or servers can be polled more frequently than others. Token-based systems can also incorporate a priority set of bits that allows assignment of different classes, to facilitate the transmission of important and time-sensitive data, like video.

Clients wishing to transmit on a network using a contention approach simply listen to determine if the network is currently being used. If the channel is free, the station transmits. Because it is possible for more than one station to attempt to transmit at virtually the same time, contention approaches must have mechanisms to deal with the resulting event, which is referred to as a collision. Carrier Sense Multiple Access (CSMA) is the dominant contention mechanism. CSMA requires that each station listen to the media (Carrier Sense), and that all stations have equal access (Multiple Access). CSMA with collision detection (CSMA/CD) systems are set up so that if a collision is detected, both stations immediately emit a jamming signal to warn all other clients that a collision has occurred and must be resolved. How do clients know a collision has occurred? A client transmitting a specific voltage level on a wire receives a voltage spike when more voltage is detected than is being transmitted. When these stations recognize a collision, they begin the binary exponential back-off algorithm—beginning with one bit which has two values (zero or one), each client randomly selects a value and waits that amount of time in milliseconds, then attempts to retransmit. If the two clients choose the same value, they move to two bits (four values) and try again. The clients continue until they either are able to transmit or reach sixteen bits, at which time they give up and send an error message to their systems.

Collision avoidance differs from collision detection in that before a client transmits it sends a short "intent to transmit" message warning other clients not to transmit. The client then waits a short time to ensure that the channel is clear, and then transmits its message, and waits for acknowledgment of receipt.

Switches and Bridges

To connect networks at the Data Link layer, specific technologies are employed. While the hub connects networks at the Physical layer, connecting two networks with a hub results in one large network (or collision domain). Connecting them with a Layer 2 switch, which is capable of bridging, maintains separate collision domains. Bridging is the process of connecting networks with the same DLL protocols while maintaining the integrity of each network, and only passing messages that need to be transmitted between the two.

Network Layer

The Network layer is the primary layer for communications between networks. This layer has three key functions: packetizing, addressing, and routing.

Packetizing

The Network layer takes the segments sent from the transport layer and organizes them into one or more packets for transmission across a network.

Addressing

The Network layer uses a network-layer address to uniquely identify a destination across multiple networks. A typical address consists of multiple components: the network ID and the host ID, as shown in Figure 2-11. In TCP/IP the IP address is the network-layer address. As shown earlier in Figure 2-10, the IP address contains a source and destination IP address along with additional information on the packet.

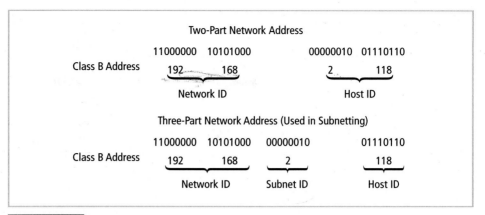

Two-Part Network Address

	11000000 10101000		00000010 01110110
Class B Address	192 ———— 168		2 118
	Network ID		Host ID

Three-Part Network Address (Used in Subnetting)

	11000000 10101000	00000010	01110110
Class B Address	192 168	2	118
	Network ID	Subnet ID	Host ID

FIGURE 2-11 Multipart Addresses

Addresses are maintained by the Internet Assigned Numbers Authority (IANA) and issued on an as-needed basis. In early years, these addresses were distributed as follows:

- Class A addresses consist of a primary octet (the netid) with three octets providing the host ID portion. This allows an organization to configure up to 16,777,214 hosts on their network. In practice, the final octet of an address of zero or 255 is not used. The eight binary zeros are used to represent the network address, and eight binary ones are used to represent a broadcast address.
- Class B addresses consist of two octets in the netid, with two octets providing 65534 host IDs.
- Class C addresses consist of three octets in the netid, with one octet providing 254 host IDs.
- Class D and Class E addresses are reserved.

TABLE 2-4 IP Address Classes

Class	Address Range	Supports
Class A	1.0.0.1 to 126.255.255.254	Approximately 16 million hosts on each of 127 networks
Class B	128.1.0.1 to 191.255.255.254	Approximately 65,000 hosts on each of 16,000 networks
Class C	192.0.1.1 to 223.255.254.254	254 hosts on each of 2 million networks
Class D	224.0.0.0 to 239.255.255.255	Reserved for multicast groups
Class E	240.0.0.0 to 254.255.255.254	Reserved

In practice this assignment method proves very inefficient. For example, a typical university was issued a Class B address, but may have at its peak only 4000–5000 devices needing a network address, which means that 61,000 or more addresses are not used. This is one reason that the Internet is moving to a new version of IP, IPv6, which uses a 128-bit address, instead of a 32-bit address. This substantially increases the number of available addresses (by a factor of 2^{128}). The "classful" method of assigning addresses shown in Table 2-4 is rather inflexible, because the size of the address blocks is determined by the "class" of the address. For example, a Class C address can only accommodate up to 254 hosts. If an organization needs 500 hosts, they need two Class C blocks, and thus two entries in all routing tables, and other supporting network infrastructure including Domain Name System, Mail Exchange addressing, and every other higher-order protocol. The solution to this problem is Classless Interdomain Routing (CIDR), wherein the netmask is specified rather than taken from the class of the address. For example, a normal Class C address would be specified as 192.168.16.0/24 in CIDR notation, which specifies that the network ID is the first 24 bits of the address. An organization that needs a block of 500 hosts might be assigned the CIDR address block 192.168.16.0/23. This "steals" one of the netmask bits of the Class C address and makes it part of the host address (more about the details of how this works in the subnet section). This allows the single CIDR address block 192.168.16.0/23 to actually refer to the two Class C network blocks 192.168.16.0 and 192.168.17.0 with a single network address.

Instead of assigning fixed addresses to each network entity, addresses can be assigned dynamically. Dynamic addressing assigns a pool of addresses to an address assignment server. When a system boots, it requests and receives an address and additional network configuration information, including the gateway address and the addresses of DNS servers. The advantages of this method are ease of administration and that it allows a large group of systems to use a smaller number of addresses. When a system shuts down, it returns the address to the pool, where it can be reused by another system.

Network Address Translation (NAT).   NAT, a network layer mechanism that helps systems manage addresses, uses a device like a router to segregate the external Internet from an internal intranet or network. The device is provided with the addresses assigned to the organization. The device then maps these addresses to different addresses inside the intranet. This provides security but can also maximize network address assignment when combined with Port Address Translation (PAT), which is mentioned later in this chapter. The internal addresses could be any address, but there are specific IP addresses reserved for use in private (non-routable) networking (RFC1918). These include:

- 10.0.0.0 — Class A networks
- 172.16.0.0 through 172.31.0.0 — Class B networks
- 192.168.0.0 — Class C networks

Routing

Routing is the process of moving a Network layer packet across multiple networks. The devices that connect networks are called routers. Routers work at the Network layer to receive packets and direct them toward their ultimate destination. The transmission links between routers work at the Data Link layer. In other words, the router has one or more types of Data Link layer protocols represented by an interface or network card. A router could have different types of Data Link protocols, as it receives the frame carrying the Network layer packet, and creates a new frame once it determines the outbound interface that represents the direction the packet needs to go. Routers accomplish this through the use of routing tables. A routing table contains information on destination addresses, outbound interfaces toward that address, and additional information such as the cost of using that route.

There are a number of categories of routing protocols. Static routing requires an administrator to manually enter the routing table information, while dynamic routing is accomplished by a router capable of updating its own table. Routers do this by transmitting their router tables to their neighbors and updating their own tables with the information they receive.

Internal Routing Protocols.   Internal routing protocols are used inside an autonomous system (AS). An AS is a system owned or managed by a single entity, and generally consisting of analogous technologies. The two dominant internal routing methods are distance-vector routing protocols and link-state routing protocols. Distance-vector protocols base their routing decisions on a simple determination of the number of hops between the router and the destination. A hop is one connection from router to router. The two dominant distance-vector protocols are the Routing Information Protocol (RIP) and the Interior Gateway Routing Protocol (IGRP). RIP is more widely used, although implementations are rapidly being replaced by link-state protocols. RIP routers originally transmitted their entire router tables every 30 seconds, resulting in a significant amount of network traffic. In order to manage the table sizes, RIP tables have a maximum hop count of 15. RIP has evolved through versions 1, 2 and next generation (ng).

Link-state protocols contain information about not only the distance to the destination but also about the states of the links, including traffic, throughput, and other components. The dominant link-state routing protocols are Open Shortest Path First (OSPF) and Intermediate System to Intermediate System (IS-IS). OSPF is superior to RIP in that the entire router table is not transmitted, only information on the immediate neighbor routers. OSPF also includes information on time to transmit and receive an update. Each neighbor router receives this information and then uses it to update its table, providing information on network traffic delays as well as being able to calculate hop counts. OSPF also doesn't broadcast routing information on a regular basis; instead, it selectively sends routing updates to select devices.

External Gateway Routing Protocols.   External routing protocols are used to communicate between ASs. They provide translation among different internal routing protocols. The dominant external routing protocol is the Border Gateway Protocol (BGP). When used as an Internal Gateway Protocol, it is referred to as IBGP, and when used externally, as EBGP.

Transport Layer

The primary function of the Transport layer is to provide reliable end-to-end transfer of data between user applications. While the lower layers focus on networking and connectivity, the upper layers, beginning with the Transport layer, focus on application-specific services. The Transport layer can also provide support for a virtual circuit, which is an extension of the connection-oriented model. In a connectionless model, individual segments (the term for packets at this level) are transmitted, each with its own addressing information. Individual segments may take different paths but end up at the same destination, where they are reassembled into the correct order. In a connection-oriented model, a connection is established between two points, and all communication occurs over that dedicated end-to-end connection. With virtual circuits, each segment has the path as well as the destination embedded into the packet, ensuring that the segment will follow the predesigned path, without the overhead of establishing an actual connection. The Transport layer is also responsible for end-to-end error control, flow control, and several other functions.

Error Control.   Error control is the process of handling problems with the transfer process, which might result in modified or corrupted segments. Error control is broken into two components, error detection and error correction. Errors typically comprise one of two formats. A single-bit error only affects a single bit—typically changing a 1 to a 0 or vice versa. Single-bit errors are easily detected. Multiple-bit errors are more complex in that they affect more than one bit, and even bits in more than one location in the segment. Bit errors are most likely the result of noise interference. Errors are detected through one of several common schemes:

- Repetition—Data is transmitted redundantly. Each block of data is repeated a predetermined number of times. Any errors may not affect each block and thus allow an error to be detected. This overly simplistic method is inefficient, and only catches basic errors.
- Parity—Additional bits are provided at the end of each byte of data; these additional "check bits" provide a measure of error detection. With odd parity, the sum of the values in a bit is expected to be odd. If they are, a zero is added to the block; if not, then a one is added, making the block sum odd. Similarly, with even parity the check bits are added to make the sum even.
- Redundancy—Parity is calculated for blocks of data rather than for an individual byte. Longitudinal redundancy checking (LRC) examines a long row of blocks, and then adds a byte of parity for the row. LRC is often used with vertical redundancy checking (VRC), which does the same task for a column of data. Placing the data into blocks and incorporating both LRC and VRC data makes it possible to detect even multi-bit errors easily. Cyclic redundancy checking (CRC) uses a long division computation, where the remainder becomes a block of data included with the segment. CRCs are often 16, 32, and 64 bits long. The receiver performs the same computation at its end, and if the remainder is different, then there is a problem with the segment, and a retransmission is requested.

For advanced error detection, especially at the message level, redundancy checking has given way to message authentication codes, where hash values of the entire message are appended onto the message.

Errors are most commonly corrected by retransmission of the damaged segment. The dominant error correction techniques are automatic repeat requests (ARQs). The three most common ARQs are Stop-And-Wait ARQ, Go-Back-N ARQ and Selective Repeat ARQ. Stop-And-Wait ARQ works on a 1-datagram (or packet) premise. For each segment transmitted there must be acknowledgment by the receiver before another segment is transmitted. This one-to-one operation is very slow and intensive. However, it is very reliable in that if an error is detected, the bad segment is requested for retransmission—most commonly by reacknowledging the last good segment received. Figure 2-12 illustrates the Stop-And-Wait ARQ.

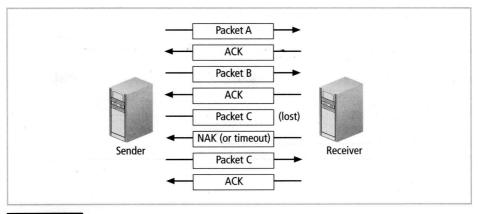

FIGURE 2-12 Stop-And-Wait ARQ

Go-Back-N ARQ requires that a number of packets be transmitted before an acknowledgment is received. The exact number—called the window size—is negotiated between the two stations, as part of the sliding window protocol described in the following section. Once the number of packets that is set by the window size is transmitted, an acknowledgment is received, and additional segments are transmitted. If an error is detected, then the recipient acknowledges the last good segment received before the error, and all segments after that point are retransmitted. While this is somewhat wasteful, in that all segments received since the bad segment are discarded, it is still much more efficient than Stop-And-Wait ARQ. Figure 2-13 illustrates the Go-Back-N ARQ.

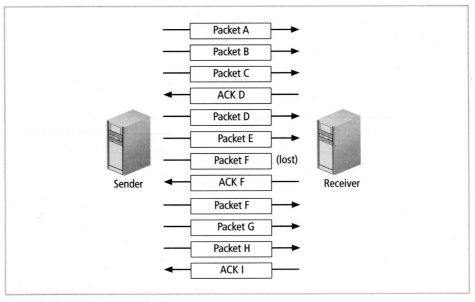

FIGURE 2-13 Go-Back-N ARQ

Selective Repeat ARQ only retransmits those segments that are determined to be bad. Figure 2-14 illustrates the Selective Repeat ARQ.

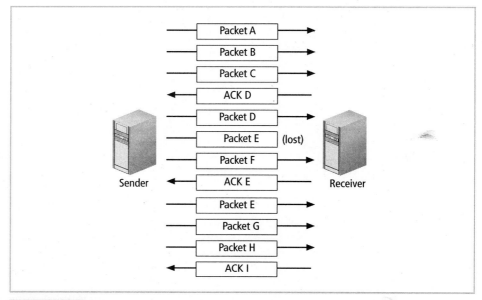

FIGURE 2-14   Selective Repeat ARQ

Flow Control.   Along with the error correction schemes, the Transport layer also provides for flow control for end-to-end transfers. The purpose of flow control is to prevent a receiver from being overwhelmed with segments preventing effective processing of each received segment. Some error correction techniques, like Stop-And-Wait ARQ, provide built-in flow control. Other techniques require some mechanism to regulate the traffic. The dominant technique for flow control is the sliding window protocol, which provides a mechanism by which a receiver can specify the number of segments (or number of bytes) it can receive before the sender must wait. In TCP this is implemented as a WIN value. A typical WIN value is 4096 (or 4K). If the sender and receiver are using a maximum segment size of 1K, then the sender could send 4 segments before waiting for permission to continue transmitting. As a receiver gains efficiency—possibly through the reduction in number of concurrent sessions, it can enlarge the window size. As the receiver gets overwhelmed with additional connection requests, it can reduce the window size, slowing down each connection. Figure 2-15 provides an illustration of the sliding window protocol process.

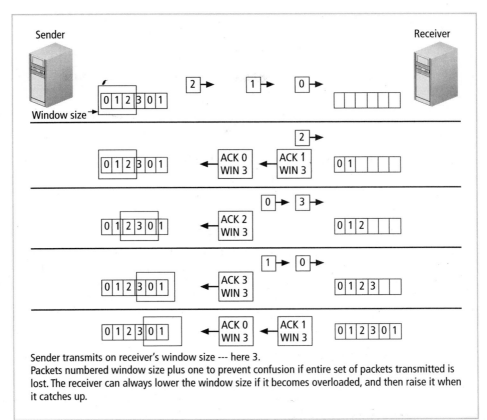

Sender transmits on receiver's window size --- here 3.
Packets numbered window size plus one to prevent confusion if entire set of packets transmitted is lost. The receiver can always lower the window size if it becomes overloaded, and then raise it when it catches up.

FIGURE 2-15 Sliding Window Protocol   *Port 80 HTTP*

Other functions.   The Transport layer is also responsible for the assignment of ports, which identify the service requested by the user. The combination of Network layer address and port is referred to as a socket. When a client wishes to establish a connection with a particular service, such as HTTP, it sends a connection request to the destination on well-known port address 80. This tells the receiving server, which may provide more than one type of service, which specific Application layer service is requested. The client system usually assigns a random port number outside of the well-known port range (that is, above 1023) as the source port of its socket, so that the response can find its way to the corresponding application. This socket combination allows an individual to open multiple versions of an application, such as multiple Web browsers. Similarly, this allows a home Internet user to have multiple systems working off a single dynamic IP address. The home router performs Port Address Translation, and assigns a unique socket to each client request, along with an internal IP address. Thus multiple users with multiple applications can request external services through a common source address.

Tunneling protocols also work at the Transport layer. These protocols work with Data Link layer protocols to provide secure connections. You learn more about tunneling later in this book.

ex: VPN

Session Layer

The Session layer is responsible for establishing, maintaining, and terminating communications sessions between two systems. It also regulates whether communications are preformed in a simplex (one way only), half-duplex (one way at a time), or full-duplex (bidirectional) mode. In other words, when one station wishes to request services from a server, it requests a session, much as a person dials a telephone. The dialing, ringing, and opening conversation ("Hello, may I speak with Mr. Smith?") are part of the establishment of a communications session. As data is transferred, the Session layer maintains the connection. Once both parties are finished communicating, the session is closed. In TCP/IP this is referred to as a half-close, because even though the client may have completed its data transfer, the server may still have data to transmit.

Presentation Layer

The Presentation layer is responsible for data translation and encryption functions. For example, if one system is using the standard ASCII (American Standard Code for Information Interchange) and another system is using EBCDIC (Extended Binary Coded Decimal Interchange Code), then the Presentation layer performs the translation. Encryption can also be part of this layer's operations. The Presentation layer also encapsulates the Application layer message prior to passing it down to the Transport layer.

Application Layer

At the Application layer, the user is provided with a number of services, perhaps most aptly called application protocols. The TCP/IP protocol suite includes applications such as e-mail (SMTP and POP), the World Wide Web (HTTP and HTTPS), file transfer (FTP and SFTP), and others. Table 2-5 provides a more comprehensive list of Application layer protocols and their uses.

TABLE 2-5   Common Application Layer Protocols

Protocol	Description
Bootstrap (BOOTP)	Used to assist a client in obtaining a network address on startup. Replaced by DHCP.
Dynamic Host Configuration (DHCP)	Used to obtain a client network address from a central pool of available addresses, as well as the subnet mask, the addresses of its gateway, and DNS servers.
Domain Name System (DNS)	Provides a translation between Application layer addresses or host names—HTTP Uniform Resource Locators (URLS)—and IP addresses. Serves as a look-up resource for the Internet.
File Transfer Protocol (FTP)	Transfers files from a server to a client and vice versa over the Internet. Also allows the user to move, modify, and delete these files.

TABLE 2-5   Common Application Layer Protocols (continued)

Protocol	Description
HyperText Transfer Protocol (HTTP) & Secure HTTP (HTTPS)	Retrieves and displays hypertext documents over the Internet. HTTP is the foundation of the World Wide Web, and is also frequently used for internal networks.
Internet Message Access Protocol, version 4 (IMAP, IMAP4)	Allows a client to access e-mail on a server.
Internet Relay Chat Protocol (IRCP)	Supports near-real-time chat support. Allows one-to-one communications between users.
Lightweight Directory Access Protocol (LDAP)	Supports the modification and querying of directory services.
Multipurpose Internet Mail Extensions (MIME) and Secure MIME (S/MIME)	Extends e-mail formats beyond basic text. Allows nontext attachments, non-ASCII character sets, and additional extensions to standard e-mail formats.
Post Office Protocol, version 3 (POP3)	Supports the retrieval of e-mail from an e-mail server. Most e-mail servers support both IMAP and POP.
Remote Login in UNIX Systems (RLOGIN)	Allows remote log on to a Unix system.
Server Message Block (SMB)	Supports the sharing of files and peripherals (printers, drives, directories, etc.) among clients on a network. Most commonly associated with Microsoft Windows systems under the name Microsoft Windows Network.
Simple Mail Transfer Protocol (SMTP), Extended SMTP (ESMTP)	Supports e-mail transfer across the Internet. Extended SMTP improves upon the base SMTP protocol to support the use of service extensions.
Simple Network Management Protocol (SNMP)	Specifies a dictionary of predefined service queries for network systems, used to determine network management issues. SNMP standard includes a Management Information Base (MIB), the database of queries; agents, remote utilities to collect information for the MIB; and a Network Management Station, a client system that serves to collect and present the information collected from the network systems.
Remote Desktop Protocol (RDP)	Enables remote operation of a system by transmitting keyboard, video, and mouse commands from a remote location.
Secure Shell (SSH)	Establishes a secure channel between two systems. Used heavily in electronic commerce. SSH uses public key encryption to support the establishment of this session.

TABLE 2-5   Common Application Layer Protocols (continued)

Protocol	Description
Terminal Emulation Protocol of TCP/IP (TELNET)	Allows terminal (command-line) access to other systems.
Trivial File Transfer Protocol (TFTP)	Provides simple FTP-like services. TFTP uses little memory, making it useful for networking devices like switches and routers.
Remote Directory Access Protocol (Whois)	Identifies the registrant (or owner) of an IP address or domain name.
Internet SCSI (iSCSI)	An Internet Protocol (IP)-based storage networking standard for linking data storage facilities by carrying SCSI commands over IP networks. It is used to facilitate data transfers over intranets and to manage storage over long distances.
Fibre[10] Channel over IP (FCIP)	An Internet Protocol (IP)-based storage networking technology, which enables the transmission of Fibre Channel (FC) information by tunneling data between storage area network (SAN) facilities over IP networks. This capacity facilitates data sharing over a geographically distributed enterprise. It is also known as Fibre Channel tunneling or storage tunneling.

The Internet and TCP/IP

The Internet incorporates millions of small, independent networks, connected by most of the major common carriers (AT&T, ITT, MCI, Sprint, etc.). Most of the services we associate with the Internet are based on Application layer protocols like e-mail, the Web, FTP, and instant messaging (IM). Because the subject of the Internet and the World Wide Web is so vast, this section will only provide a brief overview of the Internet and its primary protocols, TCP and IP.

In late 2007, Internet World Stats reported that 1.244 billion people were using the Internet. Writing in the *Harvard International Review*, philosopher N. J. Slabbert, a writer on policy issues for the Washington, D.C.-based Urban Land Institute, has asserted that the Internet is fast becoming a basic feature of global civilization, so that what has traditionally been called "civil society" is now becoming identical with information technology society, as defined by Internet use.[11]

The World Wide Web

It is important to distinguish the Internet from the World Wide Web (WWW). The Internet is a physical set of networks, while the Web is a set of applications that runs on top of the Internet. Specifically, the Web is a series of hyperlinked documents that allow simple creation and retrieval of information from a number of locations using Domain Name based Uniform Resource Identifiers (URIs). The ubiquitous Uniform Resource Locator, or URL, is the best-known type of URI. The Web was created in 1989 by Sir Tim Berners-Lee, while working at CERN in Geneva, Switzerland. Berners-Lee has since actively guided the development of many Web standards, including markup languages like HTML and XML.

The Web works via a Web browser (Mozilla, Firefox, Internet Explorer), an application that takes the requested information from the user or a Web resource, and presents it by integrating text, video, graphics, and sound through hyperlinks. The Web is used to access a document via a browser when the user seeks to find a specific Web page. DNS plays a key role in finding this information. First, the root-level Web servers provide information on the primary name server responsible for containing the information about the specific host containing the requested resource, including its IP address. Next, the primary name server points the browser to the IP address of the host, where the browser goes for the actual resource. By separating the resolution of the primary domain from that of the secondary and tertiary domains, significantly fewer changes are made to the root servers. Any changes beyond the assignment of the primary domain name are the responsibility of the primary (and secondary) name server. ISPs frequently provide this service for small networks. Many organizations may provide their own primary and secondary name services. Once a browser has visited a specific site, it can cache this information to facilitate subsequent visits.

TCP/IP

TCP/IP is actually a suite of protocols used to facilitate communications across the Internet. Developed before the OSI reference model, the TCP/IP suite is similar in concept, but different in detail, as shown in Table 2-6.

TABLE 2-6 TCP/IP Layers Compared to OSI Layers

	OSI Layers	Included Protocols		TCP/IP Layers
7	Application	SNMP TFTP	FTP Telnet	Application
6	Presentation	NFS	Finger	Application
5	Session	DNS BOOTP	SMTP POP	Application
4	Transport	UDP	TCP	Host-to-Host Transport
3	Network	IP		Internet
2	Data Link	Network Interface Cards		Network Interface
1	Physical	Transmission Media		Network Interface

The TCP/IP model is less formal than the OSI reference model. Each of the four layers of the TCP/IP model represents a section of one or more layers of the OSI model.

Application Layer

The TCP/IP Application layer consists of the utility protocols that provide value to the end user. Data from the users and use of these utilities are passed down to the Transport layer for processing, as shown in Figure 2-16.

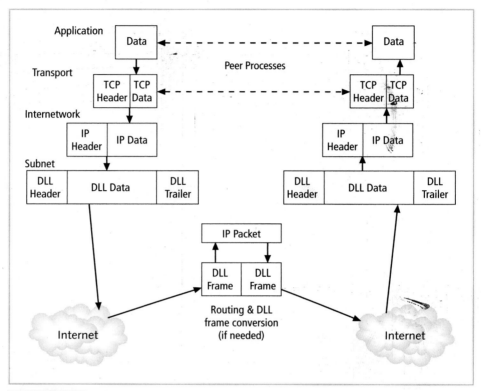

FIGURE 2-16   Application Layer Interconnection

There are a wide variety of Application layer protocols that support Internet users—SMTP and POP for e-mail, FTP for data transfer, and HTTP for the transfer of Web content. The Application layers on each host interact directly with corresponding applications on the other hosts to provide the requisite communications support.

Transport Layer

The Transport layer is responsible for the basic capacity of transferring messages, including resolution of errors, managing necessary fragmentation, and the control of message flow, regardless of the underlying network. At this layer, two basic message approaches are used: (1) a connection-oriented approach such as that implemented in the Transmission Control Protocol (TCP), or (2) a connectionless-oriented approach such as the one used in the User Datagram Protocol (UDP). The Transport layer can be considered literally as a mechanism of transport, perhaps like a delivery truck that takes on the responsibility for the delivery of its contents (goods) to the specified destination without risk, unless a higher or lower layer is responsible for that sure delivery. The Transport layer provides the service of connecting applications through the use of the ports, and the Transport layer is the lowest layer of the TCP/IP stack to offer any form of reliability.

TCP is a connected protocol that tackles many questions of reliability. It provides a reliable mechanism such that data packets will arrive in sequence, with a minimum level of errors, without redundancy, without loss, and able to handle congestion concerns found in networks.

UDP is a connectionless protocol. Like the IP, it is a best-effort or an unreliable protocol. UDP is typically employed for applications such as streaming media (audio, video, Voice over IP) where the on-time arrival is more important than reliability, or for simple query/response functions such as those found in DNS, where the overhead to install a reliable connection is disproportionately large.

Internetwork Layer

The Internetwork layer addresses the problem of moving packets in a single network. Examples of such protocols are X.25 and the ARPANET's Host/IMP Protocol. The Internet Protocol (IP) performs the basic task of moving packets of data from a source host to a destination host. IP carries data for many different upper-layer protocols.

Some of the protocols carried by IP, such as the Internet Control Management Protocol (ICMP) (which is used to transmit diagnostic information about IP transmission) and the Internet Group Management Protocol (IGMP) (which is used to manage IP Multicast data) function on top of IP but perform other Internetwork layer functions. This illustrates an incompatibility between the Internet model (and its implementation as the IP stack) and the OSI model. All routing protocols are also part of the network layer.[12] Discussions about the specifics on IP packets are provided in other chapters throughout the text.

Subnet Layers

The TCP/IP Subnet layers include the Data Link and Physical layers. TCP/IP relies on whatever native network subnet layers are present. If the user's network is Ethernet, then the IP packets are encapsulated into Ethernet frames. As such, TCP/IP provides no specification for the Data Link layer or Physical layer.

Chapter Summary

- Communication can only occur when the recipient is able to receive, process, and comprehend the message. This one-way flow of information is referred to as a channel. Any communications medium may be subject to various types of interference, which is commonly called noise.

- Data communications and networking go hand in hand. Data communications is the exchange of messages across a medium, and networking is the interconnection of groups or systems with the purpose of exchanging information. Networks come in a variety of types and can be characterized by size (LAN, MAN, WAN) or topology (bus, ring, star) or by other criteria.

- A number of organizations promote standardized components of data communications. Some standards are formal, or de jure; these formal standards have been reviewed by a group of experts, and endorsed by a standards body. Other standards are informal, or de facto, and have simply been widely adopted without having been formally reviewed.

- Among the agencies that work on data communications standards are the Internet Society (ISOC), the American National Standards Institute (ANSI), The International Telecommunications Union (ITU), the Institute of Electrical and Electronics Engineers (IEEE), the Telecommunications Industry Association, and the International Organization for Standardization (ISO).

- The OSI reference model is a vendor-neutral, nonproprietary set of network standards that was established to act as a method of creating networking components that used common protocols. The fundamental premise of the model is that information from one host is translated and encoded through the various layers, then sent to another host where the process is reversed. The seven layers are Physical, Data Link, Network, Transport, Sessions, Presentation, and Application.

- The Internet comprises millions of small, independent networks, connected by common carriers. Most of the services of the Internet are based on Application layer protocols like e-mail, the Web, FTP, and instant messaging (IM) which operate over the fundamental protocols of the Internet Protocol, the Transmission Control Protocol, and the User Datagram Protocol.

Review Questions

1. What are the two parties to any communication channel called?
2. What is interference in communications channels called?
3. List and describe the various types of noise.
4. What are the reasons to create a computer network?
5. What are the various ways in which networks can be categorized?
6. List and describe the various sizes of networks.
7. List and describe network physical topologies.
8. What is the ISOC? Name the organizations related to ISOC.
9. What is IANA? What role does it play in the operation of the Internet?
10. What is ANSI? How and why does it have influence and impact outside of the United States?
11. List and describe the various networking standards-setting organizations.
12. What is the OSI reference model?
13. List and describe the layers of the OSI reference model.
14. List and describe the various network media types.
15. What is Wi-Fi? List and describe the various Wi-Fi protocol standards.
16. What is multiplexing and when is it used? What are the various forms of multiplexing?
17. What is a packet? At which layer of the OSI reference model are packets formed?
18. What are the IP address classes? How many hosts can be addressed in each?
19. What is the World Wide Web? How is it the same or different from the Internet?
20. What is TCP/IP? What is it used for?

Exercises

1. Using an Internet search engine, look up "world Internet usage." What is the most recent estimate of worldwide Internet usage, and when was it assessed? What percentage of the world's population is using the Internet?

2. Using an Internet search engine, look up "Ethernet Standards." Read content from at least two of the resulting links and then answer these questions:
   a. Who invented Ethernet and when?
   b. What is the IEEE standard number for all Ethernet standards?
   c. What is the highest rated speed for Ethernet?

3. Using an Internet search engine, look up "Overview of the IETF." Read the page "IETF Overview" and then answer these questions:
   a. Where can you find the IETF mission statement?
   b. What is an IETF working group area? What working group areas are currently defined?

4. Using an Internet search engine, go to *www.protocols.com/protocols.htm*.
   a. What is your estimate of how many protocols are shown on this page?
   b. How many 'Families' of protocols are listed on the right side of the page?
   c. Select one of the protocol families that interests you. Now, select one of the protocols on that page. Identify the protocol you have chosen, and then describe the section headings for that protocol.

5. Using an Internet search engine, look up "PPP." After reading at least two pages about the Point-to-Point Protocol, define it in your own words.

6. Using an Internet search engine, look up "Network Access Control." After reading at least two pages from the search results, define NAC in your own words.

Case Exercises

Eliana waited for the student's reply.

He said, "Well, I've had some coursework in networking, and I've used networks a lot in several classes, including one on network defense. I wouldn't call myself a network expert, but I'm well-grounded in the theory and am willing to learn."

Eliana smiled back at the student's infectious grin and said, "Well, if you have the basic skills we need, we would make a competitive offer, and we are willing to train. It sounds like you might fit, so let me have a copy of your résumé."

Questions:

1. Do you think this student is a good choice for ATI in today's employment market?

2. How else could the student have explained his networking background to Eliana?

3. Did the student come across too strongly, bringing up salary from the beginning?

Endnotes

1. Forouzan, B. *Business Data Communications* © 2002 McGraw-Hill Professional.
2. *www.isoc.org/isoc*
3. *www.ansi.org/about_ansi/overview/overview.aspx?menuid=1*
4. *www.itu.int/net/home/index.aspx*
5. *www.ieee.org/web/aboutus/home/index.html*
6. *www.tiaonline.org/business/about/*
7. *www.iso.org/iso/about/discover-iso_meet-iso.htm*
8. Use of different frequency lasers and different types of cables, coupled with repeaters if necessary, can extend these ranges significantly.
9. Bialoglowy, M. "Bluetooth Security Review, Part I: Introduction to Bluetooth." Accessed 15 April, 2007, from www.securityfocus.com/infocus/1830.
10. Perhaps one of the most confusing things about fibre channel is the spelling "fibre." This was a deliberate decision during development of the protocol to clearly distinguish the fibre channel protocol from the fiber-optic media it commonly used.
11. *www.edchange.org/multicultural/quiz/quiz_key.pdf*
12. *http://en.wikipedia.org/wiki/TCP/IP_model*

Security Policies, Standards, and Planning

3

MATTHIAS WAS READY TO APPLY THE FIREWALL scripts to protect the servers belonging to ATI's clients. The *Linen Planet* had hired ATI to design, configure, and operate the network and defenses used to implement the electronic commerce startup's business plan. Matthias had a text file with more than 300 scripted instructions that had to be added to the firewall.

Since this change would affect the client's entire network, it was being tested in tonight's third-shift change-window, a time-slot during which network technicians could interrupt the normal operation of the network for a short time. Even though Matthias had only recently become involved in this project, it had been under development for several weeks, and the activities planned for tonight had been approved by the change control committees at *Linen Planet* and at ATI.

The plan was for Matthias to update the firewall command interface and be ready to commit the new rules at 2:30 AM. He had already made the connection and edited the file, and he was waiting to commit the new rules so the quality assurance testing team could spend an hour furiously testing the new configuration. At the first sign of a test failure, they would tell Matthias to back out the changes and reset the firewall to its original configuration.

He had a few minutes to wait, and Al sat down next to him to monitor the event.

Matthias said, "Hi Al. I have a question."

Al looked over his arm at the monitor to review Matthias's work. Seeing it was all in order and that the commit time was still a few minutes away, he said, "OK. Shoot."

Matthias pointed at the work order with the attached script of complex firewall rules and said, "Who writes these rules, and how do they know what the rules should do?"

Al looked at him and said, "One word—policy."

"Huh," said Matthias. "What does that mean?"

"Well," said Al, "Every company has a set of policies that let everyone know what they can and can't do with the company network. *Linen Planet* has an enterprise policy and a network usage policy that specify how they manage their network. Also, they have certain technical control systems in place, like intrusion detection systems that need to operate on their network. Our engineers take all of these factors into account and write rules that they hope will make it all work."

"Oh," said Matthias. "Well, it's time to commit these rules."

He pressed the Enter button on his keyboard.

LEARNING OBJECTIVES:

Upon completion of this material, you should be able to do the following:

- Define management's role in the development, maintenance, and enforcement of information security policy, standards, practices, procedures, and guidelines
- Describe an information security blueprint, identify its major components, and explain how it is used to support a network security program
- Discuss how an organization institutionalizes policies, standards, and practices using education, training, and awareness programs
- Explain contingency planning, and describe the relationships among incident response planning, disaster recovery planning, business continuity planning, and contingency planning

Introduction

In order to most effectively secure its network environment, an organization must establish a functional and well-designed information security program. Firewalls, network security, and intrusion detection systems can only succeed within the context of a well-planned and fully defined information security program. Uncoordinated security initiatives are seldom as effective as those that operate under a complete and effective policy environment. The creation of an information security program begins with the creation or review of the organization's information security policies, standards, and practices, followed by the selection or creation of information security architecture and a detailed information security blueprint. Without policy, blueprints, and planning, the organization will not be able to meet the information security needs of the various communities of interest. The role of planning in the modern organization is hard to overemphasize. All but the smallest organizations undertake at least some planning: strategic planning to manage the allocation of resources, and contingency planning to prepare for the uncertainties of the business environment.

Information Security Policy, Standards, and Practices

Management must make policies the basis for all information security planning, design, and deployment. Policies direct how issues are addressed and how technologies are used. Policies do not specify the proper operation of equipment or software—this information should be placed in the standards, procedures, and practices of users' manuals and systems documentation. In addition, *policy should never contradict law*, because this can create a significant liability for the organization.

Because information security is primarily a management problem, not a technical one, quality security programs begin and end with policy.[1] Policy obliges personnel to function in a manner that adds to the security of information assets, rather than threatening them. Security policies are the least expensive control to design and disseminate— they require only the time and effort of the management team—but the most difficult to implement *properly*. Even if the management team hires an outside consultant to assist in the development of policy, the costs are minimal compared to those of technical controls. However, shaping policy is difficult because policy must:

- Never conflict with laws
- Stand up in court, if challenged
- Be properly administered through dissemination and documented acceptance

For a policy to be considered effective and legally enforceable, it must meet the following criteria:

- Dissemination (distribution)—The organization must be able to demonstrate that the relevant policy has been made readily available for review by the employee. Common dissemination techniques include hard-copy and electronic distribution.

- Review (reading)—The organization must be able to demonstrate that it disseminated the document in an intelligible form, including versions for illiterate, non-English reading, and reading-impaired employees. Often organizations record versions of the policy in English and alternate languages.

- Comprehension (understanding)—The organization must be able to demonstrate that employees understood the requirements and content of the policy. Common techniques include quizzes and other assessments.

- Compliance (agreement)—The organization must be able to demonstrate that employees agree to comply with the policy, through act or affirmation. Common techniques include logon banners that require a specific action (mouse click or keystroke) to acknowledge agreement, or requiring employees to sign a document clearly indicating that they have read, understood, and agreed to comply with the policy.

- Uniform enforcement—The organization must be able to demonstrate that the policy has been uniformly enforced.

Definitions

Before examining the various types of information security policies, it is important to understand exactly what policy is and how it can and should be used.

A **policy** is a set of guidelines or instructions that an organization's senior management implements to regulate the activities of the members of the organization who make decisions, take actions, and perform other duties. Policies are organizational laws in that they dictate acceptable and unacceptable behavior within the organization. Like laws, policies define what is right and what is wrong, what the penalties are for violating policy, and what the appeal process is. **Standards**, though they have the same compliance requirement as policies, are more detailed descriptions of what must be done to comply with policy. The standards may be informal, or part of an organizational culture, as in **de facto standards**. Or standards may be published, scrutinized, and ratified by a group, as formal or **de jure standards**. Practices, procedures, and guidelines effectively explain how to comply with policy. Figure 3-1 shows policies as the force that drives standards, which in turn drive practices, procedures, and guidelines.

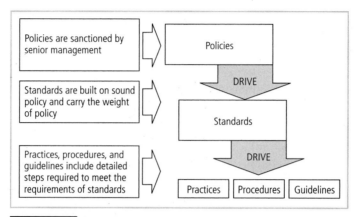

FIGURE 3-1 Policies, Standards, and Practices

Policies are put in place to support the organization's mission, vision, and strategic planning. The **mission** of an organization is a written statement of an organization's purpose. The **vision** of an organization is a written statement of the organization's long-term goals—where will the organization be in five years? In ten? **Strategic planning** is the process of moving the organization towards its vision.

The meaning of the term **security policy** depends on the context in which it is used. Governmental agencies discuss security policy in terms of national security and national policies to deal with foreign states. A security policy can also be a credit card agency's method of processing credit card numbers. In general, a security policy is a set of rules that protect an organization's assets. An **information security policy** provides rules for the protection of the information assets of the organization.

Management must define three types of security policies, according to The National Institute of Standards and Technology's Special Publication 800-14:

1. Enterprise information security policies
2. Issue-specific security policies
3. System-specific security policies

Each of these management policies is examined in greater detail in the sections that follow.

Enterprise Information Security Policy (EISP)

An **enterprise information security policy (EISP)** is also known as a general security policy, IT security policy, or information security policy. The EISP is based on and directly supports the mission, vision, and direction of the organization and sets the strategic direction, scope, and tone for all security efforts. The EISP is an executive-level document, usually drafted by, or in cooperation with, the chief information officer of the organization. This policy is usually two to ten pages long and shapes the philosophy of security in the IT environment. The EISP usually needs to be modified only when there is a change in the strategic direction of the organization.

The EISP guides the development, implementation, and management of the security program. It specifies the requirements to be met by the information security blueprint or framework. It defines the purpose, scope, constraints, and applicability of the security program in the organization. It also assigns responsibilities for the various areas of security, including systems administration, maintenance of the information security policies, and the practices and responsibilities of the users. Finally, it addresses legal compliance. According to the National Institute of Standards and Technology, the EISP typically addresses compliance in two areas:

(1) General compliance to ensure meeting the requirements to establish a program and the responsibilities assigned therein to various organizational components and (2) the use of specified penalties and disciplinary action.[2]

When the EISP has been developed, the CISO (chief information security officer) begins forming the security team and initiating the necessary changes to the information security program.

EISP Elements

Although the specifics of EISPs vary from organization to organization, most EISP documents should include the following elements:

- An overview of the corporate philosophy on security
- Information on the structure of the information security organization and individuals who fulfill the information security role
- Fully articulated security responsibilities that are shared by all members of the organization (employees, contractors, consultants, partners, and visitors)
- Fully articulated security responsibilities that are unique to each role within the organization

The components of a good EISP are shown in Table 3-1.[3]

TABLE 3-1 Components of the EISP

Component	Description
Statement of Purpose	Answers the question, "What is this policy for?" Provides a framework that helps the reader to understand the intent of the document. For example: "This document will:
	Identify the elements of a good security policy
	Explain the need for information security
	Specify the various categories of information security
	Identify the information security responsibilities and roles
	Identify appropriate levels of security through standards and guidelines
	This document establishes an overarching security policy and direction for our company. Individual departments are expected to establish standards, guidelines, and operating procedures that adhere to and reference this policy while addressing their specific and individual needs."[4]
Information Technology Security Elements	Defines information security. For example: "Protecting the confidentiality, integrity, and availability of information while in processing, transmission, and storage, through the use of policy, education and training, and technology…"
	This section can also lay out security definitions or philosophies to clarify the policy.
Need for Information Technology Security	Provides information on the importance of information security in the organization and the obligation (legal and ethical) to protect critical information about customers, employees, and markets.
Information Technology Security Responsibilities and Roles	Defines the organizational structure designed to support information security. Identifies categories of individuals with responsibility for information security (IT department, management, users) and their information security responsibilities, including maintenance of this document.
Reference to Other Information Technology Standards and Guidelines	Lists other standards that influence and are influenced by this policy document, perhaps including relevant laws (federal and state) and other policies.

Issue-Specific Security Policy (ISSP)

As an organization executes various technologies and processes to support routine operations, it must instruct employees on the proper use of those technologies and processes. In general, the **issue-specific security policy**, or **ISSP**, (1) addresses specific areas of technology as listed below, (2) requires frequent updates, and (3) contains a statement on the organization's position on a specific issue.[5] An ISSP may cover the following topics, among others:

- Use of company-owned networks and the Internet
- Use of telecommunications technologies (fax and phone)
- Use of electronic mail
- Specific minimum configurations of computers to defend against worms and viruses
- Prohibitions against hacking or testing organization security controls
- Home use of company-owned computer equipment
- Use of personal equipment on company networks
- Use of photocopy equipment

There are a number of approaches to creating and managing ISSPs within an organization. Three of the most common are to create the following types of ISSP documents:

1. Independent ISSP documents, each tailored to a specific issue
2. A single comprehensive ISSP document covering all issues
3. A modular ISSP document that unifies policy creation and administration, while maintaining each specific issue's requirements

The independent ISSP document typically has a scattershot effect. Each department responsible for a particular application of technology creates a policy governing its use, management, and control. This approach may fail to cover all of the necessary issues, and can lead to poor policy distribution, management, and enforcement.

The single comprehensive ISSP is centrally managed and controlled. With formal procedures for the management of ISSPs in place, the comprehensive policy approach establishes guidelines for issue coverage and clearly identifies processes for the dissemination, enforcement, and review of these guidelines. Usually, comprehensive ISSPs are developed by those responsible for managing the information technology resources. Unfortunately, they tend to overly generalize the issues and skip over vulnerabilities.

The optimal balance between the independent and comprehensive ISSP is the modular ISSP. It is also centrally managed and controlled but tailored to the individual technology issues. The modular approach provides a balance between issue orientation and policy management. The policies created via this approach comprise individual modules, each created and updated by individuals responsible for the issues addressed. These individuals report to a central policy administration group that incorporates specific issues into an overall comprehensive policy.

Table 3-2 shows an outline of a sample ISSP, which can be used as a model. An organization should add to this structure any security procedures not covered by these general guidelines.

TABLE 3-2   Components of an Effective Use Policy

1. Statement of policy
   a. Scope and applicability
   b. Definition of technology addressed
   c. Responsibilities

2. Authorized access and usage
   a. User access
   b. Fair and responsible use
   c. Protection of privacy

3. Prohibited usage
   a. Disruptive use or misuse
   b. Criminal use
   c. Offensive or harassing materials
   d. Copyrighted, licensed, or other intellectual property
   e. Other restrictions

4. Systems management
   a. Management of stored materials
   b. Employee monitoring
   c. Virus protection
   d. Physical security
   e. Encryption

5. Violations of policy
   a. Procedures for reporting violations
   b. Penalties for violations

6. Policy review and modification
   a. Scheduled review of policy and procedures for modification

7. Limitations of liability
   a. Statements of liability or disclaimers

The components of each of the major categories presented in the sample issue-specific policy shown in Table 3-2 are discussed below. Even though the details may vary from policy to policy and some sections of a modular policy may be combined, it is essential for management to address and complete each section.

Statement of Policy

The policy should begin with a clear statement of purpose. Consider a policy that covers the issue of fair and responsible use of the Internet. The introductory section of this policy should outline these topics: What is the scope of this policy? Who is responsible and accountable for policy implementation? What technologies and issues does it address?

Authorized Access and Usage

This section of the policy statement addresses *who* can use the technology governed by the policy, and *what* it can be used for. Remember that an organization's information systems are the exclusive property of the organization, and users have no general rights of use. Each technology and process is provided for business operations. Use for any other purpose constitutes misuse. This section defines "fair and responsible use" of the covered technology and other organizational assets, and should also address key legal issues, such as protection of personal information and privacy.

Prohibited Use

Unless a particular use of technology is clearly prohibited, the organization cannot penalize its employees for using it in that fashion. The following can be prohibited: personal use, disruptive use or misuse, criminal use, offensive or harassing materials, and infringement of copyrighted, licensed, or other intellectual property. An alternative approach collapses categories 2 and 3 of Table 3-2 into a single category—appropriate use. Many organizations use an ISSP titled "Appropriate Use" to cover both categories.

Systems Management

The systems management section of the ISSP policy statement focuses on users' relationships to systems management. Specific management rules include regulating the use of e-mail, the storage of materials, authorized monitoring of employees, and the physical and electronic scrutiny of e-mail and other electronic documents. It is important that all such responsibilities be designated to either the systems administrators or the users; otherwise, both parties may infer that the responsibility belongs to the other party.

Violations of Policy

Once guidelines on use have been outlined and responsibilities have been assigned, the policy must specify the penalties for, and repercussions of, policy violation. Violations should incur appropriate, not draconian, penalties. This section of the policy statement should specify the penalties for each category of violation as well as instructions on how individuals in the organization can report observed or suspected violations. Many people think that powerful individuals in the organization can discriminate, single out, or otherwise retaliate against someone who reports violations. Allowing anonymous submissions is often the only way to convince users to report the unauthorized activities of other, more influential employees.

Policy Review and Modification

Because a document is only useful if it is up to date, each policy should contain procedures and a timetable for periodic review. As the organization's needs and technologies change, so must the policies that govern their use. This section should specify a methodology for the review and modification of the policy, to ensure that users do not begin circumventing it as it grows obsolete.

Limitations of Liability

If an employee is caught conducting illegal activities with organizational equipment or assets, management does not want the organization held liable. The policy should state that the organization will not protect employees who violate a company policy or any law using company technologies, and that the company is not liable for such actions. It is understood that such violations are without the organization's knowledge or authorization.

System-Specific Policy (SysSP)

While issue-specific policies are written documents readily identifiable as policy, system-specific security policies (SysSPs) sometimes have a different look. SysSPs often function as standards or procedures to be used when configuring or maintaining systems. For example, a

SysSP might describe the configuration and operation of a network firewall. This document could include a statement of managerial intent; guidance to network engineers on the selection, configuration, and operation of firewalls; and an access control list that defines levels of access for each authorized user. SysSPs can be separated into two general groups, **managerial guidance** and **technical specifications**, or they can be combined into a single policy document.

Managerial Guidance SysSPs

A managerial guidance SysSP document is created by management to guide the implementation and configuration of technology as well as to regulate the behavior of people in the organization. For example, while the method for implementing a firewall belongs in the technical specifications SysSP, the firewall's configuration must follow guidelines established by management. An organization might not want its employees to have access to the Internet via the organization's network, for instance; in that case, the firewall would have to be implemented accordingly.

Firewalls are not the only technology that may require system-specific policies. Any system that affects the confidentiality, integrity, or availability of information must be assessed to evaluate the trade-off between improved security and restrictions.

System-specific policies can be developed at the same time as ISSPs, or they can be prepared in advance of their related ISSPs. Before management can craft a policy informing users what they can do with the technology and how they can accomplish this, it might be necessary for system administrators to configure and operate the system. Some organizations may prefer to develop ISSPs and SysSPs in tandem, so that operational procedures and user guidelines are created simultaneously.

Technical Specifications SysSPs

While a manager can work with a systems administrator to create managerial policy, the system administrator may in turn need to create a policy to implement the managerial policy. Each type of equipment requires its own set of policies to translate the managerial intent into an enforceable technical approach. For example, an ISSP may require that user passwords be changed quarterly; a systems administrator can implement a technical control within a specific application to enforce this policy. There are two general methods of implementing such technical controls: access control lists and configuration rules.

Access control lists (ACLs) consist of the user access lists, matrices, and capability tables that govern the rights and privileges of users. ACLs can control access to file storage systems, software components, or network communications devices. A **capability table** specifies which subjects and objects users or groups can access; in some systems, capability tables are called user profiles or user policies. These specifications frequently take the form of complex matrices, rather than simple lists or tables. The **access control matrix** includes a combination of tables and lists, such that organizational assets are listed along the column headers, while users are listed along the row headers. The resulting matrix contains ACLs in columns for a particular device or asset, while a row contains the capability table for a particular user.

Operating systems translate ACLs into sets of configurations that administrators use to control access to their systems. The level of detail may differ from system to system, but in general ACLs can restrict access for a particular user, computer, time, duration—even a particular file. This specificity provides powerful control to the administrator. In general ACLs regulate:

- *Who* can use the system
- *What* authorized users can access

- *When* authorized users can access the system
- *Where* authorized users can access the system from

The *who* of ACL access may be determined by a person's identity or by a person's membership in a group. Restricting *what* authorized users are permitted to access—whether by resource type (printers, files, communication devices, or applications), name, or location—is achieved by adjusting the resource privileges for a person or group to Read, Write, Create, Modify, Delete, Compare, or Copy. To control *when* access is allowed, some organizations implement time-of-day and/or day-of-week restrictions for some network or system resources. To control *where* resources can be accessed from, many network-connected assets block remote usage and also have some levels of access that are restricted to locally connected users. When these various ACL options are applied concurrently, the organization has the ability to govern how its resources can be used. The implementation of ACLs to manage firewalls is fully explored in other chapters of this book.

Configuration rule policies are the specific instructions entered into a security system, to regulate how it reacts to the data it receives. Rule-based policies are more specific to the operation of a system than ACLs are, and they may or may not deal with users directly. Many security systems, for example firewalls, intrusion detection systems (IDSs), and proxy servers, use specific configuration scripts that represent the configuration rule policy, to determine how the system handles each data element it processes.

Combination SysSPs

Many organizations create a single document that combines the management guidance SysSP and the technical specifications SysSP. While this document can be somewhat confusing to casual users, it is practical to have the guidance from both managerial and technical perspectives in a single place. If this approach is employed, care should be taken to clearly articulate the required actions. Some might consider this type of policy document a procedure, but it is actually a hybrid that combines policy with procedural guidance for the convenience of the implementers of the system being managed. This approach is successfully used by organizations that have multiple technical control systems of different types, and by smaller organizations that are seeking to document policy and procedure in a compact format.

Policy Management

Policies are living documents that must be managed and nurtured. It is unacceptable to create such an important set of documents and then shelve them. These documents must be properly disseminated (distributed, read, understood, and agreed to) and managed. How they are managed relates directly to the policy management section of the issue-specific policy described earlier. Good management practices for policy development and maintenance make for a more resilient organization. For example, all policies, including security policies, undergo tremendous stress when corporate mergers and divestitures occur; in such situations employees are faced with uncertainty and many distractions. System vulnerabilities can arise if, for instance, incongruous security policies are implemented in different parts of a new, merged organization. When two companies merge but retain separate policies, the difficulty of implementing security controls increases. Likewise, when one company with unified policies splits in two, each new company may require different policies.

To remain viable, security policies must have one or more responsible individuals assigned to manage them, a schedule of reviews, a method for making recommendations for reviews, and a policy issuance and revision date. Each of these is examined in additional detail below.

Responsible Individual

Just as information systems and information security projects must have champions and managers, so must policies. The policy champion and manager is called the **policy administrator**. Typically the policy administrator is a mid-level staff member and is responsible for the creation, revision, distribution, and storage of the policy. Note that the policy administrator position does not necessarily require technical expertise. While practicing information security professionals require extensive technical knowledge; policy management and policy administration require only a moderate technical background. It is good practice, however, for policy administrators to solicit input both from the technically adept information security experts and from the business-focused managers in each community of interest when making revisions to security policies. The administrator should also notify all affected members of the organization when the policy is modified.

It is disheartening when a policy that required hundreds of staff-hours to develop and document is ignored. Thus, someone must be responsible for placing the policy and all subsequent revisions into the hands of those who are accountable for its implementation. The policy administrator must be clearly identified on the policy document as the primary point of contact for additional information or for revision suggestions to the policy.

Schedule of Reviews

Policies can only retain their effectiveness in a changing environment if they are periodically reviewed for currency and accuracy and modified accordingly. Out-of-date policies can become liabilities, as outdated rules are enforced (or not), and new requirements are ignored. In order to demonstrate due diligence, an organization must demonstrate that it is actively trying to meet the requirements of the market in which it operates. This applies to both public (government, academic, and nonprofit) and private (commercial and for-profit) organizations. A properly organized schedule of reviews should be defined and published as part of the document. Typically a policy should be reviewed at least annually to ensure that it is still an effective control.

Review Procedures and Practices

To facilitate policy reviews, the policy manager should implement a mechanism to enable people to make recommendations for revisions. Recommendation methods can involve e-mail, office mail, and an anonymous drop box. If the policy is controversial, the policy administrator may feel that anonymous submission of information is the best way to solicit staff opinions. Many employees are intimidated by management and hesitate to voice honest opinions about a policy unless they can do so anonymously. Once the policy has come up for review, all comments should be examined, and management-approved improvements should be implemented. Additional review methods can include representative users in the revision process and solicit direct comment on the revision of the policy. In reality, most policies are drafted by a single, responsible individual and then reviewed by a higher-level manager. But even this method should not preclude the collection and review of employee input.

Policy and Revision Date

The simple act of dating the policy is often skipped. When policies are published without dates, confusion can arise. If policies are not reviewed and kept current, or if members of the organization are following undated versions, disastrous results and legal headaches can ensue. These problems are particularly common in high-turnover environments. It is therefore important that the policy contain the date of origin, along with the date(s) of any revisions. Some policies may also need a **sunset clause**, which provides an expiration date—particularly in policies that govern information use in short-term business associations or in agencies that become involved with the organization. Establishing a policy end date prevents a temporary policy from mistakenly becoming permanent, and it also enables an organization to gain experience with a given policy before adopting it permanently.

Automated Policy Management

Recent years have seen the emergence of a new category of software for managing information security policies. This type of software was developed in response to needs articulated by information security practitioners. While there have been many software products that meet the need for a specific technical control, there is now software that meets the need for automating some of the busywork of policy management. Automation can streamline the process of writing policy, tracking the workflow of policy approvals, publishing policy once it is written and approved, and tracking policy distribution and compliance agreement. Using techniques from computer-based training and testing, organizations can train staff members and also improve the organization's awareness program. Once an organization has developed its information security policies and standards, the information security community can begin developing the blueprint for the information security program. If one or more components of policies, standards, or practices are incomplete, management must determine whether or not to nonetheless proceed with the development of the blueprint.

Frameworks and Industry Standards

After the information security team has inventoried the organization's information assets and assessed and prioritized the threats to those assets, it must conduct a series of risk assessments using quantitative or qualitative analyses, as well as feasibility studies and cost-benefit analyses. These assessments, which include determining each asset's current protection level, are used to decide whether or not to proceed with any given control. Armed with a general idea of the vulnerabilities in the information technology systems, the security team develops a design blueprint for security, which is used to implement the security program.

This **security blueprint** is the basis for the design, selection, and implementation of all security program elements, including policy implementation, ongoing policy management, risk management programs, education and training programs, technological controls, and maintenance of the security program. The security blueprint, built on top of the organization's information security policies, is a scalable, upgradable, comprehensive plan to meet the organization's current and future information security needs. It is a detailed version of the **security framework**, which is an outline of the overall information security strategy and a roadmap for planned changes to the organization's information security environment. The blueprint specifies the tasks in the order in which they are to be accomplished.

To select a methodology by which to develop an information security blueprint, you can adapt or adopt a published information security model or framework. This framework can be an outline of steps to take to design and implement information security in the organization. There are a number of published information security frameworks, including ones from government sources, which are presented later in this chapter. Because each information security environment is unique, the security team may need to modify or adapt pieces from several frameworks; what works well for one organization may not precisely fit another.

The ISO 27000 Series

One of the most widely referenced security models is the *Information Technology—Code of Practice for Information Security Management*, which was originally published as British Standard BS7799. In 2000, this Code of Practice was adopted as an international standard framework for information security by the International Organization for Standardization (ISO) and the International Electrotechnical Commission (IEC) as ISO/IEC 17799. The document was revised in 2005 (becoming ISO 17799:2005), and it was renamed ISO 27002 in 2007, to align it with the document ISO 27001, discussed later in this chapter. While the details of ISO/IEC 27002 are available to those who purchase the standard, its structure and general organization are well known. For a summary description, see Table 3-3. For more details on ISO/IEC Sections, see *www.praxiom.com/iso-17799-2005.htm*.

TABLE 3-3   The Sections of the ISO/IEC 27002[6]

1.	Risk Assessment and Treatment
2.	Security Policy
3.	Organization of Information Security
4.	Asset Management
5.	Human Resource Security
6.	Physical and Environmental Security
7.	Communications and Operations
8.	Access Control
9.	Information Systems Acquisition, Development and Maintenance
10.	Information Security Incident Management
11.	Business Continuity Management
12.	Compliance

The stated purpose of ISO/IEC 27002 is to "give recommendations for information security management for use by those who are responsible for initiating, implementing, or maintaining security in their organization. It is intended to provide a common basis for developing organizational security standards and effective security management practice and to provide confidence in inter-organizational dealings."[7] Where ISO/IEC 27002 offers a broad overview of the various areas of security, providing information on 127 controls over ten broad areas, ISO/IEC 27001 provides information on how to implement ISO/IEC 27002 and how to set up an information security management system (ISMS). The overall methodology for this process and its major steps are presented in Figure 3-2.

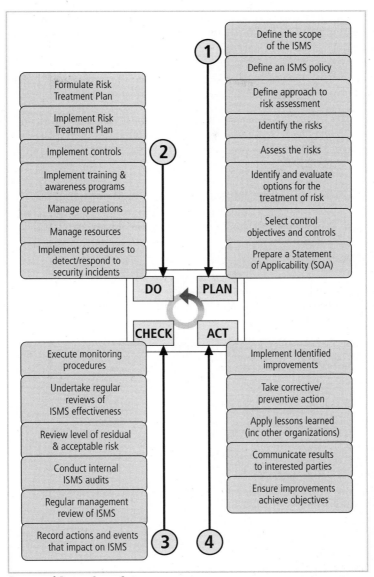

Courtesy of Gamma Secure Systems

FIGURE 3-2   BS7799:2 Major Process Steps[8]

In the United Kingdom, correct implementation of these standards (both volumes), as determined by a BS7799 certified evaluator, allows organizations to obtain system (ISMS) certification and accreditation. When the standard first came out, several countries including the United States, Germany, and Japan refused to adopt it, on the grounds that there are several fundamental problems, including:

- The global information security community has not defined any justification for a code of practice as was identified in the ISO/IEC 17799.

- ISO/IEC 17799 lacked "the necessary measurement precision of a technical standard."[9]
- There is no reason to believe that ISO/IEC 17799 was more useful than any other approach.
- ISO/IEC 17799 was not as complete as other frameworks.
- ISO/IEC 17799 was hurriedly prepared given the tremendous impact its adoption could have on industry information security controls.[10]

ISO/IEC 27002 is an interesting framework for information security, but aside from those relatively few U.S. organizations that operate in the European Union (or are otherwise obliged to meet its terms), most U.S. organizations are not expected to comply with this standard.

ISO/IEC 27001:2005: The Information Security Management System

ISO/IEC 27001 provides implementation details using a Plan-Do-Check-Act cycle, as described in Table 3-4 and shown in Figure 3-3 in abbreviated form:

TABLE 3-4   The ISO/IEC 27001:2005 Plan-Do-Check-Act Cycle

Plan:

1.	Define the scope of the ISMS.
2.	Define an ISMS policy.
3.	Define the approach to risk assessment.
4.	Identify the risks.
5.	Assess the risks.
6.	Identify and evaluate options for the treatment of risk.
7.	Select control objectives and controls.
8.	Prepare a Statement of Applicability (SOA).

Do:

9.	Formulate a Risk Treatment Plan.
10.	Implement the Risk Treatment Plan.
11.	Implement controls.
12.	Implement training and awareness programs.
13.	Manage operations.
14.	Manage resources.
15.	Implement procedures to detect and respond to security incidents.

TABLE 3-4   The ISO/IEC 27001:2005 Plan-Do-Check-Act Cycle (continued)

Check:

16.	Execute monitoring procedures.
17.	Undertake regular reviews of ISMS effectiveness.
18.	Review the level of residual and acceptable risk.
19.	Conduct internal ISMS audits.
20.	Undertake regular management review of the ISMS.
21.	Record actions and events that impact an ISMS.

Act:

22.	Implement identified improvements.
23.	Take corrective or preventive action.
24.	Apply lessons learned.
25.	Communicate results to interested parties.
26.	Ensure improvements achieve objectives.[11]

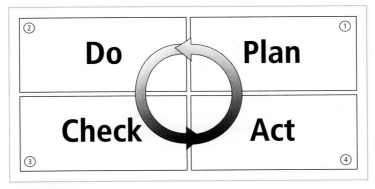

FIGURE 3-3   BS7799:2 —Plan-Do-Check-Act

Although ISO/IEC 27001 provides some implementation information, it simply specifies *what* must be done—not *how* to do it. As noted by Gamma Secure Systems, "The standard has an appendix that gives guidance on the use of the standard, in particular to expand on the Plan-Do-Check-Act concept. It is important to realize that there will be many Plan-Do-Check-Act cycles within a single ISMS all operating asynchronously at different speeds." [12]

As stated earlier, ISO/IEC 27001's primary purpose is to enable organizations that adopt it to obtain certification, and thus serves better as an assessment tool than an implementation framework.

In 2007, the International Organization for Standardization announced the plans for the numbering of current and forthcoming standards related to information security issues and topics, as shown in table 3-5.

TABLE 3-5 ISO 27000 Series Current and Planned Standards

ISO 27000 Series Standard	Status	Title or Topic	Comment
27000	Planned	Series Overview and Terminology	Typically when ISO releases a series of standards, the first defines series terminology and vocabulary.
27001	2005	Information Security Management System Specification	Drawn from BS 7799:2.
27002	2007	Code of Practice for Information Security Management	Was renamed from ISO/IEC 17799, drawn from BS 7799:1.
27003	Planned	Information Security Management Systems Implementation Guidelines	Expected 2008.
27004	Planned	Information Security Measurements and Metrics	Expected 2008.
27005	Planned	ISMS Risk Management	Expected in 2008 or later.
27006	2007	Requirements for Bodies Providing Audit and Certification of an ISMS	Is largely intended to support the accreditation of certification bodies providing ISMS certification.

NIST Security Models

Another possible approach is described in documents available from the Computer Security Resource Center of the National Institute for Standards and Technology (*csrc.nist.gov*). Because the NIST documents are publicly available, free, and have been available for some time, they have been broadly reviewed by government and industry professionals, and were among the references cited by the federal government when it decided not to select the ISO/IEC 17799 standards. The following NIST documents can assist in the design of a security framework:

- SP 800-12: *An Introduction to Computer Security: The NIST Handbook*
- SP 800-14: *Generally Accepted Principles and Practices for Securing Information Technology Systems*
- SP 800-18 Rev. 1: *Guide for Developing Security Plans for Federal Information Systems*
- SP 800-26: *Security Self-Assessment Guide for Information Technology Systems*
- SP 800-30: *Risk Management Guide for Information Technology Systems*

NIST Special Publication SP 800-12

SP 800-12, *An Introduction to Computer Security: The NIST Handbook*, is an excellent reference and guide for the security manager or administrator in the routine management of information security. It provides little guidance, however, on design and implementation of new security systems, and therefore should be used only as a precursor to understanding an information security blueprint.

NIST Special Publication 800-14

Generally Accepted Principles and Practices for Securing Information Technology Systems provides best practices and security principles that can direct the security team in the development of a security blueprint. In addition to detailing security best practices across the spectrum of security areas, it provides philosophical principles that the security team should integrate into the entire information security process. The document can guide the development of the security framework and should be combined with other NIST publications providing the necessary structure to the entire security process.

NIST Special Publication 800-18 Rev. 1

The *Guide for Developing Security Plans for Federal Information Systems* can be used as the foundation for a comprehensive security blueprint and framework. This publication provides detailed methods for assessing, designing, and implementing controls and plans for applications of varying size. SP 800-18 Rev. 1 can serve as a useful guide to the information security planning process. It also includes templates for major application security plans. As with any publication of this scope and magnitude, SP 800-18 Rev. 1 must be customized to fit the particular needs of an organization.

IETF Security Architecture

The Security Area Working Group acts as an advisory board for the protocols and areas developed and promoted by the Internet Society and the Internet Engineering Task Force (IETF), and while the group endorses no specific information security architecture, one of its requests for comment (RFC), RFC 2196: *Site Security Handbook*, offers a good discussion of important security issues. RFC 2196: *Site Security Handbook* covers five basic areas of security with detailed discussions on development and implementation. There are also chapters on such important topics as security policies, security technical architecture, security services, and security incident handling.

Benchmarking and Best Business Practices

Benchmarking and best practices are reliable methods used by some organizations to assess security practices. Benchmarking and best practices don't provide a complete methodology for the design and implementation of all the practices needed by an organization; however, it is possible to put together the desired outcome of the security process, and to work backwards toward an effective design. The Federal Agency Security Practices (FASP) site, *fasp.nist.gov*, is a popular place to look up best practices. FASP is designed to provide best practices for public agencies, but these practices can be adapted easily to private institutions. The documents found in this site include specific examples of key policies and planning documents, implementation strategies for key technologies, and position descriptions for key security personnel. Of particular value is the section on program management, which includes:

- A summary guide: public law, executive orders, and policy documents
- Position description for computer system security officer
- Position description for information security officer
- Position description for computer specialist

- Sample of an information technology (IT) security staffing plan for a large service application (LSA)
- Sample of information technology (IT) security program policy
- Security handbook and standard operating procedures
- Telecommuting and mobile computer security policy

In the later stages of information security blueprint creation, these policy documents are particularly useful.

A number of other public and semipublic institutions provide information on best practices. One of these groups is the EDUCAUSE Computer and Network Security Task Force (*http://www.educause.edu/content.asp?SECTION_ID=30*), which is a non-profit group that provides resources for higher education. This group focuses on the impact of Internet security in higher education, but provides valuable resources for any organization that uses the Internet, including many recommendations for security implementations. Another widely referenced source is the Computer Emergency Response Team Coordination Center (CERT/CC) at Carnegie Mellon University (*www.cert.org*). CERT/CC provides detailed and specific assistance on how to implement a sound security methodology.

Professional societies often provide information on best practices to their members. The Technology Managers Forum (*www.techforum.com*) has an annual best practice award in a number of areas, including information security. The Information Security Forum (*www.isfsecuritystandard.com*) has a free publication titled "Standard of Good Practice." This publication outlines information security best practices.

Many organizations hold seminars and classes on best practices for implementing security; in particular the ISACA (*www.isaca.org*) hosts regular seminars. The International Association of Professional Security Consultants (*www.iapsc.org*) has a listing of best practices, as does the Open Grid Forum (*www.ogf.org*). At a minimum, information security professionals can peruse Web portals for posted security best practices. There are several free portals dedicated to security that have collections of best practices, such as SearchSecurity.com, and NIST's Computer Resources Center. These are but a few of the many public and private organizations that promote solid best security practices. Investing a few hours searching the Web reveals dozens of locations for additional information.

Security Architecture

To further the discussion of information security program architecture and to illustrate industry best practices, the following sections outline a few key security architectural components. Many of these components are examined in detail in later chapters, but an overview is provided here.

Spheres of Security

The spheres of security, shown in Figure 3-4, are the foundation of the security framework. Generally speaking, the spheres of security illustrate how information is under attack from a variety of sources. The sphere of use, on the left-hand side of Figure 3-4, illustrates the ways in which people access information; for example, people read hard copies of documents, and can also access information through systems. Information, as the most important asset in this model, is at the center of the sphere. Information is always at risk from the people and computer systems that have access to it. Networks and the Internet represent indirect threats, because a person attempting to access information from the Internet must first go through the local networks and then access systems that contain the information. The sphere of protection, on the right-hand side of Figure 3-4, illustrates that between each layer of the sphere of use there must exist a layer of protection to prevent access to the inner layer from the outer layer. Each shaded band is a layer of protection and control. For example, the items labeled "Policy & law" and "Education & training" are located between people and the information. Controls are also implemented between systems and the information, between networks and the computer systems, and between the Internet and internal networks. This reinforces the concept of defense in depth. As illustrated in the sphere of protection, a variety of controls can be used to protect the information. The items of control shown in the figure are not intended to be comprehensive, but illustrate individual safeguards that can protect the various systems that are located closer to the center of the sphere. However, because people can directly access each ring as well as the information at the core of the model, the side of the sphere of protection that attempts to control access by relying on people requires a different approach to security than the side that uses technology. The members of the organization must become a safeguard that is effectively trained, implemented, and maintained, or they too represent a threat to the information.

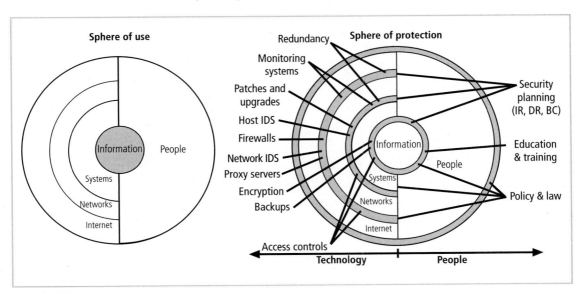

FIGURE 3-4   Spheres of Security

Information security is designed and implemented in three layers: policies, people (education, training, and awareness programs), and technology. While the design and implementation of the people layer and the technology layer overlap, both must follow the sound management policies discussed earlier in this chapter. Each of the layers contain controls and safeguards that protect the valuable information and information system assets. But before any technical controls or other safeguards are put into place, the policies defining the management philosophies that guide the security process must already be in place.

Defense in Depth

One of the basic tenets of security architectures is the layered implementation of security. This layered approach is called **defense in depth**. To achieve defense in depth, an organization must establish multiple layers of security controls and safeguards, which can be organized into policy, training and education, and technology, as per the NSTISSC model presented in Chapter 1. While policy itself may not prevent attacks, it certainly prepares the organization to handle them, and coupled with other layers, it can deter attacks. This is true of training and education, which can also provide some defense against attacks stemming from employee ignorance and social engineering. Technology is also implemented in layers, with detection equipment working in tandem with reaction technology, all operating behind access control mechanisms. Implementing multiple types of technology and thereby preventing the failure of one system from compromising the security of information is referred to as **redundancy**. Redundancy can be implemented at a number of points throughout the security architecture, such as firewalls, proxy servers, and access controls. Figure 3-5 illustrates the concept of building controls in multiple, sometimes redundant layers. The figure shows the use of firewalls and intrusion detection systems (IDS) that use both packet-level rules (shown as the header in the diagram) and data content analysis (shown as 0100101011 in the diagram).

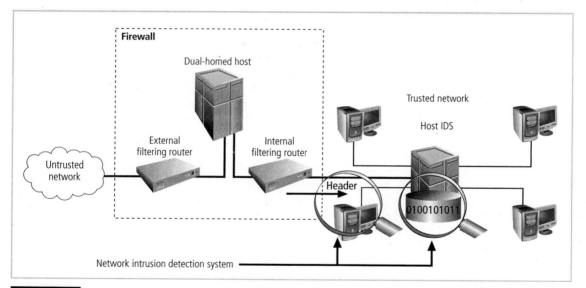

FIGURE 3-5   Defense in Depth

Security Perimeter

A **security perimeter** defines the boundary between the outer limit of an organization's security and the beginning of the outside world. A security perimeter protects all internal systems from outside threats, as pictured in Figure 3-6. Unfortunately, the perimeter does not protect against internal attacks from employee threats or on-site physical threats. There can be both an electronic security perimeter, usually at the organization's exterior network or Internet connection, and a physical security perimeter, usually at the gate to the organization's offices. Both require perimeter security. Security perimeters can be implemented as multiple technologies that segregate the protected information from potential attackers. Within security perimeters the organization can establish **security domains,** or areas of trust within which users can freely communicate. The assumption is that if individuals have access to one system within a security domain, they have authorized access to all systems within that particular domain. The security perimeter is an essential element of the overall security framework, and its implementation details are the core of the completed security blueprint. The key components used for planning the perimeter include firewalls, DMZs, proxy servers, and intrusion detection systems.

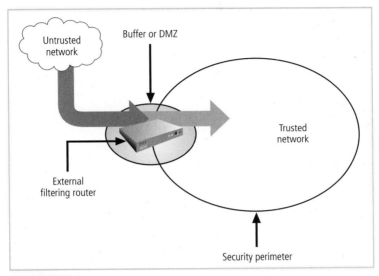

FIGURE 3-6   Security Perimeter

It should be noted that the proliferation of endpoints such as mobile devices are challenging the traditional definition of an organization's perimeter.[13] Enterprises must carefully consider how these new technologies can redefine where the perimeter actually falls.

Security Education, Training, and Awareness Program

Once your organization has defined the polices that will guide its security program, selected an overall security model by creating or adapting a security framework, and established a corresponding detailed blueprint for implementation, it is time to implement a **security education, training, and awareness (SETA)** program. The SETA program is the responsibility of the CISO and is a control measure designed to reduce the incidences of accidental security breaches by employees. Employee errors are among the top threats to information assets, so it is worth expending the organization's resources to develop programs to combat this threat. SETA programs are designed to supplement the general education and training programs that many organizations have in place to educate staff on information security. For example, if an organization detects that many employees are opening e-mail attachments inappropriately, those employees must be retrained. As a matter of good practice, systems development life cycles must include user training during the implementation phase.

The SETA program consists of three elements: security education, security training, and security awareness. An organization may not be able or willing to undertake all three of these elements; in this case, it may outsource elements to local educational institutions. The purpose of SETA is to enhance security by:

- Improving awareness of the need to protect system resources
- Developing skills and knowledge so computer users can perform their jobs more securely
- Building in-depth knowledge, as needed, to design, implement, or operate security programs for organizations and systems[14]

Table 3-6 compares the features of security education, training, and awareness within the organization.

TABLE 3-6 Comparative Framework of SETA (from NIST SP800-12[15])

	Education	Training	Awareness
Attribute	Why	How	What
Level	Insight	Knowledge	Information
Objective	Understanding	Skill	Exposure
Teaching method	Theoretical instruction • Discussion seminar • Background reading • Hands-on practice	Practical instruction • Lecture • Case study workshop • Posters	Media • Videos • Newsletters
Test measure	Essay (interpret learning)	Problem solving (apply learning)	• True or false • Multiple choice (identify learning)
Impact timeframe	Long-term	Intermediate	Short-term

Security Education

Everyone in an organization needs to be trained and made aware of information security, but not every member of the organization needs a formal degree or certification in information security. When management agrees that formal education is appropriate, an employee can investigate available courses from local institutions of higher learning or continuing education. A number of universities have formal coursework in information security. Those interested in researching formal information security programs can use resources such as the NSA-identified National Centers of Academic Excellence in Information Assurance Education (*www.nsa.gov/ia/academia/caemap.cfm?MenuID=10.1.1.2*). The Centers of Excellence program identifies outstanding universities with both coursework in information security and an integrated view of information security in the institution itself. Other local resources can also provide security education information, such as Kennesaw State's Center for Information Security Education (*http://infosec.kennesaw.edu*).

Security Training

Security training provides detailed information and hands-on instruction to employees to prepare them to perform their duties securely. Management of information security can develop customized in-house training or outsource the training program.

Alternatives to formal training programs are industry training conferences and programs offered through professional agencies such as SANS (*www.sans.org*), ISC² (*www.isc2.org*), ISSA (*www.issa.org*), and CSI (*www.gocsi.com*). Many of these programs are too technical for the average employee, but may be perfect for the continuing education requirements of information security professionals.

A number of SETA resources offer assistance in the form of sample topics and structures for security classes. The Computer Security Resource Center at NIST provides several useful documents free of charge in their special publications area (*http://csrc.nist.gov*).

Security Awareness

One of the least frequently implemented but most beneficial programs is the security awareness program. A security awareness program is designed to keep information security at the forefront of users' minds. These programs don't have to be complicated or expensive. Good programs can include newsletters, security posters (see Figure 3-7 for an example), videos, bulletin boards, flyers, and trinkets. Trinkets can include security slogans printed on mouse pads, coffee cups, T-shirts, pens, or any object frequently used during the workday that reminds employees of security. In addition, a good security awareness program requires a dedicated individual willing to invest the time and effort into promoting the program, and a champion willing to provide the needed financial support.

FIGURE 3-7 Example Security Awareness Poster

The security newsletter is the most cost-effective method of disseminating security information and news to the employee. Newsletters can be distributed via hard copy, e-mail, or intranet. Newsletter topics can include information about new threats to the organization's information assets, the schedule for upcoming security classes, and security personnel updates. The goal is to keep the idea of information security in users' minds and to stimulate users to care about security. If a security awareness program is not actively implemented, employees may begin to neglect security matters and the risk of employee accidents and failures is likely to increase.

Continuity Strategies

A key role for all managers is planning. Managers in the IT and information security communities are usually called on to provide strategic planning to ensure the continuous availability of information systems.[16] Unfortunately for managers, however, the probability that some form of attack will occur, whether from inside or outside, intentional or accidental, human or nonhuman, annoying or catastrophic, is very high. Thus, managers from each community of interest within the organization must be ready to act when a successful attack occurs.

There are various types of plans for events of this type: business continuity (BC) plans, disaster recovery (DR) plans, incident response (IR) plans, and contingency plans. In some organizations, these might be handled as a single integrated plan. In large, complex organizations, each of these plans may cover separate but related functions that differ in scope, applicability, and design. In a small organization, the security administrator (or systems administrator) may have one simple plan that consists of a straightforward set of media backup and recovery strategies, and a few service agreements from the company's service providers. But the sad reality is that many organizations have a level of planning that is woefully deficient.

Incident response, disaster recovery, and business continuity planning are components of contingency planning, as shown in Figure 3-8. A **contingency plan** is prepared by the organization to anticipate, react to, and recover from events that threaten the security of information and information assets in the organization, and, subsequently, to restore the organization to normal modes of business operations. The discussion of contingency planning begins with an explanation of the differences among its various elements, and an examination of the points at which each element is brought into play.

An **incident** is any clearly identified attack on the organization's information assets that would threaten the assets' confidentiality, integrity, or availability. An **incident response (IR) plan** addresses the identification and classification of, response to, and recovery from an incident. A **disaster recovery (DR) plan** addresses the preparation for and recovery from a disaster, whether natural or man-made. A **business continuity (BC) plan** ensures that critical business functions continue, if a catastrophic incident or disaster occurs. The primary functions of these three types of planning are as follows:

- The IR plan focuses on immediate response, but if the attack escalates or is disastrous (e.g., fire, flood, earthquake, or total blackout), the process moves on to the disaster recovery and BC plans.
- The DR plan typically focuses on restoring systems at the original site after disasters occur, and as such is closely associated with BC plan.
- The BC plan occurs concurrently with DR plan when the damage is major or long-term, requiring more than simple restoration of information and information resources. The BC plan establishes critical business functions at an alternate site.

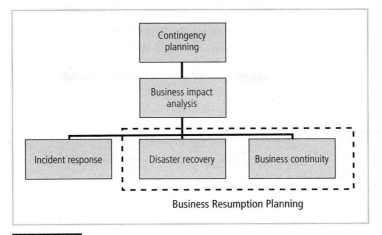

FIGURE 3-8   Components of Contingency Planning

Some experts argue that the DR plans and BC plans are so closely linked that they are indistinguishable. However, each has a distinct role and planning requirement. The following sections detail the tasks necessary for each of these three types of plans. You can also further distinguish the three types of planning by examining when each comes into play during the life of an incident. Figure 3-9 shows a sample sequence of events and the overlap between when each plan comes into play. Disaster recovery activities typically continue even after the organization has resumed operations at the original site.

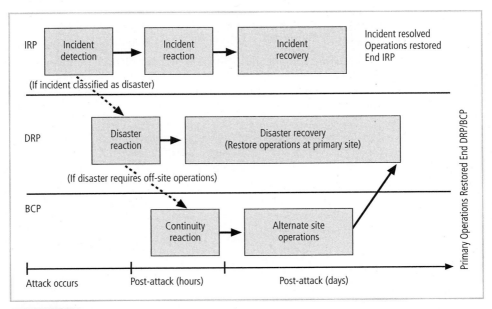

FIGURE 3-9   Contingency Planning Timeline

Contingency planning is similar to another process—one that you may have heard about and are likely to encounter in your education or future employment—called the risk management process. The contingency plan is a microcosm of risk management activities, and it focuses on the specific steps that must be taken to restore all information assets to their pre-incident or disaster states. As a result, the planning process closely emulates the risk management process.

Before any planning can begin, an assigned person or a planning team must begin the process. Typically, a contingency planning team is assembled for that purpose. A roster for this team may consist of the following members:

- Champion—As with any strategic function, the contingency planning project must have a high-level manager to support, promote, and endorse the findings of the project. In a contingency planning project, this could be the CIO, or ideally the CEO.

- Project manager—A project manager, possibly a mid-level manager or even the CISO, must lead the project and make sure a sound project-planning process is used, a complete and useful project plan is developed, and project resources are prudently managed to reach the goals of the project.

- Team members—The team members for this project should be the managers or their representatives from the various communities of interest: business, information technology, and information security. Representative business managers, familiar with the operations of their respective functional areas, should supply details on their activities and provide insight into the criticality of their functions to the overall sustainability of the business. Information technology managers on the project team should be familiar with the systems that could be at risk and with the IR plans, DR plans, and BC plans that are needed to provide technical content within the planning process. Information security managers must oversee the security planning of the project and provide information on the threats, vulnerabilities, attacks, and recovery requirements needed in the planning process.

The major project work modules performed by the contingency planning project team are shown in Figure 3-10. As you read the remainder of this chapter, it may help you to return to this diagram, since many of the upcoming sections correspond to the steps depicted in the diagram.

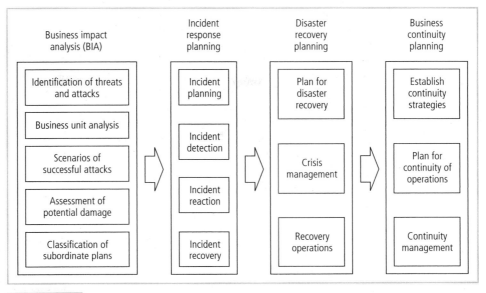

FIGURE 3-10   Major Steps in Contingency Planning

Business Impact Analysis

The first phase in the development of the contingency planning process is the **business impact analysis (BIA)**. A BIA is an investigation and assessment of the impact that various attacks can have on the organization. BIA takes up where the risk assessment process leaves off. It begins with a prioritized list of threats and vulnerabilities and adds information about the criticality of the systems involved and detailed assessments of the threats and vulnerabilities in the context in which the systems are used. The BIA is a crucial component of the initial planning stages, as it provides detailed analyses of the potential impact each attack could have on the organization. The BIA therefore adds insight into what the organization must do to respond to the attack, minimize the damage from the attack, recover from the effects, and return to normal operations. One of the fundamental differences between a BIA and the risk management processes is that the risk management approach identifies the threats, vulnerabilities, and attacks to determine what controls can protect the information. The BIA assumes that these controls have been bypassed, have failed, or have proven otherwise ineffective, that an attack has succeeded, and attempts to answer the question, *what* do you do then?

The contingency planning team conducts the BIA in the following stages, which are shown in Figure 3-10 and described in the sections that follow:

1. Threat attack identification and prioritization
2. Business unit analysis
3. Attack success scenario development
4. Potential damage assessment
5. Subordinate plan classification

Threat Attack Identification and Prioritization

Organizations that have a well-established risk management process will not need to develop this aspect of the BIA and need only to update the threat list from their risk management process with new developments and add one additional piece of information, the attack profile. An **attack profile** is a detailed description of the activities that occur during an attack. The content items in an attack profile, shown in Table 3-7, include preliminary indications of an attack, as well as actions and outcomes. These profiles must be developed for every serious threat the organization faces, natural or manmade, deliberate or accidental. It is as important to know the typical hacker's profile as it is to know what kind of data entry mistakes employees make, or the weather conditions that indicate an imminent tornado or hurricane. The attack profile is useful in later planning stages to provide indicators of attacks. It is used here to determine the extent of damage that could result to a business unit if a given attack were successful.

TABLE 3-7 Attack Profile

Date of analysis	June 21, 2008
Attack name and description	Mako worm
Threat and probable threat agent	Malicious code via automated attack
Known or possible vulnerabilities	All desktop systems not updated with all latest patches
Likely precursor activities or indicators	Attachments to e-mails
Likely attack activities or indicators of attack in progress	Systems sending e-mails to entries from address book, activity on port 80 without browser being used
Information assets at risk from this attack	All desktop and server systems are at risk
Damage or loss to information assets likely from this attack	Business partners and others connected to our networks
Other assets at risk from this attack	None identified at this time
Damage or loss to other assets likely from this attack	Will vary depending on severity, minimum disruption will be needed to repair worm infection

Business Unit Analysis

The second major task within the BIA is the analysis and prioritization of the business functions within the organization's departments, sections, divisions, groups, or other units to determine which are most vital to continued operations. Each unit must also be evaluated to determine how important its functions are to the organization as a whole. For example, recovery operations would probably focus on the IT department and network operation before addressing the personnel department and hiring activities. Likewise, it is more urgent to reinstate a manufacturing company's assembly line than the maintenance tracking system for that assembly line. This is not to say that personnel functions and assembly line maintenance are not important to the business; however, the reality is that if the organization's main revenue-producing operations cannot be restored quickly, there may cease to be a need for other functions.

Attack Success Scenario Development

Once the threat attack profiles have been developed and the business functions prioritized, the business impact analysis team must create a series of scenarios depicting the impact of a successful attack from each threat on each prioritized functional area. This can be a long and detailed process, as threats that succeed can affect many functions. Attack profiles should include scenarios depicting a typical attack with details on the method, the indicators, and the broad consequences of the attack. Once the attack profiles are completed, the business function details can be integrated with the attack profiles, after which more details are added to the attack profile, including alternate outcomes. These alternate outcomes should describe a best, worst, and most likely case that could result from each type of attack on a particular business functional area. This level of detail allows planners to address each business function in turn.

Potential Damage Assessment

Using the attack success scenarios, the BIA planning team must estimate the cost of the best, worst, and most likely cases. At this stage, you are *not* determining how much to spend on the protection of information assets, rather, you are identifying what must be done to recover from each possible case. These costs include the actions of the response team(s), which are described in subsequent sections, as they act to recover quickly and effectively from an incident or disaster. These cost estimates can also inform management representatives from all the organization's communities of interest of the importance of the planning and recovery efforts. The final result of the assessment is referred to as an **attack scenario end case**.

Subordinate Plan Classification

Once the potential damage has been assessed, and each scenario and attack scenario end case has been evaluated, a subordinate plan must be developed or identified from among existing plans already in place. These subordinate plans take into account the identification of, reaction to, and recovery from each attack scenario. An attack scenario end case is categorized either as disastrous or not disastrous. Most attacks are not disastrous and therefore fall into the category of incident. Those scenarios that do qualify as disastrous are addressed in the disaster recovery plan. The qualifying difference is whether or not an organization is able to take effective action during the attack to combat its effects. Attack end cases that are disastrous find members of the organization waiting out the attack with hopes to recover effectively after it is over. In a typical disaster recovery operation, the lives and welfare of the employees are the most important priority *during* the attack, as most disasters are fires, floods, hurricanes, and tornadoes. Please note that there are attacks that are not natural disasters that fit this category as well, for example:

- Electrical blackouts
- Attacks on service providers that result in a loss of communications to the organization (either telephone or Internet)
- Massive, malicious code attacks that sweep through an organization before they can be contained

The objective of this process is that each scenario should be classified as a probable incident or disaster, and then the corresponding actions required to respond to the scenario should be built into either the IR plan or DR plan.

Incident Response Planning

Incident response planning includes the identification of, classification of, and response to an incident. The IR plan is made up of activities that are to be performed when an incident has been identified. Before developing such a plan, you should understand the philosophical approach to incident response planning.

What is an incident? What is incident response? As stated earlier, an incident is an attack against an information asset that poses a clear threat to the confidentiality, integrity, or availability of information resources. If an action that threatens information is confirmed, the action is classified as an incident. All of the threats identified in earlier chapters could result in attacks that would be classified as information security incidents. For purposes of this discussion, however, attacks are only classified as incidents if they have the following characteristics:

- They are directed against information assets.
- They have a realistic chance of success.
- They could threaten the confidentiality, integrity, or availability of information resources.

Incident response (IR) is therefore the set of activities taken to plan for, detect, and correct the impact of an incident on information assets. Prevention is purposefully omitted, as this activity is more a function of information security in general than of incident response. In other words, IR is more reactive than proactive, with the exception of the planning that must occur to prepare the IR teams to be ready to react to an incident.

IR consists of the following four phases:

1. Planning
2. Detection
3. Reaction
4. Recovery

Disaster Recovery Planning

An event can be categorized as a disaster when the following happens: (1) the organization is unable to mitigate the impact of an incident during the incident, and (2) the level of damage or destruction is so severe that the organization is unable to recover quickly. The difference between an incident and a disaster may be subtle; the contingency planning team must make the distinction between disasters and incidents, and it may not be possible to make this distinction until an attack occurs. Often an event that is initially classified as an incident is later determined to be a disaster. When this happens, the organization must change how it is responding and take action to secure its most valuable assets to preserve value for the longer term, even at the risk of more disruption in the short term.

Disaster recovery (DR) planning is the process of preparing an organization to handle and recover from a disaster, whether natural or man-made. The key emphasis of a DR plan is to reestablish operations at the primary site, the location at which the organization performs its business. The goal is to make things whole, or as they were before the disaster.

The Disaster Recovery Plan

Similar in structure to the IR plan, the DR plan provides detailed guidance in the event of a disaster. It is organized by the type or nature of the disaster, and specifies recovery procedures during and after each type of disaster. It also provides details on the roles and responsibilities of the people involved in the disaster recovery effort, and identifies the personnel and agencies that must be notified. Just as the IR plan must be tested, so must the DR plan, using the same testing mechanisms. At a minimum, the DR plan must be reviewed during a walk-through or talk-through on a periodic basis.

Many of the same precepts of incident response apply to disaster recovery:

1. Priorities must be clearly established. The first priority is always the preservation of human life. The protection of data and systems immediately falls to the wayside if the disaster threatens the lives, health, or welfare of the employees of the organization or members of the community in which the organization operates. Only after all employees and neighbors have been safeguarded can the disaster recovery team attend to nonhuman asset protection.
2. Roles and responsibilities must be clearly delineated. Everyone assigned to the DR team should be aware of his or her expected actions during a disaster. Some people are responsible for coordinating with local authorities, such as fire, police, and medical staff. Others are responsible for the evacuation of personnel, if required. Still others are tasked simply to pack up and leave.
3. Someone must initiate the alert roster and notify key personnel. Those to be notified may be the fire, police, or medical authorities mentioned earlier. They may also include insurance agencies, disaster teams like the Red Cross, and management teams.
4. Someone must be tasked with the documentation of the disaster. Just as in an IR reaction, someone must begin recording what happened to serve as a basis for later determination of why and how the event occurred.
5. If and only if it is possible, attempts must be made to mitigate the impact of the disaster on the operations of the organization. If everyone is safe, and all needed authorities have been notified, some individuals can be tasked with the evacuation of physical assets. Some can be responsible for making sure all systems are securely shut down to prevent further loss of data.

Recovery Operations

Reaction to a disaster can vary so widely that it is impossible to describe the process with any accuracy. Each organization must examine the scenarios developed at the start of contingency planning, and determine how to respond.

If the physical facilities are spared, the disaster recovery team should begin the restoration of systems and data to reestablish full operational capability. If the organization's facilities do not survive, alternative actions must be taken until new facilities can be acquired. When a disaster threatens the viability of the organization at the primary site, the disaster recovery process transitions into the process of business continuity planning.

Business Continuity Planning

Business continuity planning prepares an organization to reestablish critical business operations during a disaster that affects operations at the primary site. If a disaster has rendered the current location unusable, there must be a plan to allow the business to continue to function. Not every business needs such a plan or such facilities. Small companies or fiscally sound organizations may have the latitude to cease operations until the physical facilities can be restored. But organizations such as manufacturers and retailers may not have this option, because they depend on physical types of commerce and may not be able to relocate operations.

Developing Continuity Programs

Once the incident response plans and disaster recovery plans are in place, the organization needs to consider finding temporary facilities to support the continued viability of the business in the event of a disaster. The development of the BC plan is somewhat simpler than that of the IR plan or DR plan, in that it consists primarily of selecting a continuity strategy and integrating the off-site data storage and recovery functions into this strategy. Some of the components of the BC plan could already be integral to the normal operations of the organization, such as an off-site backup service. Others require special consideration and negotiation. The first part of business continuity planning is performed when the joint DR/BC plan is developed. The identification of critical business functions and the resources needed to support them is the cornerstone of the BC plan. When a disaster strikes, these functions are the first to be reestablished at the alternate site. The contingency planning team needs to appoint a group of individuals to evaluate and compare the available alternatives, and recommend which strategy should be selected and implemented. The strategy selected usually involves some form of off-site facility, which should be inspected, configured, secured, and tested on a periodic basis. The selection should be reviewed periodically to determine if a superior alternative has emerged or if the organization needs a different solution.

Crisis Management

Disasters are, of course, larger in scale and less manageable than incidents, but the planning processes are the same, and in many cases are conducted simultaneously. What may truly distinguish an incident from a disaster is the actions of the response teams. An incident response team typically rushes to duty stations or to the office from home. The first act is to reach for the IR plan. A disaster recovery team may not have the luxury of flipping through a binder to see what must be done. Disaster recovery personnel must know their roles without any supporting documentation. This is a function of preparation, training, and rehearsal. You probably all remember the frequent fire, tornado, or hurricane drills—and even the occasional nuclear blast drills—from your public school days. Fire or disaster is no less likely in the business world.

The actions taken during and after a disaster are referred to as **crisis management**. Crisis management differs dramatically from incident response, as it focuses first and foremost on the people involved. It also addresses the viability of the business. The disaster recovery team works closely with the crisis management team. According to Gartner Research, the crisis management team is

> responsible for managing the event from an enterprise perspective and covers the following major activities:
> - Supporting personnel and their loved ones during the crisis
> - Determining the event's impact on normal business operations and, if necessary, making a disaster declaration

- Keeping the public informed about the event and the actions being taken to ensure the recovery of personnel and the enterprise
- Communicating with major customers, suppliers, partners, regulatory agencies, industry organizations, the media, and other interested parties.[17]

The crisis management team should establish a base of operations or command center to support communications until the disaster has ended. The crisis management team includes individuals from all functional areas of the organization, to facilitate communications and cooperation. Some key areas of crisis management include:

- Verifying personnel head count: Everyone must be accounted for, including those on vacations, leaves of absence, and business trips.
- Checking the alert roster: Alert rosters and general personnel phone lists are used to notify individuals whose assistance may be needed, or simply to tell employees not to report to work until the disaster is over.
- Checking emergency information cards: It is important that each employee have two types of emergency information cards. The first is personal emergency information that specifies whom to notify in case of an emergency (next of kin), medical conditions, and a photocopy of the employee's driver's license or other identification. The second is a set of instructions on what to do in the event of an emergency. This mini-snapshot of the disaster recovery plan should contain, at a minimum, a contact number or hot line, emergency services numbers (fire, police, medical), evacuation and assembly locations (storm shelters, for example), the name and number of the disaster recovery coordinator, and any other needed information.

Crisis management must balance the needs of the employees with the needs of the business in providing personnel with support for personal and family issues during disasters.

Chapter Summary

- In order to most effectively secure its networks, an organization must establish a functional and well-designed information security program in the context of a well-planned and fully defined information policy and planning environment. The creation of an information security program requires information security policies, standards and practices, an information security architecture, and a detailed information security blueprint.
- Management must make policy the basis for all information security planning, design, and deployment in order to direct how issues are addressed and how technologies are used. Policy must never conflict with laws, but should stand up in court, if challenged, and should be properly administered through dissemination and documented acceptance. For a policy to be considered effective and legally enforceable, it must be disseminated, reviewed, understood, complied with, and uniformly enforced. Policy is implemented with an overall enterprise information security policy and as many issue-specific and system-specific policies as are indicated to meet the management team's policy needs.

- After the information security team identifies the vulnerabilities in the information technology systems, the security team develops a design blueprint for security used to implement the security program. The security blueprint is a detailed version of the security framework, an outline of steps to take to design and implement information security in the organization. There are a number of published information security frameworks, but since each information security environment is unique, the security team may need to modify or adapt pieces from several frameworks.

- Each organization should implement a security education, training, and awareness (SETA) program to supplement the general education and training programs that many organizations have in place to educate staff on information security. A SETA program consists of three elements: security education, security training, and security awareness. The purpose of SETA is to enhance security by: improving awareness of the need to protect system resources, developing skills and knowledge so computer users can perform their jobs more securely, and building in-depth knowledge to design, implement, or operate security programs for organizations and systems.

- Managers in the IT and information security communities must ensure the continuous availability of information systems. This is achieved with various types of contingency planning such as: incident response, disaster recovery, and business continuity planning. An incident response (IR) plan addresses the identification and classification of, response to, and recovery from an incident. A disaster recovery (DR) plan addresses the preparation for and recovery from a disaster, whether natural or man-made. A business continuity (BC) plan ensures that critical business functions continue, if a catastrophic incident or disaster occurs.

Review Questions

1. What is management's role with regard to information security policies and practices?
2. What are the differences between a policy, a standard, and a practice? What are the three types of security policies? Where would each be used? What type of policy would be needed to guide use of the Web? E-mail? Office equipment for personal use?
3. For a policy to be considered effective and legally enforceable, what must it accomplish?
4. What are the components of an effective EISP?
5. What are the components of an effective ISSP?
6. What is an ACL and how does it fit into the discussion about policy? Hint: look at the SysSP.
7. Who is ultimately responsible for managing a technology? Who is responsible for enforcing policy that affects the use of a technology?
8. What must occur for a security policy to remain viable?
9. What is the difference between a security framework and a security blueprint?
10. How can a security framework assist in the design and implementation of a security infrastructure?
11. Where can a security administrator find information on established security frameworks?
12. What is the ISO 27000 series of standards? What individual standards make up the series?
13. Briefly describe the history of the standard now known as ISO 27002. In which country did it originate? Has it had any other names?
14. What documents are available from the NIST Computer Resource Center, and how can they support the development of a security framework?
15. Define benchmarking. What is it used for?

16. Briefly describe the spheres of security. Who could benefit from understanding this approach to security?

17. What is defense in depth? Why is this so often encountered in information security technical control settings?

18. What resources are available on the Web that can aid an organization in developing best practices as part of a security framework?

19. What is SETA? Which organizations should have a SETA program?

20. What is contingency planning? How is it different from routine management planning?

21. What are the components of contingency planning, and what are the major steps used for contingency planning?

22. When is IR planning used?

23. When is DR planning used?

24. When is BC planning used? How do you determine when to use the IR plan, DR plan, or BC plan?

25. What are the elements of a business impact analysis?

Exercises

1. Using a graphics program, design several security awareness posters on the following themes: updating antivirus signatures, protecting sensitive information, watching out for e-mail viruses, prohibiting the personal use of company equipment, changing and protecting passwords, avoiding social engineering, and protecting software copyrights. What other areas can you come up with?

2. Search the Web for a listing of security education and training programs in your area. Keep a list and see which category has the most examples. See if you can determine the costs associated with each example. Which do you feel would be more cost-effective in terms of both time and money?

3. Search the Web for examples of issue-specific security policies. What types of policies can you find? Draft a simple issue-specific policy using the format provided in the text that outlines "Fair and Responsible Use of College Computers" and is based on the rules and regulations you have been provided with in your institution. Does your school have a similar policy? Does it contain all the elements listed in the text?

4. Use your library or the Web to find a reported natural disaster that occurred within the last 180 days. From the news accounts, determine if local or national officials had prepared disaster plans and if these plans were used. See if you can determine how the plans helped the officials improve the response to the disaster. How do the plans help the recovery?

5. Classify each of the following occurrences as an incident or disaster. If an occurrence is a disaster, determine whether or not business continuity plans would be called into play.

   a. A hacker gets into the network and deletes files from a server.

   b. A fire breaks out in the storeroom and sets off sprinklers on that floor. Some computers are damaged, but the fire is contained.

   c. A tornado hits a local power company, and the company will be without power for three to five days.

   d. Employees go on strike, and the company could be without critical workers for weeks.

   e. A disgruntled employee takes a critical server home, sneaking it out after hours.

   For each of the scenarios (a–e), describe the steps necessary to restore operations. Indicate whether or not law enforcement would be involved.

Case Exercises

Matthias and Al watched the monitor for a few more minutes. The firewall at *Linen Planet* seemed to be running just fine.

Al stood up and went on to his next task, and Matthias also moved on to his next task. After an hour, he picked up the phone and called the number for the QA team.

"Hello, QA Test Team, Debbie speaking."

"Hi Debbie," said Matthias. "What's the word on the Linen Planet firewall project?"

"Oh, we just finished," said Debbie. "We're good to go. The new rules can stay in place."

Matthias said, "OK. We won't roll back. Thanks for the info."

Debbie replied, "OK. I'll put a note on the test log. Thanks for your help."

They both hung up the phone. As Al walked across the room, Matthias called out to him, "Is it always this easy?"

Al shook his head. "Not hardly, you must be having beginner's luck."

Questions:

1. What are some of the things that might have gone wrong in the test?

2. If the test had failed, what do you think the rollback plan would have entailed?

3. What is the relationship between the EISP, the network usage ISSP, and the rules that Matthias entered in the updated firewall?

Endnotes

1. Charles Cresson Wood. "Integrated Approach Includes Information Security." *Security* 37, no. 2 (February 2000): 43–44.

2. National Institute of Standards and Technology. *An Introduction to Computer Security: The NIST Handbook*. SP 800-12.

3. Derived from a number of sources, the most notable of which is *www.wustl.edu/policies/infosecurity.html*.

4. Robert J. Alberts, Anthony M. Townsend, and Michael E. Whitman. "Considerations for an Effective Telecommunications Use Policy." *Communications of the ACM* 42, no. 6 (June 1999): 101–109.

5. National Institute of Standards and Technology. *An Introduction to Computer Security: The NIST Handbook*. SP 800-12.

6. National Institute of Standards and Technology. *Information Security Management, Code of Practice for Information Security Management*. ISO/IEC 17799 (6 December 2001).

7. National Institute of Standards and Technology. *Information Security Management, Code of Practice for Information Security Management*. ISO/IEC 17799 (6 December 2001).

8. National Institute of Standards and Technology. *Information Security Management, Code of Practice for Information Security Management*. ISO/IEC 17799 (6 December 2001).

9. National Institute of Standards and Technology. *Information Security Management, Code of Practice for Information Security Management*. ISO/IEC 17799 (6 December 2001).

10. T. Humphries. The Newly Revised Part 2 of BS 7799. Accessed May 27, 2003. *www.gammassl.co.uk/bs7799/ The%20Newly%20Revised%20Part%202%20of%20BS%207799ver3a.pdf*.

11. How 7799 Works. WWW Document [Cited 27 May, 2003] available from *www.gammassl.co.uk/bs7799/works.html*.

12. Kadrich, M. *Endpoint Security* (Boston: Addison-Wesley, 2007).

13. National Institute of Standards and Technology, *An Introduction to Computer Security: The NIST Handbook.* SP 800-12.

14. National Institute of Standards and Technology, *An Introduction to Computer Security: The NIST Handbook.* SP 800-12.

15. William R. King and Paul Gray, *The Management of Information Systems* (Chicago: Dryden Press, 1989), 359.

16. Roberta Witty, "What Is Crisis Management?" *Gartner Online* (19 September 2001). Accessed 30 April, 2007 from *www.gartner.com/DisplayDocument?id=340971.*

Finding Network Vulnerabilities

4

> Once we know our weaknesses they cease to do us any harm.
>
> **G.C. (GEORG CHRISTOPH) LICHTENBERG**

THE ELEVATOR CHIMED AS IT OPENED and Virginia Burnett, who worked at the ATI reception area on the 14th floor, straightened a little in her chair. A tall dark-haired man dressed in coveralls and carrying a large toolbox walked off the elevator and then around Virginia's desk with a confident stride.

"Can I help you?" asked Virginia, smiling.

He walked a few more steps until he was almost past her desk.

Virginia raised her voice a little. "Stop! What do you want?"

He stopped. "Yes. Hi. My name is Greg Reiner; I'm a contractor working for building maintenance. Someone reported a water leak in the break room."

"Can I see your photo ID and maintenance work order, please?" asked Virginia.

The man turned toward her and sank his hand into his front pocket. It came out empty. Then he looked at the clipboard he was carrying. "Well, it looks like I left them in the van." He smiled and said, "Surely you can see that I'm no thief, though."

Virginia said tightly, "I don't know anything about a leak, and in any case ATI has very strict policies about who can come and go in our offices. I really need your credentials before I can allow you through. I'll be right here when you get back."

The man looked exasperated. "Well, I would hate for your attitude about my badge to cause property damage—that leak isn't going to stop itself, so I'm sure you can make an exception." He started to walk toward the office area.

LEARNING OBJECTIVES:

Upon completion of this material, you should be able to do the following:

- Name the common categories of vulnerabilities
- Discuss common system and network vulnerabilities
- Locate and access sources of information about emerging vulnerabilities
- Identify the names and functions of the widely available scanning and analysis tools

Introduction

To maintain secure networks, information security professionals must be prepared to identify system vulnerabilities, whether by hiring system assessment experts, or by conducting self-assessments using scanning and penetration tools. The term vulnerability, like so many in information security, has a variety of meanings. To a systems developer, a vulnerability may be a poorly designed input buffer that is subject to an overflow attack, or a badly designed exception handler that allows an escalation of user privileges. To system administrators, vulnerabilities may be things like the presence of unneeded services or easily guessed passwords.

A network security vulnerability is, in general, a defect in a product, process, or procedure that, if exploited, may result in a violation of security policy, which in turn might lead to a loss of revenue, a loss of information, or a loss of value to the organization.

Common Vulnerabilities

Common vulnerabilities fall into two broad classes:

- Defects in software or firmware
- Weaknesses in processes and procedures

Defects in Software or Firmware

Defects in software or firmware (software that is embedded in a device such as a router or network switch) are common; an industry has grown up around researching, identifying, and fixing them, and then deploying the fixes across an organization's infrastructure.

Michael Howard, David LeBlanc, and John Viega in their excellent book *19 Deadly Sins of Software Security*[1] catalog 19 types of common programming flaws that create most vulnerabilities. Some of the more common vulnerabilities that result from programming faults are buffer overruns, injection attacks, eavesdropping on network traffic, and cross-site scripting.

Buffer overruns (also called buffer overflows) arise when the quantity of input data exceeds the size of the available data area (buffer). The most innocuous of these will cause the program or application to crash, but an attacker can craft instructions that are executed by the computer when the buffer overruns. These instructions might insert a back door for later access, or they might consist of malicious code (usually referred to as arbitrary code execution).

Injection attacks can occur when the programmer does not properly validate user input, and they allow an attacker to include input that, when passed to a database, can give rise to SQL injection vulnerabilities. Consider this simple example using a Windows command script:

```
echo off
set /p newdir = "Directory to be created>"
mkdir %newdir%
```

This simple script requests the user input of a directory name, and then creates that directory. However, if a malicious user types `mynewdir&cmd` at the script's prompt, the content beginning with "&", which is the command chaining character, opens another command window, which can be used to execute commands of the attacker's choice. SQL injection works similarly, by appending the attacker's SQL command(s) to a programmer's intended user input of a simple query variable, allowing the attacker to execute SQL commands that are different from those the developer intended.

Network traffic is vulnerable to eavesdropping because a network medium is essentially an open channel. Traditional wired networks can be just as vulnerable as wireless networks to sniffing through active network taps and other attacks. Once attackers have access to the communications medium, they can also record (and later replay) traffic, modify it, or hijack a communications session. The cross-site scripting (XSS) vulnerability has enabled users of social networking sites to embed HTML or script (JavaScript, for example) into portions of the site under their control (such as their profile page). The content appears to be provided by the site but is actually controlled by a possibly hostile user. One user ("samy") of the popular MySpace social networking site used XSS to amass more than one million "friends" in a 24-hour period.[2]

An excellent catalog of common vulnerabilities in Web applications is maintained by the Open Web Application Security Project (OWASP) at *www.owasp.org/index.php/ OWASP_Top_Ten_Project*.

OFFLINE

Who You Gonna Tell?

There are two general approaches to handling announcements of vulnerabilities: Announce immediately and publicly upon discovery (full disclosure); or, disclose only after a fix is available.

The advantages and disadvantages of these two approaches have been hotly debated since the early 1990s.[3] While well-known security experts such as Bruce Schneier advocate full disclosure[4] because it is likely that attackers already know about the vulnerabilities, and because public disclosure encourages vendors to provide fixes in a timely fashion and improve their products, others allege that publicly disclosing the vulnerability only encourages the production of automated attack tools which allow "script kiddies" to mount the attacks.

continued

A successful example of the "disclose after fix" approach was the sendmail vulnerability discovered in 2003.[5] This vulnerability was quietly communicated to the affected vendors and only publicly disclosed when a fix was available. In fact, the first public exploit of the vulnerability appeared the day after its existence became public.

Full disclosure adherents are quick to point out that there is really no way to ensure that a vulnerability has not also been discovered in the hacker underground, and argue that there are often measures that can be taken to prevent a successful exploit in advance of the fix.

Another complicating factor is that the person who discovers the vulnerability controls to whom it is released. While many security researchers follow the "responsible disclosure" approach of communicating the vulnerability to the affected vendor and withholding public disclosure until a vendor fix is released (or a reasonable amount of time has passed), others may disclose the vulnerability immediately, within the hacker underground, on public Web sites, or via full disclosure mailing lists.

This debate shows no sign of a speedy solution; wise security professionals carefully monitor both vendor security announcements and the full disclosure mailing lists.

How can security professionals remain abreast of all the vulnerabilities? First and perhaps foremost, they must know the following:

- Their organization's security policies—the existence of a vulnerability is not in and of itself a cause for concern. The danger arises from the risk of the vulnerability being exploited to create a policy violation. Consider a Web server with a known vulnerability that operates only on a protected network, and that provides data of limited value. If that same vulnerability existed on an Internet-exposed e-commerce server, it would be essential to repair it immediately.

- What software and hardware devices the organization uses—if the organization does not use a vulnerable piece of software, then the risk is minimal. If a new vulnerability for Microsoft Internet Information Server is announced, this is of little concern to a company that uses only Apache Web servers.

Information security professionals should regularly consult the following types of public disclosure lists:

- Vendor announcements
- Full disclosure mailing lists
- CVE, the common vulnerabilities and exposures database maintained by Mitre Corporation for the Department of Homeland Security

Vendor Announcements

Most of the major vendors maintain mailing lists that they use to announce vulnerabilities, fixes, and any compensating actions that can be taken (for example, closing the network port associated with a vulnerable network service, or disabling script execution in a vulnerable Web browser). A Microsoft security bulletin is shown in Figure 4-1.

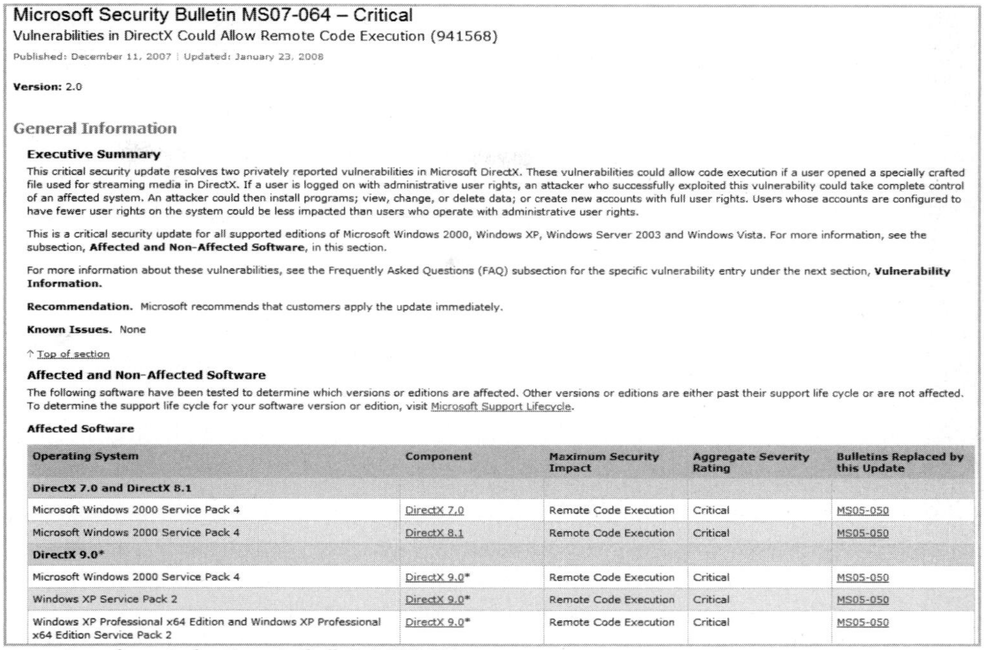

Microsoft Security Bulletin MS07-064 – Critical
Vulnerabilities in DirectX Could Allow Remote Code Execution (941568)
Published: December 11, 2007 | Updated: January 23, 2008

Version: 2.0

General Information

Executive Summary

This critical security update resolves two privately reported vulnerabilities in Microsoft DirectX. These vulnerabilities could allow code execution if a user opened a specially crafted file used for streaming media in DirectX. If a user is logged on with administrative user rights, an attacker who successfully exploited this vulnerability could take complete control of an affected system. An attacker could then install programs; view, change, or delete data; or create new accounts with full user rights. Users whose accounts are configured to have fewer user rights on the system could be less impacted than users who operate with administrative user rights.

This is a critical security update for all supported editions of Microsoft Windows 2000, Windows XP, Windows Server 2003 and Windows Vista. For more information, see the subsection, **Affected and Non-Affected Software**, in this section.

For more information about these vulnerabilities, see the Frequently Asked Questions (FAQ) subsection for the specific vulnerability entry under the next section, **Vulnerability Information.**

Recommendation. Microsoft recommends that customers apply the update immediately.

Known Issues. None

↑ Top of section

Affected and Non-Affected Software

The following software have been tested to determine which versions or editions are affected. Other versions or editions are either past their support life cycle or are not affected. To determine the support life cycle for your software version or edition, visit Microsoft Support Lifecycle.

Affected Software

Operating System	Component	Maximum Security Impact	Aggregate Severity Rating	Bulletins Replaced by this Update
DirectX 7.0 and DirectX 8.1				
Microsoft Windows 2000 Service Pack 4	DirectX 7.0	Remote Code Execution	Critical	MS05-050
Microsoft Windows 2000 Service Pack 4	DirectX 8.1	Remote Code Execution	Critical	MS05-050
DirectX 9.0*				
Microsoft Windows 2000 Service Pack 4	DirectX 9.0*	Remote Code Execution	Critical	MS05-050
Windows XP Service Pack 2	DirectX 9.0*	Remote Code Execution	Critical	MS05-050
Windows XP Professional x64 Edition and Windows XP Professional x64 Edition Service Pack 2	DirectX 9.0*	Remote Code Execution	Critical	MS05-050

www.microsoft.com/technet/security/bulletin/MS07-064.mspx

FIGURE 4-1 Example Microsoft Security Bulletin

Security professionals should subscribe to the relevant vendor mailing lists and conduct risk assessments on each new announcement to determine the appropriate actions to be taken.

OFFLINE

Risk Assessment for Patches

Managing and installing security fixes (patches) for all the products used by an organization can be an overwhelming task. Keep in mind that each announced vulnerability may pose some risk to the organization, but that the remediation effort must be in proportion to the assessed risk.

Vendors commonly assign a priority to their fixes. For example, the fix for a vulnerability that poses significant risk that an attacker could take control of a system, and that already has publicly available exploit code, may be rated "critical." Less dangerous vulnerabilities may receive a fix priority rating of "recommended."

continued

Additional factors that must be taken into account when conducting a risk assessment for a vulnerability include:

- Exposure—how susceptible is the organization to an exploit of the vulnerability? A critical defect in an Internet-facing router or firewall leads to much more exposure than a vulnerability in a Web server only accessible from within the organization.
- Criticality of the affected assets—patches are produced by the same human developers who introduced the problem in the first place, and must be tested to ensure they do not have undesirable side effects when installed on the organization's infrastructure. Loss of access to a critical asset is equally disruptive to an organization whether the cause is a malicious attack or a bad software patch.
- Compensating factors—there may be other ways to prevent the vulnerability from being exploited before the fix can be tested and installed. For example, it might be possible to close the network port associated with a vulnerable network service, or disable script execution in a vulnerable Web browser.
- Downtime requirements—many patch installations require the server to be restarted during installation. This restart will impact the availability of the services hosted by the server and may require special scheduling, failover to alternate servers, or other accommodations.

A risk assessment takes into account all these factors to determine what percentage of an organization's scarce IT resources should be dedicated to the deployment of any given fix.

Full Disclosure Lists

Vendors tend to delay announcing vulnerabilities until they've had time to research them and develop a fix or identify compensating actions. This can create a "window of vulnerability"[6] for organizations, if the problem has been discovered elsewhere or disclosed to someone besides the affected vendor.

Unfortunately, the hacker community and some security researchers release details of vulnerabilities as soon as they are discovered, either in local chat rooms or in a full disclosure mailing list such as Bugtraq or the CVE list.

The Bugtraq mailing list is widely known as one of the major sources of public vulnerability announcements. As a founding member of the "full disclosure" movement, Bugtraq disseminates vulnerability information as soon as it is discovered, regardless of whether vendors have been notified or a fix is available. Bugtraq has been alternately praised for improving software quality, by focusing public attention on the prevalence of security flaws, and castigated for informing potential attackers of methods for compromising systems.

A sample Bugtraq posting is shown in Figure 4-2.

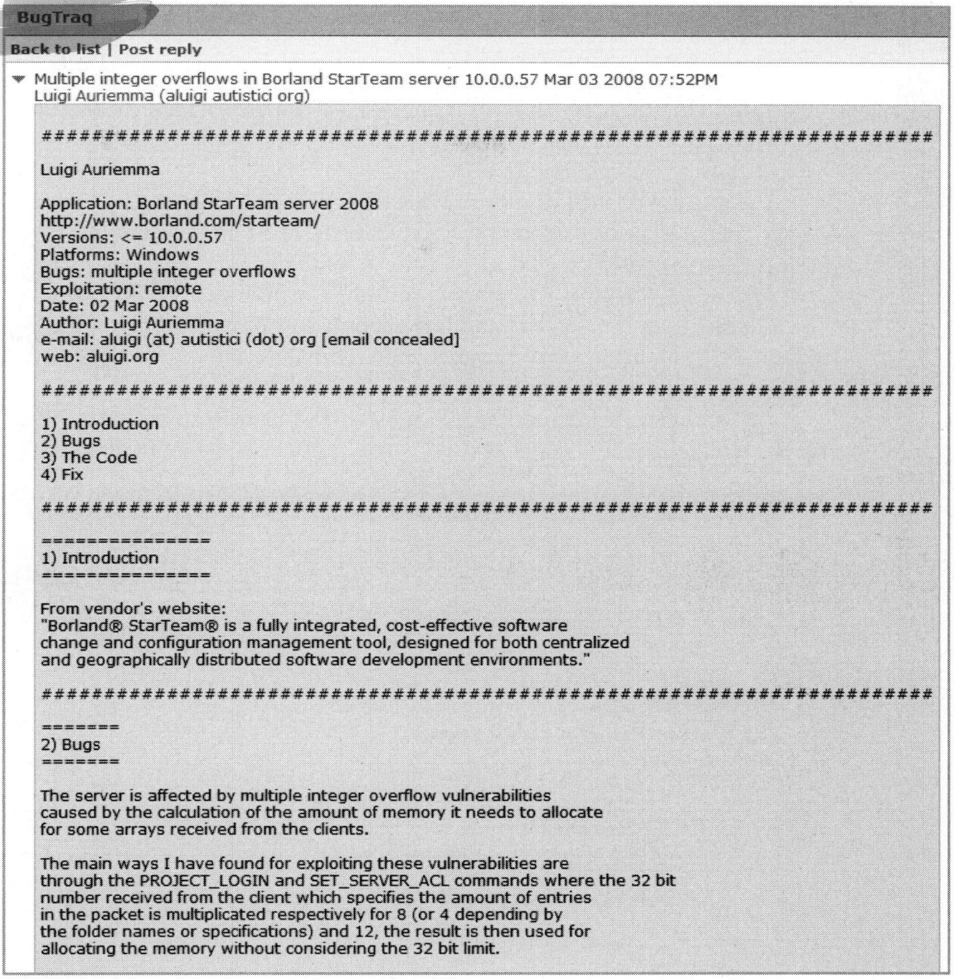

```
BugTraq

Back to list | Post reply

▼  Multiple integer overflows in Borland StarTeam server 10.0.0.57 Mar 03 2008 07:52PM
   Luigi Auriemma (aluigi autistici org)

   ######################################################################

   Luigi Auriemma

   Application: Borland StarTeam server 2008
   http://www.borland.com/starteam/
   Versions: <= 10.0.0.57
   Platforms: Windows
   Bugs: multiple integer overflows
   Exploitation: remote
   Date: 02 Mar 2008
   Author: Luigi Auriemma
   e-mail: aluigi (at) autistici (dot) org [email concealed]
   web: aluigi.org

   ######################################################################

   1) Introduction
   2) Bugs
   3) The Code
   4) Fix

   ######################################################################

   ===============
   1) Introduction
   ===============

   From vendor's website:
   "Borland® StarTeam® is a fully integrated, cost-effective software
   change and configuration management tool, designed for both centralized
   and geographically distributed software development environments."

   ######################################################################

   =======
   2) Bugs
   =======

   The server is affected by multiple integer overflow vulnerabilities
   caused by the calculation of the amount of memory it needs to allocate
   for some arrays received from the clients.

   The main ways I have found for exploiting these vulnerabilities are
   through the PROJECT_LOGIN and SET_SERVER_ACL commands where the 32 bit
   number received from the client which specifies the amount of entries
   in the packet is multiplicated respectively for 8 (or 4 depending by
   the folder names or specifications) and 12, the result is then used for
   allocating the memory without considering the 32 bit limit.
```

www.securityfocus.com/archive/1/485458/30/0/threaded

FIGURE 4-2   Example Bugtraq Posting

The CVE list, in addition to announcing vulnerabilities, assigns identifiers to individual vulnerabilities. For example, suppose two Microsoft Word buffer overflow vulnerabilities are announced at the same time, or a Linux kernel overflow prompts the creation of fixes from Debian and Red Hat. The CVE identifiers help security professionals distinguish vulnerabilities and their fixes.

For more details on the CVE process or to subscribe to their regular vulnerability updates, visit their website at *http://cve.mitre.org/cve/index.html.*

OFFLINE

The Internet Storm Center

The SANS Institute, which hosts many respected network security conferences and also provides paths to various security certifications, also operates the Internet Storm Center (ISC, at *http://isc.sans.org*).

The mission of the ISC is to provide detection and analysis of network threats, while providing assessments of their severity and advice on how to counter the threat. Perhaps the most useful portion of the site is the "Handler's Diary," which is a daily log written by the volunteer intrusion analysts that staff the storm center.

Because it accepts firewall and intrusion logs from many sources, the ISC is often one of the first organizations to spot network anomalies, and often traces them to specific malware or vulnerability exploits.

For example, an advisory issued on December 24, 2007, which describes the beginning of an anticipated attack by the "Storm Botnet," is shown in Figure 4-3.

isc.sans.org/diary.html?date=2007-12-24

FIGURE 4-3   Example SANS Alert

The ISC Handler's Diary is available as an RSS feed (*http://isc.sans.org/xml.html*) and also includes a facility for forwarding the entries to a pager.

Weaknesses in Processes and Procedures

While generating much less buzz than software vulnerabilities, weaknesses in processes and procedures are just as hazardous, and are more difficult to detect and fix, because they typically involve the weakest link in our security defenses, the human element. These "soft" vulnerabilities often arise when a policy is violated, or when the processes and procedures that implement the policy are inadequate or fail.

For example, consider the password: almost all organizations have policies that specify password complexity (must be at least eight characters long, include at least one alphabetic character, etc.), as well as a required change schedule and restrictions on how often a password can be reused. However, if this policy is not enforced by means of process and procedure, then it does nothing to protect an organization against a dictionary attack on access credentials.

To ensure that security policy is implemented, organizations should hold regular security awareness training for all employees (including contractors and business partners). However, training by itself is not sufficient and must be supplemented with a regular review of the policies and their implementation. These reviews have many names, but a common one is the policy compliance audit.[7]

Audits verify that an organization's security policies are prudent (cover the right issues) and are being implemented correctly. For example, to verify the implementation of the password policy, an auditor would seek evidence that employees are required to change their passwords on a regular basis and that the complexity and reuse standards are enforced as part of that process.

The auditor typically looks at two things: the relevant policy and the evidence that the policy is being implemented. If the compliance is not documented, you are not in compliance with the policy.

Security professionals view the process of implementing policy and auditing (verifying) compliance with that policy as an integral part of policy development. Some resources on policy and compliance are the Computer Security Resource Center at the U.S. National Institute of Standards and Technology (*http://csrc.nist.gov*) and textbooks like *Management of Information Security* by Michael Whitman and Herbert Mattord (Course Technology).

Scanning and Analysis Tools

To truly assess the risk within a computing environment, you must deploy technical controls using a strategy of defense in depth, which is likely to include intrusion detection/prevention systems (IDPS), active vulnerability scanners, passive vulnerability scanners, automated log analyzers, and protocol analyzers (commonly referred to as sniffers). The IDPS helps to secure networks by detecting intrusions; the scanners and analyzers help secure networks by helping administrators identify where the network needs securing. More specifically, scanners and analysis tools can find vulnerabilities in systems, holes in security components, and unsecured aspects of the network.

Scanners, sniffers, and other such vulnerability analysis tools are invaluable because they enable administrators to see what the attacker sees. Some of these tools are extremely complex, and others are rather simple; some are expensive commercial products, but many of the best scanning and analysis tools were developed by the security research community, and are available free on the Web. There is nothing wrong with a security administrator using the tools that potential attackers use in order to examine network defenses and find areas that require additional attention. In the military, there is a long and distinguished history of generals inspecting the troops under their command before battle, walking down the line to inspect the equipment and mental preparedness of each soldier. In a similar way, the security administrator can use vulnerability analysis tools to inspect the units (host computers and network devices) under his or her command. A word of caution, though: many of these scanning and analysis tools have distinct signatures, and some Internet service providers (ISPs) watch for these signatures, and might pull the access privileges of those who use them. Administrators should establish a working relationship with their ISPs, and notify them when planning to scan the external network.

Scanning tools are typically used as part of an attack protocol to collect information that an attacker would need to launch a successful attack. The **attack protocol** is a series of steps or processes used by an attacker, in a logical sequence, to launch an attack against a target system or network. One of the preparatory parts of the attack protocol is the collection of publicly available information about a potential target, a process known as footprinting. **Footprinting** is the organized research of the Internet addresses owned or controlled by a target organization. The attacker uses public Internet data sources to perform searches to identify the network addresses of the organization.

gathering info. To prepare the Attack.

OFFLINE

Fingerprinting Ficticious.com

The first step in footprinting our target, fictitious.com, is to identify its assigned address range. One common way to start is to determine the IP address of the Web site, which is easily done using the nslookup command (note that these examples are contrived to use RFC1918 addresses rather than publicly routable addresses):

```
:nslookup www.ficticious.com
Server: mynameserver.hackersrus.com
Address: 10.1.2.100
Non-authoritative answer:
Name:  www.ficticious.com
Address: 192.168.3.100
```

The next step is to consult the responsible domain registrar to see what IP address ranges are registered to the organization. Assuming ficticious.com is located in North America, you use the ARIN database at *http://ws.arin.net/whois*.

A query on 192.168.3.100 reveals the following information about ficticious.com:

```
OrgName:    Ficticious.com
OrgID:      FC-7
Address:    126 Anywhere Lane
City:       Somecity
StateProv:  Somestate
PostalCode: 99999
Country:    US
```

continued

```
NetRange:  192.168.3.0 - 192.168.3.255
CIDR:    192.168.3.0/24
NetName: FC-8
NetHandle: NET-192-168-3-0-1
Parent:   NET-192.168.0.0.0
NetType:  Direct Assignment
NameServer: NS1.ficticious.com
NameServer: NS2.ficticious.com
NameServer: NS3.ficticious.com
NameServer: NS4.ficticious.com
Comment:
RegDate:  2007-12-20
Updated:  2007-12-23

RTechHandle: XV191-ARIN
RTechName:  Doe, John
RTechPhone: +1-999-999-9999
RTechEmail: jdoe@ficticious.com
```

*Most importante info Range of IP Address (handwritten annotation)

The most important information for footprinting purposes is the "NetRange," which shows ficticious.com has been assigned the addresses 192.168.3.0–192.168.3.255. All publicly accessible services will be offered on one of those addresses, so when you begin the fingerprinting process, you will look at all those addresses.

Another piece of useful information is the name, phone number, and e-mail address of the technical contact. You might be able to make use of this information in a social engineering attack on the organization. For this reason, it is a recommended practice to provide generic information rather than actual employee names (e.g., network operator, the phone number of the help desk, and an e-mail such as *netops@ficticious.com*).

This research is augmented by browsing the organization's Web pages, since the Web pages usually contain quantities of information about internal systems, individuals developing Web pages, and other tidbits, which can be used for social engineering attacks. The View Source command, available on most popular Web browsers, allows users to see the source code behind the page. Details in this source code can provide clues for potential attackers and give them insight into the configuration of an internal network, such as the locations and directories for Common Gateway Interface (CGI) scripts and the names or addresses of computers and servers. In addition, public business Web sites (such as Forbes or Yahoo Business) often reveal information about company structure, commonly used company names, and other information that attackers find useful. Furthermore, common search engines allow attackers to query for any site that links to their proposed target. By doing a little bit of initial Internet research into a company, an attacker can often find additional Internet locations that are not commonly associated with the company—that is, business-to-business (B2B) partners and subsidiaries. Armed with this information, the attacker can find the weakest link into the target network.

For an example, consider Company X, which has a large datacenter located in Atlanta. The datacenter has been secured, and thus it is very hard for an attacker to break into the datacenter via the Internet. However, the attacker has run a "link:" query on the search engine *www.altavista.com* and found a small Web server that links to Company X's main Web server. After further investigation the attacker learns that the small Web server was set up by an administrator at a remote facility, and that the remote facility has, via its own leased lines, an unrestricted internal link into Company X's corporate datacenter. The attacker can now attack the weaker site at the remote facility and use this compromised network—which is an internal network—to attack the true target. If a company has a trusted network connection with 15 business partners, one weak business partner can compromise all 16 networks.

To assist in the footprint intelligence collection process, you can use an enhanced Web scanner that, among other things, can scan entire Web sites for valuable pieces of information, such as server names and e-mail addresses. One such scanner is called Sam Spade, the details of which can be found at *www.samspade.org*. A sample screenshot from Sam Spade is shown in Figure 4-4. Sam Spade can also do a host of other scans and probes, such as sending multiple ICMP information requests (pings), attempting to retrieve multiple and cross-zoned DNS queries, and performing network analysis queries (known, from the commonly used UNIX command for performing the analysis, as traceroutes). All of these are powerful diagnostic and hacking activities. Sam Spade is not, however, considered hackerware (or hacker-oriented software), but rather is a utility that happens to be useful to network administrators and miscreants alike.

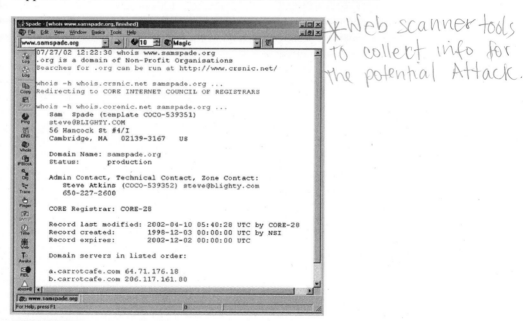

FIGURE 4-4 Sam Spade

Linux or BSD systems support a tool called "wget" that allows a remote individual to "mirror" entire Web sites. With this tool, attackers can copy an entire Web site and then go through the source HTML, JavaScript, and Web-based forms at their leisure, collecting and collating all of the data from the source code that will be useful to them for their attack.

The next phase of the attack protocol is a data-gathering process called **fingerprinting.** This is a systematic survey of all of the target organization's Internet addresses (which are collected during the footprinting phase described above); the survey is conducted to identify the network services offered by the hosts in that range. By using the tools discussed in the next section, fingerprinting reveals useful information about the internal structure and operational nature of the target system or network for the anticipated attack. Since these tools were created to find vulnerabilities in systems and networks quickly and with a minimum of effort, they are valuable for the network defender, since they can quickly pinpoint the parts of the systems or network that need a prompt repair to close the vulnerability.

Port Scanners

Port-scanning utilities (or **port scanners**) are tools used by both attackers and defenders to identify (or fingerprint) the computers that are active on a network, as well as the ports and services active on those computers, the functions and roles the machines are fulfilling, and other useful information. These tools can scan for specific types of computers, protocols, or resources, or their scans can be generic. It is helpful to understand the environment that exists in the network you are using, so that you can use the tool most suited to the data collection task at hand. For instance, if you are trying to identify a Windows computer in a typical network, a built-in feature of the operating system, nbtstat, may be able to get the answer you need very quickly, without the installation of a scanner. This tool does not work on other types of networks, however, so you must know your tools in order to make the best use of the features of each.

The more specific the scanner is, the better and more useful the information it provides to attackers and defenders. However, you should keep a generic, broad-based scanner in your toolbox, as well, to help locate and identify rogue nodes on the network that administrators may be unaware of. Probably the most popular port scanner is Nmap, which runs on both UNIX and Windows systems. You can find out more about Nmap at *http://insecure.org*. As of version 4.5, Nmap includes the Zenmap GUI front end, which simplifies use of the tool.

A port is a network channel or connection point in a data communications system. Within TCP/IP, TCP, and User Datagram Protocol (UDP), port numbers differentiate the multiple communication channels that are used to connect to the network services being offered on the same network device. Each application within TCP/IP has a unique port number. Some have default ports but can also use other ports. Some of the well-known port numbers are presented in Table 4-1. In all, there are 65,536 port numbers in use for TCP and another 65,536 port numbers for UDP. Services using the TCP/IP protocol can run on any port; however, the services with reserved ports (also called well-known ports) generally run on ports 1–1023. Port 0 is not used. Ports greater than 1023 are typically referred to as ephemeral ports and may be randomly allocated to server and client processes.

Why secure open ports? Simply put, an open port is an open door, and can be used by an attacker to send commands to a computer, potentially gain access to a server, and possibly exert control over a networking device. The general policy statement is to remove from service or secure any port not absolutely necessary to conducting business. For example, if a business doesn't host Web services, there is no need for port 80 to be available on its servers.

Most common ports:

TABLE 4-1 Commonly Used Port Numbers

TCP Port Numbers	TCP Service
20 and 21	File Transfer Protocol (FTP)
22	Secure Shell (SSH)
23	Telnet
25	Simple Mail Transfer Protocol (SMTP)
53	Domain Name Services (DNS)
67 and 68	Dynamic Host Configuration Protocol (DHCP)
80	Hypertext Transfer Protocol (HTTP)
110	Post Office Protocol (POP3)
161	Simple Network Management Protocol (SNMP)
194	IRC chat port (used for device sharing)
443	HTTP over SSL
8080	Used for proxy services

Firewall Analysis Tools

Understanding exactly where an organization's firewall is located and learning what the existing rule sets on the firewall do are very important steps for any security administrator. There are several tools that automate the remote discovery of firewall rules and assist the administrator (or attacker) in analyzing the rules to determine exactly what they allow and what they reject.

The Nmap tool mentioned earlier has some advanced options that are useful for firewall analysis. The Nmap option called *Idle scanning* (which is run with the -I switch) will allow the Nmap user to bounce your scan across a firewall by using one of the IDLE DMZ hosts as the initiator of the scan. More specifically, as most operating systems do not use truly random IP packet identification numbers (IP IDs), if there is more than one host in the DMZ and one host uses non-random IP IDs, then the attacker can query the server (server X) and obtain the currently used IP ID, as well as the known algorithm for incrementing the IP IDs. The attacker can then spoof a packet that is allegedly from server X and destined for an internal IP address behind the firewall. If the port is open on the internal machine, the internal machine replies to server X with a SYN-ACK packet, which forces server X to respond with a TCP RESET packet. In responding with the TCP RESET, server X increments its IP ID number. The attacker can now query server X a second time to see if the IP ID has incremented. If it has, the attacker knows that the internal machine is alive and that the internal machine has the queried service port open. In a nutshell, running the Nmap Idle scan allows an attacker to scan an internal network as if he or she were physically located on a trusted machine inside the DMZ.

Another tool that can be used to analyze firewalls is Firewalk. Written by noted author and network security expert Mike Schiffman, Firewalk uses incrementing Time-To-Live (TTL) packets to determine the path into a network, as well as the default firewall policy. Running Firewalk against a target machine reveals where routers and firewalls are filtering traffic to the target host. More information on Firewalk can be obtained from *http://packetstormsecurity.org/UNIX/audit/firewalk/*.

Another firewall analysis tool is hping, which is a modified ping client. It supports multiple protocols, and you can use a command line to specify nearly any of the ping parameters. For instance, you can use hping with modified TTL values to determine the infrastructure of a DMZ. You can use hping with specific ICMP flags in order to bypass poorly configured firewalls (i.e., firewalls that allow all ICMP traffic to pass through) and find internal systems. You can find hping at *www.hping.org*.

Administrators who are wary of using the same tools that attackers use should remember two important points: regardless of the nature of the tool that is used to validate or analyze a firewall's configuration, it is the intent of the user that dictates how the information gathered will be used; in order to defend a computer or network, it is necessary to understand the ways it can be attacked. Thus, a tool that can help close up an open or poorly configured firewall helps the network defender minimize the risk from attack.

Operating System Detection Tools

Identifying a target computer's operating system is very valuable to an attacker, because once the OS is known, it is easy to determine all of the vulnerabilities to which it is susceptible. There are many tools that use networking protocols to determine a remote computer's OS. One such tool is XProbe, which uses ICMP to determine the remote OS. This tool can be found at *http://sourceforge.net/projects/xprobe/*. XProbe sends a lot of different ICMP queries against the target host. As reply packets are received, XProbe matches these responses from the target's TCP/IP stack with its own internal database of known responses. Because most OSs have a unique way of responding to ICMP requests, Xprobe is able to find matches and thus detect the operating systems of remote computers. System and network administrators should take note of this, and restrict the use of ICMP through their organization's firewalls and, when possible, within its internal networks.

The port scanner Nmap also includes a version detection engine, which attempts to identify the operating system version and version information for any running services, as shown in Figure 4-5.

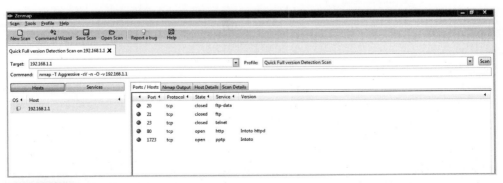

FIGURE 4-5   Version Detection with Nmap

Vulnerability Scanners

Active vulnerability scanners scan networks for highly detailed information. An *active* scanner is one that initiates traffic on the network in order to identify security holes. As a class, this type of scanner identifies exposed usernames and groups, shows open network shares, and exposes configuration problems and other vulnerabilities in servers. An example of a vulnerability scanner is GFI LANguard Network Security Scanner (NSS), which is available as freeware for noncommercial use. Another vulnerability scanner is Nessus, which is a professional freeware utility that uses IP packets to identify available hosts, the services (ports) each host is offering, the operating system and OS version they are running, the type of packet filters and firewalls in use, and dozens of other network characteristics. Figures 4-6 and 4-7 show sample LANguard and Nessus result screens.

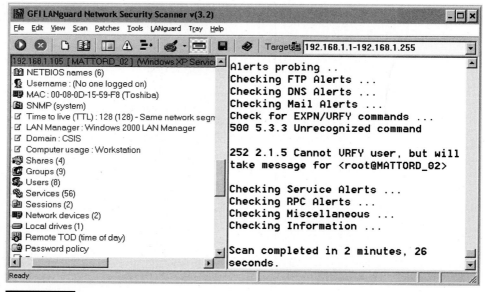

FIGURE 4-6   LANguard

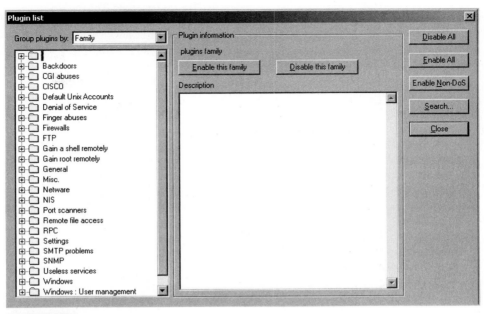

FIGURE 4-7 Nessus

Vulnerability scanners are proficient at finding known, documented holes, but what happens if the Web server is from a new vendor, or the application was developed by an internal development team? There is a class of vulnerability scanners called blackbox scanners, or fuzzers. Fuzz testing is a straightforward testing technique that looks for vulnerabilities in a program or protocol by feeding random input to the program or to a network running the protocol. Vulnerabilities can be detected by measuring the outcome of the random inputs. One fuzz scanner is SPIKE, which has two primary components. The first is the SPIKE Proxy, which is a full-blown proxy server. As Web site visitors utilize the proxy, SPIKE builds a database of each of the traversed pages, forms, and other Web-specific information. When the Web site owner determines that enough history has been collected to fully characterize the Web sites, SPIKE can check the Web site for bugs—that is, administrators can use the usage history collected by SPIKE to traverse all known pages, forms, and active programs (e.g., asp, cgi-bin), and can test the system by attempting overflows, SQL injection, cross-site scripting, and many other classes of Web attacks.

SPIKE can "fuzz" any protocol that utilizes TCP/IP. By sniffing a session and building a SPIKE script, or building a full-blown C program using the SPIKE API, a user can simulate and fuzz nearly any protocol. Figure 4-8 shows a sample SPIKE script being prepared to fuzz the ISAKAMP protocol (which is used by VPNs). Figure 4-9 shows the SPIKE program, generic_send_udp, fuzzing an IKE server using the SPIKE script. As you can see, SPIKE can be used to quickly fuzz and find weaknesses in nearly any protocol.[8]

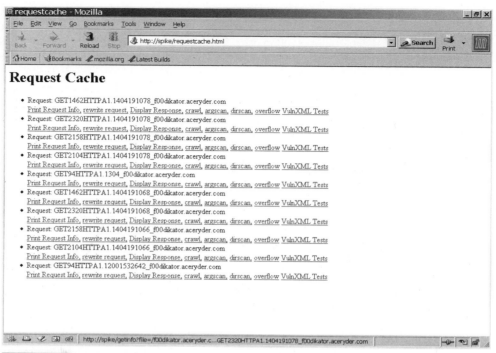

FIGURE 4-8   SPIKE in Action

```
root@f00dikator:~/SPIKE/src/IKE
[root@f00dikator IKE]# more ike_generic.spk
// jwlampe@aceryder.com

s_block_start("ikky");
s_binary("FF 00 FE 01 FD 02 FC 03"); //8 byte initiator cookie
s_binary("00 00 00 00 00 00 00 00"); // 8 byte responder cookie
s_binary_block_size_byte_variable("NP"); //next payload
s_binary_block_size_byte_variable("majorminor"); //major version (hi order bits)/ minor version (lo order bits)
s_binary_block_size_byte_variable("ET");    // exchange type, make this a static 0x04 for quicker rezults ;-)
s_binary("00");              // IKE flag (upper 3 bits, unused lower 5)
s_binary("00 00 00 00");         // message ID
s_binary_block_size_halfword_bigendian_variable("lenhi");    // do *not* set a Len...this is half the fun
s_binary_block_size_halfword_bigendian_variable("lenlo");    // len is, btw, 0x00 0x00 0x01 0x7B

s_binary_block_size_byte_variable("SANP");        // security association next payload
s_binary("00");                 // reserved
s_binary_block_size_byte_variable("PLEN");       // total len of all payloads...
s_binary("00 00 00");             // first 3 bytes of DOI
s_binary_block_size_byte_variable("DOI");       // last byte of DOI
s_binary("00 00 00");             // first 3 bytes of Situation
s_binary_block_size_byte_variable("SIT");      // last byte of situation
s_binary("00 00");                     // proposal next payload == 0/last proposal | reserved
s_binary_block_size_halfword_bigendian_variable("plen");  // proposal len
--More--(36%)
```

FIGURE 4-9   SPIKE vs. IKE

The Nessus scanner has a class of attacks called *DESTRUCTIVE*. If enabled, Nessus attempts common overflow techniques against a target host. Fuzzers or black-box scanners and Nessus in destructive mode can be very dangerous tools and should only be used in a lab environment. In fact, these tools are so powerful that even system defenders who use them are not likely to use them in the most aggressive modes on their production networks. At the time of this writing, the most popular are Nessus (a commercial version of Nessus for Windows is available), Retina, and Internet Scanner. The Nessus scanner is available at no cost; the other two require a license fee.

Often, members of an organization require proof that a system is actually vulnerable to a certain attack. They may require such proof in order to avoid having system administrators attempt to repair systems that are not in fact broken, or because they have not yet built a satisfactory relationship with the vulnerability assessment team. There exists a class of scanners that actually exploit the remote machine and allow the vulnerability analyst (sometimes called a penetration tester) to create an account, modify a Web page, or view data. These tools can be very dangerous and should only be used when absolutely necessary. Three tools that can perform this action are Core Impact, Immunity's CANVAS, and the Metasploit Framework.

Of these three tools, only the Metasploit Framework is available without a license fee (see *www.metasploit.com*). The Metasploit Framework is a collection of exploits coupled with an interface that allows you to customize exploitation of vulnerable systems. For instance, you can customize the overflow to exploit a Microsoft Exchange server and enable the specific attack script to insert a unique command, perhaps to create a new user and add that user to the administrators group. See Figure 4-10 for a screenshot of the Metasploit Framework in action.

```
        =[ msf v3.1-release
+ -- --=[ 268 exploits - 118 payloads
+ -- --=[ 17 encoders - 6 nops
        =[ 52 aux
msf > use exploit/windows/dcerpc/ms03_026_dcom
msf exploit(ms03_026_dcom) > set PAYLOAD windows/shell/bind_tcp
PAYLOAD => windows/shell/bind_tcp
msf exploit(ms03_026_dcom) > set RHOST 192.168.1.20
RHOST => 192.168.1.20
msf exploit(ms03_026_dcom) > exploit
[*] Started bind handler
[*] Trying target Windows NT SP3-6a/2000/XP/2003 Universal...
[*] Binding to 4d9f4ab8-7d1c-11cf-861e-0020af6e7c57:0.0@ncacn_ip_tcp:192.168.1.20[135] ...
[*] Bound to 4d9f4ab8-7d1c-11cf-861e-0020af6e7c57:0.0@ncacn_ip_tcp:192.168.1.20[135] ...
[*] Sending exploit ...
[*] The DCERPC service did not reply to our request
[*] Sending stage (474 bytes)
[*] Command shell session 1 opened (192.168.1.3:2535 -> 192.168.1.20:4444)
msf exploit(ms03_026_dcom) >
```

FIGURE 4-10   Metasploit

A **passive vulnerability scanner** listens in on the network and identifies vulnerable versions of both server and client software. There are currently two primary vendors offering this type of scanning solution: Tenable Network Security, which offers a product called NeVO, and Sourcefire, which offers a product called RNA. Passive scanners are advantageous in that they do not require vulnerability analysts to get approval prior to testing. These tools simply monitor the network connections to and from a server to obtain a list of vulnerable applications. Furthermore, passive vulnerability scanners can find client-side vulnerabilities that are typically not found by active scanners. For instance, an active scanner operating without DOMAIN Admin rights would be unable to determine the version of Internet Explorer running on a desktop machine, but a passive scanner can observe the traffic to and from the client to make that determination. See Figure 4-11 for a screenshot of the NeVO passive vulnerability scanner running on Windows XP.

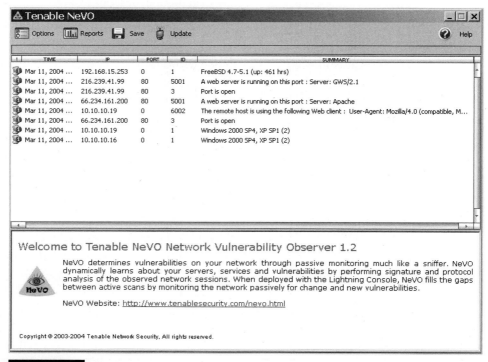

FIGURE 4-11 NeVO

Table 4-2 provides World Wide Web addresses for the products mentioned in the vulnerability scanners section.

TABLE 4-2 Vulnerability Scanner Products and Web Pages

Product	Web Page
Nessus	*www.nessus.org*
Nessus for Windows	*www.tenablesecurity.com*
GFI LANguard Network Security Scanner	*www.gfi.com/languard*
SPIKE – SPIKE Proxy	*www.immunitysec.com*
Retina	*www.eeye.com*
Internet Scanner	*www.iss.net*
Core Impact	*www.coresecurity.com/*
CANVAS	*www.immunitysec.com/*
Metasploit Framework	*www.metasploit.com*

Packet Sniffers

A **packet sniffer** (sometimes called a network protocol analyzer) is a network tool that collects copies of packets from the network and analyzes them. It can provide a network administrator with valuable information for diagnosing and resolving networking issues. In the wrong hands, however, a sniffer can be used to eavesdrop on network traffic. There are both commercial and open-source sniffers—more specifically, Sniffer is a commercial product, and Snort is open-source software. An excellent free, client-based network protocol analyzer is Ethereal (*www.ethereal.com*). Ethereal allows the administrator to examine data from both live network traffic and captured traffic. Ethereal has several features, including a language filter and TCP session reconstruction utility. Figure 4-12 shows a sample screen from Ethereal. Typically, to use these types of programs most effectively, the user must be connected to a network from a central location. Simply tapping into an Internet connection floods you with more data than can be readily processed, and technically constitutes a violation of the wiretapping act. To use a packet sniffer legally, the administrator must: (1) be on a network that the organization owns, (2) be under direct authorization of the owners of the network, and (3) have knowledge and consent of the content creators. If all three conditions are met, the administrator can selectively collect and analyze packets to identify and diagnose problems on the network. Conditions 1 and 2 are self-explanatory. The third, consent, is usually handled by having all system users sign a release when they are issued a user ID and password. Incidentally, these three items are the same requirements for employee monitoring in general, and packet sniffing should be construed as a form of employee monitoring.

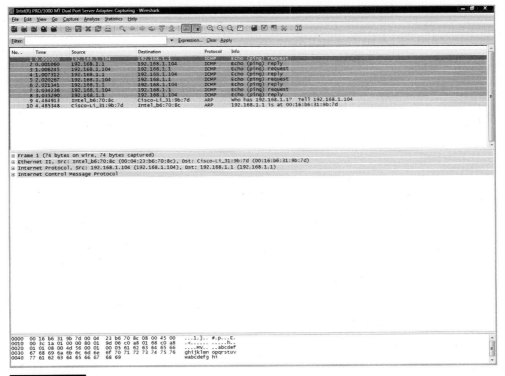

FIGURE 4-12   Ethereal

Many administrators feel that they are safe from sniffer attacks when their computing environment is primarily a switched network environment. This couldn't be further from the truth. There are a number of open-source sniffers that support alternate networking approaches that can, in turn, enable packet sniffing in a switched network environment. Two of these alternate networking approaches are ARP-spoofing and session hijacking (which uses tools like ettercap). To secure data in transit across any network, organizations must use encryption to be ensured of content privacy.

Wireless Security Tools

802.11 wireless networks have sprung up as subnets on nearly all large networks. A wireless connection, while convenient, has many potential security holes. An organization that spends all of its time securing the wired network and leaves wireless networks to operate in any manner is opening itself up for a security breach. As a security professional, you must assess the risk of wireless networks. A wireless security toolkit should include the ability to sniff wireless traffic, scan wireless hosts, and assess the level of privacy or confidentiality afforded on the wireless network. There is a suite of tools from dachb0den labs (*www.dachb0den.com/projects/bsd-airtools.html*) called bsd-airtools that automates all of the items noted above. The tools included within the bsd-airtools toolset are an access point detection tool, a sniffer, and a tool called dstumbler used to crack Wired Equivalent Protocol (WEP) encryption keys. A Windows version of the dstumbler tool called NetStumbler is also offered as freeware and can be found at *www.netstumbler.org*. Figure 4-13 shows NetStumbler running on a Windows XP machine. Another wireless tool is AirSnare, a free tool that can be run on a low-end wireless workstation. AirSnare monitors the airwaves for any new devices or access points. When it finds one, AirSnare sounds an alarm alerting the administrators that a new, potentially dangerous, wireless apparatus is attempting access on a closed wireless network. Figure 4-14 shows AirSnare in action.

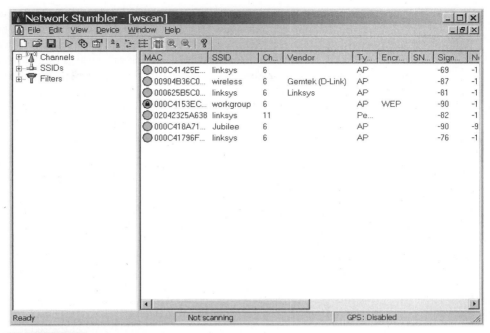

FIGURE 4-13 NetStumbler

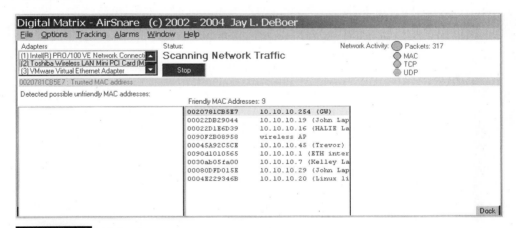

FIGURE 4-14 AirSnare

Penetration Testing

Many organizations use a specialized service called a penetration test to assess their security posture on a regular basis. A penetration test essentially involves using all the techniques and tools available to an attacker in order to attempt to compromise or penetrate an organization's defenses.

Penetration tests can be performed in a variety of ways and with different scopes. For example, the organization might only wish to assess the quality of their network defenses, and would therefore limit the scope of the test to their externally accessible network resources (Web sites, e-commerce sites, wireless networking infrastructure, etc.). For a more complete assessment, the scope may include all the organization's defenses, including physical security.

The scope should also identify the goal of the test–for example, should the compromise stop at the identification of an exploitable vulnerability, or should the exploit actually be carried out? There are advantages and disadvantages to either decision. For example, stopping at the identification phase has minimal impact on the organization, while carrying out a full exploit exercises the organization's incident detection and response plans.

Penetration testing can be performed by an internal group (so called "red teams") or outsourced to an external organization. Needless to say, when a penetration (or "pen") test is outsourced, the agreement must carefully specify the scope and limitations of the test, and ensure absolute confidentiality of the results.

A variable of the penetration test, whether performed internally or outsourced, is the amount of information provided to the red team. There are three categories of testing:

- Black box—the red team is given no information whatsoever about the organization, and approaches the organization as an external attacker. While this is the most realistic type of test, it also requires the most work on the part of the red team and is therefore the most expensive. This is also the most difficult type of test for an organization to do internally, as its employees cannot really approach the organization as if they knew nothing about it.
- Gray box—the red team is given some general information about the organization such as general structure, network address ranges, software, and versions. This reduces the level of effort for the red team and reduces the cost of the exercise.
- White box—the red team has full information on the organization and its structure. They are provided with detailed network maps, software documentation, details on alarm systems, etc. This type of test is perhaps easiest to perform and can serve the very useful purpose of verifying that the controls in place are actually installed and operating correctly and, most importantly, actually do what they are supposed to.

The tools used in a penetration test are the same tools that security professionals use to defend the organization (a fine example of dual-use technology). Where a defender uses the tools to identify potential weaknesses that can be remediated, the red team uses them as an attacker would, to identify portals and methods of entry.

Remember that not all attacks against an organization's assets are technical attacks. For example, using the domain registration information for ficticious.com, an attacker could call the help desk impersonating the network technical contact in order to have their password reset.

OFFLINE

The Doughnut Lady

One software development organization's physical security was penetrated by a young woman with the aid of some pillows and several bags of doughnuts. She used the pillows under a maternity outfit and presented herself at the security checkpoint with several bags of doughnuts "for the break room" at a few minutes past 4 pm. The company had recently been the subject of a news story about a behind-schedule software project and the maximum effort being made to deliver the product on time; the doughnuts were therefore for the people working late. The guard informed her that she couldn't deliver the doughnuts without authorization, and the woman—who was a penetration tester—made a great show of trying to get the guard to help her read a handwritten delivery order that clearly specified the company name and the number of doughnuts, but the name of the person ordering them was blurred.

She said she was late for an appointment with her obstetrician—her baby was due in a few days. The guard gave in, and directed her to the break room.

While some might say that this was "dirty pool," remember that penetration testers can use any means available to violate security policy.

Tools can also be combined to form a quite effective penetration solution. For example, Nmap can identify open network ports and make a good guess as to the software versions running on the servers. This information can then be used with the Metasploit Framework to run all available exploits for that software and version. This operation is shown as the "hack-o-matic" in Figure 4-15.

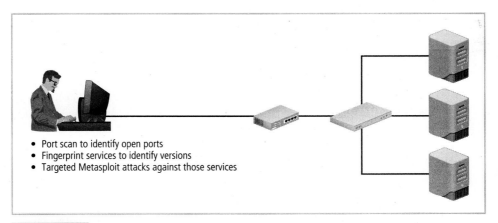

- Port scan to identify open ports
- Fingerprint services to identify versions
- Targeted Metasploit attacks against those services

FIGURE 4-15   Hack-o-Matic

For this technique to succeed, there only has to be one server accessible to the attacker somewhere in the infrastructure.

Chapter Summary

- To maintain secure networks, information security professionals must be prepared to systematically identify system vulnerabilities. This is often done by performing self-assessment using scanning and penetration tools testing.

- Common vulnerabilities fall into two broad classes: Defects in software or firmware, and weaknesses in processes and procedures, which typically involve the weakest link in your security defenses, the human element.

- To keep abreast of emerging vulnerabilities, information security professionals should regularly consult vendor announcements, full disclosure mailing lists, and CVE—the common vulnerabilities and exposures database maintained by Mitre Corporation for the Department of Homeland Security.

- To assess the risk within a computing environment, network professionals must use tools such as intrusion/prevention detection systems (IDPS), active vulnerability scanners, passive vulnerability scanners, automated log analyzers, and protocol analyzers, commonly referred to as sniffers.

- Many organizations use a service called a penetration test to assess their security posture on a regular basis. A penetration test team, called a red team, uses all the techniques and tools available to attackers in order to attempt to compromise or penetrate an organization's defenses.

Review Questions

1. What is a vulnerability? Does it differ from a threat? How so?
2. What are the two major classes of vulnerability?
3. What is a buffer overflow? What can occur when software has a buffer overflow vulnerability?
4. What is an injection attack? What kind of vulnerability gives rise to this type of attack?
5. What kinds of vulnerabilities can occur when programmers assume all network connections are secure?
6. What is a cross-site scripting attack? How is it used to compromise a network service?
7. Why is an organization's policy important to how it defends itself against network attacks?
8. What are the most significant sources of vulnerability information, and what do they provide?
9. What is an attack protocol, and how is it used to attack a network?
10. What is network footprinting? What is network fingerprinting? How are they related?
11. Why do many organizations ban port-scanning activities on their internal networks? Why would ISPs ban outbound port scanning by their customers?
12. What is an open port? Why is it important to limit the number of open ports a system has to only those that are absolutely essential?
13. What is a vulnerability scanner? How is it used to improve security?
14. What is the difference between active and passive vulnerability scanners?
15. What is a fuzz tester? How is it used to find network vulnerabilities?
16. What is a firewall analysis tool used for?
17. What kind of data and information can be found using a packet sniffer?
18. What capabilities should a wireless security toolkit include?
19. What is penetration testing, and how is it used in most organizations?
20. What are the three categories of penetration testing? Describe each of them.

Exercises

1. Visit the Open Web Application Security Project (OWASP) at *www.owasp.org/index.php/OWASP_Top_Ten_Project*. Answer these questions:
   a. What is the most recent annual Top 10 ranking?
   b. What is the primary aim of the OWASP Top 10?
   c. What is the next scheduled OWASP event? When and where is it?

2. Use a Web search engine to find out more about Nessus. Use the search results to answer these questions:
   a. Who started the "Nessus project"? When was it begun?
   b. What does Nessus do?

3. Visit the Web site at *www.securityfocus.com/archive/1*. Answer the following questions:
   a. What is the most recent announcement? When was it posted?
   b. Click the Vulnerabilities tab. What is the most recent vulnerability announcement you can see? When was it posted?

4. Visit the Web site at *cve.mitre.org/cve/index.html*. Answer these questions:
   a. What is a CVE?
   b. When did the CVE process start?
   c. Who owns a CVE?

5. Search for "Internet Storm Center" using a Web search engine. Answer the following questions:
   a. What is the ISC?
   b. When was it established?
   c. Which organization is the primary sponsor of the ISC?

Case Exercises

Virginia got the man's attention by shouting, "Stop!" When he turned around, she said, "Sir, unless you leave this floor immediately, I will call security. Please get your badge and work order, and then you can do your job. I'm just doing mine."

He said, "Obviously, this is getting us nowhere." He turned on his heel and left.

Questions:

1. Without knowing the ATI policy on visitors, do you think Virginia handled this situation correctly?
2. What do you think she should do now?

Endnotes

1. Michael Howard, David Leblanc, and John Viega (2005). 19 *Deadly Sins of Software Security: Programming Flaws and How to Fix Them*. New York: McGraw-Hill.
2. *www.betanews.com/article/CrossSite_Scripting_Worm_Hits_MySpace/1129232391*
3. *http://en.wikipedia.org/wiki/Full_disclosure*
4. Schneier, B. (2000). *Secrets & Lies: Digital Security in a Networked World*. New York: John Wiley & Sons.
5. Verton, D. (2003, March 3). *Major Internet vulnerability discovered in e-mail protocol*. Retrieved December 15, 2007, from *www.computerworld.com/securitytopics/security/holes/story/0,10801,78991,00.html*.

6. *http://en.wikipedia.org/wiki/Window_of_vulnerability*

7. While "compliance audit" may mean an audit to verify compliance with SOX, GLBA, HIPAA, or other legislative mandates, in its more general sense it is quite appropriate to the task of verifying compliance with an organization's security policies.

8. For more information on fuzzers and their use in vulnerability research, see Michael Sutton, Adam Greene, and Pedram Amini, *Fuzzing: Brute Force Vulnerability Discovery*. 2007. Upper Saddle River: Addison-Wesley.

Firewall Planning and Design

5

> A goal without a plan is just a wish.
>
> **ANTOINE DE SAINT-EXUPERY**

MATTHIAS WAS GRINNING WHEN HE ENTERED THE conference room. Earlier in the week he had been given his first design assignment. A new client had hired ATI to build a network for them, and as part of his training, Matthias was going to work with the design team to plan the new client's network. This meeting was the kickoff for the project.

Matthias was eager to meet with the experienced network engineers from ATI. He had already begun to consider the options for this new client. Would they need to use a proxy server? Would they have to provide a reverse proxy? Would the firewall need to use a state table?

Austin Tuck, a network engineer and the project manager, came into the meeting room next. He didn't greet Matthias, and sat at the head of the table and started collating handouts for the meeting. The rest of the attendees came as a group and all of them sat down. It was obvious they all knew each other quite well.

Austin called them to order and began, "Hi everyone. Let me introduce our trainee. This is Matthias Paul. He is a third-shift network admin who is training for network security design. He'll be joining us for the project, which is why we'll always meet at 8:30 in the morning— he meets with us after his regular shift."

Austin continued, "Let's handle the rest of the introductions first."

The woman to Austin's left said, "Hi Matthias, my name is Keesha Williams. I'm the security engineer for this project. I work for Andy Ying, the manager of the security consulting group."

The man to her left said, "Hello. I'm Jeff Noak, security architect."

The next person to the left said, "My name is Kaz, and I'm the senior network architect."

Andy said, "OK. That's it for introductions. Here's the initial design packet and the customer specs. I think this is a 'number 3' with a volume rating of 4. Please check out my specs and let me know what you think. I have it set for first reading at change control this Thursday."

Andy stood up and said, "Thanks everyone."

Everyone but Andy and Matthias left the room.

LEARNING OBJECTIVES:
Upon completion of this material, you should be able to do the following:

- Identify common misconceptions about firewalls
- Explain why a firewall is dependent on an effective security policy
- Discuss what a firewall does
- Describe the types of firewall protection
- Identify the limitations of firewalls
- Evaluate and recommend suitable hardware and software for a firewall application

Introduction

Achieving network security is a process that imposes controls on an organization's network resources, with the goal of balancing the risks and rewards that come from network usage. The controls are a continually evolving set of policies, programs, and technologies. Networks that connect to the Internet for communications or commerce are perceived as being particularly vulnerable; attacks that get lots of publicity are usually portrayed as being accomplished by network-based hackers who gain access from remote network locations. In this light, firewalls and associated technical controls have become a fundamental security tool. They are now a required component of virtually every network, and serve as part of the Defense in Depth strategy by protecting many individual computers.

No security system can ensure with absolute certainty that it can protect all of an organization's information all of the time. But firewalls—used in conjunction with other technical controls and security policies and programs, deployed according to the needs of the businesses they protect, and maintained and upgraded on a regular basis—are one of the most effective security tools a network administrator has. This chapter provides an overview of the issues involved in planning and designing firewalls. First, you learn what a firewall is *not* so that you can begin to understand what it actually is. Then you learn about security policies and the rules and procedures that govern how a firewall works. You then learn about types of firewall protection, the limitations of firewalls, and hardware firewall implementations. The chapter finishes with evaluations of firewall software packages.

Throughout this book the term "firewall" is used in the singular, but a firewall is not necessarily a single router, computer, VPN gateway, or software program. Any individual firewall is actually a combination of multiple software and hardware components. This chapter assumes that you have a working knowledge of TCP/IP, the basics of network infrastructures, IP addressing and the domain system, and the Internet and Web-based software. If you're a bit rusty on the basics of TCP/IP or other aspects of network infrastructure, please visit *www.course.com* to find resources to refresh your skills.

Misconceptions About Firewalls

Most people have heard of the term "firewall," but not in connection with the Internet. They may know about the fireproof barrier between the engine of a car and its interior, or have heard the term used to describe a brick wall or other fireproof barrier. Such firewalls are intended to keep even the smallest amount of a dangerous element—specifically, fire—from passing from one side to the other.

Comparisons with structural firewalls have led to the false notion that a firewall is designed to prevent all attackers, viruses, and would-be intruders from entering a computer or computer network. In fact, firewalls are simply designed to enable authorized traffic to pass through and to block unauthorized traffic.

Some managers may also think that once you deploy a firewall, you can let it operate on its own. The fact is that firewalls aren't perfect. They are, after all, designed and configured by people, who are fallible. Firewalls also need constant maintenance to keep up with the latest security threats. They work best when they are part of a multi-layered approach to network security called **defense in depth**, which encompasses a security policy, the firewall, intrusion detection software, virus scanners, and encryption.

Firewalls Explained

In general, a **firewall** is anything, whether hardware or software (or a combination of hardware and software), that can filter the transmission of packets of digital information as they attempt to pass through a boundary of a network.
Firewalls perform two basic security functions:

- Packet filtering: First and foremost, a firewall must be able to determine whether to allow or deny the passage of packets of digital information, based on established security policy rules.

- Application proxy: In some cases, a firewall may provide network services to users while shielding individual host computers. This is done by breaking the IP flow (which is the traffic into and out of the network) between the network being protected and the network outside.

Firewalls can be complex, but if you thoroughly understand only these two functions, you'll make a lot of progress toward being able to choose the right firewall and configure it to protect a computer or network. Figure 5-1 illustrates the basic nature of a firewall stationed at a network perimeter.

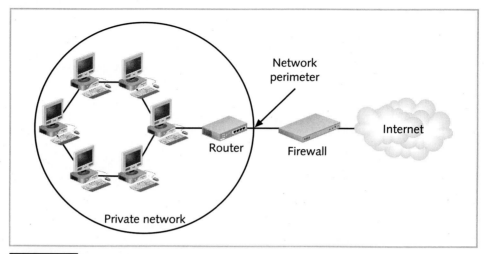

FIGURE 5-1   Firewall at the Perimeter

An Analogy: Office Tower Security Guard

A firewall is like a security guard at a guardhouse or checkpoint. Suppose you have taken a job as a security guard at a big, modern office tower. Thousands of people pass into and out of the building's security checkpoint every day. (For security reasons, there's only *one* security checkpoint.) How do you know who's an authorized employee and who's an intruder? To enable you to make decisions about who gets in and who does not, the security department has set up these rules:

- All personnel must enter and leave through Entrance 1.
- Staff wearing a green ID card can go through the checkpoint without signing in.
- Individuals wearing blue ID cards must sign in when entering and sign out when leaving.
- Everyone must pass through the metal detector and surrender knives or other potentially harmful devices.
- If someone passes through the checkpoint without being checked, push the red security button to alert the response team.

A firewall performs the same types of functions that a security checkpoint does—plus it may be able to undertake a few advanced gimmicks that a real-life security guard would never handle, like filtering unacceptable content or **caching** data (storing it on disk). In fact, these security rules have an equivalent in the digital realm of the firewall:

- Entry and exit points (called ports) are specified for different types of content. (Web page content typically travels through port 80, for instance.)
- Information that meets specified security criteria (such as an IP address) is allowed to pass, while other data is filtered—it can't pass through freely.

- Data in some cases must pass through firewall software that functions as a sort of electronic metal detector, scanning for viruses and repairing infected files before they invade the network.
- Firewalls can be configured to send out alert messages if viruses are detected and to notify staff of break-ins.

Firewall Security Features

As firewalls become more widely used, their manufacturers compete more fiercely to make their products stand out from the competition. Some companies have added a number of advanced security functions, such as the following:

- Logging unauthorized (as well as authorized) accesses both into and out of a network
- Providing a virtual private network (VPN) link to another network
- Authenticating users who provide usernames and passwords so that they can be identified and given access to the services they need
- Shielding hosts inside the network so that attackers cannot identify them and use them as staging areas for sustained attacks
- Caching data so that files that are repeatedly requested can be called from cache to reduce server load and improve Web-site performance
- Filtering content that is considered inappropriate, such as video streams, or dangerous, such as executable mail attachments

Firewall User Protection

For a single home user who regularly surfs the Web and uses e-mail and instant messaging, a firewall's primary job is to keep viruses from infecting files and prevent Trojan horses from entering the system and installing hidden openings called **back doors**, which can be used for access at a later time. Norton Internet Security, for instance, has an antivirus program that alerts users when an e-mail attachment or file containing a known virus is found.

Firewall Network Perimeter Security

A perimeter is a boundary between two zones of trust. For example, an organization's internal network is more trusted than the Internet, and it is common to install a firewall at this boundary to inspect and control the traffic that flows across it. There are additional zones of trust within the organization's network, such as among the Web, application, and database tiers of a three-tiered application.

If you have an extranet, an extended network that shares part of an organization's network with a third party (for example, a business partner), the location of the "perimeter" becomes a bit murky. If the extranet operates over a VPN, the VPN should have its own perimeter firewall because your network boundary technically extends to the end of the VPN. To be really secure, you should install a firewall on the partner's VPN host (as shown in Figure 5-2).

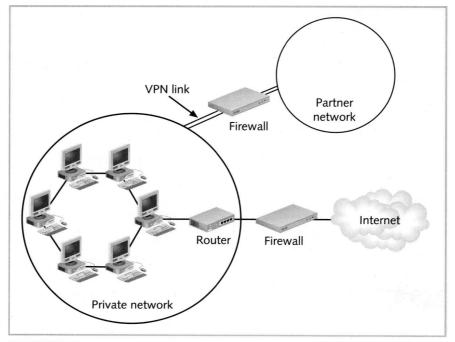

FIGURE 5-2 VPN Perimeter

Mobile devices such as laptops, PDAs, and SmartPhones blur the perimeter boundary even more as these mobile endpoints may extend the organization's network into Internet cafes, coffee shops, etc.

Locating the firewall at the perimeter has one obvious benefit: it enables you to set up a checkpoint where you can block viruses and infected e-mail messages before they get inside. However, it has less obvious benefits, too. A perimeter firewall enables you to log passing traffic, protecting the whole network at one time. If an attack does occur, having defined network boundaries—especially those that include firewalls—can minimize the damage.

As a professional network administrator or security expert, you also need to become familiar with firewalls that function as checkpoints, protecting large companies or other organizations from attackers and thieves. The firewall is positioned at the border of the network (zone of trust), providing security for all the computers within it, so each individual server or workstation need not provide its own security.

Firewall Components

A firewall can contain many components, including a packet filter, a proxy server, an authentication system, and software that performs Network Address Translation (NAT). Some firewalls can encrypt traffic, and some help establish VPNs. Some firewalls are packaged in a hardware device that also functions as a router. Firewalls themselves are often part of multiple-component security setups. The most effective protection systems used by large corporate networks employ not just one but several firewalls. They combine the firewalls with routers and other components to delineate zones of trust such as a screened subnet, also known as a demilitarized zone (DMZ), which is positioned between the internal network and the outside world.

Many firewalls make use of a bastion host, a machine that has no unnecessary services—only the bare essentials. A network that needs to connect to the Internet might have a bastion host and a service network (another term for screened subnet). Together, they are the only part of the organization exposed to the Internet. Figure 5-3 shows such a configuration.

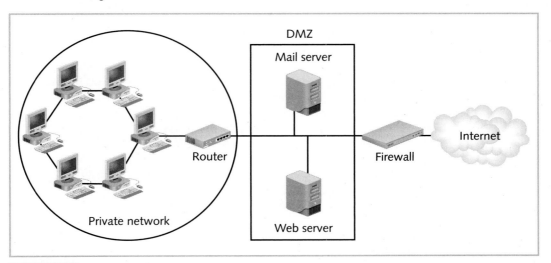

FIGURE 5-3 DMZ Networks

Firewall Security Tasks

To understand how a firewall works, you need to have a general idea of the range of threats against which you need to protect your network, and which security tasks the firewall can perform.

Restricting Access from Outside the Network

The most obvious goal of a firewall is to regulate which packets of information can enter the network. To do so, a firewall examines each packet to determine whether it meets the necessary "authorized" criteria. The criteria might be protocols or IP addresses on an "approved" list. Anything not on the list is excluded. Such packet filtering is discussed in more detail later in this chapter.

A firewall that does packet filtering (and virtually all do) protects networks from port scanning attacks. A port is a network sub-address (assigned a number between 0 and 65,535) through which a particular type of data is allowed to pass. In a port scanning attack, special software scans a series of network addresses, attempting to connect to each one. If a connection is made, it gives the attacker a target. A properly configured firewall only allows authorized connection attempts to the ports on the network it protects.

Technical Details

Ports

Ports work like apartment numbers in that they allow many network services to share a single network address. Just as Bob, Alice, and Eve each have their own apartment numbers in the building at 324 Evergreen Terrace, network services are like the apartments within the building at that address, each having its own port number.

To address a specific letter to Bob, a sender would address the envelope with the street address and then add the apartment number. The sender then adds their own address to the envelope, including the apartment number of their own building. This combination of a sender's full address (network address plus port) and receiver's address (network address plus port) makes up what is called a *socket*. To initiate a connection to a network service, the user specifies both the IP address and the port number.

Port numbers come in two flavors: well-known ports (those numbered at 1023 and below) and ephemeral ports (those numbered from 1024 through 65535). Well-known ports are defined for most common services such as the Web (port 80), SSH (port 22), Simple Mail Transport Protocol (port 25), or POP Mail (port 110) among many others. So, for example, when a user requests a connection to a Web server running at address 192.168.5.203, the Web browser would know to attempt the connection at port 80. Ephemeral port numbers are dynamically assigned as needed and have no special meaning outside the connection using them.

Exposed network services—such as an unplanned mail server running on a corporate Web server—are one of the biggest vulnerabilities that firewalls can protect against. A firewall can block external access to such unplanned services, so that, for example, mail server connection requests are always routed to the actual mail server and not any other systems that may have inadvertently set up a mail server.

Technical Details

Netstat on Windows

To find out how many connections are open on a Windows-based computer that is connected to the Internet, run the built-in network application netstat.exe, which displays network connections. Follow these general steps:

1. Click Start, point to Programs, point to Accessories, and then click Command Prompt to open a command prompt window.
2. Type netstat –an. (Note that if you launch netstat.exe and type netstat –an5, you'll refresh the display every five seconds. Periodically refreshing the display enables you to track connections as new services are launched or stopped.)
3. Press Enter to view command prompt information such as that shown in Figure 5-4.

continued

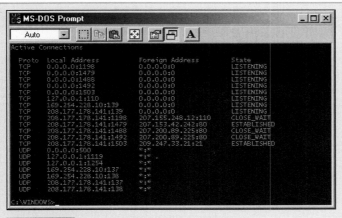

FIGURE 5-4 Listening on Multiple Ports

As you can see, you might have one or more services listening on ports that you don't even use. For example, if you are working at a Windows XP computer, you can determine which program is listening on a given port by typing netstat -b. The resulting information allows you to turn off the service, which closes the port.

Restricting Unauthorized Access from Inside the Network

It is sometimes easier to protect a network from the Internet than from an *inside* attack. Whether they are disgruntled, dishonest, or just ignorant of the proper security procedures, employees can be a major source of trouble. Be aware of the following:

- Staff who bring to the office mobile media (memory sticks, CD/DVDs, etc.) that contain virus-infected files.
- Staff who access office computers from home using remote access software that bypasses the perimeter firewall.
- **Social engineering**, in which an attacker obtains confidential information by contacting employees and deceiving them into giving up passwords, IP addresses, server names, and so on.
- Poorly trained firewall administrators; the better the instructions, the more effective the firewall. A firewall, for instance, can be configured to filter out certain IP packets, but it might pass those packets if they arrive in fragments.
- Employees who receive e-mail messages with executable attachments. If the employee downloads and executes that attachment it may launch a program that could spread to other computers using the recipient's e-mail address book. It might begin to damage files on the host machine or undertake any number of harmful activities.

Firewalls can help prevent some, but not all, of these internal threats. You can configure a firewall to recognize packets or to prevent access to protected files from internal as well as external hosts. Note, however, that remote access and social engineering attacks can be prevented only by means of training and raising awareness about security procedures.

Limiting Access to External Hosts

Along with restricting unauthorized external traffic from entering the network, firewalls can selectively permit traffic to go from inside the network to the Internet or other networks to provide more precise control of how employees inside the network use external resources. In other words, the firewall can act as a **proxy server** that makes high-level application connections on behalf of internal hosts and other machines. A single firewall product can provide both outbound packet filtering (shown in Figure 5-5) and outbound proxy services.

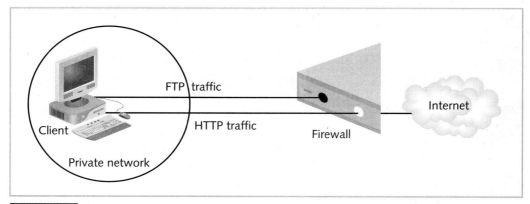

FIGURE 5-5   Outbound Packet Filtering

Application proxies can restrict internal users who want to gain unrestricted access to the Internet. Some technically sophisticated users might be able to circumvent the security measures you set up. They might, for instance, dial into the office using remote access, thus opening a security hole. They might use a remote access program like gotomypc.com, which provides client software they install on both their home and work computers. The software is configured so that every 15 or 20 seconds the work computer sends out a query "Does anyone want to connect to me?" (The target port used is TCP port 80, the commonly used HTTP port.) Such traffic may well go through the firewall unchecked, and it presents an obvious security risk since home networks are seldom as well defended as corporate networks, and attackers may be able to first attack a user's home network and thus gain access to the more valuable corporate network.

Protecting Critical Resources

Attacks on critical resources are becoming all too common: Worms, viruses and other types of malicious code—collectively known as malware—represent one type of attack. Malware can arrive in an e-mail attachment or as a downloaded file. A worm differs from a virus in that a worm can replicate itself, whereas a virus requires a software environment in order to run on a computer and thus infect it and to spread. Trojan horses are types of malware (virus or worm) that contain malicious code that is hidden inside supposedly harmless programs. **Distributed denial-of-service (DDoS)** attacks occur when an attacker floods a server with requests coming from many different sources under their control. These attacks are just as harmful, shutting down the server and making Web sites and networks that depend on that server unreachable.

Protecting Against Hacking

Hacking, in general, is the practice of infiltrating computers or networks to steal data, cause harm, or simply claim bragging rights. Such attacks can also have tangible impact on a larger organization, including the following:

- Loss of data: Many organizations now use the Internet to run their business. They calculate payroll online, record health insurance information, maintain staff directories, and may even keep their books online. Personnel and financial information is among a company's most valuable assets and, if compromised, can have a big impact on its bottom line.

- Loss of time: The time spent recovering files, rebuilding servers, and otherwise dealing with security breaches can be extensive, far outweighing the time spent preventing trouble.

- Staff resources: In response to a security incident, many staff may need to take time away from their regular business activities to recover data.

- Confidentiality: E-business customer data, such as contact information and credit card numbers, is a valuable asset that must be kept secure; such information has been obtained by hackers, and even published online.

Providing Centralization

A firewall centralizes security for the organization it protects. It simplifies the security-related activities of the network administrator, who typically has many other responsibilities. Having a firewall on the perimeter gives the network administrator a single location from which to configure security policies and monitor arriving and departing traffic.

Enabling Documentation

Every firewall should be configured to provide information to the network administrator in the form of log files. These log files record attempted intrusions and other suspicious activity, as well as mundane events like legitimate file accesses, unsuccessful connection attempts, and the like. Looking through log files is tedious, but they can help a network administrator to identify weak points in the security system so they can be strengthened. Log files can also identify intruders so that they can be apprehended in case theft or damage actually occurs. Regular review and analysis of the log file data they accumulate is what makes firewalls effective because methods of attack change all the time. The firewall rules must be evaluated and adjusted to account for the many new and emerging threats.

Providing for Authentication

You are probably familiar with authentication—the process of logging in to a server with a username and a password before being allowed access to protected information. Only users who have registered their username and password are recognized by the server and allowed to enter. The authentication process can also be performed at the firewall and make use of encryption to protect the usernames and passwords transmitted from client to server (or client to firewall).

Contributing to a VPN

A firewall is an ideal endpoint for a VPN, which connects two companies' networks over the Internet. A VPN is one of the safest ways to exchange information online. You find out more about VPNs later in this chapter.

Types of Firewall Protection

Firewalls work at many different levels of the seven-layer OSI networking model, which is one reason why they're so effective. Table 5-1 gives some examples of firewall functions and the corresponding layers at which they operate.

TABLE 5-1 Network Layers and Firewalls

Layer Number	OSI Reference Model Layer	Firewall Functions
1	Application	Application-level gateway
2	Presentation	Encryption
3	Session	SOCKS proxy server
4	Transport	Packet filtering
5	Network	NAT
6	Physical	N/A
7	Data Link	N/A

Packet Filtering

Packet filtering is a key function of any firewall. In fact, packet filters were one of the first types of firewalls. Packet filters are an effective element in any perimeter security setup.

As you learned in Chapter 2, a packet (which is sometimes called a **datagram**) is the basic quantum of network data and contains two types of information:

- The **header**, which consists of general information about the size of the packet, the protocol that was used to send it, and the IP address of both the source computer and its destination.

- The data, which is the information you view and use; it's the text of an e-mail message, the contents of a Web page, a piece of a file being transferred, or the bits of a digital photograph.

A packet-filtering firewall installed on a TCP/IP-based network typically functions at the IP level and determines whether to drop a packet (deny) or forward it to the next network connection (allow) based on the rules programmed into the firewall. Packet-filtering firewalls examine every incoming packet header and can selectively filter packets based on header information such as destination address, source address, packet type, and other key information. Figure 5-6 shows the structure of an IPv4 packet.

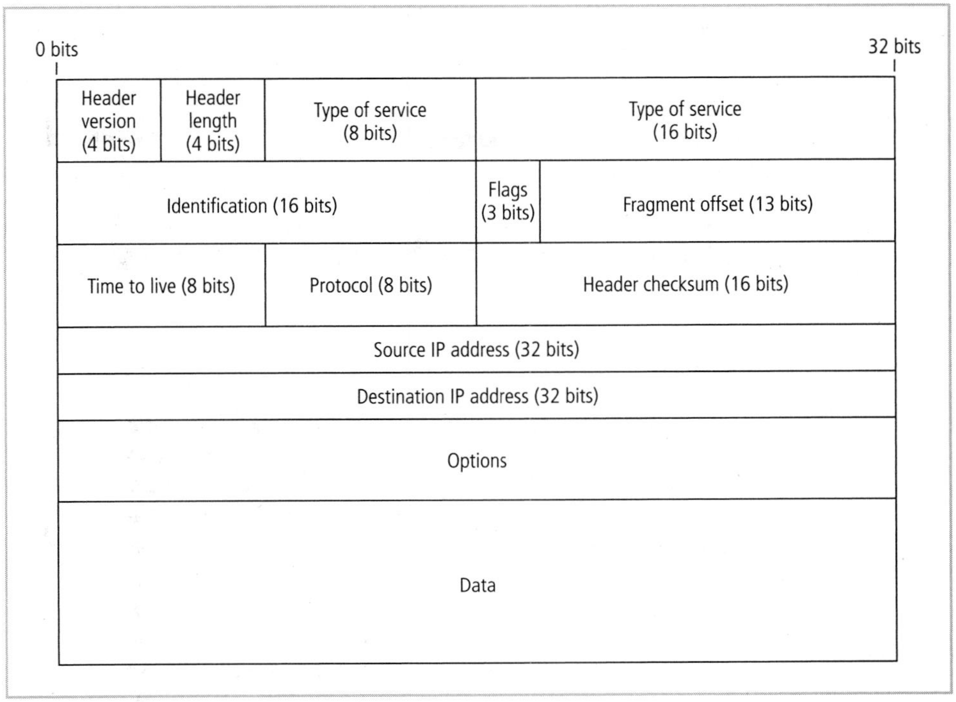

0 bits				32 bits

Header version (4 bits)	Header length (4 bits)	Type of service (8 bits)	Type of service (16 bits)	
Identification (16 bits)			Flags (3 bits)	Fragment offset (13 bits)
Time to live (8 bits)		Protocol (8 bits)	Header checksum (16 bits)	
Source IP address (32 bits)				
Destination IP address (32 bits)				
Options				
Data				

FIGURE 5-6   IPv4 Packet Structure

Packet-filtering firewalls scan network data packets looking for compliance with, or violation of, the rules of the firewall's database. Filtering firewalls inspect packets at the network layer, or Layer 3, of the OSI model. If the device finds a packet that violates a rule, it stops the packet from traveling from one network to another. The restrictions most commonly implemented in packet-filtering firewalls are based on a combination of the following:

- IP source and destination address
- Direction (inbound or outbound)
- Transmission Control Protocol (TCP) or User Datagram Protocol (UDP) source and destination port

Packet structure varies, depending on the nature of the packet. The server that receives the packet makes use of the details of its packet structure when it processes the packet. The two primary service types are TCP and UDP (as noted above). Figures 5-7 and 5-8 show the structures of these two major elements of the combined protocol known as TCP/IP.

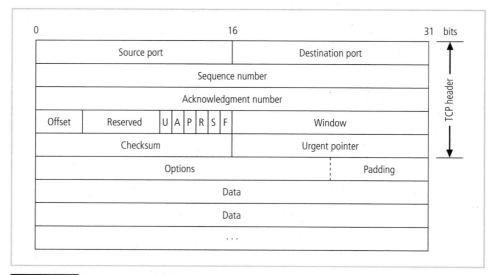

FIGURE 5-7   TCP Packet Structure

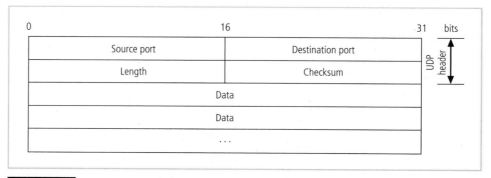

FIGURE 5-8   UDP Packet Structure

Simple firewall models examine two components of the packet header: the destination and source addresses. They enforce address restrictions—rules designed to prohibit packets with specific addresses or incomplete addresses from passing through the device. These restrictions are defined in access control lists (ACLs), which are created and modified by the firewall administrators. Figure 5-9 shows how a packet-filtering router can be used as a simple firewall to filter data packets from inbound connections and allow outbound connections unrestricted access to the public network.

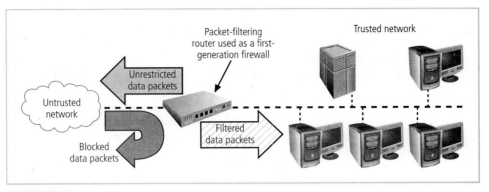

FIGURE 5-9   Packet-Filtering Router

The ability to restrict a specific service is now standard in most routers and is invisible to the user. Unfortunately, such routers are unable to detect whether packet headers have been modified, which occurs in some advanced attack methods, including IP spoofing attacks. IP spoofing is the falsification of the source IP address in a packet's header, so that it appears to have come from a trusted or legitimate sender. In some cases attackers spoof using a source IP address that belongs to the target, to make it look as though the file is coming from a computer within the organization.

Stateless Packet-Filtering Firewalls

Stateless inspection, also called stateless packet filtering, is firewall packet inspection that ignores the state of the connection between the internal computer and the external computer. A firewall that conducts stateless packet filtering simply blocks or allows a packet based on the information in the header.

Stateful Packet-Filtering Firewalls

Stateful inspection, also called stateful packet filtering, is an examination of the data contained in a packet as well as the state of the connection between internal and external computers. This information, known as the state table, is kept in a memory location called the cache. Stateful inspection is superior to stateless inspection because it uses the connection state to make decisions on whether to allow the traffic.

A state table tracks the state and context of each packet in the conversation by recording which station sent what packet and when. Whereas simple packet-filtering firewalls allow or deny certain packets based only on their addresses, a stateful packet filtering can allow incoming packets that have been sent in response to internal requests. If the stateful firewall receives an incoming packet that it cannot match in its state table, it defaults to its ACL to determine whether to allow the packet to pass. The primary disadvantage of this type of firewall is the additional processing required to manage and verify packets against the state table, which can leave the system vulnerable to a DoS or DDoS attack. In such an attack, the system receives a large number of external packets, which slows the firewall because it attempts to compare all of the incoming packets first to the state table and then to the ACL. On the positive side, these firewalls can track connectionless packet traffic, such as UDP and remote procedure calls (RPC) traffic. Dynamic stateful filtering firewalls maintain a dynamic state table, making changes (within predefined limits) to the filtering rules based on events as they happen. A sample state table is shown in Table 5-2. The state table contains the source IP and port, and destination IP and port, and adds information on the protocol used (i.e., UDP or TCP), total time in seconds, and time remaining in seconds. Many state table implementations allow a connection to remain in place for up to 60 minutes without any activity before the state entry is deleted. The state table in Table 5-2 shows this in the column labeled Total Time in Seconds. The Time Remaining in Seconds column shows the number of seconds left until the entry is deleted.

TABLE 5-2 State Table Entries

Source Address	Source Port	Destination Address	Destination Port	Time Remaining in Seconds	Total Time in Seconds	Protocol
192.168.2.5	1028	10.10.10.7	80	2725	3600	TCP

Stateful inspection also blocks packets that are sent from an external computer that does not have a currently active connection to an internal computer.

Here's an example of how stateful inspection works. Suppose you have set up a firewall for a company and an employee attempts to connect to the U.S. White House Web site. When the employee's request packet arrives at the stateful firewall, the following events occur:

1. The firewall checks a list of active connections—the state table—to see if an active connection exists.
2. Because a connection does not yet exist, the firewall then checks its list of rules (called a **rulebase**). The firewall is configured so that users inside the network are allowed to access the Internet on TCP port 80 and are allowed to access any host on the Internet. The packet is allowed to go on its way—after the firewall makes an entry to the state table recording the connection attempt.
3. When the packet is received by the White House server (probably after passing through one or more firewalls), a reply packet is generated and returned to the source company's firewall.
4. At the company's firewall, the state table is checked, and the inbound packet's header is inspected. The header conveys the following information:
   - *Source IP*: *www.whitehouse.gov*
   - *Source port*: 80
   - *Destination IP*: the originating user's computer address
   - *Protocol*: TCP
5. Because there's nothing suspicious about this packet, the firewall sends it to the computer that made the request.

Now, suppose a very different scenario. An attacker at IP address *hack.yourcomputer.net* tries to access your system through port 80. The packet header contains the following:

- *Source IP*: *hack.yourcomputer.net*
- *Source port*: 80
- *Destination IP*: The address of a computer on your system that the attacker has previously uncovered through address or port scanning
- *Destination port*: 2400

The firewall's stateful packet inspector first checks its state table to see if such a request matches a previous entry. Because no such entry exists, the firewall consults its rulebase. Because the only rule specified is that only internal users can connect to port 80, the packet is blocked.

Packet-Filtering Rules

Packet filtering depends on the establishment of rules. Among the most general rules are the following:

- Any outbound packet must have a source address that is in your internal network.
- Any outbound packet must not have a destination address that is in your internal network.
- Any inbound packet must not have a source address that is in your internal network.
- Any inbound packet must have a destination address that is in your internal network.
- Any packet that enters or leaves your network must have a source or destination address that falls within the range of addresses in your network. Your network may use (but does not have to use) private addresses or addresses listed in RFC1918 reserved space. These include 10.x.x.x/8, 172.16.x.x/12, or 192.168.x.x/16, and the loopback network 127.0.0.0/8.

To better understand an address restriction scheme, consider Table 5-3. If an administrator were to configure a simple rule based on the content of Table 5-3, any attempt to connect that was made by an external computer or network device in the 192.168.x.x address range (192.168.0.0-192.168.255.255) would be allowed. The ability to restrict a specific service, rather than just a range of IP addresses, is available in a more advanced version of this first-generation firewall. Additional details on firewall rules and configuration are presented in a later section of this chapter.

TABLE 5-3 Sample Firewall Rule and Format

Source Address	Destination Address	Service (HTTP, SMTP, FTP, Telnet)	Action (Allow or Deny)
172.16.x.x	10.10.x.x	Any	Deny
192.168.x.x	10.10.10.25	HTTP	Allow
192.168.0.1	10.10.10.10	FTP	Allow

Filter rules affect the transmission of packets. These rules encompass an understanding of how the various protocols of the Internet function:

- *Internet Control Message Protocol (ICMP)*: IP, by itself, has no way of letting the host that originated a request know whether a packet was received at its destination in its entirety. It can, however, use ICMP to report any errors that occurred in the transmission. Utilities like Ping and Traceroute use ICMP. The danger is that ICMP packets can be filled with false information that can trick your hosts into redirecting or stopping communications.
- *User Datagram Protocol (UDP)*: This protocol is similar to TCP in that it handles the addressing of a message. UDP breaks a message into numbered segments so that it can be transmitted. UDP then reassembles it when it reaches the destination computer.

Unlike TCP, UDP is connectionless: it simply sends segments of messages without performing error checking or waiting for an acknowledgment that the message has been received. Such a protocol is useful for video and audio broadcasts on the Internet. TCP and UDP are often mentioned together in discussions of firewalls because both transmit data through ports and thus open up vulnerabilities. It's useful to set up rules to block UDP traffic on ports 21 and below and to block traffic on ports that control hardware such as keyboards, hubs, and routers; see Chapter 2 for more information.

- *TCP filtering*: The rules used to control filtering of TCP packets are similar to those used for UDP packets. For example, you should block packets that use ports below 20, and you can block specific protocols, for example Telnet connections on port 23.

- *IP filtering*: The rules used for all parts of the IP protocol control the overall flow of IP traffic through your network. If you have identified a computer or network that you want to block from your company's network, you would specify Source IP or Destination IP rule criteria. These rules will affect all the TCP/IP suite of protocols (ICMP, UDP, or TCP).

Packet filtering has limitations. Filtering does not hide the IP addresses of the hosts that are on the network inside the filter. The IP addresses are contained in the outbound traffic, which makes it easy for attackers to target individual hosts behind the filter to attack them. Packet-filtering firewalls don't check to make sure the protocols inside packets are legitimate either. Packet filtering can limit addresses based only on the source IP address listed in the packet's header, and thus it does not protect against IP spoofing. For these reasons, firewalls that perform only packet filtering do not provide adequate network protection.

Larger organizations use multiple packet filters in a DMZ perimeter security setup. They might use a router that functions as a static packet filter, a stateful packet filter that has been set up in a bastion host, and firewall software (as shown in Figure 5-10).

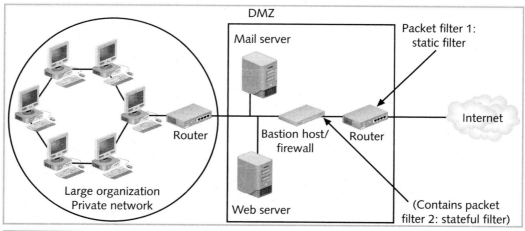

FIGURE 5-10 Multiple Packet Filters

PAT and NAT

Each computer on a network is assigned an IP address. One approach to assigning these numbers is to use static, routable IP addresses for all computers, where each computer is configured to use one IP address and that address can be reached by outside computers to make a connection directly to it. When an address is static, it's relatively easy for an attacker to find it and gain access to the computer. A computer with a static IP address that can be accessed via the Internet is an easy target for an attacker, who might also use it as a staging area for launching long, sustained attacks.

Port Address Translation (PAT) and Network Address Translation (NAT) are addressing methods that make internal network addresses invisible to outside computers. PAT and NAT hide the TCP/IP information of hosts in the network being protected to prevent attackers from getting the address of an actual host on your internal network; thus, they are unable to send a malformed packet or virus-laden message to that machine.

PAT and NAT function as an outbound network-level proxy, acting as a single host that makes requests on behalf of all the internal hosts on the network. PAT uses one external address as the proxy for all internal systems, assigning random and high-order port numbers to each internal computer. NAT uses a pool of valid external IP addresses, assigning one of these actual addresses to each internal computer requesting an outside connection. Both techniques convert the IP addresses of internal hosts to the IP address assigned by the proxy router. To someone on the Internet or other outside network, it appears that all information is coming from a single computer when PAT is used, or from a small number of computers (IP numbers that do not change) when NAT is used. This is sometimes called IP masquerading, because the individual machines can be assigned IP addresses in a private address range—for example, 10.0.0.1, 10.0.0.2, 10.0.0.3, and so on. But when the PAT/NAT-equipped router receives a request from one of these computers, it replaces the real IP address with the one from the outbound pool (for NAT) or its own address (for PAT). The remote computer outside the network that receives the request gets a packet whose header includes a source IP address of, say, 24.33.9.100, not 10.0.0.3, as shown in Figure 5-11.

The internal network addresses assigned by PAT or NAT are drawn from three differ-ent ranges (specified by the IETF as published in RFC1918). Organizations that need a large group of internal addresses use the Class A address range of 10.x.x.x, which has over 16.5 million usable addresses. Organizations that need smaller groups of internally assigned addresses can select from the reserved group of 16 Class B address blocks found in the 172.16.x.x to 172.31.x.x range, or about 1.05 million total addresses. Those with smaller needs can use Class C addresses, in the 192.168.x.x range, each of which has approximately 65,500 addresses. See Table 5-4 for the IP address ranges reserved for non-public networks. Messages sent with internal addresses within these three reserved ranges cannot be routed externally, so if a computer with one of these internal-use addresses is directly connected to the external network, and avoids the PAT/NAT server, its traffic can-not be routed on the public network. Therefore, PAT/NAT prevents external attacks from reaching internal machines with addresses in specified ranges.

TABLE 5-4 Reserved Non-Routable Address Ranges

Class	From	To	CIDR Mask	Decimal Mask
Class "A" or 24 Bit	10.0.0.0	10.255.255.255	/8	255.0.0.0
Class "B" or 20 Bit	172.16.0.0	172.31.255.255	/12 or /16	255.240.0.0 or 255.255.0.0
Class "C" or 16 Bit	192.168.0.0	192.168.255.255	/16 or /24	255.255.0.0 or 255.255.255.0

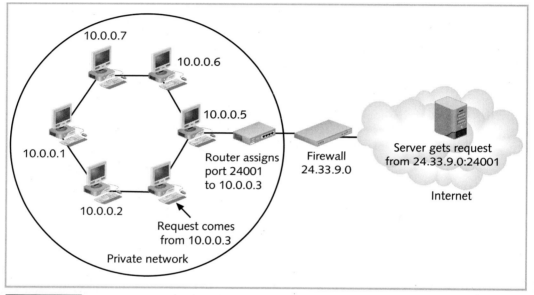

FIGURE 5-11 Port Address Translation (PAT)

Technical Details

PAT/NAT

PAT/NAT capabilities are built into Linux and many UNIX operating systems. In Windows 2000/98/ Me/XP, a simpler form of PAT/NAT is part of Internet Connection Sharing (ICS). Another feature, Routing and Remote Access, gives you more control. However, you should avoid enabling PAT/NAT using both ICS and Routing and Remote Access—you're essentially telling Windows to route the same IP address to two different addresses. Pick one or the other feature, not both.

Application Layer Gateways

Another type of firewall protection is the application layer gateway, also known as a proxy server. The application layer gateway works at the application layer, the top layer of the OSI model of network communications, which is described in Chapter 2.

Application layer gateways can control the way applications inside the network access external networks by setting up proxy services. This service acts as a substitute (i.e., as a proxy) for the client, making requests for Web pages or sending and receiving e-mail on behalf of individual users, who are thus shielded from directly connecting with the Internet. This shielding minimizes the effect of viruses, worms, Trojan horses, and other malware.

The application layer gateway runs special software that enables it to act as a proxy for a specific service request. For example, an organization that runs a Web server can avoid exposing the server to direct user traffic by installing such a proxy server, configured with the registered domain's URL. This proxy server receives requests for Web pages, accesses the Web server on behalf of the external client, and returns the requested pages to the users. These servers can store the most recently accessed pages in their internal cache, and are also called cache servers. The benefits of this type of implementation are significant. For one, the proxy server is placed in an unsecured area of the network or in the demilitarized zone (DMZ)—an intermediate area between a trusted network and an untrusted network—so that it, rather than the Web server, is exposed to the higher levels of risk from the less trusted networks. Additional filtering routers can be implemented behind the proxy server, limiting access to the more secure internal system, and thereby further protecting internal systems.

One common example of a proxy server implementation is a firewall that blocks all requests for and responses to requests for Web pages and services from the organization's internal computers, and instead makes all such requests and responses go to intermediate computers (or proxies) in the less protected areas of the organization's network. This technique is still widely used to implement electronic commerce functions, although most users of this technology have upgraded to take advantage of the DMZ approach discussed later.

The primary disadvantage of application-level firewalls is that they are designed for a specific protocol and cannot easily be reconfigured to protect against attacks on other protocols. Since application firewalls work at the application layer (hence the name), they are typically restricted to a single application (e.g., FTP, Telnet, HTTP, SMTP, SNMP). The processing time and resources necessary to read each packet down to the application layer diminish the ability of these firewalls to handle multiple types of applications.

An application layer gateway provides you with one especially valuable security benefit. Unlike a packet filter, which decides whether to allow or deny a request based on the information contained in the packet header, the gateway understands the contents of the requested data. It can be configured to allow or deny (both of which are actions that can be taken as a result of filtering) specific content, such as viruses and executables.

Such content filtering is only one of the complex tasks that enable application layer gateways to accomplish security tasks that go far beyond blocking specified IP addresses. Among these other tasks are:

- *Load balancing*: If the big office building described in the beginning of this chapter has two secure entrances, the number of people passing through each can be reduced substantially. In the same way, large organizations commonly install more than one firewall and divide the traffic load between them.

- *IP address mapping*: This is a type of NAT in which a static IP address assigned by an ISP is mapped to the private IP address of a computer on the local network; it is sometimes called address vectoring or static IP mapping. The benefit of this to an internal network is to shield actual internal IP addresses from the prying eyes of unauthorized external clients.

- *Filtering content*: An application proxy server can be set up to filter on some detailed criteria. You can block files that have a certain filename or part of a filename, a keyword, an e-mail attachment, or content type.

- *URL filtering*: This can be used to block a site's Domain Name System (DNS) name, such as *www.criminalactivity.com*.

Most of these application-level security techniques are discussed in more detail in later parts of this book.

Firewall Categories

Firewalls can be categorized by processing mode, generation, or structure. Firewalls categorized by level of technology are identified by generation, with the later generations being more complex and more recently developed. Firewalls categorized by intended structure are typically divided into categories including residential- or commercial-grade, hardware-based, software-based, or appliance-based devices.

Processing Mode

There are five major processing-mode categories for firewalls: (1) packet-filtering firewalls, (2) application gateways, (3) circuit gateways, (4) MAC layer firewalls, and (5) hybrids.[1] Hybrid firewalls use a combination of the other four methods, and in practice, most firewalls fall into this category, since most use multiple approaches within the same device. The section that follows recaps the types of firewalls already described and provides a short overview of the other variants.

Packet-Filtering Firewalls

There are three subsets of packet-filtering firewalls: static filtering, dynamic filtering, and stateful inspection. Static filtering requires that the filtering rules are developed and installed with the firewall. The rules are created and sequenced either by a person directly editing the rule set, or by a person using a programmable interface to specify the rules and the sequence. Any changes to the rules require human intervention. This type of filtering is common in network routers and gateways.

A dynamic filtering firewall can react to an emergent event and update or create rules to deal with that event. This reaction could be positive, as in allowing an internal user to engage in a specific activity upon request, or negative, as in dropping all packets from a particular address when an increase in the presence of a particular type of malformed packet is detected. While static filtering firewalls allow entire sets of one type of packet to enter in response to authorized requests, the dynamic packet-filtering firewall allows only a particular packet with a particular source, destination, and port address to enter through the firewall. It does this by opening and closing "doors" in the firewall based on the information contained in the packet header, which makes dynamic packet filters an intermediate form, between traditional static packet filters and application proxies.

Stateful inspection firewalls, as described earlier in this chapter, are also called stateful firewalls, and keep track of each network connection between internal and external systems using a state table.

Application Gateways

The application gateway, described earlier, is also known as an application-level firewall, proxy server, or application firewall. It is frequently installed on a dedicated computer, separate from the filtering router, but is commonly used in conjunction with a filtering router.

Circuit Gateways

The circuit gateway firewall operates at the transport layer. Connections are authorized based on addresses. Like filtering firewalls, circuit gateway firewalls do not usually examine traffic flowing between one network and another, but they do prevent direct connections between one network and another. They accomplish this by creating tunnels connecting specific processes or systems on each side of the firewall, and then allowing only authorized traffic, such as a specific type of TCP connection for only authorized users, in these tunnels. A circuit gateway is a firewall component often included in the category of application gateway, but it is in fact a separate type of firewall. Writing for NIST in SP 800-10, John Wack describes the operation of a circuit gateway as follows:

A circuit-level gateway relays TCP connections but does no extra processing or filtering of the protocol. For example, the TELNET application gateway example provided here would be an example of a circuit-level gateway, since once the connection between the source and destination is established, the firewall simply passes bytes between the systems. Another example of a circuit-level gateway would be for NNTP, in which the NNTP server would connect to the firewall, and then internal systems' NNTP clients would connect to the firewall. The firewall would, again, simply pass bytes.[2]

MAC Layer Firewalls

While not as well known or widely referenced as the firewall approaches above, MAC layer firewalls are designed to operate at the media access control sub-layer of the data link layer (Layer 2) of the OSI network model. This enables these firewalls to consider the specific host computer's identity, as represented by its MAC or network interface card (NIC) address in its filtering decisions. Using this approach, the MAC addresses of specific host computers are linked to ACL entries that identify the specific types of packets that can be sent to each host, and all other traffic is blocked.

Figure 5-12 shows where in the OSI model each of the firewall processing modes inspects data.

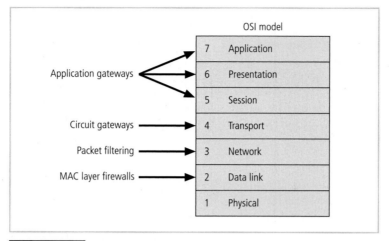

FIGURE 5-12 Firewalls in the OSI Model

Hybrid Firewalls

Hybrid firewalls combine the elements of various types of firewalls—that is, the elements of packet filtering and proxy services, or of packet filtering and circuit gateways. A hybrid firewall system may actually consist of two separate firewall devices; each is a separate firewall system, but they are connected so that they work in tandem. For example, a hybrid firewall system might include a packet-filtering firewall that is set up to screen all acceptable requests then pass the requests to a proxy server, which, in turn, requests services from a Web server deep inside the organization's networks. An added advantage to the hybrid firewall approach is that it enables an organization to make security improvements without completely replacing its existing firewalls.

Firewall Generation

Firewalls are also frequently categorized by their position on a developmental continuum—that is, by generation. The first generation of firewall devices consists of routers that perform only simple packet-filtering operations. More recent generations of firewalls offer increasingly complex capabilities, including the increased security and convenience of creating a DMZ—"demilitarized zone." At present, there are five generally recognized generations of firewalls, and these generations can be implemented in a wide variety of architectures.

- First-generation firewalls are static packet-filtering firewalls—that is, simple networking devices that filter packets according to their headers as the packets travel to and from the organization's networks.

- Second-generation firewalls are application-level firewalls or proxy servers—that is, dedicated systems that are separate from the filtering router and that provide intermediate services for requestors.

- Third-generation firewalls are stateful inspection firewalls, which, as described previously, monitor network connections between internal and external systems using state tables.

- Fourth-generation firewalls, which are also known as dynamic packet-filtering firewalls, allow only a particular packet with a particular source, destination, and port address to enter.

- Fifth-generation firewalls are the kernel proxy, a specialized form that works under Windows NT Executive, which is the kernel of Windows NT. This type of firewall evaluates packets at multiple layers of the protocol stack, by checking security in the kernel as data is passed up and down the stack. Cisco implements this technology in the security kernel of its Centri Firewall. The Cisco security kernel contains three component technologies:[3] the Interceptor/Packet Analyzer, the Security Verification Engine (SVEN), and Kernel Proxies. The Interceptor captures packets arriving at the firewall server and passes them to the Packet Analyzer, which reads the header information, extracts signature data, and passes both the data and the packets to the SVEN. The SVEN receives this information and determines whether to drop the packet, map it to an existing session, or create a new session. If a current session exists, the SVEN passes the information through a custom-built protocol stack created specifically for that session. The temporary protocol stack uses a customized implementation of the approach widely known as Network Address Translation (NAT). The SVEN enforces the security policy that is configured into the Kernel Proxy as it inspects each packet.

Firewall Structures

Firewalls can also be categorized by the structures used to implement them. Most commercial-grade firewalls are dedicated appliances. That is, they are stand-alone units running on fully customized computing platforms that provide both the physical network connection and firmware programming necessary to perform their function, whatever that function (static packet filtering, application proxy, etc.) may be. Some firewall appliances use highly customized, sometimes proprietary hardware systems that are developed exclusively as firewall devices. Other commercial firewall systems are actually off-the-shelf general-purpose computer systems that use custom application software running either over standard operating systems like Windows or Linux/Unix or on specialized variants of these operating systems. Most small office or residential-grade firewalls are either simplified dedicated appliances running on computing devices, or application software installed directly on the user's computer.

Commercial-Grade Firewall Appliances

Firewall appliances are stand-alone, self-contained combinations of computing hardware and software. These devices frequently have many of the features of a general-purpose computer with the addition of firmware-based instructions that increase their reliability and performance and minimize the likelihood of their being compromised. The customized software operating system that drives the device can be periodically upgraded, but can only be modified using a direct physical connection or using extensive authentication and authorization protocols. The firewall rule sets are stored in non-volatile memory, and thus they can be changed by technical staff when necessary but are available each time the device is restarted.

These appliances may be manufactured from stripped-down, general-purpose computer systems, and/or designed to run a customized version of a general-purpose operating system. These variant operating systems are tuned to meet the type of firewall activity built into the application software that provides the firewall functionality.

Commercial-Grade Firewall Systems

A commercial-grade firewall system consists of application software that is configured for the firewall application and run on a general-purpose computer. Organizations can install firewall software on an existing general-purpose computer system, or they can purchase hardware that has been configured to specifications that yield optimum firewall performance. These systems exploit the fact that firewalls are essentially application software packages that use common general-purpose network connections to move data from one network to another. Full-featured, enterprise-grade firewall packages include:

- *Check Point FireWall-1*: FireWall-1, by Check Point Software Technologies Ltd., is considered by many security experts to be the product of choice when it comes to software firewalls. The product is notable for being among the first to use stateful packet inspection to monitor network traffic.

  FireWall-1 includes a full array of security tools, including authentication, virus checking (via a third-party application that is integrated into the FireWall package), intrusion detection, and packet filtering. FireWall-1 is the only firewall that is compliant with the OPSEC security standard. It's an especially good choice for large networks. A high availability feature enables a corporate network to run two parallel installations of FireWall-1 in tandem. If one firewall goes down, the other remains functioning, keeping the network connected and maintaining current connections, thus making it especially good for large-scale networks.

  FireWall-1's software engine has been incorporated into a number of firewall appliances. FireWall-1 also comes in several variations, including a wireless model and a VPN-1 version for VPNs (though the standard version of FireWall-1 includes VPN capabilities as well).

- *Cisco PIX*: PIX is not a single product but a name given to a series of secure, self-contained hardware devices that contain full-featured firewalls. The line ranges from the PIX 535, which is able to handle up to 500,000 concurrent connections, to the PIX 501 for home office environments.

  The Cisco PIX firewalls are notable for competitive pricing, extensive online documentation, and highly regarded customer support. Cisco's firewall products have been available for several years and are reliable and feature-rich, including high availability, an intrusion detection system, and protection against DoS attacks.

- *Microsoft Internet Security & Acceleration Server*: Internet Security & Acceleration Server (ISA) 2000 is an application-level firewall from Microsoft Corporation. ISA 2000 features include authentication through integration with Active Directory, virus scanning (through integrated third-party products), data-aware filtering capabilities, and IP packet-filtering functionality. ISA also supports the Cache Array Routing Protocol (CARP) so that the product can be scaled to fit larger traffic requirements.

- *NAI Gauntlet*: Gauntlet is one of the longest-established firewall products available today. It is a flexible product, supporting application proxies, packet filtering, and the ability to adjust the speed of the firewall as needed. Gauntlet is integrated by McAfee's anti-virus software.

Small Office/Home Office (SOHO) Firewall Appliances

As more and more small businesses and residences obtain fast Internet connections with digital subscriber lines (DSL) or cable modem connections, they become more and more vulnerable to attacks. What many small business and work-from-home users don't realize is that, unlike dial-up connections, these high-speed services are always on, and thus the computers connected to them are much more likely to be visible to the scans performed by attackers than those connected only for the duration of a dial-up session. Coupled with the typically lax security capabilities of home computing operating systems like Windows 95, Windows 98, and even Windows Millennium Edition, most of these systems are wide open to outside intrusion. Even a home computing operating system with secure capabilities, like Windows XP Home Edition, is rarely configured securely by its users. Newer operating systems like Windows Vista have improved security "out of the box," but users can still benefit from having solid SOHO networking security in place. Just as organizations must protect their information, residential users must also implement some form of firewall to prevent loss, damage, or disclosure of personal information.

One of the most effective methods of improving computing security in the SOHO setting is by means of a SOHO or residential-grade firewall. These devices, also known as broadband gateways or DSL/cable modem routers, connect the user's local area network or a specific computer system to the Internet working device—in this case, the cable modem or DSL router provided by the Internet service provider (ISP). The SOHO firewall serves first as a stateful firewall to enable inside to outside access and can be configured to allow limited TCP/IP port forwarding and/or screened subnet capabilities (see the later sections of this chapter for definitions of these terms).

In recent years, the broadband router devices that can function as packet-filtering firewalls have been enhanced to combine the features of wireless access points (WAPs) as well as small stackable LAN switches in a single device. These convenient combination devices give the residential/SOHO user the strong protection that comes from the use of Network Address Translation (NAT) services. NAT assigns non-routing local addresses to the computer systems in the local area network and uses the single ISP-assigned address to communicate with the Internet. Since the internal computers are not visible to the public network, they are very much less likely to be scanned or compromised. Many users implement these devices primarily to allow multiple internal users to share a single external Internet connection. Figure 5-13 shows a few examples of the SOHO firewall devices currently available on the market.

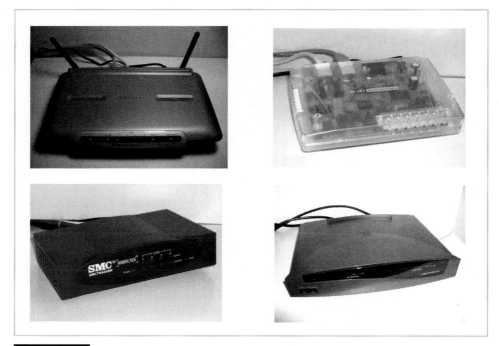

FIGURE 5-13 Example SOHO Firewalls

Many of these firewalls provide more than simple NAT services. As illustrated with the example screen shots in Figures 5-14 through 5-17, some SOHO/residential firewalls include packet filtering, port filtering, and simple intrusion detection systems, and some can even restrict access to specific MAC addresses. Users may be able to configure port forwarding and enable outside users to access specific TCP or UDP ports on specific computers on the protected network.

Figure 5-14 shows the MAC Address filter setup screen from the SMC Barricade residential broadband router, which can be used to identify which computers inside the trusted network may access the Internet.

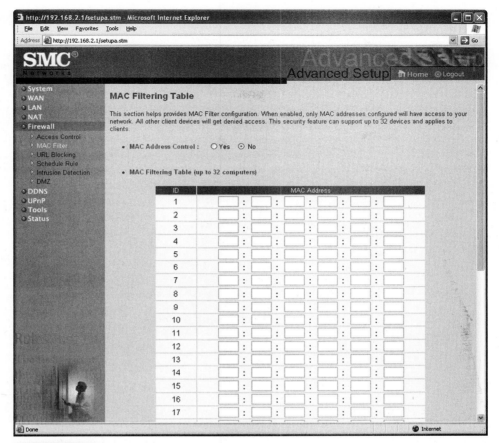

FIGURE 5-14 Filtering MAC Addresses

Some firewall devices provide a limited intrusion detection capability. Figure 5-15 shows the configuration screen from the SMC Barricade residential broadband router that enables the intrusion detection feature. When enabled, this feature detects specific intrusion attempts that are defined in the currently installed detection library—that is, attempts to compromise the protected network that are known to the device manufacturer and are detectable based on the nature of the attack. In addition to recording intrusion attempts, the router can be configured to use the contact information to notify the firewall administrator when an intrusion attempt occurs.

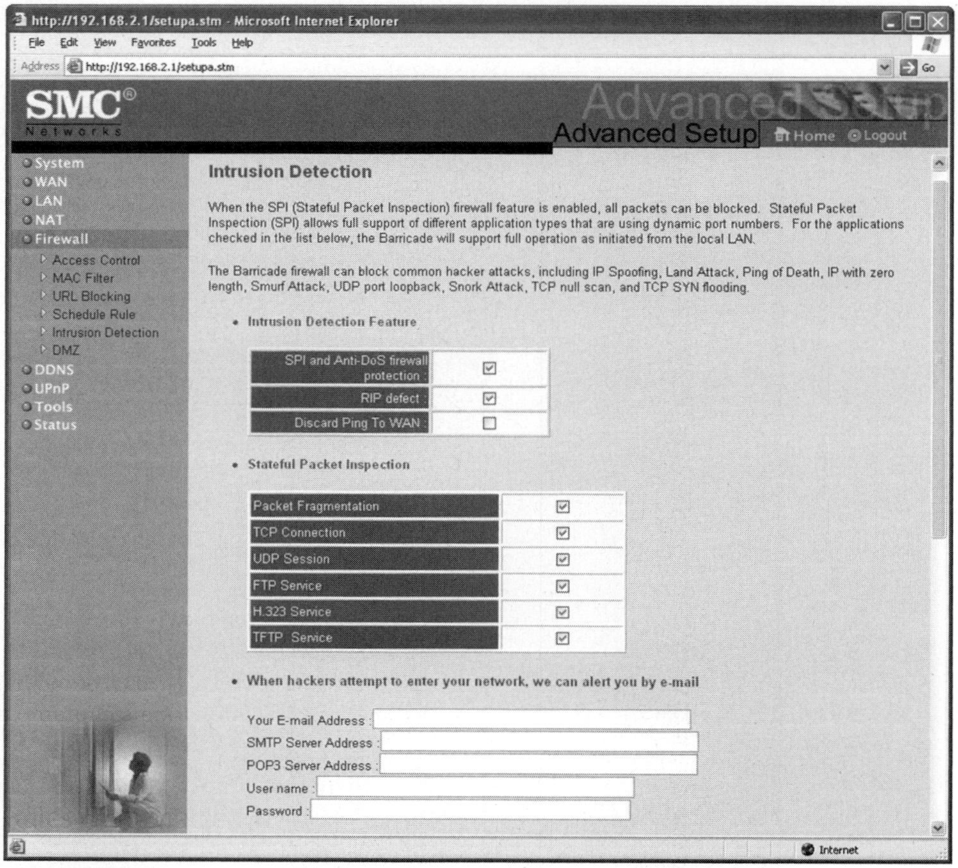

FIGURE 5-15 Configuring Intrusion Detection

Figure 5-16 shows a continuation of the configuration screen for the intrusion detection feature. Note that the intrusion criteria are limited in number, but the actual threshold levels of the various activities detected can be customized by the administrator.

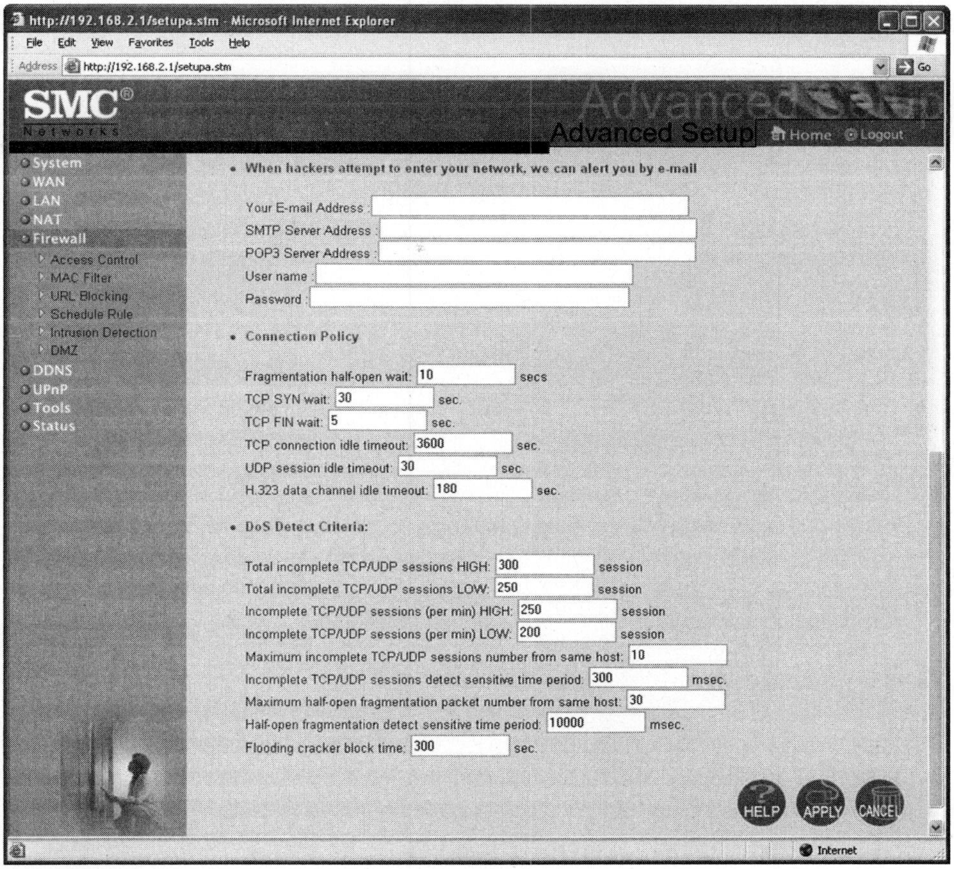

FIGURE 5-16   Configuring Intrusion Detection (Cont.)

Figure 5-17 illustrates that even simple residential firewalls can be used to create a logical screened subnetwork (often called a demilitarized zone, or DMZ) that can provide Web services. This screen shows how the Barricade can be configured to allow port forwarding to be established so that Internet users can be allowed access to servers inside the trusted network for services at specific port numbers. The network administrator is expected to ensure that the exposed servers are sufficiently secured for this type of exposure.

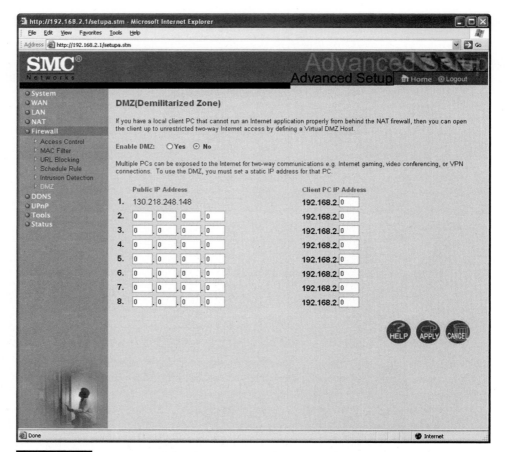

FIGURE 5-17   Configuring Port Forwarding

Residential-Grade Firewall Software

Many people have installed on their systems residential-grade software-based firewalls (some of which also provide anti-virus or intrusion detection capabilities), but, unfortunately, they may not be as fully protected as they think. Many software programs available offer local-system firewall capabilities. The Web site *www.firewallguide.com/ software.htm* offers a complete list along with current reviews and additional information about current versions of the software. Some of these options are listed in Table 5-5. These applications claim to detect and prevent intrusion into the user's system, without affecting usability. However, many of the freeware applications that provide firewall capabilities are not fully functional, and the old adage "you get what you pay for" certainly applies to software in this category. Users who implement this free, less-capable software often find that it delivers less than complete protection.

TABLE 5-5 Common Software Firewalls

Recommended: Sunbelt Personal Firewall
Recommended: CheckPoint ZoneAlarm Pro
Reviewed: CA Personal Firewall 2007
Reviewed: F-Secure Internet Security
Reviewed: Jetico Personal Firewall for 32/64-bit Windows v.2.0.0.33
Reviewed: Microsoft Windows Firewall
Reviewed: Agnitum OutpostPro Firewall
Reviewed: Matousec Tall Emu Online-Armor
Reviewed: Deefield VisNetic Firewall
Reviewed: Webroot Desktop Firewall

Free Firewall Tools on the Internet

Most of the free firewall software on the Internet, including the packet filter IP Chains and TIS Firewall Toolkit, also run on a free operating system, such as Linux, The Berkeley Software Design variety of UNIX (BSD), or DOS.

Free firewall programs aren't perfect. Their logging capabilities aren't as robust as some commercial products, they can be difficult to configure, and they usually don't include a way to monitor the firewall in real time. Nonetheless, they have a place in networking because of their convenience, simplicity, and unbeatable price.

Among the free firewall products are:

- *Pretty Good Privacy (PGP)*: PGP is a program that's highly regarded for providing e-mail and disk encryption. Created by Phil Zimmerman, it was originally released for free on the Internet; a commercial version of PGP has also been developed by Network Associates. Although the commercial version of PGP is available through the NAI Web site, the freeware version is still available from MIT at *http://web.mit.edu/network/pgp.html*. The latest versions of PGP work with Windows 95/98/NT/2000, Macintosh, AIX/HP-UX/Linux, and Solaris. PGP is noteworthy not only for its ability to encrypt files but for its firewall and VPN functions. The fact that it's available for free makes it a good program to use to learn about cryptography, and it is often used in academic exercises, including in a few places in this book.

- *Netfilter*: Netfilter is the firewall software that comes with the Linux 2.4 kernel and is a powerful (and freely available) solution for stateless and stateful packet filtering, NAT, and packet processing. Netfilter doesn't have all the features of commercial programs such as VPN, but it does one thing very well: logging. Netfilter records copious information about the traffic that passes through it, but that information is well organized and easy to review.

There are limits to the level of configurability and protection that software firewalls can provide. Many of the applications in Table 5-5 have very limited configuration options ranging from none to low to medium to high security. With only three or four levels of configuration, users may find that the application becomes increasingly difficult to use in everyday situations. They find themselves sacrificing security for usability, because at higher levels of security the application constantly asks for instruction on whether to allow a particular application, packet, or service to connect internally or externally. The Microsoft Windows 2000, XP, and Vista versions of Internet Explorer have similar configuration settings that allow users to choose from a list of preconfigured options, or choose a custom setting with a more detailed security configuration.

Software vs. Hardware: The SOHO Firewall Debate

Which type of firewall should the residential user implement? Many users swear by their software firewalls. Personal experience will produce a variety of opinionated perspectives. Ask yourself this question: Where would you rather defend against an attacker? When you use software only, the attacker is inside your computer, battling a piece of software (free software, in many cases) that may not have been correctly installed, configured, patched, upgraded, or designed. If the software happens to have a known vulnerability, the attacker could bypass it and then have unrestricted access to your system. When you use the hardware device, even if the attacker manages to crash the firewall system, your computer and information are still safely behind the now disabled connection, which is assigned a non-routable IP address making it virtually impossible to reach from the outside. A former student of one of the authors responded to this debate by installing a hardware firewall, and then visiting an attacker chat room. He challenged the group to penetrate his system. A few days later, he received an e-mail from an attacker claiming to have accessed his system. The attacker included a graphic of a screen showing a C:\ prompt, which he claimed was from the student's system. After doing a bit of research, the student found out that the firewall had an image stored in firmware that was designed to distract attackers. It was an image of a command window with a DOS prompt. The hardware (NAT) solution had withstood the challenge.

Firewall Architectures

Each of the firewall devices described earlier can be configured in a number of network connection architectures. These approaches are sometimes mutually exclusive and sometimes can be combined.

The configuration that works best for a particular organization depends on three factors: the objectives of the network, the organization's ability to develop and implement the architectures, and the budget available for the function. Although literally hundreds of variations exist, there are four common architectural implementations of firewalls. These implementations are packet-filtering routers, screened host firewalls, dual-homed firewalls, and screened subnet firewalls. Each of these is examined in more detail in the following sections.

Packet-Filtering Routers

Most organizations with an Internet connection have some form of a router at the perimeter between the organization's internal networks and the external service provider. Many of these routers can be configured to reject packets that the organization does not allow into the network. This is a simple but effective way to lower the organization's risk from external attack. The drawbacks to this type of system include a lack of auditing and strong authentication. Also, the complexity of the access control lists used to filter the packets can degrade network performance.

Screened Host Firewalls

Screened host firewalls combine the packet-filtering router with a separate, dedicated firewall, such as an application proxy server. This approach allows the router to prescreen packets to minimize the network traffic and load on the internal proxy. The application proxy examines an application layer protocol, such as HTTP, and performs the proxy services. This separate host is often referred to as a bastion host; it can be a rich target for external attacks, and should be very thoroughly secured. Even though the bastion host/application proxy actually contains only cached copies of the internal Web documents, it can still present a promising target, because compromise of the bastion host can disclose the configuration of internal networks and possibly provide external sources with internal information. Since the bastion host stands as a sole defender on the network perimeter, it is also commonly referred to as the sacrificial host. To its advantage, this configuration requires the external attack to compromise two separate systems before the attack can access internal data. In this way, the bastion host protects the data more fully than the router alone. Figure 5-18 shows a typical configuration of a screened host architecture.

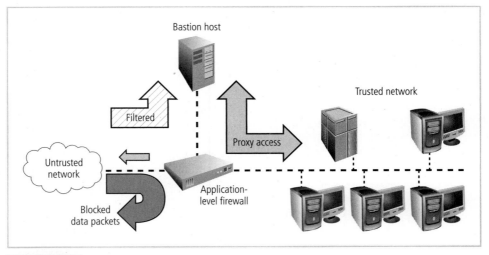

FIGURE 5-18 Screened Host Architecture

Dual-Homed Host Firewalls

The next step up in firewall architectural complexity is the dual-homed host. When this architectural approach is used, the bastion host contains two NICs (network interface cards) rather than one, as in the bastion host configuration. One NIC is connected to the external network, and one is connected to the internal network, providing an additional layer of protection. With two NICs, all traffic must physically go through the firewall to move between the internal and external networks. This architecture often makes use of NAT—mapping real, valid, external IP addresses to special ranges of non-routable internal IP addresses—thereby creating yet another barrier to intrusion from external attackers.

If the NAT server is a multi-homed bastion host, it translates between the true, external IP addresses assigned to the organization by public network naming authorities and the internally assigned, non-routable IP addresses. NAT translates by dynamically assigning addresses to internal communications and tracking the conversations with sessions to determine which incoming message is a response to which outgoing traffic. Figure 5-19 shows a typical configuration of a dual-homed host firewall that uses NAT and proxy access to protect the internal network.

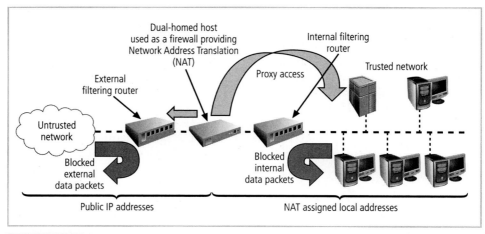

FIGURE 5-19 Dual-Homed Host

Another benefit of a dual-homed host is its ability to translate many different protocols at their respective data link layers, including Ethernet, Token Ring, Fiber Distributed Data Interface (FDDI), and Asynchronous Transfer Method (ATM). On the downside, if this dual-homed host is compromised, it can disable the connection to the external network, and as traffic volume increases, it can become overloaded. Compared to more complex solutions, however, this architecture provides strong overall protection with minimal expense.

Screened Subnet Firewalls (with DMZ)

The dominant architecture used today is the screened subnet firewall. The architecture of a screened subnet firewall provides a DMZ. The DMZ can be a dedicated port on the firewall device linking a single bastion host, or it can be connected to a screened subnet, as shown in Figure 5-20. Until recently, servers providing services through an untrusted network were commonly placed in the DMZ. Examples of these include Web servers, File Transfer Protocol (FTP) servers, and certain database servers. More recent strategies using proxy servers have provided much more secure solutions.

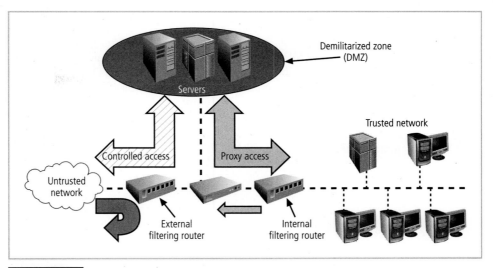

FIGURE 5-20   Screened Subnet

A common arrangement is a subnet firewall consisting of two or more internal bastion hosts behind a packet-filtering router, with each host protecting the trusted network. There are many variants of the screened subnet architecture. The first general model consists of two filtering routers, with one or more dual-homed bastion hosts between them. In the second general model the connections are routed as follows:

- Connections from the outside or untrusted network are routed through an external filtering router.
- Connections from the outside or untrusted network are routed into—and then out of—a routing firewall to the separate network segment known as the DMZ.
- Connections into the trusted internal network are allowed only from the DMZ bastion host servers.

The screened subnet is an entire network segment that performs two functions: it protects the DMZ systems and information from outside threats by providing a network of intermediate security (more secure than the general public networks but less secure than the internal network); and it protects the internal networks by limiting how external connections can gain access to them. Although extremely secure, the screened subnet can be expensive to implement and complex to configure and manage. The value of the information it protects must justify the cost.

Another facet of the DMZ is the creation of an area known as an extranet. An extranet is a segment of the DMZ where additional authentication and authorization controls are put into place to provide services that are not available to the general public. An example is an online retailer that allows anyone to browse the product catalog and place items into a shopping cart, but requires extra authentication and authorization when the customer is ready to check out and place an order.

Limitations of Firewalls

Firewalls can do a lot, but they can't be expected to do it all. Firewalls should not be the only form of protection for a network. They should be part of an overall security plan and should be used in conjunction with other forms of protection, including ID cards, passwords, and employee rules of conduct. Even the most elaborate firewall can't protect against an employee who brings a floppy disk to work containing files that have been infected with a virus, or employees who use a host inside the firewall to gain unauthorized access to sensitive information.

Chapter Summary

- Achieving network security is a process that imposes controls on an organization's network resources in order to balance the risks and rewards that come from network usage. The controls are a continually evolving set of policies, programs, and technologies.

- A firewall is anything, whether hardware or software (or a combination of hardware and software), that can filter the transmission of packets of digital information as they attempt to pass through a boundary of a network. They perform two basic security functions: packet filtering and/or application proxying.

- A firewall can contain many components, including a packet filter, a proxy server, an authentication system, and software that performs Network Address Translation or Port Address Translation (NAT or PAT). Some firewalls can encrypt traffic, and some help establish VPNs.

- Packet filtering is a key function of any firewall. In fact, packet filters were one of the first types of firewalls. Packet filters are an effective element in any perimeter security setup. A packet-filtering firewall may be stateless or stateful. Stateless packet filtering ignores the state of the connection between the internal computer and the external computer. Stateful packet filtering is an examination of the data contained in a packet with a memory of the state of the connection between client and internal and external computers.

- Port Address Translation (PAT) and Network Address Translation (NAT) are addressing methods that are specific approaches that make internal network addresses invisible to outside computers. PAT and NAT are used to hide the TCP/IP information of hosts in the network being protected.

- Application layer gateways, also known as proxy servers, control the way applications inside the network access external networks by setting up proxy services. This service acts as a substitute (i.e., as a proxy) for the client, making requests for Web pages or sending and receiving e-mail on behalf of individual users, who are thus shielded from directly connecting with the Internet.

- Firewalls can be categorized by processing mode, generation, or structure. Firewalls categorized by level of technology are identified by generation, with the later generations being more complex and more recently developed. Firewalls categorized by intended structure are typically divided into categories including residential- or commercial-grade, hardware-based, software-based, or appliance-based devices.

- Each of the firewall devices described earlier can be configured in a number of network connection architectures. The configuration that works best for a particular organization depends on three factors: the objectives of the network, the organization's ability to develop and implement the architectures, and the budget available for the function. There are four common architectural implementations of firewalls: packet-filtering routers, screened host firewalls, dual-homed firewalls, and screened subnet firewalls.

Review Questions

1. Why is it important that a firewall provide a centralized security checkpoint for a network?
2. What are the two basic functions of a firewall?
3. What advanced security features can be incorporated into a firewall?
4. What technology was used in the earliest firewalls?
5. What components are found in many firewalls?
6. Why is packet filtering alone inadequate for security purposes?
7. When does packet filtering offer an advantage over other security methods, such as proxy services?
8. What actions are taken by a firewall when a request from a user is received?
9. Web site requests are routed to which TCP port by default?
10. What can TCP do that UDP cannot do?
11. How is a firewall configured to allow Web access to a Web server?
12. At how many ports can a computer offer services?
13. What is a stateless firewall?
14. What is a stateful firewall?
15. List the benefits of locating your firewall on the perimeter of a network.
16. What network information do attackers initially try to find?
17. Name two reasons why a hardware firewall solution is a good choice compared with software-only solutions.
18. Which protocol is connectionless?
19. For what kinds of communications is a connectionless protocol useful?
20. What is a proxy server and what can it do?

Exercises

1. There are many different network monitoring tools, many that are free, and some that are built into operating systems. Using an Internet search engine, look up the term "monitor network activity using Windows." You should find several Web sites with instructions on how to perform this activity in Windows. Read at least two Web pages that describe the process, then write a short instruction guide on looking at your local network on a Windows platform.

2. Using an Internet search engine, look up the term "monitor network activity using Linux." Read at least two Web pages that describe the process, then write a short instruction guide on how to look at your local network on a Linux platform.

3. Using an Internet search engine, look up the term "monitor network activity using Mac OS X." Read at least two web pages that describe the process, then write a short instruction guide on how to look at your local network on a Mac OS X platform.

4. When you need to assign private IP addresses or perform other network-related tasks, it's important to get the correct information. The most complete source of information about the Internet and IP addresses is RFC document 1918, which is maintained by the Internet Engineering Task Force (IETF), a group dedicated to providing standardized solutions to the technical problems of running the Internet. You can locate an RFC document when you know the RFC number by using a Web browser connected to the Internet to access the IETF library of RFC document. Look up the term "IETF RFC Library." Find the Web page titled RFC Index. What date does it have at the top? What is the highest numbered RFC on the list?

5. Whois is a service that looks up the information submitted when registering a domain name. Whois information is widely accessible. Use your Internet connected web browser to access *www.whois.net*. Enter the name of your own school or university into the Search by domain or keyword box (as in myuniversity.edu), and click the GO button. A Search Results page appears containing the registration information for your institution. What is the name server address for your target? What other kinds of information can you see?

6. Any networked computer has access to as many as 65,535 ports through which it can exchange information. When configuring firewalls, it's often important to record those port numbers on which you want to block traffic. Certain port numbers are frequently used by attackers, and you should be aware of what they are. You can research these vulnerable ports, and many others, online at the IANA Web site. Use an Internet connected Web browser to access *www.iana.org/assignments/port-numbers* and look at the text file that is displayed. Which are the well known ports? The registered ports? The dynamic ports and/or private ports? Using the document, identify which ports are used for HTTP, FTP, SMTP, POP3, Telnet, and DNS. Which port would be used for a Nimbus Gateway?

7. You are assigned to purchase a firewall and hardware, but first you have to prepare a report that (1) describes your organization's network, (2) lists three primary goals for the firewall, and (3) compares two different candidate firewall packages. Prepare the report based on either your home network (if you have one), your classroom, or lab network.

8. Create a diagram of your home network (if you have one), your classroom, or lab network. Be sure to determine where the network connects with the larger network—your ISP, your school's network, or the Internet. Indicate on the diagram where a firewall would go by drawing a miniature brick wall.

Case Exercises

Matthias asked, "Andy, what happened? We spent more time on introductions than on the project work. Did I miss something?"

Andy said, "Nope. That's just the way it works. In fact, the project kick-off didn't require a face-to-face meeting; we probably could have done this one by e-mail. There are only so many ways you can set up a network, and when you have set up and secured a hundred or so like we have in the past two years, it goes pretty quick."

Matthias nodded. Then he said, "But I was hoping to learn something from this, and that meeting didn't really give me anything except a few new names and faces and a packet of papers."

Andy said, "That should be a start. Every one of the people you met today really knows their stuff and will be ready to help you understand the proposed design."

Questions:

1. Make a list of the meeting attendees and describe what role you think each would play in a more elaborate network design project.

2. For each of the meeting attendees, list one or two questions that Matthias could ask about the proposed system design.

Endnotes

1. Avolio, Frederic. "Firewalls and Internet Security, the Second Hundred (Internet) Years." Accessed 6 May 2007 from *www.cisco.com/web/about/ac123/ac147/ac174/ac200/ about_cisco_ipj_archive_article09186a00800c85ae.html.*

2. Wack, John. "Keeping Your Site Comfortably Secure: An Introduction to Internet Firewalls." 16 Oct 2002. Accessed 7 March 2007 from *www.windowsecurity.com/whitepaper/ Keeping_Your_Site_Comfortably_Secure__Introduction_to_Firewalls.html.*

3. Cisco Systems, Inc. "Inside the Cisco Centri Firewall." Cisco Online. Accessed 14 May 2007 from *www.cisco.com/univercd/cc/td/doc/product/iaabu/centri4/user/ scf4ch5.htm#xtocid157876.*

Packet Filtering

6

> The supreme end of education is expert discernment in all things—the power to tell the good from the bad, the genuine from the counterfeit, and to prefer the good and the genuine to the bad and the counterfeit.
>
> **CHARLES GROSVENOR OSGOOD**

KIARA SPRING WAS BORED. SHE WAS A SMART seventh grader who made excellent grades and enjoyed a variety of after school activities. Since her parents worked late quite often and her older brothers were usually out, she spent a lot of time on her own, in front of her computer.

Kiara had made a discovery at school that day. When she was in the guidance office to pick up her course-planning packet for next year's classes, she saw a Post-it note on the secretary's desk. She had a pretty good memory, and after she left the office she made a note of the Web address, the username, and the password that were written on the sticky note.

Kiara just wanted to see if she could connect to the school system and see her own records—she had no desire to change anything, since she had good grades, but getting into the system seemed like a fun and challenging thing to do. She had watched the guidance office secretary use this program on several occasions. The same screen opened up for her now. She typed in the username and password she had written down.

Instead of a screen allowing her to pick out a student record to view, a window opened that said "OFF NETWORK ACCESS ATTEMPTED – PLEASE USE DISTRICT APPROVED VPN FOR CONNECTION." About five seconds later, the browser program on her computer was automatically redirected to the school district's home page.

Kiara's attempt to hack the school district was over before it had really started.

LEARNING OBJECTIVES:

Upon completion of this material, you should be able to do the following:

- Describe packets and packet filtering
- Explain the approaches to packet filtering
- Recommend specific filtering rules

Introduction

To understand how firewalls work, you must first understand packets. Packets are discrete blocks of data, and are the basic unit of data handled by a network—all network traffic is broken down into packets for network transmission, and then reassembled into its original form at its destination. A **packet filter** is hardware or software that is designed to block or allow transmission of packets of information based on criteria such as port, IP address, and protocol.

Packet filters not only help you learn about firewalls but also provide a basis for understanding TCP/IP network communications. To figure out how to control the movement of traffic through the network perimeter, you should know how packets are structured and what goes into packet headers. In this chapter, you will learn how packet header criteria can be used to filter traffic, as well as various approaches to packet filtering and the configuration of specific packet-filtering rules.

Understanding Packets and Packet Filtering

A packet filter acts like a ticket-taker in a multiplex movie theatre. The ticket-taker's task is to admit only those with valid tickets—that is, tickets for a particular film, on a particular day, at a particular time. Similarly, a packet filter reviews the **packet header** before sending it on its way to a specific location within the network.

Packet-Filtering Devices

There are a variety of hardware devices and software programs that perform packet filtering. Here are a few examples:

- *Routers*: These are probably the most common packet filters.
- *Operating systems*: Some systems, like Windows and Linux, have built-in utilities that can filter packets on the TCP/IP stack of the server software. Linux has a kernel-level packet filter called IPtables; Windows has TCP/IP Filtering.
- *Software firewalls*: Most enterprise-level programs, such as Check Point FireWall-1, filter packets, as do personal firewalls like ZoneAlarm and Sygate Personal Firewall, though in general personal firewalls use less sophisticated methods than enterprise-level.

Anatomy of a Packet

Packets are part of Transport Control Protocol/Internet Protocol (TCP/IP), the collection of protocols that computers use to communicate with one another on the network and, increasingly, in local area networks (Windows 2000 and Windows XP use TCP/IP as the basis for file sharing and communications). TCP/IP provides for the transmission of data in small, manageable chunks called **packets**.

Each packet (also called a **datagram**) consists of two parts: the header and the data. The header contains information that is normally only read by computers, such as where the packet is coming from and its destination. The data is the part that end users actually see—the body of an e-mail message or a Web page.

Understanding exactly what goes in a packet header is important because it can help you configure packet filters against possible attacks. Some firewall programs can give you a glimpse of the contents of a packet. When Sygate Personal Firewall detects a packet for which a rule has not been established, for instance, it presents you with an alert box asking whether it should allow the packet to pass. When you click the Details button, you can view the header contents, as shown in Figure 6-1, to decide if anything is suspicious.

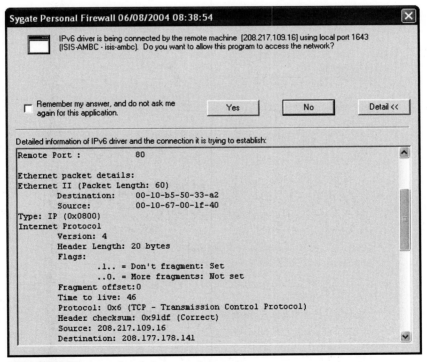

FIGURE 6-1   Firewall View of Packet Data

To find out more about headers and their contents, go to the original Internet Protocol specification at *www.ietf.org*, click RFC Pages, and search for RFC 791.

The header of an IP packet is commonly illustrated according to the layers of information within it, as in Figure 6-2.

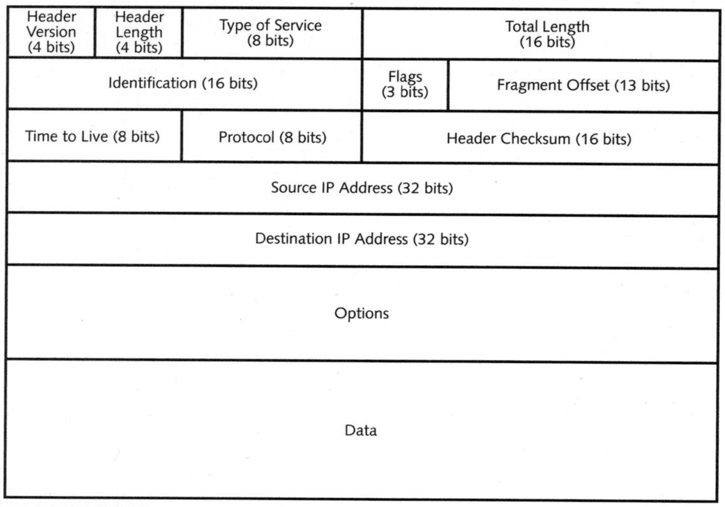

Header Version (4 bits)	Header Length (4 bits)	Type of Service (8 bits)	Total Length (16 bits)	
Identification (16 bits)			Flags (3 bits)	Fragment Offset (13 bits)
Time to Live (8 bits)		Protocol (8 bits)	Header Checksum (16 bits)	
Source IP Address (32 bits)				
Destination IP Address (32 bits)				
Options				
Data				

FIGURE 6-2 IP Packet Header

The packet elements shown in this figure are:

- *Version*: This identifies the version of IP that was used to generate the packet. As of early 2008, TCP/IP version 4 is still in common use. However, some larger organizations and ISPs have begun to deploy IPv6 on their internal networks.

- *Internet Header Length*: This describes the length of the header in 32-bit words and is a 4-bit value. The default value is 20.

- *Type of Service*: This indicates which of four service options is used to transmit the packet: minimize delay, maximize throughput, maximize reliability, and minimize cost. This field is of limited value, however, because most IP network setups don't enable an application to set this value.

- *Total Length*: This 16-bit field gives the total length of the packet, to a maximum of 165,535 bytes.

- *Identification*: This 16-bit value aids in the division of the data stream into packets of information. The receiving computer (possibly a firewall) uses each packet's identification number to reassemble in the correct order the packets that make up the data stream.

- *Flags*: This 3-bit value tells whether this packet is a **fragment** of a whole packet and, more specifically, whether it's the last fragment or whether more fragments are to follow.

- *Fragment Offset*: If the data received is a fragment, this value indicates where the fragment belongs in the sequence of fragments so that a packet can be reassembled.

- *Time to Live (TTL)*: This 8-bit value identifies the maximum time the packet can remain in the system before it is dropped. Each router or device through which the packet passes reduces the TTL by a value of one. Having a TTL prevents a packet from getting caught in loops because it is undeliverable. When the value reaches zero, the packet is destroyed, and an ICMP message is transmitted to the sender.

- *Protocol*: This identifies the IP protocol that was used in the data portion of the packet and should receive the data at its destination (for example, TCP, UDP, or ICMP).

- *Header Checksum*: This is a summing up of all of the 16-bit values in the packet header in a single value.

- *Source Address*: This is the address of the computer or device that sent the IP packet.

- *Destination Address*: This is the address of the computer or device that is to receive the IP packet.

- *Options*: This element can contain a Security field, which enables the sender to assign a classification level to the packet (such as Secret, Top Secret, and so on), as well as several source routing fields by which the sender can supply routing information that gateways can use to send the packet to its destination.

- *Data*: This is the part that the end user actually sees, such as the body of an e-mail message.

Some packets have an additional segmented section at the end that is either called a trailer or footer, which contains data that indicates the end of the packet. The data needed to support an error-checking procedure called a **Cyclical Redundancy Check (CRC)** might also be added.

Packet-Filtering Rules

Packet-filtering devices evaluate information in packet headers and compare it to one or more sets of rules that have been established to conform to network usage policy. If a packet appears to satisfy one of the "Allow" rules, the packet is allowed to pass. On the other hand, if the information matches one of the "Deny" rules, the packet is dropped. Note that packet filters only examine packet headers, in contrast to application proxies, which examine packet data and then forward the packet to its destination on behalf of the originating host.

Some of the more common rules for packet filtering are as follows:

- Drop all inbound connections; allow only outbound connections on Ports 80 (HTTP), 25 (SMTP), and 21 (FTP).

- Eliminate packets bound for all ports that should not be available to the Internet, such as NetBIOS, but allow Internet-related traffic, such as SMTP, to pass.

- Filter out any ICMP redirect or echo (ping) messages, which may be used by attackers attempting to locate open ports or host IP addresses.

- Drop all packets that use the IP header **source routing** feature. In IP source routing, the originator of a packet can attempt to partially or completely control the path through the network to the destination. Source routing is widely considered a suspect activity from a security standpoint, since this is a favorite technique of network attackers, and few legitimate uses exists for this kind of route control.

Although small-scale, software-only "personal" firewall programs can protect one computer, they can cause problems in a network situation. Often, they block traffic between networked computers unless rules are set up to enable communications. Thus, you need to set up an access list that includes all of the computers in your local network by name or IP address so communications can flow between them.

Norton Internet Security 2002's built-in firewall has an easy way to identify computers on the local network: it puts them in a list of machines in a trusted zone. The software can detect other networked machines that have IP addresses in one of the private ranges (10.0.0.1 and so on), or you can add IP addresses of networked machines yourself, as shown in Figure 6-3.

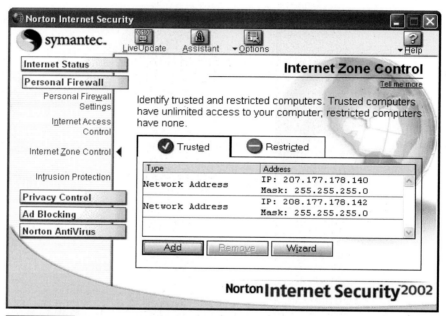

FIGURE 6-3   Trust Rules

Other firewall programs require you to set up rules yourself. Typically, you start with a protocol such as ICMP, UDP, or HTTP. A good practice is to block all the traffic that uses that protocol on all ports and then add back in specific ports or programs to enable only the functionality that is needed. The subsequent rules identify the specific types of communication you want to permit. The allowances may be based on a specific program being executed, a precise time of day, a specific port, a known IP address, or other specific criteria. Sygate Personal Firewall, for example, lets you identify hosts yourself and set up the filtering criteria that the program uses to block or allow packets (see Figure 6-4).

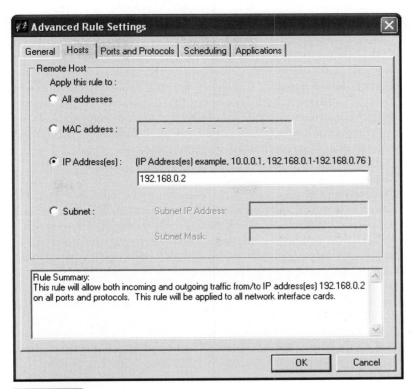

FIGURE 6-4 Adding Rules

Packet-Filtering Methods

The simplest packet-filtering method, **stateless packet filtering** (also called static packet filtering), reviews packet header content and makes decisions on whether to allow or drop the packets based on whether a connection has actually been established between an external host and an internal one. A more sophisticated and secure method, stateful packet filtering, maintains a record of the state of a connection and can thus make informed decisions—for example, allowing traffic that is a genuine reply to an established connection. A third method performs packet filtering based on the contents of the data part of a packet and the header.

Stateless Packet Filtering

It's easy to jump to the conclusion that stateless packet filtering is of no value at all because, unlike stateful packet filtering, it doesn't pay attention to the state of the connection when making decisions about blocking or allowing packets. However, stateless packet filters are useful for completely blocking traffic from a subnet or other network.

Some of the most common criteria that a stateless filter can be configured to use are IP header information, the TCP or UDP port number being used, the ICMP message type, fragmentation flags such as ACK and SYN, and suspect inbound IP addresses (an external packet that contains an internal address).

Filtering on IP Header Criteria

A stateless filter looks at each packet's header individually. It compares the header data against its **rule base** and forwards each packet as a rule is found to match the specifics of that packet. For instance, if the filter has a rule stating that all connections from outside the network are to be blocked, and it receives a request from an external host, it drops the packet(s) associated with that request. Or, if it has a rule that all incoming HTTP traffic needs to be routed to the public Web server at IP address 192.168.100.2, it sends any HTTP packets to 192.168.100.2. Suppose you set up a filter to allow TCP packets to pass through for a session that has already been established. Such sessions make use of one or more identifiers called flags. Flags that identify the status of a session are found in the TCP header section of a packet. Figure 6-5 shows detailed packet information from the packet log of Sygate Personal Firewall. The upper part of the log shows attributes of the packet, such as source IP, destination IP, and so on. The TCP header information is shown in the box in the lower-left corner. The Flags section shows that the **Acknowledgment (ACK) flag** has been set, signifying that the destination computer has received the packets that were previously sent.

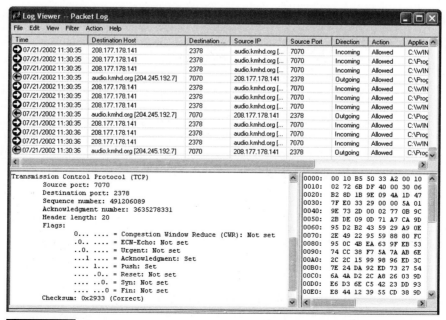

FIGURE 6-5   TCP Flags

However, an attacker can craft a false TCP header that contains an ACK flag (and, presumably, a Trojan horse or other harmful software). The stateless packet filter would allow such a packet to pass through even though no connection has actually been established.

One of the first IP header criteria you can filter on is the packet's source IP address. If someone tries to access your database server from IP address 62.10.100.6, however, it doesn't do any good to simply set up a single rule blocking all access from 62.10.100.6. If this is a hack attempt, the attacker will make another attempt from a different host. In addition, so many attackers will attempt to come at you from so many different addresses that it will be impossible to keep up with all of them. A much more effective approach is to allow only certain source IP addresses to access your resources; denying all hosts except for a group of trusted IP addresses is the most effective security approach for a stateless packet filter. You can use a stateless filter to block all access from untrusted networks or subnets.

You can also set up filter rules based on the destination or target IP address. The most obvious example is to enable external hosts to connect to your public servers in the DMZ but not to hosts in the internal LAN.

You can also go a step further and specify which protocols are available. For instance, you could set up a rule that allows all external hosts to access your Web server at TCP Port 80, but that limits internal addresses to TCP Port 23 (Telnet).

Table 6-1 shows the filtering rules that combine IP addresses and port numbers to control how hosts gain access to your internal network.

TABLE 6-1 Filtering by Destination IP and Port Number

Protocol	Transport Protocol	Source IP	Source Port	Destination IP	Destination Port	Action
HTTP	TCP	Any	Any	192.168.0.1	80	Allow
HTTPS	TCP	Any	Any	192.168.0.1	443	Allow
Telnet	TCP	10.0.0.1/24	Any	192.168.0.5	23	Allow

Packets can also be filtered based on the IP protocol ID field in the header. The filter can use the data to allow or deny traffic attempting to connect to a particular service, including the following:

- TCP (Protocol number 6)
- UDP (Protocol number 17)
- IGMP (Protocol number 2)
- ICMP (Protocol number 1)

Internet Group Management Protocol (IGMP) enables a computer to identify its multicast group membership to routers so that it can receive a multicast (a broadcast of streaming media, newsletters, or other content) from another computer. You can find a complete list of protocol numbers at *www.iana.org/assignments/protocol-numbers*.

Most simple packet filters cannot store lists of hosts that are permitted to access a particular protocol. They can only block or allow traffic for an entire designated protocol. Filtering by protocol might work if you can block all traffic for one protocol—all UDP traffic on a public FTP server, for instance. The Options field in an IP header can be set by both hosts and routers. Options, though, are rarely used. Source routing, for instance, is not required by any protocol or ISP. Yet, source routing is a tempting tool to attackers, who only need to enter their own IP addresses in the destination to have the packet returned to them, using this method to gain valuable intelligence about the internal network they would otherwise be unable to gain.

Filtering by TCP or UDP Port Number

Filtering by TCP or UDP port number is commonly called port filtering or protocol filtering. Using TCP or UDP port numbers can help you filter a wide variety of information, including SMTP and POP e-mail messages, NetBIOS sessions, DNS requests, and Network News Transfer Protocol (NNTP) newsgroup sessions. For instance, you can block everything but TCP Port 80 for Web, TCP Port 25 for e-mail, and TCP Port 21 for FTP.

Filtering by ICMP Message Type

Internet Control Message Protocol (ICMP) is a general management protocol for TCP/IP, helping networked systems and administrators diagnose various communication problems and communicate certain status information. From a security standpoint, ICMP packets have a downside: they may be used in some situations by attackers to crash computers on your network. Because ICMP packets cannot be verified as to the recipient of a packet, attackers may attempt to engineer man-in-the-middle attacks, in which they redirect network traffic using the ICMP Redirect message. This might trick users into believing a rogue network server is a trusted server by directing traffic to a computer the attacker controls that is outside the protected network. The users think they are using a known and trusted computer.

A firewall/packet filter must be able to determine, based on message type, whether an ICMP packet should be allowed to pass. Some of the more common ICMP message types are shown in Table 6-2.

TABLE 6-2 ICMP Message Codes

ICMP Type	Name	Possible Cause
0	Echo reply	Normal response to a ping
3	Destination unreachable	Destination unreachable
3 code 6	Destination network unknown	Destination network unknown
3 code 7	Destination host unknown	Destination host unknown
4	Source quench	Router receiving too much traffic
5	Redirect	Faster route located
8	Echo request	Normal ping request
11	Time exceeded	Too many hops to destination
12	Parameter problem	There is a problem with a parameter

You'll find a complete list of ICMP message types at *www.iana.org/assignments/ icmp-parameters.*

One type of network protocol attack takes advantage of the ICMP Echo Request message type, by flooding a target computer with a constant stream of ICMP echo requests. The receiving machine is so busy fielding requests that it can't process any other network traffic. If the computer that goes down is providing important services such as DNS, an ICMP Redirect packet can point target computers to the attacker's computer where the attacker can attempt to access confidential information such as passwords.

Firewall logs indicate whether a large number of echo messages are being received. You can configure your firewall to drop ICMP packets that change network behavior (for example, that do ICMP Redirect) and that have come from sources outside your own network.

Filtering by Fragmentation Flags

Fragmentation of IP packets isn't bad in theory. Fragmentation was originally developed as a means of enabling large packets to pass through early routers that had frame size limitations. Routers were able to divide packets into multiple fragments and send them along the network, where receiving routers would reassemble them in the correct order and pass them to their destination.

The problem with fragmentation is that because the TCP or UDP port number is provided only at the beginning of a packet, it appears only in fragments numbered 0. Fragments numbered 1 or higher pass through the filter because they don't contain any port information. All an attacker has to do is modify the IP header to start all fragment numbers of a packet at 1 or higher.

To be safe, you should have the firewall reassemble fragmented packets before making the admit/drop decision.

Filtering by ACK Flag

A single bit of information in a TCP packet—the ACK bit or ACK flag—indicates whether a packet is requesting a connection or whether a connection has already been established. Packets requesting a connection have the ACK bit set to 0; those that are part of an ongoing connection have the ACK bit set to 1. An attacker can insert a false ACK bit of 1 into a packet to fool a host into thinking a connection is ongoing. You should configure the firewall to allow packets with the ACK bit set to 1 to access only the ports you specify and only in the direction you want.

Filtering Suspicious Inbound Packets

If a packet arrives at the firewall from the external network but containing an IP address that is inside the network, the firewall should send an alert message. In Figure 6-6, Tiny Personal Firewall has encountered a request from an external host to access the protected host's SQL server.

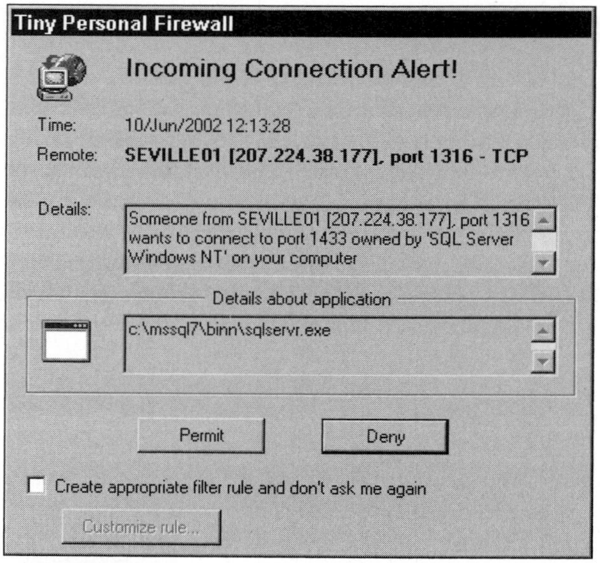

Tiny Personal Firewall

Incoming Connection Alert!

Time: 10/Jun/2002 12:13:28

Remote: **SEVILLE01 [207.224.38.177], port 1316 - TCP**

Details:
```
Someone from SEVILLE01 [207.224.38.177], port 1316
wants to connect to port 1433 owned by 'SQL Server
Windows NT' on your computer
```

Details about application

`c:\mssql7\binn\sqlservr.exe`

[Permit]   [Deny]

☐ Create appropriate filter rule and don't ask me again

[Customize rule...]

FIGURE 6-6 Firewall Alert

This firewall, like others, lets users graphically decide whether to permit or deny the packet on a case-by-case basis, or automatically, by setting up a rule to cover all future instances of such connection attempts.

Most firewalls customize rules to work with all ports or all protocols, if you wish. If you receive an alert message like the one shown in Figure 6-6, click the Customize rule button at the bottom of the alert window. You can then customize the rule to apply to specific ports or addresses, as shown in Figure 6-7.

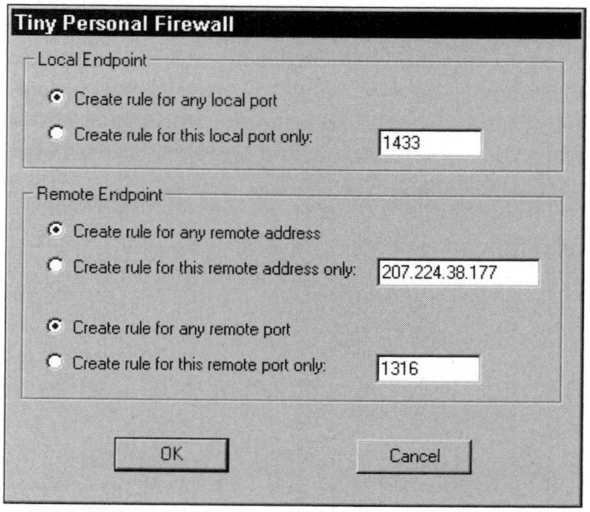

Tiny Personal Firewall

Local Endpoint
- ⦿ Create rule for any local port
- ○ Create rule for this local port only: `1433`

Remote Endpoint
- ⦿ Create rule for any remote address
- ○ Create rule for this remote address only: `207.224.38.177`

- ⦿ Create rule for any remote port
- ○ Create rule for this remote port only: `1316`

[OK]   [Cancel]

FIGURE 6-7 Customizing Rules

You can also set up other common rules for inbound packets, such as:

- Dropping any inbound packets that have a source IP address that is within your internal network
- Dropping all inbound traffic that has the loopback address 127.0.0.1 as the source IP address
- Dropping traffic that has a source IP address that has not yet been allocated to any network, such as 0.x.x.x, 1.x.x.x, or 2.x.x.x

You may encounter repeated alerts if you block packets individually rather than setting up rules so that the firewall can handle them automatically. However, it can also be enlightening to track how many connection attempts are made, what ports and services are being accessed, and where the attempts are originating—provided you have the time to review them.

Stateful Packet Filtering

Stateful packet filtering takes the concept of packet filtering a step further than stateless filtering. A stateful filter can do everything a stateless filter can, but with one significant addition: the ability to maintain a record of the state of a connection. By "remembering" which packets are part of an active connection and which are not, the stateful filter can make "intelligent" decisions to allow traffic that is a true reply to an established connection and to deny packets that contain false information. The more powerful enterprise firewalls such as those in the Cisco PIX series or Check Point FireWall-1 do stateful packet filtering. However, versions 1 and 2 of FireWall-1 do stateful filtering only on UDP. More recent versions handle UDP, TCP, and some ICMP packets.

In addition to a rule base, a stateful filter has a state table, which is a list of current connections. The packet filter compares the packet with the state table as well as the rule base. Entries that match criteria in both the state table and rule base are allowed to pass; all others are dropped. Figure 6-8 illustrates steps involved in processing a single request from a computer within your network to access the Web site *www.course.com*.

A stateful packet filter has to consult its state table and its rule base when a packet is encountered. However, it's worth noting that when the packet shown in Figure 6-8 arrives at the router, the state table is consulted but the rule base is not. It is not consulted because the rule base was consulted when the state table entry for the session was created. Also, stateful packet filters don't require a rule that allows reply packets to pass, but a stateless filter does.

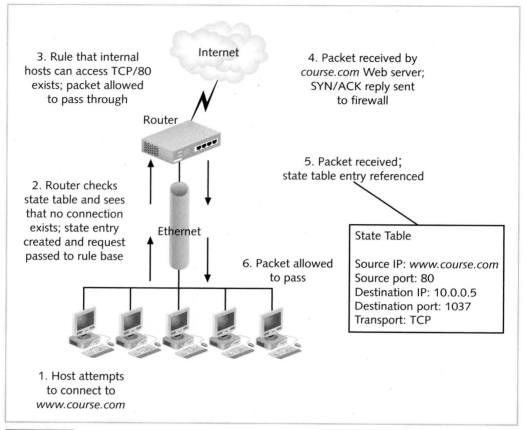

FIGURE 6-8 Stateful Packet Filtering

If an attacker tries to craft a packet with a false ACK bit set to 1, the stateful filter passes it to the rule base because no entry exists in the state table, and the rule base drops the packet since there would be no rule in place to allow it to pass. There's no need to create a special rule for packets that have the ACK bit set to 1.

Two of the flags that are part of a packet's TCP header information, and that indicate whether a session is beginning or ending, are RST (Reset, which tells a host to immediately terminate a connection) and FIN (Finished, which tells a host to gracefully end a connection). If a session ends abnormally (if one system goes offline or a computer crashes), and no RST or FIN flag is received, the filter uses a timer to determine when to remove state table entries. The timer can be set to remove entries as soon as 60 seconds or as late as several days after a session ends.

Note that stateful packet filtering has limitations. It inspects only header information and doesn't verify the packet data. It works by controlling the type of transport and the port number being used. If one of your servers is set up to listen for inbound communications on a nonstandard but well-known port, such as TCP/25 for SMTP, the filter might let in traffic that is bound for the well-known port but block traffic bound for other ports.

Filtering Based on Packet Content

As mentioned, both stateless and stateful packet filters examine the header of a packet. Some traffic, such as ICMP traffic, uses packets that are difficult to filter reliably for various reasons, including ICMP packets that don't always originate from the same source and destination IP addresses. If a server has become unreachable, a status message is created by an intermediary device instead. Because this message comes from a different source IP address than was recorded in the original state table entry, the message would be dropped by a stateful filter, even though it's part of a legitimate session.

To handle such cases, some stateful firewalls examine the contents of packets as well as the headers for signs that they are legitimate. Such content filtering is sometimes called stateful inspection. For example, active FTP might use ports that are determined as a session is initiated. A stateless or stateful packet filter that supports active FTP must allow all traffic coming from TCP Port 20 as well as outbound traffic coming from ports above 1023. However, a stateful inspection looks at the data part of the FTP command packets to determine which ports are to be used for this session—instead of opening all possible FTP ports, the packet filter opens ports as needed. After the session is done, the ports are again closed.

There are two other types of firewall-related programs that examine packet content. One type is the proxy gateway. It looks at the data within a packet and decides which application should handle it. The other type is the specialty firewall, such as MailMarshal (*www.mailmarshall.com*), which looks at the body of e-mail messages or Web pages for profanities or other content identified as offensive. It then blocks the transmission of such information based on the presence of such terms. Such specialty firewalls are primarily designed to prevent employees within an organization from visiting inappropriate Web sites and from sending or receiving inappropriate e-mail messages.

Setting Specific Packet Filter Rules

Once you have a general idea of how packet filtering works, you can establish the actual packet filter rules that control traffic to various resources. The following sections describe the types of rules that can block potentially harmful packets, as well as rules that pass packets that contain legitimate traffic.

Best Practices for Firewall Rules

In practice, configuring firewall rule sets can be something of a nightmare. Logic errors in the preparation of the rules can cause unintended behavior, such as allowing access instead of denying it, specifying the wrong port or service type, or causing the network to misroute traffic. These and a myriad of other mistakes can turn a device designed to protect communications into a choke point. For example, a novice firewall administrator might improperly configure a virus-screening e-mail gateway (think of it as a type of e-mail firewall), thus blocking all incoming e-mail, instead of only e-mail that contains malicious code. Each firewall rule must be carefully crafted, placed into the list in the proper sequence, debugged, and tested. The proper rule sequence ensures that the most resource-intensive actions are performed after the most restrictive ones, thereby reducing the number of packets that undergo intense scrutiny.

Some of the best practices for firewall use are:

- All traffic from the trusted network is allowed out. This allows members of the organization to access the services they need. Filtering and logging outbound traffic is possible when indicated by specific organizational policy.

- The firewall device is never accessible directly from the public network. Almost all access to the firewall device is denied to internal users as well. Only authorized firewall administrators access the device via secure authentication mechanisms, with preference for a method based on cryptographically strong authentication using two-factor access control techniques.

- Simple Mail Transport Protocol (SMTP) data is allowed to pass through the firewall, but all of it is routed to a well-configured SMTP gateway to securely filter and route messaging traffic.

- All Internet Control Message Protocol (ICMP) data is denied. Known as the ping service, it is a common method for attacker reconnaissance and should be turned off to prevent snooping.

- Telnet (terminal emulation) access to all internal servers from the public networks is blocked. At the very least, Telnet access to the organization's Domain Name Service (DNS) server should be blocked to prevent illegal zone transfers, and to prevent attackers from taking down the organization's entire network. If internal users need to reach an organization's network from outside the firewall, use a virtual private network (VPN) client or other secure authentication system to allow this kind of access.

- When Web services are offered outside the firewall, HTTP traffic is prevented from reaching your internal networks via the implementation of some form of proxy access or DMZ architecture. That way, any Web servers running on employees' desktops for internal use are invisible to the Internet. If your Web server is located behind the firewall, you need to allow HTTP or HTTPS (SHTTP) data through for the Internet at large to view it. The best solution is to place the Web servers containing critical data inside the network and to use proxy services from a DMZ (screened network segment). It is also advisable to restrict incoming HTTP traffic to internal network addresses such that the traffic must be responding to requests originating at internal addresses. This restriction can be accomplished through NAT or firewalls that can support stateful inspection or are directed at the proxy server itself. All other incoming HTTP traffic should be blocked. If the Web servers contain only advertising, they should be placed in the DMZ and rebuilt when (not if) they are compromised.

Test all firewall rules before they are placed into production use. Testing should include what is called regression testing, when all rules are tested with a representative set of traffic. The practice of testing just the new rules should be avoided, since it is necessary to test all of the rules together in order to ferret out any unexpected interactions. Tools such as the open-source tool Firewall Tester (Ftester, found at *http://dev.inversepath.com/trac/ftester*) are available for this purpose.

Rules That Cover Multiple Variations

Packet filter rules must account for all possible ports that a type of communication might use, or for all variations within a particular protocol (for instance, passive and active FTP, or standard HTTP and secure HTTP). This is a tricky process; rules are often created and modified as a result of trial and error, for example, an employee complains that he or she can't communicate with someone using MSN Messenger, and you adjust the packet filter's rule base accordingly (after consulting the security policy, of course).

Consider the network shown in Figure 6-9, which will serve as a basis for the discussion in this section.

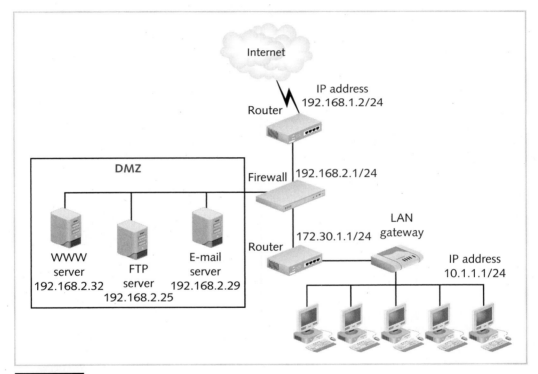

FIGURE 6-9   Sample Network

Figure 6-9 illustrates a typical LAN that is protected by a firewall and two routers. A DMZ connected to the firewall provides services that the public network can access, such as a Web server, FTP server, and e-mail server. Accordingly, packet filter rules need to be set up to allow Web, FTP, e-mail, and other services, while blocking potentially harmful packets from getting to the internal LAN.

Rules for ICMP Packets

ICMP rules are especially important because ICMP packets can be easily forged and used to redirect other communications.

The most common ICMP command is Packet Internet Groper (commonly called ping). The command determines if a host is unreachable on the network. You send a packet to a host you're trying to reach, and the host responds with an ICMP response packet that tells you the host is "alive." Many attackers begin attacks by using ping to see whether a host is reachable by them as well. If all of your hosts respond to the ping command, you could be opening up your network to an attack.

To prevent attackers from using the ping command to identify some of your resources, you need to establish specific ICMP commands that cover common ICMP messages. Table 6-3 gives some rules that enable you to send and receive the ICMP packets you need while blocking those that open your internal hosts to intruders.

TABLE 6-3 ICMP Packet Filter Rules

Rule	Protocol	Transport Protocol	Source IP	Destination IP	ICMP Message	Action
1	ICMP	ICMP	Any	Any	Source Quench	Allow inbound
2	ICMP	ICMP	192.168.2.1/24	Any	Echo Request	Allow outbound
3	ICMP	ICMP	Any	192.168.2.1/24	Echo Reply	Allow inbound
4	ICMP	ICMP	Any	192.168.2.1/24	Destination Unreachable	Allow inbound
5	ICMP	ICMP	Any	192.168.2.1/24	Service Unavailable	Allow inbound
6	ICMP	ICMP	Any	192.168.2.1/24	Time to Live (TTL)	Allow inbound
7	ICMP	ICMP	Any	192.168.2.1/24	Echo Request	Drop inbound
8	ICMP	ICMP	Any	192.168.2.1/24	Redirect	Drop inbound
9	ICMP	ICMP	192.168.2.1/24	Any	Echo Reply	Drop outbound
10	ICMP	ICMP	192.168.2.1/24	Any	TTL Exceeded	Drop outbound
11	ICMP Block	ICMP	Any	Any	All	Drop

The rules shown in Table 6-3 serve the following purposes:

- *Rule 1 (Source Quench)*: Lets external hosts tell your internal hosts if the network is saturated
- *Rule 2 (Echo Request)*: Gives your computers the ability to ping external computers
- *Rule 3 (Echo Reply)*: Enables your computers to receive ping replies from external hosts
- *Rule 4 (Destination Unreachable)*: Lets your hosts receive packets that an external resource is unreachable
- *Rule 5 (Service Unavailable)*: Lets your hosts receive packets that an external resource is unavailable
- *Rule 6 (Time to Live Exceeded)*: Lets your hosts know that an exterior resource is too many "hops" away
- *Rule 7 (Echo Request)*: Blocks ping packets that might be used to locate internal hosts
- *Rule 8 (Redirect)*: Prevents attackers or others from changing your **routing tables**
- *Rule 9 (Echo Reply)*: Prevents attackers from receiving replies to ping requests
- *Rule 10 (Time to Live Exceeded)*: Prevents attackers from determining the number of hops inside your network
- *Rule 11 (ICMP Block)*: After setting your rules, drops all other ICMP packets for extra security; that is, all ICMP packets not listed in the preceding rules will be dropped at the firewall

Rules That Enable Web Access

The first priority of employees in a protected network is (not surprisingly) to be able to surf the Web and exchange e-mail messages. The rules for accessing the Web need to cover both standard HTTP traffic on TCP Port 80 as well as Secure HTTP (HTTPS) traffic on TCP Port 443. The rules for the Internet-accessible Web server in our test network would look like those shown in Table 6-4. The rules in the table assume that the firewall uses a Deny-all policy. All packets are denied except for those that meet the rules listed in the rule base.

TABLE 6-4 HTTP Access Rules

Rule	Protocol	Transport Protocol	Source IP	Source Port	Destination IP	Destination Port	Action
12	HTTP	TCP	Any	Any	192.168.2.32	80	Allow inbound
13	HTTPS	TCP	Any	Any	192.168.2.32	443	Allow inbound
14	HTTP	TCP	192.168.1.2/24	Any	Any	80	Allow outbound
15	HTTPS	TCP	192.168.2.32	Any	Any	443	Allow outbound

Rules That Enable DNS

To connect to Web sites, the employees in our sample organization need to be able to resolve the fully qualified domain names (FQDNs) they enter, such as course.com, to their corresponding IP addresses using the Domain Name System (DNS). Internal users connect to external hosts using a DNS server located in the DMZ of the security perimeter. DNS uses either UDP Port 53 or TCP Port 53 for connection attempts. In addition, you need to set up rules that enable external clients to access computers in your own network using the same TCP and UDP ports, as shown in Table 6-5.

TABLE 6-5 Rules that Enable DNS Resolution

Rule	Protocol	Transport Protocol	Source IP	Source Port	Destination IP	Destination Port	Action
16	DNS	TCP	192.168.2.31	Any	Any	53	Allow outbound
17	DNS	UDP	192.168.2.31	Any	Any	53	Allow outbound
18	DNS	TCP	Any	Any	192.168.2.31	53	Allow inbound
19	DNS	UDP	Any	Any	192.168.2.31	53	Allow inbound

If your network uses DNS forwarding to an ISP's DNS server, enter the IP address of the ISP's DNS server as the destination IP and your own DNS server as the source IP. Some security administrators believe that allowing their company's DNS server to communicate with any DNS server is a security risk, and thus they direct all DNS traffic to a single DNS server operated by an ISP.

Rules That Enable FTP

As stated, FTP transactions can be either active or passive. The rules you set up for FTP need to support two separate connections: TCP Port 21, which is the FTP control port, and TCP 20, which is the FTP data port. If some clients in your network support active FTP, you can't specify a particular port because the client can establish a connection with the FTP server at any port above 1023. Instead, you specify the IP address of your FTP server, as shown in Table 6-6.

TABLE 6-6 Rules to Enable Active and Passive FTP

Rule	Protocol	Transport Protocol	Source IP	Source Port	Destination IP	Destination Port	Action
20	FTP Control	TCP	Any	Any	192.168.1.25	21	Allow inbound
21	FTP Data	TCP	192.168.1.25	20	Any	Any	Allow inbound
22	FTP PASV	TCP	Any	Any	192.168.1.25	Any	Allow
23	FTP Control	TCP	192.168.1.25	Any	Any	21	Allow outbound
24	FTP Data	TCP	Any	20	192.168.1.25	Any	Allow outbound

Some administrators prefer to drop incoming active FTP connections because of the danger of FTP port scanning. They allow only passive connections to go through.

Rules That Enable E-Mail

Setting up firewall rules that filter e-mail messages can be difficult. One reason is the variety of e-mail protocols that might be used:

- Post Office Protocol 3 (POP3) and Internet Message Access Protocol version 4 (IMAP4) for inbound mail transport
- Simple Mail Transfer Protocol (SMTP) for outbound mail transport
- Lightweight Directory Access Protocol (LDAP) for looking up e-mail addresses
- Hypertext Transfer Protocol (HTTP) and/or TLS (HTTPS) for Web-based mail service

To keep things simple, our sample configuration only uses POP3 and SMTP for inbound and outbound e-mail, respectively. However, SSL encryption is used for additional security. Some sample rules are found in Table 6-7.

TABLE 6-7 POP3 and SMTP E-mail Rules

Rule	Protocol	Transport Protocol	Source IP	Source Port	Destination IP	Destination Port	Action
25	POP3	TCP	192.168.2.1/24	Any	Any	110	Allow outbound
26	POP3/S	TCP	192.168.2.1/24	Any	Any	995	Allow outbound
27	POP3	TCP	Any	Any	192.168.2.1/24	110	Allow inbound
28	POP3/S	TCP	Any	Any	192.168.2.1/24	995	Allow inbound
29	SMTP	TCP	192.168.2.29	Any	Any	25	Allow outbound
30	SMTP/S	TCP	192.168.2.29	Any	Any	465	Allow outbound
31	SMTP	TCP	Any	Any	192.168.2.29	25	Allow inbound
32	SMTP/S	TCP	Any	Any	192.168.2.29	465	Allow inbound

To set up your own configuration rules, you need to assess whether your organization needs to accept incoming e-mail messages at all, whether internal users can access mail services outside your company (such as Hotmail), and what e-mail clients are supported by your company. By identifying the e-mail clients your company will support, you can provide the highest level of security without blocking e-mail access.

Case Exercises

A few days after her attempt to connect to the school system, Kiara was back in the guidance office. She noticed the secretary was not her usual happy self. The sticky note with all the connection information was gone. Trying to be her normal, friendly self, Kiara asked the secretary, "Why so glum, Ms. Simpson?"

Ms. Simpson answered, "It seems somebody tried to access the school district mainframe from the Internet and they used my username. I got in trouble for failure to properly secure my login credentials and had to go take a special security awareness class yesterday. My manager is really upset with me, and I'm worried about keeping my job."

Kiara said, "I'm sorry, Ms. Simpson. Do they know who did it?"

Ms. Simpson said, "They didn't really tell me, except they said something about firewalls and audit logs and some kind of investigation."

Kiara left the office quickly.

Questions:

1. What kind of packet filtering rule might have been set up to detect Kiara's hacking attempt?

2. Is it possible Kiara will be found out from this hacking attempt? Is it likely?

7

Working with Proxy Servers and Application-Level Firewalls

> Your representative owes you, not his industry only, but his judgment; and he betrays instead of serving you if he sacrifices it to your opinion.
> **EDMUND BURKE**

RON HALL WAS DREAMING OF HIS NEXT VACATION. He had been working for Andy Ying, the manager of the security consulting group, on a very demanding project for nearly six months. Today he finally finished the work and had a few minutes to surf the Web to plan his upcoming trip to New Zealand.

Ron knew that ATI did not allow indiscriminate Web surfing and that they used a proxy server to ensure compliance with this policy, but he felt he had earned this treat and believed that Andy would have no problems with a little recreational Web surfing. Besides, it was almost 5:00 and nearly time to go home.

Google was allowed by the proxy server, so Ron went there to start his search. He typed in

```
new zealand vacation spots
```

Faster than he could blink, the giant search engine Google came back with a list of relevant links. The first entry looked promising: "New Zealand Tourism Online: New Zealand Travel Guide." But the second one looked even better: "New Zealand Pictures." He clicked that URL.

No pictures opened up. No green valleys. No coral reefs. No gorgeous mountains. Just a plain white screen with black letters that read:

```
ACCESS PROHIBITED—CONTACT PROXY SERVER ADMINISTRATOR
FOR INSTRUCTIONS ON HOW TO ACCESS THE REQUESTED CONTENT.
```

Ron was not surprised, but he had hoped. He clicked the "Back" button and tried the next link. He got the same message. He tried three or four more times and then realized he was not getting any pictures today.

LEARNING OBJECTIVES:

Upon completion of this material, you should be able to do the following:

- Discuss proxy servers and how they work
- Identify the goals your organization can achieve using a proxy server
- Make recommendations from among proxy server configurations
- Choose a proxy server and work with the SOCKS protocol
- Evaluate the most popular proxy-based firewall products
- Explain how to deploy and use reverse proxy
- Determine when a proxy server isn't the correct choice

Introduction

Proxy servers were originally developed as a way to speed up communications on the Web by storing a site's most popular pages in a cache. Since then, they have become a formidable security solution. Proxies can conceal the end users in a network, filter out undesirable Web sites, and block harmful content in much the same manner as packet filters. Today, most proxy servers function as firewalls at the boundary of a network, performing packet filtering, Network Address Translation (NAT), and other services. In this chapter, you will learn what proxy servers are, how they work, and in what ways they are vulnerable. You will also learn about the different kinds of proxy servers you can install, so that you can make an informed decision about the one that's right for you.

Overview of Proxy Servers

Proxy servers—also called **proxy services**, **application-level gateways**, or **application proxies**—consist of software that runs on a network device or appliance, or on a dedicated, general-purpose computer. Proxy servers evaluate the data portion of an IP packet (unlike packet filters, which examine only the header of an IP packet) to determine whether to allow the packet to pass into or out of the network.

How Proxy Servers Work

Proxies function as a software go-between, forwarding data between internal users and external hosts or external users and internal hosts. They screen all traffic into and out of the relevant ports and decide whether to block or allow traffic based on rules set up by the proxy server administrator.

In a typical transaction, a proxy server intercepts a request from a user on the internal network and passes it along to a destination computer on the Internet. This might seem like a complex and time-consuming process, but it takes only a matter of seconds for the following steps to occur:

1. An internal host makes a request to access a Web site.
2. The request goes to the proxy server, which examines the header and data of the packet against rules configured by the firewall administrator.
3. The proxy server recreates the packet in its entirety, with a different source IP address.
4. The proxy server sends the packet to its destination; the packet appears to be coming from the proxy server, not the original end user who made the request.
5. The returned packet is sent to the proxy server, which inspects it again and compares it against its rule base.
6. The returned packet is rebuilt by the proxy server and sent to the originating computer; when received, the packet appears to have come from the external host, not the proxy server.

Figure 7-1 illustrates these steps, which describe an inside to out transaction. Proxy servers are also used for outside to in transactions.

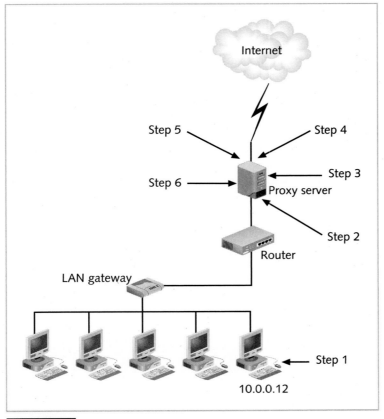

FIGURE 7-1   Steps in an Example Proxy Transaction

The main complaint about proxy servers is the time they take to inspect, compare, and rebuild packets. However, in return, they conceal clients, translate network addresses, and filter content, among other tasks.

How Proxy Servers Differ from Packet Filters

Proxy servers and packet filters are used together in a firewall to provide multiple layers of security of different varieties. Both inspect different parts of IP packets and act on them in different ways.

It's useful to contrast proxies and packet filters so that you understand the different types of network security they provide:

- Because proxy servers scan the entire data portion of IP packets, they create much more detailed log file listings than packet filters.
- If a packet matches one of the packet filter's rules, the filter simply acts as directed by the rule for that packet, allowing it to pass or blocking it from entering the destination network. A proxy server also rebuilds the packet with new source IP information, which shields internal users from those on the outside.
- Because a proxy server rebuilds all packets that pass between the Internet and the internal host, attacks that can start with mangled packet data never reach the internal host.
- Proxy servers are far more critical to network communications than packet filters. If a packet filter fails, all packets might be allowed through to the internal network. If a proxy server **gateway** or firewall were to crash, all network communications would cease. Of course, if a failover or backup firewall is in place, it keeps network communications up and running while the primary device is being serviced.

Sample Proxy Server Configurations

A proxy server is positioned between the hosts in the internal LAN and the outside network to provide services on behalf of both internal and external users. A proxy server has two interfaces: one between itself and the external network, the other between itself and the internal network. The dual-interface nature of a proxy server suggests that a dual-homed host computer—that is, a computer that has two separate network interfaces, one to the external Internet and one to the internal LAN—provides an ideal setup for hosting (see Figure 7-2).

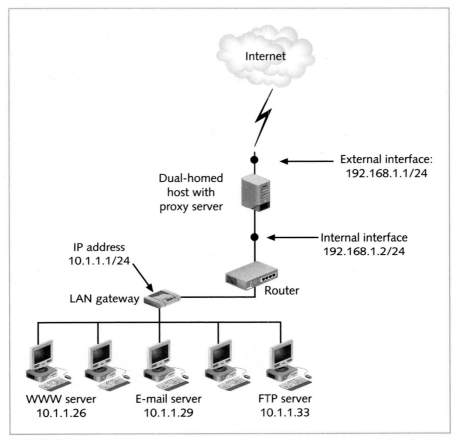

FIGURE 7-2 Proxy Using a Dual-Homed Host

You can also configure a proxy server on a screened host and install routers that function as packet filters on either side.

In Figure 7-3, the packet filter that has an interface on the Internet is configured so that external traffic is allowed to pass only if it is destined for a service provided on the proxy server, which sits on the protected side of the perimeter.

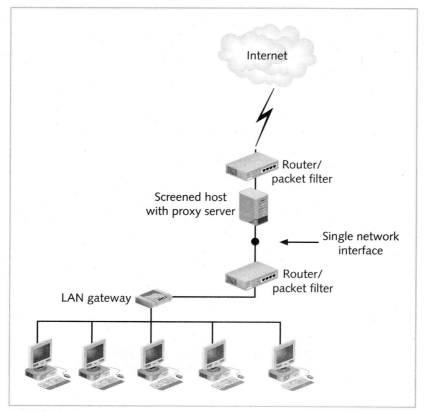

FIGURE 7-3   Proxy Using a Screened Host

Note that although the screened host/proxy server in Figure 7-3 has a direct interface on the Internet, in practice, it's far better to use a proxy server behind a firewall or at least some form of router. As a rule, it is better for a firewall to have the direct interface to the Internet and to protect the proxy server by placing it behind the firewall, because if the proxy is compromised, hackers can disguise themselves as internal clients, and the results can be disastrous for the organization being protected. The only reason you should place a proxy server directly on the Internet is if the proxy is intended to serve as a reverse proxy, which is described later in this chapter. If you use proxy servers in conjunction with stateful or stateless packet filters, make sure you disable IP forwarding so that the proxy server handles packet delivery from one network to another.

Goals of Proxy Servers

When you consider setting up a proxy system to protect a network, you should understand the goals that proxy systems can help you achieve. These goals—from concealing internal clients to redirecting URLs—are described in the following sections.

Concealing Internal Clients

Perhaps the most important benefit of a proxy server is its ability to conceal internal clients from external clients who try to gain access to the internal network. Rather than connecting directly to internal hosts, external clients see a single machine—the one that hosts the proxy server software (see Figure 7-4). This concealment of the internal network is useful to you because if external users cannot detect hosts on your internal network, they cannot initiate direct attacks against those hosts.

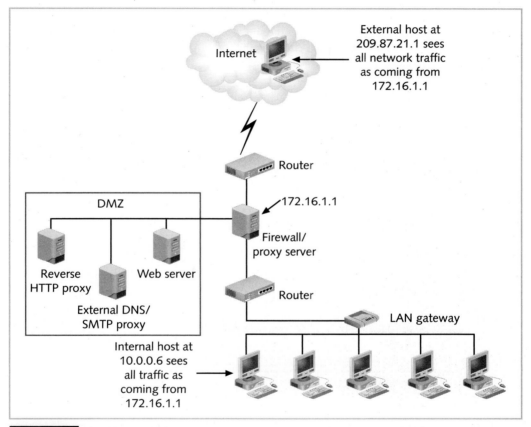

FIGURE 7-4   Concealing the Local Network

The concealment that proxy servers perform resembles NAT and PAT; however, proxy servers don't simply insert a new source IP into the headers of the packets they send out in response to a request. Rather, the proxy server receives requests as though it was the destination server, and then generates a new request, which is sent to its destination.

Because proxy servers route all client requests through a single gateway, they are commonly used to share Internet connections. Simple proxy servers such as WinGate (Windows) or Squid (UNIX) are used to provide Internet connection sharing in small office or home environments.

Blocking URLs

Network administrators and managers like the fact that they can block users from certain URLs. This feature is frequently used to keep employees from visiting Web sites that offer content that management regards as unsuitable. URLs can be specified as either IP addresses or DNS names.

However, in practice, blocking URLs is unreliable, mainly because URLs are typically blocked by proxy servers as full-text URLs. The simple proxy server NetProxy, for example, lets you enter the URLs of sites that you want to block from passing through the WWW proxy gateway (see Figure 7-5). However, if you only enter the domain name of the site, users can still access the site using the IP address that corresponds to the URL. Security policy is a more effective method of preventing employees from visiting certain Web sites, because URLs change frequently.

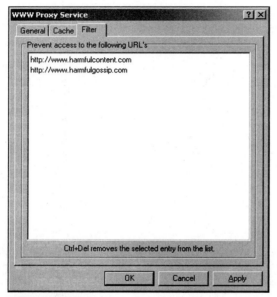

FIGURE 7-5   NetProxy Domain Name Blocking

Blocking and Filtering Content

Proxy servers can be configured to scan packets for questionable content. The proxy can be set up to not only block but also to strip out Java applets or ActiveX controls if you don't want them to enter the internal network. In addition, you should certainly have the proxy delete executable files attached to e-mail messages. When an organization must send file attachments via e-mail, the organization should take specific steps to allow this without enabling the free flow of executables or even large attachments via uncontrolled e-mail. The control approach could include using specific compression or encryption approaches and appropriate levels of authentication and/or approval. Proxy servers, like packet filters, can filter out content based on rules that contain a variety of **parameters**, including time, IP address, and port number. Virtually all proxy server products scan the payload of a packet and provide some sort of content-filtering system. Typically, this is used to block children (in a home environment) or employees (in a work environment) from viewing Web sites that are considered unsuitable.

E-Mail Proxy Protection

Casual users often assume that a proxy server exists primarily to protect users who are surfing the Web or to limit outside Web users' access to internal Web servers. However, proxy servers can be used to support and protect other network services, including e-mail. Figure 7-6 shows a configuration that provides e-mail protection for a network with a proxy Simple Mail Transfer Protocol (SMTP) server.

In Figure 7-6, a sendmail server has been placed in the DMZ where it receives e-mail from the Internet. It passes requests on to the real mail server, which is the Exchange Server located on the internal network. Mail that originates on an internal host is sent from the Exchange Server to the sendmail server, which strips out the IP source address information when it rebuilds the packets and sends them on to the Internet. External e-mail users never interact directly with internal hosts, which is the great advantage of this configuration.

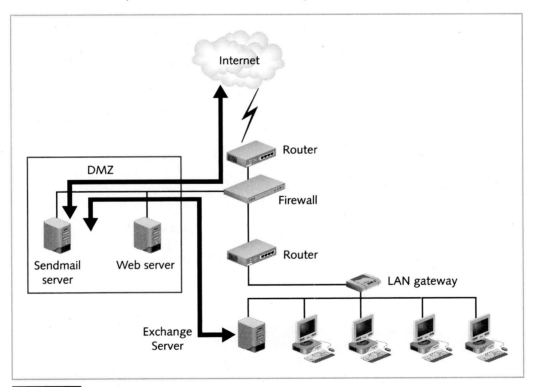

FIGURE 7-6 E-mail Proxy Protection

Improving Performance

Although proxy servers can slow down some requests for information, they can also speed up access to documents that have been requested repeatedly. For instance, they can be configured to store Web pages in a disk **cache**. When someone requests a previously accessed Web page, the proxy server can retrieve it from the cache. This lightens the load on the Web server, which doesn't have to serve up the same documents repeatedly.

Ensuring Security

Log files, which maintain records of events such as logon attempts and accesses to files, might be tedious and time consuming to review, but they can serve many different functions to help ensure the effectiveness of a firewall:

- *Detect intrusions*: By reviewing the firewall logs in detail, you can determine whether an unauthorized user has accessed resources that should be protected.
- *Uncover weaknesses*: Log files can point to ports, machines, or other vulnerable computers through which hackers can gain entry. These entry points are known as **holes**.
- *Provide documentation*: If intrusions occur, log files record when the attacks occurred and provide indications of the method that was used.

As stated, proxy servers provide very complete log files. The fact that proxies require all communications to flow through a single gateway means you have a reliable checkpoint from which to monitor network activity. To keep log files from getting unwieldy and eating up an inordinate amount of disk space, you should log only the services and events you view as most critical. (Events you want to log should certainly include unauthorized connection attempts.)

NetProxy, like other proxy servers, lets you select services from a list for logging (see Figure 7-7). Note that the applications and events you are going to log should be spelled out in your organization's security policy, as described in Chapter 3.

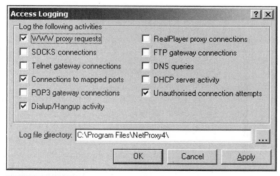

FIGURE 7-7 NetProxy Logging Services

Some proxy servers have an alerting feature: they can notify you when a possible attack is in progress. An example of a possible attack is an attempted connection at the external interface of the proxy server.

Providing User Authentication

If user authentication is used in combination with a proxy server, you enhance security even more. Most proxy server products can prompt users who connect to the server for a username and password, which the server then checks against a database in your system. Authentication is discussed in more detail in Chapter 10.

Redirecting URLs

Some proxies can scan specific parts of the data part of an HTTP packet and redirect it to a specific location. The proxy can be configured to recognize two types of content (and perform **URL redirection** to send them to other locations):

- Files or directories requested by the client

- The name of the host with which the client wants to communicate

The second method, which involves scanning the HTTP host field, is the most popular. It enables you to direct clients to a different Web server based on the host being requested. Suppose you have a single machine with a static IP address that hosts half a dozen or more virtual Web servers. Requests for the host *www.widgets.org* can be directed to one server, requests for *www.knicknacks.org* can be directed to another, and so on.

Many Web servers, such as the popular freeware program Apache or Microsoft Internet Information Server, have URL redirection built in, thus alleviating the need for a proxy server to do redirection.

Proxy Server Configuration Considerations

Proxy servers offer many security-related benefits, but they also require you to perform special tasks, for example, configuring each piece of client software that uses the proxy server, maintaining a separate proxy service for each network protocol, and creating packet filter rules. Also, proxy servers carry with them potential security vulnerabilities, particularly in that they present a single point of failure for the network.

Providing for Scalability

As the number of users on the network grows, the machine that hosts the proxy server should be upgraded. The capacity of the server that hosts the proxy service must be sized to match the amount of traffic that has to flow through each gateway.

One way to cope with the issue of proxy server slowdown is to add multiple proxy servers to the same network connection. The servers can be configured in such a way that they share the total network traffic load. One server can handle traffic for one network service or from one subnet of users, one can handle another, and so on.

Before building out a complex of multiple proxy servers, make sure your Internet connection throughput is robust enough to handle the amount of traffic your network is expected to process.

Working with Client Configurations

You have to configure each client program to work with the proxy server. For example, when you set up a proxy server, you must configure a Web browser to support the connection. A typical setup for Internet Explorer is shown in Figure 7-8. No proxy server is specified for FTP and Gopher connections because the browser can use the **SOCKS** standard—a set of protocols that enable proxy server access to applications without an assigned proxy server—to make connections via the proxy server's gateway.

Proxy Settings
Servers
Type
Proxy address to use
Port
HTTP:
192.168.0.1
8080
Secure:
192.168.0.1
8080
FTP:
Gopher:
Socks:
192.168.0.1
1080
Use the same proxy server for all protocols
Exceptions
Do not use proxy server for addresses beginning with:
Use semicolons (;) to separate entries.
OK
Cancel

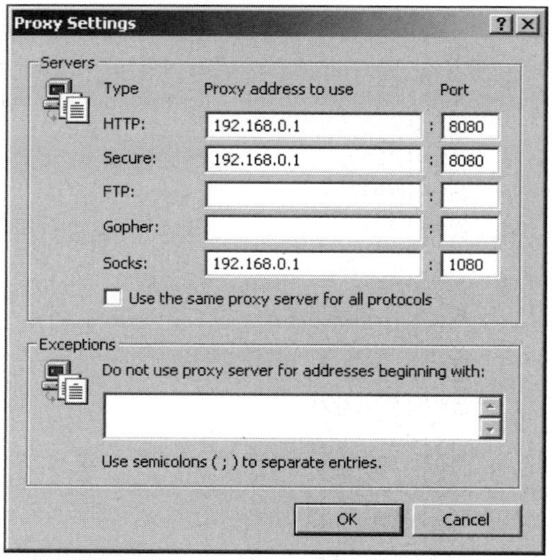

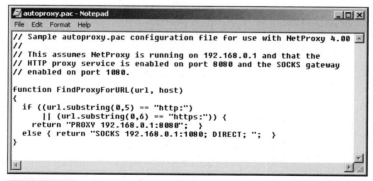

FIGURE 7-8 Internet Explorer Configuration Example

Such configurations are easy to perform once or twice, but when multiplied across dozens or even hundreds of client computers, the time and effort involved can be substantial. Most proxy servers will let you access a configuration file from which the browsers on your network can automatically retrieve the proxy settings. The file shown in Figure 7-9 contains the default settings for NetProxy; you can edit the JavaScript to include the static IP address (if you have one) of the server that hosts the proxy server(s).

autoproxy.pac - Notepad
File Edit Format Help
// Sample autoproxy.pac configuration file for use with NetProxy 4.00
//
// This assumes NetProxy is running on 192.168.0.1 and that the
// HTTP proxy service is enabled on port 8080 and the SOCKS gateway
// enabled on port 1080.
function FindProxyForURL(url, host)
{
if ((url.substring(0,5) == "http:")
|| (url.substring(0,6) == "https:")) {
return "PROXY 192.168.0.1:8080"; }
else { return "SOCKS 192.168.0.1:1080; DIRECT; "; }
}

FIGURE 7-9 NetProxy Configuration Script Example

Working with Service Configurations

A network must have one or more proxy servers available for each service protocol proxied on the network. The exact mixture of servers will depend on the needs of the configuration. For instance, a dedicated proxy can handle one type of traffic that is especially vulnerable to attack, such as SMTP. Services that receive an especially heavy load, such as HTTP, might also run more efficiently if given a dedicated proxy server—such as the proxy server Squid—designed to work especially with HTTP.

More commonly, though, organizations use a general-purpose firewall that includes a proxy server that monitors all inbound and outbound traffic. You should certainly configure HTTP and DNS, as well as SMTP and POP3, for e-mail. The range of options available with NetProxy is shown in Figure 7-10. Services for which no proxy server is available can make use of the SOCKS generic proxy.

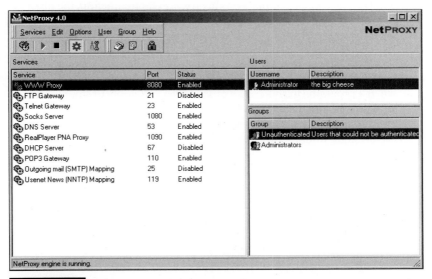

FIGURE 7-10   NetProxy Configuration Options

Creating Filter Rules

Firewall rules should be established to optimize the performance of the proxy environment. While the details of how such rules should be created and managed are very complex, consider that rules can be established to enable known hosts to bypass the proxy. Also, it is possible to filter out specific URLs, and set up rules that enable internal users to send outbound requests only at certain times. In an organization that only works during daylight hours, cutting off communications (except e-mail messages that might come in overnight) can be an important security level in the evening and overnight hours. During those hours, the protection ensures that no Trojan horses that may have found their way into a system can try to connect to the Internet. You can also set up rules governing the length of time a session can last. Cutting off a session after a lengthy period, such as an hour, can stall hackers who manage to get into your system and attempt to run executables from one of your host machines.

Recognizing the Single Point of Failure

A proxy server that routes all traffic into and out of a network is a single point of ingress and egress and thus has the potential to be a single point of failure for the network. If the proxy server crashes due to a hardware failure or a hacker's efforts, your network could be totally cut off from the Internet.

This problem isn't unique to proxies, of course. Routers and firewalls that lie between your internal network and the Internet can provide the same failure point. Most network architectures include alternate means of enabling traffic to flow with a limited amount of protection in the event the primary protection controls have failed. This might mean that the network falls back to simple packet filtering if the proxy servers go offline. You can also use load-balancing systems, such as the Windows Network Load Balancing feature, to create multiple proxies that are in use simultaneously and thus make your system less vulnerable—if one proxy ceases to function, the others will still work.

Recognizing Buffer Overflow Vulnerabilities

Proxy servers can be subject to a number of problems that result from misconfiguration or other vulnerabilities. The most common problem is a buffer overflow, which occurs when a program (in this case, a proxy server) attempts to store more data in a temporary storage area (a buffer) than that area can hold. The resulting overflow of data (some of which might even contain executable code intended to cause harm to a network) renders the program nonfunctional.

Some proxy servers have been known to fall victim to buffer overflow problems which might cause the proxy server to crash or allow an attacker to assume administrative rights for the server. The only way to combat such vulnerabilities is to check the Web site of the manufacturer of the proxy server you are using and install all available security patches.

Choosing a Proxy Server

Proxy servers come in different varieties. Some, like WinGate, are commercial products primarily used by home and small business users. Others, like Squid, are designed to protect one type of service (Web or FTP) and to serve cached Web pages. Most proxy systems are part of a **hybrid firewall**—a firewall that combines several different security technologies, such as packet filtering, application-level gateways, and VPNs. Others, like NetProxy, are true stand-alone proxy servers.

The following sections give you an overview of the different types of proxy servers with which you should be familiar—transparent, nontransparent, and SOCKS-based.

Transparent Proxies

Transparent proxies can be configured such that they are totally invisible to end users. A transparent proxy sits between two networks like a router. The firewall intercepts outgoing traffic and directs it to a specific computer, such as a proxy server. The individual host does not know its traffic is being intercepted; in addition, the client software doesn't have to be configured, which makes network administrators very happy.

Nontransparent Proxies

Nontransparent proxies, also called explicit proxies, require that the client software be configured to use them. Every FTP client, chat program, browser, or e-mail software you use must be able to house a proxy server. All target traffic is forwarded to the proxy at a single target port, typically by means of the SOCKS protocol.

Nontransparent proxies are more complicated to configure because each client program must be set up to route all requests to a single port. However, nontransparent proxies provide greater security. Clients can have their routing entries removed so that only the proxy server knows how to reach the Internet. Figure 7-11 shows a configuration that uses a nontransparent proxy.

Notice that in Figure 7-11 an exception has been made for local networks. If you have a local network that does not need to go through the proxy, such as a branch of your own company, you should list it as shown. All traffic from that network will access resources directly.

FIGURE 7-11   Nontransparent Proxy Configuration Example

SOCKS-Based Proxies

SOCKS is a protocol that enables the establishment of generic proxy applications—applications designed to act on behalf of many different services, such as FTP, NetMeeting, and other programs. SOCKS is known for its flexibility; it can help developers set up firewalls and virtual private networks (VPNs) as well as proxies. The term SOCKS is derived from sockets, a TCP/IP protocol used to establish a communication session. A socket is also an identifier consisting of an IP address and port number, such as 172.16.0.1:80. WinSock, for instance, is the name of a DLL that implements Sockets for Windows.

SOCKS Features

SOCKS is typically used to direct all traffic from the client to the proxy, using a target port of TCP/1080. (TCP 8080 may be used as well.) SOCKS acts as a transparent proxy.

SOCKS is important because it provides a number of security-related advantages, including the following:

- It functions as a **circuit-level gateway**, at the Session layer, filtering internal traffic that leaves the network being protected. Because it functions at the Session layer, it can work with virtually any TCP/IP application.
- It can encrypt data passing between client and proxy.
- It uses a single protocol to both transfer data via TCP and UDP and to authenticate users.

SOCKS has one disadvantage, and it's a big one: it does not examine the data part of a packet. It does hide IP addresses of internal clients, however, and it does recreate packets before passing them on. Thus, it does provide some protection against malformed packets.

SocksCap

SocksCap, a free SOCKS application available from Permeo Technologies (the originators of the SOCKS protocol), has a graphical interface that enables you to quickly configure applications to use SOCKS. In Figure 7-12, a chat application has been configured, and Microsoft Messenger is about to be added.

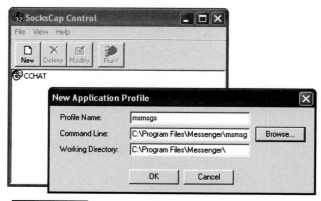

FIGURE 7-12   SocksCap Configuration Example

Proxy Server-Based Firewalls Compared

You can choose from a number of firewalls that are based on proxy servers (that is, proxy servers either play an important role in their makeup or are their primary function). Your choice depends on the platform you are running and the number of hosts and services you need to protect.

T.REX Open-Source Firewall

T.REX (*www.opensourcefirewall.com/*) is an open-source UNIX-based firewall solution based on the well-known open-source product Trusted Information System Firewall Toolkit (TIS Firewall Toolkit). It can handle URL blocking as well as encryption and authentication. The firewall's CD-ROM contains installation scripts that can help expedite installation, but configuration can be a complex and lengthy process. T.REX runs on AIX 4.2.x and later, Solaris 2.6 and later, and Linux Red Hat 7.1 and later. Choose T.REX only if you are looking for a free UNIX-based solution and you are already proficient with proxy server configuration.

Squid

Squid (*www.squid-cache.org/*) is a high-performance and free open-source application that is specially designed to act as a proxy server and cache files for Web and FTP servers. Squid isn't a full-featured firewall. It performs access control and filtering, and it is especially good at quickly serving cached files.

Squid runs on all UNIX-based systems. One nice feature is that the program is popular and well known enough that developers have come up with plug-in applications that enhance its functionality. Add-on applications include a banner ad filter created by the privacy organization Junkbusters; a log analyzer called Calamaris (*http://cord.de/tools/ squid/calamaris/*), and a content filter called Jeanne (*www.ists.dartmouth.edu/IRIA/ projects/d_jeanne.htm*). Squid is an excellent choice if you want to protect a UNIX-based network and you are on a budget.

WinGate

WinGate by Deerfield.com is the most popular proxy server for home and small business environments. Early versions suffered from a default configuration that enabled external users to connect to the proxy as though their computers were internal clients. In particular, the default configuration allowed the port used for administering WinGate (Port 808) to be open to an outside attack. Current versions don't have that problem.

Currently, WinGate comes in three versions: Home for home users, Standard for small businesses, and Pro for larger enterprises. The Home version is primarily intended to provide Internet connection sharing (a feature that is built in to more recent versions of Windows anyway). The Standard version adds a proxy server, URL redirection, logging, and authentication. The Pro version adds database integration and remote administration. Choose WinGate (*www.wingate.com*) if you want to protect a small network and are looking for a well-documented Windows-based program that offers customer support and frequent upgrades.

Symantec Enterprise Firewall

Formerly known by the name Raptor, Symantec Enterprise Firewall by Symantec Corp. (*http://enterprisesecurity.symantec.com/products/products.cfm?ProductID=47*) combines proxy services with encryption, authentication, load balancing, and packet filtering in a single full-featured firewall package. It filters content using a technology it calls WebNOT, which enables administrators to limit access to Web sites that contain unauthorized content. It also contains one nice feature for Windows users: configuration can be handled through a snap in to the Microsoft Management Console (MMC). Choose this product if you are looking for a commercial firewall that has proxy servers built in and that is a little more full featured than WinGate.

Microsoft Internet Security & Acceleration Server

Microsoft Internet Security & Acceleration Server (ISA) is Microsoft's proxy server product (*www.microsoft.com/isaserver*); it replaces the earlier Microsoft Proxy Server. It's a complex, full-featured firewall that includes stateful packet filtering as well as proxy services, NAT, and intrusion detection. ISA is designed to compete with FireWall-1, Symantec Enterprise Firewall, and other high-performance firewall products.

ISA does more than cache files and provide an application proxy gateway. It comes in two editions: Standard Edition and Enterprise Edition. The Standard Edition is a standalone product that supports up to four processors; the Enterprise Edition is a multiserver product with centralized management and no limit on the number of processors supported. However, both versions can be installed on a stand-alone basis for networks that don't use Active Directory.

Reverse Proxies

Most proxies act primarily on behalf of their internal hosts—receiving, rebuilding, and forwarding outbound requests. However, you can improve security as well as enhance performance by setting up a **reverse proxy**, which is a service that acts as a proxy for *inbound* connections. It can be used outside the firewall as a secure content server to outside clients, preventing direct, unmonitored access to your server's data from outside your company. A reverse proxy setup is shown in Figure 7-13.

Chapter Summary

- Proxy servers are a formidable security solution that can conceal the end users in a network, filter out undesirable Web sites, and block harmful content. Most proxy servers function as firewalls at the boundary of a network, performing packet filtering, Network Address Translation (NAT), and other services.

- Proxy servers consist of software that runs on a network device or appliance, or on a dedicated, general-purpose computer. Proxy servers evaluate the data portion of an IP packet (unlike packet filters, which examine only the header of an IP packet) to determine whether to allow the packet to pass into or out of the network.

- Proxies function as a software go-between, forwarding data between internal users and external hosts or external users and internal hosts, screening all traffic into and out of the relevant ports to decide whether to block or allow traffic based on rules set up by the proxy server administrator. In a typical transaction, a proxy server intercepts a request from a user on the internal network and passes it along to a destination computer on the Internet.

- When establishing a proxy system to protect a network, understand the goals that proxy systems achieve, such as: concealing internal clients, blocking URLs, blocking and filtering content, e-mail proxy protection, improving performance, ensuring security, providing user authentication, and redirecting URLs.

- Proxy servers require the performance of several special tasks—configuring each piece of client software that uses the proxy server, maintaining a separate proxy service for each network protocol, and creating packet filter rules. In addition, proxy servers carry the risk of being a single point of failure for the network.

- Proxy servers come in different varieties, some being enterprise solutions and others being oriented to the smaller business. Some are designed to protect one type of service, while most are part of a hybrid firewall—a firewall that combines several different security technologies, such as packet filtering, application-level gateways, and VPNs.

- Most proxies act primarily on behalf of their internal hosts, but some act as a reverse proxy, a service that acts as a proxy for *inbound* connections.

Review Questions

1. Why were application-level proxies originally developed?
2. What proxy server functions are similar to packet-filtering firewall functions?
3. What things can proxy servers do better than packet filters?
4. Why do proxy servers reassemble packets before sending them on their way?
5. Which is the most effective way proxy servers conceal internal clients?
6. What are the disadvantages or complications of using a proxy server gateway?
7. Why would load balancing be used in conjunction with a proxy server gateway?
8. What type of proxy server receives traffic from all services at a single port, such as a SOCKS server?
9. When would you want to dedicate a proxy server to a single service?
10. What is a nontransparent proxy?

11. When a proxy server focuses on an HTTP header to redirect a request to a specific URL, what will it use as its most critical determinant?

12. Consider the following: You run an external Web site that lists catalog items for sale. The overwhelming number of requests your company receives from the Internet are HTTP requests. You need to distribute the traffic load more evenly, and you need to protect sensitive client information contained on your Web server. What two proxy server approaches could help you achieve these goals?

13. Should a proxy server be located so that it has a direct interface to the Internet? If so, under what circumstances?

14. What functions are performed at the Session layer of the OSI model?

15. What are the disadvantages of using a reverse proxy?

16. What is the disadvantage of using SOCKS?

17. Why is authentication required when a proxy server completely separates internal clients from the Internet?

18. How might you protect an internal network overnight when no employees are present?

19. Within application-level firewalls, what is the purpose of parameters such as time, IP address, or port number?

20. When is a proxy server the wrong protection mechanism for a network?

Exercises

1. Using an Internet search engine, look up "proxy server." Access several Web sites that define the term. After reading at least two definitions, write your own, original definition of the term.

2. Using an Internet search engine, look up "TCP/IP socket." Access several Web sites that define the term. After reading at least two definitions, write your own, original definition of the term.

3. Using an Internet search engine, look up "SOCKS protocol." Access several Web sites that define the term. After reading at least two definitions, write your own, original definition of the term.

4. Using a drawing program, sketch a SOHO network with three computers on the local network that uses PAT. Assume you use an ISP that issues your router an address of 172.16.101.123. You plan to use 192.168.1.* for your local, non-routable address pool. Label the router with its inside and outside addresses. Label each computer with a possible set of assigned addresses.

5. You decide to add a personal Web server accessible from the Internet to the local network described in Exercise 4. What router feature would you use for this capability? Describe how that configuration could be done and how it would function.

6. Telnet is widely considered to be insecure. Why do you think this is the case? What could be done to make Telnet secure? What are the alternatives that might replace Telnet?

Case Exercises

Ron Hall got to his desk a little early the next morning. He turned on his PC and went to get a cup of coffee while it booted up. When he got back he opened his e-mail program. In the list of new e-mail was a note from the network security group. He opened the message and saw it had been addressed to him and to Andy Ying, his boss. It also had a CC to the HR department. The message said:

Recently, your account was used to access Web content that has not been approved for use inside ATI. We are asking you to explain your actions to your supervisor. You are encouraged to enroll in a class on appropriate use of the Internet at ATI at your earliest convenience. Until you complete the class or your supervisor contacts this office, your network privileges have been suspended.

If this access attempt was for legitimate business purposes, please have your supervisor notify us at once so that this Web location can be added to the ATI approved Web locations list.

What a hassle. Ron did not look forward to his conversation with Andy.

Questions:

1. Does the ATI policy on Web usage seem harsh to you? Why or why not?
2. Do you think Ron was justified in his actions?
3. How should Andy react to this situation if Ron is known to be a reliable and a diligent employee?

Firewall Configuration and Administration

8

> Computers are like Old Testament gods; lots of rules and no mercy.
>
> **JOSEPH CAMPBELL**

IT WAS A NONDESCRIPT BUILDING, in an area full of nondescript buildings. It was featureless on the outside and even though it was larger than 20,000 square feet it seldom had more than 15 people in it. Its hard-working air-conditioning system blew a plume of heat exhaust that could be detected by thermal imaging cameras in orbit.

Inside this structure was a room, a big room, which was filled with rack upon rack of quietly humming equipment. Some of the machines processed electricity to make it more reliable. Some of the machines were hooked to the exterior air conditioning compressors to maintain a stable temperature of 21.5 degrees Celsius.

In one rack was a computer. This computer was configured to run as a firewall. It was as much like its neighboring firewalls as its designers could make it. The company that owned this equipment, ATI, tried to keep all of the systems that performed a given function as much alike as possible. Standardized hardware and standardized software was the mantra at ATI. This specific computer had been running without pause for 116 days, since it was last rebooted as part of a scheduled maintenance routine. A few weeks ago, the firewall rule set was updated during a routine change window. The testing of that update seemed to show the revised rules were correct, but somehow, something went wrong.

One of the rules was meant to allow customers of Linen Planet, a Web-based business, to make secure connections to the commerce server, and then, a reverse proxy connection would connect to the Web server behind the firewall, in the protected network leased by Linen Planet from ATI. This was what the firewall engineer had written. This is what was typed into the script file that was applied by Matthias Paul. These were the rules tested by Debbie Masters. This was exactly what everyone wanted to result from the change control process so carefully set up by ATI to keep Linen Planet in business.

Too bad it didn't work.

LEARNING OBJECTIVES:

Upon completion of this material, you should be able to do the following:

- Set up firewall rules that reflect an organization's overall security approach
- Identify and implement different firewall configuration strategies
- Update a firewall to meet new needs and threats
- Adhere to proven security principles to help the firewall protect network resources
- Use a remote management interface
- Track firewall log files, and follow the basic initial steps in responding to security incidents
- Understand the nature of advanced firewall functions

Introduction

In this chapter, you learn how to design perimeter security for a network that integrates firewalls with a variety of other software and hardware components. Firewalls aren't intended to do just one thing or to block just one type of threat. By using one or more firewalls in conjunction with routers, gateways, hubs, and switches, you can block many common attacks while permitting hosts inside the network to access the Internet.

This chapter provides an overview of the various approaches to firewall configuration. It begins with a review of the kinds of rules and restrictions that influence how you configure a security perimeter. Then, it presents a variety of security configurations that can either perform firewall functions or be used to permit firewalls to create protected areas.

Setting up a firewall is only the start of an effective perimeter security effort. Ongoing firewall administration ensures that the network is actually protected and that intrusions are detected and thwarted. Without routine log reviews, firewall performance evaluation, and regular hardware and software upgrades, the best firewall configuration in the world can quickly become useless.

In addition, you'll learn about the various administrative tasks that are required to keep a firewall running smoothly as the network it protects continues to grow and as new security threats arise. You will learn how to expand a firewall to meet new needs, and about the importance of observing fundamental principles of network security when maintaining your firewall. You will learn how to manage a firewall remotely, how to review log files, and how to respond to security incidents when they occur. Finally, you'll examine advanced firewall functions, some of which require the firewall to work in tandem with third-party products for added security.

Establishing Firewall Rules and Restrictions

After you have established a security policy as described in Chapter 3, you can begin to implement the strategies that policy specifies. One way to configure a firewall is by setting rules. Rules give the firewall specific criteria on which to make decisions on whether to allow packets through or drop them.

The firewall rules that are written will tell the firewall what types of traffic to let in and out of your network. All firewalls have a rules file; it is the most important firewall configuration file.

The Role of the Rules File

The specific packet-filtering rules that are used to set up a firewall will implement the security approach specified in the organization's security policy. A restrictive approach is reflected in a set of rules that blocks all access by default, then permits only specific types of traffic to pass through. A permissive or connectivity-based approach has fewer rules because its primary intent is to let all traffic through and then block specific types of traffic.

The rules implemented by the firewall will not only block traffic coming from outside the protected network, but can also enable internal traffic to get outside the network. Rules that permit traffic to your DNS server, for instance, are essential if your internal users are going to access other computers on the Internet using domain name resolution.

Finally, the rules are important because they establish an execution order that the firewall should follow. Firewalls should process rules in top-to-bottom order, so the first rules cover the most basic types of traffic, such as ICMP messages that computers use to establish basic communications. Rules are almost always processed in sequential order to avoid confusion about which is most important.

Restrictive Firewalls

If the primary goal of your planned firewall is to block unauthorized access, the emphasis needs to be on restricting rather than enabling connectivity. In such a "Deny-All" approach, the firewall blocks *everything* by default and only specifically allows those services you need on a case-by-case basis. Deny-all and other primarily restrictive approaches are described in Table 8-1.

TABLE 8-1 Restrictive Firewall Approaches

Approach	What It Does	Advantage	Disadvantage
Deny-All	Blocks all packets except those specifically permitted	More secure; requires fewer rules	May result in user complaints
In Order (sometimes called "first fit")	Processes firewall rules in top-to-bottom order	Good security	Incorrect order can cause chaos
Best Fit	The firewall determines the order in which the rules are processed—usually it starts with the most specific rules and goes to the most general	Easy to manage; reduces risk of operator error	Lack of control

If you decide to first restrict all transmissions through the gateway except a specific set of services, you are following the **principle of least privilege**—the practice of designing operational aspects of a system to operate with minimum system privileges. Least privilege reduces the number of authorization level at which various actions are performed and decreases the chance that a process or user with high privileges will perform unauthorized activity, resulting in a security breach.

There are other ways in which you can implement the overall approaches described in an organization's security policy. You can carry out specific elements of the policy in the firewall by following strategies such as these:

- Spell out which services employees cannot use. On the firewall, you can block services such as FTP or Telnet. You can use authentication to enable such services to be used only by a network administrator.

- Use and maintain passwords. Enable authentication on the firewall so users can only surf the Web or use e-mail after they successfully authenticate themselves—this forces employees to keep track of passwords and to remember them.

- Follow an "open" approach to security. Set the firewall to allow all traffic to pass through by default, but block specific Web sites or specific services as needed.

- Follow an "optimistic" approach to security. Set up a stateful packet filter configured to let most packets pass but to block traffic from troublesome or questionable IP addresses, or deny access to specific database servers on the internal network.

- Follow a "cautious" approach to security. Set up a stateful instead of (or in addition to) a stateless packet filter.

- Follow a "strict" approach to security. Set up application proxy gateways that forward requests on behalf of internal users.

- Follow a "paranoid" approach to security. Set up one or more packet filters to protect a pool of workstations set aside to allow access to the Web and e-mail only and that are not connected to the internal network, which has no connection at all to any external networks.

Connectivity-Based Firewalls

If the primary orientation of your firewall is permissive—that is, permitting connectivity through the gateway—the burden is on you, in your role as security administrator, to educate your coworkers on how to use the network responsibly. Most employees don't want to put the company's assets at risk, but they do want to access data and be productive. It's your job to help them understand how to get their work done in a secure manner.

Table 8-2 lists the advantages and disadvantages of a firewall that enforces a restrictive policy or one that emphasizes connectivity.

TABLE 8-2 Connectivity-based Firewall Approaches

Approach	What It Does	Advantage	Disadvantage
Allow-All	Allows all packets to pass through except those identified as to be blocked	Easy to implement	Provides minimal security; requires complex rules
Port 80/ Except Video	Allows Web surfing without restrictions, except for video files	Lets users surf Web	Opens network to Web vulnerabilities

In almost all instances, this is not an either/or question. Most firewalls are partly restrictive and partly permissive (connective). Your job is to strike a balance between the two.

The order in which rules are set can be critical. The rules on a firewall must be placed in a very specific order or they will not work properly. Some firewalls can order the rules automatically, but be sure you can turn this feature off unless you have a high degree of confidence that it will work as expected. If the algorithms and code used to make the order-independent rule-setting decisions are not completely bug-free, using this feature could open up security holes in your network. In a perfect world, automatic order-independent rule setting is a great feature, because if you have a lot of firewall rules, it can help you understand how to order the rules properly. However, there is no substitute for human knowledge and experience in setting up your firewall rules.

Firewall Configuration Strategies

A firewall must be scalable so it can grow with the network it protects. It needs to take into account the communication needs of individual employees, who see Web surfing and e-mail as must-haves to be productive. Because TCP/IP is the protocol of choice for internal networks as well as the Internet itself, the firewall also needs to deal with the IP address needs of the organization—to enable port forwarding or Network / Port Address Translation, for instance.

Scalability

A firewall needs to adapt to the changing needs of the organization whose network it protects. More Internet business and a growing staff are likely to increase the need for firewall resources. Be sure to provide for the firewall's growth by recommending a periodic review and upgrading software and hardware as needed.

Productivity

The stronger and more elaborate your firewall, the slower data transmissions are likely to be. Productivity is definitely a concern if you use a proxy server, which tends to slow down communications for users inside the company who are trying to access the Internet.

Two important features of the firewall are the processing and memory resources available to the **bastion host**. A bastion host, though it may not be the only hardware component in firewall architecture, is of central importance to the operation of the firewall software that it hosts. If the host machine runs too slowly or doesn't have enough memory to handle the large number of packet-filtering decisions, proxy service requests, and other traffic, the productivity of the entire organization can be adversely affected. That's because the bastion host resides on the perimeter of the network and—unless other bastion hosts and firewalls have been set up to provide the network with load balancing—it is the only gateway through which inbound and outbound traffic can pass. Scalability and security are important not only to the firewall but to its bastion host machine as well. Your bastion host needs sufficient memory (RAM) to support every instance of every program necessary to service the load placed on the machine.

A **critical resource** is defined as a software- or hardware-related item that is indispensable to the operation of a device or program. Table 8-3 lists critical resources for a firewall's successful operation. Restricting the items in the second column of the table will conserve critical resources.

TABLE 8-3 Critical Resources for Firewall Services

Critical Resource	Service To Be Restricted
Disk I/O	E-mail
Disk I/O	News
Bastion Host OS Performance	IP Routing
Bastion Host OS Performance	Web Cache
Bastion Host OS Performance	Web

Dealing with IP Address Issues

The more complex a network becomes, the more IP-addressing complications arise. It's important to plan out the installation, including IP addressing, before you start purchasing or installing firewalls.

Both a **demilitarized zone (DMZ)** and a service network need IP addresses. If your service network needs to be privately rather than publicly accessible, which DNS will its component systems use? You can ask your ISP for more addresses if they are available. If not, you may need to do NAT and convert the internal network to private addressing.

However, when you mix public and private addresses, this brings up more questions. How will your Web server and DNS servers communicate? If the Web server uses a public IP address that is stored in your external DNS server, and the local subnet uses private addressing, communications may fail. You can solve the problem by switching to public addresses on the private network or by binding two IP addresses—one public and one private—to each network. Be sure to consider and resolve such issues before you've purchased and installed your hardware.

IP forwarding enables a packet to get from one network's OSI stack of interfaces to another. Most operating systems are set up to perform IP forwarding. Many operating systems perform IP forwarding, as do routers. Proxy servers that handle the movement of data from one external network to another perform the same function; however, if a proxy server is in service, IP forwarding should be disabled on routers and other devices that lie between the networks. It's better to let the proxy server do the forwarding because it's the security device—having routers do the IP forwarding will defeat the purpose of using the proxy and make communications less secure.

The need for advance planning applies not only to firewalls but to servers and other hardware. There may be specific aspects of your design that influence your hardware selection. For example, suppose you want your firewall to include a proxy server function. You have to make sure you have the hardware to support a proxy server that provides services for the Web, e-mail, FTP, chat, instant messaging, and other means of network communication. Assess the hardware that will host the firewall or proxy server. If you expect high traffic volume—for instance, if you run a busy e-commerce Web server—you may be better off avoiding a proxy server and sticking with packet filters, which don't require as much memory and processor speed. Proxy servers quickly consume memory and processor time, so if you plan to run them, buy a machine that has as much of these resources as you can afford.

Approaches That Add Functionality to Your Firewall

Network security setups can become incrementally more complex when specific functions are added. Each function is discussed separately in the following sections; however, you should assume that any or all of the following can be part of a perimeter security system that includes a firewall.

NAT/PAT

A router or firewall that performs **Network Address Translation (NAT)** or **Port Address Translation (PAT)** converts publicly accessible IP addresses to private ones and vice versa, thus shielding the IP addresses of computers on the protected network from those on the outside. For more on NAT and PAT, you can review the relevant section in Chapter 5.

Encryption

A firewall or router that can do Secure Sockets Layer (SSL) or some other type of encryption takes a request, encrypts it using a private key, and exchanges the public key with the recipient firewall or router. The recipient then decrypts the message and presents it to the end user in readable form (see Figure 8-1).

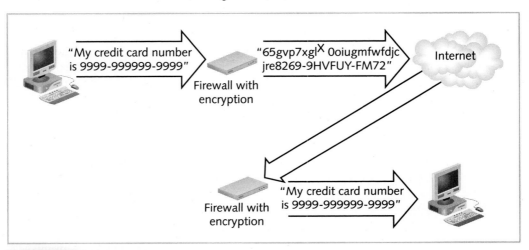

FIGURE 8-1 Using Encryption

Application Proxies

An application proxy is software that acts on behalf of a host, receiving requests, rebuilding them completely from scratch, and forwarding them to the intended location as though the request originated with it (the proxy). It can be set up with either a dual-homed host or a screened host system. In a dual-homed host setup, the host that contains the firewall or proxy server software has two interfaces, one to the Internet and one to the internal network being protected (see Figure 8-2).

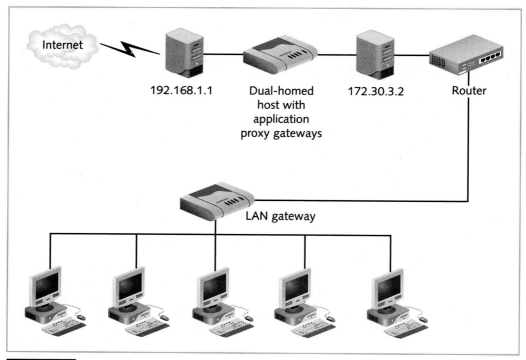

FIGURE 8-2 Using Application Proxies

Because the dual-homed host lies between the internal LAN and the Internet, the hosts on the internal network never access the Internet directly. (At least, they shouldn't; some employees may get frustrated with the slower functioning of the proxy system and try to establish their own independent Internet connections, and you should be on the alert for this.) The proxy server software on the dual-homed host makes requests on their behalf and forwards packets from the Internet to them.

In a screened subnet system, the host that runs the proxy server software has a single network interface; packet filters on either side of the host filter out all traffic except that which is destined for the proxy server software.

VPNs

Many companies use the Internet to enable a virtual private network (VPN) that connects internal hosts with specific clients in other organizations. The advantage to a VPN over a conventional Internet-based connection is that VPN connections are encrypted and limited to machines with specific IP addresses. The VPN gateway can go in a screened subnet (sometimes called a DMZ), or the gateway can bypass the firewall and connect directly to the internal LAN, as shown in Figure 8-3. VPNs are discussed in greater detail in Chapter 11.

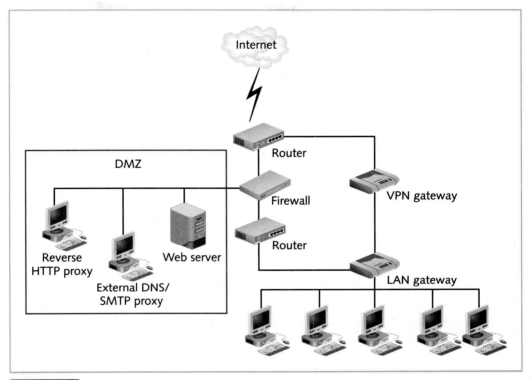

FIGURE 8-3   Virtual Private Networking

Intrusion Detection and Prevention Systems

An intrusion detection and prevention system (IDPS)—software that can detect possible intrusion attempts and notify administrators when they occur—can be installed in the external and/or the internal routers at the perimeter of a network (see Figure 8-4). IDPS capability is also built into many popular software firewall packages, including Sidewinder by Secure Computing.

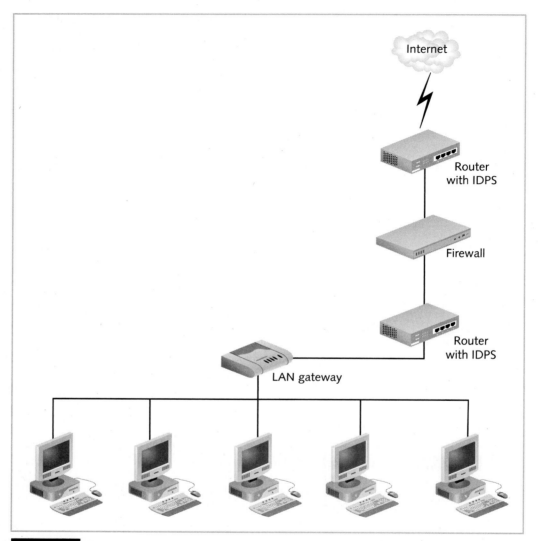

FIGURE 8-4   Intrusion Detection and Protection Systems

Why install IDPS on both routers? An external router with IDPS can notify you of intrusion attempts from the Internet. An internal router with IDPS can notify you when a host on the internal network attempts to access the Internet via a suspicious port or using an unusual service, which may be a sign that a Trojan horse has entered the system. An IDPS might also be configured to look for a large number of TCP connection requests (SYN) to many different ports on a target machine, thus discovering if someone is attempting a TCP port scan. The IDPS sends the alert so an administrator can either prevent it or cut the attack short before too much damage occurs.

The Cisco CIDS intrusion detection system works in a different way. It monitors the area between the firewall and the Internet. It can be configured to tell you when an attack on the firewall from the Internet occurs (see Figure 8-5).

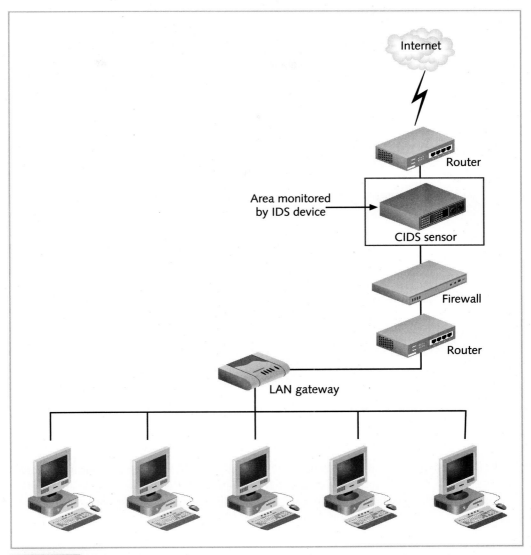

FIGURE 8-5   Example IDS Placement

Enabling a Firewall to Meet New Needs

You need to consistently upgrade your firewall architecture and add new components to keep your perimeter protected and traffic running smoothly. Overall, you need to gain and maintain the following:

- *Throughput*: Because the firewall is the point through which all traffic flows, you need to make sure traffic flows quickly through it and it is not slowing down the network.

- *Scalability*: Very few networks get smaller. It's almost inevitable that your network will grow, either in terms of the number of hosts that need to be protected or in the amount of traffic you receive from the external Internet. Your firewall and other security systems need to be able to grow along with your needs.

- *Security*: This is the effectiveness with which the firewall blocks traffic that has been identified as unacceptable based on its rule base and—if the firewall is also full-featured enough to provide some intrusion detection functions—the effectiveness with which it detects and provides notifications of intrusion attempts.

- *Recoverability*: The firewall is critical not only to the network's security but to the network's connection with outside networks. If the firewall crashes, you need to restart it, recover the original security configuration, and get back online quickly.

- *Manageability*: The firewall should be easy to manage, either from within the organization or from a remote location.

To achieve these goals, you might need to upgrade your security software or hardware, or even add new layers of security to your overall firewall perimeter. The process that you'll go through as you make these decisions is described in the following sections.

Verifying Resources Needed by the Firewall

You have to test how well the firewall is working and evaluate its performance so that you can make network traffic move more efficiently. One of the factors that can be easily evaluated for software-only firewalls is memory and CPU usage. You can check just how much memory you need in one of two ways. The first way is to make use of vendor recommendations such as the following formula provided for Check Point's NG firewall:

```
MemoryUsage = ((ConcurrentConnections)/(AverageLifetime))
*(AverageLifetime + 50 seconds)*120
```

This formula indicates that the memory needed by the firewall equals the following:

1. The number of **concurrent connections**—the number of connections made to hosts in the internal network at any one time—is divided by the **average lifetime** of a typical connection (how long a connection to a host lasts) as indicated by your log files.
2. The number resulting from Step 1 is multiplied by the average lifetime plus 50 seconds times 120.

For example, if there are 100 connections and the average lifetime of a connection is 10 minutes, the memory needed to run Check Point NG is (100/10) * 10+50 * 120 = 72000, or 72MB of RAM.

A second way to keep track of the memory and system resources being consumed is to use the software's own monitoring feature. For example, Figure 8-6 illustrates the Status Manager module in Check Point NG. If you open the module and select your own network, you get data that tells you how much memory is being consumed and how much of your available system resources are being used by the firewall. For a small network, the memory and system resources being used may be relatively small. But in a large enterprise in which hundreds or even thousands of users may send traffic through the firewall at any one time, such data can be invaluable to the network administrator attempting to track down network bottlenecks. CPU usage that climbs to a high level (perhaps as much as 60 percent, although this depends on the operating system being used) should be a warning to the administrator that some kind of load balancing is needed, which might require adding another firewall to the network.

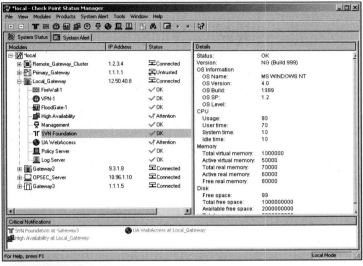

FIGURE 8-6　Check Point Status Manager

Identifying New Risks

A firewall needs regular care and attention to keep up with the new threats that are constantly appearing. It's a good idea, after you first get your firewall up and running, to monitor its activities for a month and store all the data that accumulates in the form of log files. Then go through the logs and analyze the traffic that passes through the firewall, paying particular attention to suspicious activity.

When administering a firewall, it's important to keep up with new threats so the firewall can meet them. Visit the sites listed in Appendix A of this book to keep informed of the latest dangers, so you can install patches and updates as they become available.

Adding Software Updates and Patches

The best way to combat the constant stream of new viruses and security threats is to install updated software that is specifically designed to meet those threats. Test updates and patches as soon as you install them to make sure the new software does not slow down your system, crash applications, or cause other problems. Ask the vendors of your firewall, VPN appliance, routers, and other security-related hardware and software to notify you when security patches become available for their products. Also check the manufacturer's Web site for security patches and software updates. Because it can be difficult to remember to check a Web site for an update on a routine basis—that is, if you aren't facing an immediate problem—you should configure a calendar or scheduling program to send you a monthly reminder. Develop a maintenance window—a period of two or three hours that is set aside every month for performing improvements such as software upgrades. It's a good way for organizations—even small ones—to manage changes to the network environment while minimizing the impact on production applications. It's also a good idea to participate in firewall-related mailing lists, not just to share ideas and ask questions of your colleagues, but to learn about new security threats as they occur and news about patches as they become available.

Some software-only firewalls provide a module that automatically updates the software you have installed. The module enables licensed users of the software to remotely install and update software by connecting to the vendor's download center (see Figure 8-7 for an example of Check Point NG SecureUpdate).

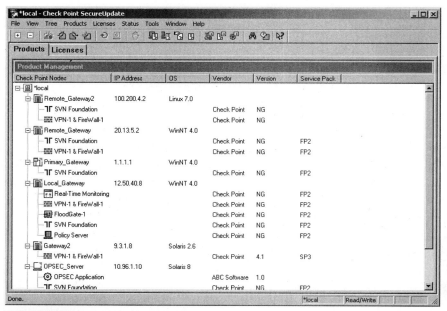

FIGURE 8-7   Check Point Update Manager

Adding Hardware

Whenever you add a piece of hardware to your network, you need to identify it in some way so your firewall can include it in its routing and protection services. Different firewalls require you to identify network hardware in different ways. Microsoft Internet Security and Acceleration Server (ISA), which functions as a proxy server, requires that you record the IP addresses of hosts or gateways on a Local Address Table. Check Point FireWall-1, requires you to "define" an object by giving it a name and recording its IP address and other information.

The need to list hardware as being part of your protected network applies not only to workstations that you add to the network, but also to the routers, VPN appliances, and other gateways you add as the network grows. This applies particularly to proxy servers such as ISA, which function as the default gateway for a network and need to know exactly how to route traffic through your different hardware devices.

Different types of hardware can be secured in different ways, but one of the most important is simply choosing good passwords that you guard closely. Some network hubs require the administrator to enter two separate passwords to manage or update those devices. One password gives the administrator read access, and the other gives the administrator write permission so he or she can change configuration files on the router if needed.

It's always a good idea, with routers and other hardware or software, to change the write password from the default value to a value of your own choosing for extra security. Switches and routers have their own passwords as well; some switches also have timeout periods that you can configure so they disconnect themselves from the network automatically from a management console if it is idle for a period of time.

Dealing with Complexity on the Network

Firewall configurations can take many forms, and they can grow in complexity as a network grows. One level of complexity you may need to manage comes from **distributed firewalls**, which are installed at all endpoints of the network, including the remote computers that connect to the network through VPNs. They add complexity because they require you to install and/or maintain a variety of firewalls that are located not only in your own corporate network but in remote locations; however, distributed firewalls also add security because they protect your network from viruses or other attacks that can originate from remote laptops or other machines that use VPNs to connect.

A firewall that is deployed on the desktop of a VPN client needs to adopt the security policy of the network to which it connects. It also needs to use Internet Protocol Security, (IPSec) which, as explained in Chapter 9, provides for encryption, encapsulation, and authentication.

If you need to configure remote users to access your network via a VPN, determine what level of firewall security (if any) they already have. If they don't have a firewall already (or if they already installed their own firewall software and you find it to be weak or improperly configured), install a more effective desktop firewall along with the VPN client software. For example, one of Check Point's two VPN clients, Secure Desktop, includes desktop firewall support along with its VPN client software (see Figure 8-8). If you have a team of administrators involved in maintaining a security system, you need to keep strict records of any changes made to the system so that everyone on the team can be informed. You should hold regular meetings and report on any changes that have been made or problems that have been identified.

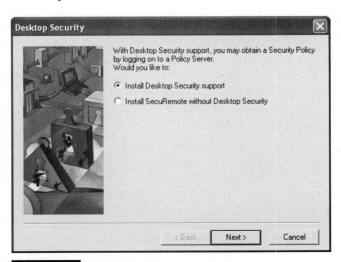

FIGURE 8-8   Check Point Secure Desktop

Adhering to Proven Security Principles

Part of firewall management—and network management in general—is adherence to principles that have been put forth by reputable organizations to ensure that you are maintaining your firewall and network security configuration correctly. The **Generally Accepted System Security Principles (GASSP)** is a set of security and information management practices put forth by the International Information Security Foundation (I2SF). The GASSP gives you some good guidelines to follow that help you manage your firewall as well as the information that passes through it.

The following sections focus on the aspects of the GASSP that apply to ongoing firewall management: securing the physical environment in which the firewall-related equipment is housed, and securing software so that unauthorized users cannot access it. The GASSP is published on the Web by the Massachusetts Institute of Technology (MIT) at *http://web.mit.edu/ist/topics/security/*.

Environmental Management

The GASSP recommends the **environmental management** of IT assets and resources: the measures taken to reduce risks to the physical environment where the resources are stored. At the most basic level, this means that you need to secure the building where your network resources are located to protect them from natural disasters such as earthquakes, floods, hurricanes, tornadoes, and other catastrophic events.

Such problems might seem unlikely, but many businesses have run up huge losses due to hurricanes and other weather-related problems. Computer systems have failed when critical computers were placed on the top floor of buildings that were poorly air-conditioned. Likewise some firms experienced water damage when they placed critical systems in basement locations that were later flooded.

To prepare for environmental problems, an organization should consider installing the following:

- Power conditioning systems to manage power quality and provide backup power when needed
- Backup hardware and software to help recover network data and services in case of equipment failure
- Sprinkler and fire alarm systems
- Locks to guard against theft

BIOS, Boot, and Screen Locks

Laptop computers that are used to connect to the main network should be secured not only by desktop firewalls but also by more low-level types of security. Some of the most basic features you should look for in a laptop include BIOS boot-up and supervisor passwords, which protect the machine while it is booting up. A screen password should also be assigned.

The GASSP document on this topic includes the suggestion that a public notice be included in the company's logon screen that advises anyone who uses the network of the existence of the organization's security policy. Such a notice might state the following: "Notice: Anyone who logs on to the *[Company Name]* network is hereby notified that the files and databases they are about to access are valued assets and that they include much proprietary information that is protected by copyright. Unauthorized access to such resources is prohibited and violators will be prosecuted."

BIOS and Boot-Up Passwords

Most computers give you the chance to set a **boot-up password**, a password that must be entered to complete the process of starting up a computer. Boot-up passwords (which are often called BIOS passwords or CMOS passwords) aren't perfect: they won't work when your computer is already on and is left unattended, for instance. In addition, a thief who can't crack your BIOS password can remove the hard drive and attach it to a computer that does not have a BIOS password, or remove the lithium battery from the computer's motherboard, thus erasing the BIOS password from memory.

Nevertheless, requiring people to enter a BIOS password on startup does add another level of defense to a computer. The BIOS password alone may discourage many thieves from putting out the effort to crack it. In addition, having a BIOS password in place prevents someone from starting up your computer and accessing your hard disk files with a floppy disk called a boot disk.

Supervisor Passwords

Some systems only use a BIOS password to enable the computer to complete booting up. On others (such as Windows NT and 2000), a second, higher-level password called a **supervisor password** is also used. In a case where a supervisor password and a BIOS password are used, the supervisor password is used to gain access to the BIOS setup program or to change the BIOS password. Take care when assigning a supervisor password. Because of its importance, it should only be assigned to an administrator. Make every effort not to lose this password: if you do, you'll have to replace the system motherboard to access the BIOS.

Screen Saver Passwords

A screen saver is an image or design that appears on a computer monitor when the machine is idle. A screen saver password is a password you need to enter to make your screen saver vanish so you can return to your desktop and resume working. Configuring a screen saver password protects your computer while you're not working on it. It's thus a good complement to a BIOS password, which protects your computer during startup but not when the machine is running, but idle for a time. A screen saver password can be easily circumvented by rebooting the computer, but a BIOS password will be needed during the reboot.

Remote Management Interface

A remote management interface is software that enables you to configure and monitor one or more firewalls that are located at different network locations. You use it to start and stop the firewall or change the rule base from locations other than your primary computer. Without it, most administrators would spend hours moving from room to room or building to building making the same changes on each of a company's firewalls.

Why Remote Management Tools Are Important

A remote management system is important because it saves many hours of time and makes the security administrator's job much easier. For instance, the Global Enterprise

Management System (GEMS) for the McAfee Gauntlet firewall enables the administrator to use the same Graphical User Interface (GUI) as a stand-alone firewall, but allows the administrator to establish rules for as many as 500 separate firewalls. Although it's unlikely that any one administrator would actually have to manage that many firewalls, it's not uncommon for dozens of firewall devices to be deployed on a large-scale network.

Besides reducing time for the administrator, remote management tools reduce the chance of configuration errors that might result if the same changes have to be made manually for each firewall in the network. Many remote management programs come with a graphical interface in which network components are highlighted with colored icons to make it easier for the manager to evaluate their activities and determine the need for load balancing.

Security Concerns

Security Information Management (SIM) is a GUI program that can be used to remotely manage a firewall. Because a SIM has access to all of the firewalls on your network, it needs to be as secure as possible to prevent unauthorized users from circumventing your security systems. The SIM offers strong security controls such as multi-factor authentication and encryption. The SIM should also be equipped with auditing features that keep track of who uses the software and when. The best remote management tools use tunneling to connect to the firewall or use certificates for authentication, rather than establishing a weak connection like a Telnet interface. Once the SIM software is installed and you begin to use it, be sure to evaluate the software to ensure that it does not introduce any new security vulnerabilities into the environment.

A remote management interface should provide the administrator with a consistent appearance and operation across multiple platforms. Both netForensics (*www.netforensics.com/*) and Novell (*www.novell.com/products/sentinel*) make such devices. The WatchGuard Central Policy Manager (CPM) tool, which is designed for use with WatchGuard's Firebox line of firewall appliances (*www.watchguard.com/products/firebox.asp*), enables administrators to monitor multiple appliances using a drag-and-drop interface.

Basic Features of Remote Management Tools

Any SIM or remote management program should enable you to monitor and configure firewalls from a single centralized location. They should also enable you to start and stop firewalls as needed. Starting and stopping a firewall is a drastic step because it can affect network communications (unless you have a hot standby or load-sharing system set up as described in the section "Configuring Advanced Firewall Functions" later in this chapter), but it's one you need to have at your disposal in case you detect an intrusion.

Remote management tools should also help you perform such remote management tasks as the following:

- View and change firewall status
- View the firewall's current activity
- View any firewall event or alert messages
- Stop or start firewall services if needed

Be careful when giving out management accounts that enable others to administer the firewall. If unauthorized users steal account passwords or usernames, the consequences can be devastating for your network.

Automating Security Checks

You can hire a service to do the ongoing checking and administration of a firewall for you. This is not simply passing the buck: if your time as a network administrator is taken up with making sure the network is up and running and adding or removing users as needed, it's more efficient to consider outsourcing the firewall administration. Be aware, though, that if you outsource your firewall management, you have to put a high level of trust in the outsourcer to maintain your network security. You can't always expect outside companies to devote as high a level of attention to your log files as in-house employees would.

Presinet (*www.presinet.com/web/firewall_services.php*) is just one of many companies that can remotely manage your firewall for you. The best way to find a company to which you can outsource your firewall management responsibilities is to ask network administrators in other organizations for their personal recommendations, or scan security-related sites such as SANS (*www.sans.org*) for recommendations.

Configuring Advanced Firewall Functions

The ultimate goal for many organizations is the development of a high-performance firewall configuration that has **high availability** (in other words, it operates on a 24/7 basis or close to it) and that can be **scaled** (that can grow and maintain effectiveness) as the organization grows. This section briefly discusses some advanced firewall functions that can keep the firewall running effectively on a day-to-day basis: data caching, redundancy, load balancing, and content filtering.

Data Caching

Caching—the practice of storing data in a part of disk storage space so it can be retrieved as needed—is one of the primary functions of proxy servers. Firewalls can be configured to work with external servers to cache data, too. Caching of frequently accessed resources such as Web page text and image files can dramatically speed up the performance of your network because it reduces the load on your Web servers. The load on the servers is reduced when end users are able to call pages from disk cache rather than having to send a request to the Web server itself.

Usually, firewalls give you a variety of options for how data is cached. First, you need to set up a server that receives requests for URLs and that filters those requests against different criteria you set up. Those criteria include whether the Web page requested can be viewed by the public as per the organization's security policy; whether the Web page requested is part of a site that has been identified as containing harmful or inappropriate content and that should not be viewed by employees; and whether the site already exists in disk cache because it has been previously viewed and its contents have not changed since the last time it was viewed. The server returns the URL to the requesting host only if a set of caching criteria is met.

Typically you choose one of four options for how data is to be cached:

- *No caching*: Caching is turned off in this instance, and every request has to go to the originating Web server. This produces a heavier load on Web servers, but you might still choose this option if your server configuration changes frequently and you want to filter each request using the most up-to-date criteria.

- *UFP server*: This option specifies the use of a **URI Filtering Protocol server**—a server that filters and processes requests for URIs and that can work in conjunction with firewalls—to call up Web pages from cache if needed. The UFP server reviews the requests, checks the URI against the contents of disk cache, and returns documents from cache if they are present.

- *VPN & Firewall (one request)*: The VPN and firewall servers, rather than the UFP server, control caching. When a Web page is requested by an end user for the first time, it is immediately sent to the UFP server after that one request and added to disk cache, which considerably improves network performance.

- *VPN & Firewall (two requests)*: URIs are sent to the UFP server two times before they are added to disk cache. Performance isn't as good as with a one-request system, but security is improved because each URI is checked by the firewall twice before being sent to cache.

Hot Standby Redundancy

One way to balance the load placed on a firewall is to set up a **hot standby** system in which one or more auxiliary or failover firewalls are configured to take over all traffic if the primary firewall fails. Usually, hot standby only involves two firewalls, the primary and the secondary systems. Only one firewall operates at any given time. The two firewalls need to be connected in what is sometimes called a **heartbeat network**: a network that monitors the operation of the primary firewall and synchronizes the state table connections so the two firewalls have the same information at any given time.

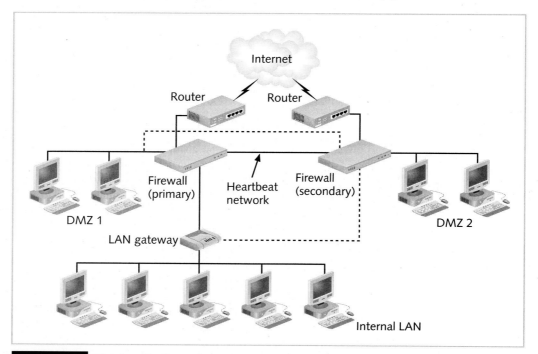

FIGURE 8-9   Hot Standby Example

Figure 8-9 shows a simplified diagram of a hot standby setup (simplified because in reality there would be more routers joining the various networks and probably more servers in the DMZs). The heartbeat network is made up of the two firewalls. The dashed line indicates the paths through which network traffic would flow if the primary firewall failed. The advantage of a hot standby system is the ease and economy with which it can be set up and the quick backup system it provides for the network. Another advantage is that one firewall can be stopped for maintenance purposes without stopping traffic to and from the network. On the downside, hot standby by itself doesn't improve network performance, and VPN connections may or may not be included in the failover system, depending on whether the firewall supports failover for VPN connections. Hot standby systems are just one aspect of incident response.

Load Balancing

As discussed in the early chapters of this book, the simplest firewalls function as gateways, monitoring all traffic as it passes into and out of a network. As organizations grow and Web, e-mail, and e-commerce services grow, it can be a liability to have a single firewall gateway that can become a single point of failure. When the firewall becomes **mission-critical**—an integral, key part of the company's core operations—everything possible must be done to maximize the firewall's uptime and smooth operation. One way to accomplish this goal is **load balancing**: the practice of balancing the load placed on the firewall so that it is handled by two or more firewall systems.

Another type of load balancing is **load sharing**: the practice of configuring two or more firewalls to share the total traffic load. Each firewall in a load-sharing setup is active at the same time. Traffic between the firewalls is distributed by routers using special routing protocols such as:

- *Open Shortest Path First (OSPF)*: This protocol can route traffic based on its IP type. It can also divide traffic equally between two routers that are equally far apart or that have an equal load already.

- *Border Gateway Protocol (BGP)*: This protocol uses TCP as its transport protocol to divide traffic among available routers.

A load-sharing setup has many advantages: total network performance is improved because the load is balanced among multiple firewalls, and the routing protocols needed to distribute traffic are present in virtually all routers. A big advantage is that maintenance can be performed on one firewall without disrupting total network traffic to the other firewall(s). On the downside, the load is usually distributed unevenly, and the configuration can be complex to administer. The connections between load-sharing firewalls may or may not include failover functions. This depends on whether the firewalls involved support failover connections. A load-balancing setup is illustrated in Figure 8-10.

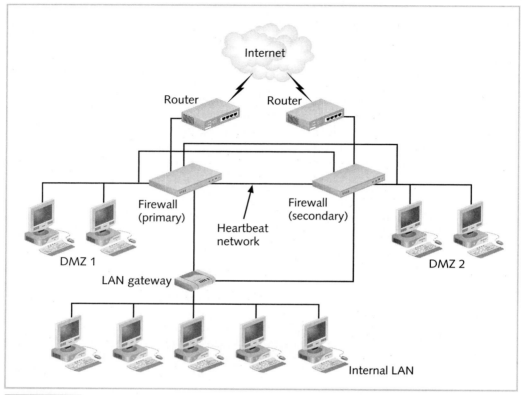

FIGURE 8-10 Load-Sharing Example

The even distribution of traffic among two or more load-sharing firewalls can be achieved through the use of **layer four switches**: network devices with the intelligence to make routing decisions based on source and destination IP address or port numbers as specified in Layer 4 of the OSI reference model.

Filtering Content

One of the most malicious and difficult to filter network attacks is the inclusion of harmful code in e-mail messages. Firewalls, by themselves, don't scan for viruses, but their manufacturers enable them to work with third-party applications to scan for viruses or perform other functions. Zone Alarm and Check Point NG, for instance, have an **Open Platform for Security (OPSEC) model** that lets you extend its functionality and integrate virus scanning into its set of abilities.

Many advanced firewalls support the **Content Vectoring Protocol (CVP)**, a protocol that enables firewalls to work with virus-scanning applications so such content can be filtered out. For instance, you can define a network object such as a server that contains anti-virus software and then have the firewall send SMTP traffic to that server using CVP. Once you define the server as a network object, you set the application properties for that server.

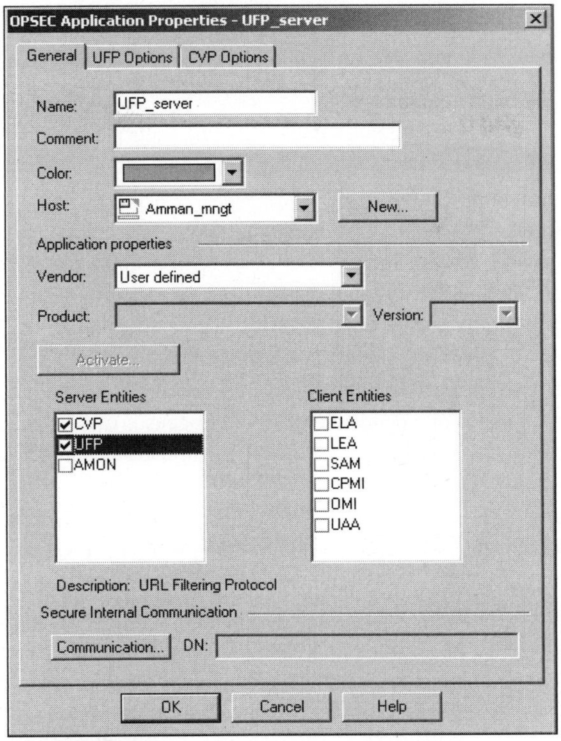

FIGURE 8-11   Content Filtering Example

In Figure 8-11, the anti-virus server is identified as an OPSEC_Server in the Host list. CVP is being identified as a server entity, and an OPSEC-compliant vendor intended for use on the anti-virus server is being chosen from the Vendor list. You then set options in the CVP Options tab to identify the server as a CVP object and identify the types of data you want to send to that server. CVP and OPSEC are two important tools you can use to help your firewall grow along with your organization's security needs.

Anti-virus protection is fast becoming one of the most important aspects of network security due to the proliferation of viruses borne by e-mail messages. For this reason, consider installing anti-virus software on your SMTP gateway in addition to providing desktop anti-virus protection for each of your computers. Be sure to choose an anti-virus gateway product that provides for content filtering, can be updated regularly to account for recent viruses, can scan the system in real time, and has detailed logging capabilities.

Chapter Summary

■ After establishing a security policy, implement the strategies that policy specifies. This is often done by setting rules for one or more firewalls. Rules give the firewall specific criteria on which to make decisions on whether to allow packets through or drop them, and inform the firewall about what types of traffic to let in and out of your network.

■ If the primary goal of your planned firewall is to block unauthorized access, you must emphasize restricting rather than enabling connectivity. In a "Deny-All" approach, the firewall blocks *everything* by default and only specifically allows those services you need on a case-by-case basis. Alternatively, if the primary orientation of your firewall is permissive, the rules should only block specific items, and the burden is shifted to one of education, training, and awareness.

■ A firewall must be scalable so it can grow with the network it protects. It needs to take into account the communication needs of individual employees. Because TCP/IP is the protocol of choice for internal networks as well as the Internet itself, the firewall also needs to deal with the IP address needs of the organization.

■ The stronger and more elaborate your firewall, the slower data transmissions are likely to be. Productivity needs of users inside the company who are trying to access the Internet must be addressed.

■ The more complex a network becomes, the more IP-addressing complications arise. It's important to anticipate how firewalls will affect this facet of network operations.

■ Network security setups can become incrementally more complex when specific functions are added. Any or all of the following can be part of a perimeter security system that includes a firewall: NAT/PAT, use of encryption, an application proxy, virtual private networks, and/or an intrusion detection and prevention system.

■ Firewalls must be maintained regularly to ensure that critical measures of success are kept within acceptable levels of performance. The firewall architecture and implementation must be maintained to ensure throughput, scalability, security, recoverability, and manageability.

■ Successful firewall management requires adherence to principles that have been put forth by reputable organizations to ensure that firewalls and network security configurations are maintained correctly. The Generally Accepted System Security Principles (GASSP) is one such set of security and information management practices. The GASSP provides guidelines that can help you manage a firewall as well as the information that passes through it. This advice encompasses the following areas: environmental management, BIOS, boot and screen locks, and others.

■ Remote management allows configuration and monitoring of one or more firewalls that are located at different network locations. These capabilities require security controls to enable their safe operation.

■ The ultimate goal for many organizations is the development of a high-performance firewall configuration that has high availability and that can be scaled as the organization grows. This is often accomplished by using data caching, redundancy, load balancing, and content filtering.

Review Questions

1. Why is a set of packet filtering rules just as important as a firewall?
2. Describe how a firewall could be configured to implement a "strict" approach to security.
3. What is a potential concern with the firewall practice of processing all rules in top-to-bottom order?
4. What is the advantage of adding a second router between a firewall and the LAN it protects in addition to a router outside the firewall?
5. Consider the following scenario: Your company operates a Web server and is promoting a new line of products. The server experiences a large number of visits from users on the Internet who want to place orders. The server needs to provide protection from viruses and harmful programs for users in the company; however, for business reasons you are instructed that commerce and revenue should take priority over security. Under these circumstances, where should the Web server be positioned?
6. Proxy servers, routers, and operating systems are all designed to perform IP forwarding. If your security configuration includes a proxy server, why should IP forwarding be disabled on routers and other devices that lie between the networks?
7. What is the most important configuration file in a firewall?
8. A "Deny-All" approach would work best in which circumstances?
9. What is the principle of "least privilege"?
10. If a firewall is primarily permissive, how does this affect the work factor of the network administrator?
11. What are the potential problems of a "Deny-All" policy?
12. What is the primary difference between a screened host and a dual-homed gateway?
13. Describe how using multiple layers of protection can add security benefits to a network.
14. Describe how placing two routers with IDPS at the perimeter of the network, rather than one, can improve the security of the network.
15. What are the primary goals you need to keep in mind when you consider upgrading your firewall architecture?
16. A network administrator should be concerned when a firewall's CPU consumption climbs above what percentage of total CPU usage?
17. What circumstances indicate that data caching should be disabled?
18. When should a company hire an outside firm to handle the ongoing administration of a firewall?
19. What features are important for a remote network management program?
20. What is the primary advantage of using a hot standby setup to achieve load balancing?

Exercises

1. You congratulate yourself on configuring your firewall. The next morning, you check the log files. You discover a number of unsuccessful attempts to log on to the FTP server. You turn on your firewall's real-time monitoring program and you immediately notice that 15MB worth of files are being transferred to an external user. You realize an attack is probably in progress. What should you do?
2. You are a network engineer who has been instructed to take a restrictive approach to firewall rules—as close to Deny-all as is practically possible. However, staff needs to look at training videos

online during regular business hours. People should be allowed to use the Web and to exchange e-mail at all times, but access to multimedia should be prohibited at night. Describe how you would structure the rules to accomplish this.

3. Sterling Silver Widgets, a manufacturer of luxury office supplies for high-powered executives, sells its products on a Web site that receives an average of a thousand visits per day. The company regularly receives shipments from Silver Supply Inc., a supplier that wants to access its own shipping and receiving information on the office network as well as transmit invoices to the Sterling Silver Widgets Accounting Department. Sterling Silver Widgets has had problems in the past with DoS attacks. Design a perimeter setup that includes stateful packet filtering, public Web server access, a firewall-protected internal network, and VPN access to the accounting department server.

4. You need to monitor different types of traffic at different times of day using your firewall-protected network. You primarily want to monitor e-mail, Web, and videoconferencing activity during the day, but in the overnight hours, branch offices around the world might connect to your network for FTP, TCP, and UDP traffic. How would you specify different monitoring parameters for different times of the day?

5. You have set up a load-sharing configuration in which three firewalls provide separate gateways for an internal network. You are alarmed to yield only a slight improvement in network traffic performance, despite the fact that you purchased and configured two new bastion hosts and firewall products. What might be the cause of the continued poor network performance? What could you do to improve the situation?

6. Despite the fact that you have installed an enterprise-class firewall, your company's employees have reported receiving e-mail messages that contain potentially harmful executable code attachments. Such attachments have been identified and isolated by the virus protection software installed on each workstation. You know, however, that the number of such harmful attachments is growing all the time, and you are worried that one will slip through that the virus protection software isn't yet configured to handle. What can you do to block such harmful e-mail messages from entering the protected network in the first place?

Case Exercises

The rule that "allowed" the reverse-proxy connection was written to forward both secured and nonsecured (ports 80 and 443) packets to the application server inside Linen Planet's network. Unfortunately one of the network administrators made a last-minute bug fix that caused the secure Web server to have a different address than the firewall rule set expected. The port 80 rule still worked, but when a customer linked to the HTTPS service, the rule that handled port 443 pointed to the wrong server. The folks at Linen Planet were only now starting to hear from customers that could not connect. Even worse, some of those customers abandoned their online shopping carts, and moved on to one of their competitors.

Questions:

1. How could ATI make sure glitches like this do not catch them unawares in the future?

2. How should the owners of the business Linen Planet protect themselves from losing business in cases like this?

9

Encryption and Firewalls

> There are no secrets that time does not reveal.
>
> **JEAN RACINE**

PADMA SANTHANAM, THE CTO OF LINEN PLANET, WAS COMMUTING TO work her usual way—riding the train from the suburban station near her home to her office in a commercial business area across town. As she turned the page of the morning paper, her cell phone rang. She looked at the caller ID and saw it was her assistant, David Kalb.

"Hello David. What's up?"

"Hi, Padma. Crisis here as usual. Our customer service rep at ATI is on the other line. He says you have to log in to the work order system and approve the change request ASAP or they'll miss the next change window for the new version of our online credit application."

Padma said, "OK. I'll be in the office in 25 minutes or so. The train just left Broadmore station."

"He says they can't wait that long. You were supposed to do this day before yesterday, and somehow it got overlooked. They say they need it now or we'll lose a week waiting for the next change window."

Padma sighed. Then she said, "OK. I want you to browse to the work order Web site, you know the one we use at linenplanet.biz/wo and log in for me. You can approve the change order and we won't miss the window. I'll change my password when I get there. My username is papa, sierra, alpha, november, tango, alpha. Got that?"

David said "Got it. Password?"

Looking both ways first, Padma lowered her voice some and said, "Romeo, lima, eight, four, bang, zulu, india, victor, dollar sign."

David repeated it back. He said, "OK, I am logged on now and just approved the work order. I'll tell our rep we're good to go."

"Thanks, David."

In the row behind Padma, Maris Heath closed her pocket notepad and clicked her ballpoint pen closed. Smiling, she hefted her laptop bag and stood up to exit the train at the next station, which she knew sat right next to an Internet cafe.

LEARNING OBJECTIVES:

Upon completion of this material, you should be able to do the following:

- Describe the role encryption plays in a firewall architecture
- Explain how digital certificates work and why they are important security tools
- Analyze the workings of SSL, PGP, and other popular encryption schemes
- Discuss Internet Protocol Security (IPSec) and identify its protocols and modes

Introduction

A firewall inspects packets of information when they reach the network perimeter, and, depending on the content of the packet and the firewall rules, sends the packet to the appropriate location or drops it.

What happens if a packet's contents have been corrupted in transit? What happens if a packet is intercepted before it gets to the firewall and mangled by a hacker? The firewall can't control what happens to packets before they arrive at or after they leave the protected network. This is one reason why firewalls and other security applications encrypt the contents of packets leaving the protected network, and are able to decrypt incoming packets.

This chapter explains why networks use encryption and explains how to use encryption in a way that complements and does not hinder the firewall. It also describes encryption applications, such as Pretty Good Privacy (PGP), Secure Sockets Layer (SSL), and Internet Protocol Security (IPSec), and schemes that can form part of a firewall architecture. By encrypting the data that passes into and out of your network, you help protect your hardware and data in a way that is different, but just as effective, as packet filtering, proxy services, and other firewall functions.

Firewalls and Encryption

Encryption is a process that turns information that is plainly readable (plaintext) into scrambled form (ciphertext) in order to preserve the authenticity, integrity, and privacy of the information that passes through the security perimeter. In other words, encryption renders information unreadable to all but the intended recipients.

Firewalls have not always been able to perform encryption-related functions. They originally focused on basic features like IP forwarding and Network Address Translation (NAT), and while these approaches provided protection at the network level, they didn't account for application-level problems, such as executable code that finds its way into a system. In fact, many of the attacks that plague companies both small and large—even those that are already protected by firewalls—are the result of executable code that is either tampered with before it reaches the firewall or, more commonly, that makes it past the firewall in malicious e-mail attachments or HTTP downloads.

Firewall vendors add encryption to their products to provide protection against "active attacks," which are also known as **session hijacks**. These are attacks involving a communication session that has already been established between a server and a client. The hacker inserts confusing or misleading commands into packets, thus disabling the server and enabling the hacker to gain control of the session. These are different from "passive attacks," such as packet sniffing, in which a program scans for open ports that can be compromised.

As you can see in Figure 9-1, the unencrypted packet is vulnerable at points A and B. With encryption, however, an attack that relies on the attacker's knowledge of the packet's content is rebuffed, as shown in Figure 9-2.

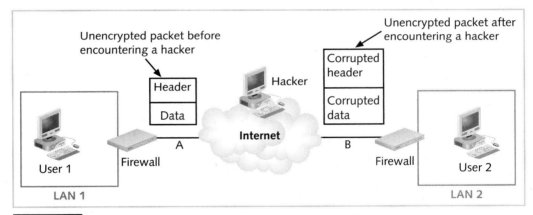

FIGURE 9-1   Unencrypted Packet

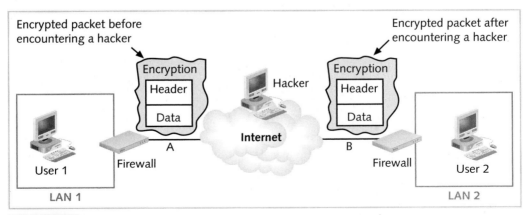

FIGURE 9-2   Encrypted Packet

The Cost of Encryption

Before you decide whether to use a firewall that has the ability to encrypt communications, be aware that encryption can be a very CPU-intensive process. The bastion host is a type of application server that has at least one networking interface on the Internet. In some situations, it may be the platform of choice to host firewall capabilities. It should be robust enough to manage encryption along with its other security functions. In addition, encrypted packets may need to be padded to uniform length to ensure that some algorithms work effectively.

Ideally, when firewalls encrypt data, the encryption is transparent to the end user. However, on busy networks, encryption can increase the time it takes to perform individual tasks. In addition, choosing an encryption method and monitoring how well encryption works is another task on a busy system administrator's list of responsibilities. An overworked system administrator can make choices and take actions that lead to insecure networks.

Preserving Data Integrity

One reason to encrypt information is to preserve its integrity. Although encryption minimizes the risk that information will be corrupted, it isn't foolproof. Even encrypted sessions can go wrong as a result of **man-in-the-middle attacks**: attacks in which a hacker intercepts part of an encrypted data session to gain control over the data being exchanged.

Another service related to data integrity that encryption can perform is nonrepudiation, which is the ability to prevent one participant in an electronic transaction from denying that it performed an action. Nonrepudiation uses encryption to document that all steps in an electronic transaction were, in fact, completed by the participating parties. Specifically, an encrypted code called a **digital signature** is attached to the files that are exchanged during the transaction so that each party can verify the other's identity. Nonrepudiation is an important aspect of trusted communications between corporations or other organizations that do business across a network rather than face to face.

Maintaining Confidentiality

The most obvious reason to encrypt data is to keep it confidential. The reason computers are stolen frequently is that the information such devices can contain is more valuable than the hardware itself. The computer insurance agency Safeware, Inc. (*www.safeware.com*) has stated that, in 1999, 319,000 laptops and 27,000 desktop computers were reported stolen. In addition, a widely reported survey by the American Society for Industrial Security claims that Fortune 1000 companies experienced data-related losses of more than $45 million in 1999. Such losses are especially hard to document or verify because many companies lose data to thieves, hackers, and disgruntled employees without even knowing it.

One memorable data-integrity incident in September 2000 indicates how quickly sensitive data can be lost: The CEO of a well-known wireless communications company had just used his laptop to make a slide show presentation at a conference in California. When the CEO left the podium to chat with members of the audience, the laptop was stolen. Although the computer was password protected, the password could conceivably be cracked using a number of specialized software programs. In addition, the computer reportedly contained proprietary information about the company's wireless technologies that would be of value to foreign governments.

Authenticating Network Clients

A cashier who accepts noncash payment from customers in a brick-and-mortar retail store can determine with reasonable certainty that customers are who they claim to be—for example, customers can be asked to show photo identification, such as a driver's license. The cashier and the store's management place trust in the state or other government agency that issued the ID.

On the Internet, requests for information reach a firewall at the perimeter of a network. The firewall, like any individual Internet user, needs to trust that the person's claimed identity is genuine. Firewalls that use encryption, as well as specialized encryption software, can also identify individuals who possess "digital ID cards" that include encrypted codes. These codes include digital signatures, **public keys**, and **private keys**—all codes that are generated by complex algorithms. Users on the Internet can exchange these codes like digital ID cards, enabling them to identify each other. The same codes can be used to encrypt and decrypt e-mail messages as well as files.

Enabling Virtual Private Networks (VPNs)

A VPN joins two separate LANs. Encryption is an integral part of VPNs and is used to accomplish two goals:

- Encryption enables the firewall to determine whether the user who wants to connect to the VPN is actually authorized to do so.
- Encryption is used to encode the payload of the information to maintain privacy.

Virtual private networking is a complex and important type of firewall function, and is discussed in greater detail in Chapter 11.

Principles of Cryptography

Although it is not a specific application or security tool, cryptography represents a sophisticated element that is often included in other information security controls. In fact, many security-related tools use embedded encryption technologies to protect sensitive information. The use of the proper cryptographic tools can ensure confidentiality by keeping private information concealed from those who do not need to see it. Other cryptographic methods can provide increased information integrity by providing a mechanism to guarantee that a message in transit has not been altered, by using a process that creates a secure message digest, or hash. In e-commerce, some cryptographic tools can be used to ensure that parties to the transaction are authentic, so that they cannot later deny having participated in a transaction, a feature often called **nonrepudiation**.

Encryption is the process of converting a message into a form that cannot be read by unauthorized individuals. An encrypted message cannot be converted back to its readable form without the specific tools and knowledge used to encrypt it. The science of encryption, known as **cryptology**, actually encompasses two disciplines: cryptography and cryptanalysis. **Cryptography**—from the Greek words *kryptos,* meaning "hidden," and *graphein,* meaning "to write"—is the processes involved in encoding and decoding messages so that others cannot understand them. **Cryptanalysis**—from *analyein,* meaning "to break up"—is the process of deciphering the original message (or **plaintext**) from an encrypted message (or **ciphertext**), without knowing the algorithms and keys used to perform the encryption.

Cryptology is a very complex field based on advanced mathematical concepts. The following sections provide a brief overview of the foundations of encryption and a short discussion of some of the related issues and tools in the field of information security. Those students who would like more information about cryptography can consult either H. X. Mel and D. Baker's *Cryptography Decrypted* for a general introduction, or Bruce Schneier's *Applied Cryptography: Protocols, Algorithms, and Source Code in C,* which provides a more technical tutorial.

Encryption Definitions

You can better understand the tools and functions popular in encryption security solutions if you know some basic terminology:

Algorithm: The mathematical formula or method used to convert an unencrypted message into an encrypted message, or vice versa

Cipher: The transformation of the individual components (characters, bytes, or bits) of an unencrypted message into encrypted components

Ciphertext or **cryptogram**: The encrypted or encoded message resulting from an encryption

Cryptosystem: The set of transformations necessary to convert an unencrypted message into an encrypted message

Decipher: To decrypt or convert ciphertext to plaintext

Encipher: To encrypt or convert plaintext to ciphertext

Key or **cryptovariable**: The information used in conjunction with the algorithm to create the ciphertext from the plaintext

Keyspace: The entire range of values that can possibly be used to construct an individual key

Plaintext: The original unencrypted message or the results from successful decryption

Work factor: The amount of effort (usually expressed in units of time) required to perform cryptanalysis on an encoded message

Cryptographic Notation

The notation used to describe the encryption process varies, depending on its source. The notation chosen for the discussion in this text uses the letter M to represent the original message, C to represent the resulting ciphertext, and E to represent the encryption process: thus, $E(M) = C^1$. This formula represents the application of encryption (E) to a message (M) to create ciphertext (C). Also in this notation scheme, the letter D represents the decryption or deciphering process, thus the formula $D[E(M)] = M$ states that if you decipher (D) an enciphered message (E(M)), you should get the original message (M).

This could also be stated as D[C]=M, or the deciphering of the ciphertext (remember that C=E(M)) results in the original message M. Finally, the letter K is used to represent the key, therefore E(M, K) = C suggests that encrypting (E) the message (M) with the key (K) results in the ciphertext (C). Similarly, D(C,K) = D[E(M,K),K] = M, or deciphering the ciphertext with key K results in the original plaintext message—or, to translate this formula even more precisely, deciphering with key K the message encrypted with key K results in the original message.

To encrypt a plaintext set of data, you can use one of two general methods: stream or block ciphers. With the stream method, each plaintext bit is transformed into a cipher bit, one after the other. With the block cipher method, the message is divided into blocks, e.g., 8-, 16-, 32- or 64-bit blocks, and then each block is transformed using the algorithm and key. Bit stream methods most commonly use algorithm functions like XOR, whereas block methods can use XOR, transposition, or substitution, described later in this chapter.

Encryption Operations

Encryption is accomplished by using algorithms to manipulate the plaintext into the ciphertext for transmission. Some widely used encryption operations are explained in the sections that follow.

Common Ciphers

In encryption the most commonly used algorithms include three functions: substitution, transposition, and XOR. In a **substitution cipher**, you substitute one value for another. For example, using the line labeled "input text," you can substitute the message character with the character three values to the right in the alphabet by looking at the aligned text in the line labeled "output text."

Input text:	ABCDEFGHIJKLMNOPQRSTUVWXYZ
Output text:	DEFGHIJKLMNOPQRSTUVWXYZABC

Thus a plaintext of BERLIN becomes EHUOLQ.

This is a simple enough method by itself, but it becomes very powerful if combined with other operations. Incidentally, this type of substitution is based on a **monoalphabetic substitution**, as it uses only one alphabet. More advanced substitution ciphers use two or more alphabets, and are called **polyalphabetic substitutions**. To continue the previous example, consider the following block of text:

Input text:	ABCDEFGHIJKLMNOPQRSTUVWXYZ
Substitution cipher 1:	DEFGHIJKLMNOPQRSTUVWXYZABC
Substitution cipher 2:	GHIJKLMNOPQRSTUVWXYZABCDEF
Substitution cipher 3:	JKLMNOPQRSTUVWXYZABCDEFGHI
Substitution cipher 4:	MNOPQRSTUVWXYZABCDEFGHIJKL

Here the plaintext is matched character by character to the input text row. The next four lines are four sets of substitution ciphers. In this example, you can encode the word TEXT as WKGF, as you select letters from the second row for the first letter, letters from the third row for the second letter, and so on. This type of encryption is substantially more difficult to decipher without the algorithm (rows of ciphers and use of the second row for the first letter, the third row for the second letter, and so on). It is also easy to completely randomize the cipher rows to create more complex substitution operations.

Another simple example of the substitution cipher is the daily cryptogram in your local newspaper, or the well-known Little Orphan Annie decoder ring. Julius Caesar reportedly used a three-character shift to the right (using the Roman alphabet), in which A becomes D and so on, giving that particular substitution cipher his name—the Caesar cipher.

Like the substitution operation, transposition is simple to understand but can be complex to decipher if properly used. Unlike the substitution cipher, the **transposition cipher** (or **permutation cipher**) simply rearranges the values within a block to create the ciphertext. This can be done at the bit level or at the byte (character) level. Here is an example:

Plaintext: 0010010101101011100101010101001001

Key: 1 > 3, 2 > 6, 3 > 8, 4 > 1, 5 > 4, 6 > 7, 7 > 5, 8 > 2

(Read as bit 1 moves to position 4, and so on, with bit position 1 being the rightmost bit.)

The following shows the plaintext broken into 8-bit blocks (for ease of discussion) and the corresponding ciphertext, based on the application of the preceding key to the plaintext:

Plaintext 8-bit blocks: 00100101 01101011 10010101 01010100

Ciphertext: 11000100 01110101 10001110 10011000

To make this easier to follow, consider the following example in character transposition:

Plaintext: MY DOG HAS FLEAS. (Spaces count as characters.)

Key: Same key as above but characters are transposed, rather than bits. (Note that spaces are transposed as well.)

Plaintext 8-character blocks: MY DOG H   AS FLEAS

Ciphertext: G YDHMO   E ASFSAL

Transposition ciphers and substitution ciphzers can be used together in multiple combinations to create a very secure encryption process. To make the encryption stronger (more difficult to cryptanalyze), the keys and block sizes can be made much larger (64 bit or 128 bit), resulting in substantially more complex substitutions or transpositions.

In the **XOR cipher conversion**, the bit stream is subjected to a Boolean XOR function against some other data stream, typically a key stream. The symbol commonly used to represent the XOR function is " ∧ ". XOR works as follows:

'0' XOR'ed with '0' results in a '0'. (0 ∧ 0 = 0)

'0' XOR'ed with '1' results in a '1'. (0 ∧ 1 = 1)

'1' XOR'ed with '0' results in a '1'. (1 ∧ 0 = 1)

'1' XOR'ed with '1' results in a '0'. (1 ∧ 1 = 0)

Simply put, if the two values are the same, you get "0"; if not, you get "1". Suppose you have a data stream in which the first byte is 01000001. If you have a key stream in which the first "byte" is '0101 1010', and you XOR them:

'0100 0001' Plaintext

'0101 1010' Key stream

'0001 1011' Ciphertext

This process is reversible. That is, if you XOR the ciphertext with the key stream, you get the plaintext.

Vernam Cipher

Also known as the one-time pad, the Vernam cipher was developed at AT&T and uses a set of characters for encryption operations only one time and then discards it. The values from this one-time pad are added to the block of text, and the resulting sum is converted to text. When the two sets of values are added, if the resulting values exceed 26, 26 is subtracted from the total (a process called modulo 26). The corresponding results are then converted back to text. The following example demonstrates how the Vernam cipher works:

Plaintext:	M	Y	D	O	G	H	A	S	F	L	E	A	S
Corresponding values:	13	25	04	15	07	08	01	19	06	12	05	01	19
One-time pad:	F	P	Q	R	N	S	B	I	E	H	T	Z	L
Pad corresponding values:	06	16	17	18	14	19	02	09	05	08	20	26	12

Results:

Plaintext:	13	25	04	15	07	08	01	19	06	12	05	01	19
One-time Pad	06	16	17	18	14	19	02	09	05	08	20	26	12
Sum:	19	41	21	33	21	27	03	28	11	20	25	27	31
Subtraction (modulo 26)		15		07		01		02				01	05
Ciphertext:	P	O	U	G	U	A	C	B	K	T	Y	A	E

Book or Running Key Cipher

Another method, one seen in the occasional spy movie, is the use of text in a book as the algorithm to decrypt a message. The key relies on two components: (1) knowing which book to use, and (2) having a list of codes representing the page number, line number, and word number of the plaintext word. For example, using a copy of a particular popular novel, one might send the following message: 67,3,1;145,9,4;375,7,4;394,17,3. Dictionaries and thesauruses are the most popular sources as they provide every needed word, although almost any book will suffice. If the receiver knows which book is used for the preceding example, he or she goes to page 67, line 3, and selects the first word from that line; then goes to page 145, line 9, and uses the fourth word; and so forth. The resulting message "cancel operation target compromised" can then be deciphered. When using dictionaries, it is necessary to use only a page and word number. An even more sophisticated version of this cipher can use multiple books, with a new book in a particular sequence for each word or phrase.

Symmetric Encryption

Each of the aforementioned encryption and decryption methods requires the same algorithm and key—a **secret key**—to be used to both encipher and decipher the message. This is known as **private key encryption**, or **symmetric encryption**. Symmetric encryption is efficient and easy to process, as long as both the sender and the receiver possess the encryption key. Of course, if either copy of the key becomes compromised, an intermediary can decrypt and read the messages. One challenge in symmetric key encryption is getting a copy of the key to the receiver, a process that must be conducted out-of-band (that is, through a different channel or band than the one carrying the ciphertext) to avoid interception. Figure 9-3 illustrates the concept of symmetric encryption.

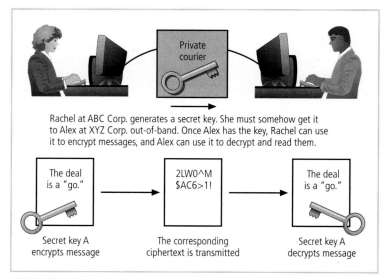

Rachel at ABC Corp. generates a secret key. She must somehow get it to Alex at XYZ Corp. out-of-band. Once Alex has the key, Rachel can use it to encrypt messages, and Alex can use it to decrypt and read them.

The deal is a "go."	2LW0^M $AC6>1!	The deal is a "go."
Secret key A encrypts message	The corresponding ciphertext is transmitted	Secret key A decrypts message

FIGURE 9-3   Symmetric Encryption

A number of popular symmetric encryption cryptosystems are available. One of the most familiar is Data Encryption Standard (DES). DES was developed in 1977 by IBM and is based on the Data Encryption Algorithm (DEA), which uses a 64-bit block size and a 56-bit key. With a 56-bit key, the algorithm has 2^{56} (more than 72 quadrillion) possible keys.

DES is a federally approved standard for nonclassified data (see Federal Information Processing Standards Publication 46-2). It was cracked in 1997 when the developers of a new algorithm, Rivest-Shamir-Adleman (RSA) (which you will learn about later in this chapter), offered a $10,000 reward for the first person or team to crack the algorithm. Fourteen thousand users collaborated over the Internet to finally break the encryption.

Triple DES (3DES) was developed as an improvement to DES and uses as many as three keys in succession. It is substantially more secure than DES, not only because it uses as many as three keys instead of one, but also because it performs three different encryption operations. As it was demonstrated that DES was not strong enough for highly classified communications, 3DES was created to provide a level of security far beyond that of standard DES. (In between, there was a 2DES; however, it was statistically shown that the double DES did not provide significantly stronger security than that of DES.) 3DES takes three 64-bit keys for an overall key length of 192 bits. Triple DES encryption is the same as that of standard DES; however, it is repeated three times. Triple DES can be employed using two or three keys, and a combination of encryption or decryption to obtain additional security. The most common implementations involve encrypting and/or decrypting with two or three different keys, a process that is described below. 3DES employs 48 rounds in its encryption computation, generating ciphers that are approximately 2^{56} (72 quadrillion) times stronger than standard DES ciphers but takes only three times longer to process. One example of 3DES encryption is illustrated here:

1. In the first operation, 3DES encrypts the message with key 1, then decrypts it with key 2, and then it encrypts it again with key 1. In cryptographic notation terms, this would

be [E{D[E(M,K1)],K2},K1]. Decrypting with a different key is essentially another encryption, but it reverses the application of the traditional encryption operations.

2. In the second operation, 3DES encrypts the message with key 1, then it encrypts it again with key 2, and then it encrypts it a third time with key 1 again, or [E{E[E(M,K1)],K2},K1].

3. In the third operation, 3DES encrypts the message three times with three different keys: [E{E[E(M,K1)],K2},K3]. This is the most secure level of encryption possible with 3DES.

The successor to 3DES is **Advanced Encryption Standard** (**AES**). Of the many ciphers that were submitted (from across the world) for consideration in the AES selection process, five finalists were chosen: MARS, RC6, Rijndael, Serpent, and Twofish. On October 2, 2000, NIST announced the selection of Rijndael as the cipher to be used as the basis for the AES, and this block cipher was approved by the Secretary of Commerce as the official federal governmental standard as of May 26, 2002. The Rijndael Block Cipher features a variable block length and a key length of either 128, 192, or 256 bits. The AES version of Rijndael can use a multiple round based system. Depending on the key size, the number of rounds varies between 9 and 13: for a 128-bit key, 9 rounds plus one end round are used; for a 192-bit key, 11 rounds plus one end round are used; and for a 256-bit key, 13 rounds plus one end round are used. Once Rijndael was adopted as the AES, the ability to use variable-sized blocks was standardized to a single 128-bit block for simplicity.

There are four steps within each Rijndael round:

1. The Byte Sub step, where each byte of the block is replaced by its substitute in an S-box (substitution box). *[Author's Note: The S-box consists of a table of computed values, the calculation of which is beyond the scope of this text.]*

2. The Shift Row step. Considering the block to be made up of bytes 1 to 16, these bytes are arranged in a rectangle, and shifted as follows:

from					to			
1	5	9	13		1	5	9	13
2	6	10	14		6	10	14	2
3	7	11	15		11	15	3	7
4	8	12	16		16	4	8	12

Other shift tables are used for larger blocks.

3. The Mix Column step. Matrix multiplication is performed: each column is multiplied by the matrix:

2	3	1	1
1	2	3	1
1	1	2	3
3	1	1	2

4. The Add Round Key step. This is simply XORs in the subkey for the current round.

The extra final round omits the Mix Column step, but is otherwise the same as a regular round."[2] In 1998, it took a special computer designed by the Electronic Frontier Foundation (www.eff.org) more than 56 hours to crack DES. It would take the same computer approximately 4,698,864 quintillion years (4,698,864,000,000,000,000,000) to crack AES.

Asymmetric Encryption

Another encryption technique is **asymmetric encryption**, also known as **public key encryption**. Whereas symmetric encryption systems use the same key to both encrypt and decrypt a message, asymmetric encryption uses two different keys. Either key can be used to encrypt or decrypt the message. However, if Key A is used to encrypt the message, then only Key B can decrypt it; conversely, if Key B is used to encrypt a message, then only Key A can decrypt it. This technique is most valuable when one of the keys is private and the other is public. The public key is stored in a public location, where anyone can use it. The private key, as its name suggests, is a secret known only to the owner of the key pair.

Consider the following example, illustrated in Figure 9-4. Alex at XYZ Corporation wants to send an encrypted message to Rachel at ABC Corporation. Alex goes to a public key registry and obtains Rachel's public key. Recall the foundation of asymmetric encryption: The same key cannot be used to both encrypt and decrypt the same message. Thus, when Rachel's public key is used to encrypt the message, only her private key can be used to decrypt it, and that private key is held by Rachel alone. Similarly, if Rachel wishes to respond to Alex's message, she goes to the registry where Alex's public key is held and uses it to encrypt her message, which of course can be read only by using Alex's private key to decrypt it.

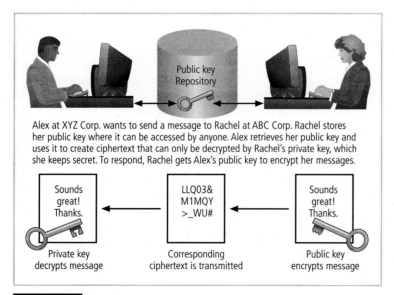

FIGURE 9-4 Public Key Encryption

The problem with asymmetric encryption is that it requires four keys to hold a single conversation between two parties. If four organizations want to frequently exchange messages, each must manage its four private keys and the four public keys from its partners. It can be confusing to determine which public key is needed to encrypt a particular message. With more organizations in the loop, the problem grows. Also, asymmetric encryption is not as efficient in its use of CPU resources as symmetric encryptions when performing the extensive mathematical calculations. As a result, the hybrid system described in the section "Public Key Infrastructure" (later in this chapter) is more commonly used.

Digital Signatures

When the asymmetric process is reversed—the private key encrypts a (usually short) message, and the public key decrypts it—the fact that the message was sent by the organization that owns the private key is difficult to refute. This nonrepudiation is the foundation of digital signatures. **Digital signatures** are encrypted messages that can be independently verified by a central facility (registry) as authentic, but can also be used to prove certain characteristics of the message or file with which they are associated. They are often used in Internet software updates (see Figure 9-5). A pop-up window shows that the downloaded files did, in fact, come from the purported agency and thus can be trusted. A **digital certificate** is similar to a digital signature and asserts that a public key is associated with a particular identity (for example, that a particular public key really belongs to Alex). A **certificate authority (CA)** is an agency that manages the issuance of certificates and serves as the electronic notary public to verify their origin and integrity.

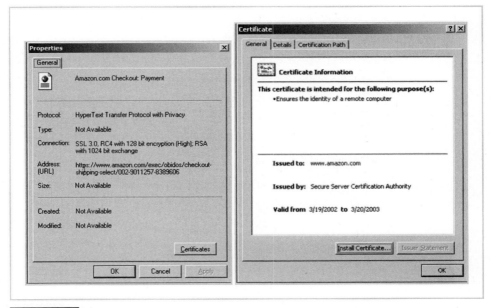

FIGURE 9-5 Digital Signature

RSA

One of the most popular public key cryptosystems is a proprietary model named Rivest-Shamir-Adleman (RSA) after the surnames of its developers. It is the first public key encryption algorithm developed for commercial use. RSA is very popular and has been integrated into both Microsoft Internet Explorer and Netscape Navigator. A number of extensions to the RSA algorithm exist, including RSA Encryption Scheme—Optimal Asymmetric Encryption Padding (RSAES-OAEP) and RSA Signature Scheme with Appendix—Probabilistic Signature Scheme (RSASSA-PSS). For more information as to how RSA's algorithm works, see the RSA Algorithm Technical Details box.

Technical Details

RSA Algorithm

If you understand modulo mathematics, you can appreciate the complexities of the RSA algorithm. The security of the RSA algorithm is based on the computational difficulty of factoring large composite numbers and computing the *eth roots modulo*, a composite number for a specified odd integer *e*. Encryption in RSA is accomplished by raising the message *M* to a nonnegative integer power *e*. The product is then divided by the nonnegative modulus *n* (n should have a bit length of at least 1024 bits), and the remainder is the ciphertext *C*. This process results in a one-way operation (shown below) when n is a very large number.

$$C = M^e \ / \ mod \ n$$

In the decryption process, the ciphertext C is raised to the power d, a nonnegative integer, as follows:

$$d = e^{-1} \ mod \ ((p-1)(q-1))$$

C is then reduced modulo n. In order for the recipient to calculate the decryption key, the p and q factors must be known. The modulus n, which is a composite number, is determined by multiplying two large nonnegative prime numbers, p and q:

$$n = p \infty q$$

In RSA's asymmetric algorithm, which is the basis of most modern public key infrastructure (PKI) systems (a topic covered later in this chapter), the public and private keys are generated as follows:

Choose two large prime numbers, p and q, of equal length, compute p x q = n, which is the public modulus.

Choose a random public key, e, so that e and (p-1)(q-1) are relatively prime.

Compute e x d = 1 mod (p − 1)(q − 1), where d is the private key.

Thus $d = e^{-1} mod[(p - 1)(q - 1)]$.

where "(d, n) is the private key; (e, n) is the public key. P is encrypted to generate ciphertext C as $C = P^e$ mod n, and is decrypted to recover the plaintext, P as $P = C^d$ mod n."[3]

Essentially. the RSA algorithm can be divided into three steps:

1. *Key generation*: Prime factors p and q are statistically selected by a technique known as probabilistic primality testing and then multiplied together to form n. The encryption exponent e is selected, and the decryption exponent d is calculated.
2. *Encryption*: M is raised to the power of e, reduced by modulo n, and remainder C is the ciphertext.
3. *Decryption*: C is raised to the power of d and reduced by modulo n.

The sender publishes the public key, which consists of modulus n and exponent e. The remaining variables d, p, and q are kept secret.

A message can then be encrypted by:	$C = M^e$(recipient) mod n(recipient)
Digitally signed by:	$C' = M'^d$(sender) mod n(sender)
Verified by:	$M' = C'^e$(sender) mod n(sender)
Decrypted by:	$M = C^d$(recipient) mod n(recipient)

Example Problems

As this Technical Details box presents complex information, the following sections contain practice examples to help you better understand the machinations of the various algorithms.

RSA Algorithm Example: [4] Work through the following steps to better understand how the RSA algorithm functions.

1. Choose randomly two large prime numbers: P, Q (usually P, Q > 10^{100}) → This means 10 to the power 100.
2. Compute:
   $$N = P \times Q$$
   $$Z = (P - 1)(Q - 1)$$
3. Choose a number relatively prime with Z and call it D.
   D < N ; relatively prime means that D and Z have no common factors, except 1.
4. Find number E, such that → E × D = 1 mod Z.
5. The public key is: (N, E); the private Key is (N, D).
6. Create Cipher (Encrypted Text):
   C = | TEXT |E (MOD N)
   C → Encrypted text → this is the text that's transmitted
   | TEXT | → Plaintext to be encrypted (its numerical correspondent)
7. Decrypt the message:
   D = Plaintext = CD (MOD N), C = Ciphertext from part 6.

Note that it is almost impossible to obtain the private key, knowing the public key, and it's almost impossible to factor N into P and Q.

RSA Numerical Example: [13] Work through the following steps to better understand RSA Numericals:

1. Choose P = 3, Q = 11 (two prime numbers). Note that small numbers have been chosen for the example, so that you can easily work with them. In real-life encryption, they are larger than 10^{100}.
2. N = P ∞ Q = 3 ∞ 11 = 33; Z = (P-1)(Q-1) = 2 ∞ 10 = 20
3. Choose a number for D that is relatively prime with Z, for example, D=7 → (20 and 7 have no common divisors, except 1).
4. E = ? such as E ∞ D = 1 MOD Z (1 MOD Z means that the remainder of E/D division is 1).
   E ∞ D / Z → E ∞ 7 / 20 → E=3
   Check E ∞ D / Z → 3 ∞ 7 / 20 → 21/20 → Remainder = 1
5. So, the public key is (N,E) = (33,3) → This key will be used to encrypt the message. The private key is (N,D) = (33,7) → This key will be used to decrypt the message.

English Alphabet and Corresponding Numbers for Each Letter:[5] In real-life applications, the ASCII code is used to represent each of the characters of a message. For this example, the position of the letter in the alphabet is used instead to simplify the calculations: A = 01, B = 02, etc... Z = 26.

Encrypt the word "Technology" as illustrated in Table 9-1:[6] Now you can use the corresponding numerical and the previous calculations to calculate values for the public key (N,E)= (33,3) and the private key (N,D)=(33,7):

Table 9-1 Encryption

Plaintext	Text Value	(Text)^E	(Text)^E MOD N = Ciphertext
T	20	8000	8000 MOD 33 = 14
E	05	125	125 MOD 33 = 26
C	03	27	27 MOD 33 = 27
H	08	512	512 MOD 33 = 17
N	14	2744	2744 MOD 33 = 05
O	15	3375	3375 MOD 33 = 09
L	12	1728	1728 MOD 33 = 12
O	15	3375	3375 MOD 33 = 09
G	07	343	343 MOD 33 = 13
Y	25	15625	15625 MOD 33 = 16

So, the cipher (encrypted message) is: 14262717050912091316. This is what is transmitted over unreliable lines. Note that there are two digits per letter. To decrypt the transmitted message we apply the private key (^D) and re-MOD the product. The result of this is the numerical equivalent of the original plaintext. See Table 9-2.

Table 9-2 Encryption

Ciphertext	(Cipher)^D	(Cipher)^D MOD N = |Text|	Plaintext
14	105413504	105413504 MOD 33 = 20	T
26	8031810176	8031810176 MOD 33 = 05	E
27	10460353203	10460353203 MOD 33 = 03	C
17	410338673	410338673 MOD 33 = 08	H
05	78125	78125 MOD 33 = 14	N
09	4782969	4782969 MOD 33 = 15	O
12	35831808	35831808 MOD 33 = 12	L
09	4782969	4782969 MOD 33 = 15	O
13	62748517	62748517 MOD 33 = 07	G
16	268435456	268435456 MOD 33 = 25	Y

As you can see in Table 9-2, although very small P and Q numbers were used, the numbers required for decrypting the message are relatively large. Now you have a good idea of what kind of numbers are needed when P and Q are large (that is, in the 10^{100} range).

If P and Q are not big enough for the cipher to be secure, P and Q must be increased. The strength of this encryption algorithm relies on how difficult it is to factor P and Q from N if N is known. If N is not known, the algorithm is even harder to break, of course.

Public Key Infrastructure

A public key infrastructure (PKI) is the entire set of hardware, software, and cryptosystems necessary to implement public key encryption. PKI systems are based on public key cryptosystems and include digital certificates and certificate authorities. Common implementations of PKI include:

- Systems to issue digital certificates to users and servers
- Encryption enrollment
- Key-issuing systems
- Tools for managing the key issuance
- Verification and return of certificates
- Key revocation services
- Other services associated with PKI that vendors bundle into their products

The use of cryptographic tools is made more manageable when using PKI. PKI can increase the capabilities of an organization in protecting its information assets by providing the following services:[7]

- Authentication: Digital certificates in a PKI system permit individuals, organizations, and Web servers to authenticate the identity of each of the parties in an Internet transaction.
- Integrity: Digital certificates assert that the content signed by the certificate has not been altered while in transit.
- Confidentiality: PKI keeps information confidential by ensuring that it is not intercepted during transmission over the Internet.
- Authorization: Digital certificates issued in a PKI environment can replace user IDs and passwords, enhance security, and reduce some of the overhead for authorization processes and controlling access privileges for specific transactions.
- Nonrepudiation: Digital certificates can validate actions, making it less likely that customers or partners can later repudiate a digitally signed transaction, such as an online purchase.

Hybrid Systems

Pure asymmetric key encryption is not widely used except in the area of certificates. For other purposes, it is typically employed in conjunction with symmetric key encryption, creating a hybrid system. In this method, asymmetric encryption is used to exchange a symmetric key, so that two organizations can conduct quick, efficient, secure communications based on symmetric encryption.

The process, which is illustrated in Figure 9-6, works like this: Because symmetric encryption is more efficient than asymmetric encryption for sending messages, and because asymmetric encryption doesn't require out-of-band key exchange, asymmetric encryption can be used to transmit symmetric keys in a hybrid approach. Suppose Alex at ABC Corporation wants to communicate with Rachel at XYZ Corporation. First, Alex creates a session key. A **session key** is a symmetric key for limited-use, temporary communications. Alex encrypts a message with the session key, and then gets Rachel's public key. He uses her public key to encrypt both the session key and the message that is already encrypted. Alex transmits the entire package to Rachel, who uses her private key to decrypt the package containing the session key and the encrypted message, and then uses the session key to decrypt the message. Rachel can then continue the electronic conversation using only the more efficient symmetric session key.

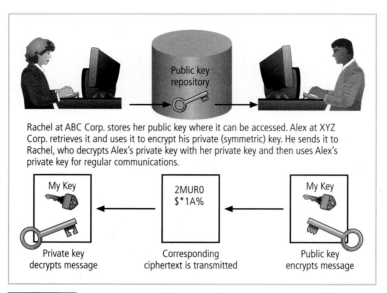

Rachel at ABC Corp. stores her public key where it can be accessed. Alex at XYZ Corp. retrieves it and uses it to encrypt his private (symmetric) key. He sends it to Rachel, who decrypts Alex's private key with her private key and then uses Alex's private key for regular communications.

| My Key | 2MUR0 $*1A% | My Key |
| Private key decrypts message | Corresponding ciphertext is transmitted | Public key encrypts message |

FIGURE 9-6 Hybrid Encryption

Using Cryptographic Controls

Cryptographic controls are often misunderstood by those new to the area of information security. While modern cryptosystems can certainly generate unbreakable ciphertext, that is possible only when the proper key management infrastructure has been constructed and when the cryptosystems are operated and managed correctly. As in many InfoSec endeavors, the technical control is valuable, as long as it remains within programs that are founded on sound policy and managed with an awareness of the fundamental objectives of the organization. Unfortunately, many vendors of cryptographic controls have sold products to organizations that have not been able to deploy them to improve their security programs. This may be due to poor project planning, errors in executing the implementation plans, or failure to put sound policies in place before acquiring the controls. Whatever the causes, many organizations have failed to make full use of their investment in cryptographic controls.

Organizations with the need and the ability to use cryptographic controls can use them to support several aspects of the business:

- Confidentiality and integrity of e-mail and its attachments
- Authentication, confidentiality, integrity, and nonrepudiation of e-commerce transactions
- Authentication and confidentiality of remote access through VPN connections
- A higher standard of authentication when used to supplement access control systems

E-mail Security

A number of cryptosystems have been adapted to help secure e-mail, a notoriously inse-cure method of communication. Some of the more popular adaptations include Secure Multipurpose Internet Mail Extensions, Privacy Enhanced Mail, and Pretty Good Privacy.

Secure Multipurpose Internet Mail Extensions (S/MIME) builds on the Multipurpose Internet Mail Extensions (MIME) encoding format by adding encryption and authentica-tion via digital signatures based on public key cryptosystems. **Privacy Enhanced Mail (PEM)** has been proposed by the Internet Engineering Task Force (IETF) as a standard that will function with public key cryptosystems. PEM uses 3DES symmetric key encryption and RSA for key exchanges and digital signatures. **Pretty Good Privacy (PGP)** was developed by Phil Zimmerman and uses the IDEA Cipher, a 128-bit symmetric key block encryption algorithm with 64-bit blocks for message encoding. Like PEM, it uses RSA for symmetric key exchange and to support digital signatures. PGP does not use a centralized certificate authority; rather, it relies on a "web of trust" model to allow its users to share key informa-tion easily, albeit with some loss in the degree of control and trust in the key information. If user A has established a trusting relationship with user B, and user B has a trusting rela-tionship with user C, then user A is presumed to have a trusting relationship with user C and can exchange encrypted information with that user.

Securing the Web

Just as PGP, PEM, and S/MIME help to secure e-mail operations, a number of cryptosystems help to secure Web activity, especially transactions between customers' browsers and the Web servers at electronic commerce sites. Among the protocols used for this purpose are Secure Electronic Transactions, Secure Sockets Layer, Secure Hypertext Transfer Protocol, Secure Shell, and IP Security.

Secure Electronic Transactions (SET) was developed by MasterCard and VISA in 1997 to provide protection from electronic payment fraud. It works by encrypting the credit card transfers with DES for encryption and RSA for key exchange, much as other algo-rithms do. SET provides the security for both Internet-based credit card transactions and the encryption of card swipe systems in retail stores.

Secure Sockets Layer (SSL) was developed by Netscape in 1994 to provide security for online electronic commerce transactions. It uses a number of algorithms, but mainly relies on RSA for key transfer and on IDEA, DES, or 3DES for encrypted symmetric key-based data transfer. If the Web connection does not automatically display the certificate, you can right-click in the window and select Properties to view the connection encryption and certificate properties. SSL has largely been replaced by TLS (Transport Layer Security) but many still refer to it as SSL, and we follow that common usage.

Secure Hypertext Transfer Protocol (SHTTP) is an encrypted solution to the unsecured version of HTTP. It provides an alternative to the aforementioned protocols and can pro-vide secure e-commerce transactions as well as encrypted Web pages for secure data transfer over the Web, using a number of different algorithms.

Secure Shell (SSH) is a popular extension to the TCP/IP protocol suite, sponsored by the IETF. It provides security for remote access connections over public networks by creating a secure and persistent connection. It provides authentication services between a client and a server and is used to secure replacement tools for terminal emulation, remote management, and file transfer applications.

IP Security (IPSec) is the primary and now dominant cryptographic authentication and encryption product of the IETF's IP Protocol Security Working Group. It is used to support a variety of applications, just as SSH does. A framework for security development within the TCP/IP family of protocol standards, IPSec provides application support for all uses within TCP/IP, including VPNs. This protocol combines several different cryptosystems:

- Diffie-Hellman key exchange for deriving key material between peers on a public network
- Public key cryptography for signing the Diffie-Hellman exchanges to guarantee the identity of the two parties
- Bulk encryption algorithms, such as DES, for encrypting the data
- Digital certificates signed by a certificate authority to act as digital ID cards[8]

IPSec has two components: (1) the IP Security protocol itself, which specifies the information to be added to an IP packet and indicates how to encrypt packet data, and (2) the Internet Key Exchange (IKE), which uses asymmetric key exchange and negotiates the security associations.

IPSec operates in two modes: transport and tunnel. In **transport mode**, only the IP data is encrypted—not the IP headers themselves. This allows intermediate nodes to read the source and destination addresses. In **tunnel mode**, the entire IP packet is encrypted and inserted as the payload in another IP packet. This requires other systems at the beginning and end of the tunnel to act as proxies to send and receive the encrypted packets. These systems then transmit the decrypted packets to their true destinations.

IPSec and other cryptographic extensions to TCP/IP are often used to support a **virtual private network (VPN)** as was described in Chapter 5 and is further discussed in Chapter 11. A VPN is a private, secure network operated over a public and insecure network. It keeps the contents of the network messages hidden from observers who may have access to public traffic. Using the VPN tunneling approach described earlier, an individual or organization can set up a network connection on the Internet and send encrypted data back and forth, using the IP-packet-within-an-IP-packet method to deliver the data safely and securely. VPN support is built into most Microsoft Server software, including Windows 2000, and client support for VPN services is included in Windows XP. While true private network services can cost hundreds of thousands of dollars to lease, configure, and maintain, a VPN can be established for much less.

Securing Authentication

A final use of cryptosystems is to provide enhanced and secure authentication. One approach to this issue is provided by **Kerberos**, named after the three-headed dog of Greek mythology (*Cerberus* in Latin) that guarded the gates to the underworld. Kerberos uses symmetric key encryption to validate an individual user's access to various network resources. It keeps a database containing the private keys of clients and servers that are in the authentication domain that it supervises. Network services running on the servers in the shared authentication domain register with Kerberos, as do clients that wish to use those services.[9] The Kerberos system knows these private keys and can authenticate one network node (client or server) to another. For example, it can authenticate a client to a print service. To understand Kerberos, think of a typical multi-screen cinema. You acquire your ticket at the box office, and the ticket-taker then lets you in to the proper screen based on the contents of your ticket. Kerberos also generates temporary session keys—that is, private keys given to the two parties in a conversation. The session key is used to encrypt all communications between these two parties. Typically a user logs into the network, is authenticated to the Kerberos system, and is then authenticated by the Kerberos system to other resources on the network.

Kerberos consists of three interacting services, all of which rely on a database library:

- Authentication Server (AS), which is a Kerberos server that authenticates clients and servers.
- Key Distribution Center (KDC), which generates and issues session keys.
- Kerberos Ticket-granting service (TGS), which provides tickets to clients who request services. An authorization ticket is an identification card for a particular client that verifies to the server that the client is requesting services and that the client is a valid member of the Kerberos system and, therefore, authorized to receive services. The ticket consists of the client's name and network address, a ticket validation starting and ending time, and the session key, all encrypted in the private key of the target server.

Kerberos operates according to the following principles:

1. The KDC knows the secret keys of all clients and servers on the network.
2. The KDC initially exchanges information with the client and server by using the secret keys.
3. Kerberos authenticates a client to a requested service on a server through TGS and by issuing temporary session keys for communications between the client and the KDC, the server and the KDC, and the client and the server.
4. Communication takes place between the client and server using the temporary session keys.[10]

Figures 9-7 and 9-8 illustrate this process.

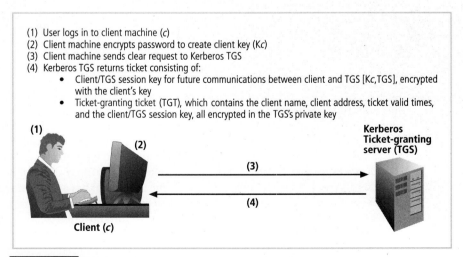

(1) User logs in to client machine (*c*)
(2) Client machine encrypts password to create client key (K*c*)
(3) Client machine sends clear request to Kerberos TGS
(4) Kerberos TGS returns ticket consisting of:
- Client/TGS session key for future communications between client and TGS [K*c*,TGS], encrypted with the client's key
- Ticket-granting ticket (TGT), which contains the client name, client address, ticket valid times, and the client/TGS session key, all encrypted in the TGS's private key

(1)
(2)
Client (*c*)

Kerberos Ticket-granting server (TGS)

(3)
(4)

FIGURE 9-7 Kerberos Login

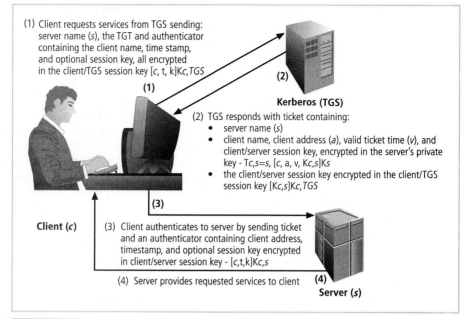

(1) Client requests services from TGS sending: server name (*s*), the TGT and authenticator containing the client name, time stamp, and optional session key, all encrypted in the client/TGS session key [*c*, t, k]K*c*,*TGS*

(1)

(2)

Kerberos (TGS)

(2) TGS responds with ticket containing:
- server name (*s*)
- client name, client address (*a*), valid ticket time (*v*), and client/server session key, encrypted in the server's private key - T*c*,*s*=*s*, [*c*, a, v, K*c*,*s*]K*s*
- the client/server session key encrypted in the client/TGS session key [K*c*,*s*]K*c*,*TGS*

(3)

Client (*c*)

(3) Client authenticates to server by sending ticket and an authenticator containing client address, timestamp, and optional session key encrypted in client/server session key - [*c*,t,k]K*c*,*s*

(4) Server provides requested services to client **(4)**

Server (*s*)

FIGURE 9-8 Kerberos Request for Service

You can obtain Kerberos free of charge from MIT at *http://itinfo.mit.edu/ product.php?name=kerberos*. If you decide to use it, however, be aware of some concerns in its operation. If the Kerberos servers are subjected to denial-of-service attacks, no client can request (or receive) any services. If the Kerberos servers, service providers, or clients' machines become compromised, their private key information may also be compromised.

Attacks on Cryptosystems

Historically, attempts to gain unauthorized access to secure communications have used brute force attacks in which the ciphertext is repeatedly searched for clues that can lead to the algorithm's structure. These attacks are known as ciphertext attacks, and involve a hacker searching for a common text structure, wording, or syntax in the encrypted message that can enable him or her to calculate the number of each type of letter used in the message. This process, known as frequency analysis, can be used along with published frequency of occurrence patterns of various languages and can allow an experienced attacker to crack quickly almost any code if the individual has a large enough sample of the encoded text. To protect against this, modern algorithms attempt to remove the repetitive and predictable sequences of characters from the ciphertext.

Occasionally, an attacker may obtain duplicate texts, one in ciphertext and one in plaintext, which enable the individual to reverse-engineer the encryption algorithm in a **known-plaintext attack** scheme. Alternatively, an attacker may conduct a **selected-plaintext attack** by sending the potential victim a specific text that they are sure the victim will forward on to others. When the victim does encrypt and forward the message, it can be used in the attack if the attacker can acquire the outgoing encrypted version. At the very least, reverse engineering can usually lead the attacker to discover the cryptosystem that is being employed.

Most publicly available encryption methods are generally released to the user community for testing of the encryption algorithm's resistance to cracking. In addition, attackers are kept informed of which methods of attack have failed. Although the purpose of sharing this information is to develop a more secure algorithm, it has the danger of preventing attackers from wasting their time—thus freeing them up to find new weaknesses in the cryptosystem or new, more challenging means of obtaining encryption keys.

In general, attacks on cryptosystems fall into four general categories: man-in-the-middle, correlation, dictionary, and timing. Although many of these attacks have been discussed elsewhere, they are reiterated here in the context of cryptosystems and their impact on these systems.

Man-in-the-Middle Attack

A **man-in-the-middle attack** is a method used to intercept the transmission of a public key or even to insert a known key structure in place of the requested public key. Thus, attackers attempt to place themselves between the sender and receiver, and once they've intercepted the request for key exchanges, they send each participant a valid public key, which is known only to them. From the perspective of the victims of such attacks, their encrypted communication appears to be occurring normally, but in fact the attacker is receiving each encrypted message and decoding it (with the key given to the sending party), and then encrypting and sending it to the originally intended recipient. Establishment of public keys with digital signatures can prevent the traditional man-in-the-middle attack, as the attacker cannot duplicate the signatures.

Correlation Attacks

As the complexities of encryption methods have increased, so too have the tools and methods of cryptanalysts in their attempts to attack cryptosystems. **Correlation attacks** are a collection of brute-force methods that attempt to deduce statistical relationships between the structure of the unknown key and the ciphertext that is the output of the cryptosystem. Differential and linear cryptanalysis, both of which are advanced methods of breaking codes that are beyond the scope of this discussion, have been used to mount successful attacks on block cipher encryptions such as DES. If these advanced approaches can calculate the value of the public key, and if this can be achieved in a reasonable time, all messages written with that key can be decrypted. The only defense against this kind of attack is the selection of strong cryptosystems that have stood the test of time and thorough key management with strict adherence to the best practices of cryptography in the frequency of changing keys.

Dictionary Attacks

In a **dictionary attack**, the attacker encrypts every word in a dictionary using the same cryptosystem as used by the target. The attacker does this in an attempt to locate a match between the target ciphertext and the list of encrypted words from the same cryptosystem.

Dictionary attacks can be successful when the ciphertext consists of relatively few characters, for example, files which contain encrypted usernames and passwords. If an attacker acquires a system password file, the individual can run hundreds of thousands of potential passwords from the dictionary he or she has prepared against the stolen list. Most computer systems use a well-known one-way hash function to store passwords in such files, but this can almost always allow the attacker to find at least a few matches in any stolen password file. After a match is located, the attacker has essentially identified a potential valid password for the system under attack.

Timing Attacks

In a **timing attack**, the attacker eavesdrops during the victim's session and uses statistical analysis of the user's typing patterns and inter-keystroke timings to discern sensitive session information. While timing analysis may not directly result in the decryption of sensitive data, it can be used to gain information about the encryption key and perhaps the cryptosystem in use. It may also eliminate some algorithms as possible candidates, thus narrowing the attacker's search. In this narrower field of options, the attacker can increase the odds of eventual success. Once the attacker has successfully broken an encryption, he or she may launch a **replay attack**, which is an attempt to resubmit a recording of the deciphered authentication to gain entry into a secure source.

Defending from Attacks

Encryption is a very useful tool in protecting the confidentiality of information that is in storage and/or transmission. However, it is just that—another tool in the information security administrator's arsenal of weapons against threats to information security. Frequently, unenlightened individuals describe information security exclusively in terms of encryption (and possibly firewalls and anti-virus software). But encryption is simply the process of hiding the true meaning of information. Over the millennia, mankind has developed dramatically more sophisticated means of hiding information from those who should not see it. No matter how sophisticated encryption and cryptosystems have become, however, they have retained the same flaw that the first systems contained thousands of years ago: If you discover the key, that is, the method used to perform the encryption, you can determine the message. Thus, key management is not so much the management of technology but rather the management of people.

Encryption can, however, protect information when it is most vulnerable—that is, when it is outside the organization's systems. Information in transit through public or leased networks is an example of information that is outside the organization's control. With loss of control can come loss of security. Encryption helps organizations secure information that must travel through public and leased networks by guarding the information against the efforts of those who sniff, spoof, and otherwise skulk around. As such, encryption is a vital piece of the security puzzle.

Chapter Summary

- Encryption is the process of rendering information unreadable to all but the intended recipients. The purpose of encryption is to preserve the integrity and confidentiality of information and/or make the process of authenticating users more effective.

- Firewalls use encryption both to provide protection for the data in transit and to help keep the firewall secure. Encryption of data incurs costs since it requires processing time to encrypt and decrypt the data being protected.

- The science of encryption is known as cryptology. Cryptography is the complex process of making and using codes. Applying these concealing techniques is called encryption, and decoding the ciphertext is called decryption. The process used to decrypt data when the process and/or keys are unknown is called cryptanalysis.

- Cryptographic controls are the techniques and tools used to implement cryptographic protections in networks and information systems. They are used to secure e-mail, Web access, Web applications, file transfers, and remote access procedures like VPNs. Other controls can be applied to secure the authentication processes, like Kerberos.

- Cryptographic control systems are often subject to attack. Many methods of attack have evolved including some that use brute computational approaches and others that make use of weaknesses that are often found in the implementation of cryptographic controls. Some attacks, known as man-in-the-middle attacks, attempt to inject themselves between the parties of a secured communication channel. Others combine multiple brute-force approaches like dictionary attacks and timing attacks into one so-called correlation attack.

Review Questions

1. What is cryptology?
2. What is cryptography?
3. How is encryption used to secure networks in general, and how is it used in firewalls?
4. Which aspect of digital data passing between networks is preserved by cryptography?
5. Which functions of a firewall might not be compatible with, or are compromised by using, encryption?
6. What problems encountered by firewalls are made worse by using encryption?
7. What name is given to an attack in which the attacker intercepts a public key exchange and acts as a go-between for the network session?
8. What name is given to an attack in which the attacker guesses a key value or password?
9. What name is given to an attack in which the attacker guesses a key value or password from a list of possible values?
10. What is the difference between a digital signature and a digital certificate?
11. What is the main advantage of using symmetric encryption?
12. What is the advantage of using asymmetric encryption?
13. You handle security for a corporation with 10 branch offices and 5,000 employees. You are tasked with issuing security keys to each of these employees. How would you handle this?
14. What is IPSec?

15. What does an IPSec policy do?

16. What is a digital certificate?

17. IPSec has two modes and two protocols. Explain which combination of modes and protocols gives you the highest level of protection.

18. What can digital certificates authenticate that IPSec cannot?

19. Digital certificates contain digital signatures and public keys as well as detailed information about the digital certificate holder. However, the quality of all that information depends on one thing that neither you nor the digital certificate holder can control. What is it?

20. What is a hybrid security control?

Exercises

1. Use a browser connected to the Internet to research Pretty Good Privacy (PGP). Be sure to read at least two different Web sites. Then answer these questions:
   a. Who is Phil Zimmerman and what is his relationship to PGP?
   b. What is a web of trust? What is the alternative to a web of trust?
   c. What year was PGP released?
   d. What is the relationship between the company Network Associates and PGP?

2. Use a browser connected to the Internet to research Secure Sockets Layer (SSL). Be sure to read at least two different Web sites. Then answer these questions:
   a. Briefly describe SSL.
   b. How is SSL different from TLS? How is it similar?
   c. What RFC first defined the TLS/SSL protocol?

3. Use a browser connected to the Internet to research Advanced Encryption Standard (AES). Be sure to read at least two different Web sites. Then answer these questions:
   a. What was this cipher's name before it was adopted as the AES?
   b. When did the National Institute of Standards and Technology announce the AES?
   c. What is the AES's fixed block size? What are its possible key sizes?

4. Use a browser connected to the Internet to research symmetric encryption and asymmetric encryption. Be sure to read at least two different Web sites for each term. Then answer these questions:
   a. Which type of encryption can be computed more quickly?
   b. In what way are the two approaches to encryption the same?
   c. How are these two approaches different?
   d. How are these two methods used together to provide a better way to do encryption?

5. Use a browser connected to the Internet to research digital signatures and digital certificates. Be sure to read at least two different Web sites for each term. Then answer these questions:
   a. What are the typical component parts of a digital certificate?
   b. What international standard controls how digital certificates are used?
   c. How are digital signatures related to digital certificates?

Case Exercises

Maris opened her laptop and connected her browser to the Linen Planet Web server. The firewall asked for her username and password. She flipped open her notepad and punched in the data she had written down while eavesdropping on Padma's cell phone call.

Her browser connected in no time. She noticed that the security icon was showing at the bottom of her browser window. The encryption between her browser and the server was now in place. At least no other hackers could watch her while she put a back door into Linen Planet's Web servers. She would spend several hours over the next few days scouting out the network and planning her raid. It looked like she would be able to buy that new game system sooner than she had planned.

Questions:

1. Was the firewall and Web server used by Linen Planet providing encryption services? If so, what kind of protection was in place?

2. How could the access to Linen Planet's Web server have been better secured?

Endnotes

1. Ronald L. Krutz and Russell Dean Vines, *The CISSP Prep Guide: Mastering the Ten Domains of Computer Security* (New York: John Wiley & Sons, Inc., 2001), 131.

2. Savard, John (1999). "The Advanced Encryption Standard (Rijndael)" Viewed online March 31, 2004, at *http://home.ecn.ab.ca/~jsavard/crypto/co040401.htm.*

3. Steve Burnett and Stephen Paine, *RSA Security's Official Guide to Cryptography* (New York: Osborne/McGraw-Hill, 2001).

4. Special thanks to our reviewer for this example: Robert Statica, Associate Director, Cryptography and Telecommunications Laboratory, New Jersey Institute of Technology.

5. Steve Burnett and Stephen Paine, *RSA Security's Official Guide to Cryptography* (New York: Osborne/McGraw-Hill, 2001).

6. Steve Burnett and Stephen Paine, *RSA Security's Official Guide to Cryptography* (New York: Osborne/McGraw-Hill, 2001).

7. Verisign. Understanding PKI. *Verisign Online.* Accessed November 22, 2006, from *verisign.netscape.com/security/pki/understanding.html.*

8. Cisco Systems, Inc. White Paper: IPSec. *Cisco Online,* November 21, 2000. Accessed November 22, 2006, from *www.cisco.com/en/US/tech/tk827/tk369/tech_white_papers_list.html.*

9. Jennifer G. Steiner, Clifford Neuman, and Jeffrey I. Schiller. An authentication service for open network systems (paper presented for Project Athena, March 30, 1988). Accessed November 22, 2006, from *www.scs.stanford.edu/nyu/05sp/sched/readings/kerberos.pdf.*

10. Ronald L. Krutz and Russell Dean Vines. *The CISSP Prep Guide: Mastering the Ten Domains of Computer Security.* New York: John Wiley & Sons, Inc., 2001:40.

Authenticating Users

10

> The reason why any one refuses his assent […] is in you: he refuses to accept you as a bringer of truth, because, though you think you have it, he feels that you have it not. You have not given him the authentic sign.
>
> **RALPH WALDO EMERSON**

NIKI SIMPSON WAS IN THE CONFERENCE ROOM WAITING for the training session to begin. She was at the session because her user account credentials had been used by an unidentified attacker, attempting to access the school computer system. She had been an employee of the local school district for 12 years, and this was her first formal training in information security.

Three hours and thirty minutes later, Niki closed her workbook. The trainer said, "And that concludes the basic information security training session for school district employees. Are there any questions?"

Niki raised her hand. When the trainer acknowledged her, she said, "OK. I understand that the district policy is to have a twelve-character password of nonsense syllables that are changed by the system every 30 days. I also understand we are not supposed to write the new passwords down on anything. Any suggestions on how I am supposed to remember this password?"

The trainer said, "I really can't say. I suppose you'll just have to memorize the new password before you clear the screen when it is assigned to you."

Niki's mouth dropped open. She said to the trainer, "That's easy for you to say, but I think I'm going to have a hard time with that."

LEARNING OBJECTIVES:

Upon completion of this material, you should be able to do the following:

- Explain why authentication is a critical aspect of network security
- Explain why firewalls authenticate and how they identify users
- Describe user, client, and session authentication
- List the advantages and disadvantages of popular centralized authentication systems
- Discuss the potential weaknesses of password security systems
- Discuss the use of password security tools
- Describe common authentication protocols used by firewalls

Introduction

Firewall security strategies, such as packet filtering, which are discussed in previous chapters, are used to authenticate machines rather than individuals. Some firewalls can perform a stronger level of authentication—that is, they can reliably determine whether persons or entities are who they claim to be. This level of authentication is important because if an unauthorized user gains access to protected resources, the whole purpose of the firewall has been defeated. For this reason, many firewalls implement user authentication schemes to support their other security approaches. In this chapter, you will learn what authentication is and why it is important to network security in general. Then you'll learn how and why firewalls perform authentication services. This chapter also introduces the main types of authentication performed by firewalls—client, user, and session authentication—as well as the different types of centralized authentication methods that firewalls can use, including Kerberos, TACACS+, and RADIUS. Because passwords are a critical part of all of the aforementioned authentication schemes, you'll explore password security issues, and learn about special password security tools, including one-time passwords. The chapter ends with a section on the different authentication protocols used by full-featured enterprise-level firewalls.

The Authentication Process in General

Authentication is the act of confirming the identity of a potential user. Once the identity is confirmed as authentic, that user is authorized to perform specific actions on the system or network. Potential users (sometimes called supplicants) first propose an identity and then verify that identity by providing:

- A piece of information known to the supplicant, such as a password or passphrase (something you know)
- Proof of physical possession of something, such as a **smart card** (a plastic card with an embedded microchip that can store data about the owner) or even a metal key (something you have)

■ A piece of information that is a measurement or evaluation of the physical nature of a supplicant (something you are)—this can be subdivided into measurements of physical attributes (fingerprints or iris scans) or pattern evaluation and recognition (perhaps a voiceprint or a keyboard typing pattern)

If you have a bank card that enables you to withdraw cash from a debit account, you have made use of a smart card. Along with the card (something you have) you also need to enter a PIN (something you know) to authenticate yourself to the bank's network. After you are authenticated, the ATM gives you access to your account. When an authentication system uses two different forms of confirming the proposed identity, it is said to use **strong authentication**.

In the field of network computing, authentication takes one of two specific forms:

■ *Local authentication*: A server maintains a local file of usernames and passwords that it refers to for matching the username-password pair being supplied by a client. This is the most common form of authentication, the weakness of which is that passwords can be forgotten, stolen, or accidentally revealed.

■ *Centralized authentication service*: A centralized server handles three separate and essential authentication practices: authentication, authorization, and auditing (AAA). Authentication, as you have already seen, is the process of identifying someone who wishes to use network services. Authorization is the process of determining what users are and are not allowed to do on the network based on their identity. **Auditing** is the recording (usually in a log file) of authentication and authorization activities.

Both types of authentication might require a user to enter a password at some point, which by itself is an example of single-factor authentication: the user only needs to know one item (the password) to initiate the authentication process. Physical objects such as smart cards or other kinds of physical **tokens** offer a more stringent level of two-factor authentication in which users need to have something (the token) and know something (the PIN or password) to gain access. Two-factor authentication can be used to strengthen either of the aforementioned systems, but it is most commonly used with a centralized authentication server.

Biometrics (retinal scans, fingerprints, and the like) is used for authentication mainly by large security-minded entities such as banking institutions and credit card centers, for regulating access to sensitive information, but its use is gaining ground in the general corporate world.

How Firewalls Implement the Authentication Process

Most operating systems are equipped with authentication schemes. Web servers can be configured to authenticate clients who want to access certain protected content. Firewalls, too, can perform **user authentication**. In fact, many organizations depend on firewalls to provide more secure authentication than conventional systems. Authentication is a key function because firewalls exist to give external users (such as mobile users and telecommuters) access to protected resources.

Authentication comes into play when a firewall is called upon to apply its set of rules to specific individuals or groups of users. For instance, the IT staff may need access to all computers in the organization, and, thus, a higher level of security is needed to ensure that only the proper individuals are granted such a level of access. On the other hand, the head of a company's accounting department may need remote access to another company once a quarter or once a year—not frequently enough to warrant the establishment of a VPN between the two companies' LANs.

A firewall uses authentication to identify individuals so that it can apply rules that have been associated with those individuals. Some firewalls use authentication to give employees access to common resources such as the Web or File Transfer Protocol (FTP). Some identify the user associated with a particular IP address; after the user is authorized, the IP address can then be used to send and receive information with hosts on the internal network.

The exact steps that firewalls follow to authenticate users may vary, but the general process is the same:

1. The client makes a request to access a resource.
2. The firewall intercepts the request and prompts the user for name and password.
3. The user submits the requested information to the firewall.
4. The user is authenticated.
5. The request is checked against the firewall's rule base.
6. If the request matches an existing allow rule, the user is granted access.
7. The user accesses the desired resources.

The "plain English" version of the exchange between external client and authenticating firewall is illustrated in Figure 10-1.

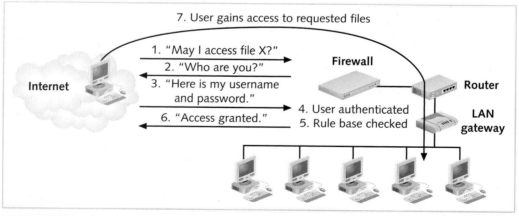

FIGURE 10-1   Basic User Authentication

Firewall Authentication Methods

Some firewalls, such as Check Point FireWall-1, provide for a variety of different authentication methods, including user, client, or session authentication.

User Authentication

User authentication is the simplest type of authentication, and the one with which you are most likely to be familiar. Upon receiving a request, a program prompts the user for a username and password. When the information is submitted, the software checks the information against a list of usernames and passwords in its database. If a match is made, the user is authenticated. User authentication for the program NetProxy is shown in Figure 10-2.

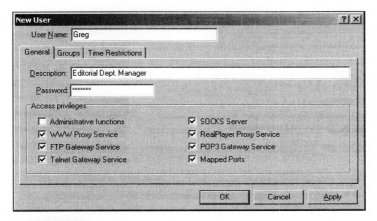

FIGURE 10-2   NetProxy Authentication

User authentication can enable the following users to access your internal servers:

- Employees who work remotely or who are traveling
- Contractors who work on-site
- Freelancers who work off-site
- Visitors who want to do some work or take a look at your system from your offices
- Employees in branch offices
- Interns
- Employees of partner companies
- Members of the public who may need to get into your internal network to make purchases, change contact information, or review account information

Authorized users should be added to your **access control lists (ACLs)**. The ACLs can be organized by directory, or even by individual files, but most often ACLs are organized by groups of users because this simplifies administration. How you organize the ACLs depends on how many users you have, how many resources you need to protect, and how much time you have to administer the ACL.

Client Authentication

Of course, not every outside user can or should gain access to everything on the network. Client authentication can help you establish limits to user access.

Client authentication is similar to user authentication but with the addition of usage limits. The firewall enables the authenticated user to access the desired resources for a specific period of time (for instance, one hour) or for a specific number of times (three accesses, for instance).

For example, NetProxy lets you assign time limits by double-clicking the name of a configured user group and then editing the settings in the Time Restrictions tab (see Figure 10-3).

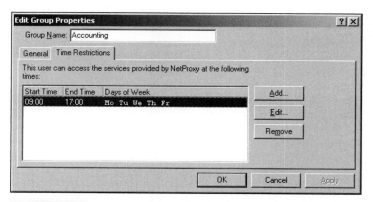

FIGURE 10-3   Example of Time Limited Authentication

To configure client authentication, you need to set up one of two types of authentication systems:

- A **standard sign-on** system, in which the client, after being successfully authenticated, is allowed to access whatever resources the user needs or perform any desired functions, such as transferring files or viewing Web pages
- A **specific sign-on** system, in which clients must authenticate each time they access a server or use a service on the protected network

Session Authentication

Session authentication requires authentication whenever a client system attempts to connect to a network resource and establish a session (a period when communications are exchanged). Session authentication can be used with any service. The client system wishing to be authenticated is usually equipped with a software agent that enables the authentication process; the server or firewall detects the agent when the connection request is made. When necessary, the firewall intercepts the connection request and contacts the agent. The agent performs the authentication, and the firewall allows the connection to the required resource.

Some advanced firewalls offer multiple authentication methods; which one should you choose? The choice depends on the client operating system and the applications you need to authenticate. Choose user authentication if the protocols you want authorized users to use include FTP, HTTP, HTTPS, rlogin, or Telnet. Client authentication or session authentication should be used when only a single user is coming from a single IP address. Table 10-1 gives the reasons for using each service.

TABLE 10-1 Authentication Methods

Method	Use When...
User Authentication	■ You want to scan the content of IP packets
	■ The protocol in use is HTTP, HTTPS, FTP, rlogin, or Telnet
	■ You need to authenticate for each session separately
Client Authentication	■ The user to be authenticated will use a specific IP address
	■ The protocol in use is not HTTP, HTTPS, FTP, rlogin, or Telnet
	■ You want a user to be authenticated for a specific length of time
Session Authentication	■ The individual user to be authenticated will come from a specific IP address
	■ The protocol in use is not HTTP, HTTPS, FTP, rlogin, or Telnet
	■ You want a client to be authenticated for each session

Centralized Authentication

Large corporations can easily develop a complex set of security requirements that are difficult to maintain, and that require different types of authentication control for different purposes. Fortunately, deploying a centralized authentication server can greatly simplify such enterprise-wide authentication. This centralized server maintains all the authorizations for users regardless of where the user is located and how the user connects to the network.

In a centralized authentication setup, a server—which is sometimes referred to as an **authentication, authorization, and auditing (AAA) server**—alleviates the need to provide each server on the network with a separate database of usernames and passwords, each of which would have to be updated individually each time a password changed or a user was added. The process of centralized authentication is illustrated in Figure 10-4: a client on a local network requests access to a program held on an application server, but first the client must be authenticated using the authentication server. Two levels of trust are involved: the client trusts that the authentication server holds the correct information, as indicated by number 2 in Figure 10-4, and the application server trusts that the authentication server can correctly identity and authorize the client, as indicated by number 3 in Figure 10-4. The scenario illustrated in Figure 10-4 has a substantial downside: the authentication server becomes a single point of failure. Organizations that use this method should also have contingency plans in place to get the server back online or provide alternative servers to limit downtime.

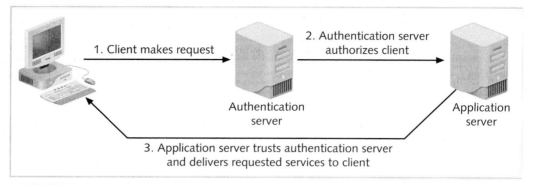

1. Client makes request
2. Authentication server authorizes client

Authentication server

Application server

3. Application server trusts authentication server and delivers requested services to client

FIGURE 10-4 Centralized Authentication

Centralized authentication can use a number of different authentication methods. The following sections examine some of the most common ones, including Kerberos, TACACS+, and RADIUS.

Kerberos

Kerberos was developed at the Massachusetts Institute of Technology (MIT) in the university's Athena Project. Kerberos is designed to provide authentication and encryption on standard clients and servers. Instead of a server having to trust a client over an untrusted network, both client and server place their trust in the Kerberos server. Kerberos provides an effective network authentication system that is used internally on Windows 2000 and XP systems. It also has backward compatibility with Microsoft's NTLM protocol, which is used in Windows NT 4.0 and earlier. Although Kerberos is useful on internal networks, it is not recommended for authentication of outside users because it uses **cleartext** passwords. Remote users should make use of encrypted transmissions or **one-time passwords**, which are discussed later in this chapter.

The Kerberos system of granting access to a client that requests a service is quite involved (and thus quite secure). The steps are as follows:

1. The client requests a file or other service.
2. The client is prompted for a username and password.
3. The client submits a username and password. The request goes to an Authentication Server (AS) that is part of the Kerberos system. The AS creates an encrypted code called a **session key** that is based on the client's password plus a random number that is associated with the service being requested. The session key functions as a **Ticket-granting ticket (TGT)**.
4. AS grants the TGT.
5. The client presents the TGT to a **Ticket-granting server (TGS)**, which is also part of the Kerberos system and that may or may not be the same server as the AS.
6. The TGS grants a session ticket. The TGS forwards the session ticket to the server holding the requested file or service.
7. The client gains access.

The Kerberos authentication server is also known as a Key Distribution Center (KDC). In Windows 2000 or XP, a domain controller also functions as an authentication server. The Kerberos server must be highly secured because of the strong level of trust placed in it.

One great advantage of using the Kerberos ticket system is that passwords are not stored on the system and thus cannot be intercepted by hackers. The tickets issued are specific to the individual user who made the request and to the services the user is attempting to access. Tickets have a time limit (typically, eight hours, though this can be configured by the security administrator). Before a ticket expires, the client may make additional requests using the same ticket without reauthenticating. Another advantage is that Kerberos is widely used in the UNIX environment, which enables authentication to take place across operating systems: a Windows client can be authenticated by a UNIX server, and vice versa. The authentication process is illustrated in Figure 10-5. You can download trial versions of both the Kerberos client and server from the U.S. Department of Defense (DoD) High Performance Computing Modernization Program (*www.hpcmo.hpc.mil/security/kerberos/*).

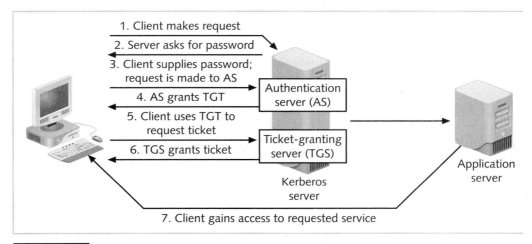

FIGURE 10-5   Kerberos Authentication

TACACS+

Terminal Access Controller Access Control System Plus (TACACS+)—commonly called "tac-plus"—is the latest and strongest version of a set of authentication protocols developed by Cisco Systems. TACACS+ replaces its less-secure predecessor protocols, TACACS and XTACACS. All of these protocols provide what Cisco has dubbed the **AAA services** that form an essential part of a dial-up environment:

- Authentication
- Authorization
- Auditing

TACACS+ and its predecessor protocols all provide authentication for dial-in users and are used primarily on UNIX-based networks. TACACS+ uses the **MD5** algorithm (a formula that produces a 128-bit code called a **message digest**) to encrypt data. It provides centralized authentication services so that a network access server such as a router or firewall doesn't have to handle dial-in user authentication. You might have to use TACACS+ or RADIUS (described in the following section) if your firewall doesn't support authentication or if your authentication needs are so extensive that they might slow down other tasks the firewall is called on to perform. For more information about the

MD5 algorithm and other security tools, visit the CERT Web site at *www.cert.org/ tech_tips/security_tools.html.*

Remote Authentication Dial-In User Service (RADIUS)

Remote Authentication Dial-In User Service (RADIUS) is the other common protocol used to provide dial-in authentication. Note that RADIUS still transmits authentication packets unencrypted across the network, which means they are vulnerable to attacks from packet sniffers. RADIUS is generally considered to provide a lower level of security than TACACS+, even though it's more widely supported.

TACACS+ and RADIUS Compared

If you authenticate remote users who connect to your network from remote locations, chances are you'll use either TACACS+ or RADIUS. The following sections examine the relative strength of security, filtering characteristics, proxy characteristics, and NAT characteristics of TACACS+ and RADIUS.

Strength of Security

Table 10-2 summarizes the characteristics of TACACS+ and RADIUS.

TABLE 10-2 Characteristics of TACACS+ and RADIUS

TACACS+	RADIUS
Uses TCP	Uses UDP
Full packet encryption between client and server	Encrypts only passwords—other information is unencrypted
Independent authentication, authorization, and auditing	Combines authentication and authorization
Passwords in the database may be encrypted	Passwords in the database are in cleartext

All the items in Table 10-2 indicate that TACACS+ provides stronger security than RADIUS. TCP is considered more secure than User Datagram Protocol (UDP), an alternative network communications protocol, because when a host sends a TCP packet, it expects a packet to be sent in response, with the ACK bit sent to show that a connection has been established. ACK (for acknowledgment), is one of the flags in the TCP header part of a packet, and indicates that the destination computer has received the packets that were previously sent. UDP, in contrast, is considered "connectionless." If a UDP packet is sent, an acknowledgment packet is not sent. If the destination host doesn't receive the packet, it simply asks for the packet to be re-sent.

TCP traffic can be filtered by firewalls based on the presence of the ACK bit. TACACS+ also does full-packet encryption, and handles accounting (that is, auditing or logging) as well as authentication and authorization; RADIUS stores passwords in cleartext. Note, however, that if you use both a firewall and an authentication server, the encryption benefits of TACACS+ aren't as dramatic because the firewall receives communications directly from the Internet, and the firewall and authentication server communicate with one another over a trusted network. RADIUS can be a viable solution in this type of network configuration.

Filtering Characteristics

TACACS+ uses TCP Port 49, so in order to use it you need to set up rules that enable clients to exchange authorization packets with the TACACS+ or RADIUS server. RADIUS uses UDP Port 1812 for authentication and UDP Port 1813 for auditing. Table 10-3 shows a set of packet-filtering rules that enables users on an internal network that is protected by a firewall to be authenticated by a TACACS+ or RADIUS server.

TABLE 10-3 Filtering Rules for TACACS+ and RADIUS

Direction	Protocol	Source Port	Destination Port	Remarks
Inbound	TCP	All ports > 1023	49	Enables external client to connect to internal TACACS+ server
Outbound	TCP	49	All ports > 1023	Allows internal TACACS+ server to respond to external client
Inbound	UDP	All ports >1023	1812	Allows external client to connect to internal RADIUS server
Outbound	UDP	1812	All ports > 1023	Allows internal RADIUS server to respond to external client
Inbound	UDP	All ports > 1023	1813	Enables auditing when external client connects to RADIUS server
Outbound	UDP	1813	All ports > 1023	Enables auditing when internal RADIUS server responds to a client

Proxy Characteristics

Note that RADIUS doesn't work with generic proxy systems. However, a RADIUS server can function as a proxy server, speaking to other RADIUS servers or other services that do authorization, such as Windows domain authentication.

TACACS+ does work with generic proxy systems. Because some TACACS+ systems use the same IP address to generate the key, you may need a dedicated proxy that has its own encryption key.

NAT Characteristics

RADIUS doesn't work with NAT. Addresses that are intended to go through NAT need to be static, not dynamic.

TACACS+ should work with NAT systems, but because TACACS+ supports encryption using a secret key shared between server and client, there is no way for the server to know which key to use if different clients make use of different keys. Static IP address mappings work best because some TACACS+ systems use the source IP address to create the encryption key.

Password Security Issues

Many authentication systems depend in part or entirely on passwords. The simplest forms of authentication require typing a username and a reusable password. This method is truly secure for controlling only outbound Internet access because password guessing and eavesdropping attacks are likely on inbound access attempts.

The following sections discuss password security issues that you need to be aware of to prevent your network from being accessed by unauthorized users.

Passwords That Can Be Cracked

Systems that rely on passwords for authentication can be **cracked**—that is, accessed by an unauthorized user—in a number of different ways. An attacker might:

- Find a way to authenticate without knowing the password
- Uncover the password from the system that holds it
- Guess the password

Passwords that are transmitted or stored in cleartext (plain, unencrypted text) are easy to crack because they are readable. Systems that exchange **hashed** passwords (passwords that have been encrypted) that a hacker can copy and reuse as is (that is, in their encrypted format) also create vulnerabilities. You can avoid both by ensuring that your network's authorized users protect passwords effectively and observe some simple security habits.

Password Vulnerabilities

Passwords have a number of built-in vulnerabilities. The more obvious ones include:

- Passwords are often easy to guess because they haven't been thought through by users.
- Passwords are often stored on sticky notes or papers displayed in readily visible areas.
- Passwords can be uncovered by "social engineering"—fooling users into giving out information.

You can reduce the chances that passwords will be stolen or guessed by telling individual users to choose passwords that are complicated enough not to be guessed easily. They should also be coached to memorize the passwords rather than store them in writing and to never give out the passwords to anyone.

Lax Security Habits

Large organizations can't keep tabs on everyone who works outside the office and who needs to access internal resources. In addition, in partner organizations, passwords might get copied and shared in ways the original organization can't control.

To maintain some level of integrity, some corporations draw up a formal **Memorandum of Understanding (MOU)** with their partner companies. In an MOU, both parties formally agree to observe a set of rules of behavior. The MOU usually states what outsiders can do on the network or with passwords and states that any other use is forbidden. An MOU spells out who bears responsibility for critical resources as well as system maintenance, and it lists whom to contact in case questions arise or help is needed.

Password Security Tools

The risks introduced by poor password management can be offset by passwords that are generated for one-time use with each session and then discarded. In addition, Linux makes use of a "shadow password system" that also makes passwords difficult, if not impossible, to crack.

One-Time Password Software

The many problems associated with passwords and the ease of cracking them are alleviated by a one-time password. Two types of one-time passwords are available:

- *Challenge-response passwords*: The authenticating computer or firewall generates a random number (the challenge) and sends it to the user, who enters a secret PIN or password (the response). If the code and PIN or password match the information stored on the authenticating server, the user gains access.

- *Password list passwords*: You enter a seed phrase, and the password system generates a list of passwords you can use. You pick one from the list and submit it along with the seed phrase to gain access.

For inbound access, one-time passwords using a scheme, such as Bellcore's S/KEY, provide a higher level of security. Users type a different password each time they connect. (See the section on S/Key later in this chapter for a more detailed description.)

An even higher level of security is realized by some firewalls that work with hardware devices called token generators, which automatically generate and display the next password the user types. (See the sections on SecurID and Axent Pathways Defender later in this chapter for more information.)

The Shadow Password System

Linux stores passwords in the **/etc/passwd** file in encrypted format. The passwords are encrypted using a one-way hash function: an algorithm that is easy to compute when encrypting passwords but very difficult to decrypt.

The algorithm begins to encrypt the password after receiving a randomly generated value called the **salt**. The salt has one of 4096 possible values. Hackers can possibly determine passwords by compiling a database of words and common passwords that can be generated with all of the 4096 possible salt values. The hacker can then compare the encrypted passwords in your /etc/passwd file with their database; if they find a match, they can gain access to your computer or network. Such an attack is called a **dictionary attack**.

The **shadow password system**, which is a feature of the Linux operating system that enables the secure storage of passwords, stores passwords in another file that has restricted access. In addition, passwords are stored only after being encrypted by a randomly generated value and an encoding formula. The key is then stored along with the encrypted password. When a user enters a password, it is encrypted using the same formula and then compared to the stored password; if the passwords match, the user is granted access to the requested system resources.

Other Authentication Systems

Most firewalls that handle authentication make use of one or more well-known systems. Check Point FireWall-1, for instance, uses the two centralized authentication protocols discussed earlier in this chapter, RADIUS and TACACS+. In addition, FireWall-1 can provide access control to other authentication systems, including those mentioned in the following sections.

Single-Password Systems

FireWall-1 supports the use of relatively simple authentication systems. The following simple authentication systems require a user to enter a single password:

- *Operating system password*: FireWall-1, like other firewall programs, gives you the option of forwarding all authentication requests to the operating system of the bastion host on which it resides.
- *Internal firewall password*: If you do not make use of a centralized authentication server, FireWall-1 can function as the repository of static usernames and passwords. In this case, users are required to enter the account name and password information associated with FireWall-1 itself to be authenticated.

One-Time Password Systems

FireWall-1 overcomes the problems associated with single-password systems. Each time the user wishes to authenticate and access resources, a different password is required. As long as the secret key used to generate the password is not divulged, the scheme is secure because hackers cannot pretend to be a particular user by intercepting a password. You should be familiar with the following three types of systems.

Single Key (S/Key)

The S/Key one-time password authentication system uses multiple-word rather than single-word passwords: the user begins by specifying a single-word password and by specifying a number (n) that represents the number of times the password is to be encrypted. The password is then processed by a hash function n times, and the resulting encrypted passwords are stored on the server.

When users attempt to log in, the server prompts them for the password. The server then processes the password $n-1$ times; the result is compared with the stored password set. If the result is the same, the user is granted access. S/Key has the great advantage that it never stores the original password on the server, so the original password cannot be intercepted or "sniffed" by a hacker.

SecurID

SecurID, an authentication system developed by RSA Security Inc., makes use of a highly touted feature called **two-factor authentication**. As the name implies, it requires two things from the user to authenticate:

- *A physical object*: In this case, a SecurID authenticator (or token) that takes the form of a card or "fob"; the token that generates a unique code that is supplied to the user. (Figure 10-6 shows some of the available tokens.)

- *A piece of knowledge*: In this case, the PIN associated with that authenticator.

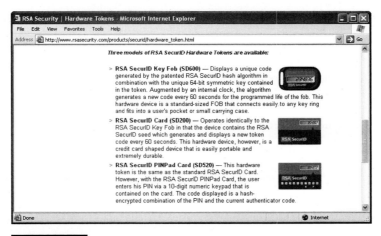

FIGURE 10-6   SecurID Tokens

The SecurID tokens from RSA generate a random code every 60 seconds; the code, along with the associated PIN, is submitted to the authentication server. SecurID is among the most frequently used one-time password solution. There are other providers of this technology, including Authenex and VeriSign. The online payment service PayPal also offers this technology for its customers.

Axent Pathways Defender

Axent Pathways Defender is another two-factor authentication system: it requires the administrator to purchase a Defender token (either a hardware keypad or a software-based keypad) that is used to enter and submit PIN numbers to the authentication server. A **challenge-response** system is used: when you log in to the network, the server responds by sending you a random password—a one-time numeric code. You respond by submitting the same numeric code along with your PIN.

Certificate-Based Authentication

FireWall-1 supports the use of digital certificates, rather than passwords, to authenticate users. An organization using FireWall-1 must set up a public-key infrastructure (PKI) that generates keys for users. The user receives a code called a public key that is generated using the server's private key and uses the public key to send encrypted information to the server. The server receives the public key and can decrypt the information using its private key.

802.1X Wi-Fi Authentication

IEEE 802.1X is one of the fastest growing standards being used in enterprise networks today. It's popular because it supports wireless Ethernet connections (sometimes called Wi-Fi).

This relatively new protocol isn't supported by FireWall-1, but it deserves mention because of the increasing popularity of wireless networks in corporate settings. Wireless networks make it easy for users to connect to the network regardless of inside wiring. At the same time, they present the security administrator with a considerable challenge: without some kind of authentication, any hacker with a laptop computer equipped with a wireless network card who ventures within a few hundred feet of the wireless network can potentially connect to it.

The 802.1X protocol provides for authentication of users on wireless networks. Windows XP can be configured to use such authentication, which also requires the use of a smart card or digital certificate (see Figure 10-7).

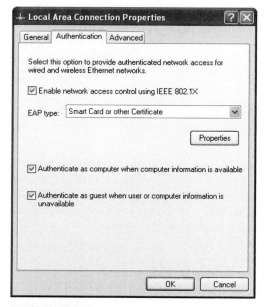

FIGURE 10-7 Wireless Authentication

Wi-Fi makes use of Extensible Authentication Protocol (EAP), which enables a system that uses Wi-Fi to authenticate users on other kinds of network operating systems. For instance, the EAP-MD5 type enables a Windows XP user to authenticate with Ethernet LANs, and the EAP-TLS type works with 802.11b WLANs.

Chapter Summary

- Firewalls authenticate when they need to assign different levels of authorization to different users and groups. By determining that users or computers are really who or what they claim to be, the firewall can then grant access to the needed network resources.

- Firewalls can make use of many different authentication schemes, including user, client, and session authentication. In general, they require a user to supply either something they have (such as a smart card) or something they know (such as a password), or both. The latest authentication systems measure or evaluate a physical attribute, such as a fingerprint or voiceprint.

- In a centralized authentication system, the firewall works in tandem with an authentication server. The authentication server handles the maintenance (or generation) of usernames and passwords as well as login requests and auditing—the process of recording who is and who is not authenticated, and what level of access is granted. Kerberos is a centralized authentication system used by Windows and UNIX, whereas TACACS+ and RADIUS are systems used to authenticate remote users who remotely connect to the network.

- Passwords are an important part of virtually every authentication system and take one of two general forms:

  - Single-word, static password systems receive a password from a user, compare it against a database of passwords, and grant access if a match is made. Such simple password security is vulnerable to the ability of hackers to determine passwords, to user error, and to bad security habits.

  - One-time passwords are generated dynamically each time the user attempts to log on to the network. A secret key is used to generate a single- or multiple-word password. Hardware devices might also generate one-time passwords that, when combined with PIN numbers previously assigned to users, provide an authentication system that is especially difficult to crack.

Review Questions

1. What is authentication? What is a supplicant as the term is used here?
2. What characteristics distinguish user authentication from the other security approaches used by firewalls?
3. What are the factors on which authentication may be based?
4. Which authentication factor is being used by an authenticating server that responds to a login request by generating a random number or code, and expecting to receive that code plus a secret password in return?
5. How is local authentication different from centralized authentication? How is it the same?
6. Identify and define the three elements associated with AAA services.
7. Which type of network environment is not suitable for Kerberos authentication services?
8. Why is Kerberos considered less secure than other authenticating methods?
9. Authentication systems such as Kerberos and RADIUS are more complex to set up and use than other systems, so what is the advantage of using them?
10. What could be the second factor in a two-factor authentication system in addition to a password?
11. What is a token? How is a token different from a biometric measurement? How is it the same?

12.   When should a firewall require authentication?

13.   How are client and session authentication the same? How are they different?

14.   What is Kerberos? Briefly describe how it works.

15.   What is the name given to the service granting tokens used in Kerberos?

16.   What is the advantage of TACACS+ over RADIUS?

17.   Why is a one-time password system considered more secure than a basic authentication system? Provide at least two reasons.

18.   If TACACS+ provides a much stronger level of security than RADIUS, why would you consider using a RADIUS server to authenticate dial-in users?

19.   Which authentication protocol creates one-time passwords that consist of multiple words?

20.   Why is authentication important in wireless networks?

Exercises

1.   You need to restrict your company's rank-and-file employees to using the Internet only during regular working hours (9 am to 5 pm, five days a week). However, as network administrator, you want to be able to access the Internet at any time of the day or night, seven days a week. How could you meet the needs of the employees and yourself?

2.   A group of freelance designers, who work at home, using DSL or cable modem connections, needs to gain access to a set of your company publication files to design them. How could you enable this?

3.   Your network employs basic authentication that centers on usernames and passwords. However, you have two ongoing problems. Usernames and passwords are frequently lost by negligent users. In addition, hackers have, on occasion, fooled employees into giving up their authentication information. Identify two things you could do to strengthen the use of basic username and password authentication.

4.   You have configured your firewall to authenticate a group of 100 users who are in your company. You set up the database of users using your firewall's own user management software. As your network grows and security items are added, other network components need to access the same database of users. What strategies could you employ to provide the other network components with access to the database of users?

5.   Using an Internet search engine, look up the term "one-time password." Access several Web sites that define the term. After reading at least two definitions, write your own, original definition of the term.

6.   Using an Internet search engine, look up the term "biometric user authentication." Access several Web sites that define the term. Write a paragraph expressing your opinion about if and when this will be the dominant way that users authenticate when using home computers.

Case Exercises

The day after her remedial security class, Niki got a call at her office from the help desk. The technician on the other end said that her account had been reset and she could log on again and her temporary password would be her employee ID number and then the last 4 digits of her social security number. A short while later, she was ready to try to connect to the system for the first time in a week—her access had been suspended until she took the training class.

She turned on her computer, and after it had booted, she entered her username and password as instructed. The next screen that opened said that her password had been reset. It displayed her new password as a series of twelve letters, numbers, and special characters, and then provided a brief mnemonic nonsense phrase. She saw:

```
HA  YU  M2  KA  Y!  I7

Hello All, You're Unhappy, Me Too, Keep Apples, Yes Bang,
It's Seven
```

Niki looked at the "helpful" nonsense phrase and just shook her head. She was going to get another one of these every month! She reached for her yellow sticky notes and started writing down her new password.

Questions:

1. Does the school district's password policy seem to be effective, considering the needs of the employees affected?

2. How would you suggest the district IT department adjust its password approach?

3. Consider how your recommendations might improve or degrade compliance with the policy. How would your suggestions alter the strength of the passwords?

11

Setting Up a Virtual Private Network

> Oh, how much is today hidden by science!
> Oh, how much it is expected to hide!
>
> **FRIEDRICH NIETZSCHE**

CONSTANTINE 'CONNIE' DIMITRIOS OPENED HIS TENT FLAP to watch the sun rise over the gentle slopes of the Virginia countryside. He had been hiking for four days on this leg of his ongoing quest to hike the roughly 2,175 miles of the Appalachian trail. He had begun his adventure in the summer of his junior year in college, but did not have the time to complete it in one go.

He listened carefully and could only hear a few birds in the nearby brush and, after a few minutes, the drone of an airplane high overhead and the dull growl of traffic on the interstate. He was considering whether to have a dry breakfast or to get started making coffee when the shrill ring of his cell phone sounded, evaporating the morning calm like an air-raid siren.

"Hello," he said, not bothering to conceal his irritation.

"Dr. Dimitrios," began a voice. "This is Debbie Masters from the QA team at ATI. I am working as part of an incident team that was formed 36 hours ago. It seems the intrusion system is not working, and no one here is able to make any progress. We worked this as long as we could without calling you, but we're out of options, and Ms. Johnson said to get you on the problem."

Connie was not surprised. He had pretty much rewritten the implementation of the commercial IDS that was in place when he took over that department eight years ago. It was good, but nothing was perfect.

"OK," he said. "I'll get online as soon as possible."

Connie now shifted his planning from coffee to finding a secure online link, as quickly as possible. It would take him 18 hours to get to the office if he left this minute. His cell phone couldn't provide enough bandwidth, and in any case couldn't provide a secure connection. He pulled out his GPS map and saw that there was a Starbucks in the next valley, about a 30 minutes' hike from where he stood. He began breaking camp immediately.

LEARNING OBJECTIVES:

Upon completion of this material, you should be able to do the following:

- Explain the components and essential operations of virtual private networks (VPNs)
- Describe the different types of VPNs
- Create VPN setups, such as mesh or hub-and-spoke configurations
- Choose the right tunneling protocol for your VPN
- Enable secure remote access for individual users via a VPN
- Recommend best practices for effective configuration and maintenance of VPNs

Introduction

Organizations routinely join two or more LANs to facilitate point-to-point communications over a secure line that can be accessed by no one else. Private **leased lines** are often used to connect remote users or branch offices to a central administrative site. However, private leased lines, such as **frame relay** high-speed network connections, don't scale well; the cost of leased lines and the complexity of the technology used to support them often make this an expensive option, although it is more reliable than using the public Internet infrastructure. The growth and widespread use of the Internet has been coupled with the use of encryption technology to produce a solution for specific types of private communication channels: **virtual private networks (VPNs)**. VPNs function like private leased lines; they encapsulate and encrypt the data being transmitted, and they use authentication to ensure that only approved users can access the VPN. However, rather than using an expensive leased line, VPNs provide a means of secure point-to-point communications over the public Internet. In this chapter, you'll learn how to set up a VPN for your organization.

VPN Components and Operations

VPNs, which are used for e-commerce and telecommuting, have become commonplace. Many telecommunications companies provide VPN services. VPNs can be set up with special hardware or with firewall software that includes VPN functionality. Many firewalls have VPN systems built into them, because the rules that apply to the VPN are part of the firewall's existing security policy. When set up correctly, a VPN can become a critical component in an organization's perimeter security configuration.

The goal of VPNs is to provide a cost-effective and secure way to connect business locations to one another, and remote workers to office networks. When each remote branch office has a secure connection using a VPN to the central office, all branches can communicate via a LAN-based file-sharing protocol, such as NetBIOS or AppleTalk.

VPN Components

VPNs consist of two different types of components: hardware devices and the software that performs security-related activities. This section briefly discusses the components that are used to create a VPN.

Each VPN tunnel has two **endpoints** or **terminators**. Endpoints are hardware devices or software modules that perform encryption to secure data, authentication to make sure the host requesting the data is an approved user of the VPN, and **encapsulation** to protect the integrity of the information being sent.

A VPN connection occurs within the context of a TCP/IP **tunnel**. A tunnel is a channel or pathway over a packet network used by the VPN and runs through the Internet from one endpoint to another. The term *tunnel* can be misleading, because it implies that there is a single cable joining one endpoint to another and that no one but approved users can send or receive data using that cable. In reality, a VPN uses a *virtual* tunnel between two endpoints; this virtual tunnel makes use of Internet-based hosts and servers to conduct data from one network station to another, just like any other TCP/IP data transmission. While using the Internet's system of networks, subnetworks, and servers keeps costs down and makes it relatively easy to set up a VPN, it also adds a level of uncertainty to VPN communications because so many systems are involved. See "Benefits and Drawbacks of VPNs" later in this chapter for a more detailed discussion on this point.

In drawings of networks that employ VPNs, you'll often see a single line used to join the two endpoints, as shown in Figure 11-1.

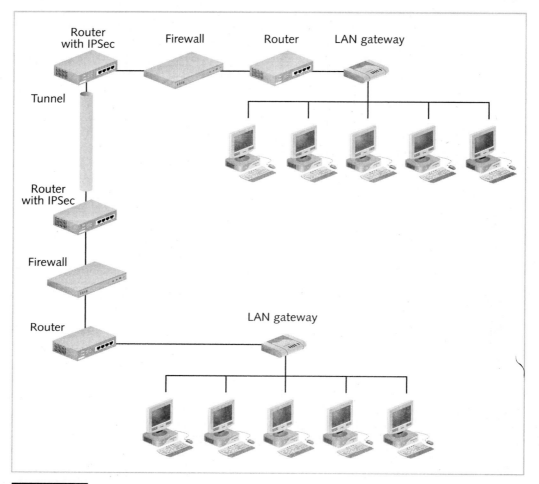

FIGURE 11-1 Simplified Model VPN

This very simplified picture illustrates that a VPN is essentially a communications path through the Internet that provides a heightened degree of security for two participants.

Figure 11-2, on the other hand, illustrates that VPNs in fact traverse the public Internet and must therefore handle the Internet's protocols and procedures. The figure shows one set of endpoints for a VPN: routers that support Internet Security Protocol (IPSec). Each LAN's communications first go to its ISP's server, then to a **Network access point** (a point that is on a high-speed part of the Internet called the backbone) and several intermediate servers.

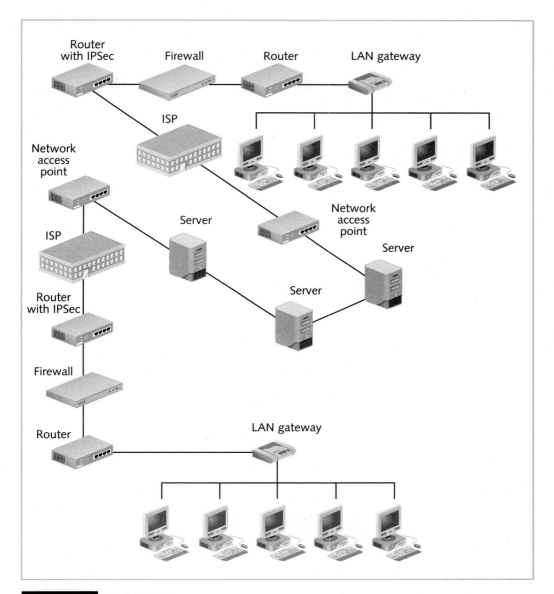

FIGURE 11-2 Model VPN

Figure 11-2 is also greatly simplified because the ISPs involved may or may not be connected to the Internet backbone, and there are probably more than three servers that lie between one LAN and the other. Not only that, more than one VPN may be involved when different offices that are part of the same corporation attempt to share information. Figure 11-3 builds on this model to attempt to illustrate the complexity of the Internet environment in which VPNs are deployed.

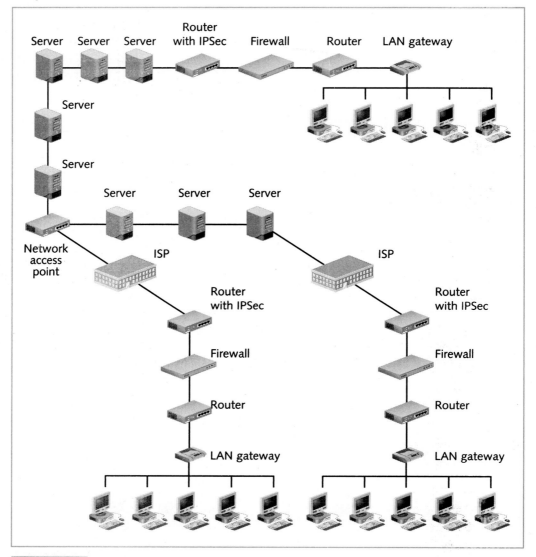

FIGURE 11-3 A Common VPN

The devices that form the endpoints of the VPN (which are often said to "termi-nate" the VPN) can be one of the following:

- A server running a tunneling protocol.
- A VPN appliance, which is a special hardware device devoted to setting up VPN communications.
- A firewall/VPN combination; many high-end firewall programs support VPN setups as part of their built-in features.

- A router-based VPN; routers that support IPSec can be set up at the perimeter of the LANs to be connected. (These are also sometimes called **IPSec concentrators.**) IPSec concentrators use a complex set of security protocols to protect information, including Internet Key Exchange (IKE), which provides for the exchange of security keys between the machines in the VPN.

The final components in a VPN scenario are certificate servers, which manage certificates if required, and client computers that run VPN client software, which lets remote users connect to the LAN over the VPN.

Essential Activities of VPNs

Because the VPN uses the Internet to transfer information from one computer or LAN to another, the data needs to be well protected. The essential activities that protect data transmitted over a VPN are:

- IP encapsulation
- Data payload encryption
- Encrypted authentication

IP Encapsulation

You already know that information that passes to and from TCP/IP-based networks travels in manageable chunks called packets. VPNs protect packets by performing IP encapsulation, the process of enclosing a packet within another one that has different IP source and destination information.

Encapsulating IP packets within other packets hides the source and destination information of the encapsulated packets—the encapsulating packet uses the source and destination addresses of the VPN gateway. The gateway might be a router that uses IPSec, or a VPN appliance, or a firewall that functions as a VPN and that has a gateway set up.

What's more, because a VPN tunnel is being used, the source and destination IP addresses of the encapsulated packets can be in the private reserved blocks that are not usually routable over the Internet, such as the 10.0.0.0/8 addresses or the 192.168.0.0/16 reserved network blocks.

Data Payload Encryption

One of the big benefits of using VPNs is that they can be implemented to fully or partially encrypt the data portion of the packets that are passing through them. The encryption can be accomplished in one of two ways:

- *Transport method*: The host encrypts traffic when it is generated; the data part of packets is encrypted, but not the headers.
- *Tunnel method*: The traffic is encrypted and decrypted in transit, somewhere between the source computer that generated it and its destination. In addition, both the header and the data portions of packets are encrypted.

The level of encryption applied by the firewall or VPN hardware device varies: the higher the number of data bits used to generate keys, the stronger the encryption. As you'll recall from Chapter 9, a key is the value used by the cryptographic formula or algorithm to either produce or decrypt ciphertext. The length of a key affects the strength of the encryption.

Encrypted Authentication

Some VPNs use the term **encryption domain** to describe everything in the protected network and behind the gateway. The same cryptographic system that protects the information within packets can be used to authenticate computers that use the VPN. Authentication is essential because hosts in the network that receive VPN communications need to know that the host originating the communications is an approved user of the VPN.

Hosts are authenticated by exchanging long blocks of code, called keys, that are generated by complex formulas called algorithms. As we learned in Chapter 9, two types of keys can be exchanged in an encrypted transaction:

- *Symmetric keys*: The keys are exactly the same. The two hosts exchange the same secret key to verify their identities to one another.
- *Asymmetric keys*: Each participant has two different keys: a private key, and a complementary public key. The participants in the transaction exchange their public keys. Each can then use the other's public key to encrypt information, such as the body of an e-mail message. When the recipient receives the encrypted message, he or she can decrypt it using the private key.

Symmetric key encryption is faster and more computationally efficient, but is more difficult to manage because each participant must have a copy of the secret key before communication can occur. The choice and implementation of a key distribution system is another complication facing anyone who wants to set up a VPN. For more on keys and symmetric/asymmetric keys, algorithms, and key distribution systems, see Chapter 9.

Benefits and Drawbacks of VPNs

One of the benefits of VPNs is secure networking without the expense of establishing and maintaining leased lines. VPNs also allow the packet encryption/translation overhead to be done on dedicated systems, decreasing the load placed on production machines. VPNs also allow you to control the physical setup, and therefore to decide upon data encryption levels, and whether to encrypt data at the physical level or at the application level.

VPNs do have some significant drawbacks. They are complex and, if configured improperly, can create significant network vulnerabilities. Leased lines may be more expensive, but the chance of introducing vulnerabilities is not as great because they create point-to-point connections. VPNs also make use of the unpredictable and often unreliable Internet. Multinational VPNs in particular can experience problems because packets being routed through various hubs can encounter slowdowns or blockages that you can neither predict nor resolve. You then have to explain to administration that the problem is occurring thousands of miles away and you'll just have to wait until it is fixed there.

Another problem involves authorization: if your VPN's authorization is not configured properly, you can easily expose your corporate network. In addition, some vendor solutions have more documented security issues than others.

VPNs Extend Network Boundaries

High-speed Internet connections such as cable modem and DSL lines are changing the role of VPNs in the corporate setting. Only a few years ago, when high-speed connections were expensive and relatively hard to come by, remote users primarily used VPNs to dial in to a network using modems. They were connected to the corporate network through the VPN only for the length of the dial-up connection. Because many ISPs charged by the minute or placed restrictions on the number of hours a customer could be connected each month, the remote user was likely to hang up as soon as business was completed.

Now, it's increasingly likely that the contractors, vendors, and telecommuters who connect to an organization's internal network through a VPN will have a high-speed connection that is "always on." Unless you specifically place limits on how long such employees can use the VPN, they can be connected to your network around the clock. Thus, each VPN connection extends your network to a location that is out of your control, and each such connection can open up your network to intrusions, viruses, or other problems. You need to take extra care with users who connect to the VPN through always-on connections. Here are some suggestions for how to deal with the increased risk:

- *Use of two or more authentication tools to identify remote users*: **Multifactor authentication** adds something the user possesses, such as a token or smart card, and something physically associated with the user, such as fingerprints or retinal scans. For such a system to work, each remote user would have to have a smart card reader, fingerprint reader, retinal scanner, or other (potentially expensive) device along with a computer.
- *Integrate virus protection*: Make sure each user's computer is equipped with up-to-date virus software that scans the computer continually, screening out any viruses as soon as they enter the system. After files are encapsulated, encrypted, and sent through the VPN tunnel, any viruses in those files will make it through the firewall into the corporate network. Virus-scanning software needs to be present on the network to catch any viruses, of course; however, requiring vendors, partners, or contractors to use their own anti-virus software will reduce the chance of viruses entering the system in the first place.
- *Use Network Access Control (NAC)*: NAC is a computer networking philosophy and a related set of protocols that are used to evaluate the trustworthiness of a client wishing to join a network. NAC solutions vary in complexity; some check for installed anti-virus software, current anti-virus updates, and relevant security patches. More sophisticated solutions can remediate identified defects by installing the appropriate items.[1]
- *Set usage limits*: Policy and practice should be to inform all VPN participants that they need to terminate VPN sessions as soon as they are done with them. Configuration of the VPN software can enforce the policy limits.

Such provisions should be supported by the organization's security policies, and requirements for their enforcement should be written into any agreements with business partners or contractors. As with all security policies, they should be explained to employees and business partners during orientation and security awareness sessions.

Types of VPNs

In general, you can set up two different types of VPNs. The first type links two or more networks and is called a **site-to-site VPN**. The second type makes a network accessible to remote users who need dial-in access and is called a **client-to-site VPN**. The two types of VPNs are not mutually exclusive—many large corporations link the central office to one or more branch locations using site-to-site VPNs, and they also provide dial-in access to the central office by means of a client-to-site VPN.

Because of their cost effectiveness, VPNs are growing steadily in popularity. Accordingly, you can choose between a number of options for configuring VPNs: hardware systems, software systems, and hybrids that combine both hardware and software. When choosing a system, keep in mind that any type of VPN, whether it consists of hardware or software or both, needs to be able to work with any number of different operating systems or types of computers.

VPN Appliances

One way to set up a VPN is to use a hardware device such as a router that has been configured to use IPSec or another VPN protocol (see the section "Tunneling Protocols Used with VPNs" later in this chapter for a rundown on these). Another option is to obtain a **VPN appliance**, a hardware device specially designed to terminate VPNs and join multiple LANs. VPN appliance can permit connections between large numbers of users or multiple networks, but they don't provide other services such as file sharing and printing.

The SonicWALL series of VPN hardware devices is composed of a variety of different VPN products. At one end is a product designed for the small business or a branch office. It can support 10, 25, or 50 simultaneous VPN connections along with stateful packet filtering, Network Address Translation (NAT), and even anti-virus protection. A Web-based interface and wizard installations make this SonicWALL product good for installations that require basic VPN support with a minimal amount of management.

At the high end of the series is a product that can support up to 500 concurrent VPN connections at speeds greater than 1.5 Gbps. Designed to deliver a high-performance VPN solution, this VPN appliance comes with redundant power supplies that can be replaced without turning the unit off. It provides mission-critical safety for large organizations that need the highest level of security.

Another widely used VPN appliance is the Symantec Firewall/VPN appliance. Similar to the SonicWall, the Symantec Firewall/VPN appliance is a series of different models. Each model is an integrated security VPN networking device that provides secure and cost-effective Internet connectivity between locations. The Symantec Firewall/VPN is designed for small businesses and remote offices, and supports up to 40 simultaneous VPN connections. For larger, dispersed organizations, Symantec Firewall/VPN offers a solution for extending firewall protection and VPN access to satellite offices or branch locations, and provides a remote VPN for traveling users.

Symantec Firewall/VPN security has a Web-based management interface that enables both remote and local administration. Because it contains a built-in local area network (LAN) auto-sense switch, system setup is easy, with no additional devices required to connect networking systems to the appliance. To ensure continuous connectivity, the Symantec Firewall/VPN appliance features an automatic backup that enables dial-up connections using an external modem in the event of a service disruption.

The advantage of using hardware systems is illustrated in Figure 11-4. They enable you to connect more tunnels and users than software systems. If the server goes offline or crashes for some reason (as shown in the left half of the figure), the hardware VPN appliance doesn't go offline (as shown in the right half of the figure).

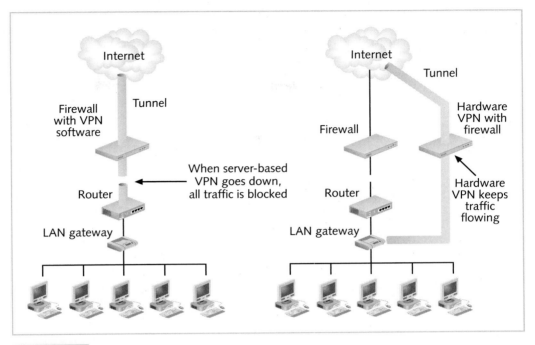

FIGURE 11-4   Hardware VPN

Software VPN Systems

Software VPNs are generally less expensive than hardware systems, and they tend to scale better on fast-growing networks. One popular software VPN product is F-Secure VPN+. This product supports traveling employees who need private access to a corporate LAN or intranet from any dial-up location, IT staff who need the ability to secure internal networks and partition parts of the network, and corporate partners who require secure connections to a company's data network for business collaboration. F-Secure VPN+ supports Windows, Linux, and Solaris Sparc clients and servers as well as gateways.

F-Secure VPN+ uses a policy manager system for enterprise-wide software distribution, policy creation, and management. Security settings for the entire corporate network using VPN can be made from the administrator's computer. Settings can be based on "role-based policies." This allows multiple configuration profiles for end users to be created; examples include "out-of-office," "at-home," or "in-office." In addition, all installations and maintenance can be performed from a single central location.

Another widely used software VPN is Novell BorderManager VPN services. This software-based VPN supports both the TCP/IP protocol and IPX/SPX (another LAN protocol), which is found on older Novell networks. BorderManager can support up to 256 sites per tunnel and can handle up to 1000 dial-in users per server. Novell BorderManager VPN clients run on Windows 95, 98, NT 4.0, 2000, Me, and XP.

In addition, Novell BorderManager VPN services integrate with Novell's directory service, known as eDirectory, to simplify VPN management and administration. Novell BorderManager authenticates all users through the Novell eDirectory to ensure that only authorized users are permitted to access the VPN. Administrators can control access through the same interface used to manage other network users, as it is not necessary to maintain a separate directory of information for VPN users.

An increasingly popular alternative for remote access to Web-enabled applications is SSL-based VPNs. These VPNs make use of the SSL protocol (instead of IPSec) but only allow access to Web-enabled applications.

VPN Combinations of Hardware and Software

You may also use VPN systems that implement a VPN appliance at the central network and use client software at the remote end of each VPN connection. Cisco offers multiple series of VPN concentrators that offer a variety of features and capabilities. Cisco VPN concentrators provide solutions for everything from the smallest office or branch location to the largest enterprise setting. Access levels can be set either for individual users or by groups, which allows for easy configuration and maintenance of company security policies.

Most VPN concentrator appliances give users the choice of operating in one of two modes: client mode and network extension mode. In client mode, the concentrator acts as a software client, enabling users to connect to another remote network via a VPN. In network extension mode, the concentrator acts as a hardware device enabling a secure site-to-site VPN connection.

Combination VPNs

You may have to operate a VPN system that is "mixed," and that uses hardware and software from different vendors. You might have one company that issues certificates, another that handles the client software, another that handles the VPN termination, and so on. The challenge is to get all of these pieces to communicate with one another successfully. To do this, pick a standard security protocol that is widely used and supported by all the devices, such as IPSec, which is described later in this chapter, and in Chapter 9.

VPN Setups

If you have only two participants in a VPN, the configuration is relatively straightforward in terms of expense, technical difficulty, and the time involved. However, when three or more networks or individuals need to be connected, there are several options—a mesh configuration, a hub-and-spoke arrangement, or a hybrid setup.

Mesh Configuration

In a **mesh configuration**, each participant (that is, network, router, or computer) in the VPN has an approved relationship, called a **security association** (**SA**), with every other participant. In configuring the VPN, you need to specifically identify each of these participants to every other participant that uses the VPN. Before initiating a connection, each VPN hardware or software terminator checks its routing table or **SA table** to see if the other participant has an SA with it. A mesh configuration is shown in Figure 11-5.

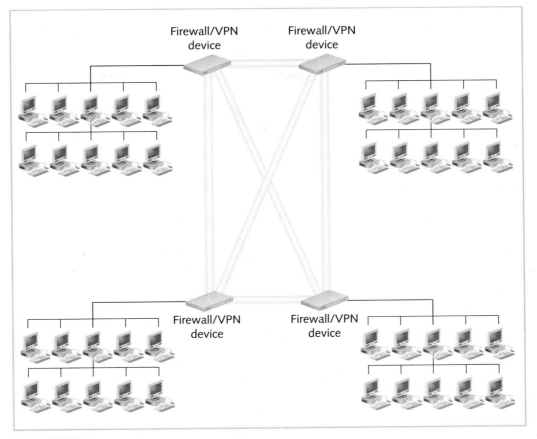

FIGURE 11-5   Mesh VPN

In Figure 11-5, four separate LANs are joined in a mesh VPN. Each LAN has the ability to establish VPN communications with all of the other participants in the LAN. If a new LAN is added to the VPN, all other VPN devices must be updated to include information about the new users in the LAN. Thus, each host can be added to the state table. In addition, every host that needs to use the VPN in each of the LANs must be equipped with sufficient memory to operate the VPN client software and to communicate with all other hosts in the VPN. The problem with VPNs is the difficulty associated with expanding the network and updating every VPN device whenever a host is added. For fast-growing networks, a hub-and-spoke configuration is preferable.

Hub-and-Spoke Configuration

In a **hub-and-spoke configuration**, a single VPN router contains records of all SAs in the VPN. Any LANs or computers that want to participate in the VPN need only connect to the central server, not to any other machines in the VPN. This setup makes it easy to increase the size of the VPN as more branch offices or computers are added. Figure 11-6 illustrates a hub-and-spoke configuration.

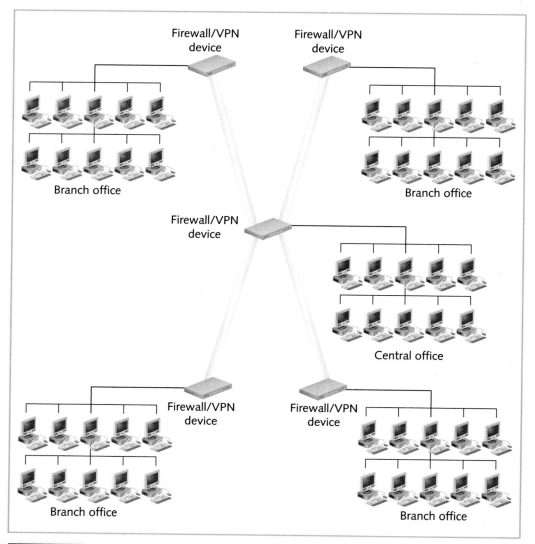

FIGURE 11-6 Hub-and-Spoke VPN

In Figure 11-6, the central VPN router resides at the organization's central office because it is most common for a hub-and-spoke VPN to have all communications go through the central office where the main IT staff resides. A hub-and-spoke VPN is ideally suited for communications within an organization that has a central main office and a number of branch offices.

The problem with hub-and-spoke VPNs is that the requirement that all communications flow into and out of the central router slows down communications, especially if branch offices are located on different continents around the world. In addition, the central router must have double the bandwidth of other connections in the VPN because it must handle both inbound and outbound traffic at the same time. The high-bandwidth charge for such a router can easily amount to several thousand dollars per month. However, in a situation where all communications need to go through the central office anyway, a hub-and-spoke configuration makes sense because of the heightened security it gives to all participants.

Hybrid Configuration

As organizations grow, a VPN that starts out as a mesh design or hub-and-spoke design often evolves into a mixture of the two. This is a common scenario, and you don't need to exclusively use one configuration or another.

Because mesh configurations tend to operate more efficiently, the central core linking the most important branches of the network should probably be a mesh configuration. However, as branch offices are added, they can be added as spokes that connect to a central VPN router at the central office.

Any time-critical communications with branch offices should be part of the mesh configuration. However, far-flung offices, such as overseas branches, can be part of a hub-and-spoke configuration. A hybrid setup that combines the two configurations benefits from the strengths of each one—the scalability of the hub-and-spoke option, and the speed of the mesh option. If at all possible, try to have the branch offices that participate in the VPN use the same ISP. That will minimize the number of "hops" between networks.

Configurations and Extranet and Intranet Access

Whether you use a hub-and-spoke, mesh, or hybrid configuration, creating VPNs that connect business partners and other branches of your own organization raises a number of questions and considerations.

Each end of the VPN represents an extension of your corporate network to a new location—you are, in effect, creating an **extranet**. The same security measures you take to protect your own network should be applied to the endpoints of the VPN. Each remote user or business partner should have firewalls and anti-virus software enabled, for instance.

VPNs can also be used to give parts of your own organization access to other areas through a corporate **intranet**—for example, a large corporation that has facilities spread across several different buildings in separate locations can use a VPN to allow the IT staff in one location to monitor servers in the other location, or accounting staff to adjust the financial records or job records in a server located in another building. Leaving the VPN connection "always on" can enable an unscrupulous staff to gain access to corporate resources that they are not allowed to use. VPN users inside your organization should have usage limits and anti-virus and firewall protection, just as outside users should, as indicated in Figure 11-7.

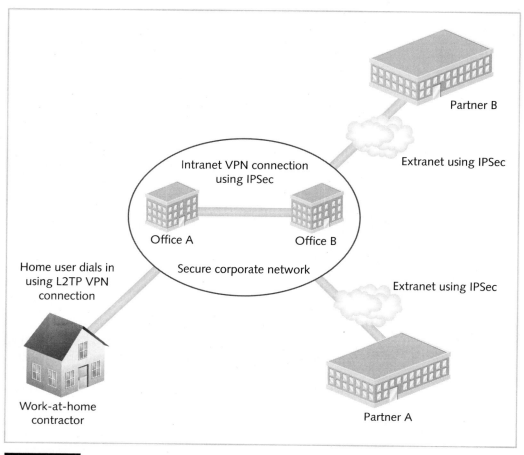

FIGURE 11-7   VPN for Intranets and Extranets

Tunneling Protocols Used with VPNs

In the past, firewalls that provided for the establishment of VPNs used **proprietary** protocols. Such firewalls would only be able to establish connections with remote LANs that used the same brand of firewall. Today, the widespread acceptance of the IPSec protocol with the Internet Key Exchange (IKE) system means that proprietary protocols are used far less often.

IPSec/IKE

IPSec is a standard for secure encrypted communications developed by the Internet Engineering Task Force (IETF). IPSec, which you learned about in detail in Chapter 9, provides for encryption of the data part of packets, authentication to guarantee that packets come from valid sources, and encapsulation between two VPN hosts.

IPSec provides two security methods: Authenticated Headers (AH) and Encapsulating Security Payload (ESP). AH is used to authenticate packets, whereas ESP encrypts the data portion of packets. You can use both methods together.

IPSec can work in two different modes: transport mode and tunnel mode. Transport mode is used to provide secure communications between hosts over any range of IP addresses. Tunnel mode is used to create secure links between two private networks. Tunnel mode is the obvious choice for VPNs; however, there are some concerns about using tunnel mode in a client-to-site VPN because the IPSec protocol by itself does not provide for user authentication. However, when combined with an authentication system like Kerberos, IPSec can authenticate users.

IPSec is commonly combined with IKE as a means of using public key cryptography to encrypt data between LANs or between a client and a LAN. IKE provides for the exchange of public and private keys. The key exchange is used to tell the hosts wishing to initiate a VPN connection that each is a valid user of the system. IKE can also determine which encryption protocols should be used to encrypt data that flows through the VPN tunnel. The process of establishing an IPSec/IKE VPN connection works like this:

1. The host or gateway at one end of the VPN sends a request to a host or gateway at the other end asking to establish a connection. (Both hosts have obtained the same key, called a pre-shared key, from the same trusted authority.)
2. The remote host or gateway generates a random number and sends a copy of the number back to the machine that made the original request.
3. The original machine encrypts its pre-shared key using the random number and sends the pre-shared key to the remote host or gateway.
4. The remote host decrypts the pre-shared key and compares it to its own pre-shared key or, if it has multiple keys, a set of keys called a keyring. If the pre-shared key matches one of its own keys, the remote host encrypts a public key using the pre-shared key and sends it back to the machine that made the original request.
5. The original machine uses the public key to establish a security association (SA) between the two machines, which establishes the VPN connection.

Even though many firewalls support IPSec and IKE, they sometimes use different versions of these protocols. If your VPN uses more than one kind of firewall and you plan to implement an IPSec/IKE VPN, check with the manufacturers of those firewalls to see if their product will work with the other firewalls you have, and ask about any special configuration you have to perform.

PPTP

Point-to-Point Tunneling Protocol (PPTP) is commonly used by remote users who need to connect to a network using a dial-in modem connection. PPTP uses Microsoft Point-to-Point Encryption (MPPE) to encrypt data that passes between the remote computer and the remote access server. It's older technology than the other dial-in tunneling protocol, L2TP, but it is useful if support for older clients is needed. It's also useful because packets sent using PPTP can pass through firewalls that perform Network Address Translation (NAT)—in contrast to L2TP, which is incompatible with NAT but provides a higher level of encryption and authentication.

L2TP

Layer 2 Tunneling Protocol (L2TP) is an extension of the protocol long used to establish dial-up connections on the Internet, **Point-to-Point Protocol (PPP)**. L2TP uses IPSec rather than MPPE to encrypt data sent over PPP. It provides secure authenticated remote access by separating the process of initiating a connection by answering a phone call from the process of forwarding the data encapsulated in PPP communications. Using L2TP, a host machine can make a connection to a modem and then have its PPP data packets forwarded to another, separate remote access server. When the data reaches the remote access server, its payload is unpacked and forwarded to the destination host on the internal network.

PPP Over SSL/PPP Over SSH

Point-to-Point Protocol (PPP) Over Secure Sockets Layer (SSL) and **Point-to-Point Protocol (PPP) Over Secure Shell (SSH)** are two UNIX-based methods for creating VPNs. Both combine an existing tunnel system (PPP) with a way of encrypting data in transport (SSL or SSH). As you probably know already, PPP can be used to establish a connection between two hosts over an IP system.

SSL is a public key encryption system used to provide secure communications over the World Wide Web (see Chapter 9 for more on SSL). SSH is the UNIX secure shell, which was developed when serious security flaws were identified in Telnet. SSH enables users to perform secure authenticated logons and encrypted communications between a client and host. SSH requires that both client and host have a secret key in advance—a **pre-shared key**—in order to establish a connection.

Which protocol should you use in a VPN you establish, and why? Table 11-1 lists the protocols mentioned in this section along with situations in which they might be used.

TABLE 11-1 VPN Protocols and Their Uses

Protocol	Recommended Usage
IPSec/IKE	Rapidly becoming the protocol of choice for VPN connections of all sorts and should be used when the other protocols are not acceptable
PPTP	When a dial-up user has an old system that doesn't support L2TP and needs to use PPP to establish a VPN connection to your network
L2TP	When a dial-up user needs to establish a VPN connection with your network (L2TP provides stronger protection than PPTP)
PPP Over SSL	When a UNIX user needs to create a VPN connection "on the fly" by connecting to the SSL port on a server
PPP Over SSH	When a UNIX user needs to create a VPN connection "on the fly" over the UNIX secure shell (SSH) and both parties know the secret key in advance

Enabling Remote Access Connections Within VPNs

If users in disparate locations need to connect to the central network via a VPN, a remote access connection is needed. A VPN is a good way to secure communications with users who need to connect remotely by dialing in to their ISP and establishing a connection to the corporate network, or by using their cable or DSL Internet connection to initiate the VPN connection. To enable a remote user to connect to a VPN, you need to issue that user VPN client software. You should also make sure the user's computer is equipped with anti-virus software and a firewall. You may need to obtain a key for the remote user if you plan to use IPSec to make the VPN connection as well.

If one or more remote users who want to make a VPN connection to you reside overseas, you may encounter the problem of having to find a phone provider that will have dial-up numbers in all locations. Some providers may not cover the foreign countries you want; you may have to sign up with several different providers to obtain dial-up access from certain locations.

Configuring the Server

One step in setting up a client-to-server VPN is configuring the server to accept incoming connections. If you use a firewall-based VPN, you need to identify the client computer. Check Point FireWall-1 calls this process defining a network object.

The major operating systems incorporate their own methods of providing secure remote access. In Linux, you use the IP Masquerade feature built into the Linux kernel to share a remote access connection. A part of IP Masquerade, called VPN Masquerade, enables remote users to connect to the Linux-based firewall using either PPTP or IPSec.

Windows XP and 2000 include a New Connection Wizard that makes it particularly easy to set up a workstation to accept incoming VPN connections, with one limitation: the remote access server that is used to provide the connection has the ability to permit only one incoming connection at a time. It's primarily intended to let one individual user connect to his or her home workstation from a remote location. However, if one connection is all you need, the wizard (see Figure 11-8) is a useful tool.

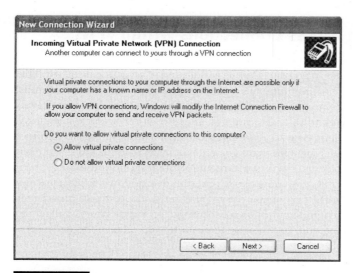

FIGURE 11-8   VPNs in Windows XP

After the remote workstation is connected, the Windows XP workstation displays a dialog box similar to the one shown in Figure 11-9. (A Windows 2000 workstation displays a network connection icon in the system tray.) Either party can terminate the connection at any time by clicking the Disconnect button.

FIGURE 11-9   Windows VPN Status

Configuring Clients

After you set up the server, you need to configure each client that wants to use the VPN. This involves installing and configuring VPN client software or, in the case of a Windows-to-Windows network, using the New Connection Wizard. FireWall-1 uses client software called SecuRemote that, when installed on a client computer, enables connections to another host or network via a VPN.

The most important things to consider are whether your client software will work with all client platforms, and whether the client workstation is itself protected by a firewall. All users who dial in to the LAN using a VPN extend the LAN and open up a new "hole" through which viruses and hackers can gain access. A requirement that remote users protect laptops and other computers with firewalls can be part of your organization's VPN policy.

VPN Best Practices

The successful operation of a VPN depends not only on its hardware and software components and overall configuration, but also on a number of best practices. These include security policy rules that specifically apply to the VPN, the integration of firewall packet filtering with VPN traffic, and auditing the VPN to make sure it is performing acceptably.

The Need for a VPN Policy

In a corporate setting, the VPN is likely to be used by many different workers in many different locations. A VPN policy is essential for identifying who can use the VPN and for ensuring that all users know what constitutes proper use of the VPN. This can be a separate stand-alone policy, or it may be a clause within a larger security policy.

The policy should spell out who should be permitted to have VPN access into your corporate network. For example, vendors might be granted access to the network through a VPN connection, but they may only be allowed to access information pertaining to their own company's accounts. The vendor VPN solution should have controls that allow the administrator to restrict where they can go on the corporate network. On the other hand, managers and full-time employees who access the network through a VPN while traveling should be granted more comprehensive access to network resources.

The policy should also state whether authentication is to be used and how it is to be used, whether **split tunneling** (two connections over a VPN line) is permitted, how long users can be connected using the VPN at any one session, whether virus protection is included, and so on. The SANS Institute provides a sample VPN Policy in PDF format (see *http://www.sans.org/resources/policies*).

Packet Filtering and VPNs

When configuring a VPN, you must decide early on where data encryption and decryption will be performed in relation to packet filtering. You can decide to do encryption and decryption either outside the packet-filtering perimeter or inside it. Figure 11-10 shows encryption and decryption outside the packet-filtering perimeter.

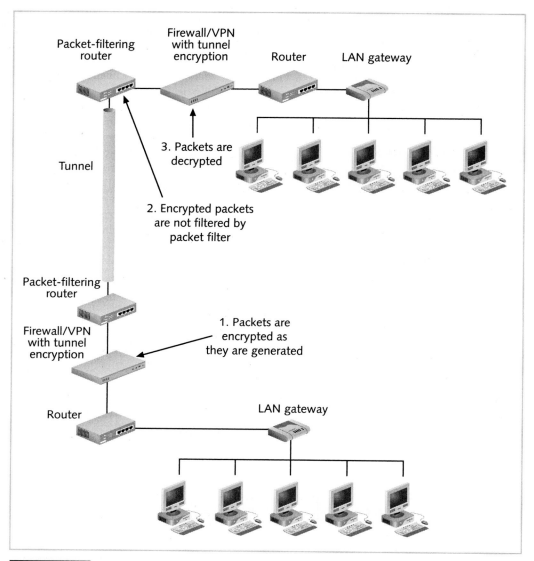

Packet-filtering router

Firewall/VPN with tunnel encryption

Router

LAN gateway

3. Packets are decrypted

Tunnel

2. Encrypted packets are not filtered by packet filter

Packet-filtering router

Firewall/VPN with tunnel encryption

1. Packets are encrypted as they are generated

Router

LAN gateway

FIGURE 11-10 External Encryption

In the scenario shown in Figure 11-10, the firewall/VPN combination is configured to perform transport encryption. Packets are encrypted at the host as soon as they are generated. Already-encrypted packets pass through the packet filters at the perimeter of either LAN and are not filtered. In this scenario, if the LAN that generates the communications has been infected by a virus or is compromised in some way, the packets that pass through the packet filters could be infected and could then infect the destination LAN.

Figure 11-11 illustrates the alternative: encryption and decryption are performed inside the packet-filtering perimeter using the tunnel method. Keep in mind that the network configurations illustrated in this figure and Figure 11-10 depict a packet filter that is separate from the firewall (this is done for clarity of explanation). In fact, packet filtering might be done by the firewall itself; the same firewall may provide VPN services, or a separate VPN appliance may be used instead of a firewall-based VPN.

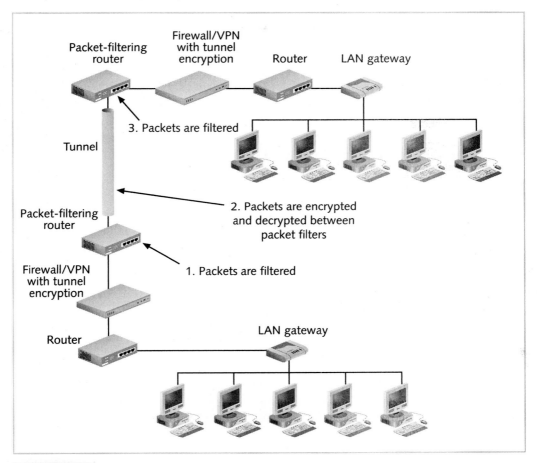

FIGURE 11-11 Internal Encryption

In Figure 11-11, packet filtering is performed before the data reaches the VPN. Mangled packets can be dropped before they reach the firewall/VPN, thus providing additional protection for the destination LAN.

PPTP Filters

PPTP is commonly used when older clients need to connect to a network through a VPN or when a tunnel must pass through a firewall that performs NAT. For PPTP traffic to pass through the firewall, you need to set up packet-filtering rules that permit such communications. Incoming PPTP connections arrive on TCP Port 1723. In addition, PPTP packets use Generic Routing Encapsulating (GRE) packets that are identified by the protocol identification number ID 47. Table 11-2 shows the filter rules that you would use for remote users at IP addresses 211.208.30.1 and 105.40.4.10.

TABLE 11-2 PPTP Packet-Filtering Rule Set

Protocol	Transport Protocol	Source IP	Source Port	Destination IP	Destination Port	Action
PPTP	TCP	211.208.30.1, 105.40.4.10	Any	*(remote access server's IP address)*	1723	Allow
GRE	ID 47	Any		*(remote access server's IP address)*		Allow

L2TP and IPSec Packet-Filtering Rules

Because L2TP uses IPSec to encrypt traffic as it passes through the firewall, you need to set up packet-filtering rules that cover IPSec traffic. Table 11-3 shows the filter rules that you would use for remote users at IP addresses 211.208.30.1 and 105.40.4.10.

TABLE 11-3 Packet-Filtering Rule Set 2

Protocol	Transport Protocol	Source IP	Source Port	Destination IP	Destination Port	Action
IKE	UDP	211.208.30.1, 105.40.4.10	500	*(remote access server's IP address)*	500	Allow
AH	ID 51	Any		*(remote access server's IP address)*		
ESP	ID 50	Any		*(remote access server's IP address)*		Allow

Auditing and Testing the VPN

After the VPN is installed, you need to test the VPN client on each computer that might use the VPN. In an organization with many different workstations, this can be a time-consuming prospect. There's no easy way around this, but you can choose client software (which is installed as part of the test) that is easy for end users to install on their own to save you time and effort.

To give you an idea of how testing of a VPN client might work, consider the following step-by-step scenario:

1. You issue VPN client software and a certificate to the remote user.
2. You call the remote user on the phone and lead him or her through the process of installing the software and storing the certificate.
3. If you are using IPSec, you verify with the remote user that the IPSec policies are the same on both the remote user's machine and your VPN gateway.
4. You tell the user to start up the VPN software and connect to your gateway. (Hopefully, you'll be able to remain on the phone while the end user connects, but if the remote user has only one telephone line and a dial-up connection to the Internet, you may have to communicate by e-mail.)

5. If there are any problems connecting to the gateway, tell the remote user to write down or report the error message exactly, to help you correctly diagnose the problem.

6. After the connection is established, the remote user should authenticate by entering his or her username and password when prompted to do so.

After the testing of the client is done, you need to check the VPN to make sure files are being transferred at an acceptable rate and that all parts of the VPN remain online when needed. To give you an idea of how testing of file transferring might work, consider the following step-by-step scenario:

1. After the remote user connects to your network, tell him or her to start up a Web browser and connect to your server.

2. Enter the username and password needed to access the server when prompted.

3. Locate the files to be transferred.

4. Copy the files from the corporate network to the remote user's computer (or vice versa).

5. Keep track of how long the file transfers take.

6. Open the files after they are transferred to make sure they transferred completely and work correctly.

7. The remote user should disconnect from the corporate network when he or she is finished transferring files.

If part of the network goes down frequently, switch to another ISP—preferably, an ISP that also serves another part of the VPN. If you find yourself needing to switch to another ISP, consider using the following questions to help determine which ones can help you (and which ones cannot):

- How often does your network go offline?

- Do you have backup servers that will keep customers like me online if the primary server goes down?

- Do you have backup power supplies in case of a power outage?

- How far are you from the network backbone? (Two or three hops is considered close; the closer to the backbone the ISP is, the faster the connection.)

OFFLINE

Connecting From Personal Computers

One of the most troublesome aspects of allowing users remote access to an organization's internal network has to do with use of personal equipment. For example, many organizations do not provide employees or contractors a separate system to use for VPN access from home. This means that access is commonly done from the user's personal PC.

In such situations, remote users must be carefully trained to understand that even when they access the organizational network from a personally owned piece of equipment, all organizational security policies (permitted use, required anti-virus measures, etc.) apply during that use.

It can also be difficult for the organization's security personnel to ensure that any monitoring they perform or agents they install in order to grant remote access function only during the duration of the VPN connection. After all, an employee may use his or her own computer for entertainment and personal uses that are not allowed for a company-owned system. It would not be appropriate for a content filter or a software license metering program to block employees from such personal uses.

Chapter Summary

- The growth and widespread use of the Internet has been coupled with the use of encryption technology to produce a solution for specific types of private communication channels: **virtual private networks (VPNs)**. VPNs provide a means of secure point-to-point communications over the public Internet.

- VPNs are used for e-commerce and telecommuting and are becoming widespread. VPNs can be set up with special hardware or with firewall software that includes VPN functionality. Many firewalls have VPN systems built into them, and VPN is a critical component in an organization's perimeter security configuration.

- Because the VPN uses the Internet to transfer information from one computer or LAN to another, the data needs to be well protected. The essential activities that protect data transmitted over a VPN are: IP encapsulation, data payload encryption, and encrypted authentication.

- In general, there are two different types of VPN: site-to-site and client-to-site, which are not necessarily mutually exclusive. To set up a VPN, you can use a hardware device—such as a router that has been configured to provide a VPN protocol—a VPN appliance, or run VPN software on a general-purpose server.

- VPN configuration for three or more networks or individuals may be a mesh configuration, a hub-and-spoke arrangement, or a hybrid setup. In a mesh configuration, each participant in the VPN has an approved relationship with every other participant. In a hub-and-spoke configuration, a single, central VPN router contains records of all associations in the VPN, and any other participants need only connect to the central server, not to any other machines in the VPN. As organizations grow, a VPN that starts out as a mesh design or hub-and-spoke design often evolves into a mixture of the two.

- Firewalls that use proprietary protocols can only establish connections with remote LANs that use the same brand of firewall. Today, the widespread acceptance of the IPSec protocol with the Internet Key Exchange (IKE) system means that proprietary protocols are used far less often. IPSec provides two security methods: Authenticated Headers (AH) and Encapsulating Security Payload (ESP). AH is used to authenticate packets, whereas ESP encrypts the data portion of packets. You can use both methods together.

- Point-to-Point Tunneling Protocol (PPTP) is commonly used by remote users who need to connect to a network using a dial-in modem connection. Layer 2 Tunneling Protocol (L2TP) is an extension of the protocol long used to establish dial-up connections on the Internet, Point-to-Point Protocol (PPP).

- Point-to-Point Protocol (PPP) Over Secure Sockets Layer (SSL) and Point-to-Point Protocol (PPP) Over Secure Shell (SSH) are two UNIX-based methods for creating VPNs. Both combine an existing tunnel system (PPP) with a way of encrypting data in transport (SSL or SSH).

- A VPN is a good way to secure communications with users who need to connect remotely by dialing into their ISP, or who use their cable or DSL Internet connection to initiate the VPN connection. To enable a remote user to connect to a VPN, you need to issue that user VPN client software. You should make sure the user's computer is equipped with anti-virus software and a firewall. You may need to obtain a key for the remote user if you plan to use IPSec to make the VPN connection as well.

- The successful operation of a VPN depends not only on its hardware and software components and overall configuration, but also on a number of best practices. These include security policy rules that specifically apply to the VPN, the integration of firewall packet filtering with VPN traffic, and auditing the VPN to make sure it is performing acceptably.

Review Questions

1. What do VPNs do that firewalls cannot do?
2. What are the disadvantages of using leased lines to set up a private network?
3. What are the disadvantages of using a VPN instead of a leased line?
4. Why would you choose a VPN that is built into a firewall rather than a VPN appliance or a router?
5. In the context of VPNs, why is the term *tunnel* often misleading?
6. What is the downside of using a proprietary VPN protocol?
7. Why is authentication an essential part of a VPN?
8. What are the ways that participants in a VPN can be authenticated?
9. Which of the VPN protocols discussed in the chapter provide for client-to-site authentication?
10. What are the benefits of setting up a VPN rather than using a leased line?
11. What special considerations need to be considered when setting up a multinational VPN?
12. Why would you consider purchasing a VPN appliance rather than installing less expensive VPN software?
13. Aside from the fact that they're less expensive, under what circumstances does using a software VPN give you an advantage over a VPN appliance?
14. Define and describe a mesh VPN configuration.
15. Under what circumstances is a mesh VPN configuration most useful?
16. Define and describe a hub-and-spoke VPN configuration.
17. When is a hub-and-spoke VPN configuration most useful?
18. Which VPN protocol is most widely used today?
19. Tunnel mode seems like the obvious choice in using IPSec to secure communications through a VPN tunnel; what's the potential drawback to using it?
20. PPTP is an older VPN protocol that is mainly used with older client computers, but it has one advantage over the more recent L2TP. What is it?

Exercises

1. You have been hired by a small company that has set up a VPN. The VPN is used by two business partners with which the company needs to communicate on a regular basis. You set up a simple mesh configuration, going from office to office to do the initial configuration, which includes SA table listings for all devices in the VPN. The VPN operates smoothly until your company purchases another business that has branch offices located overseas. You are given the assignment of expanding the VPN to include the new employees. You are told that all internal LANs should be able to communicate with one another and are informed in confidence that more acquisitions may be in store. You are happy about the prospect of traveling overseas to extend the VPN, but the prospect of updating four or more VPN devices around the world on a regular basis seems impractical. What should you do to help the VPN grow?
2. Your company (the same one mentioned in the previous exercise) does indeed follow through with the purchase of a distribution center located in another state. You are told, however, that only the central office and one branch office will need to communicate with the distribution center, to send delivery instructions and maintain shipping records. You are told that speed is of the essence in getting updated records, particularly at budget time each spring. What is the best way to expand this VPN?

3. Once the expanded VPN mentioned in the previous exercises is up and running, you notice significant slowdowns in communications, particularly with one Asian branch office. What are your options for speeding up communications with this single office? Give two alternatives.

4. Your VPN uses transport mode to send traffic to other VPN participants. The network administrator of one of the LANs in the VPN e-mails you an alert stating that his network has been infected with the W32.Storm virus. Because all communications between your LAN and his LAN go through a VPN, you feel reasonably confident that you won't be infected. Nevertheless, the next day a computer on your machine reports that its anti-virus software has isolated the same virus. How could this have happened, and what steps can you take to reduce the chances of it happening again?

5. Using an Internet search engine, look up the term *split tunneling*. Be sure to read at least two of the resulting definitions, and then write your own definition of this term. What kinds of attacks can split tunneling help prevent?

Case Exercises

Connie walked into Starbucks and ordered a Venti drip coffee. He found a table that could reach a power outlet and started his laptop. He started the VPN client software and authenticated using his user ID, his PIN, and the numbers from his cryptographic security token.

Once a secure connection was in place, he ran the remote desktop software, and it was as if he were sitting in his office. He plugged in his headset and ran the virtual meeting software.

He saw that there was a standing conference for the incident team. He clicked into the meeting.

Questions:

1. Are Connie's communications, which are being carried over a public network, going to be safe?

2. What kind of authentication do you think is being used by this VPN?

3. Using the terminology and concepts from this chapter, describe the VPN configuration Connie is using.

Endnotes

[1] For more information, see Mark Kadrich, *Endpoint Security*, Addison-Wesley, 2007.

Contingency Planning

12

> Court disaster long enough, and it will accept your proposal.
>
> **MASON COOLEY**

IT WAS FRIDAY NIGHT. ALL THE EMPLOYEES had long since left for the day, except for a select group of senior staff who were crowded around the conference table with binders open and index cards in hand. Hedda Linn, who was facilitating the meeting, turned to Al Agostino, who was the acting incident manager for this meeting, and said, "It's your turn."

Al looked at the next index card in his deck. The two words made him grimace: "Power out."

Al asked, "How widespread and for how long?"

"Beats me," Hedda replied. "That's all I know."

Al flipped through his tattered copy of the disaster recovery plan, finally settling on a page. He looked for the communications coordinator, Jeffrey Noak. Jeffrey, a more experienced security architect, was responsible for all communications during this disaster recovery practice session.

"Okay, Jeff," he said. "Please call the power company and ask how widespread the outage is."

Jeff, who was reading the same binder page as Al, looked up. "Okay, I'll let you know as soon as I have an answer. Anything else?"

"Just a minute." As Al looked for the next step, Tana Stainforth, the second shift supervisor, said, "We've got about 45 minutes of battery time, but the generators need to be manually started. I'm going to need power to maintain network operations."

"Right!" Al said. He turned to Meredith Isaacs, who represented the building management company that leased space to ATI. "Can you get a team to the generator and get it going?"

Meredith said, "Okay. I'm on it. We already turned on the heaters. It takes 10 to 15 minutes from a cold start, and in this weather it's a very cold start. We need five to seven more minutes before we can crank the motor, and three to four minutes after that we can generate power."

Everyone at the table laughed. The weather outside was 92 degrees and humid, but the disaster scenario they were rehearsing was a massive snowstorm impacting operations.

"How long will the generators run?" Al asked.

Meredith flipped a page in her binder and replied, "Days. If we have to, we can siphon gas from employee vehicles! With the reserve tank, supplemented by gas from employee vehicles, we have plenty of fuel, provided the generator doesn't break down."

"Whew! That's a relief." Al smiled as he leaned back in his seat. "OK, what's our next step?" He glanced over at Hedda.

Hedda said, "Good job everybody. Al, flip the next card."

LEARNING OBJECTIVES:

Upon completion of this material, you should be able to do the following:

- Recognize the need for contingency planning
- Describe the major components of contingency planning
- Create a simple set of contingency plans, using business impact analysis
- Prepare and execute a test of contingency plans
- Explain the unified contingency plan approach
- Discuss the reasons for sound backup and recovery practices, and know the elements that constitute backup and recovery techniques

Introduction

Networks are susceptible to many outside events and internal failures as well as deliberate attacks from hostile parties. In fact, many network outages are the unintended consequences of actions taken by friendly parties. When the network is disrupted, business operations often come to a standstill. NIST Special Publication 800-18, *Guide for Developing Security Plans for Information Technology Systems,* specifies that when an unexpected event occurs, "Procedures are required that will permit the organization to continue essential functions if information technology support is interrupted."[1] Some organizations—particularly, for national security reasons, federal agencies—are charged by law or other mandate to have such procedures in place at all times.

Organizations in the private and nonprofit sectors should also prepare for the unexpected. In general, an organization's ability to weather losses caused by an unexpected event depends on proper planning and execution of such a plan; without a workable plan, an unexpected event can cause severe damage to an organization's information resources and assets from which it may never recover. As noted by The Hartford insurance company: "On average, over 40% of businesses that don't have a disaster plan go out of business after a major loss like a fire, a break-in, or a storm."[2]

What Is Contingency Planning?

The overall process of preparing for unexpected events is called **contingency planning (CP)**. CP is the process by which the information technology and information security communities of interest position their organizations to prepare for, detect, react to, and recover from events—both human and natural—that threaten the security of information resources and assets. The main goal of CP is to restore normal modes of operation with minimal cost and disruption to normal business activities after an unexpected event—in other words, to make sure things get back to the way they were within a reasonable period of time. Ideally, CP should ensure continuous information systems availability to the organization even in the face of the unexpected.

CP consists of four major components:

- Business impact analysis (BIA)
- Incident response plan (IR plan)
- Disaster recovery plan (DR plan)
- Business continuity plan (BC plan)

Depending on the size and business philosophy of an organization, information technology and information security managers can either (1) create and develop these three CP components as one unified plan or (2) create the three separately in conjunction with a set of interlocking procedures that ensure continuity. Typically, larger, more complex organizations create and develop the CP components separately, as the functions of each component differ in scope, applicability, and design. Smaller organizations tend to adopt a one-plan method, consisting of a straightforward set of recovery strategies.

Four teams of individuals are involved in contingency planning and contingency operations:

- The *CP team* collects information about information systems and the threats they face, conducts the business impact analysis, and then creates the contingency plans for incident response, disaster recovery, and business continuity. The CP team often consists of a coordinating manager and representatives from each of the other three teams.

- The *incident response team* manages and executes the incident response plan by detecting, evaluating, and responding to incidents.

- The *disaster recovery team* manages and executes the disaster recovery plan by detecting, evaluating, and responding to disasters, and by reestablishing operations at the primary business site.

- The *business continuity team* manages and executes the business continuity plan by setting up and starting off-site operations in the event of an incident or disaster.

Incident response focuses on immediate response, but if the incident escalates into a disaster, the IR plan may give way to the DR plan and BC plan, as illustrated in Figure 12-1. The DR plan typically focuses on restoring systems after disasters occur, and therefore is closely associated with the BC plan. The BC plan occurs concurrently with the DR plan when the damage is major or long term, requiring more than simple restoration of information and information resources, as illustrated in Figure 12-2.

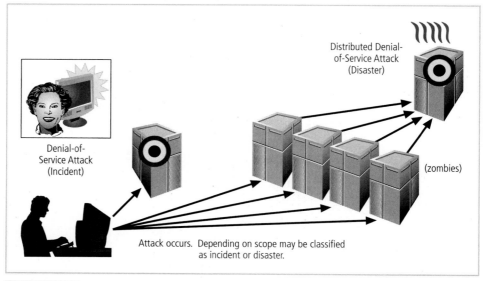

FIGURE 12-1   Incident Response and Disaster Recovery

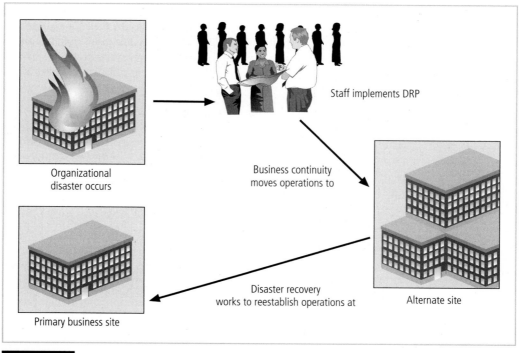

FIGURE 12-2   Disaster Recovery and Business Continuity Planning

Some experts argue that the three elements of CP are so closely linked that they are indistinguishable. In fact, each has a distinct place, role, and planning requirement. Furthermore, each component (IR, DR, and BC) comes into play at a specific time in the life of an incident. Figure 12-3 illustrates this sequence and shows the overlap that may occur. How the plans interact and the ways in which they are brought into action are discussed in the sections that follow.

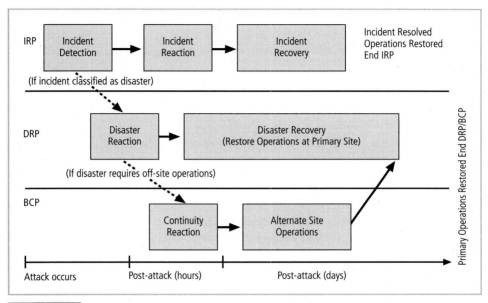

FIGURE 12-3 Contingency Planning Implementation Timeline

Components of Contingency Planning

The major project components performed during contingency planning efforts are business impact analysis, incident response planning, disaster recovery planning, and business continuity planning, as shown in Figure 12-4.

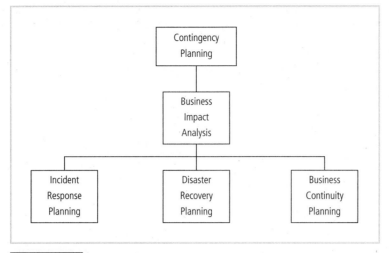

FIGURE 12-4   Contingency Planning Hierarchies

Business Impact Analysis

The **business impact analysis (BIA)**, the first phase in the CP process, provides the CP team with information about systems and the threats they face. The BIA is a crucial component of the initial planning stages, as it provides detailed scenarios of the effects that each potential attack could have on the organization.

The CP team conducts the BIA in the following stages, which are shown in Figure 12-5:

1. Threat attack identification and prioritization: In this stage, organizations update the prioritized threat list created during the risk assessment process, and add one piece of information, the **attack profile**, a detailed description of the activities that occur during an attack that includes preliminary indications of the attack, as well as the actions taken and the outcome.
2. Business unit analysis: The second major task is the analysis and prioritization of business functions within the organization. Each business department, unit, or division must be independently evaluated to determine how important its functions are to the organization as a whole.
3. Attack success scenario development: The BIA team next creates a series of scenarios depicting the effects of an occurrence of each threat on each prioritized functional area. **Attack success scenarios** are added to the attack profile developed earlier, including alternative outcomes—best, worst, and most likely.
4. Potential damage assessment: From these detailed scenarios, the BIA planning team must estimate the cost of the best, worst, and most likely outcomes by preparing an **attack scenario end case**, which allows the organization to identify the costs associated with recovering from each possible case.
5. Subordinate plan classification: Once the potential damage has been assessed, and each scenario and attack scenario end case has been evaluated, a subordinate plan must be developed or identified from among existing plans already in place. Some of these related plans may already be part of standard operating procedures, such as file recovery from backup. Because most attacks are not disastrous and therefore fall into

the category of incident response, the BIA team will likely develop a number of subordinate plans that are meant to be exclusively used at the incident level.

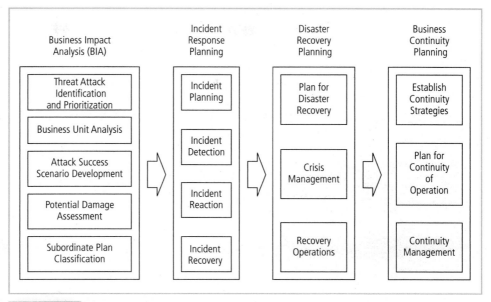

FIGURE 12-5 Major Tasks in Contingency Planning

Incident Response Plan

The actions an organization can and perhaps should take while the incident is in progress should be defined in a document referred to as the **incident response (IR) plan**. An **incident** is any clearly identified attack on the organization's information assets that would threaten the assets' confidentiality, integrity, or availability. The IR plan deals with the identification of, classification of, response to, and recovery from an incident. The IR plan provides answers to questions victims might pose in the midst of an incident, such as, "What do I do now?" As was noted in the opening scenario, the IT organization was ready to respond to the unusual events that had alerted Al to an unusual situation. In that example, a simple process is used, based on documented procedures that were prepared in advance. In another scenario, a systems administrator may notice that someone is copying information from the server without authorization, signaling a policy violation by a potential hacker or an employee. What should the administrator do first? Whom should they contact? What should be documented? The IR plan supplies the answers.

For example, in the event of a serious virus or worm outbreak, the IR plan may be used to assess the likelihood of imminent damage and to inform key decision makers in the various communities of interest (IT, information security, organization management, and users). The IR plan also enables the organization to take coordinated action that is either predefined and specific, or ad hoc and reactive. The intruders that, in some instances, cause the incidents constantly scan for new weaknesses in operating systems, network services, and protocols. According to the Carnegie Mellon Software Engineering Institute, "[Intruders] actively develop and use sophisticated programs to rapidly penetrate systems. As a result, intrusions, and the damage they cause, are often achieved in a matter of seconds."[3]

The same source also reports that organizations "will not know what to do in the event of an intrusion if the necessary procedures, roles, and responsibilities have not been defined and exercised in advance. The absence of systematic and well-defined procedures can lead to:

- Extensive damage to data, systems, and networks due to not taking timely action to contain an intrusion. This can result in increased costs, loss of productivity, and loss of business.

- The possibility of an intrusion affecting multiple systems both inside and outside your organization because staff did not know who else to notify and what additional actions to take.

- Negative exposure in the news media that can damage your organization's stature and reputation with your shareholders, your customers, and the community at large.

- Possible legal liability and prosecution for failure to exercise an adequate standard of due care when your systems are inadvertently or intentionally used to attack others."[4]

Disaster Recovery Plan

The next vital part of contingency planning is the disaster recovery plan. The IT community of interest, under the leadership of the CIO, is often made responsible for disaster recovery planning, including aspects that are not necessarily technology-based.

Disaster recovery planning (DRP) entails the preparation for and recovery from a disaster, whether natural or human-made. For example, if a malicious program evades containment actions and infects or disables many or most of an organization's systems and its ability to function, the DR plan is activated. Sometimes incidents are, by their nature, immediately classified as disasters, such as an extensive fire, flood, damaging storm, or earthquake.

In general, a disaster has occurred when either of two criteria is met: (1) the organization is unable to contain or control the impact of an incident or (2) the level of damage or destruction from an incident is so severe that the organization cannot quickly recover from it. The distinction between an incident and a disaster may be subtle. The CP team must document in the DR plan whether an event is classified as an incident or a disaster. This determination is critical because it determines which plan is activated. The key role of a DR plan is defining how to reestablish operations at the location where the organization is usually located.

Business Continuity Plan

Business continuity planning (BCP) ensures that critical business functions can continue if a disaster occurs. Unlike the DR plan, which is usually managed by the IT community of interest, the business continuity plan (BC plan) is most properly managed by the CEO of an organization. The BC plan is activated and executed concurrently with the DR plan when the disaster is major or long term and requires fuller and complex restoration of information and IT resources. If a disaster has rendered the current business location unusable, there must be a plan to allow the business to continue to function. While the BC plan reestablishes critical business functions at an alternate site, the DR plan team focuses on the reestablishment of the technical infrastructure and business operations at the primary site. Not every business needs such a plan, or such facilities. Some small companies or fiscally sound organizations may be able to simply cease operations until the primary facilities are restored. Manufacturing and retail organizations, however, depend on continued operations for revenue. Thus these entities must have a BC plan in place so as to quickly relocate operations with minimal loss of revenue.

Incident Response: Preparation, Organization, and Prevention

In an organization, unexpected activities occur periodically and are referred to as **events**. In CP, events that indicate a threat to the security of the organization's information are called incidents. An incident occurs when an attack (natural or human-made) affects information resources and/or assets, causing actual damage or other disruptions. **Incident response (IR)**, then, is a set of procedures that commence when an incident is detected. IR must be carefully planned and coordinated, because organizations heavily depend on the quick and efficient containment and resolution of incidents. As was noted earlier in this chapter, the incident response plan (IR plan) comprises a detailed set of processes and procedures that anticipate, detect, and mitigate the effects of an unexpected situation that might compromise information resources and assets. Incident response planning (IRP) is therefore the preparation for such a situation.

To provide an overview of the ways that IR is performed at other organizations, two examples of the IR life cycle are shown in Figures 12-6 and 12-7. Figure 12-6 shows how the U.S. National Institute of Standards and Technology (NIST) defines the IR process. Figure 12-7 provides a slightly broader perspective, showing how the Computer Emergency Response Team Coordinating Center (CERT/CC) approach to IR planning fits into its overall IR model.

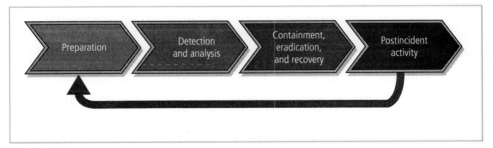

FIGURE 12-6 The NIST Incident Response Life Cycle[5]

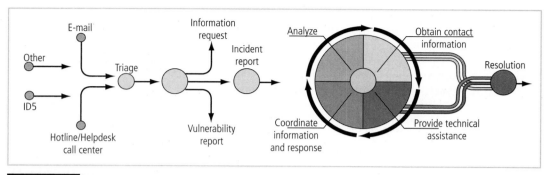

FIGURE 12-7 The CERT Incident Handling Life Cycle[6]

When the contingency planning management committee (CPMC) completes the business impact analysis, it begins to transfer the information gleaned from the organization to the various subordinate committees. To assist in their subordinate planning, the incident response committee, disaster recovery committee, and business continuity committee each get overlapping information on the attacks they could face, the prioritization of those attacks, and the attack scenario end cases. In fact, each committee gets as much of the overall contingency plan as the CPMC has prepared. Once committee members have this information, they begin their subordinate plans. In the case of incident planning, the group follows these general stages:

- Form the IR planning team
- Develop the IR policy
- Organize the security incident response team (SIRT)
- Develop the IR plan
- Develop IR procedures

Organizing the incident response planning process begins with staffing the IR planning team. Much of the preliminary organizing effort is done by the CP team, but the IR team needs to be organized as a separate entity, and that process begins by identifying and engaging a collection of stakeholders, meaning a representative collection of individuals with a stake in the successful and uninterrupted operation of the organization's information infrastructure. These stakeholders are used to collect vital information on the roles and responsibilities of the SIRT team. Stakeholders include representatives from general management, IT management, InfoSec management and operations, and other specialized groups like legal affairs, public relations, etc.

One of the first deliverables to be undertaken by the IR planning committee should be the incident response policy.

The incident response policy defines the roles and responsibilities for incident response for the SIRT and others who will be mobilized in the activation of the plan. Table 12-1 provides an overview of the structure of a typical IR policy.

TABLE 12-1 Incident Response Policy Elements
(Source: NIST SP 800-61)[7]

• Statement of management commitment

• Purpose and objectives of the policy

• Scope of the policy (to whom and what it applies and under what circumstances)

• Definition of information security incidents and their consequences within the context of the organization

• Organizational structure and delineation of roles, responsibilities, and levels of authority; should include the authority of the incident response team to confiscate or disconnect equipment and to monitor suspicious activity, and the requirements for reporting certain types of incidents

• Prioritization or severity ratings of incidents

• Performance measures (as discussed in later chapters)

• Reporting and contact forms

IR policy, like all well-written policies, must gain the full support of top management and be clearly understood by all affected parties. It is especially important to gain the support of those communities of interest that will be required to alter business practices or make changes to their information technology infrastructures.

The responsibility for creating an organization's IR plan usually falls to the chief information security officer (CISO). Planning for an incident and the responses to it requires a detailed understanding of the information systems and the threats they face. The IR planning team and SIRT seek to develop a series of predefined responses that will guide the team and information security staff through the incident response steps. Predefining incident responses enables the organization to react to a detected incident quickly and effectively, without confusion or wasted time and effort.

For every attack scenario end case, the IR team creates the incident plan, made up of three sets of incident-handling procedures to be deployed during, after, and before the incident.

Although it may not seem logical to prepare the documentation of the IR plan in the order given, when the members of the IR team reach for the documentation, the primary concern is what is to be done now, during the incident. This is followed by the need to engage in the follow-up activities. The final section on the procedures used for IR readiness and the steps needed to maintain the plan are included in the final section, which is used only when an incident response is not underway.

Planning for the Response During the Incident

Beginning with the end in mind is useful in most planning activities. However, in the case of IR, you begin with the middle in mind, the actual incident response. The most important phase of the IR plan is the reaction to the incident.

Each viable attack scenario end case is examined in turn by the IR team. Representatives from the SIRT assist as part of this team, once the SIRT has been formed. The IR team discusses the end cases and begins to understand the actions that must be taken to react to the incident. The discussion begins with the **trigger**, or the circumstances that cause the IR team to be activated and the IR plan to be initiated. This trigger could be a number of situations or circumstances, including the following:

- A phone call from a user to the help desk about unusual computer or network behavior
- Notification from a systems administrator about unusual server or network behavior
- Notification from an intrusion detection device
- Review of system log files indicating unusual pattern of entries
- Loss of system connectivity
- Device malfunctions
- Other specific identifiable situations that result in the invocation of the IR plan

OFFLINE

Event Detection and Notification

While the triggers for some types of incidents are obvious (smoke, fire alarm), the triggers for others can be subtle. A large enterprise with a complex infrastructure might need to centralize the responsibility for identifying and reporting events into an event detection and notification (EDN) function.

The EDN function is responsible for identifying and correlating the sources of information, and for determining when that information constitutes an event needing additional scrutiny rather than just unusual activity. According to NIST's Draft publication 800-61, "Computer Security Incident Handling Guide," common sources of information include:

- Intrusion detection systems
- Anti-virus, anti-spyware, and anti-spam software
- File integrity checking software
- Operating system and application logs
- Network device logs

The EDN function would, for example, determine that a rate of invalid logon attempts, as indicated by the log records from an AAA server, indicates that a brute force attack may be underway. Similarly, the use of prohibited network protocols, as reported by an IDS (for example, an outgoing FTP session from one of the servers in the Web tier), or a threefold increase in network traffic between the application and database tiers, as reported by an enterprise performance monitoring product, might be considered an indicator of attack or possible intrusion.

The EDN function can improve the quality of the information that the incident response team uses to determine if the reported events indicate an actual incident.

The IR team lead, or IR duty officer, determines when the IR plan must be activated. An **IR duty officer** is a SIRT team member, other than the team leader, who is scanning the organization's information infrastructure for signs of an incident.

The next planning component is the determination of what must be done to react to the particular situation. First, you must identify or verify the source of the problem; for example, in the event of a virus infestation, you examine the antivirus software, system logs, and other monitoring systems. The next step is to determine the extent of the exposure or damage.

Once the extent is determined, the team must determine how to stop the incident if it is ongoing, for example by disconnecting infected systems from the network or by isolating network segments, terminating server sessions, disconnecting the Internet connection, or shutting down the network servers.

The final phase is to eliminate the source of the problem—for example, in the case of a virus; the team begins disinfecting systems by running antivirus software, searching for spyware, and so on. Should antivirus software be functional and up to date, the presence of a new virus should be documented.

Planning for After the Incident

Once the incident has been contained, the "actions after" phase begins. During this phase, the goal is to return each system to its previous state. The IR plan thus must describe the stages necessary to recover from the most likely events of the incident. It should also detail other events needed for the "actions after" phase, like the protection from follow-on incidents, forensic analysis, and the after-action review.

Follow-on incidents are highly probable in the case of infection or hacker attack. By identifying and resolving the avenues of attacks using forensic analysis, the organization can prevent these incidents from reoccurring.

Forensic analysis is the process of examining information assets for evidentiary material on how the incident transpired, while preserving the information's potential to be used as evidence in legal proceedings. Forensic analysis is covered in detail in Chapter 14.

Before returning to routine duties, the IR team must also conduct an **after-action review (AAR)**. An AAR is a detailed examination of the events that occurred from first detection to final recovery. All key players review their notes and verify that the IR documentation is accurate and precise. All team members review their actions during the incident and identify areas where the IR plan worked, didn't work, or should be improved. This allows the team to update the IR plan. The AAR can serve as a training case for future staff. It also brings to a close the actions of the IR team.

Planning for Before the Incident

"Before" actions include both preventative measures to manage the risks associated with a particular attack, and activities that ensure the preparedness of the IR team. As described in the opening scenario, it is only by means of routine rehearsal that the team can maintain a state of readiness to respond to attacks. This process includes training the SIRT, testing the IR plan, selecting and maintaining the tools used by the SIRT, and training users of the systems and procedures controlled by the organization.

Training the SIRT

Training incident response personnel can be conducted in a number of ways. There are several national training programs that focus on incident response tools and techniques. SANS offers a number of national conferences designed to train the information security professional (see *www.sans.org*), and includes incident response topics. SANS even has a dedicated set of conferences—SANS Forensics and Incident Response Education (SANSFIRE) specifically focused on incident response. In addition to formal external training, the organization can set up its own training program, wherein more experienced staff members share their knowledge with less experienced employees. An ongoing training program should include this mentoring-type training to prevent organizational knowledge from leaving when certain employees depart.

IR Plan Testing

An untested plan is no plan at all. Very few plans are executable as written; they must be tested to identify weaknesses, faults, and inefficient processes. Once problems are identified during the testing process, improvements can be made, and the resulting plan can be relied on in times of need. Six strategies that can be used to test contingency plans are:[8]

- Desk check—Each member of the SIRT performs a desk check by reviewing the IR plan and creating a list of correct and incorrect components. While not a true test, it is a good way to review the perceived feasibility and effectiveness of the plan.

- Structured walk-through—All involved individuals walk through the steps they would take during an actual event. This can consist of an on-site walk-through, in which the team discusses their actions at each location and juncture, or it may be more of a "chalk talk," in which team members sit together and discuss in turn their responsibilities as the incident unfolds.

- Simulation—Each team member works separately, simulating the performance of each task. The simulation stops short of the physical tasks—installing the backup, or disconnecting a communications circuit. The major difference between a walk-through and a simulation is that individuals work on their own tasks, and are responsible for identifying the faults in their own procedures.

- Parallel testing—Team members act as if an incident occurred, performing their required tasks and executing the necessary procedures, without interfering with the normal operations of the business. Great care must be taken to ensure that the procedures performed do not halt the operations of the business functions, creating an actual incident.

- Full interruption—Team members follow each and every procedure—interrupting service, restoring data from backups, and notifying of appropriate individuals. This type of testing is often performed after normal business hours in organizations that cannot afford to disrupt business functions. Although full interruption testing is the most rigorous, it is unfortunately too risky for most businesses.

- War gaming—Team members act as defenders, using their own equipment or a duplicate environment, against realistic attacks, executed by external information security professionals. This valid, effective training technique is so popular there are national competitions at conferences like Black Hat (*http://blackhat.com*) and DEFCON (*www.defcon.org*).[9] War gaming competition at the collegiate level is held at the West Point Military Training Academy (*www.cs.ucsb.edu/~vigna/CTF*). A national collegiate CyberDefense exercise has been held annually since 2005, and details can be found at *http://www.nationalccdc.org*.

At a minimum, organizations should conduct periodic walk-throughs (or chalk talks) of each of the CP component plans. A failure to update each of these plans as the business and its information resources change can erode the team's ability to respond to an incident, and possibly cause greater damage than the incident itself.

Training the Users

Training the end user to assist in the process of incident response is primarily the responsibility of those individuals who provide security education training and awareness (SETA) for the organization. As part of the ongoing employee training program, SETA trainers should instruct end users on:

- What is expected of them as members of the organization's security team
- How to recognize an attack; each user should be instructed on what to look for, and be apprised of the key attack indicators
- How to report a suspected incident, and whom to report it to—the help desk, and information security hotline or e-mail address (abuse@myorganization.com), or another designated mechanism
- How to mitigate the damage of attacks on the desktop by disconnecting the system from the network if they suspect an attack in progress, and by reporting suspected incidents promptly
- Good information security practices that prevent attacks on the desktop, such as:
  - Keeping antivirus software up to date
  - Using spyware detection software
  - Working with system administrators to keep the operating system and applications up to date with patches and updates
  - Not opening suspect e-mail attachments
  - Avoiding social engineering attacks by not providing critical information over the phone or e-mail
  - Not downloading and installing unauthorized software or software from untrusted sources
  - Protecting passwords and classified information

Incident Classification and Detection

Among the earliest challenges incident response planners face is determining how to classify events as they occur. Some events are the product of routine system activities, while others are indicators of situations needing an urgent response. **Incident classification** is the process of evaluating organizational events, determining which events are possible incidents, or **incident candidates**, and then determining whether or not the incident candidate is an actual incident or a nonevent, also called a false positive incident candidate.

Designing the process used to make this judgment is the role of the IR design team; the process of actually classifying an event is the responsibility of the IR team. Some organizations have a single incident center where all incident candidates are sent as soon as they are recognized. Others have geographically separate review locations, perhaps based on time zones, wherein preliminary determinations about the status of an incident candidate can be assessed. Still other organizations handle incident candidate evaluation by business unit, product line, or some other criterion.[10]

Initial reports from a variety of sources, including end users, intrusion detection systems, virus management software, and systems administrators are all ways to detect and track incident candidates. Careful training in incident candidate reporting allows end users, the help desk staff, and all security personnel to relay vital information to the IR team.

Classifying Incidents

A number of different events occurring in and around an organization signal the presence of an incident candidate. Unfortunately, these same events may occur when a network becomes overloaded, a computer or server encounters an error, or some normal operation of an information asset mimics an incident candidate. To help make the detection of actual incidents more reliable, D. L. Pipkin has identified three broad categories of incident indicators: *possible*, *probable*, and *definite*.[11] This categorization enables an organization to expedite the decision-making process of incident classification and ensure the proper IR plan is activated as early as possible.

Possible Indicators of an Incident

Four types of *possible* actual incidents are:

1. Presence of unfamiliar files—Users might discover unfamiliar files in their home directories or on their office computers. Administrators might find files that are not in a logical location or owned by an authorized user.
2. Presence or execution of unknown programs or processes—Users or administrators might detect unfamiliar programs running, or processes executing, on office machines or network servers. For more information on processes and services, see the Technical Details on processes and services.
3. Unusual consumption of computing resources—Memory consumption or hard disk usage might suddenly spike or fall. Many computer operating systems, including Windows 2000, Windows XP, and many UNIX variants, allow users and administrators to monitor CPU and memory consumption. Most computers also have the ability to monitor hard drive space. In addition, servers maintain logs of file creation and storage.
4. Unusual system crashes—Older operating systems running newer programs are notorious for locking up or spontaneously rebooting whenever the operating system is unable to execute a requested process or service. You are probably familiar with systems error messages such as "Unrecoverable Application Error," "General Protection Fault," and the infamous Windows Blue Screen of Death. However, if a computer system seems to be crashing, hanging, rebooting, or freezing more frequently than usual, the cause could be an incident candidate.

Probable Indicators of an Incident

Pipkin identifies four types of *probable* indicators of actual incidents:

1. Activities at unexpected times—If traffic levels on an organization's network exceed the baseline values, an incident candidate is probably present. If this activity surge occurs when few members of the organization are at work, the probability becomes much greater. Similarly, if systems are accessing drives, such as CD-ROM drives, in the absence of user actions, an incident may also be occurring.
2. Presence of new accounts—The presence of an account (or accounts) that the administrator did not create or that are not logged in the administrator's journal signal an incident candidate. An unlogged new account with root or other special privileges has an even higher probability of being an actual incident.
3. Reported attacks—If users of the system report a suspected attack, there is a high probability that an attack has occurred, which constitutes an incident. The technical sophistication of the person making the report should be considered.

4. Notification from IDS—If the organization has installed and correctly configured a host- or network-based intrusion detection system (IDS), then notification from the IDS indicates that an incident might be in progress. However, IDSs are seldom configured optimally and, even when they are, tend to issue many false positives or false alarms. The administrator must determine whether the notification indicates an incident, or is the result of a routine operation by a user or other administrator.

Definite Indicators of an Incident

Five types of events are *definite* indicators of an actual incident. That is, they clearly and definitively signal that an incident is in progress or has occurred. In these cases, the IR plan must be activated immediately.

1. Use of dormant accounts—Many network servers maintain default accounts, and quite often accounts exist from former employees, employees on a leave of absence or sabbatical without remote access privileges, or dummy accounts set up to support system testing. If any of these accounts begins accessing system resources, querying servers, or engaging in other activities, an incident is almost certain to have occurred.
2. Modified or missing logs—Log records are a valuable source of information, particularly when centralized for purposes of consolidation and analysis. Unfortunately, attackers are well aware of this value and often delete or modify log records to conceal their activities. For this reason, unexplained gaps in records or modifications to records are definite indicators of an incident.
3. Presence of hacker tools—Network administrators sometimes use system vulnerability and network evaluation tools to scan internal computers and networks to determine what a hacker can see. These tools are also used to support research into attack profiles. Too often the tools are used by employees, contractors, or outsiders with local network access to hack into systems. To combat this problem, many organizations explicitly prohibit the use of these tools without written permission from the CISO, making any unauthorized installation a policy violation. Therefore if unauthorized hacker tools are detected on a system, an incident has occurred.
4. Notifications by partner or peer—If a business partner or another connected organization reports an attack from your computing systems, then an incident has occurred.
5. Notification by hacker—Some hackers enjoy taunting their victims. If an organization's Web pages are defaced, it is an incident. If an organization receives an extortion request for money in exchange for its customers' credit card files, an incident is in progress.

In addition, the following events indicate that an incident is under way:

- Loss of availability: Information or information systems become unavailable.
- Loss of integrity: Users report corrupt data files, garbage where data should be, or data that just looks wrong.
- Loss of confidentiality: You are notified of sensitive information leaks or information you thought was protected has been disclosed.
- Violation of policy: If organizational policies addressing information or information security have been violated, an incident has occurred.
- Violation of law: If the law has been broken and the organization's information assets are involved, an incident has occurred.

Data Collection

The routine collection and analysis of data is required to properly detect and declare incidents. Even if an incident is not detected in real time, the data collected by automatic recording systems assists the teams in better understanding the normal and routine operations of the systems that process, transmit, and store information. As part of "knowing yourself," understanding the norm assists in the detection of the abnormal. Information that should be collected is presented in Table 12-2.[12]

TABLE 12-2 Data Categories and Types of Data to Collect

Data Category	Data to Be Collected
Network performance	■ Total traffic load in and out over time (packet, byte, and connection counts) and by event (new product or service release) ■ Traffic load (percentage of packets, bytes, connections) in and out over time sorted by protocol, source address, destination address, other packet header data ■ Error counts on all network interfaces
Other network data	■ Service initiation requests ■ Name of the user/host requesting the service ■ Network traffic (packet headers) ■ Successful connections and connection attempts (protocol, port, source, destination, time) ■ Connection duration ■ Connection flow (sequence of packets from initiation to termination) ■ States associated with network interfaces (up, down) ■ Network sockets currently open ■ Whether or not network interface card is in promiscuous mode ■ Network probes and scans ■ Results of administrator probes ■ Protocols in use
System performance	■ Total resource use over time (CPU, memory (used, free), disk (used, free)) ■ Status and errors reported by systems and hardware devices ■ Changes in system status, including shutdowns and restarts ■ File system status (where mounted, free space by partition, open files, biggest file) over time and at specific times ■ File system warnings (low free space, too many open files, file exceeding allocated size) ■ Disk counters (input/output, queue lengths) over time and at specific times ■ Hardware availability (modems, network interface cards, memory)
Other system data	■ Actions requiring special privileges ■ Successful and failed logins ■ Modem activities ■ Presence of new services and devices ■ Configuration of resources and devices

TABLE 12-2 Data Categories and Types of Data to Collect (continued)

Data Category	Data to Be Collected
Process performance	▪ Resources used (CPU, memory, disk, time) by specific processes over time; top resource-consuming processes ▪ System and user processes and services executing at any given time
Other process data	▪ User executing the process ▪ Process startup time, arguments, filenames ▪ Process exit status, time, duration, resources consumed ▪ The means by which each process is normally initiated (administrator, other users, other programs or processes), with what authorization and privileges ▪ Devices used by specific processes ▪ Files currently open by specific processes
Files and directories	▪ List of files, directories, attributes ▪ Cryptographic checksums for all files and directories ▪ Accesses (open, create, modify, execute, delete), time, date ▪ Changes to sizes, contents, protections, types, locations ▪ Changes to access control lists on system tools ▪ Additions and deletions of files and directories ▪ Results of virus scanners
Users	▪ Login/logout information (location, time): successful attempts, failed attempts, attempted logins to privileged accounts ▪ Login/logout information on remote access servers that appears in modem logs ▪ Changes in user identity ▪ Changes in authentication status, such as enabling privileges ▪ Failed attempts to access restricted information (such as password files) ▪ Keystroke monitoring logs ▪ Violations of user quotas

Applications	▪ Application- and service-specific information such as network traffic (packet content), mail logs, FTP logs, Web server logs, modem logs, firewall logs, SNMP logs, DNS logs, intrusion detection system logs, database management system logs
	   ▪ Services-specific information could be:
	   ▪ For FTP requests: Files transferred and connection statistics
	   ▪ For Web requests: Pages accessed, credentials of the requestor, connection statistics, user requests over time, which pages are most requested, and who is requesting them
	   ▪ For mail requests: Sender, receiver, size, and tracing information; for a mail server, number of messages over time, number of queued messages
	   ▪ For DNS requests: Questions, answers, and zone transfers
	   ▪ For a file system server: File transfers over time
	   ▪ For a database server: Transactions over time

TABLE 12-2 Data Categories and Types of Data to Collect (continued)

Data Category	Data to Be Collected
Log files	▪ Results of scanning, filtering, and reducing log file contents ▪ Checks for log file consistency (increasing file size over time; use of consecutive, increasing time stamps with no gaps)
Vulnerabilities	▪ Results of vulnerability scanners (presence of known vulnerabilities) ▪ Vulnerability patch logging

Managing Logs and Other Data Collection Mechanisms

When the data sources used for incident detection and classification are individual or aggregated log files, the management of those sources becomes more critical. The aggregated log files from network devices, servers, and even critical workstations can contain both indicators and documentation of the intrusion events. To be effective, logs must first be enabled. (Some types of logging are enabled by default; others must specifically be activated.) Logs should typically be stored off the entity that generates them (for example on a central syslogd server), and this storage area must be suitably hardened to protect the information.[13]

Managing logs involves the following:

▪ Be prepared to handle the amount of data generated by logging. Some systems may create literally gigabytes of data that must be stored or otherwise managed.

▪ Rotate logs on a schedule. As indicated, some systems overwrite older log entries with newer entries to comply with the space limitations of the system. Ensure that the rotation of log entries is acceptable, rather than accepting system defaults.

▪ Archive logs. Log systems can copy logs periodically to remote storage locations. There is a debate among security administrators as to how long log files should be maintained. Some argue that log files may be subpoenaed during legal proceedings and thus should be routinely destroyed to prevent unwanted disclosure during this process. Others argue that the information to be gained from analyzing legacy and archival logs outweighs the risk. Still others take the middle ground and aggregate the log information, then destroy the individual entries. Regardless of the method employed, some plan must be in place to handle these files or risk loss.

▪ Encrypt logs. If the organization does decide to archive logs, they should be encrypted in storage. Should the log file system be compromised, this prevents unwanted disclosure.

▪ Dispose of logs. Once log files have outlived their usefulness, they should be disposed of using a routine and secure process. [14]

Detecting Compromised Software

Who watches the watchers? (*Sed quis custodiet ipsos custodes?*) If the systems that monitor the network, servers, or other components are compromised, then the organization's incident detection is compromised. Some organizations use a separate intrusion detection system (IDS) sensor, or agents monitor the IDS itself. If you suspect the detection systems have been compromised, you can quarantine them and examine the installation by comparing them to either the original installation files, or to an insulated installation.

Challenges in Intrusion Detection

It should be painfully obvious by this point that the detection of intrusions can be a tedious and technically demanding process. Only those with advanced technical skills within a certain set of hardware and software can manually detect signs of an intrusion through reviews of logs, system performance, user feedback, and system processes and tasks. This underscores the value of two key facets of incident detection: (1) effective use of technology to assist in detection, and (2) the necessity of cooperation between incident response and information security professionals and the entire information technology department. The former is discussed in sufficient detail in the sections on IDS. With regard to the latter, the IT staff is best prepared to understand the day-to-day operations of the hardware, software, and networking components that support organizational operations on an ongoing basis. They can then work with the SIRT and information security teams to identify anomalies in the system performance and administration. This should underscore the necessity to integrate IT systems and network administrators as part of SIRT operations, if not SIRT team building.

Incident Reaction

An organization may have spent great effort in developing an incident response plan yet still be unprepared when an incident occurs. It is not enough to simply prepare plans; it is necessary to alter the culture of the organization to make the organization more responsive and resilient when incidents occur. The best plans may not always be the most thorough or the most elaborate; the best plans are those that improve the outcome when an incident occurs.

How and when to activate IR plans is determined by the IR strategy the organization chooses to pursue. Whether a one-size-fits-all IR strategy or a more complex and responsive multipart approach is chosen, the organization must make sure the outcome from the planned response meets the organization's strategic and tactical needs.

Selecting an IR Strategy

Once an actual incident has been confirmed, the IR team moves from the detection phase to the reaction phase. Once activated, the IR plan is designed to stop the incident, mitigate its effects, and provide information that facilitates recovering from the incident. Determining what an organization should do in any given incident requires that the organization have in place one or more IR strategies. Some organizations may choose to have a single IR strategy in place for all incidents. Others may choose to have several optional plans to handle different circumstances.

In formulating an incident response strategy, there are a number of factors that influence the organization's decision process:

- Are the affected systems impacting profitable operations?
- If information was stolen, what was the level of sensitivity or classification?
- Which business functions are being impacted and at what level?
- Has the incident been contained, or is it continuing?
- What is the origin of the emergency? Is it internal or external to the organization?
- Is the incident public knowledge?

- What are the legal reporting requirements? Does the law require this matter to be reported immediately to authorities? Who are those authorities? Should this matter be handled as a human resources function? Should this matter be handled as a civil suit?
- What, if any, steps should be immediately taken to discover the identity of an outside-agency attacker?
- As of the moment the incident is contained, what are the financial losses?[15]

Two general categories of strategic approaches or philosophies at either extreme in the range of options available to an organization as it responds to an incident are *protect and forget*—the simplest of strategies—and *apprehend and prosecute*, which requires a greater and more complex effort.[16] The response to the incident is the same regardless of which strategy is employed, but the data collection tasks differ dramatically.

Tasks performed when pursuing *protect and forget* focus on the detection, logging, and analysis of events for the purpose of determining how they happened and preventing reoccurrence. Once the current incident is over, who caused it or why is immaterial except insofar as it is relevant to the prevention of future incidents. Tasks performed when pursuing *apprehend and prosecute* focus on the identification and apprehension of the intruder (if a human threat-agent is involved), with additional attention given to the collection and preservation of potential evidentiary materials that might support administrative or criminal prosecution.

The key steps that are used in *protect and forget* and in *apprehend and prosecute* are shown in Table 12-3.

TABLE 12-3 Key Steps in Reaction Strategies

Key Steps in *Protect and Forget*	Key Steps in *Apprehend and Prosecute*
1. Determine if the event is a real incident.	1. Determine if the event is a real incident.
2. If the event is an incident, terminate the current intrusion.	2. If the event is an incident, and the circumstances warrant doing so, contact law enforcement.
3. Discover how access was obtained and how many systems were compromised.	3. Document each action taken, including the date and time, as well as who was present when the action was taken.
4. Restore the compromised systems to their pre-incident configuration.	4. Isolate the compromised systems from the network.
5. Secure the method of unauthorized access by the intruder on all systems.	5. If the organization has the capability, it should entice the intruder into a safe system that seemingly contains valuable data.
6. Document steps taken to deal with the incident.	6. Discover the identity of the intruder while documenting his or her activity.
7. Develop lessons learned.	7. Discover how the intruder gained access to the compromised systems, and secure these access points on all uncompromised systems.
8. Conduct brief evaluation by upper management in the incident aftermath.[17]	8. As soon as sufficient evidence has been collected, or when vital information or vital systems are endangered, terminate the current intrusion.

TABLE 12-3 Key Steps in Reaction Strategies (continued)	
Key Steps in *Protect and Forget*	Key Steps in *Apprehend and Prosecute*
	9. Document the current state of compromised systems.
	10. Restore the compromised systems to their pre-incident configuration.
	11. Secure the method of unauthorized access by the intruder on all compromised systems.
	12. Document in detail the time in man-hours, as well as the cost of handling the incident.
	13. Secure all logs, audits, notes, documentation, and any other evidence gathered during the incident, and appropriately identify it to secure the "chain of custody" for future prosecution.
	14. Develop lessons learned.
	15. Conduct brief evaluation by upper management in the incident's aftermath.[18]

CERT Intrusion Response Strategies

Intrusion response, a subcategory of incident response, focuses on those incidents that involve incursions into an organization's information infrastructure. CERT provides nine best practices for intrusion response:

- Establish policies and procedures for responding to intrusions
- Prepare to respond to intrusions
- Analyze all available information to characterize an intrusion
- Communicate with all parties that need to be aware of an intrusion and its progress
- Collect and protect information associated with an intrusion
- Apply short-term solutions to contain an intrusion
- Eliminate all means of intruder access
- Return systems to normal operation
- Identify and implement security lessons learned

Notification

As soon as the IR team determines that an incident is in progress, the right people must be immediately notified in the right order. Most response organizations, such as firefighters or the military, maintain an alert roster for all emergencies. An **alert roster** is a document containing contact information for the individuals who need to be notified in the event of an incident.

There are two ways to activate an alert roster: sequentially and hierarchically. A **sequential roster** requires that a contact person call each and every person on the roster. A **hierarchical roster** has the first person call certain other people on the roster, who in turn call other people, and so on. Each approach has advantages and disadvantages. The hierarchical system is quicker, because more people are calling at the same time, but the message can become distorted as it is passed from person to person. The sequential system is more accurate, but slower because a single contact person provides each responder with the message.

The **alert message** is a scripted description of the incident and consists of just enough information so that each responder knows what portion of the IR plan to implement without impeding the notification process. It is important to recognize that not everyone is on the alert roster—only those individuals who must respond to a specific actual incident. As with any part of the IR plan, the alert roster must be regularly maintained, tested, and rehearsed if it is to remain effective.

During this phase, other key personnel not on the alert roster, such as general management, must be notified of the incident as well. This notification should occur only after the incident has been confirmed, but before media or other external sources learn of it. In addition, some incidents are disclosed to the employees in general, as a lesson in security, and some are not, as a measure of security. Furthermore, other organizations may need to be notified, if it is determined that the incident is not confined to internal information resources, or if the incident is part of a larger-scale assault. For example, during Mafiaboy's distributed denial-of-service attack on multiple high-visibility Web-based vendors in late 1999, many of the target organizations reached out for help. In general, the IR planners should determine in advance whom to notify and when, and should offer guidance about additional notification steps to take as needed.

Documenting an Incident

As soon as an incident has been confirmed and the notification process is under way, the team should begin to document it. The documentation should record the *who, what, when, where, why,* and *how* of each action taken while the incident is occurring. This documentation serves as a case study after the fact to determine whether the right actions were taken and if they were effective. It also proves, should it become necessary, that the organization did everything possible to prevent the spread of the incident. Legally, the standards of due care protect the organization should an incident adversely affect individuals inside and outside the organization or other organizations that use the target organization's systems. Incident documentation can also be used as a simulation in future training sessions on future versions of the IR plan.

Incident Containment Strategies

One of the most critical components of IR is stopping the incident or containing its scope or impact. Incident containment strategies vary depending on the incident and on the amount of damage caused. Before an incident can be stopped or contained, however, the affected areas must be identified. During an incident is not the time to conduct a detailed analysis of the affected areas; those tasks are typically performed after the fact, in the forensics process. Instead, simple identification of what information and systems are involved determines the containment actions to be taken. Incident containment strategies focus on two tasks: stopping the incident and recovering control of the affected systems.

The IR team can attempt to stop the incident and try to recover control by means of several strategies. If the incident originates outside the organization, the simplest and most straightforward approach is to disconnect the affected communication circuits. Of course, if the organization's lifeblood runs through that circuit, this step may be too drastic; if the incident does not threaten critical functional areas, it may be more feasible to monitor the incident and contain it another way. One approach used by some organizations is to dynamically apply filtering rules to limit certain types of network access. For example, if a threat agent is attacking a network by exploiting a vulnerability in the Simple Network Management Protocol (SNMP), then applying a blocking filter for the commonly used IP ports for that vulnerability stops the attack without compromising other services on the network. Depending on the nature of the attack and the organization's technical capabilities, ad hoc controls can sometimes gain valuable time to devise a more permanent control strategy. Other containment strategies include the following:

- Disabling compromised user accounts
- Reconfiguring a firewall to block the problem traffic
- Temporarily disabling the compromised process or service
- Taking down the conduit application or server—for example, the e-mail server
- Stopping all computers and network devices

Obviously, the final strategy is used only when all system control has been lost, and the only hope is to preserve the data stored on the computers so that operations can resume normally once the incident is resolved. The IR team, following the procedures outlined in the IR plan, determines the length of the interruption.

Interviewing Individuals Involved in the Incident

Part of determining the scale, scope, and impact of an incident is the collection of information from those reporting the incident and responsible for the systems impacted by the incident. This can be potentially dangerous when you consider that one of the individuals interviewed during incident response may in fact be the cause, in the case of an internal incident. Interviews involve three groups of stakeholders: end users, help desk personnel, and systems administrators. Each group can provide a different perspective on the incident as well as clues to its origin, cause, and impact. Interviews with end users require the SIRT to collect information in a manner that does not intimidate the end user or overwhelm the end user with technical jargon and questions. The interview should make the user feel that he or she is contributing to the incident response capacity. Interviews with the help desk tend to be more technical and intense, and often seek information beyond that gained from the one or two individual users who initially contacted the help desk. Interviewers frequently ask the help desk staff to review previous trouble tickets, looking for signs of similar attacks that could indicate a previous incident or attempted incident by the same attacker. Interviews with systems administrators similarly seek additional information, specifically logs from the affected systems, and possibly online or offline forensic images, to be analyzed in a lab.

Recovering from Incidents

Once an incident has been contained, and system control has been regained, incident recovery can begin. As in the incident response phase, the first task is to inform the appropriate human resources. Almost simultaneously, the IR team must assess the full extent of the damage to determine what must be done to restore the systems. Each individual involved should begin recovery operations based on the appropriate incident recovery section of the IR plan.

The immediate determination of the scope of the breach of confidentiality, integrity, and availability of information and information assets is called *incident damage assessment*.

Incident damage assessment can take days or weeks, depending on the extent of the damage. The damage can range from minor (a curious hacker snooped around) to severe (the infection of hundreds of computer systems by a worm or virus). System logs, intrusion detection logs, configuration logs, as well as the documentation from the incident response provide information on the type, scope, and extent of damage. Using this information, the IR team assesses the current state of the information and systems and compares it to a known state. Individuals who document the damage from actual incidents must be trained to collect and preserve evidence in case the incident is part of a crime or results in a civil action.

The following sections detail the appropriate steps to be taken in the recovery process.[19]

Identify and Resolve Vulnerabilities

Although it may appear simple, identifying and resolving vulnerabilities could prove to be a major challenge in reestablishing operations. Forensic analysis, used as a tool for both intrusion analysis and evidentiary purposes, can also help organizations best assess how the incident occurred and what vulnerabilities were exploited. In some cases, such as disasters, computer forensics may not be necessary, but when hackers, worms, and other systems violations are involved, organizations can benefit greatly from better understanding exactly what occurred.

However, if the incident data is to be used in legal proceedings, it is imperative that the individuals performing the forensic collection and analysis be trained to recognize and handle the material in a way that does not violate its value as evidence in civil or criminal proceedings.

After any incident, address the safeguards that failed to stop or limit the incident, or were missing from the system in the first place, and install, replace, or upgrade them. Whether due to a faulty, malfunctioning, or misconfigured network security device such as a firewall, router, or VPN connection, or whether due to a breach in policy or data protection procedures, the safeguards that were already in place must be examined to determine if they were part of the incident. If the incident was due to a missing safeguard, an assessment as to why the safeguard was not in place should be conducted. It may be determined that the incident occurred because a planned safeguard had not been procured yet, or it may be determined that a safeguard that could have prevented or limited the incident was assessed as being unnecessary.

Evaluate monitoring capabilities, if present. Improve detection and reporting methods, or install new monitoring capabilities. Many organizations do not have automated intrusion detection systems. Some feel that the performance does not justify the cost, especially when perceptions of "it can't happen to me" cloud the judgment of those responsible for the recommendation. Unfortunately, some decision makers must witness firsthand or secondhand the damage, destruction, or loss caused by an incident before they are willing to commit to the expenses of intrusion monitoring. This is especially unfortunate because, in some cases, open source software can provide many of the capabilities needed with little or no additional hardware or software expense (for example, Snort, found at *www.snort.org*). Although each set of circumstances needs to be carefully analyzed, in many cases the expense of training staff and providing support for open source solutions costs much less than replacing existing proprietary solutions.

If you don't have monitoring capabilities, get them. If you have them, review the implementation and configuration to determine if they failed to detect the incident. Network or host IDSs won't detect all incidents, especially attacks that are not network-based. Burglar and fire alarm systems are also needed to detect physical forms of incidents.

Restore Data

The IR team must understand the backup strategy used by the organization, restore the data contained in backups, and then use the appropriate recovery processes from incremental backups or database journals to recreate any data that was created or modified since the last backup. Backup strategies and procedures are discussed in detail later in this chapter.

Restore Services and Processes

Compromised services and processes must be examined, verified, and then restored. If services or processes were interrupted in the course of regaining control of the systems, they need to be brought back online.

Continuously monitor the system. If an incident happened once, it could easily happen again. Hackers frequently boast of their exploits in chat rooms and dare their peers to match their efforts. If word gets out, others may be tempted to try the same or different attacks on your systems. It is therefore important to maintain vigilance during the entire IR process.

Restore Confidence Across the Organization

The IR team may wish to issue a short memorandum outlining the incident and assuring all that the incident was handled and the damage was controlled. If the incident was minor, say so. If the incident was major or severely damaged systems or data, reassure the users that they can expect operations to return to normal as soon as possible. The objective of this communication is to prevent panic or confusion from causing additional disruption to the operations of the organization.

IR Plan Maintenance

The ongoing maintenance of the IR plan includes procedures to conduct effective after-action reviews, plan review and maintenance, train staff that will be involved in incident response, and rehearse the process that maintains readiness for all aspects of the incident plan.

The After-Action Review

Before returning to its routine duties, the IR team must conduct one last process, the after-action review (AAR). The **after-action review** entails a detailed examination of the events that occurred, from first detection to final recovery. All key players review their notes and verify that the IR documentation is accurate and precise. All team members review the actions taken during the incident and identify areas where the IR plan worked, didn't work, or should improve. This exercise allows the team to update the IR plan. AARs are conducted with all role players in attendance. The SIRT team leader presents a timeline of events and highlights who was involved at each stage, with a summary of their actions.

Ideally, each involved person relates what they discovered or did, and any discrepancies between documentation and the verbal case are noted. The entire AAR is recorded for use as a training case for future staff. All parties should treat the AAR not as an inquisition, but as a discussion group. If properly structured and conducted, the AAR can have a positive effect on the organization's IR capacity and employee confidence in responding to incidents. If poorly handled, the AAR can actually reduce the organization's ability to react because individuals, especially users, may prefer to sweep potential incidents under the rug rather than risk improperly responding and having to face a punitive-seeming AAR.

AAR as Review Tool

The AAR serves as a review tool, allowing the team to examine how it responded to the incident. Examining the documentation of the incident should reveal the point at which the incident was first detected, the point at which the IR plan was enacted, and how the first responders and SIRT reacted. This is to ensure that the best methods were employed, and that any mistakes made during the process, whether from a failure to follow the IR plan or from errors in the IR plan, are not made again. The IR plan is continually reexamined during AARs to ensure the procedures are in fact the best method of responding to incidents. Should the AAR reveal that the incident represents a new type or variation of incident, additional material can be added to the IR plan to better prepare the team for future interactions.

AAR as Historical Record

An additional use of the AAR is as a historical record of events. Such a record may or may not be a requirement for legal proceedings, depending on the laws that apply to your organization. In any case, it is useful to be able to establish a timeline of events, drawn from a number of different sources, to show the evolution of the incident, from first identification to final resolution. This timeline then serves other purposes, as described in the following sections.

AAR as Case Training Tool

One of the positive aspects of an incident is that it can improve an organization's ability to respond to future incidents; that is, "That which does not kill us, makes us stronger."[20] By examining previous attacks, students of information security and incident response can learn from others' actions, whether correct or incorrect. You can learn as much from mistakes as from successes. As Thomas Edison is credited with saying, "I have not failed. I've just found 10,000 ways that won't work."

Honest effort in the pursuit of one's goals is not failure. By studying the AAR reports from an organization's past incidents, not only do the new information security professionals and incident response team members become familiar with the system, plans, and responses of the organization, but they also get a lesson in how to deal with the challenges of incident response in general. Part of knowing yourself is knowing how you and your team handle victories as well as defeats. But even in defeat, as in the case of a successful and consequential attack, the organization must continue, recover, and rebuild its defenses.

AAR as Closure

One final quote on the AAR and its reports, this one from Yogi Berra: "It ain't over til it's over." People require closure, especially in the wake of traumatic events. The AAR serves as a closure to organizational incidents, although there may still be a great deal of systems data and recovery and training to be done.

IR Plan Review and Maintenance

The specific processes for maintaining the IR plan vary from one organization to another, but there are some commonly used maintenance techniques. When shortcomings are noted, the plan should be reviewed and revised to remediate the deficiency. Deficiencies may come to light based on after-action reviews, when the plans are used for actual incidents, during rehearsals when the plan is used in simulated incidents, or by review during periodic maintenance. At periodic intervals, such as one year or less, an assigned member of management should undertake a review of the incident response plan that addresses the following questions:

- Has the plan been used since the last review?
- Were any AAR meetings held, and have the minutes of any such meetings been reviewed to note deficiencies that may need attention?
- Have any other notices of deficiency been submitted to the plan owner, and have they been addressed?

Depending on the answer to the questions above, the plan may need to be reviewed and amended by the CPMC. All changes proposed to the IR plan must be coordinated with the CPMC so that the plan remains aligned with the organization's other contingency planning documents.

Training

Because the nature of the IR plan dictates that any number of people may be called upon to fill the roles identified in the plan, the organization must undertake training programs to ensure that a sufficient pool of qualified staff members are available to execute the plan when it is activated.

The training plan should include references to the provisioning of actual or contingent credentials needed to execute the containment and recovery steps in the plan. It does little good to have trained and qualified staff on hand to restart servers if said staff does not have the credentials to authorize those actions.

Cross-training is also needed to make assurances that enough staff with the proper skills are available for all reasonably realistic scenarios. Remember that in some cases the IR plan, the DR plan, and the BC plan may all be functioning concurrently. Staff should be sufficiently cross-trained and authorization provisioning should be in place to allow a sufficient employee response to all likely scenarios.

Rehearsal

This ongoing and systematic approach to planning requires that plans be rehearsed until responders are prepared for the actions they are expected to perform. When structured properly, rehearsals can also supplement training by pairing less experienced staff members with more experienced staff members.

Data and Application Resumption

There are a number of data backup and management methods that aid in the preparation for incident response. The most commonly used varieties, disk backup and tape backup, are presented here. Backup methods must be founded in an established policy that meets organizational needs. In general, data files and critical system files should be backed up daily, with nonessential files backed up weekly.

Equally important is the determination of how long data should be stored. Some data must, according to law, be stored for specific lengths of time. If data is not covered by law or regulation, it may be in the organization's best interest to destroy it quickly. Management should create a formal data retention plan that includes recommendations from legal counsel that conform to the applicable laws, regulations, and standards. For routine data backups of critical data, the organization only needs to retain the one or two most recent copies (daily backups) and at least one off-site copy. For full backups of entire systems, at least one copy should be stored in a secure location, such as a bank vault, security deposit box, remote branch office, or other secure data storage facility.

Disk-to-Disk-to-Tape

With the decrease in the costs of storage media, including hard drives and tape backups, more and more organizations are creating massive arrays of independent but large-capacity disk drives to store information at least temporarily. In fact, many home users are using similar methods, adding external USB-mounted ATA drives, in the 200–300 GB range, and simply copying critical files to these external and portable devices as routine backup. The availability of these devices not only precludes the need for time-consuming tape backups, but also avoids the costs and implementation challenges of tape at the user level. It also allows quick and easy recovery of individual files and directories, unlike extractions from tape.

Individuals and organization alike can then build libraries of these devices, or massively connected storage area networks, to support larger-scale data backup and recovery. The problem with this technology is the lack of redundancy should both the online and backup versions fail, due to a virus or hacker intrusion. This is why the secondary data disk series should be backed up to tape or other removable media periodically.

Backup Strategies

There are three basic types of backups: full, differential, and incremental. A **full backup** is just that, a full and complete backup of the entire system, including all applications, operating systems components, and data. The advantage of a full backup is that it takes a comprehensive snapshot of the organization's system. The primary disadvantages are that it can require large amounts of media, and it can be time consuming. A **differential backup** is the storage of all files that have changed or been added since the last full backup. The differential backup is faster and uses less storage space than the full backup, but each daily differential backup is larger and slower than that of the day before. For example, if you conduct a full backup on Sunday, then Monday's backup contains all the files that have changed since Sunday, and Tuesday's backup contains all the files that have changed since Sunday as well, including Monday. By Friday, the quantity of data to back up has increased substantially. If one backup is corrupt, the previous day's backup contains almost all of the same information. An **incremental backup** only archives the data that have been modified that day, and thus requires less space and time than the differential. The downside to incremental backups is that if an incident occurs, multiple backups are needed to restore the full system. In general, incremental backups are designed to complete the backup in the shortest elapsed time. An incremental backup also requires less storage space.

Regardless of the strategy employed, the following guidelines apply: first, all on-site and off-site storage must be secured. It is common practice to use media-certified fire-proof safes or filing cabinets to store backup media. The off-site storage in particular must be in a safe location, such as a safety deposit box in a bank or at a professional backup and recovery service. The trunk of the administrator's car is not secure off-site storage. It is also important to provide a conditioned environment for the media, preferably an airtight, humidity-controlled, static-free storage container. Each media unit must be clearly labeled, and write protected. Because media wear out, it is important to retire individual media units before they reach the end of their useful life.

Tape Backup and Recovery

There is still value in tape backups as a cost-effective method for organizations with large quantities of data. Traditionally, tape has been able to store larger quantities of data in smaller containers. The most common types of tape media include digital audio tapes (DATs), quarter-inch cartridge (QIC) drives, 8 mm tape, digital linear tape (DLT) and Linear Tape Open (LTO). The media types differ in their capacity, lifetime, and performance characteristics, and a type will be chosen based on the capacity and performance requirements of the organization's backup processes.

The most common backup schedule is a daily on-site, incremental or differential backup, with a weekly off-site full backup. Most backups are conducted during twilight hours, when systems activity is lowest, and the probability of user interruption is limited. There are also some classic methods for selecting the files to back up. These include the six-tape rotation method, Grandfather-Father-Son, and the Towers of Hanoi.

OFFLINE

The Disappearing Backup Window

The time available to take servers and applications down for backup is called the backup window. The backup window used to be any time after daily online processing and nightly batch processing had been completed. However, with the rise of the global, Internet-connected, always-on enterprise, the backup window is a rapidly shrinking commodity.

The driving forces behind new backup modalities—online backups, disk-to-disk-to-tape backups—as well as the proliferation of new media types, have been the sharp decrease in the available backup window and the continuing increase in the amount of data to be backed up.

Six-Tape Rotation

The **six-tape rotation** method of backup uses a rotation of six sets of media and is perhaps the most simple and well known. It uses five media sets per week and offers roughly two weeks of recovery capability in a five-step process:

If a recovery is needed, the organization first attempts to recover the file(s) using the Monday through Thursday tapes, if they are on hand. If the file that needs to be restored is not contained within the backups that are on hand, the last full backup that was stored off-site is retrieved, and the file(s) recovered from that medium. For additional ease of use and redundancy, an organization can make a copy of each full backup so that an on-site version can be kept in the data center and an off-site set of full backup (Friday) tapes can be sent to the secure storage location. This prevents the need to retrieve the off-site set.

Grandfather-Father-Son

The Grandfather-Father-Son (GFS) method of backup uses five media sets *per week* and allows recovery of data for the previous three weeks.

Every second or third month, a group of media sets are taken out of the cycle for permanent storage, and a new set is brought in. This method equalizes the wear and tear on the tapes and helps to prevent tape failure.

The Towers of Hanoi

The Towers of Hanoi is a more complex approach than the previous two methods and is based on statistical principles to optimize media wear. This 16-step strategy assumes that five media sets are used per week, with a backup each night.

Selecting a Rotation Method

Which rotation method is best? Table 12-4 lists the advantages and disadvantages of each method.

TABLE 12-4 Selecting the Best Rotation Method[21]

Rotation Method	Advantages	Disadvantages
Six-tape rotation	Requires only a few tapes, therefore is an easy and cheap rotation method; ideal for small data volumes (as much capacity as one tape can hold).	Keeps only a week's worth of data, unless you regularly archive the full backup tapes.
Grandfather-Father-Son (GFS)	Provides the most secure data protection and implements monthly archival of tapes; it is also a simple method, which most software supports.	Requires more tapes, which can become expensive.
The Towers of Hanoi	Allows for easy full-system restores (no shuffling through tapes with partial backups on them); ideal for small businesses that wish to do full restores. Also, it is more cost effective than GFS (uses fewer tapes).	Requires a difficult rotation strategy, which is not as straightforward to implement as the other rotation methods. Unless your backup software supports it, this method is too complex to track tape rotation manually. Also requires a time-consuming full backup every session.

OFFLINE

The Threats to Stored Information

While most organizations understand very well the need to back up their information, fewer have recognized the risks of storing backups. Backup media holds copies of much, if not all, of an organization's information assets, and are commonly moved around outside the secured confines of the data center (transferred to a different data center, subsidiary, business partner, or offsite storage facility). If this media is lost or misplaced, this may constitute unauthorized disclosure of the information and trigger notifications as required by CA SB 1386 and other privacy legislation. Careful processes and the use of professional bonded couriers are among various techniques organizations can use to avoid accidental loss of backup media. New technologies such as tape encryption can also provide valuable protection for externalized data.

Another risk derives from the persistent nature of backup media—once written, the data remains until it is erased or overwritten with fresh data. Consider, for example, a magnetic tape containing the backup of a sensitive database. When the contents of the backup are replaced by newer backups, it is a common practice to return the tape to the "scratch pool" where it is available for reuse. If the contents of the medium are not erased before being returned to the pool, its contents are still available on the tape and can be accessed in violation of security policy. For this reason, it is a good practice to erase backup tapes before returning them to the scratch pool.

Backup and Recovery Elapsed Time

One of the drawbacks of tape backups is the time required to store and retrieve information. Even differential or incremental backups to tape can take some time to complete.

For planning purposes, remember that it typically requires at least twice as much time to restore information from backup media as it does to produce the backup. This additional time is required because disks usually write more slowly than they read.

Redundancy-Based Backup and Recovery Using RAID

Another form of data protection is provided through usage of **redundant array of independent**[22] **disks (RAID)** systems. RAID can overcome some of the limits of magnetic tape backup systems, and as seen later in the section titled Real-Time Protection, Server Recovery, and Application Recovery, RAID systems provide enhanced capabilities. Unlike tape backups, RAID uses a number of hard drives to store information across multiple drive units. For operational redundancy, this can spread out data and, when coupled with checksums, can eliminate or reduce the impact of a hard drive failure. There are many RAID configurations (called levels); the nine most common are covered in the following sections.

RAID Level 0

RAID 0 creates one larger logical volume across several available physical hard disk drives and stores the data in segments, called stripes, across all the disk drives in the array. This is also often called **disk striping** without parity, and is frequently used to combine smaller drive volumes into fewer, larger volumes to gain the advantages that larger volumes offer as well as offer increased I/O throughput. Unfortunately, failure of one drive makes all data inaccessible. In fact, this level of RAID does not improve the risk situation when using disk drives, but rather increases the risk of losing data from a single drive failure. Some RAID configurations combine RAID level 0 with RAID level 5 or RAID level 1 to provide both data protection and improved I/O throughput.

RAID Level 1

Commonly called **disk mirroring**, RAID level 1 uses two drives where data is written to both drives simultaneously, providing a backup if the primary drive fails. It is a rather expensive and inefficient use of media. Mirroring is often used to create duplicate copies of operating system volumes for high-availability systems, for example by splitting disk mirrors to create highly available copies of critical system drives.

RAID Level 2

This is a specialized form of disk striping with parity, and is not widely used (there are no commercial implementations). It uses a specialized parity coding mechanism known as the Hamming code to store stripes of data on multiple data drives and corresponding redundant error correction on separate error-correcting drives. This approach allows the reconstruction of data in the event some of the data or redundant parity information is lost.

RAID Levels 3 and 4

RAID 3 uses byte-level striping of data, and RAID 4 uses block-level striping of data. These approaches use a process in which the data is stored in segments on dedicated data drives, and parity information is stored on a separate drive. As in RAID 0, one large volume is used for the data, but the parity drive operates independently to provide error recovery.

RAID Level 5

This form of RAID is most commonly used in organizations that balance safety and redundancy against the costs of acquiring and operating the systems. It is similar to RAID 3 and 4 in that it stripes the data across multiple drives, but there is no dedicated parity drive. Instead, segments of data are interleaved with parity data and are written across all of the drives in the set.

RAID Level 6

This is a combination of RAID 1 and RAID 5 in that it "performs two different parity computations or the same computation on overlapping subsets of the data."[23]

RAID Level 7

This is a proprietary variation on RAID 5 in which the array works as a single virtual drive. RAID level 7 is sometimes performed by running special software over RAID 5 hardware.

RAID Level 10 or RAID Level 50

This is a combination of RAID 1 and RAID 0 or RAID 5. Raid 0 is used for its performance, and RAID 1/ RAID 5 is used for its fault tolerance.

Some of the more common implementations of RAID are illustrated in Figure 12-8.

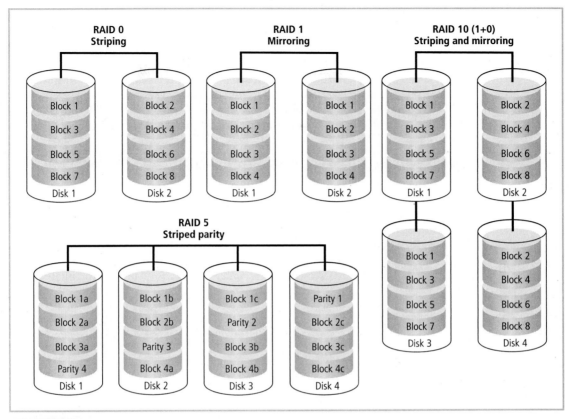

FIGURE 12-8　Popular RAID Implementations

Database Backups

Systems that make use of databases, whether hierarchical, relational, or object-oriented, require special backup and recovery procedures. Depending on the type of database and the software vendor, you may or may not be able to back up the database with the utilities that are provided with the server operating systems. A further consideration is whether or not system backup procedures can be used without interrupting the use of the database. In most databases, a system backup can work correctly only if all user access to the database is stopped (or quiesced). Using these databases while they are being backed up requires additional backup tools. Administrators also need to know whether the database being safeguarded is using special journal file systems, such as run-unit journals or after-image journals that enable database concurrency functions. If these file systems and the files they use are not backed up properly, the backup tapes or disk images may be unusable when they are used to restore the prior state of the system.

Application Backups

Some applications use file systems and databases in ways that invalidate the customary way of doing backup and recovery. In some cases applications write large binary objects as files and manage pointers, and they handle internal data structures in ways that make routine backups unable to handle the concurrency or complexity of the application. Make sure that members of the application support and development teams are part of the planning process when these systems' backup plans are made, and that these team members are included in training, testing, and rehearsal activities.

Real-Time Protection, Server Recovery, and Application Recovery

Some strategies that are employed seek to improve the robustness of a server or system, in addition to or instead of performing data backups. One approach that provides real-time protection as well as data backup is the use of mirroring. Mirroring provides duplication of server data storage by using multiple hard drive volumes, as described earlier in the section on RAID level 1. RAID level 1 can be achieved with software or hardware, writing data to other drives, even if they are located on other systems. This concept of mirroring can be extended to vaulting and journaling, which are discussed later in this chapter.

OFFLINE

Disk-to-Disk-to-Tape

One multinational enterprise needed to provide backups for its very large e-mail servers. Tape backups, even using the fastest drives available, were far too slow. To solve this problem, the enterprise used the capabilities provided by its enterprise disk arrays to provide three-way mirroring. The primary e-mail server storage area was mirrored to two copies. On Sundays, the first copy was broken out of the mirror to provide the weekly view of the server and written off to tape, while the primary and tertiary mirrors continued operation. For the daily backup, the tertiary mirror was broken off and backed up to tape while the primary cached all changes in a journal. When the tape backup of the tertiary was complete, the mirror was reestablished with the primary, and the cached changes were applied to re-sync the mirrors without the need to copy the entire server storage area.

On Saturday, the secondary mirror was reestablished and copied the contents of the primary.

This solution allowed the e-mail servers to operate without interruption while providing the tape backups required for disaster recovery.

This very expensive solution demonstrates that meeting the availability needs of the connected enterprise can be a challenging exercise.

One way to implement server recovery and redundancy through mirroring servers uses hot, warm, and cold servers. In this strategy, the online primary server is the hot server, and provides the services necessary to support operations. The warm server serves as an ancillary or secondary server that services requests when the primary is busy or down. The cold server is the administrator's test platform, and it should be identically configured to the hot and warm servers. Before a patch, upgrade, or new application is applied to the hot and warm servers, it is first tested on the cold server. Should the hot server go down, the warm server automatically takes over as the hot server, and the cold server can be used as the new warm server while the hot server is taken offline for repair. Recent advances in server recovery have developed **bare metal recovery** technologies designed to replace operating systems and services when they fail. These applications allow you to restart the affected system from a CD-ROM or other remote drive, and quickly restore your operating system by providing images backed up from a known stable state. Linux and UNIX have been able to use boot CDs such as Knoppix or Helix for some time, but Microsoft has only recently developed its Preinstallation Environment (Win PE) to provide similar capabilities. Use of bare metal recovery applications, in conjunction with routine backups, allows the recovery of entire servers quickly and easily.

Another option for online backup and application availability is server clustering. Clustering works similarly to the hot/warm server model described earlier. The simpler clustering model is active/passive clustering, where two identically configured servers share access to the application data storage. At any point in time, only the active server is controlling the storage and responding to requests. If the active server crashes or hangs, the passive server takes control of the application storage and begins servicing requests. Active/active clustering is a more complex model where all members of a cluster simultaneously provide application services. As noted earlier, mirroring of data, whether through the use of RAID level 1 or alternative technologies, can increase the reliability of primary systems and also enhance the effectiveness of business resumption strategies. Vaulting and journaling dramatically increase the level of protection and are discussed in the sections that follow.

Electronic Vaulting

The bulk transfer of data in batches to an off-site facility is called **electronic vaulting** and is illustrated in Figure 12-9. This transfer is usually conducted via dedicated network links or data communications services provided for a fee. The receiving server archives the data as it is received. Some disaster recovery companies specialize in electronic vaulting services. The primary criteria for selecting an electronic vaulting (or e-vaulting) solution are the cost of the service and the required bandwidth. If the organization does not currently have enough bandwidth to support e-vaulting, it must select a vendor to obtain the additional bandwidth needed.[24]

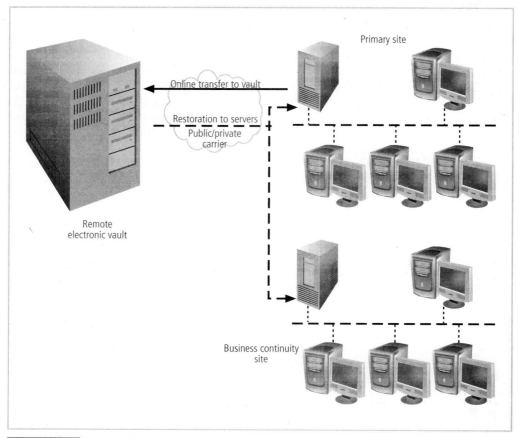

Online transfer to vault

Primary site

Restoration to servers
Public/private
carrier

Remote
electronic vault

Business continuity
site

FIGURE 12-9 Electronic Vaulting

Electronic vaulting can be more expensive than tape backup and slower than data mirroring, so should be used only for data that warrants the additional expense, such as critical transactional data and customer databases. While e-vaulting can be performed over public infrastructure, the data must be encrypted while in transit, which can slow the data transfer rate.

For managed solutions from vendors, typically a software agent is installed on all servers to be included into the e-vaulting process. Once installed, the software initiates a full backup of data to the remote vault and then prepares to continuously copy data as it is created or modified. The vendor is then responsible for the maintenance and protection of the data. Data can be accessed via a Web interface or by using installed software to facilitate restoration or validation of transferred data. Different applications can facilitate the transfer of organizationally owned equipment over public or private communications links, for organizations that want to transfer data to their own vaults.

Remote Journaling

Remote journaling (RJ) is the transfer of live transactions to an off-site facility. RJ was first developed by IBM in 1999 for its AS/400 – V4R2 operating system. RJ differs from electronic vaulting in that only transaction data is transferred, not archived data, and the transfer is performed online and much closer to real time. Although electronic vaulting is much like a traditional backup with a dump of data to the off-site storage, remote journaling involves online activities on a systems level, much like server fault tolerance, in which data is written to two locations simultaneously or asynchronously, as preferred. RJ facilitates the recovery of key transactions in nearly real time. Figure 12-10 shows an overview of the remote journaling process.

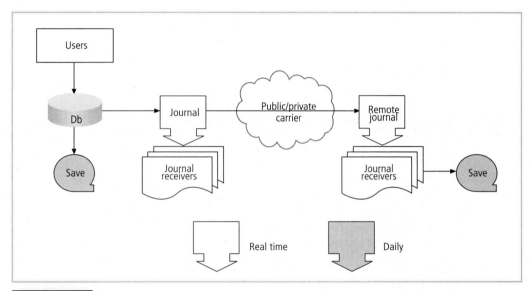

FIGURE 12-10   Remote Journaling[25]

When journaling is enabled, the operating system initiates a process that creates a record of changes to the object being journaled. These changes are recorded as a journal entry, which is stored in a journal receiver, similar to storing a record in a database file. Once the journal receiver is full, or reaches a preset level, a new journal receiver is linked to the journal, and the full receiver is available for storage. To recover data, the stored receivers can be pulled from tape and applied to the data in the production database, restoring the data to a known stable point. Remote journaling involves the transference of journal entries to a remote journal, which in turn stores them to a remote journal receiver. This remote journal receiver is transferred to remote tape or other storage when full, creating a virtual real-time backup of the entries.[26]

Database Shadowing

Database shadowing is the propagation of transactions to a remote copy of the database. It combines electronic vaulting with remote journaling, applying transactions to the database simultaneously in two separate locations. This technology can be used with multiple databases on a single drive in a single system, or with databases in remote locations across a public or private carrier, as shown in Figure 12-11. Shadowing techniques are generally used by organizations needing immediate data recovery after an incident or disaster. The "shadowed" database is available for reading as well as writing, and thus serves as a dynamic off-site backup. Database shadowing also works well for read-only functions, such as the following:

- Data warehousing and mining
- Batch reporting cycles (for example, quarterly and year-end reports)
- Complex SQL queries
- Local online access at the shadow site
- Load balancing[27]

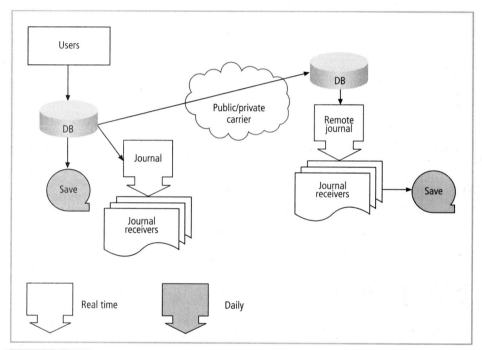

FIGURE 12-11 Database Shadowing

Network-Attached Storage and Storage Area Networks

Two other advances in data storage and recovery are **Network-Attached Storage (NAS)** and **Storage Area Networks (SANs)**. NAS is usually implemented via a single device or server that attaches to a network, and uses common communications methods, such as Windows file sharing, NFS, CIFS, HTTP directories, or FTP, to provide an online storage environment. NAS, which is often used for additional storage, is configured to allow users or groups of users to access data storage. NAS does not work well with real-time applications because of the latency of the communication methods.

SANs are similar in concept but differ in implementation. NAS uses TCP/IP-based protocols and communications methods, but SANs use fibre channel or iSCSI connections between the systems needing the additional storage and the storage devices themselves. This difference is illustrated in Figure 12-12 and described in Table 12-5.[28]

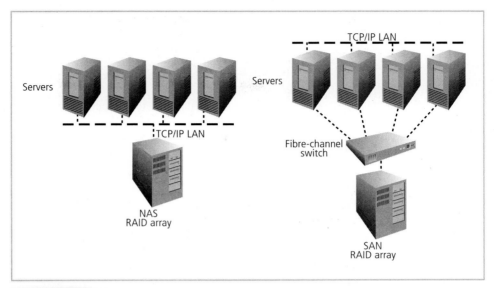

FIGURE 12-12   NAS Versus SAN

TABLE 12-5   NAS Versus SAN

Concern	NAS	SAN
Connectivity	Any machine that can connect to a LAN and use standard protocols (such as NSF, CIFS, or HTTP)	Only server-class devices with iSCSI or fibre channel; has a topology limit of 10 km
Addressing, identification and file transfer	By filename with NAS handling security, including permissions, authentication, and file locking	By disk block number, with no individual security control

For general file sharing or data backup, NAS provides a less expensive solution. For high-speed and higher-security solutions, SANs may be preferable.

Service Agreements

When an organization is making arrangements for an off-site support option, the terms and conditions of that site should be made known to all parties, by negotiating and executing a service agreement. **Service agreements** are the contractual documents guaranteeing certain minimum levels of service provided by vendors.

An effective service agreement should contain the following sections:

1. Definition of applicable parties—Identifies to whom the document applies
2. Services to be provided by the vendor—Specifies exactly what the client is to receive in exchange for the payments
3. Fees and payments for these services—Specifies what the vendor receives in exchange for the services rendered

4. Statements of indemnification—Declares that the vendor is not liable for actions taken by the client
5. Nondisclosure agreements and intellectual property assurances—Obligates the vendor to protect the confidentiality of the client's information from everyone except authorized law enforcement officials or other parties that serve legal papers directing the vendor to provide such information
6. Noncompetitive agreements (covenant not to compete)—States that the client will not use the vendor's services to compete directly with the vendor, and that the client will not use vendor information to gain a better deal with another vendor

Chapter Summary

- Contingency planning is the process of positioning an organization to prepare for, detect, react to, and recover from events that threaten the security of information resources and assets. The goal of CP is to restore normal operations after an unexpected event—in other words, to make sure things get back to the way they were within a reasonable period of time.

- The business impact analysis (BIA), the first phase in the CP process, provides the CP team with information about systems and the threats they face.

- The actions an organization should take while the incident is in progress should be defined in an incident response plan (IR plan).

- Disaster recovery planning (DRP) entails the preparation for and recovery from a disaster, whether natural or human-made.

- Business continuity planning (BCP) ensures that critical business functions can continue if a disaster occurs.

- Incident classification is the process of determining which events are possible incidents. Three broad categories of incident indicators have been established: possible, probable, and definite. The routine collection and analysis of data is required to properly detect and declare incidents.

- How and when to activate IR plans is determined by the IR strategy the organization chooses to pursue. The organization must make sure the outcome from the planned response meets the organization's strategic and tactical needs. Two general strategies govern how an organization responds to an incident: protect and forget or apprehend and prosecute.

- One of the most critical components of IR is stopping the incident or containing its scope or impact. Incident containment strategies vary depending on the incident and on the amount of damage caused.

- Once an incident has been contained, and system control has been regained, incident recovery can begin. The IR team must assess the full extent of the damage to determine what must be done to restore the systems.

- The ongoing maintenance of the IR plan includes effective after-action reviews, planned review and maintenance, training staff that will be involved in incident response, and rehearsing the process that maintains readiness for all aspects of the incident plan.

■ There are a number of data backup and management methods that aid in the preparation for incident response. The most commonly used varieties are disk backup and tape backup. Backup methods must be founded in an established policy that meets organizational needs.

Review Questions

1. What are the phases of the incident response development process? What are the critical elements of each?
2. Who are the typical stakeholders in the incident response process?
3. What is the security incident response team (SIRT)?
4. What stages should be used in the development of the SIRT?
5. What are the recommended structural categories of models that might be used to develop incident response teams? What is an incident candidate?
6. What are the three broad categories of incident indicators? What types of events are considered possible indicators of actual incidents? What types of events are considered probable indicators of actual incidents? What types of events are considered definite indicators of actual incidents?
7. What types of events indicate that an incident is in progress?
8. What is a false positive?
9. What is noise? Is noise different from a false positive event?
10. What are the components of an incident response plan?
11. Would you say that IR requires a lot of organizational commitment, or a little? What are the major commitments an effective IR requires?
12. What are the key factors that influence an organization's selection of an IR strategy?
13. What are the key steps included in the *protect and forget* IR strategy? What are the key steps included in the *apprehend and prosecute* IR strategy?
14. What is the primary objective of recovery operations during an incident response?
15. What are the key steps used to accomplish recovery?
16. Why is the restoration of user confidence an important step in the recovery process?
17. What is an after-action review? What are the primary reasons for undertaking an after-action review?
18. What are the primary techniques used for plan review and maintenance?
19. What is the difference between training and cross-training? Why are both necessary?
20. What purpose does rehearsal serve? Why should organizations continue to rehearse once a plan is known to work?

Exercises

1. Using a Web browser, search for the term "CERT Intruder Detection Checklist." Locate and review the module on Detecting Signs of Intrusions. What information should be included in a training program for (a) information security technicians, (b) systems administrations, and (c) business personnel?
2. Using a Web browser, search for the term "CERT Intruder Detection Checklist." Locate and review the module on Responding to Intrusions. What information should be included in a training program for (a) information security technicians, (b) systems administrations, and (c) business personnel?

3. Using a Web browser, go to *www.us-cert.gov/current*. Identify the top current incident threats. Categorize the incidents as either technical or behavioral (such as phishing). What is the largest group?

4. Using a Web browser, go to *www.sans.org/rr*, the SANS reading room. What headings are available that would benefit someone preparing to organize and train an incident response team? Select one of these headings and then select a paper from within it. Summarize the paper and bring your summary to class to discuss.

5. Using the list of possible, probable, and definite indicators of an incident, draft a recommendation to assist a typical end user in identifying these indicators. Alternatively, using a graphics package such as PowerPoint, create a poster to make the user aware of the key indicators.

Case Exercises

Review the opening scenario, and then consider these questions:

1. In the scenario, the group was practicing for a snow emergency. What other incident cards would you expect to see in addition to power outage?

2. For each of the incident cards you listed, what would be the proper response?

3. How often should an organization rehearse its contingency plans?

4. Who should coordinate rehearsal of the contingency plans? Why is that the appropriate person?

5. What degree of cross-training among the various roles in the plans is most effective?

6. Identify the advantages and disadvantages of such a cross-training plan. What trade-offs do you think exist between extensive and minimal cross-training?

7. Notice that the corporate CIO and CEO were not at this rehearsal. Do you think it is important that the CIO, or even the CEO, participate in this kind of readiness exercise? Why or why not?

8. How can you make progress in contingency planning in the face of resistance from upper management?

Endnotes

1. NIST. *Special Publication 800-18: Guide for Developing Security Plans for Information Technology Systems.* December 1998. Accessed January 2, 2008. *http://csrc.nist.gov/publications/nistpubs/800-18-Rev1/sp800-18-Rev1-final.pdf.*

2. *Why You Need a Disaster Recovery Plan.* Accessed May 13, 2003. *http://sb.thehartford.com/reduce_risk/disaster_recovery.asp.*

3. Carnegie Mellon University, "Detecting Signs of Intrusion" (2000), accessed February 17, 2005, from *www.cert.org/security-improvement/modules/m09.html.*

4. Carnegie Mellon University, "Detecting Signs of Intrusion," (2000), accessed February 17, 2005, from *www.cert.org/security-improvement/modules/m06.html.*

5. NIST. *Special Publication 800-61* (2004).

6. Carnegie Mellon University, *Handbook for Computer Security Incident Response Teams (CSIRT), 77* (2003), accessed February 17, 2005, from *www.cert.org/archive/pdf/csirt-handbook.pdf.*

7. See note 1 above.

8. Ronald L. Krutz and Russell Dean Vines, *The CISSP Prep Guide: Mastering the Ten Domains of Computer Security* (New York: John Wiley and Sons, 2001), 288.

9. While the authors emphatically denounce the actions of hackers and the criminal acts associated with hacking, these conferences typically are attended not only by hackers, but also by information security professionals and representatives of law enforcement and the military. In keeping with our philosophy of "know your enemy," one cannot pass up the opportunity to visit the enemy's camp and observe them preparing for battle, learning their strategies and tactics firsthand.

10. V. Masurkar, "Responding to a Customer's Security Incidents—Part 2: Executing a Policy," Sun Microsystems Web site, March 2003, accessed July 3, 2004, from *www.sun.com/blueprints/0403/817-1796.pdf*.

11. Donald L. Pipkin, *Information Security: Protecting the Global Enterprise* (Upper Saddle River, NJ: Prentice Hall PTR, 2000), 256.

12. CERT, "Identify Data that Characterize Systems and Aid in Detecting Signs of Suspicious Behavior," CERT Security Improvement Modules, accessed May 25, 2005, from *www.cert.org/security-improvement/practices/p091.html*.

13. NIST. *Special Publication 800-92. Guide to Computer Security Log Management.*

14. Phillip Maier, *Audit and Trace Log Management* (Boca Raton, FL: Auerbach, 2006).

15. A. Sterneckert, *Critical Incident Management.* (Boca Raton, FL: Auerbach/CRC Press LLC, 2004).

16. D. Adler and K. Grossman, "Establishing a Computer Incident Response Plan," accessed July 17, 2004, from *www.fedcirc.gov/library/documents/82-02-70.pdf*.

17. See note 2.

18. See note 2.

19. Donald L. Pipkin. *Information Security: Protecting the Global Enterprise* (Upper Saddle River, NJ: Prentice Hall PTR, 2000), 285.

20. Friedrich Nietzsche, "Friedrich Nietzsche Quotes," accessed May 20, 2005, from *www.brainyquote.com/quotes/quotes/f/friedrichn101616.html*.

21. Exabyte, "The Basic Backup Guide," accessed July 6, 2005, from *http://www.exabyte.com/support/online/documentation/whitepapers/basicbackup.pdf*.

22. The original title of Patterson, Gibson, and Katz's 1988 paper had "inexpensive" rather than "independent" to highlight the differences in cost between the expensive mainframe disks of the time and the much less expensive mass market disks used in their RAID implementation. Eventually, this was changed to "independent."

23. Answers.com, "RAID," accessed October 12, 2005, from *www.answers.com/RAID*.

24. Rick Cook, "Deciding on Electronic Vaulting," January 22, 2002, accessed July 7, 2005, from *http://searchstorage.techtarget.com/tip/1,289483,sid5_gci797551,00.html?bucket=ETA*.

25. Based in part on graphics from Chris Hird and Shield, "Remote Journaling and Data Recovery," accessed July 8, 2005, from *www.shield.on.ca/download/Remote%20Journaling%20and%20Data%20Recovery.pdf*.

26. iTera, "The Benefits of Remote Journaling in iSeries High-Availability Solutions," accessed July 8, 2005, from *http://advgroup.com/NEWpdfs/Benefits%20of%20Remote%20Journaling%20-%20whitepaper.pdf*.

27. ENet, "Data Recovery Without Data Loss," accessed July 11, 2005, from *www.enet.com/enet.com.nsf/PAGES_RRDF_Recov.html?OpenPage&charset=iso-8859-1*.

28. NAS vs SAN, "Technology Overview," accessed July 11, 2005, from *www.nas-san.com/differ.html*.

Intrusion Detection and Prevention Systems

13

> Bloody hell, Ma'am, what's he doing in here?
>
> **ELIZABETH ANDREWS, BUCKINGHAM PALACE MAID, ON DISCOVERING AN EARLY-MORNING INTRUDER IN THE BEDROOM OF QUEEN ELIZABETH II, QUOTED IN LONDON *OBSERVER* 18 JULY, 1982**

MATTHIAS PAUL, AT THE END OF his graveyard shift, was reviewing and finalizing the automated intrusion event recognition report for one of ATI's many customers, the Springdale Independent School District (SISD), for whom ATI provided hosting services and limited intrusion prevention services. SISD had its own in-house information security group, but the work of screening the automated intrusion detection and prevention system had been outsourced to ATI.

Matthias opened up the intrusion event resolution application. The system correlated all of the various system logs and event recordings from the many services that ATI provided to SISD. As he worked his way through the false alarms, he came across a log entry from a Web server indicating that an external network location had tried to connect to the intranet-based student records application. The system had refused entry. Since Matthias knew that SISD only allowed remote access to student records using a VPN connection with two-factor authorization, he thought he would look at the log files from the VPN concentrator, and also at the log from the VPN authentication server.

The logs showed that the user who had tried to connect to the student records system had not attempted to set up a VPN connection. Either someone was trying to hack the system, or an authorized user had forgotten all of their training about security policy and remote access.

Matthias looked at the connection attempt and found the TCP/IP address of the person who had tried to access the student records system. It was registered to a pool of addresses used by the biggest Internet service provider (ISP) in the city where SISD was located. It would take a court order to get access to the detailed ISP records to find out who had tried to access the system. On the other hand, it was easy to identify the user account that had been used to attempt access.

Matthias mumbled, "Hmmm…looks like a user just forgot to follow the rules."

He pulled up the screen in the intrusion event resolution system to escalate the event from a candidate incident to an actual incident. He provided all of the facts he had discovered and then moved on to the next item. He knew someone would be getting an unpleasant contact from the SISD security group in the near future.

LEARNING OBJECTIVES:

Upon completion of this material, you should be able to do the following:

- Describe the various technologies that are used to implement intrusion detection and prevention
- Define honey pots, honey nets, and padded cell systems
- Describe the technologies used to create honey pots, honey nets, and padded cell systems

Introduction

Many organizations deploy systems that enable them to detect and even prevent an intrusion into their information systems. This chapter explains basic intrusion detection and prevention concepts and terminology, and then describes the function and methodology of the available intrusion/extrusion detection and prevention systems. The chapter goes on to describe some powerful tools that go beyond routine intrusion detection and prevention, and which are known as honey pots, honey nets, and padded cell systems.

Intrusion Detection and Prevention

An **intrusion** occurs when an attacker attempts to gain entry or disrupt the normal operations of an information system, almost always with the intent to do harm. Even when such attacks, are self-propagating, as in the case of viruses and distributed denial-of-service attacks, they are almost always instigated by an individual whose purpose is to harm an organization. Often, the differences among intrusion types lie with the attacker: some intruders don't care which organizations they harm and prefer to remain anonymous, while others crave notoriety. In recent years the term *extrusion* has been used to describe the release of sensitive data from organizations. The detection and prevention of data extrusion is one of the control objectives of a modern information security system.

OFFLINE

Extrusion Detection

Many organizations monitor the traffic entering their networks for signs of attacks, but fewer examine the traffic leaving their networks. In his book *Extrusion Detection*, Richard Bejtlich makes the important observation that it may be easier to detect intrusions by examining the traffic leaving the network. For example, a successful compromise of a Web server may be followed by the transfer of a large number of files to the attacker's server. Therefore, monitoring the *outgoing* FTP traffic from the Web server could help organizations identify a compromised system.

Intrusion detection consists of procedures and systems that identify system intrusions. **Intrusion reaction** encompasses the actions an organization takes when an intrusion is detected. Intrusion *prevention* consists of activities that deter an intrusion. Some important intrusion prevention activities are writing and implementing good enterprise information security policy, planning and performing effective information security programs, installing and testing technology-based information security countermeasures (such as firewalls and intrusion detection/prevention systems), and conducting and measuring the effectiveness of employee training and awareness activities. These actions of intrusion detection and prevention seek to limit the loss from an intrusion, and return operations to a normal state as rapidly as possible. **Intrusion correction** activities finalize the restoration of operations to a normal state, and seek to identify the source and method of the intrusion in order to ensure that the same type of attack cannot occur again.

Information security **intrusion detection systems (IDSs)** became commercially available in the late 1990s. An IDS works like a burglar alarm in that it detects a violation (some system activity analogous to an opened or broken window) and activates an alarm. This alarm can be audible and/or visual (producing noise and lights, respectively), or it can be silent (an e-mail message or pager alert). With almost all IDSs, system administrators can choose the configuration of the various alerts and the alarm levels associated with each type of alert. Many IDSs enable administrators to configure the systems to notify them directly of trouble via e-mail or pagers. The systems can also be configured—again like a burglar alarm—to notify an external security service organization of a "break-in." The configurations that enable IDSs to provide customized levels of detection and response are quite complex. A current extension of IDS technology is the **intrusion prevention system (IPS)**, which can detect an intrusion, and also prevent that intrusion from *successfully* attacking the organization by means of an active response. Because the two systems often coexist, the combined term **intrusion detection/ prevention system (IDPS)** is used to describe current anti-intrusion technologies.

IDPS Terminology

In order to understand IDPS operational behavior, you must first become familiar with some IDPS terminology. The following is a list of IDPS terms and definitions drawn from the marketing literature of a well-known information security company, TruSecure, which are in common use across the industry:

- **Alert** or **alarm**: An indication that a system has just been attacked or is under attack. IDPS alerts and alarms take the form of audible signals, e-mail messages, pager notifications, or pop-up windows.

- **Evasion:** The process by which attackers change the format and/or timing of their activities to avoid being detected by the IDPS.

- **False attack stimulus:** An event that triggers an alarm when no actual attack is in progress. Scenarios that test the configuration of IDPSs may use false attack stimuli to determine if the IDPSs can distinguish between these stimuli and real attacks.

- **False negative:** The failure of an IDPS to react to an actual attack event. This is the most grievous failure, since the purpose of an IDPS is to detect and respond to attacks.

- **False positive:** An alert or alarm that occurs in the absence of an actual attack. A false positive can sometimes be produced when an IDPS mistakes normal system activity for an attack. False positives tend to make users insensitive to alarms, and thus reduce their reactivity to actual intrusion events.

- **Noise:** Alarm events that are accurate and noteworthy but that do not pose a significant threat to information security. Unsuccessful attacks are the most common source of IDPS noise, and some of these may in fact be triggered by scanning and enumeration tools deployed by network users without intent to do harm.

- **Site policy:** The rules and configuration guidelines governing the implementation and operation of IDPSs within the organization.

- **Site policy awareness:** An IDPS's ability to dynamically modify its configuration in response to environmental activity. A so-called *smart* IDPS can adapt its reactions in response to administrator guidance over time and to circumstances of the current local environment. A smart IDPS logs events that fit a specific profile instead of minor events, such as file modification or failed user logins. The smart IDPS knows when it does *not* need to alert the administrator—for example, when an attack is using a known and documented exploit that the system is protected from.

- **True attack stimulus:** An event that triggers alarms and causes an IDPS to react as if a real attack is in progress. The event may be an actual attack, in which an attacker is at work on a system compromise attempt, or it may be a drill, in which security personnel are using hacker tools to conduct tests of a network segment.

- **Tuning:** The process of adjusting an IDPS to maximize its efficiency in detecting true positives, while minimizing both false positives and false negatives.

- **Confidence value:** A value placed upon an IDPS's ability to detect and identify certain types of attacks correctly. The confidence value an organization places in the IDPS is based on experience and past performance measurements. The confidence value, which is based upon *fuzzy logic*, helps an administrator determine how likely it is that an IDPS alert or alarm indicates an actual attack in progress. For example, if a system deemed 90 percent capable of accurately reporting a denial-of-service attack sends a denial-of-service alert, there is a high probability that an actual attack is occurring.

- **Alarm filtering:** The process of classifying IDPS alerts in order to help an IDPS administrator set up alarm filtering by running the system for a while to track what types of false positives it generates and then adjusting the alarm classifications. For example, the administrator may set the IDPS to discard alarms produced by false attack stimuli or normal network operations. Alarm filters are similar to packet filters in that they can filter items by their source or destination IP addresses, but they can also filter by operating systems, confidence values, alarm type, or alarm severity.

■ **Alarm clustering and compaction:** A process of grouping almost identical alarms that happen at close to the same time into a single higher-level alarm. This consolidation reduces the number of alarms generated, thereby reducing administrative overhead, and also identifies a relationship among multiple alarms. This clustering may be based on combinations of frequency, similarity in attack signature, similarity in attack target, or other criteria that are defined by the system administrators.

Why Use an IDPS?

According to the NIST's documentation on industry best practices, there are several compelling reasons to acquire and use an IDPS:

1. To prevent problem behaviors by increasing the perceived risk of discovery and punishment for those who would attack or otherwise abuse the system
2. To detect attacks and other security violations that are not prevented by other security measures
3. To detect and deal with the preambles to attacks (commonly experienced as network probes and other "doorknob rattling" activities)
4. To document the existing threat to an organization
5. To act as quality control for security design and administration, especially of large and complex enterprises
6. To provide useful information about intrusions that do take place, allowing improved diagnosis, recovery, and correction of causative factors[1]

One of the best reasons to install an IDPS is that these systems serve as deterrents by increasing the fear of detection among would-be attackers. If internal and external users know that an organization has an intrusion detection system, they are less likely to probe or attempt to compromise it, just as criminals are much less likely to break into a house that has been clearly marked as having a burglar alarm.

Another reason to install an IDPS is to cover the organization when its network cannot protect itself against known vulnerabilities or is unable to respond to a rapidly changing threat environment. There are many factors that can delay or undermine an organization's ability to make its systems safe from attack and subsequent loss. For example, even though popular information security technologies such as scanning tools allow security administrators to evaluate the readiness of their systems, they may still fail to detect or correct a known deficiency, or administrators may perform the vulnerability-detection process too infrequently. In addition, even when a vulnerability is detected in a timely manner, it cannot always be corrected quickly. Also, because such corrective measures usually require that the administrator install patches and upgrades, they may be subject to fluctuations in the administrator's workload, server maintenance windows, etc. To further complicate the matter, sometimes services known to be vulnerable cannot be disabled or otherwise protected because they are essential to ongoing operations. At such times—that is, when there is a known vulnerability or deficiency in the system—an IDPS can be set up to detect attacks or attempts to exploit existing weaknesses, and thus becomes an important part of the strategy of defense in depth.

IDPSs can also help administrators detect the preambles to attacks. Most attacks begin with an organized and thorough probing of the organization's network environment and its defenses. This initial estimation of the defensive state of an organization's networks and systems is called *doorknob rattling* and is conducted first through activities collectively known as **footprinting** (which involves gathering information about the organization and its network activities and assets), and then through another set of activities collectively known as **fingerprinting** (identifies the network services and their software versions offered by the active host systems). A system capable of detecting the early warning signs of footprinting and fingerprinting functions like a neighborhood watch that spots potential burglars testing doors and windows, and enables administrators to prepare for a potential attack or to take actions to minimize potential losses from an attack.

A fourth reason for acquiring an IDPS is threat documentation. The implementation of security technology usually requires that project proponents document the threat from which the organization must be protected. IDPSs are one means of collecting such data.

OFFLINE

IDPS Metrics

Raw counts of IDS/IPS alerts have lost their glamour with upper management as justification for a security budget.[2] The raw counts provided by an IDPS need to be translated into business relevant metrics—the percentage of total attacks that were successfully blocked, the number of successful attacks, the number of hours security personnel spend analyzing IDPS alerts and actions, the number of successful attacks that were not detected by the IDPS, and so on.

These types of metrics provide much more meaningful information on the effectiveness of the security program.

Data collected by an IDPS can also help management with quality assurance and continuous improvement; the IDPS consistently picks up information about attacks that have successfully compromised the outer layers of information security controls, such as a firewall. This information can be used to identify and repair emergent or residual flaws in the security and network architectures.

Finally, even if an IDPS fails to prevent an intrusion, it can still assist in the after-attack review by providing information on how the attack occurred, what the intruder accomplished, and which methods the attacker employed. This information can be used to remedy deficiencies, and to prepare the organization's network environment for future attacks. The IDPS may also provide forensic information that may be useful should the attacker be caught and prosecuted or sued. [3]

The NIST 800-94 guide distinguishes between IPS and IDS as follows:

IPS technologies are differentiated from IDS technologies by one characteristic: IPS technologies can respond to a detected threat by attempting to prevent it from succeeding. They use several response techniques, which can be divided into the following groups:

- The IPS stops the attack itself. Examples of how this could be done are as follows:
  - Terminate the network connection or user session that is being used for the attack.
  - Block access to the target (or possibly other likely targets) from the offending user account, IP address, or other attacker attribute.
  - Block all access to the targeted host, service, application, or other resource.

- The IPS changes the security environment. The IPS could change the configuration of other security controls to disrupt an attack. Common examples are reconfiguring a network device (e.g., firewall, router, switch) to block access from the attacker or to the target, and altering a host-based firewall on a target to block incoming attacks. Some IPSs can even cause patches to be applied to a host if the IPS detects that the host has vulnerabilities.
- The IPS changes the attack's content. Some IPS technologies can remove or replace malicious portions of an attack to make it benign. A simple example is an IPS removing an infected file attachment from an e-mail and then permitting the cleaned e-mail to reach its recipient. A more complex example is an IPS that acts as a proxy and normalizes incoming requests, which means that the proxy repackages the payloads of the requests, discarding header information. This might cause certain attacks to be discarded as part of the normalization process.[4]

IDPSs commonly operate as either network- or host-based systems. A network-based IDPS functions at the network level to protect information assets. Two specialized sub-types of network-based IDPS are the wireless IDPS and the network behavior analysis (NBA) IDPS. The wireless IDPS focuses on wireless networks, while the NBA IDPS examines network traffic flows in an attempt to recognize abnormal patterns like DDoS, malware, and policy violations.

A host-based IDPS operates on the hosts themselves to protect information assets; the example shown in Figure 13-1 monitors both network connection activity and current information states on host servers. The application-based model works on one or more host systems that support a single application and defends that specific application from special forms of attack.

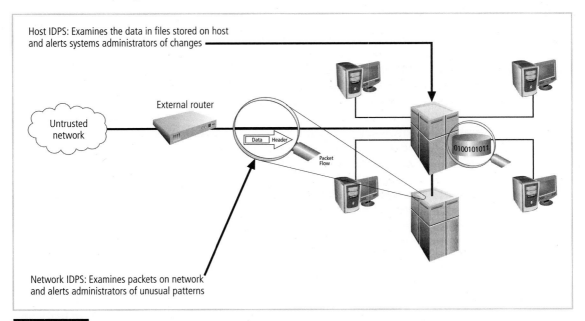

Host IDPS: Examines the data in files stored on host and alerts systems administrators of changes

Untrusted network

External router

Data   Header

Packet Flow

0100101011

Network IDPS: Examines packets on network and alerts administrators of unusual patterns

FIGURE 13-1   Intrusion Detection and Prevention Systems

Network-Based IDPS

A **network-based IDPS (NIDPS)** resides on a computer or appliance connected to a segment of an organization's network and monitors network traffic on that segment. When the NIDPS identifies activity that it is programmed to recognize as an attack, it responds by sending notifications to administrators. When examining incoming packets, an NIDPS looks for patterns in network traffic such as large collections of related items of a certain type, which could indicate that a denial-of-service attack is under way, or the exchange of a series of related packets in a certain pattern, which could indicate that a port scan is in progress. An NIDPS can detect many more types of attacks than a host-based IDPS, but it requires a much more complex configuration and maintenance program.

An NIDPS is installed at a specific place in the network (such as on the inside segment of an edge router) where it is possible to monitor the traffic going into and out of a particular network segment. The NIDPS can be deployed to monitor a specific grouping of host computers on a specific network segment, or to monitor all traffic between the systems that make up an entire network. When placed next to a hub, switch, or another key networking device, the NIDPS may use that device's monitoring port. The **monitoring port**, also known as a switched port analysis (SPAN) port or mirror port, is a specially configured connection on a network device that is capable of viewing all of the traffic that moves through the entire device. While SPAN ports are less expensive and work well for moderate traffic flows, since they consolidate the traffic from multiple ports onto a single port (e.g., the traffic flowing across 10 gigabit ports onto a single gigabit SPAN port), high-traffic links require active network taps to ensure that the NIDPS is able to see all the traffic. In the early 1990s, before switches became standard for connecting networks in a shared-collision domain, hubs were used. Hubs receive traffic from one node, and retransmit it to all other nodes. This configuration allows any device connected to the hub to monitor all traffic passing through the hub. Unfortunately, it also represents a security risk, since anyone connected to the hub can monitor all the traffic that moves through that network segment. Switches, on the other hand, create dedicated point-to-point links between their ports. These links create a higher level of transmission security and privacy, and make it more difficult for someone to capture or eavesdrop on the traffic passing through the switch.

To determine whether an attack has occurred or is under way, NIDPSs compare measured activity to known signatures in their knowledge base. This is accomplished by means of a special implementation of the TCP/IP stack that reassembles the packets and applies protocol stack verification, application protocol verification, or other verification and comparison techniques.

In the process of **protocol stack verification**, the NIDPSs look for invalid data packets—packets that are malformed under the rules of the TCP/IP protocol. A data packet is verified when its configuration matches that defined by the various Internet protocols. The elements of these protocols (IP, TCP, UDP, and application layers such as HTTP) are combined in a complete set called the *protocol stack* when the software is implemented in an operating system or application. Some types of intrusions, especially DoS and DDoS attacks, rely on the creation of improperly formed packets to take advantage of weaknesses in the protocol stack in certain operating systems or applications.

In **application protocol verification**, the higher-order protocols (HTTP, FTP, Telnet) are examined for unexpected packet behavior, or improper use. Sometimes an attack uses valid protocol packets but in excessive quantities (in the case of the Tiny Fragment Packet attack, the packets are also excessively fragmented). While the protocol stack verification looks for violations in the protocol packet *structure*, the application protocol verification looks for violations in the protocol packet *use*. One example of this kind of attack is DNS cache poisoning, in which valid packets exploit poorly configured DNS servers to inject false information to corrupt the servers' answers to routine DNS queries from other systems on the network. Unfortunately, this higher-order examination of traffic can have the same effect on an IDPS as it can on a firewall—that is, it slows the throughput of the system. It may be necessary to have more than one NIDPS installed, with one of them performing protocol stack verification and one performing application protocol verification.

The advantages of NIDPSs, taken from Bace and Mell, are:

1. Good network design and placement of NIDPS devices can enable an organization to use a few devices to monitor a large network.
2. NIDPSs are usually passive devices and can be deployed into existing networks with little or no disruption to normal network operations.
3. NIDPSs are not usually susceptible to direct attack and, in fact, may not be detectable by attackers.[5]

The disadvantages of NIDPSs, taken from Bace and Mell, are:

1. An NIDPS can become overwhelmed by network volume and fail to recognize attacks it might otherwise have detected. Some IDPS vendors are accommodating the need for ever faster network performance by improving the processing of detection algorithms in dedicated hardware circuits to gain a performance advantage. Additional efforts to optimize rule set processing may also reduce overall effectiveness in detecting attacks.
2. NIDPSs require access to all traffic to be monitored. The broad use of switched Ethernet networks has replaced the ubiquity of shared collision domain hubs. Since many switches have limited or no monitoring port capability some networks are not capable of providing aggregate data for analysis by an NIDPS. Even when switches do provide monitoring ports, they may not be able to mirror all activity with a consistent and reliable time sequence.
3. NIDPSs cannot analyze encrypted packets, making some of the network traffic invisible to the process. The increasing use of encryption that hides the contents of some or all of the packets by some network services (such as SSL, SSH, and VPN) limits the effectiveness of NIDPSs.
4. NIDPSs cannot reliably ascertain if an attack was successful or not. This requires the network administrator to be engaged in an ongoing effort to evaluate the results of the logs of suspicious network activity.
5. Some forms of attack are not easily discerned by NIDPSs, specifically those involving fragmented packets. In fact, some NIDPSs are particularly susceptible to malformed packets and may become unstable and stop functioning.[6]

Wireless NIDPS

A wireless IDPS monitors and analyzes wireless network traffic, looking for potential problems with the wireless protocols (Layers 2 and 3 of the OSI model). Unfortunately, wireless IDPSs cannot evaluate and diagnose issues with higher-layer protocols like TCP and UDP. Wireless IDPS capability can be built into a device that provides a wireless access point.[7]

OFFLINE

Sensitivity Versus Accuracy

An NIDPS is subject to two types of errors: not identifying a real attack as such, or identifying benign traffic as an attack. These errors arise because it is difficult to balance accuracy and sensitivity.

Increasing the NIDPS's ability to accurately identify attacks requires increasing its sensitivity, but increasing its sensitivity results in a great number of false alarms. Consider a police officer who is determined to crack down on speeding drivers on a particular stretch of road. To catch every violator, the officer pursues anyone going even 1 mile above the posted 25MPH speed limit. However, the manufacturer of the "radar gun" specifies that the measured speed be within 10–20% of the real speed. Thus the police officer tickets some motorists who were actually going 25 but registered as 30 (25 + 20%), and lets go some speeders who were going 30 but registered 24 (30–20%). Therefore the officer has actually decreased accuracy by increasing sensitivity.

The configuration an organization implements in its NIDPS will reflect the sometimes difficult compromise between accuracy and sensitivity.

Sensors for wireless networks can be placed at the access points, installed on specialized sensor components, or incorporated into selected mobile stations. Centralized management stations collect information from these sensors, much as other network-based IDPs do, and aggregate information into a comprehensive assessment of wireless network intrusions. Some issues associated with the implementation of wireless IDPSs include:

- Physical security—Unlike wired network sensors, which can be physically secured, many wireless sensors are located in public areas like conference rooms, assembly areas, and hallways in order to attain the widest possible network range. Some of these locations may even be outdoors, as more and more organizations are deploying networks in external locations. Physically securing these devices may require additional configuration of access point hardware and require ongoing monitoring.

- Sensor range—A wireless device's range can be affected by atmospheric conditions, building construction, and the quality of both the wireless network card and access point. Some IDPS tools allow an organization to identify the optimal location for sensors by modeling the wireless footprint based on signal strength. Sensors are most effective when their footprints overlap.

- Access point and wireless switch locations—Wireless components with bundled IDPS capabilities must be carefully deployed to optimize the IDPS sensor detection grid. The minimum range is just that; you must guard against the possibility of an attacker connecting to a wireless access point from a range far beyond the minimum. Note that the range can vary greatly depending on the sophistication of the attacker—an AP may have a stated range of 100 meters, but an attacker using a specialized antenna and receiver may be able to intercept traffic from distances of several hundred meters.

- Wired network connections—Wireless network components work independently of the wired network when sending and receiving between stations and access points. However, a network connection eventually integrates wireless traffic into the organization's wired network. Where there is no available wired network connection, it may be impossible to deploy a sensor.

- Cost—The more sensors deployed, the more expensive the configuration. Wireless components typically cost more than wired counterparts; thus, the total cost of ownership of both wired and wireless varieties of IDPS should be carefully considered.[8]

In addition to the traditional types of intrusions detected by other IDPSs, the wireless IDPS can also detect the following:

- Unauthorized WLANs and WLAN devices
- Poorly secured WLAN devices
- Unusual usage patterns
- The use of wireless network scanners
- Denial-of-service (DoS) attacks and conditions
- Impersonation and man-in-the-middle attacks[9]

Wireless IDPSs are unable to detect certain passive wireless protocol attacks, in which the attacker monitors network traffic without active scanning and probing. They are also susceptible to evasion techniques, which are described earlier in this chapter. By simply looking at a wireless device, which is often visible in public areas, attackers can custom-design evasion methods to exploit the system's channel-scanning scheme. Wireless IDPSs are designed to protect the WLAN that they are assigned to defend, but may be susceptible to logical and physical attacks against the wireless access point or wireless IDPS devices themselves. The best-configured IDPS in the world cannot withstand an attack from a well-placed brick.[10]

Network Behavior Analysis System

Network Behavior Analysis (NBA) systems examine network traffic in order to identify problems related to the flow of traffic. It uses a version of the anomaly detection method described later in this section to identify excessive packet flows such as might occur in the case of equipment malfunction, denial-of-service attacks, virus and worm attacks, and some forms of network policy violations. NBA IDPSs typically monitor internal networks but occasionally monitor connections between internal and external networks. Typical flow data particularly relevant to intrusion detection and prevention includes the following:

- Source and destination IP addresses
- Source and destination TCP or UDP ports or ICMP types and codes
- Number of packets and bytes transmitted in the session
- Starting and ending timestamps for the session[11]

Most NBA sensors can be deployed in **passive mode** only, using the same connection methods (e.g., network tap, switch spanning port) as network-based IDPSs. Passive sensors that are performing direct network monitoring should be placed so that they can monitor key network locations, such as the divisions between networks, and key network segments, such as demilitarized zone (DMZ) subnets. **Inline sensors** are typically intended for network perimeter use, so they would be deployed in close proximity to the perimeter firewalls, often between the firewall and the Internet border router to limit incoming attacks that could overwhelm the firewall. The types of events most commonly detected by NBA sensors include the following:

- Denial-of-service (DoS) attacks (including distributed denial-of-service [DDoS] attacks)
- Scanning

- Worms
- Unexpected application services (e.g., tunneled protocols, backdoors, use of forbidden application protocols)
- Policy violations

NBA sensors offer various intrusion prevention capabilities, including the following (grouped by sensor type):

- Passive Only
- Ending the Current TCP Session. A passive NBA sensor can attempt to end an existing TCP session by sending TCP reset packets to both endpoints
- Inline Only
- Performing Inline Firewalling. Most inline NBA sensors offer firewall capabilities that can be used to drop or reject suspicious network activity
- Both Passive and Inline
- Reconfiguring Other Network Security Devices. Many NBA sensors can instruct network security devices such as firewalls and routers to reconfigure themselves to block certain types of activity or route it elsewhere, such as a quarantine virtual local area network (VLAN)
- Running a Third-Party Program or Script. Some NBA sensors can run an administrator-specified script or program when certain malicious activity is detected[12]

Host-Based IDPS

While a network-based IDPS resides on a network segment and monitors activities across that segment, a **host-based IDPS** resides on a particular computer or server (the host) and monitors activity only on that system. HIDPSs are also known as **system integrity verifiers**[13] because they benchmark and monitor the status of key system files and detect when an intruder creates, modifies, or deletes monitored files. An HIDPS has an advantage over NIDPS in that it can access encrypted information that is traveling over the network after it has been decrypted at the host, and use it to make decisions about potential or actual attacks. Also, since the HIDPS works on only one computer system, all the traffic it monitors must come to the system on which the HIDPS is running. The nature of the network packet delivery mechanism (whether it is switched or in a shared-collision domain) is not a factor.

An HIDPS is also capable of monitoring system configuration databases, such as Windows registries, in addition to stored configuration files like .ini, .cfg, and .dat files. Most HIDPSs work on the principle of configuration or change management, which means that they record the sizes, locations, and other attributes of system files. The HIDPS triggers an alert when one of the following occurs: file attributes change, new files are created, or existing files are deleted. An HIDPS can also monitor system logs for predefined events. The HIDPS examines these files and logs to determine if an attack is under way or has occurred, and if the attack is succeeding or was successful. The HIDPS maintains its own log file so that an audit trail is available even when hackers modify files on the target system to cover their tracks. Once properly configured, an HIDPS is very reliable. The only time an HIDPS produces a false positive alert is when an authorized change occurs for a monitored file. The action can be quickly reviewed by an administrator who may choose to disregard subsequent changes to the same set of files. If properly configured, a HIDPS can also detect when users attempt to modify or exceed their access authorization level.

An HIDPS classifies files into various categories and then sends notifications when changes occur. Most HIDPSs provide only a few general levels of alert notification. For example, an administrator can configure an HIDPS to report changes in a system folder (such as in C:\Windows or C:\WINNT), and changes to a security-related application (such as C:\TripWire). The configuration rules may classify changes to a specific application folder (such as C:\Program Files\Office) as normal, and hence unreportable. Administrators can configure the system to log all activity but to page or e-mail them only if a reportable security event occurs. Since internal application files, such as dictionaries and configuration files, and data files are frequently modified, a poorly configured HIDPS can generate a large volume of false alarms.

Managed HIDPSs can monitor multiple computers simultaneously by creating a configuration file on each monitored host and by making each HIDPS report back to a master console system, which is usually located on the system administrator's computer. This master console monitors the information provided by the managed hosts and notifies the administrator when it senses recognizable attack conditions. Figure 13-2 provides a sample screen from Tripwire, a popular host-based IDPS (see *www.tripwire.com*).

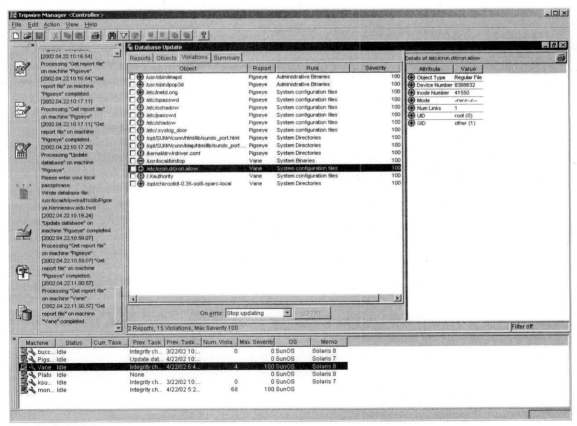

Courtesy of Tripwire®

FIGURE 13-2 Tripwire HIDS

One of the most common methods of categorizing folders and files is by color. Critical systems components are coded red, and usually include the system registry, any folders containing the OS kernel, and application software. Critically important data should also be included in the red category. Support components, such as device drivers and other relatively important files, are generally coded yellow; and user data is usually coded green, not because it is unimportant, but because monitoring changes to user data is difficult, and strategically less urgent. User data files are frequently modified, but systems kernel files, for example, should only be modified during upgrades or installations. If the three-tier system is too simplistic, an organization can implement a system that uses a scale of 0–100, with 100 being most mission-critical and zero being unimportant. It is not unusual, however, for such systems to result in confusion over issues such as how to respond to level 67 and 68 intrusions. Sometimes simpler is better.

The advantages of NIDPSs, taken from Bace and Mell, are:
1. An HIDPS can detect local events on host systems and also detect attacks that may elude a network-based IDPS.
2. An HIDPS functions on the host system, where encrypted traffic will have been decrypted and is available for processing.
3. The use of switched network protocols does not affect an HIDPS.
4. An HIDPS can detect inconsistencies in how applications and systems programs were used by examining the records stored in audit logs. This can enable it to detect some types of attacks, including Trojan Horse programs.[14]

The disadvantages of NIDPSs, taken from Bace and Mell, are:
1. HIDPSs pose more management issues since they are configured and managed on each monitored host. This means that it requires more management effort to install, configure, and operate an HIDPS than a comparably sized NIDPS solution.
2. An HIDPS is vulnerable both to direct attacks and to attacks against the host operating system. Either circumstance can result in the compromise and/or loss of HIDPS functionality.
3. An HIDPS is not optimized to detect multi-host scanning, nor is it able to detect the scanning of non-host network devices, such as routers or switches. Unless complex correlation analysis is provided, the HIDPS will not be aware of attacks that span multiple devices in the network.
4. An HIDPS is susceptible to some denial-of-service attacks.
5. An HIDPS can use large amounts of disk space to retain the host OS audit logs; to function properly, it may require disk capacity to be added to the system.
6. An HIDPS can inflict a performance overhead on its host systems, and in some cases may reduce system performance below acceptable levels.[15]

IDPS Detection Methods

IDPSs use a variety of detection methods to monitor and evaluate network traffic. Three methods dominate: the signature-based approach, the statistical-anomaly-based approach, and the stateful packet inspection approach.

Signature-Based IDPS

A **signature-based IDPS** (sometimes called a **knowledge-based IDPS, or a misuse-detection IDPS**) examines network traffic in search of patterns that match known **signatures**—that is, preconfigured, predetermined attack patterns. Signature-based IDPS technology is widely used because many attacks have clear and distinct signatures, for example: (1) footprinting and fingerprinting activities, described in detail earlier in this chapter, have an attack pattern that includes the use of ICMP, DNS querying, and e-mail routing analysis, (2) exploits involve a specific attack sequence designed to take advantage of a vulnerability to gain access to a system, (3) denial-of-service (DoS) and distributed denial-of-service (DDoS) attacks, during which the attacker tries to prevent the normal usage of a system, entail overloading the system with requests so that the system's ability to process them efficiently is compromised/disrupted, and it begins denying services to authorized users.[16]

The problem with the signature-based approach is that the IDPS's database of signatures must be continually updated with new attack strategies; otherwise, attacks that use these strategies will not be recognized and might succeed. Another weakness of the signature-based method is that a slow, methodical attack might escape detection, if the relevant IDPS attack signature has a shorter time frame. The only way for a signature-based IDPS to resolve this vulnerability is for it to collect and analyze data over longer periods of time, a process that requires substantially larger data storage capability, as well as additional processing capacity.

Statistical-Anomaly-Based IDPS

The **statistical-anomaly-based IDPS (stat IDPS)** or **behavior-based IDPS** collects statistical summaries by observing traffic that is known to be normal. This normal period of evaluation establishes a performance baseline. Once the baseline is established, the stat IDPS periodically samples network activity, and, using statistical methods, compares the sampled network activity to this baseline. When the measured activity is outside the baseline parameters—exceeding what is called the **clipping level**—the IDPS sends an alert to the administrator. The baseline data can include variables such as host memory or CPU usage, network packet types, and packet quantities.

The advantage of the statistical-anomaly-based approach is that the IDPS can detect new types of attacks, since it looks for abnormal activity of any type. Unfortunately, these systems require much more overhead and processing capacity than signature-based IDPSs, because they must constantly compare patterns of activity against the baseline. Another drawback is that these systems may not detect minor changes to system variables and may generate many false positives. If the actions of the users or systems on a network vary widely, with periods of low activity interspersed with periods of heavy packet traffic, this type of IDPS may not be suitable, because dramatic swings from one level to another will almost certainly generate false alarms. Because of its complexity and impact on the overhead computing load of the host computer, as well as the number of false positives it can generate, this type of IDPS is less commonly used than the signature-based type.

Stateful Protocol Analysis IDPS

As you learned in Chapter 6, stateful inspection firewalls track each network connection between internal and external systems using a state table to record which station sent which packet and when, essentially pairing communicating parties. An IDPS extension of this concept is stateful protocol analysis. According to SP 800-94, "**Stateful protocol**

analysis (SPA) is a process of comparing predetermined profiles of generally accepted definitions of benign activity for each protocol state against observed events to identify deviations. Stateful protocol analysis relies on vendor-developed universal profiles that specify how particular protocols should and should not be used."[17] Essentially, the IDPS knows how a protocol, such as FTP, is supposed to work, and therefore can detect anomalous behavior. By storing relevant data detected in a session and then using that data to identify intrusions that involve multiple requests and responses, the IDPS can better detect specialized, multi-session attacks. This process is sometimes called *deep packet inspection* because SPA closely examines packets at the Application layer for information that indicates a possible intrusion.

Stateful protocol analysis can also examine authentication sessions for suspicious activity, as well as for attacks that incorporate "unexpected sequences of commands, such as issuing the same command repeatedly or issuing a command without first issuing a command upon which it is dependent, as well as 'reasonableness' for commands such as minimum and maximum lengths for arguments."[18]

The models used for SPA are similar to signatures in that they are provided by vendors. These models are based on industry protocol standards established by such entities as the Internet Engineering Task Force, but they vary along with the protocol implementations in such documents. Also, proprietary protocols are not published in sufficient detail to enable the IDPS to provide accurate and comprehensive assessments.

Unfortunately, the analytical complexity of session-based assessments is the principal drawback to this type of IDPS method, which is further complicated by the amount of processing overhead in tracking multiple, simultaneous connections. Additionally, unless the protocol violates its fundamental behavior, this type of IDPS method may completely fail to detect the intrusion. One final issue is the possibility that the IDPS may in fact cause problems with the protocol it's examining, especially with client- and server-differentiated operations.[19]

Log File Monitors

A **log file monitor (LFM)** IDPS is similar to an NIDPS. Using LFM, the system reviews the log files generated by servers, network devices, and even other IDPSs, looking for patterns and signatures that may indicate that an attack or intrusion is in process or has already occurred. While an individual host IDPS is only able to examine the activity in one system, the LFM is able to look at multiple log files from a number of different systems. The patterns that signify an attack can be subtle and hard to distinguish when one system is examined in isolation, but they may be much easier to identify when the entire network and its systems are viewed. Of course this holistic approach requires the allocation of considerable resources since it involves the collection, movement, storage, and analysis of very large quantities of log data.

IDPS Response Behavior

Each IDPS responds to external stimulation in different ways, depending on its configuration and function. Some respond in active ways, collecting additional information about the intrusion, modifying the network environment, or even taking action against the intrusion. Others respond in passive ways, for example by setting off alarms or notifications, or collecting data in SNMP traps.

IDPS Response Options

When an IDPS detects a possible intrusion, it has a number of response options, depending on the organization's policy, objectives, and system capabilities. When configuring an IDPS's responses, the system administrator must exercise care to ensure that a response to an attack (or potential attack) does not inadvertently exacerbate the situation. For example, if an NIDPS reacts to suspected DoS attacks by severing the network connection, the attack is a success, and such attacks repeated at intervals will thoroughly disrupt an organization's business operations.

An analogy to this approach is the tactic of a potential car thief who walks up to a desirable target in the early hours of a morning, strikes the car's bumper with a rolled-up newspaper, and then ducks into the bushes. When the car alarm is triggered, the car owner wakes up, checks the car, determines there is no danger, resets the alarm, and goes back to bed. The thief repeats the triggering actions every half-hour or so until the owner disables the alarm. The thief is now free to steal the car without worrying about triggering the alarm.

IDPS responses can be classified as active or passive. An active response is a definitive action automatically initiated when certain types of alerts are triggered, and can include collecting additional information, changing or modifying the environment, and taking action against the intruders. Passive response IDPSs simply report the information they have collected and wait for the administrator to act. Generally, the administrator chooses a course of action after analyzing the collected data. The passive IDPS is the most common implementation, although most systems allow some active options that are disabled by default.

The following list illustrates some of the responses an IDPS can be configured to produce. Note that some of these apply only to a network-based or a host-based IDPS, while others are applicable to both.[20]

- Audible/visual alarm: The IDPS can trigger a .wav file, beep, whistle, siren, or other audible or visual notification to alert the administrator of an attack. The most common type of such notifications is the computer pop-up window. This display can be configured with color indicators and specific messages, and it can also contain specifics about the suspected attack, the tools used in the attack, the level of confidence the system has in its own determination, and the addresses and/or locations of the systems involved.

- SNMP traps and plug-ins: The Simple Network Management Protocol contains trap functions, which allow a device to send a message to the SNMP management console indicating that a certain threshold has been crossed, either positively or negatively. The IDPS can execute this trap, telling the SNMP console an event has occurred. Some of the advantages of this operation include the relatively standard implementation of SNMP in networking devices, the ability to configure the network system to use SNMP traps in this manner, the ability to use systems specifically to handle SNMP traffic, including IDPS traps, and the ability to use standard communications networks.

- E-mail message: The IDPS can respond to certain events by sending e-mail; many administrators use personal digital assistants (PDAs) to check their e-mail frequently. Organizations should use caution in relying on e-mail systems as the primary means of communication between the IDPS and security personnel—e-mail is inherently unreliable, and an attacker could compromise the e-mail system and block such messages.

- Page or phone message: The IDPS can be configured to dial a phone number, and produce an alphanumeric page or a modem noise.

- Log entry: The IDPS can enter information about the event (e.g., addresses, time, systems involved, protocol information, etc.) into an IDPS system log file, or an operating system log file. These files can be stored on separate servers to prevent skilled attackers from deleting entries about their intrusions.

- Evidentiary packet dump: Organizations that require an audit trail of the IDPS data may choose to record all log data in a special way. This method allows the organization to perform further analysis on the data and also to submit the data as evidence in a civil or criminal case. Once the data has been written using a cryptographic hashing algorithm, it becomes evidentiary documentation—that is, suitable for criminal or civil court use. This packet logging can, however, be resource-intensive, especially in denial-of-service attacks.

- Take action against the intruder: It has become possible, although not advisable, to take action against an intruder. Known as trap and trace, back hacking, or traceback, this response option involves configuring intrusion detection systems to trace the data from the target system to the attacking system in order to initiate a counter-attack. While this may sound tempting, it is ill-advised and may not be legal. An organization only owns a network to its perimeter, and conducting traces or back-hacking to systems outside that perimeter may make the organization just as criminally liable as the original attacker. Also, in some cases the "attacking system" is in fact a compromised intermediary system, and in other cases attackers use address spoofing; either way, any counter-attack would actually only harm an innocent third party. Any organization planning to configure a retaliation effort into an automated intrusion detection system is strongly encouraged to seek legal counsel.

- Launch program: An IDPS can be configured to execute a specific program when it detects specific types of attacks. A number of vendors have specialized tracking, tracing, and response software that could be part of an organization's intrusion response strategy.

- Reconfigure firewall: An IDPS could send a command to the firewall to filter out suspected packets by IP address, port, or protocol. (It is, unfortunately, still possible for a skilled attacker to break in by simply spoofing a different address, shifting to a different port, or changing the protocols used in the attack.) While it may not be easy, an IDPS can block or deter intrusions by one of the following methods:
    - Establishing a block for all traffic from the suspected attacker's IP address, or even from the entire source network from which the attacker appears to be operating. This blocking might be set for a specific period of time and be reset to normal rules after that period has expired.
    - Establishing a block for specific TCP or UDP port traffic from the suspected attacker's address or source network, blocking only the services that seem to be under attack.
    - Blocking all traffic to or from a network interface (such as the organization's Internet connection) if the severity of the suspected attack warrants that level of response.[21]

- Terminate session: Terminating the session by using the TCP/IP protocol specified packet *TCP close* is a simple process. Some attacks would be deterred or blocked by session termination, but others would simply continue when the attacker issues a new session request.
- Terminate connection: The last resort for an IDPS under attack is to terminate the organization's internal or external connections. Smart switches can cut traffic to/from a specific port, should that connection be linked to a system that is malfunctioning or otherwise interfering with efficient network operations. As indicated earlier, this response should be the last resort to protect information, as it may be the very goal of the attacker.

[The following sections were adapted from NIST SP 800-31, "Intrusion Detection Systems."]

Reporting and Archiving Capabilities

Many, if not all, commercial IDPSs provide capabilities to generate routine reports and other detailed information documents. Some of these can output reports of system events and intrusions detected over a particular reporting period (for example, a week or a month). Some provide statistics or logs generated by the IDPSs in formats suitable for inclusion in database systems or for use in report-generating packages.

Failsafe Considerations for IDPS Responses

Another factor to consider is the failsafe features of the IDPS design or product. Failsafe features protect the IDPSs from being circumvented or defeated by an attacker. For instance, IDPSs need to provide silent, reliable monitoring of attackers. Should the response function of an IDPS break this silence by broadcasting alarms and alerts in plaintext over the monitored network, attackers can detect the presence of the IDPS, and might then directly target the IDPS as part of the attack. Encrypted tunnels or other cryptographic measures that hide and authenticate IDPS communications are excellent ways to secure and ensure the reliability of the IDPS.

Selecting IDPS Approaches and Products

The wide array of intrusion detection products available today addresses a broad range of organizational security goals and considerations; the process of selecting products that represent the best fit for any particular organization is challenging. The following considerations and questions may help you prepare a specification for acquiring and deploying an intrusion detection product.

Technical and Policy Considerations

In order to determine which IDPS best meets an organization's needs, first consider the organizational environment, in technical, physical, and political terms.

What Is Your Systems Environment?   The first hurdle a potential IDPS must clear is functioning in your systems environment. This is important; if an IDPS is not designed to accommodate the information sources that are available on your systems, it will not be able to see anything that goes on—neither normal activity nor an attack—on your systems.

- What are the technical specifications of your systems environment?
  First, specify the technical attributes of your systems environment—network diagrams and maps specifying the number and locations of hosts; operating systems for each host; the number and types of network devices such as routers, bridges, and switches; number and types of terminal servers and dial-up connections; and descriptors of any network servers, including types, configurations, and application software and versions running on each. If you run an enterprise network management system, specify it here.
- What are the technical specifications of your current security protections?
  Describe the security protections you already have in place. Specify numbers, types, and locations of network firewalls, identification and authentication servers, data and link encryption, anti-virus packages, access control products, specialized security hardware (such as cryptographic accelerators or appliances), virtual private networks, and any other security mechanisms on your systems.
- What are the goals of your enterprise?
  Some IDPSs have been developed to accommodate the special needs of certain industries or market niches such as electronic commerce, health care, or financial services. Define the functional goals of your enterprise (there can be several goals associated with a single organization) that are supported by your systems.
- How formal is the system environment and management culture in your organization?
  Organizational styles vary, depending on the function of the organization and its traditional culture. For instance, the military and other organizations that deal with national security issues tend to operate with a high degree of formality, especially when contrasted with university or other academic environments. Some IDPSs support enforcement of formal use policies, with configuration options built into them by the manufacturer that can handle the particulars from commonly used issue-specific security policies or system-specific security policies, as well as providing a library of reports for commonly encountered policy violations along with other reporting capabilities.

What Are Your Security Goals and Objectives?   Once you've specified the technical landscape of your organization's systems as well as its existing security mechanisms, it's time to articulate the goals and objectives you wish to attain by using an IDPS.

- Is the primary concern of your organization protection from threats originating outside your organization?
  Perhaps the easiest way to identify security goals is by categorizing your organization's threat concerns. Identify the concerns that your organization has regarding external threats.
- Is your organization concerned about insider attack?
  Repeat the previous step, this time addressing concerns about threats that originate from within your organization, encompassing not only a user who attacks the system from within (such as a shipping clerk who attempts to access and alter the payroll system) but also the authorized user who exceeds his privileges, thereby violating organizational security policy or laws (such as a customer service agent who, driven by curiosity, accesses earnings and payroll records for public figures).

- Does your organization want to use the output of your IDPS to determine new needs? System usage monitoring is sometimes provided as a generic system management tool to determine when system assets require upgrading or replacement. When such monitoring is performed by an IDPS, the needs for upgrade can show up as anomalous levels of user activity.
- Does your organization want to use an IDPS to maintain managerial control (non-security related) over network usage?
  In some organizations, system use policies may be classified as personnel management rather than system security. These policies might prohibit accessing questionable Web sites (such as ones containing pornography) or using organizational systems to send e-mail or other messages for the purpose of harassing individuals. Some IDPSs provide features that detect such violations of management controls.

What Is your Existing Security Policy?   You should review your existing organization security policy. This will serve as the template against which features of your IDPS will be configured. You may find you need to augment the policy, or else derive the following items from it.

- How is your security policy structured?
  It is helpful to articulate the goals outlined in the security policy in terms of the standard security goals (integrity, confidentiality, and availability) as well as more generic management goals (privacy, protection from liability, manageability).
- What are the general job descriptions of your system users?
  List the general job functions of system users (there are commonly several functions assigned to a single user) as well as the data and network accesses that each function requires.
- Does the policy include reasonable use policies or other management provisions? As mentioned above, many organizations have system use policies included as part of security policies.
- Has your organization defined processes for dealing with specific policy violations? If the organization doesn't intend to react to violations, it may not make sense to configure the IDPS to detect them. If, on the other hand, the organization wishes to actively respond to such violations, the IDPS's operational staff should be informed of the response policy.

Organizational Requirements and Constraints

Your organization's operational goals, constraints, and culture will affect the selection of the IDPS and other security tools and technologies to protect your systems. Consider the following organizational requirements and limitations.

What Requirements Are Levied from Outside the Organization?

- Is your organization subject to oversight or review by another organization? If so, does that oversight authority require IDPSs or other specific system security resources?
- Are there requirements for public access to information on your organization's systems? Do regulations or statutes require that information on your system be accessible by the public during certain hours of the day, or during certain date or time intervals?

- Are there other security-specific requirements levied by law? Are there legal requirements for protection of personal information (such as earnings information or medical records) stored on your systems? Are there legal requirements for investigation of security violations that divulge or endanger that information?

- Are there internal audit requirements for security best practices or due diligence? Do any of these audit requirements specify functions that the IDPSs must provide or support?

- Is the system subject to accreditation? If so, what is the accreditation authority's requirement for IDPSs or other security protection?

- Are there requirements for law enforcement investigation and resolution of security incidents? Do these specify any IDPS functions, especially those having to do with collection and protection of IDPS logs as evidence?

What Are Your Organization's Resource Constraints? IDPSs can protect the systems of an organization, but at a price. It makes little sense to incur additional expense for IDPS features if your organization does not have sufficient systems or personnel to handle the alerts generated by the system.

- What is the budget for acquisition and life cycle support of intrusion detection hardware, software, and infrastructure? Remember that the acquisition of IDPS software is not the only element that counts toward the total cost of ownership; you may also have to acquire a system on which to run the software, obtain specialized assistance to install and configure the system, and train your personnel. Ongoing operations may also require additional staff or outside contractors.

- Is there sufficient staff to monitor an intrusion detection system full time? Some IDPSs require that systems personnel attend them around the clock. If you do not have such personnel available, you may wish to explore those systems that accommodate unattended use.

- Does your organization have authority to instigate changes based on the findings of an intrusion detection system? It is critical that your organization be clear about what to do about the problems uncovered by an IDPS. If you are not empowered to handle the incidents that arise as a result of the monitoring, you should consider coordinating your selection and configuration of the IDPS with the party who is empowered.

IDPSs Product Features and Quality

IDPSs provide a bewildering array of capabilities and features that may or may not be relevant to the needs of a particular organization. In selecting a specific product or set of product features, the organization should consider the following questions.

Is the Product Sufficiently Scalable for Your Environment? Many IDPSs cannot function within large or widely distributed enterprise network environments.

How Has the Product Been Tested? Simply asserting that an IDPS has certain capabilities is not sufficient to demonstrate that those capabilities are real. You should request demonstrations of the suitability of a particular IDPS to your environment and goals.

- Has the product been tested against functional requirements? Ask the vendor about the assumptions made regarding the goals and constraints of customer environments.

■ Has the product been tested against attack? Ask vendors for details of the security testing to which its products have been subjected. If the product includes network-based vulnerability assessment features, ask also whether test routines that produce system crashes or other denials of service have been identified and flagged in system documentation and interfaces.

What Is the User Level of Expertise Targeted by the Product? Different IDPS vendors target users with different levels of technical and security expertise. Ask the vendor what their assumptions are regarding the users of their products.

Is the Product Designed to Evolve as the Organization Grows? One important product design goal is the ability to adapt to your needs over time.

■ Can the product adapt to growth in user expertise? Ask here whether the IDPS's interface can be configured (with shortcut keys, customizable alarm features, and custom signatures) on the fly. Ask also whether these features are documented and supported.
■ Can the product adapt to growth and change of the organization's systems infrastructure? This question has to do with the ability of the IDPS to scale to an expanding and increasingly diverse network. Most vendors have experience in adapting their products as target networks grow. Ask also about commitments to support new protocol standards and platform types.
■ Can the product adapt to growth and change of the security threat environment? This question is especially critical given the current Internet threat environment, in which 30–40 new attacks are posted to the Web every month.

What Are the Support Provisions for the Product? Like other systems, IDPSs require maintenance and support over time. These needs should be identified and prepared in a written report.

■ What are the commitments for product installation and configuration support? Many vendors provide expert assistance to customers installing and configuring IDPSs; others expect that your own staff will handle these functions, and provide only telephone or e-mail help desk functions.
■ What are the commitments for ongoing product support? Ask about the vendor's commitment to supporting your use of their IDPS product.
■ Are subscriptions to signature updates included? Most IDPSs are misuse-detectors, so the value of the product is only as good as the signature database against which events are analyzed. Most vendors provide subscriptions to signature updates for some period of time (a year is typical).
■ How often are subscriptions updated? In today's threat environment, in which 30–40 new attacks are published every month, this is a critical question.
■ How quickly after a new attack is made public will the vendor ship a new signature? If you are using IDPSs to protect highly visible or heavily traveled Internet sites, it is critical that you receive the signatures for new attacks as soon as possible.
■ Are software updates included? Most IDPSs are software products and therefore subject to bugs and revisions. Ask the vendor about software update and bug patch support, and determine to what extent they are included in the product you purchase.
■ How quickly will software updates and patches be issued after a problem is reported to the vendor? As software bugs in IDPSs can allow attackers to nullify their protective effect, it is extremely important that problems be fixed, reliably and quickly.

- Are technical support services included? What is the cost? In this category, technical support services mean vendor assistance in tuning or adapting your IDPS to accommodate special needs, be they monitoring a custom or legacy system within your enterprise, or reporting IDPS results in a custom protocol or format.
- What are the provisions for contacting technical support (e-mail, telephone, online chat, Web-based reporting)? The contact provisions will likely tell you whether these technical support services are accessible enough to support incident handling or other time-sensitive needs.
- Are there any guarantees associated with the IDPS? As with other software products, IDPSs traditionally have few guarantees associated with them; however, in an attempt to gain market share, some vendors are initiating guarantee programs.
- What training resources does the vendor provide? Once an IDPS is selected, installed, and configured, it must still be operated and maintained by your personnel. In order for these people to make optimal use of the IDPS, they should be trained in its use. Some vendors provide this training as part of the product package.
- What additional training resources are available from the vendor and at what cost? If the IDPS's vendor does not provide training as part of the IDPS package, you should budget for training your operational personnel.

Strengths and Limitations of IDPSs

Although intrusion detection systems are a valuable addition to an organization's security infrastructure, there are things they do well, and other things they do not do well. As you plan the security strategy for your organization's systems, it is important that you understand what IDPSs should be trusted to do and what goals might be better served by other security mechanisms.

Strengths of Intrusion Detection and Prevention Systems

Intrusion detection and prevention systems perform the following functions well:

- Monitoring and analysis of system events and user behaviors
- Testing the security states of system configurations
- Baselining the security state of a system, then tracking any changes to that baseline
- Recognizing patterns of system events that correspond to known attacks
- Recognizing patterns of activity that statistically vary from normal activity
- Managing operating system audit and logging mechanisms and the data they generate
- Alerting appropriate staff by appropriate means when attacks are detected
- Measuring enforcement of security policies encoded in the analysis engine
- Providing default information security policies
- Allowing non-security experts to perform important security monitoring functions

Limitations of Intrusion Detection and Prevention Systems

Intrusion detection systems cannot perform the following functions:

- Compensating for weak or missing security mechanisms in the protection infrastructure, such as firewalls, identification and authentication systems, link encryption systems, access control mechanisms, and virus detection and eradication software
- Instantaneously detecting, reporting, and responding to an attack, when there is a heavy network or processing load

- Detecting newly published attacks or variants of existing attacks
- Effectively responding to attacks launched by sophisticated attackers
- Automatically investigating attacks without human intervention
- Resisting all attacks that are intended to defeat or circumvent them
- Compensating for problems with the fidelity of information sources
- Dealing effectively with switched networks

There is also the considerable challenge of configuring an IDPS to respond accurately to a perceived threat. Once a device is empowered to react to an intrusion by filtering or even severing a communication session, or by severing a communication circuit, the impact from a false positive becomes increasingly significant. It's one thing to fill an administrator's e-mail box or compile a large log file with suspected attacks; it's quite another to shut down critical communications. Some forms of attacks, conducted by attackers called **IDPS terrorists**, are designed to trip the organization's IDPS, essentially causing the organization to conduct its own DoS attack, by overreacting to an actual, but insignificant, attack.

[The preceding sections were adapted from NIST SP 800-31, "Intrusion Detection Systems" and NIST SP 800-94, "Guide to Intrusion Detection and Prevention Systems."]

Deployment and Implementation of an IDPS

Deploying and implementing an IDPS is not always a straightforward task. The strategy for deploying an IDPS should take into account a number of factors, the foremost being how the IDPS will be managed and where it will be placed. These factors will determine the number of administrators needed to install, configure, and monitor the IDPS, as well as the number of management workstations, the size of the storage needed for retention of the data generated by the systems, and the ability of the organization to detect and respond to remote threats.

IDPS Control Strategies

An IDPS can be implemented via one of three basic control strategies. A control strategy determines how an organization exerts influence and maintains the configuration of an IDPS. It also determines how IDPS input and output are managed. The three commonly utilized control strategies are: centralized, partially distributed, and fully distributed. The IT industry has been exploring technologies and practices to enable the distribution of computer processing cycles and data storage for many years. These explorations have long considered the advantages and disadvantages of the centralized strategy versus strategies with varying degrees of distribution. In the early days of computing, all systems were fully centralized, resulting in a control strategy that provided high levels of security and control, as well as efficiencies in resource allocation and management. During the 1980s and 1990s, a period of rapid growth in networking and computing capabilities, the trend was to implement a fully distributed strategy. In the mid-1990s, however, the high costs of a fully distributed architecture became apparent, and the IT industry shifted toward a mixed strategy of partially distributed control. A strategy of partial distribution, where some features and components are distributed and others are centrally controlled, has now emerged as the recommended practice for IT systems in general and for IDPS control systems in particular.

Centralized Control Strategy. As illustrated in Figure 13-3, in a **centralized IDPS control strategy** all IDPS control functions are implemented and managed in a central location, shown in the figure as the large square symbol labeled "IDPS Console." The IDPS console includes management software, which collects information from the remote sensors (appearing in the figure as triangular symbols), analyzes the systems or networks monitored, and makes the determination as to whether the current situation has deviated from the preconfigured baseline. All reporting features are also implemented and managed from this central location. The primary advantages of this strategy are cost and control. With one central implementation, there is one management system, one place to go to monitor the status of the systems or networks, one location for reports, and one set of administrative management tools. This centralization of IDPS management supports task specialization, since all managers are either located near the IDPS management console or can acquire an authenticated remote connection to it, and technicians are located near the remote sensors. This means that each person can focus on the assigned task. In addition, the central control group can evaluate the systems and networks as a whole, and since it can compare pieces of information from all sensors, the group is better positioned to recognize a large-scale attack.

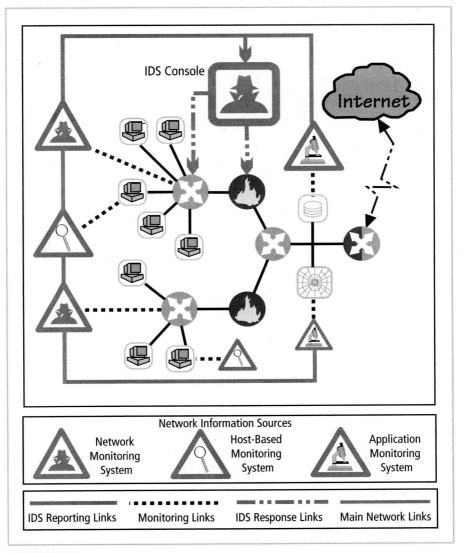

FIGURE 13-3 Centralized IDS Control

Fully Distributed Control Strategy.   As presented in Figure 13-4, a **fully distributed IDPS control strategy** is the opposite of the centralized strategy. Note in the figure that all control functions (which appear as small square symbols enclosing a computer icon) are applied at the physical location of each IDPS component. Each monitoring site uses its own, paired sensors to perform its own control functions to achieve the necessary detection, reaction, and response functions. Thus, each sensor/agent is best configured to deal with its own environment. Since the IDPSs do not have to wait for a response from a centralized control facility, their reaction to individual attacks is greatly speeded up.

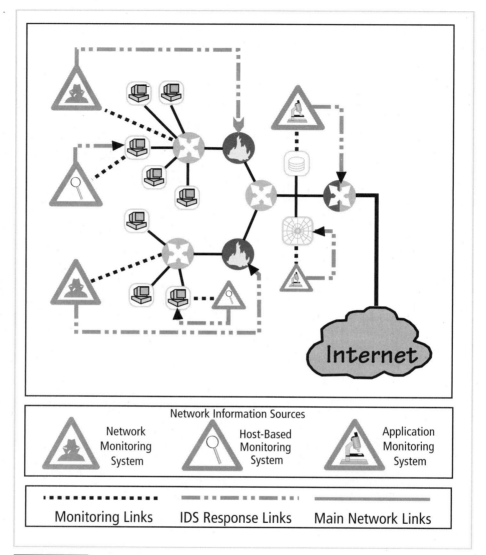

FIGURE 13-4 Fully Distributed IDS Control

Partially Distributed Control Strategy. A partially distributed IDPS control strategy, as depicted in Figure 13-5, combines the best of the other two strategies. While the individual agents can still analyze and respond to local threats, their reporting to a hierarchical central facility enables the organization to detect widespread attacks. This blended approach to reporting is one of the more effective methods of detecting intelligent attackers, especially those who probe an organization through multiple points of entry, trying to scope out the systems' configurations and weaknesses, before they launch a concerted attack. The partially distributed control strategy also allows the organization to optimize for economy of scale in the implementation of key management software and personnel, especially in the reporting areas. When the organization can create a pool of security managers to evaluate reports from multiple distributed IDPS systems, it becomes better able to detect these distributed attacks before they become unmanageable.

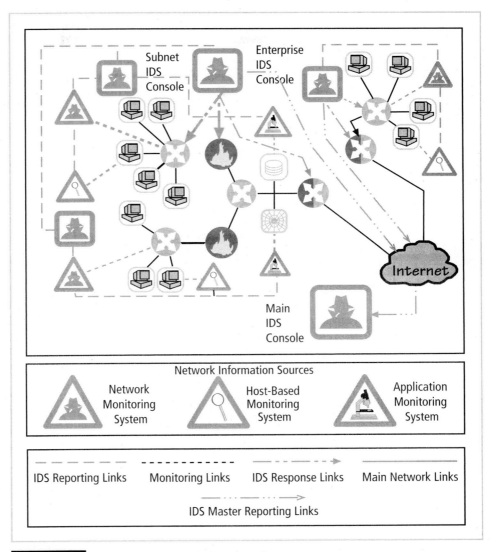

Network Information Sources

Network Monitoring System

Host-Based Monitoring System

Application Monitoring System

IDS Reporting Links   Monitoring Links   IDS Response Links   Main Network Links

IDS Master Reporting Links

FIGURE 13-5 Partially Distributed IDS Control

IDPS Deployment

Given the highly technical skills required to implement and configure IDPSs and the imperfection of the technology, great care must be taken in making the decisions about where to locate the components, both in their physical connection to the network and host devices and in how they are logically connected to each other and the IDPS administration team. Since IDPSs are designed to detect, report, and even react to anomalous stimuli, placing IDPSs in an area where such traffic is common can result in excessive reporting.

Moreover, the administrators monitoring systems located in such areas can become desensitized to the information flow and may fail to detect actual attacks in progress.

OFFLINE

Location, location, location

An IDPS works by detecting anomalies, and is most effective when deployed in an area where traffic types are well understood and fairly stable. For example, the Web tier of an organization has well-known types of expected traffic: incoming requests on port 80 or 443, and some other protocols such as incoming FTP, outgoing connections to the application tier, etc. When unusual traffic conditions, such as an outbound FTP session or Telnet connections, are detected, they are easily identified as anomalies worthy of further investigation.

Contrast this situation with a network segment used primarily by software developers. The types of protocols and traffic patterns are much more diverse and variable, making detection of anomalies much more difficult.

For these reasons, choosing the placement point for an IDPS probe or sensor is much like purchasing real estate—it's all location, location, location.

An IDPS is a complex system in that it involves numerous remote-monitoring agents (on both individual systems and networks) that require proper configuration to gain the proper authentication and authorization. As the IDPS is deployed, each component should be installed, configured, fine-tuned, tested, and monitored. A mistake in any step of the deployment process may produce a range of problems—from a minor inconvenience to a network-wide disaster. Thus, both the individuals installing the IDPS and the individuals using and managing the system require proper training.

NIDPS and HIDPS can be used in tandem to cover both the individual systems that connect to an organization's networks and the networks themselves. When doing so, it is important that an organization use a phased implementation strategy so as not to affect the entire organization all at once. A phased implementation strategy also allows security technicians to resolve the problems that do arise without compromising the very information security the IDPS is installed to protect. The organization should first implement the network-based IDPSs, as they are less problematic and easier to configure than their host-based counterparts. After the NIDPSs are configured and running without issue, the HIDPSs can be installed to protect the critical systems on the host server. Next, after both are operational, it would be advantageous to scan the network using a tool like Nmap or Nessus to determine if (a) the scanners pick up anything new or unusual, and (b) the IDPS can detect the scans.

Deploying Network-Based IDPSs.   As discussed above, the placement of the sensor agents is critical to the operation of all IDPSs, but this is especially critical in the case of Network IDPSs. NIST recommends four locations for NIDPS sensors:

Location 1: Behind each external firewall, in the network DMZ (See Figure 13-6, location 1)

Advantages:
- IDPS sees attacks that originate from the outside world and may penetrate the network's perimeter defenses.
- IDPS can identify problems with the network firewall policy or performance.
- IDPS sees attacks that might target the Web server or ftp server, both of which commonly reside in this DMZ.
- Even if the incoming attack is not detected, the IDPS can sometimes recognize, in the outgoing traffic, patterns that suggest that the server has been compromised.

Location 2: Outside an external firewall (See Figure 13-6, location 2)

Advantages:
- IDPS documents the number of attacks originating on the Internet that target the network.
- IDPS documents the types of attacks originating on the Internet that target the network.

Location 3: On major network backbones (See Figure 13-6, location 3)

Advantages:
- IDPS monitors a large amount of a network's traffic, thus increasing its chances of spotting attacks.
- IDPS detects unauthorized activity by authorized users within the organization's security perimeter.

Location 4: On critical subnets (See Figure 13-6, location 4)

Advantages:
- IDPS detects attacks targeting critical systems and resources.
- Location allows organizations with limited resources to focus these resources on the network assets considered of greatest value.[22]

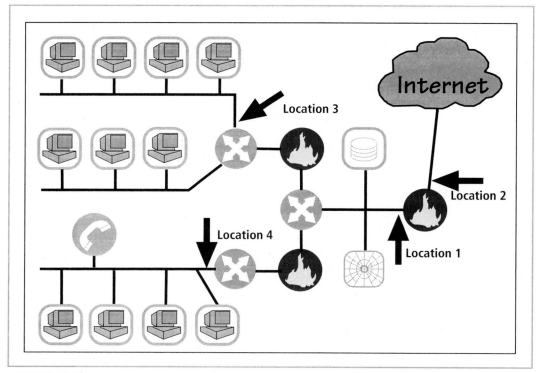

FIGURE 13-6   Network IDS Sensor Locations

Deploying Host-Based IDPSs.   The proper implementation of HIDPSs can be a painstaking and time-consuming task, as each HIDPS must be custom-configured to its host systems. Deployment begins with implementing the most critical systems first. This poses a dilemma for the deployment team, since the first systems to be implemented are mission-critical, and any installation problems could be catastrophic to the organization. As such, it may be beneficial to practice an implementation on one or more test servers configured on a network segment that resembles the mission-critical systems. Practicing will help the installation team gain experience and also help determine if the installation might trigger any unusual events. Gaining an edge on the learning curve by training on nonproduction systems will benefit the overall deployment process by reducing the risk of unforeseen complications.

Installation continues until either all systems are installed, or the organization reaches the planned degree of coverage it is willing to live with, with regard to the number of systems or percentage of network traffic. To provide ease of management, control, and reporting, each HIDPS should, as discussed earlier, be configured to interact with a central management console.

Just as technicians can install the HIDPS on offline systems to develop expertise and identify potential problems, users and managers can gain expertise and understanding of the operation of the HIDPS by using a test facility. This test facility could use the offline systems configured by the technicians, but also be connected to the organization's backbone to allow the HIDPS to process actual network traffic. This setup will also enable technicians to create a baseline of normal traffic for the organization. During the system testing process, training scenarios can be developed that enable users to recognize and respond to common attack situations. To ensure effective and efficient operation, the management team can establish policy for the operation and monitoring of the HIDPS.

Measuring the Effectiveness of IDPSs

When selecting an IDPS one typically looks at four measures of comparative effectiveness:

- Thresholds. A threshold is a value that sets the limit between normal and abnormal behavior. Thresholds usually specify a maximum acceptable level, such as x failed connection attempts in 60 seconds, or x characters for a file-name length. Thresholds are most often used for anomaly-based detection and stateful protocol analysis.

- Blacklists and Whitelists. A blacklist is a list of discrete entities, such as hosts, TCP or UDP port numbers, ICMP types and codes, applications, usernames, URLs, filenames, or file extensions, that have been previously determined to be associated with malicious activity. Blacklists, also known as hot lists, are typically used to allow IDPSs to recognize and block activity that is highly likely to be malicious, and may also be used to assign a higher priority to alerts that match entries on the blacklists. Some IDPSs generate dynamic blacklists that are used to temporarily block recently detected threats (e.g., activity from an attacker's IP address). A whitelist is a list of discrete entities that are known to be benign. Whitelists are typically used on a granular basis, such as protocol-by-protocol, to reduce or ignore false positives involving known benign activity from trusted hosts. Whitelists and blacklists are most commonly used in signature-based detection and stateful protocol analysis.

- Alert Settings. Most IDPS technologies allow administrators to customize each alert type. Examples of actions that can be performed on an alert type include the following:

    Toggling it on or off
    Setting a default priority or severity level
    Specifying what information should be recorded and what notification
        methods (e.g., e-mail, pager) should be used
    Specifying which prevention capabilities should be used

    Some products also suppress alerts if an attacker generates many alerts in a short period of time, and may also temporarily ignore all future traffic from the attacker. This is to prevent the IDPS from being overwhelmed by alerts.

- Code Viewing and Editing. Some IDPS technologies permit administrators to see some or all of the detection-related code. This is usually limited to signatures, but some technologies allow administrators to see additional code, such as programs used to perform stateful protocol analysis.[23]

Once implemented, IDPSs are evaluated using two dominant metrics: first, administrators evaluate the number of attacks detected in a known collection of probes; second, the administrators examine the level of use, commonly measured in megabits per second of network traffic, at which the IDPSs fail. An evaluation of an IDPS might read something like this: *at 100 Mb/s, the IDPS was able to detect 97% of directed attacks*. This is a dramatic change from the previous method used for assessing IDPS effectiveness, which was based on the total number of signatures the system was currently running—a sort of "more is better" approach. This evaluation method was flawed for several reasons. Not all IDPSs use simple signature-based detection. Some systems, as discussed earlier, can use the almost infinite combination of network performance characteristics of statistical-anomaly-based detection to detect a potential attack. Also, some more sophisticated signature-based systems actually use *fewer* signatures/rules than older, simpler versions—which, in direct contrast to the signature-based assessment method, suggests that less may actually be more. The recognition that the size of the signature base is an insufficient measure of an IDPS's effectiveness led to the development of stress test measurements for evaluating IDPS performance. These only work, however, if the administrator has a collection of known negative and positive actions that can be proven to elicit a desired response. Since developing this collection can be tedious, most IDPS vendors provide testing mechanisms that verify that their systems are performing as expected. Some of these testing processes enable the administrator to:

- Record and retransmit packets from a real virus or worm scan
- Record and retransmit packets from a real virus or worm scan with incomplete TCP/IP session connections (missing SYN packets)
- Conduct a real virus or worm scan against an invulnerable system

This last measure is important, since future IDPSs will probably include much more detailed information about the overall site configuration. According to one expert in the field, "it may be necessary for the IDPSs to be able to actively probe a potentially vulnerable machine, in order to either pre-load its configuration with correct information, or perform a retroactive assessment. An IDPS that performed some kind of actual system assessment would be a complete failure in today's generic testing labs, which focus on replaying attacks and scans against nonexistent machines."[24]

With the rapid growth in technology, each new generation of IDPSs will require new testing methodologies. However, the measured values that will continue to be of interest to IDPS administrators and managers will, most certainly, include some assessment of how much traffic the IDPS can handle, the numbers of false positives and false negatives it generates, and a measure of the IDPS's ability to detect actual attacks. Vendors of IDPS systems could also include a report of the alarms sent and the relative accuracy of the system in correctly matching the alarm level to the true seriousness of the threat. Some planned metrics for IDPSs may include the flexibility of signatures and detection policy customization.

IDPS administrators may soon be able to purchase tools that test IDPS effectiveness. Until these tools are available from a neutral third party, the diagnostics from the IDPS vendors will always be suspect. No vendor, no matter how reliable, would provide a test that their system would fail.

One note of caution: IDPS administrators tend to use common vulnerability assessment tools, like Nessus, to evaluate the capabilities of an IDPS. While this may seem like a good idea, it may not work as expected, because many IDPS systems are equipped to recognize the differences between a locally implemented vulnerability assessment tool and a true attack.

In order to perform a true assessment of the effectiveness of IDPS systems, the test process should be as realistic as possible in its simulation of an actual event. This means coupling realistic traffic loads with realistic levels of attacks. You cannot expect an IDPS to respond to a few packet probes as if they represent a denial-of-service attack. In one reported example, a program was used to create a synthetic load of network traffic made up of many TCP sessions, with each session consisting of a SYN (or synchronization) packet, a series of data, and ACK (or acknowledgment) packets, but no FIN or connection termination packets. Of the several IDPS systems tested, one of them crashed due to lack of resources while it waited for the sessions to be closed. Another IDPS passed the test with flying colors because it did not perform state tracking on the connections. Neither of the tested IDPS systems worked as expected, but the one that didn't perform state tracking was able to stay operational and was, therefore, given a better score on the test.[25]

Honey Pots, Honey Nets, and Padded Cell Systems

A class of powerful security tools that go beyond routine intrusion detection is known variously as honey pots, honey nets, or padded cell systems. To understand why these tools are not yet widely used, you must first understand how they differ from a traditional IDPS. **Honey pots** are decoy systems designed to lure potential attackers away from critical systems. In the industry, they are also known as decoys, lures, and fly-traps. When a collection of honey pots connects several honey pot systems on a subnet, it may be called a **honey net**. A honey pot system (or in the case of a honey net, an entire subnetwork) contains pseudo-services that emulate well-known services, but is configured in ways that make it look vulnerable to attacks. This combination is meant to lure potential attackers into committing an attack, thereby revealing themselves—the idea being that once organizations have detected these attackers, they can better defend their networks against future attacks against real assets. In sum, honey pots are designed to:

- Divert an attacker from critical systems
- Collect information about the attacker's activity
- Encourage the attacker to stay on the system long enough for administrators to document the event and, perhaps, respond

Because the information in a honey pot appears to be valuable, any unauthorized access to it constitutes suspicious activity. Honey pots are instrumented with sensitive monitors and event loggers that detect attempts to access the system and collect information about the potential attacker's activities. A screenshot from a simple IDPS that specializes in honey pot techniques, called Deception Toolkit, is shown in Figure 13-7. This screenshot shows the configuration of the honey pot as it is waiting for an attack.

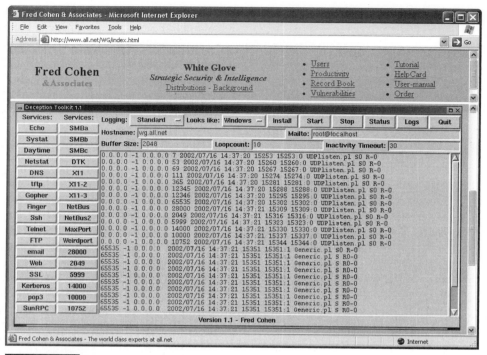

FIGURE 13-7   Deception Toolkit

A **padded cell** is a honey pot that has been protected so that it cannot be easily compromised—in other words, a hardened honey pot. In addition to attracting attackers with tempting data, a padded cell operates in tandem with a traditional IDPS. When the IDPS detects attackers, it seamlessly transfers them to a special simulated environment where they can cause no harm—the nature of this host environment is what gives the approach the name padded cell. As in honey pots, this environment can be filled with interesting data, which can convince an attacker that the attack is going according to plan. Like honey pots, padded cells are well instrumented and offer unique opportunities for a target organization to monitor the actions of an attacker.

IDPS researchers have used padded cell and honey pot systems since the late 1980s, but until recently no commercial versions of these products were available. It is important to seek guidance from legal counsel before deciding to use either of these systems in your operational environment, since using an attractant and then launching a back hack or counterstrike might be illegal, and could expose the organization to a lawsuit or a criminal complaint.

The advantages and disadvantages of using the honey pot or padded cell approach are summarized below:

Advantages:

- Attackers can be diverted to targets that they cannot damage.
- Administrators have time to decide how to respond to an attacker.

- Attackers' actions can be easily and more extensively monitored, and the records can be used to refine threat models and improve system protections.
- Honey pots may be effective at catching insiders who are snooping around a network.

Disadvantages:

- The legal implications of using such devices are not well defined.
- Honey pots and padded cells have not yet been shown to be generally useful security technologies.
- An expert attacker, once diverted into a decoy system, may become angry and launch a more hostile attack against an organization's systems.
- Administrators and security managers need a high level of expertise to use these systems.[26]

Trap and Trace Systems

Trap and trace applications, which are an extension of the attractant technologies discussed in the previous section, are growing in popularity. These systems use a combination of techniques to detect an intrusion and then to trace it back to its source. The trap usually consists of a honey pot or padded cell and an alarm. While the intruders are distracted, or trapped, by what they perceive to be successful intrusions, the system notifies the administrator of their presence. The trace feature is an extension to the honey pot or padded cell approach. The trace—which is similar to caller ID—is a process by which the organization attempts to determine the identity of someone discovered in unauthorized areas of the network or systems. If the intruder is someone inside the organization, the administrators are completely within their rights to track the individual and turn him or her over to internal or external authorities. If the intruder is outside the security perimeter of the organization, then numerous legal issues arise. One of the most popular professional trap and trace software suites is ManHunt, by Symantec (*www.symantec.com*). It includes a companion product, ManTrap, which is the honey pot application that presents a virtual network running from a single server. ManHunt is an intrusion detection system with the capability of initiating a trackback function that can trace an intruder as far as the administrator wishes. Although administrators usually trace an intruder back to their organization's information security boundary, it is possible, with this technology, to coordinate with an ISP that has similar technology and thus hand off a trace to an upstream neighbor.

On the surface, trap and trace systems seem like an ideal solution. Security is no longer limited to defense. Now the security administrators can go on the offense. They can track down the perpetrators and turn them over to the appropriate authorities. Under the guise of justice, some less scrupulous administrators may even be tempted to **back hack**, or hack into a hacker's system to find out as much as possible about the hacker. Vigilante justice would be a more appropriate term for these activities, which are in fact deemed unethical by most codes of professional conduct. In tracking the hacker, administrators may end up wandering through other organizations' systems, especially when the hacker has used IP spoofing, compromised systems, or a myriad of other techniques to throw trackers off the trail. The back-hacking administrator becomes the hacker.

There are more legal drawbacks to trap and trace. The trap portion frequently involves the use of honey pots or honey nets. When using honey pots and honey nets, administrators should be careful not to cross the line between enticement and entrapment.

Enticement is the process of attracting attention to a system by placing tantalizing information in key locations. **Entrapment** is the action of luring an individual into committing a crime to get a conviction. Enticement is legal and ethical, whereas entrapment is not. It is difficult to gauge the effect such a system can have on the average user, especially if the individual has been nudged into looking at the information. Administrators should also be wary of the *wasp trap syndrome*. In this syndrome, a concerned homeowner installs a wasp trap in his back yard to trap the few insects he sees flying about. Because these traps use scented bait, however, they wind up attracting far more wasps than were originally present. Security administrators should keep the wasp trap syndrome in mind before implementing honey pots, honey nets, padded cells, or trap and trace systems.

Active Intrusion Prevention

Some organizations would like to do more than simply wait for the next attack and implement active countermeasures to stop attacks. One tool that provides active intrusion prevention is known as LaBrea (*http://labrea.sourceforge.net/labrea-info.html*). LaBrea works by taking up the unused IP address space within a network. When LaBrea notes an ARP request, it checks to see if the IP address requested is actually valid on the network. If the address is not currently being used by a real computer or network device, LaBrea pretends to be a computer at that IP address and allows the attacker to complete the TCP/IP connection request, known as the three-way handshake. Once the handshake is complete, LaBrea changes the TCP sliding window size to a low number to hold open the TCP connection from the attacker for many hours, days, or even months. Holding the connection open but inactive greatly slows down network-based worms and other attacks. It allows the LaBrea system time to notify the system and network administrators about the anomalous behavior on the network.

Chapter Summary

- An intrusion occurs when an attacker attempts to gain entry or disrupt the normal operations of an information system, almost always with the intent to do harm.

- Intrusion detection consists of procedures and systems that identify system intrusions. Intrusion reaction encompasses the actions an organization takes when an intrusion is detected. Intrusion prevention consists of activities that deter an intrusion.

- An intrusion detection system (IDS) works like a burglar alarm in that it detects a violation and activates an alarm. An intrusion prevention system (IPS) can also prevent that intrusion from successfully attacking the organization by means of some form of active response. Because the two systems often coexist, the combined term intrusion detection/prevention system (IDPS) is used to describe current anti-intrusion technologies.

- IDPSs commonly operate as either network- or host-based systems. A network-based IDPS functions at the network level to protect information assets. A host-based IDPS operates on the hosts themselves to protect information assets. Systems that use both approaches are called hybrid IDPSs.

- IDPSs use a variety of detection methods to monitor and evaluate network traffic. Three methods dominate: the signature-based approach, the statistical-anomaly approach, and the stateful packet inspection approach.

- A log file monitor (LFM) IDPS is similar to an NIDPS. Using LFM, the system reviews the log files generated by servers, network devices, and even other IDPSs, looking for patterns and signatures that may indicate that an attack or intrusion is in process or has already occurred.

- Honey pots are decoy systems designed to lure potential attackers away from critical systems. When a collection of honey pots connects several honey pot systems on a subnet, it may be called a honey net. A honey pot is configured in ways that make it look vulnerable, to lure potential attackers into committing an attack, thereby revealing themselves.

- Trap and trace applications use a combination of techniques to detect an intrusion and then to trace it back to its source.

Review Questions

1. What are the relative recommended backup frequencies for various types of organizational information?
2. What are the dominant types of backups?
3. What is encompassed in a full backup?
4. What is encompassed in a differential backup?
5. What is encompassed in an incremental backup?
6. What is a redundant array of independent disks (RAID), and what are its primary uses? How can it be used as part of a backup strategy?
7. In what way are the backup needs of database systems different from those of ordinary backups?
8. Other than simply identifying what to back up, when to back it up, and how to restore it, a complete backup and recovery plan should include what other elements?
9. What is electronic vaulting, and how is it used as part of a backup strategy?
10. What is remote journaling, and how is it used as part of a backup strategy?
11. What are service agreements and what are their important components?
12. Which common security system is an IDPS most like? In what ways are these systems similar?
13. How does a false positive alarm differ from a false negative one? From a security perspective, which is least desirable?
14. How does a network-based IDPS differ from a host-based IDPS?
15. How does a signature-based IDPS differ from a behavior-based IDPS?
16. What is the optimal location for a network-based IDPS? Host-based IDPS?
17. What is a monitoring (or SPAN) port? What is it used for?
18. List and describe the three control strategies proposed for IDPS control.
19. What is a honey pot? How is it different from a honey net?
20. How does a padded cell system differ from a honey pot?

Exercises

1. A key feature of hybrid IDPS systems is event correlation. After researching event correlation online, define the following terms as they are used in this process: compression, suppression, and generalization.

2. ZoneAlarm is a PC-based firewall and IDPS tool. Visit the product manufacturer at *www.zonelabs.com*, and find the product specification for the IDPS features of ZoneAlarm. Which of the ZoneAlarm products offer these features?

3. Using the Internet, search for commercial IDPS systems. What classification systems and descriptions are used, and how can these be used to compare the features and components of the different IDPSs? Create a comparison spreadsheet identifying the classification systems you find.

4. Many home routers also offer firewall capabilities. Use the Internet to look at the cable/DSL routers offered by D-Link and Linksys. Which of the current models provide IDPS capabilities?

5. Use a browser connected to the Internet to visit the honeynet.org Web site. Find and read the most recent status report. Describe one interesting thing you read in that report.

Case Exercises

Review the Chapter 6 opening scenario, which describes the events that led to the IDPS alert that Matthias deals with in the opening scenario of this chapter. Review also the Chapter 10 opening scenario, which describes the consequences of Niki Simpson's habit of posting her password on sticky notes.

Questions:

1. What type of IDPS system is ATI using for this contract?

2. Was this event the result of a honeypot or honeynet? Why or why not?

3. How realistic do you think this case is? Can and do events like this happen in real networked applications?

Endnotes

1. Scarfone, K. & Mell, P. (2007) "Guide to Intrusion Detection and Prevention Systems (IDPS)" NIST Special Publication 800-94. Accessed 21 June, 2007, from csrc.nist.gov/ publications/nistpubs/800-94/SP800-94.pdf.

2. Andrew Jaquith, *"Security Metrics: Replacing Fear, Uncertainty and Doubt."* (2007)Upper Saddle River: Addison-Wesley.

3. Scarfone, K. & Mell, P. (2007) "Guide to Intrusion Detection and Prevention Systems (IDPS)" NIST Special Publication 800-94. Accessed 21 June, 2007, from csrc.nist.gov/ publications/nistpubs/800-94/SP800-94.pdf.

4. Scarfone, K. & Mell, P. (2007) "Guide to Intrusion Detection and Prevention Systems (IDPS)" NIST Special Publication 800-94. Accessed 21 June, 2007, from csrc.nist.gov/ publications/nistpubs/800-94/SP800-94.pdf.

5. Scarfone, K. & Mell, P. (2007) "Guide to Intrusion Detection and Prevention Systems (IDPS)" NIST Special Publication 800-94. Accessed 21 June, 2007, from csrc.nist.gov/ publications/nistpubs/800-94/SP800-94.pdf.

6. Scarfone, K. & Mell, P. (2007) "Guide to Intrusion Detection and Prevention Systems (IDPS)" NIST Special Publication 800-94. Accessed 21 June, 2007, from csrc.nist.gov/publications/nistpubs/800-94/SP800-94.pdf.

7. Scarfone, K. & Mell, P. (2007) "Guide to Intrusion Detection and Prevention Systems (IDPS)" NIST Special Publication 800-94. Accessed 21 June, 2007, from csrc.nist.gov/publications/nistpubs/800-94/SP800-94.pdf.

8. Scarfone, K. & Mell, P. (2007) "Guide to Intrusion Detection and Prevention Systems (IDPS)" NIST Special Publication 800-94 Accessed 21 June, 2007, from csrc.nist.gov/publications/nistpubs/800-94/SP800-94.pdf.

9. Scarfone, K. & Mell, P. (2007) "Guide to Intrusion Detection and Prevention Systems (IDPS)" NIST Special Publication 800-94 Accessed 21 June, 2007, from csrc.nist.gov/publications/nistpubs/800-94/SP800-94.pdf.

10. Scarfone, K. & Mell, P. (2007) "Guide to Intrusion Detection and Prevention Systems (IDPS)" NIST Special Publication 800-94 Accessed 21 June, 2007, from csrc.nist.gov/publications/nistpubs/800-94/SP800-94.pdf.

11. Scarfone, K. & Mell, P. (2007) "Guide to Intrusion Detection and Prevention Systems (IDPS)" NIST Special Publication 800-94 Accessed 21 June, 2007, from csrc.nist.gov/publications/nistpubs/800-94/SP800-94.pdf.

12. Scarfone, K. & Mell, P. (2007) "Guide to Intrusion Detection and Prevention Systems (IDPS)" NIST Special Publication 800-94 Accessed 21 June, 2007, from csrc.nist.gov/publications/nistpubs/800-94/SP800-94.pdf.

13. Graham, R. (2000). "FAQ: Intrusion Detection Systems." March 2000. Viewed online on 4/9/07. Accessed 21 June 2007 from linuxsecurity.com/resource_files/intrusion_detection/network-intrusion-detection.html.

14. Scarfone, K. & Mell, P. (2007) "Guide to Intrusion Detection and Prevention Systems (IDPS)" NIST Special Publication 800-94 Accessed 21 June, 2007, from csrc.nist.gov/publications/nistpubs/800-94/SP800-94.pdf.

15. Scarfone, K. & Mell, P. (2007) "Guide to Intrusion Detection and Prevention Systems (IDPS)" NIST Special Publication 800-94 Accessed 21 June, 2007, from csrc.nist.gov/publications/nistpubs/800-94/SP800-94.pdf.

16. Graham, R. (2000). "FAQ: Intrusion Detection Systems." March 2000. Viewed online on 4/9/07. Accessed 21 June 2007 from linuxsecurity.com/resource_files/intrusion_detection/network-intrusion-detection.html.

17. Scarfone, K. & Mell, P. (2007) "Guide to Intrusion Detection and Prevention Systems (IDPS)" NIST Special Publication 800-94 Accessed 21 June, 2007, from csrc.nist.gov/publications/nistpubs/800-94/SP800-94.pdf.

18. Scarfone, K. & Mell, P. (2007) "Guide to Intrusion Detection and Prevention Systems (IDPS)" NIST Special Publication 800-94 Accessed 21 June, 2007, from csrc.nist.gov/publications/nistpubs/800-94/SP800-94.pdf.

19. Scarfone, K. & Mell, P. (2007) "Guide to Intrusion Detection and Prevention Systems (IDPS)" NIST Special Publication 800-94 Accessed 21 June, 2007, from csrc.nist.gov/publications/nistpubs/800-94/SP800-94.pdf.

20. Graham, R. (2000). "FAQ: Intrusion Detection Systems." March 2000. Viewed online on 4/9/07. Accessed 21 June 2007 from linuxsecurity.com/resource_files/intrusion_detection/network-intrusion-detection.html.

21. Scarfone, K. & Mell, P. (2007) "Guide to Intrusion Detection and Prevention Systems (IDPS)" NIST Special Publication 800-94. Accessed 21 June, 2007, from csrc.nist.gov/publications/nistpubs/800-94/SP800-94.pdf.

22. Scarfone, K. & Mell, P. (2007) "Guide to Intrusion Detection and Prevention Systems (IDPS)" NIST Special Publication 800-94. Accessed 21 June, 2007, from csrc.nist.gov/publications/nistpubs/800-94/SP800-94.pdf.

23. Scarfone, K. & Mell, P. (2007) "Guide to Intrusion Detection and Prevention Systems (IDPS)" NIST Special Publication 800-94 Accessed 21 June, 2007, from csrc.nist.gov/publications/nistpubs/800-94/SP800-94.pdf.

24. Ranum, Marcus J. (2003) "False Positives: A User's Guide to Making Sense of IDS Alarms" for ICSA Labs IDSC. February. Accessed 15 March, 2004, from www.icsalabs.com/html/communities/ids/whitepaper/FalsePositives.pdf.

25. Scarfone, K. & Mell, P. (2007) "Guide to Intrusion Detection and Prevention Systems (IDPS)" NIST Special Publication 800-94. Accessed 21 June, 2007, from csrc.nist.gov/publications/nistpubs/800-94/SP800-94.pdf.

26. Scarfone, K. & Mell, P. (2007) "Guide to Intrusion Detection and Prevention Systems (IDPS)" NIST Special Publication 800-94. Accessed 21 June, 2007, from csrc.nist.gov/publications/nistpubs/800-94/SP800-94.pdf.

Digital Forensics

> If the law has made you a witness, remain a man of science, you have no victim to avenge, no guilty or innocent person to convict or save—you must bear testimony within the limits of science.
>
> **DR. P. C. BROUARDEL**

IT WAS A FEW MINUTES BEFORE 5:00 PM on one of the worst Fridays that Mary Lewis, senior storage administrator for ATI, had ever experienced. The rumors of downsizing had been circulating for some time, and that afternoon three of her colleagues had been called to meet with Human Resources, and were then escorted out of the building by the corporate security team. Her team had been understaffed for the past year; she was still juggling work and on-call schedules to accommodate its reduced size when the phone rang.

"Mary, this is Delmar in Eastern Operations. The server support crew says that the engineering programs are aborting left and right—something about drives not being available. They say each server is fine; can you take a look?" She sighed as she hung up; it was always a storage area network (SAN) problem until she proved it wasn't.

She pointed her Web browser at the Eastern Operations server SAN switch and determined that the disks were hosted on disk array Charlie. She connected her computer to the management console for array Charlie and immediately saw that something was terribly wrong—the disks assigned to the Eastern Operations server had been deleted.

Mary faced a serious situation—had the disks been deleted accidentally, or was it a retaliatory act by one of the dismissed storage administrators? How would she collect the information that would enable ATI to pursue legal action if it was sabotage? In other words, Mary had just found herself in the midst of a forensic investigation.

LEARNING OBJECTIVES:

Upon completion of this material, you should be able to do the following:

- Describe the roles and responsibilities of the members of the digital forensic team
- Enumerate the key processes involved in collecting digital evidence
- Explain the difference between search and seizure in the public and private sectors
- Identify the goals of forensic analysis

Introduction

The word "forensics" comes from the Latin word *forensis*, which in the time of the Romans referred to the public forum—the precursor to today's courts of law.[1] When an organization's information resources have been interfered with in the course of an incident, and the organization decides to apprehend and prosecute the offender(s), it must collect information in such a way that it will be usable in a criminal or civil proceeding. This information is usually called "evidence," but in fact nothing is evidence until a judge admits it as such in court. During legal proceedings, opposing counsel can (and usually will) challenge this admission on every available grounds. Even something as simple as just taking a look at a compromised computer may allow opposing counsel to challenge the information gathered from that computer on the grounds that it might have been modified or otherwise tainted.[2]

What we really mean, then, is that the organization is collecting "items of potential evidentiary value."[3] **Digital forensics** is thus defined as the use of sound investigation and analysis techniques to identify, collect, preserve, and analyze electronic items of potential evidentiary value so that they may be admitted as evidence in a court of law, or used to support administrative action. This definition has been interpreted as applying almost exclusively to computers and computer-based media; the term digital forensics, a broader term, applies to all modern electronic devices, including mobile phones, personal digital assistants (PDAs), portable music players, and other electronic devices capable of storing digital information.

In this chapter, you will learn the requirements for digital evidence, the processes involved in identifying and acquiring it, and the general process of analyzing digital evidence.

The Digital Forensic Team

What type of digital forensic team should an organization have? It really depends on the size and nature of the organization, and the available resources. Sometimes the need for a forensics unit is obvious, as in the case of large enterprises that are subject to frequent network attacks (governmental agencies or high-profile companies like Microsoft), but with the increasing criticality of digital information for business operations, organizations of all types and sizes may be required to engage in some form of forensic investigation (as is Mary Lewis in the opening scenario of this chapter).

When setting out to plan for an organization's commitment to forensic operations, you should consider the following:[4]

- Costs. These will include costs such as those for the tools, hardware, and other equipment used to collect and examine digital information, as well as for staffing and training.
- Response time. While an outside forensic consultant may seem cheaper because the service is only paid for when actually used, the interruption to normal business operations while the consultant gets into place and up to speed may turn out to be more expensive than maintaining an in-house forensic capability.
- Data sensitivity concerns. These may complicate the use of outside consultants. Forensic data collection can expose highly sensitive information such as personal health records, credit card information, business plans, etc.

Resolving these issues can be challenging, so many organizations divide the forensic functions as follows:

1. First response—Assesses the "scene," identifying the sources of relevant digital information and preserving it for later analysis, using sound processes.
2. Analysis and presentation—Analyzes the collected information to identify material facts that bear on the subject of the investigation, and prepares and presents the results of the analysis to support possible legal action.

While analysis and presentation requires significant expertise (gained through extensive training and experience) and specialized tools that are not usually found within the repertoire of most IT professionals, the first response skills are much easier to come by; they are more common IT skills that are supplemented by sound processes and documentation to preserve the collected information's evidentiary potential, which is sought in the second phase.

The First Response Team

The size and makeup of a first response team will vary based on the size of the organization and other factors, but it often includes the following roles:

- Eyes—Surveys the scene and identifies sources of relevant information. Eyes orchestrates the work of the other team members and usually produces any photographic documentation.
- Fingers—Under the direction of eyes, fingers moves things around, disassembles equipment, etc.
- Scribe—Produces the written record of the team's activities as well as maintaining control of the field evidence log and locker.
- Image the geek—Collects copies, or images, of digital evidence.

Consider a situation where a forensics team has the objective of performing an onsite data collection at an employee's corporate office. After securing the scene, the scribe begins the written record, and eyes enters the scene to make the overall photographic survey and to identify and photographically document major loci of evidence (computers, disk arrays, etc.).

An important part of this survey is prioritizing the sources of information. Some considerations that guide this prioritization are[5]:

- Value—The likely usefulness of the information
- Volatility—The stability of the information over time; some types of information are lost when the power is cut, and others by default over time (for example, log records are overwritten with newer data)
- Effort required—Amount of time required to acquire a copy of the information

Eyes then identifies a safe area for image the geek to set up equipment and directs fingers in removing items for the geek to image.

Removals are documented, both photographically and in the written record, by the scribe. As the geek finishes imaging an item, its integrity assurance (hash and other information) is documented in the written record, the image is logged into the field evidence locker, and the original item is returned to fingers for reinstallation.

When all the items have been imaged, as part of the exit process eyes will compare the scene's appearance to the initial photographic survey to ensure that the team has left no trace of its presence.

The Analysis Team

Whether performed in-house or outsourced to a third party, the analysis and reporting phases are performed by persons specially trained in the use of forensic tools to analyze the collected information and provide answers to the question(s) that gave rise to the investigation.

These forensic tools help forensic analysts to recover deleted files, reassemble file fragments, and interpret operating system artifacts.

The forensic analysis function is sometimes broken into two parts: examination and analysis. The **examination phase** involves the use of forensic tools to recover deleted files, retrieve and characterize operating system artifacts, and other relevant material, while the **analysis phase** uses those materials to answer the question(s) that gave rise to the investigation.

OFFLINE

The Forensic Question

While it is very easy to get lost in the gigabytes of data, the thousands of images, and the veritable storm of network packets that are the raw data of a forensic investigation, it is critical to remember that the investigation is about making a determination of fact in the real world.

As Inman and Rudin note, forensics is really about translating a real-world problem into one or more questions that can be answered by means of forensic analysis.[6] In the physical world, Joe may be suspected of having violated his organization's intellectual property policy by disclosing details of a new product to a competitor, in hopes of

continued

gaining a position with that competitor. The challenge for the forensic analyst is to translate the question "Did Joe violate the IP policy by disclosing the product details to a competitor?" into a series of questions answerable by digital forensic investigation, such as:

- Did Joe access the new product information during the relevant time period?
- Are there indications of a quid pro quo agreement between Joe and the competitor?
- Did Joe send e-mails to the competitor containing that information?
- Did Joe transmit the information to the competitor over the network?

The answers to these questions might be found on the disk image of Joe's computer, network logs, access logs for a file server, or within other digital sources.

Larger organizations may even delineate these two functions as job descriptions–forensic examiners are skilled in the operations of particular tools, while forensic analysts know operating systems and networks, as well as how to interpret the information gleaned by the examiners.

The analysis function is also responsible for reporting and presenting the investigation's findings. Forensic reports serve a variety of audiences, ranging from upper management to legal professionals and other forensic experts who may use the findings to build a case in court; therefore, they must clearly communicate highly technical matters without sacrificing critical details.

Effective communication becomes even more critical when the forensic analyst is called into court, where the audience includes a judge and jury who likely have only a nodding acquaintance with technology, and an opposing counsel whose job it is to undermine the analyst's findings and expertise.

OFFLINE

Critical Analogies

Presenting a forensic analysis to a nontechnical audience can be quite challenging. If the analyst's presentation is ineffective, the findings are likely to be regarded as technical gobbledygook, or worse, members of the jury may perceive that the analyst is talking down to them.

Analogies play an important part in communication; a common analogy is using the library card catalog to illustrate how deleted files are recovered.

A computer disk is rather like a large library wherein books (files) are shelved according to the information in a card catalog (file system directory). Deleting a file is rather like removing the book's card from the card catalog. The pointer to the book is gone, but the book itself can still be found in the library stacks, though it might take some searching.

This analogy aptly illustrates how a technical process can be explained to a nontechnical audience. Sometimes the most challenging part of presenting the results of forensic analysis is finding a relevant analogy that helps the audience grasp the technical details.

Digital Forensics Methodology

The overall flow of a digital investigation is shown in Figure 14-1.

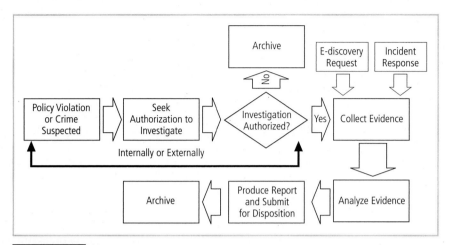

FIGURE 14-1   Digital Investigation Flow

Usually, the digital investigation begins with some allegation of wrongdoing–either a policy violation or commission of a crime. Based on that allegation, authorization is sought to begin the investigation proper by collecting relevant evidence. In the public sector, this authorization may take the form of a **search warrant**; in the private sector, it takes whatever form is specified by the organization's policy. Many private sector organizations require a formal statement, called an **affidavit**, which furnishes much of the same information usually found in a public sector search warrant. In the private sector, it is more common to authorize the collection of images of digital information, but in the public sector, the search warrant authorizes seizure of the relevant items *containing* the information.

Affidavits and Search Warrants

The laws governing private sector search and seizure are somewhat more straightforward than the ones that govern public sector search and seizure. Certain conditions must be met in order to ensure that any evidentiary material found is admissible in any legal proceedings that follow, whether administrative or judicial. In general, law enforcement agents must have a search warrant or the employer's consent to search for evidentiary materials. A private organization wishing to search an employee's computer must generally meet the following conditions:

1. The employee has been made aware of organizational policy that such a search may occur.

2. The search must be justified at its inception. That is, there is a legitimate business reason for the search—it is conducted by an authorized individual to locate legitimate work product, or it is conducted to investigate suspected misconduct involving organizational resources. If an organization routinely searches every employee's computer, or conducts truly random searches and uncovers potential evidentiary material, then the findings are admissible.

3. The search must also be permissible in its scope, meaning the search has a specific focus and was constrained to that focus. This requirement does not prohibit the use of materials found during a normal business search, but it precludes a total inventory search when the identified area of interest is confined to one or two folders or directories.

4. The organization has clear ownership over the container the material was discovered in. This precludes searches of the employee's person, personal belongings, and personal technologies, but does not exclude those containers provided by the organization for the employee's use, such as a PDA, cell phone, laptop, and so on. Gray areas include employee-purchased briefcases, satchels, and backpacks used to transport work, and personally owned computers, PDAs, and cell phones used by telecommuters.

5. The search must be authorized by the responsible manager or administrator. For systems, the senior system administrator must allow the search, unless of course that person is a suspect in an internal investigation. For most organizational equipment, a designated manager must provide authorization. Forward-thinking organizations designate a senior executive officer, such as the chief information officer, as a magistrate to authorize organizational searches. Even then, the search itself should be conducted by a designated, disinterested individual, such as the CISO, or other individual recommended by legal council.

Once these conditions are met, an organization should have a reasonable degree of confidence in its right to search for and collect potentially evidentiary material. This does not mean that any administrative or judicial actions will go unchallenged; however, it does mean that the organization has much stronger grounds to refute any allegations of impropriety.

An organization's incident response policy must spell out the procedures for initiating the investigative process, including management approvals. This is particularly critical in the private sector, as private organizations do not enjoy the broad immunity accorded to law enforcement investigations. In general, a law enforcement organization cannot be sued for its conduct during an investigation; a private organization can become the target of a retaliatory lawsuit for damages arising from an investigation that proves to be groundless.

OFFLINE

An Adversarial Legal System

Perhaps one of the most confusing things about the U.S. legal system is the recognition that it is an adversarial system. Two parties come into the proceeding holding opposing views on a question of fact and attempt to prove their view is correct, either beyond a reasonable doubt (criminal proceeding) or with a preponderance of the evidence (civil proceeding).

continued

Within the rules of the court, everything is open to challenge by opposing counsel. Consider a criminal case on possession of child pornography. During her analysis, the prosecutor's forensic investigator examined the defendant's computer and found 14 images of prepubescent children engaging in sexual acts; the defense would likely challenge this finding on some of the following grounds:

- Was the prosecution forensic expert properly trained and qualified?
- Did the evidence collection process follow established procedure to ensure that the evidence was not modified in any way during its collection and analysis?
- At all times was the evidence under proper controls, and is the chain of custody complete?
- Were the images actually downloaded by the defendant, or were they downloaded by a hacker, virus, or other malware?

These types of issues are what laypeople commonly call technicalities and usually connote a sly attorney getting a guilty person off. However, the adversarial role of opposing counsel actually functions to ensure that all parties "follow the rules." Thus, the wise forensic practitioner never thinks in terms like "if this is challenged," but rather "when this is challenged."

Acquiring the Evidence

Once the authorization to conduct an investigation is obtained, the collection of evidence can begin. As shown earlier, this is also the point where incident response begins to interface with the forensics process.

At its heart, digital evidence collection follows a simple four-step methodology:

1. Identify sources of evidentiary material.
2. Authenticate the evidentiary material.
3. Collect the evidentiary material.
4. Maintain a documented chain of custody.

Identifying Sources

While identifying sources of evidence is somewhat straightforward in the physical world of bloodstains and fingerprints, it's much more complex in the digital world. Simple data collection in a suspect's corporate office may involve hundreds of gigabytes of information that resides on:

- Disks in a desktop or laptop computer (or both)
- Disks in external storage enclosures
- Memory sticks or cards
- A PDA (possibly with additional removable memory cards installed)
- A cellular phone (including any memory cards installed in it)
- Storage devices such as MP3 players
- Optical storage such as CDs and DVDs
- Networked storage

When identifying evidence in a data center (perhaps as part of an intrusion or complex fraud investigation), the sources of potential evidence multiply to include:

- Disks attached to servers
- Storage attached to a storage network such as a fibre channel or iSCSI SAN
- Files on NAS (Network Attached Storage) devices
- Logs on servers, routers, firewalls, or centralized logging servers

One of the more perplexing problems in collecting digital data concerns so-called volatile information, such as the contents of a computer's memory. Traditional forensic practice calls for photographing a running computer's screen and then disconnecting the power, but this leads to loss of volatile information. Should investigators sacrifice the evidence stored on disk by running tools to collect the volatile information, or should they sacrifice the volatile information in favor of the information on disk? In time, better tools will make this less of a quandary, but currently it is a challenge.

OFFLINE

Thou Shalt Make No Change

The emphasis on making no change whatsoever to the evidence during a digital forensic investigation may seem overstated, but in fact it is justified by the potentially serious consequences of the investigation. Digital forensic findings can cost (or save) an organization millions of dollars, can deprive a person of a job if a policy violation leads to termination of employment, and if used in criminal proceedings, can even deprive a person of freedom or life.

When a piece of digital information is altered, the question arises as to just exactly what was changed. Did an investigator inadvertently start up a computer, or did the investigator plant evidence and cover the modification by starting up the computer? While it is possible to minutely describe every change that occurred during the computer start-up, to verify that only those changes were made in the image, such an effort is not likely to be rewarded, given the time and expertise involved, the difficulty in explaining these changes to the judge and jury, and the possibility of lingering doubts that will cause the evidence to be discounted.

Authenticating Evidence

Unlike objects in the physical world that have characteristics that set them apart from other similar items, one binary digit looks pretty much like another. This presents a significant challenge in the practice of digital forensics, as the legal system demands assurances that the information presented in court is demonstrably authentic (that is, the genuine image of the disk in John Doe's workstation or a true copy of the log records from the RADIUS server collected on January 15th). In the following discussion of collecting digital evidence, one of the core concerns is being able to demonstrate that the particular collection of bits being prepared is a true and accurate copy of the original.

One way to identify a particular digital item (collection of bits) is by means of a cryptographic hash. These mathematical functions have important properties that make them ideal for this purpose:

- Regardless of the size of their input, they produce a fixed size output (128 bits for MD5 and 160 bits for SHA-1).
- It is computationally infeasible to find another input that could produce the same output value.
- It is computationally infeasible to find an input that would produce a particular hash value.

These properties make cryptographic hashes good candidates for use as digital fingerprints.

As the following example shows, simply changing the case of two letters generates very different hash values:

```
:echo hello there > test.txt

:md5sum test.txt
782a482a8ba848cec578e3006678860c *test.txt

:echo Hello There > test.txt

:md5sum test.txt
937e9f428b23c367247b2c29318093b0 *test.txt
```

When a piece of digital evidence is collected, its hash value is calculated and recorded. At any subsequent point, the hash value can be recalculated to show that the item has not been modified since its collection. This technique can also authenticate copies of the original item as true and accurate copies.

Two commonly used hashes are MD-5 and SHA-1. Command-line and GUI tools for calculating hashes are widely available.

Recently some attacks[7] on these hash algorithms have been described in the research literature, and in one case in Australia[8] these attacks were successfully used to challenge digital evidence, but the general consensus is that hashes are still acceptable for demonstrating the integrity of digital evidence.[9] NIST is developing new hash algorithms that will be more resistant to these types of attacks in the future.

Collecting Evidence

There are many considerations and processes that surround digital evidence collection. The investigator must decide upon the mode of acquisition (live or dead), and on how to package and image the collected material. The investigator must also accurately and thoroughly document all activities undertaken.

Live Acquisition

When an investigator is faced with a running system that may have been compromised, valuable information such as open network connections and other running processes may reveal the intentions and mode of entry of the attacker. The investigator may conclude that this volatile information is important enough to conduct a live acquisition, and thus sacrifice the durable information that might be obtained by powering the system down.[10]

In a **live acquisition**, the investigator cannot know what the attacker did to the system during the compromise—common system tools may have been replaced with malicious versions, or various traps may have been put in place to destroy information if the system is disturbed. For these reasons, the investigator will typically use a trusted set of tools from a CD such as Knoppix-STD, F.I.R.E., or Helix.

A live acquisition typically uses scripts to automate the process of running a series of tools and preserving their output. One well-known script for Windows systems is the Windows Forensic Toolchest, or WFT (*www.foolmoon.net/security/wft/*); this tool can capture volatile information that might be useful in investigating a system compromise.

OFFLINE

STERILE MEDIA

One possible ground for challenging results from a digital investigation is contamination —that is, the relevant evidence came from somewhere else. For this reason, media that are used to collect digital evidence must be forensically sterile, meaning that they contain no residue from previous use.

There are various ways to prepare sterile media, but a common method is to write zeroes to every block on the device to erase any previous contents, and then, if needed, format the device with a file system.

All sterilization procedures must be codified, and all media sterilization processes must be documented. Most forensic practices maintain an inventory of sterilized media for such uses, which should be packaged and sealed as shown in Figure 14-2 to preclude possibility of tampering before use.

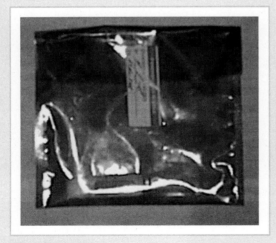

FIGURE 14-2   "Sterile" Thumb Drive

WFT is essentially a driver script that runs a series of tools that identifies and lists running processes, active network connections, and other activity, and saves the output on an external medium such as a thumb drive. It is designed for forensic use and includes a number of integrity checks such as verifying the tools before they are run, as shown in Figure 14-3.

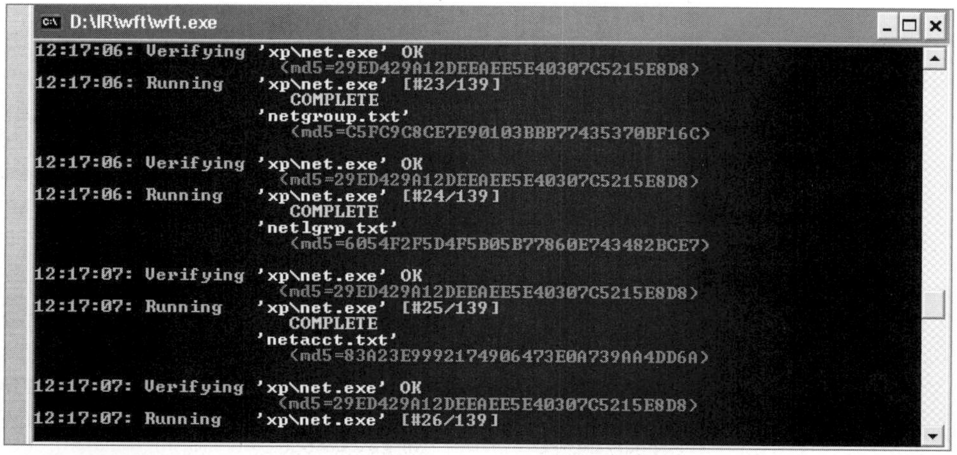

FIGURE 14-3 WFT Verification

At the completion of WFT, the files logging its execution are also hashed and their values displayed to provide an integrity reference. This is shown in Figure 14-4.

FIGURE 14-4 WFT Hash Verification

While live acquisition is usually thought of in the context of a running server, the need to acquire the state of an active process arises in at least two other situations:

- Logs—log records are generated on a continuous basis, and capturing their state at a point in time for an investigation typically requires a live acquisition
- Active devices such as PDAs and cell phones

A continuously changing process presents challenges in acquisition as there is not a "fixed" state that can be collected, hashed, etc. This has given rise to the concept of "snapshot forensics"[11] which captures a point-in-time picture of a process, much as a photograph freezes the action of a running child.

Consider the log files on a centralized syslogd server that is continually receiving log records from firewalls, intrusion detection systems, authentication servers, application servers, and other sources. Because log records are arriving on a more or less continual basis, there is no "fixed" state of the log file that can be collected and hashed.

For this reason, a snapshot is taken of the active log file by copying it using perhaps a normal file copy. This copy is then acquired (perhaps by another copy) and hashed to verify that a true and accurate copy has been acquired. The investigator should be prepared to produce good documentation and fully justify the actions in testimony, if necessary (perhaps using the analogy of extracting a single frame from a motion picture or taking a still photo of a running child, or explaining and demonstrating that a copy operation does not "add" information to the item copied, etc.).

As seen in the chapter's opening scenario, often an intrusion is detected by its end effect (such as the disk devices being deleted), and the investigator must work backwards to identify sources of evidence. In situations like this, the information in log records often provides critical evidence of how the situation developed over time. For example, logs from the VPN and authentication servers might show an intruder logging in from outside the corporate network, and records generated by management applications might reveal the exact operations performed in deleting the disks from the storage array.

Active devices[12] such as PDAs and cell phones present similar challenges because as long as they have power, they are active (monitoring the status of tasks and appointments, checking for e-mail or instant messages, managing connections with the cellular network), so their internal state is continually changing. They also maintain a lot of volatile information in memory that is lost if the batteries are removed.

These types of small wireless devices are increasingly critical to modern forensic investigations because almost everyone has at least one, and they are increasingly used for a variety of business and personal communications (including e-mail and instant messaging).

They are also fairly promiscuous—if there is a compatible network available, they will connect to it. A PDA seized from a suspect might be accessed wirelessly to modify or delete information, and a cell phone could continue to receive calls, instant messages, and e-mails after its seizure.

For these reasons, it is critical to protect wireless devices from accessing (or being accessed though) the network after seizure and during analysis. Since removing power to the device would lose the volatile information, a better solution is to block wireless access using a Faraday Cage. For example, Paraben Corporation developed the "Wireless StrongHold Bag" (shown in Figure 14-5) to protect wireless devices from wireless access while being transported or stored.

FIGURE 14-5   Paraben Wireless StrongHold Bag

This bag has a metallic coating that prevents the enclosed device from receiving or sending wireless signals.

To provide similar protection while an investigator works with the device, Paraben designed the StrongHold Box, which is shown in Figure 14-6.

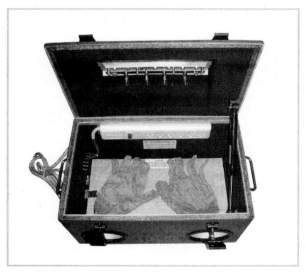

FIGURE 14-6   Paraben Wireless Stronghold Box

This enclosure provides a Faraday Cage to shield the device from network connectivity, enables investigator access, and includes shielded connections so that investigators can use external devices for imaging and analysis.

Equipping an organization to handle forensics for these types of devices can easily cost $10,000–$20,000 just in specialized hardware and software. For reasons of cost and the rapid changes in technology in these devices, forensic analysis is an excellent candidate for outsourcing to a specialist consultant.

Packaging for Protection

Two types of items used in evidence packaging are shown in Figures 14-7 and 14-8.

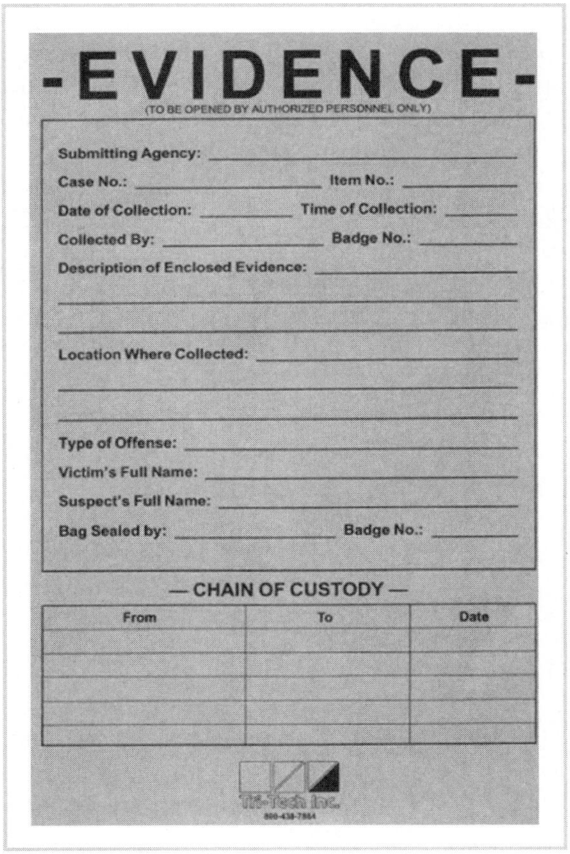

-EVIDENCE-
(TO BE OPENED BY AUTHORIZED PERSONNEL ONLY)

Submitting Agency: _____

Case No.: _____   Item No.: _____

Date of Collection: _____   Time of Collection: _____

Collected By: _____   Badge No.: _____

Description of Enclosed Evidence: _____

_____

_____

Location Where Collected: _____

_____

_____

Type of Offense: _____

Victim's Full Name: _____

Suspect's Full Name: _____

Bag Sealed by: _____   Badge No.: _____

— CHAIN OF CUSTODY —

From	To	Date

Ti-Tech Inc.
800-438-7884

FIGURE 14-7   Evidence Envelope

FIGURE 14-8   Evidence Seal

While any secure package will serve, the use of packaging specifically designed for this purpose aids proper documentation and storage. The evidence envelope is pre-printed with a form that collects the relevant information for establishing where, by whom, and when the information was collected. The evidence seal is designed for single use and is very difficult to remove without breaking it.

Dead Acquisition

In a dead acquisition, the computer is typically powered off so that its disk drives can be removed for imaging; the information on the devices is static ("dead") and durable.

While dead acquisition processes and procedures were developed for computer disks, they apply equally well to disk-like devices such as thumb drives, memory cards, MP3 players, and others.

In dead acquisition, an investigator seeks to obtain a forensic image of the disk or device. This image must include active files and directories as well as deleted files and file fragments. Consider the illustration of a small filesystem shown in Figure 14-9.

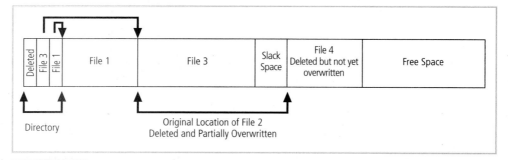

FIGURE 14-9 Example File System

A normal filesystem copy of the disk shown in Figure 14-9 would obtain File 1 and File 3, which are the only active files. However, there is more information on the device, including:

- The Deleted entry in the directory, which might contain useful information about the deleted file
- The remnant of File 2 that was not overwritten by File 3, which might retain useful file fragments
- File 4, which has been deleted but not yet overwritten, so its contents should still be recoverable
- The free space, which might contain other files or fragments

To make sure this potentially valuable information is acquired, forensic investigators use bit stream (or sector-by-sector) copying when making a forensic image of a device. Bit stream copying reads a sector (or block; 512 bytes on most devices) from the source drive and writes it to the target drive; this process continues until all sectors on the suspect drive have been copied.

Forensic imaging can be accomplished using specialized hardware tools or software running on a laptop or other computer. Hardware tools, specialized for the single purpose of copying disks, are faster. When performing a large imaging task (for example, imaging disks from 150 desktop computers involved in a complex fraud investigation), a hardware imaging solution will speed the process. A common type of hardware imaging solution is the Image MASSter Solo, shown in Figure 14-10.

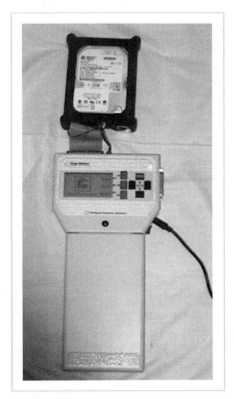

FIGURE 14-10   Image MASSter

The disadvantages of hardware imaging platforms are cost and the fact that they support only certain interfaces. For example, an IDE imaging device might require an expensive upgrade to support SATA drives.

Software imaging and other forensic tools are sold by many vendors. These tools run on a standard laptop or other system and support any disk interface supported by the host. A laptop-based imaging solution is shown in Figure 14-11.

FIGURE 14-11   Laptop Imaging System

Here the suspect drive on the left (enclosed for imaging in a protective rubber "boot") is connected to the laptop through a forensic bridge, which serves two purposes:

- It bridges the IDE drive interface to the laptop USB interface.
- It blocks any write requests the laptop might generate.

OFFLINE

Write Blockers

It is critical that the information on the suspect media not be changed during the imaging process, or its value as evidentiary material may be compromised. Since Helix is specialized for forensic use, it does not mount filesystems or create swap partitions on any of the attached disks; an experienced investigator following correct procedure should not need any additional write block protection.

However, investigators are human, and most will admit to having at least once confused the suspect and destination disks when performing imaging (say, at 4:00 am, while imaging the 72nd of 83 disks). For this reason, and to preclude any grounds for challenging the image output, it is common practice to protect the suspect media using a write blocker.

Write blockers have traditionally been hardware devices, but software write blockers are beginning to emerge. Hardware write blockers have the advantage of longer use in practice (and are better understood by the legal community) and also can perform the bridging function described above. For example, a write blocker kit (such as the UltraKit sold by Digital Intelligence) may contain bridges for IDE, SCSI, and SATA devices that both provide the write blocking function to protect the suspect media and "bridge" the connection to a USB or FireWire connection compatible with the laptop.

The Imaging Process

Before imaging a piece of disk media, its origin and description (vendor, model, and serial number) are documented in both written and photographic form. This establishes the provenance of the disk image and helps to ensure its authenticity. Also, the medium used as the target for forensic imaging should be forensically sterile and that fact documented.

Once the suspect medium is attached to the imaging setup, the general imaging process is:

- Calculate and record a baseline cryptographic hash of the suspect medium.
- Perform a bit stream image of the suspect medium.
- Calculate and record a hash of the target (and optionally another hash of the suspect medium to verify it was not modified by the imaging process).
- Compare the hashes to verify they match.
- Package the target medium for transport.

The screenshot shown in Figure 14-12 shows the imaging process being carried out with a simple naming convention for the files produced:

- The prefix PI indicates a pre-image hash.
- The prefix DI indicates the disk image.
- The prefix AI indicates a post-image hash.

FIGURE 14-12 Imaging Using Helix

Case numbers are of the form YYYY-BK-PAGE, where the case numbers are assigned from a standard record book of numbered pages. In the example, the case number assigned is for the year 2008, book 1, and page 0011. The four-digit item number just provides a reference number for this particular item of evidence and can be cross-referenced in the "field evidence log."

As is shown, the hash for the image file matches the hash for the device, and thus you can be confident that you have obtained a true and accurate image of the device.

Once the imaging is completed, the target medium must be securely packaged. The target medium is marked for identification, sealed in a static bag, and sealed in an evidence envelope, as shown in Figure 14-13.

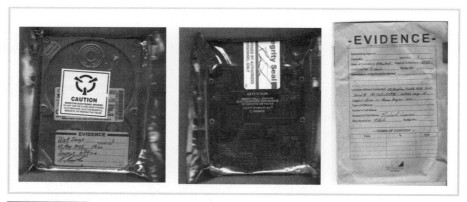

FIGURE 14-13   Securing a Drive

Note the practice of signing across the seals to ensure that someone else doesn't break the seal and replace it.

Digital Photography

Photography plays a major role in documenting evidence and its provenance. The digital camera offers much more convenience than the traditional field camera but does require some preparation and sound process, as follows:

1. Sterilize the digital photographic medium (memory card). Forensic sterilization can easily be performed by formatting the card to destroy the directory information, then using a tool such as SDelete from Sysinternals (*www.sysinternals.com*) to clear all free space on the card of any existing content.
2. Set the camera's clock to ensure that the dates/times recorded for the digital photographs are accurate.
3. Make the photographic medium "self-documenting" by taking the first exposure of a "Begin Digital Photography" marker.
4. Ensure that the :DPM (Digital Photographic Media) number—a tracking number assigned to the particular card—is identified in the digital photography log as each photograph is taken.
5. At the conclusion of the onsite activities, make an "end of photography" exposure.

6. Remove the card from the camera, package it in a static bag, and seal it in an evidence envelope like any other piece of digital evidence.
7. Do not make hashes of digital photographs until the first time the evidence envelope is opened.

Field Documentation

A series of standard forms is commonly used to document the collection of evidence in the field. An example of a scene sketch form is shown in Figure 14-14.

The scene sketch is the only item that can be done in pencil. Its purpose is to show the general locations of items. The field activity log, which documents the activities of the team during evidence collection, is shown in Figure 14-15.

Case Number
Investigator
Scene Sketch
Signature
Date
Witness
Date

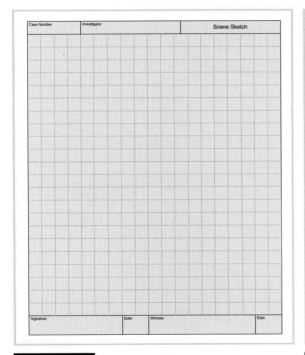

FIGURE 14-14 Scene Sketch Form

Case Number
Investigator
Field Activity Log
Continued from Page:
Page:
Signature
Date
Witness
Date

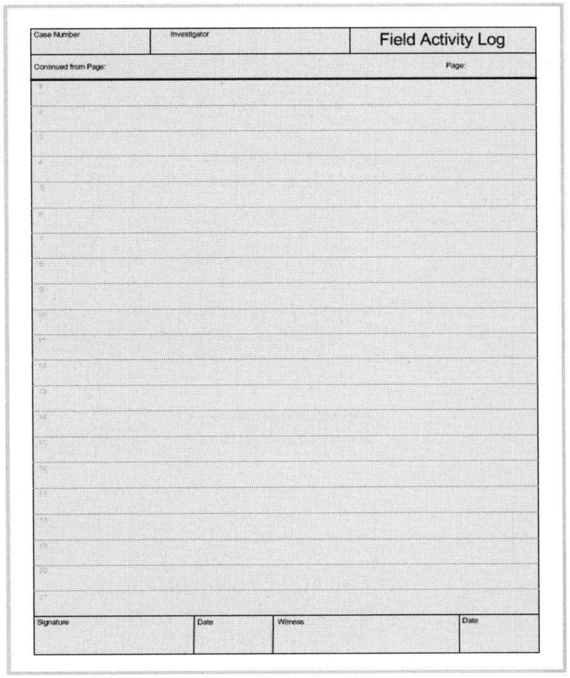

FIGURE 14-15 Field Activity Log

The field evidence log, which identifies by filename number each item collected, is shown in Figure 14-16.

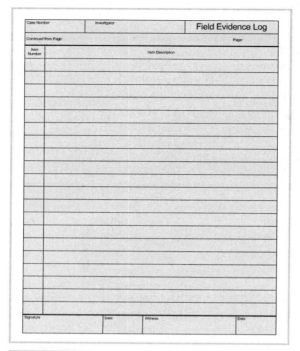

FIGURE 14-16 Field Evidence Log

These forms are normally assembled into a case file that travels with the investigation team and becomes a permanent part of the documentary record of the investigation.

The Field Forensic Kit

The field kit is typically as personal as the individual investigator, but the photograph shown in Figure 14-17 is a fairly standard kit.

FIGURE 14-17 The Field Forensic Kit

The kit includes:

- Write blockers
- Extension cord and power strip
- Evidence envelopes and seals
- Photographic markers and scales
- Gloves (vinyl)
- Tool kit
- Security bits (for dealing with specialized fasteners)
- Tie-on labels (for identifying cables, etc.)
- Assortment of screws, etc. (to replace that one screw or nut that somehow always disappears)
- Digital camera
- Pens, permanent markers
- ESD workstation and static strap

Maintaining the Chain of Custody

While documentation of process and procedures, digital fingerprints, and use of secure packaging help demonstrate the authenticity of digital evidence, there are additional requirements for demonstrating that the evidence has been protected from accidental or purposeful modification at every point from its collection through analysis to presentation in court. This protection is called maintaining the chain of custody.

In principle, the chain of custody is quite simple; basically, it is a legal record of where the evidence was at each point in its lifetime and documentation of each and every access to it.

An example of an access log is shown in Figure 14-18.

CHAIN of CUSTODY LOG

| Case Number | | Item Number | | | PAGE _____ CONTINUED FROM _____ |

ITEM DESCRIPTION

		WARNING	Receiver's signature warrants that evidence seal was intact with no visible sign of tampering except as noted under Notes at time of receipt		
Relinquished By	**Date / Time**		**Received By**	**Date / Time**	**Notes**
PRINTED			PRINTED		
SIGNATURE			SIGNATURE		
PRINTED			PRINTED		
SIGNATURE			SIGNATURE		
PRINTED			PRINTED		
SIGNATURE			SIGNATURE		
PRINTED			PRINTED		
SIGNATURE			SIGNATURE		
PRINTED			PRINTED		
SIGNATURE			SIGNATURE		
PRINTED			PRINTED		
SIGNATURE			SIGNATURE		
PRINTED			PRINTED		
SIGNATURE			SIGNATURE		
PRINTED			PRINTED		
SIGNATURE			SIGNATURE		

FIGURE 14-18   Chain of Custody Log

The usual process is that the field investigator maintains personal custody and control of the sealed item until it is logged into the chain of custody book at the evidence storage room. Each time the item is removed (for analysis, copying, etc.) it is logged out, forming a documented trail of who accessed the information and when that access occurred.

Collected evidence must be stored and handled appropriately to protect its value, especially since in some cases items may be stored for weeks or months before they are analyzed. If the investigation results in legal proceedings, the evidence may be stored for years before the matter is heard in court.

Proper storage requires a protected, controlled access environment, coupled with sound processes governing access to its contents (for example, access is limited to specifically authorized personnel, and documentation of each and every access is maintained in the chain of custody book).

The storage facility must also maintain the proper environment for holding digital information, which requires:

- Controlled temperature and humidity
- Freedom from strong electrical and magnetic fields that might damage the items
- Protection from fire and other physical hazards

The evidence storage facility can be a specialized evidence room, a locked filing cabinet in an office, or something in between.

Analyzing Evidence

To answer the question that originated in the physical world and triggered the digital investigation, an analyst must translate that question into a series of questions that are answerable through forensic analysis. These "digital world" questions will set the scope of and guide the analysis.

The first step in the analysis process is to obtain the evidence from the storage area (signing it out in the chain of custody book) and perform a physical authentication. This involves verifying the written documentation against the actual item of evidence (that is, verifying the manufacturer, serial number, and other identifying information). After successful completion of that step, a copy of the evidence is made for analysis, and the original is returned to storage—sound practice is to never work on the original evidence.

The copy of the evidence can then be authenticated by recomputing its hash and comparing it to the written record to verify that a true and accurate copy of the original evidence has been obtained.

Disk images must be loaded into the particular forensic tool used by the organization. This typically involves processing the image into the format used by the tool, performing preprocessing such as undeleting files, data carving (recovering files, images, etc., from fragments in free space), and comparison against known hashes.

Two of the major tools used in forensic analysis are EnCase (Guidance Software) and Forensic Toolkit (FTK, from AccessData), and while largely similar in function, they take different approaches to the analysis task.

FTK does extensive preprocessing of the evidence items, as shown in Figure 14-19, and organizes the various items into a tabbed display. It is common for an analyst to start this preprocessing late in the day and leave it running overnight so that it will be complete at the beginning of the following workday.

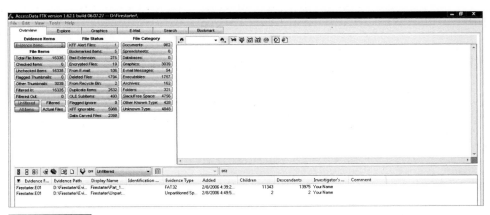

FIGURE 14-19 AccessData's FTK

Deleted files are recovered and present little challenge to a forensic tool. The tool also extracts e-mail messages and makes them available under the "E-Mail" tab.

EnCase Forensic Edition takes a slightly different approach in that it presents an extensible forensic platform that makes it easy for trained investigators to carry out their tasks. For example, rather than finding all the deleted files and folders during lengthy pre-processing, EnCase provides a right-click menu function, as shown in Figure 14-20.

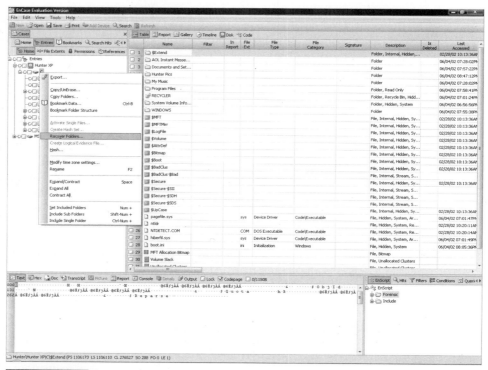

FIGURE 14-20 EnCase Forensic Edition

EnCase also supports EnScripts, which are written in a C-like language and which automate additional tasks not provided by the main program. There is a very active user community that develops and contributes these scripts, and some of the functionality has been incorporated into recent versions of EnCase. One type of EnScript is the "filter" which searches for particular types of information. Running the "Deleted Files" filter produces the list of deleted files shown in Figure 14-21.

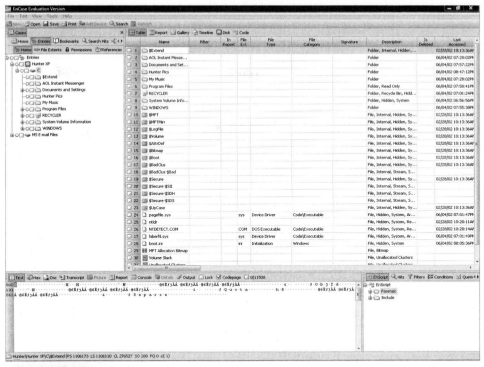

FIGURE 14-21 EnCase Deleted Files

Searching for Evidence

With the increasing sizes of disk devices, identifying relevant information is one of the more important analyst tasks. For example, when investigating a computer image in a case involving widespread identity theft, credit and social security numbers are highly relevant.

As part of its preprocessing, FTK constructs an index of terms found in the image. The results are available under the Search tab, and Figure 14-22 shows the occurrences of the word "arson" and the context of one of the search hits.

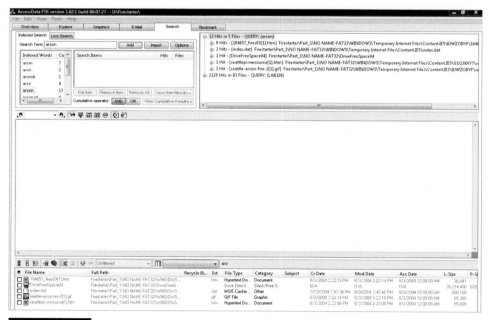

FIGURE 14-22 Search in FTK

FTK also includes the "Live Search" tab, which allows searching on user-specified terms.

Developing relevant search terms can be challenging; a technique from the legal profession called cartwheeling,[13] in which a term is extended with links to subsidiary terms, can help. For example, when investigating the unauthorized use of a keylogger, the cartwheel diagram shown in Figure 14-23 shows how someone can approach the process of developing search terms.

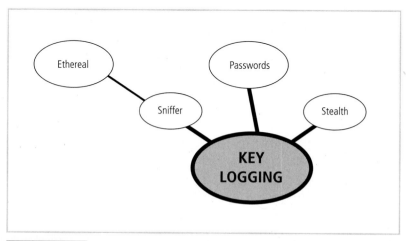

FIGURE 14-23 Cartwheel Diagram for Developing Search Terms

EnCase also offers a flexible search interface and includes predefined filters for common items such as e-mail and Web addresses and social security numbers. As relevant items are located, they are "bookmarked" for inclusion in the final report.

Reporting the Findings

Once the analysis is complete, the findings must be reported in written and often verbal form, in either a presentation or legal testimony. This report must communicate the findings clearly to the various audiences that will use the report:

- Upper management is typically interested in the recommendations as to whether or not the allegations were correct, the scope of a data breach, and the impact and cost of that breach.
- A forensic expert retained by the opposition is interested in the details of evidence collection and analysis in order to judge if the analysis was proper and identify weaknesses that could be used to challenge it in court.
- Attorneys, judges, and juries are interested in compliance with the legal requirements and the real meaning of the evidence in deciding a question of fact.
- Other professionals (auditors, human resources departments, and others) are interested in compliance with organizational policies, and in identifying possible changes to those policies.

It is a temptation to prepare a series of reports, each tailored to a particular audience. However, if the investigation leads to legal proceedings, all these various reports are discoverable (that is, must be disclosed) by the opposing side. Any differences among the various versions could cast doubt on the conclusions.

The safest approach is to prepare a single report with an index to point the parties to their particular area of interest. The report should identify what gave rise to the investigation, the sources of the evidence that was analyzed, the tools and processes that were used to analyze the evidence, the specific findings, and finally an interpretation of the findings (in other words, did the evidence support or disprove the allegation).

In general terms, the report summarizes the detailed records contained in the case file, the analyst's notebooks, and other documentation, which can be produced to address detailed questions.

Interacting with Law Enforcement

When an incident violates civil or criminal law, it is the organization's responsibility to notify the proper authorities. Selecting the appropriate law enforcement agency depends on the type of crime committed. The Federal Bureau of Investigation (FBI), for example, handles computer crimes that are categorized as felonies. The U.S. Secret Service investigates crimes involving U.S. currency and counterfeiting, and certain cases involving credit card fraud and identity theft. The U.S. Treasury Department has a bank fraud investigation unit, and the Securities and Exchange Commission has investigation and fraud control units as well. However, the heavy case loads of these agencies mean that they typically give priority to those incidents that affect the national critical infrastructure or that have significant economic impact. The FBI Web site, for example, states that the FBI Computer Intrusion Squad:

> pursues the investigation of cyber-based attacks, primarily unauthorized access (intrusion) and denial-of-service, directed at the major components of this country's critical information, military, and economic infrastructures. Critical infrastructure includes the nation's power grids and power-supply systems, transportation control systems, money transfer and accounting systems, defense-related systems, and telecommunications networks. Additionally, the Squad investigates cyber attacks directed at private industry and public institutions that maintain information vital to national security and/or the economic success of the nation.[14]

In other words, if the crime is not directed at or doesn't affect the national infrastructure, the FBI may not be able to assist an organization as effectively as state or local agencies. However, in general, if a crime crosses state lines, it becomes a federal matter. The FBI may also become involved at the request of a state agency, if it has the available resources.

Each state, county, and city in the United States has its own law enforcement agencies. These agencies enforce all local and state laws, handle suspects, and secure crime scenes for state and federal cases. Local law enforcement agencies rarely have computer crimes task forces, but the investigative (detective) units are quite capable of processing crime scenes; handling most common criminal violations, such as physical theft, trespassing, and damage to property; and apprehending and processing suspects in computer-related crimes.

Involving law enforcement agencies has advantages and disadvantages. Such agencies are usually much better equipped for processing evidence than a business organization. Unless the security forces in the organization have been trained in processing evidence and computer forensics, they may do more harm than good when attempting to extract information that can lead to the legal conviction of a suspected criminal. Law enforcement agencies are also prepared to handle the warrants and subpoenas necessary when documenting a case. They are adept at obtaining statements from witnesses, affidavits, and other required documents. For all these reasons, law enforcement personnel can be a security administrator's greatest allies in prosecuting a computer crime. It is therefore important to become familiar with the appropriate local and state agencies before you have to make a call announcing a suspected crime. Most state and federal agencies offer awareness programs, provide guest speakers at conferences, and offer programs such as the InfraGard program of the FBI (*www.infragard.net*). These agents clearly understand the challenges facing security administrators.

The disadvantages of law enforcement involvement include possible loss of control of the chain of events following an incident, including the collection of information and evidence and the prosecution of suspects. An organization that wishes to simply reprimand or dismiss an employee should not involve a law enforcement agency in the resolution of an incident. Additionally, the organization may not hear about the case for weeks or even months because of heavy caseloads or resource shortages. A very real issue for commercial organizations when involving law enforcement agencies is the tagging of equipment vital to the organization's business as evidence. This means that assets can be removed, stored, and preserved to prepare the criminal case. Despite these difficulties, if the organization detects a criminal act, it has the legal obligation to notify the appropriate law enforcement officials. Failure to do so can subject the organization and its officers to prosecution as accessories to the crimes or for impeding the course of an investigation. It is up to the security administrator to ask questions of law enforcement agencies to determine when each agency needs to be involved and specifically which crimes are addressed by each agency.

Anti-Forensics

Forensic tools excel at retrieving information that has been deleted through normal means or resides in hidden places used by the operating system. This deleted or hidden data is a valuable source of information for investigators, but its recovery can pose a significant threat to the privacy and confidentiality of an organization's information assets.

Actions in the digital world leave many traces (such as records of Web sites visited, or archived e-mail messages), and these items can be easily retrieved from discarded or recycled computer equipment. Simson Garfinkel did an empirical study in which he purchased used computers and disks from online merchants and analyzed what was left on the devices by their previous owners (either inadvertently or due to poor deletion processes).[15] He found medical and business records, and many other types of confidential information.

NIST has documented recommended practices in Special Publication 800-88 "Guidelines for Media Sanitization," which range from overwriting disk media with zeroes or random data to physical destruction.

Organizations must be aware that forensic tools are not just in the hands of the honest professionals, but are available to everyone. Therefore organizations must have policies and procedures to ensure that discarded digital information is destroyed beyond forensic recovery.

An increasing concern for privacy and the widespread availability of encryption products have led to the widespread use of encryption for individual files or entire devices. While some encryption is poorly done and is easily broken, quality products are increasingly available that use good encryption algorithms that are beyond our current capability to break by "brute force." Encrypted files can present challenges to forensic investigators because they conceal information. A fairly common encryption product accepts the encryption key when the user logs on and decrypts information on the fly. When the system goes into screen saver mode or is powered down, the encryption key is destroyed and must be reentered. Unfortunately, data collected by a forensic investigator is encrypted, and will not be readable without the key.

Some forensic products offer brute force attacks against the encrypted information using dictionaries of common pass phrases. They are sometimes successful but can be defeated by a good pass phrase. Also, encrypted information may exist in unencrypted form in temporary "work files" or the paging file.

Chapter Summary

- Computer forensics is the use of computer investigation and analysis techniques to identify, collect, preserve, and analyze electronic items of potential evidentiary value so that they may be admitted as evidence in a court of law, or used to support administrative action. The term digital forensics applies to all modern electronic devices, including mobile phones, personal digital assistants (PDAs), portable music players, and other electronic devices capable of storing digital information.

- A digital investigation will begin with some allegation of wrongdoing—either a policy violation or commission of a crime. Based on that allegation, authorization is sought to begin the investigation properly by collecting relevant evidence, and once the authorization to conduct an investigation is obtained, the collection of evidence can begin.

- The first response digital forensics team secures and collects the devices, media, or media images that are evidentiary. Later, analysis and reporting techniques are performed by persons specially trained in the use of forensic tools. They analyze the collected information and provide answers to the question(s) that gave rise to the investigation.

- To answer the underlying question that prompted the investigation, an analyst must translate that overall question into a series of specific questions that are answerable through forensic analysis, and then use the proper tools to determine the answers to the detailed questions.

- When an incident violates civil or criminal law, it is the organization's responsibility to notify the proper authorities and work with them throughout the investigation and resolution of the matter.

- Forensic tools can be used by investigators to obtain information, even deleted information, from digital media. This poses risks when such tools are used for illegitimate purposes to obtain private or proprietary information from discarded digital media.

Review Questions

1. What is the primary goal of digital forensics?
2. What are the factors that guide an organization that is setting up a forensic capability?
3. What are two practical divisions in the practice of digital forensics?
4. What are the four common roles in a digital forensic team?
5. What factors determine the priority in collecting digital evidence?
6. What are the differences between forensic examination and forensic analysis?
7. What is a good analogy for explaining how deleted files can still be recovered?
8. What part does an affidavit play in obtaining authorization for a search?
9. What is a main difference between search and seizure in the public vs. the private sector?
10. What are the four steps in collecting digital evidence?
11. What two hash functions are commonly used as digital fingerprints?
12. What is the purpose of sterile media?
13. What type of forensics is used for active devices and continuous processes?
14. What is a critical concern when seizing a device such as a cell phone?

15. What types of information are missed by a normal copying process but included in a forensic image?

16. What are two required characteristics of an evidence storage facility?

17. What are two well-known commercial tools used in forensic analysis?

18. What is the relationship between forensics and anti-forensics, and why is it important to the forensics investigator?

19. Why is cryptography a good thing for IT workers but a bad thing for forensic investigators?

20. When is the involvement of law enforcement optional, recommended, or required in a forensics investigation? Who should make this determination?

Exercises

1. Using a Web search engine, look up the "Trojan Defense." How can it be used to question the conclusions drawn from a forensic investigation?

2. At the end of 2006, a new edition of the Federal Rules of Civil Procedure (FRCP) went into effect. What likely effect will the emphasis on electronically stored information (ESI) have on an organization's need for a digital forensic capability?

3. Using a Web search tool, identify some common certifications for digital forensic practitioners and determine whether they are available to public or private sector organizations.

4. When investigating a virus outbreak within an organization, what part might digital forensics play?

5. Using a Web search tool, identify cases where private information was disclosed when computer equipment was discarded.

Case Exercise

Mary resisted the temptation to try to recover the disks. Destroying critical business information is a serious matter, and ATI and its customers might want to prosecute if it could be shown that the fired staff members were responsible. She sat back down at her desk and began sketching out a fault tree that identified the ways the data might have been deleted. She quickly identified two main branches: human error and malicious intent. Since the management applications used to create and delete storage devices log each action on the central log server, if an authorized user had accidentally deleted the devices, Mary knew there should be a record of it.

She thought further down the malicious intent branch and developed two scenarios:

- The fired administrators used their credentials to delete the devices.
- The fired administrators set up a "logic bomb" to delete the devices if they were terminated.

Since the administrators were escorted from the building immediately upon termination, they would have had to access the network remotely in order to delete the devices manually. The VPN server logs and the authentication server would have recorded any access by the administrators after they were removed from the building. Also, the management application logs would trace the deletions to the terminated administrators' credentials.

A logic bomb could have been concealed in many places, but Mary concluded the most likely location would be on the workstations assigned to the administrators.

Questions:

1. What information should Mary collect first to support her investigation?

2. What forensic methods and processes will Mary have to use on the log servers and the administrators' workstations?

3. Can you think of other places Mary might look for relevant information?

Endnotes

1. *Merriam-Webster's Collegiate Dictionary* (10ed), s.v.

2. Paul G. Lewis, *Curiosity may kill the case.* New Jersey Law Journal, 182:11. Pp 1030–1031.

3. Christopher L. T. Brown, Computer Evidence Collection and Preservation, 2006. Hingham, MA: Charles River Media.

4. NIST Special Publication 800-86, "Guide to Integrating Forensic Techniques into Incident Response.

5. Ibid.

6. Keith Inman and Norah Rudin (2001). *Principles and Practice of Criminalistics: The Profession of Forensic Science.* Boca Raton, FL: CRC Press.

7. *www.schneier.com/blog/archives/2005/03/more_hash_funct.html.*

8. *www.news.com/8301-10784_3-5829714-7.html.*

9. *http://support.accessdata.com/ics/support/default.asp?deptID=5445.*

10. Note that the investigator can later shut the computer down and image its disk(s) to gather information that may be useful in identifying the mode of entry and other activities of the attacker. However, since the live response tools modified that state of the system, it is very unlikely that the information collected from the disks would be admissible in any legal proceeding.

11. Gregory Kipper (2007). *Wireless Crime and Forensic Investigation.* Boca Raton, FL: Auerbach.

12. Tyler Cohen and Amber Schroader (2007). *Alternate Data Storage Forensics.* Burlington, MA: Elsevier.

13. William P. Statsky (1982). *Legal Research and Writing.* St. Paul, MN: West Publishing.

14. Federal Bureau of Investigation, "Technology Crimes (San Francisco)," accessed from *www.fbi.gov/contact/fo/sanfran/sfcomputer.htm.*

15. *www.blackhat.com/presentations/bh-federal-06/BH-Fed-06-Garfinkel.pdf.*

Glossary

A

/etc/passwd Encrypted file in which Linux stores passwords.

AAA services Authentication, authorization, and accounting.

access control list (ACL) A method of implementing technical specifications which utilizes user access lists, matrices, and capability tables to govern the rights and privileges of users.

access control matrix A combination of tables and lists, in which organizational assets are listed along the column headers, while users are listed along the row headers. The resulting matrix contains access control lists in columns for a particular device or asset, while a row contains the capability table for a particular user.

accuracy Indicates that information is free from mistakes or errors, and has the value that the end user expects.

acknowledgment (ACK) flag Part of a data packet's flag section that, when set, signifies that the destination computer has received the packets that were previously sent.

active vulnerability scanner Tool that initiates traffic on the network in order to identify security holes. As a class, this type of scanner identifies exposed usernames and groups, shows open network shares, and exposes configuration problems and other vulnerabilities in servers.

Advanced Encryption Standard (AES) The successor to 3DES.

affidavit A formal statement issued by a private organization which furnishes much of the same information usually found in a public sector search warrant, and grants similar authorization to collect relevant evidence.

after-action review (AAR) A detailed examination of events that occurred from first detection of an incident to final recovery. This is conducted by the IR team before it returns to routine duties.

alarm *See* "alert."

alarm clustering and compaction A process of grouping almost identical alarms that happen at close to the same time into a single higher-level alarm.

alarm filtering The process of classifying IDPS alerts by running the system for a while to track what types of false positives it generates, and then adjusting the alarm classifications.

alert An indication that a system has just been attacked or is under attack.

alert message A scripted description of an incident that consists of just enough information so that each responder knows which portion of the IR plan to implement without impeding the notification process.

alert roster A document containing contact information for the individuals who need to be notified in the event of an incident.

algorithm The mathematical formula or method used to convert an unencrypted message into an encrypted message, or vice versa.

American National Standards Institute (ANSI) An organization that serves to reinforce the position of the U.S. government and industry while helping to ensure the safety and the health of consumers and ensuring environmental protection.

analysis phase Second part of the forensic analysis function, which uses materials discovered during the examination phase to answer the question(s) that gave rise to the investigation.

Application-layer gateway A device that controls the way applications inside the network access external networks by setting up proxy services. *See* "proxy server."

application-level gateway   *See* "proxy server."

application protocol verification   Process in which an NIDPS inspects the higher-order protocols (HTTP, FTP, Telnet) for unexpected packet behavior, or improper use.

application proxy   *See* "proxy server."

asymmetric encryption   *See* "public key encryption."

attack   An act or action that takes advantage of a vulnerability to compromise a controlled system.

attack profile   A detailed description of the activities that occur during an attack.

attack protocol   A series of steps or processes used by an attacker, in a logical sequence, to launch an attack against a target system or network.

attack scenario end case   The final result of the business impact analysis, which utilizes attack success scenarios to estimate the cost of the best, worst, and most likely cases.

attack success scenario   Part of a business impact analysis which is added to the attack profile and depicts the effects of an occurrence of each threat on each prioritized functional area. These typically include alternative outcomes—best, worst, and most likely.

attenuation   The loss of signal strength as a signal moves across media.

auditing   The recording (usually in a log file) of authentication and authorization activities.

authentication   The act of confirming the identity of a potential user.

authentication, authorization, and accounting (AAA) server   A server, used in a centralized authentication setup, that alleviates the need to provide each server on the network with a separate database of usernames and passwords, each of which would have to be updated individually each time a password changed or a user was added.

authenticity   The quality or state of being genuine or original, rather than a reproduction or fabrication. Information is authentic when it is the information that was originally created, placed, stored, or transferred.

availability   Enables authorized users—persons or computer systems—to access information without interference or obstruction, and to receive it in the required format.

availability disruption   A product or service not being delivered to an organization as expected. The exact causes and consequences of an availability disruption are numerous and varied, but all contribute to a degradation in the expected level of a service.

average lifetime   How long a connection to a host lasts.

B

back door   Vulnerability created in a system by a virus or worm which allows the attacker to access the system at will with special privileges.

back hack   The act of hacking into an attacker's system to find out as much as possible about the hacker.

bare metal recovery   Technologies designed to replace operating systems and services when they fail.

bastion host   Computer in a network that is fortified against illegal entry and attack because it is exposed to external networks so it can screen the internal network from security exposure. It is typically the only computer an organization allows to be addressed directly from outside the network.

behavior-based IDPS   *See* "statistical-anomaly-based IDPS."

biometrics   The use of retinal scans, fingerprints, and the like for authentication.

blackout   A lengthy complete loss of power.

boot-up password   Password that must be entered to complete the process of starting up a computer.

boot virus   A virus that infects the key operating system files located in a computer's boot sector.

bots   *See* "zombies."

brownout   A prolonged drop in voltage.

brute force attack   The application of computing and network resources to try every possible combination of options of a password.

buffer overflow   An application error that occurs when more data is sent to a buffer than it can handle.

business continuity (BC) plan   A method that ensures that critical business functions continue, if a catastrophic incident or disaster occurs.

business continuity planning   Activities that prepare an organization to reestablish critical business operations during a disaster that affects operations at the primary site.

business impact analysis (BIA)   An investigation and assessment of the impact that various attacks can have on an organization.

C

cache   The storage of frequently accessed data on a disk, or a reference to the storage media or location itself.

caching   Storing frequently accessed data on disk.

capability table   A type of access control list that specifies which subjects and objects users or groups can access. In some systems, capability tables are called user profiles or user policies.

centralized IDPS control strategy   Strategy in which all IDPS control functions are implemented and managed in a central location.

certificate authority (CA)   Agency that manages the issuance of certificates and serves as the electronic notary public to verify their origin and integrity.

challenge-response   System in which the server sends a random password to users attempting to log in. The user then responds by submitting the same code along with appropriate additional information.

champion   A senior executive who promotes a project and ensures that it is supported, both financially and administratively, at the highest levels of the organization.

channel   One-way flow of information.

chief information officer (CIO)   This individual is often the senior technology officer and is primarily responsible for advising the chief executive officer, president, or company owner on the strategic planning that affects the management of information in the organization.

chief information security officer (CISO)   The individual primarily responsible for the assessment, management, and implementation of information security in the organization. The CISO usually reports directly to the CIO, although in larger organizations it is not uncommon for one or more layers of management to exist between the two.

C.I.A. triangle   A concept developed by the computer security industry which has been the industry standard since the development of the mainframe. It is based on the three characteristics of information that make it valuable to organizations: confidentiality, integrity, and availability.

cipher   The transformation of the individual components (characters, bytes, or bits) of an unencrypted message into encrypted components.

ciphertext   The encrypted or encoded message resulting from an encryption.

circuit   Two-way flow of information.

circuit-level gateway   A type of firewall that works at the Session layer of the OSI model, filtering internal traffic that leaves the network being protected.

cleartext   An unencrypted message or transmission.

client authentication   Authentication method similar to user authentication but with the addition of usage limits.

client-to-site VPN   One of two different types of VPNs. This type makes a network accessible to remote users who need dial-in access.

clipping level   A predetermined limit that, when exceeded, will cause a statistical-anomaly-based IDPS to send an alert to the administrator.

communications security   The protection of an organization's communications media, technology, and content.

competitive intelligence   Legal information-gathering techniques.

concurrent connections   The number of connections made to hosts in the internal network at any one time.

confidence value   A value placed upon an IDPS's ability to correctly detect and identify certain types of attacks.

confidentiality   Exists when information is protected from disclosure or exposure to unauthorized individuals or systems. This means that only those with the rights and privileges to access the information are able to do so.

configuration rule policies   The specific instructions entered into a security system, to regulate how it reacts to the data it receives.

Content Vectoring Protocol (CVP)   Protocol that enables firewalls to work with virus-scanning applications so certain content can be filtered out.

contingency plan   A method prepared by the organization to anticipate, react to, and recover from events that threaten the security of information and information assets in the organization, and, subsequently, to restore the organization to normal modes of business operations.

contingency planning (CP)   The overall process of preparing for unexpected events.

correlation attack Collection of brute force methods that attempt to deduce statistical relationships between the structure of the unknown key and the ciphertext that is the output of the cryptosystem. If these advanced approaches can calculate the value of the public key, and if this can be achieved in a reasonable time, all messages written with that key can be decrypted.

cracked Accessed by an unauthorized user.

cracker An individual who "cracks" or removes software protection that is designed to prevent unauthorized duplication.

cracking Attempting to reverse-calculate a password.

crisis management The actions taken during and after a disaster.

critical resource A software- or hardware-related item that is indispensable to the operation of a device or program.

crosstalk The interference of one communications channel with another. This occurs when one transmission "bleeds" over to another.

cryptanalysis The process of deciphering the original message from an encrypted message, without knowing the algorithms and keys used to perform the encryption.

cryptogram See "ciphertext."

cryptography The processes involved in encoding and decoding messages so that others cannot understand them.

cryptology The science of encryption, which actually encompasses the two disciplines of cryptography and cryptanalysis.

cryptosystem The set of transformations necessary to convert an unencrypted message into an encrypted message.

cryptovariable See "key."

cyberactivist See "hacktivist."

cyberterrorism Activities conducted by individuals for the purpose of hacking systems to conduct terrorist activities through network or Internet pathways.

cyclical redundancy check (CRC) An error-checking procedure.

D

database shadowing The propagation of transactions to a remote copy of the database.

data custodians Individuals responsible for the storage, maintenance, and protection of the data owner's information. The custodian could be a dedicated position, or it may be an additional responsibility of a systems administrator or other technology manager.

datagram A data packet, the basic quantum of network data, which contains two types of information: the header and the data.

data owners Those responsible for the security and use of a particular set of information. Usually members of senior management and sometimes even CIOs, data owners usually determine the level of data classification associated with the data, and work with subordinate managers to oversee the day-to-day administration of that data.

data users End users who work with the information to perform their daily jobs supporting the mission of the organization.

decipher To decrypt or convert ciphertext to plaintext.

de facto standards Standards that are informal or part of an organizational culture.

defense in depth One of the basic tenets of security architectures; the layered implementation of security.

de jure standards Standards that are published, scrutinized, and ratified by a group.

demilitarized zone (DMZ) A computer or small subnetwork between an organization's trusted internal network and an untrusted, external network.

denial-of-service (DoS) An attack in which the attacker sends a large number of connection or information requests to a target. So many requests are made that the target system cannot handle them along with other, legitimate requests for service. The system may crash, or may simply be unable to perform ordinary functions.

dictionary attack A variation on the brute force attack, this attack narrows the field by selecting specific target accounts and using a list of commonly used passwords (the dictionary) instead of random combinations.

differential backup The storage of all files that have changed or added data since the last full backup.

digital certificate Similar to a digital signature, it asserts that a public key is associated with a particular identity.

digital forensics   The use of sound investigation and analysis techniques to identify, collect, preserve, and analyze electronic items of potential evidentiary value so that they may be admitted as evidence in a court of law, or used to support administrative action.

digital signature   An encrypted code attached to files that are exchanged during a transaction so that each party can verify the other's identity.

direct attack   An attack in which a hacker uses a personal computer to break into a system.

disaster recovery (DR) plan   A method that addresses the preparation for and recovery from a disaster, whether natural or man-made.

disaster recovery planning   The preparation for and recovery from a disaster, whether natural or human-made.

disk mirroring   Term referring to RAID 1, which uses two drives where data is written to both drives simultaneously, providing a backup if the primary drive fails.

disk striping   Term used in reference to the RAID 0 method of creating one large logical volume across several available physical hard disk drives and storing the data in segments, called stripes, across all the disk drives in the array.

distortion   The unintentional variation of the communication over the medium.

distributed denial-of-service (DDoS)   A coordinated attack in which streams of requests are launched against a target from many locations at the same time. Most DDoS attacks are preceded by a preparation phase in which many systems, perhaps thousands, are compromised.

distributed firewalls   An environment in which firewalls are installed at all endpoints of the network, including the remote computers that connect to the network through VPNs.

E

echo   The reflection of a signal due to equipment malfunction or poor design.

electronic vaulting   The bulk transfer of data in batches to an off-site facility.

elite hacker   *See* "expert hacker."

encapsulation   The inclusion of one data structure inside another data structure.

encipher   To encrypt or convert plaintext to ciphertext.

encryption   The process of converting a message into a form that cannot be read by unauthorized individuals.

encryption domain   Phrase used to describe everything in the protected network and behind the gateway of a VPN.

endpoint   Hardware devices or software modules that perform encryption to secure data, authentication to make sure the host requesting the data is an approved user of the VPN, and encapsulation to protect the integrity of the information being sent.

end users   Those who will be most directly affected by new implementations and changes to existing systems. Ideally, a selection of users from various departments, levels, and degrees of technical knowledge who assist a project team in focusing on the application of realistic controls applied in ways that do not disrupt the essential business activities they seek to safeguard.

enterprise information security policy (EISP)   An executive-level document that guides the development, implementation, and management of the security program. It is based on and directly supports the mission, vision, and direction of the organization and sets the strategic direction, scope, and tone for all security efforts.

enticement   The process of attracting attention to a system by placing tantalizing information in key locations.

entrapment   The action of luring an individual into committing a crime.

environmental management   Measures taken to reduce risks to the physical environment where IT assets and resources are stored.

evasion   The process by which attackers change the format and/or timing of their activities to avoid being detected by an IDPS.

event   An activity that occurs unexpectedly.

examination phase   First part of the forensic analysis function, involving the use of forensic tools to recover deleted files, and to retrieve and characterize operating system artifacts and other relevant material.

expert hacker   One who develops software scripts and program exploits used by novice or unskilled hackers. The expert hacker is usually a master of several programming languages, networking protocols, and operating systems, and also exhibits a mastery of the technical environment of the chosen targeted system.

extranet   An extension of the corporate network to a new location.

F

false attack stimulus   An event that triggers an alarm when no actual attack is in progress.

false negative   The failure of an IDPS to react to an actual attack event.

false positive   An alert or alarm that occurs in the absence of an actual attack.

fault   Complete loss of power for a moment.

fingerprinting   A systematic survey of all the target organization's Internet addresses (which are collected during the footprinting phase) to identify the network services offered by the hosts in that range.

firewall   In general, anything, whether hardware or software (or a combination of hardware and software), that can filter the transmission of packets of digital information as they attempt to pass through a boundary of a network.

footprinting   The organized research of the Internet addresses owned or controlled by a target organization.

fragment   Packet that is part of a larger, whole packet.

frame relay   A cost-efficient telecommunication technique designed for data transmission in intermittent traffic and used to send data in a relay of frames between local area networks (LANs) and between endpoints in a wide area network (WAN).

full backup   A full and complete backup of an entire system, including all applications, operating systems components, and data.

fully distributed IDPS control strategy   Strategy in which all IDPS control functions are applied at the physical location of each IDPS component.

G

gateway   A system that joins one device or network to another device or network and controls access between the two.

Generally Accepted System Security Principles (GASSP)   A set of security and information management practices put forth by the International Information Security Foundation (I2SF).

H

hackers   The classic perpetrators of espionage or trespass, these are people who use and create computer software to gain access to information illegally.

hacktivist   Someone who interferes with or disrupts systems to protest the operations, policies, or actions of an organization or government agency.

hashed   Encoded into a relatively small alphanumeric string for the purposes of encryption, indexing, or both.

header   The first part of a datagram, which consists of general information about the size of the packet, the protocol that was used to send it, and the IP address of both the source computer and its destination.

heartbeat network   Network that monitors the operation of the primary firewall and synchronizes state table connections so the two, or more, firewalls have the same information at any given time.

hierarchical roster   An alert roster activation scheme that has the first person call certain other people on the roster, who in turn call other people, and so on.

high availability   Operation on a 24/7 basis, or close to it.

hole   A port, machine, or other vulnerable computer through which hackers can gain entry.

honey net   A collection of honey pots connecting several honey pot systems on a subnet.

honey pot   Decoy system designed to lure potential attackers away from critical systems. They are also known as decoys, lures, and fly-traps.

host-based IDPS   An IDPS that resides on a particular computer or server (the host) and monitors activity only on that system.

hot standby   System in which one or more auxiliary or failover firewalls are configured to take over all traffic if the primary firewall fails.

hub-and-spoke configuration   Arrangement in which a single VPN router contains records of all SAs in the VPN. Any LANs or computers that want to participate in the VPN need only connect to the central server, not to any other machines in the VPN.

hybrid firewall   Firewall that combines several different security technologies, such as packet filtering, application-level gateways, and VPNs.

I

IDPS terrorist   Attacker who utilizes tactics designed to trip the organization's IDPS, essentially causing the organization to conduct its own DoS attack, by overreacting to an actual, but insignificant, attack.

impulse noise   A sudden, short-lived increase in signal frequency or amplitude, also known as a spike. Like distortion, impulse noise causes a temporary loss in signal clarity.

incident   Any clearly identified attack on the organization's information assets that would threaten the assets' confidentiality, integrity, or availability.

incident candidate   Term referring to a possible incident before it is determined to be either an actual incident or a nonevent.

incident classification   The process of evaluating organizational events, determining which events are possible incidents, or incident candidates, and then determining whether or not the incident candidate is an actual incident or a false positive incident candidate.

incident response (IR)   The set of activities taken to plan for, detect, and correct the impact of an incident on information assets.

incident response (IR) plan   A method that addresses the identification, classification, response to, and recovery from an incident.

incremental backup   Backup strategy that only archives the data that has been modified that day.

indirect attack   An attack in which a system is compromised and used to attack other systems.

industrial espionage   Employing information-gathering techniques that cross the threshold of what is legal or ethical.

information security (InfoSec)   The protection of information and its critical elements, including the systems and hardware that use, store, and transmit that information.

information security policy   A set of rules that provides for the protection of the information assets of the organization.

inline sensor   Type of sensor deployed in such a way that the network traffic it is monitoring must pass through it.

integrity   Indicates that information remains whole, complete, and uncorrupted. The integrity of information is threatened when the information is exposed to corruption, damage, destruction, or other disruption of its authentic state.

intranet   A private network contained within an organization.

intrusion   When an attacker attempts to gain entry or disrupt the normal operations of an information system, almost always with the intent to do harm.

intrusion detection system (IDS)   Device similar to a burglar alarm in that it detects a violation and activates an alarm.

intrusion detection/prevention system (IDPS)   Term used to describe current anti-intrusion technologies that combine both an intrusion detection system (IDS) and an intrusion prevention system (IPS).

intrusion prevention system (IPS)   A current extension of IDS technology that can detect an intrusion, and also prevent that intrusion from successfully attacking the organization, by means of an active response.

IP forwarding   Process that causes all requests to a certain URL to be redirected to a specified IP address.

IPSec concentrators   Routers that support IPSec that are set up at the perimeter of connected LANs.

IP security (IPSec)   Primary and now dominant cryptographic authentication and encryption product of the IETF's IP Protocol Security Working Group. It provides application support for all uses within TCP/IP, including VPNs.

IR duty officer   A SIRT team member, other than the team leader, who is scanning the organization's information infrastructure for signs of an incident.

issue-specific security policy (ISSP)   A statement of the organization's position which functions to instruct employees on the proper use of technologies and processes as they pertain to a specific issue.

J

jitter   Signal modification caused by malfunctioning equipment.

K

Kerberos   Authentication system that uses symmetric key encryption to validate an individual user's access to various network resources.

key   The information used in conjunction with the algorithm to create the ciphertext from the plaintext.

keyspace The entire range of values that can possibly be used to construct an individual key.

knowledge-based IDPS *See* "signature-based IDPS."

known-plaintext attack Scheme in which an attacker obtains duplicate texts, one in ciphertext and one in plaintext, which then enables the individual to reverse-engineer the encryption algorithm.

L

Layer 2 Tunneling Protocol (L2TP) An extension of the Point-to-Point Protocol (PPP).

layer four switches Network devices with the intelligence to make routing decisions based on source and destination IP address or port numbers as specified in layer four of the OSI reference model.

leased lines Point-to-point communications used by organizations to join two or more LANs. These lines are often used to connect remote users or branch offices to a central administrative site.

live acquisition The act of collecting forensic evidence from a system that is still powered up and active.

load balancing The practice of balancing the load placed on a device so that it is handled by two or more devices.

load sharing The practice of configuring two or more devices to share the total traffic load. Each device in a load-sharing setup is active at the same time.

local area network (LAN) A network containing a dedicated server that connects systems within or between a few buildings, over a small geographic space.

log file Records of events such as logon attempts and accesses to files.

log file monitor (LFM) An IDPS that reviews log files generated by servers, network devices, and even other IDPSs, looking for patterns and signatures that may indicate that an attack or intrusion is in process or has already occurred.

M

macro virus Virus that is embedded in the automatically executing macro code common in word processors, spreadsheets, and database applications.

mail bomb A form of e-mail attack that is also a DoS attack in which an attacker routes large quantities of e-mail to the target system.

malicious code Software deliberately designed to cause a system or a program to malfunction, causing unintended results.

malicious software *See* "malicious code."

malware *See* "malicious code."

managerial guidance A type of systems-specific policy created by management to guide the implementation and configuration of technology, as well as to regulate the behavior of people in the organization.

man-in-the-middle In this well-known type of attack, an attacker monitors (or sniffs) packets from the network, modifies them using IP spoofing techniques, and inserts them back into the network, allowing the attacker to eavesdrop as well as to change, delete, reroute, add, forge, or divert data.

McCumber Cube A comprehensive model for information security that is becoming the evaluation standard for the security of information systems. It provides a graphical description of the architectural approach widely used in computer and information security. The McCumber Cube uses a representation in three dimensions of a 3×3×3 cube with 27 cells representing areas that must be addressed to secure today's information systems.

MD5 Algorithm used by TACACS+ to encrypt data.

Memorandum of Understanding (MOU) A formal agreement drawn up by some corporations with their partner companies to maintain a level of integrity. In this agreement, both parties formally agree to observe a set of rules of behavior.

mesh configuration VPN arrangement in which each participant in the VPN has an approved relationship with every other participant.

message digest A 128-bit code generated by the MD5 algorithm during data encryption.

metropolitan area network (MAN) A network that typically covers a region the size of a municipality, county, or district. The informal definition is a network that is larger than a LAN but smaller than a WAN.

mission A written statement of an organization's purpose.

mission-critical An integral, key part of an organization's core operations.

misuse-detection IDPS *See* "signature-based IDPS."

monitoring port A specially configured connection on a network device that is capable of viewing all of the traffic that moves through the entire device. This type of port is also known as a switched port analysis (SPAN) port or mirror port.

monoalphabetic substitution Substitution cipher that utilizes only one alphabet.

multifactor authentication Use of two or more authentication tools to identify remote users.

N

network access point A point that is on a high-speed part of the Internet called the backbone.

Network Address Translation (NAT) Conversion of publicly accessible IP addresses to private ones and vice versa, thus shielding the IP addresses of computers on the protected network from those on the outside. NAT functions on a one-to-one conversion; one external IP address references one internal IP address.

Network-Attached Storage (NAS) Data storage method, usually implemented via a single device or server attached to a network, which uses common communications methods, such as Windows file sharing, NFS, CIFS, HTTP directories, or FTP, to provide an online storage environment.

network-based IDPS (NIDPS) IDPS that resides on a computer or appliance connected to a segment of an organization's network and monitors network traffic on that segment.

network security The protection of networking components, connections, and contents.

noise (1) One of any of the various types of interference to which a communications medium may be subject. (2) Alarm events that are accurate and noteworthy but that do not pose a significant threat to information security.

nonrepudiation A method used to ensure that parties to the transaction are authentic, so that they cannot later deny having participated in a transaction.

O

object of an attack A computer that is the entity being attacked.

one-time password Password that is generated for one-time use with each session and then discarded.

Open Platform for Security (OPSEC) model Design with the capability to extend functionality and integrate virus scanning and other functions into its set of abilities.

operations security The protection of the details of a particular operation or series of activities.

P

packets Small, manageable chunks of data that computers use to communicate with one another.

packet filter Hardware or software that is designed to block or allow transmission of packets of information based on criteria such as port, IP address, and protocol.

packet header *See* "header."

packet monkeys Script kiddies who use automated exploits to engage in distributed denial-of-service attacks.

packet sniffer A name frequently used to describe a sniffer operating on TCP/IP networks.

padded cell A honey pot that has been protected so that it cannot be easily compromised. It operates in tandem with a traditional IDPS so when the IDPS detects attackers, it seamlessly transfers them to a special simulated environment where they can cause no harm.

parameter Criterion used by proxy servers, firewalls, and similar devices to filter content and control access.

passive mode State in which most network behavior analysis (NBA) sensors perform network monitoring, using the same connection methods (e.g., network tap, switch spanning port) as a network-based IDPS.

passive vulnerability scanner Tool that listens in on the network and identifies vulnerable versions of both server and client software.

password attack Repeatedly guessing passwords to commonly used accounts.

permutation cipher *See* "transposition cipher."

personal security The protection of the people who are authorized to access the organization and its operations.

phreaker One who hacks the public telephone network to make free calls or disrupt services.

physical security The protection of the physical items, objects, or areas of an organization from unauthorized access and misuse.

plaintext An original unencrypted message, or the results from successful decryption.

Point-to-Point Protocol (PPP)   Protocol long used to establish dial-up connections on the Internet.

Point-to-Point Protocol (PPP) over Secure Shell (SSH)   A UNIX-based method for creating VPNs.

Point-to-Point Protocol (PPP) over Secure Sockets Layer (SSL)   A UNIX-based method for creating VPNs.

Point-to-Point Tunneling Protocol (PPTP)   A protocol commonly used by remote users who need to connect to a network using a dial-in modem connection.

policy   A set of guidelines or instructions that an organization's senior management implements to regulate the activities of the members of the organization who make decisions, take actions, and perform other duties.

policy administrator   The policy champion and manager responsible for the creation, revision, distribution, and storage of the policy.

polyalphabetic substitution   Substitution cipher that utilizes two or more alphabets.

polymorphic threat   A threat that changes over time, making it undetectable by techniques that look for preconfigured signatures.

Port Address Translation (PAT)   Conversion of publicly accessible IP addresses to private ones and vice versa, thus shielding the IP addresses of computers on the protected network from those on the outside. Generally, there is only one exposed IP address, and incoming packets from the external network are routed by reference to a table that tracks public and private port pairs.

port scanner   Tool used by both attackers and defenders to identify (or fingerprint) the computers that are active on a network, as well as the ports and services active on those computers, the functions and roles the machines are fulfilling, and other useful information.

possession   The ownership or control of some object or item of information. Information is said to be in one's possession if one obtains it, independent of format or other characteristics.

pre-shared key   A requirement of SSH in order to establish a connection; it is a secret key that both client and host have in advance.

Pretty Good Privacy (PGP)   Method to secure e-mail that was developed by Phil Zimmerman and uses the IDEA Cipher, a 128-bit symmetric key block encryption algorithm with 64-bit blocks for message encoding.

principle of least privilege   The practice of designing operational aspects of a system to operate with minimum system privileges.

Privacy Enhanced Mail (PEM)   A method to secure e-mail proposed by the Internet Engineering Task Force (IETF) as a standard that will function with public key cryptosystems. It uses 3DES symmetric key encryption and RSA for key exchanges and digital signatures.

private key   Used in some encrypted communications by a recipient to decode a message encoded using their public key. This key is not shared publicly.

private key encryption   A method of encrypting communications which utilizes the same algorithm and secret key to both encipher and decipher a message.

project team   Group responsible for designing and implementing information security projects. It should consist of a number of individuals who are experienced in one or multiple facets of the vast array of required technical and nontechnical areas.

proprietary   Privately owned.

protocol stack verification   Process in which an NIDPS looks for invalid data packets—packets that are malformed under the rules of the TCP/IP protocol.

proxy server   Network device that makes high-level application connections on behalf of internal hosts and other machines.

proxy service   *See* "proxy server."

public key   Used in some encrypted communications to encode a message to a particular recipient. This key is known to everyone. However, it is virtually impossible to deduce a private key using someone's public key.

public key encryption   An encryption system that utilizes two different keys to encrypt and decrypt a message. Either key can be used to encrypt or decrypt the message. However, if one key is used to encrypt the message, then only the other key can decrypt it.

R

redundancy   Implementing multiple types of technology and thereby preventing the failure of one system from compromising the security of information.

redundant array of independent disks (RAID)   A number of hard drives that store information across multiple drive units.

Remote Authentication Dial-In User Service (RADIUS)   Common protocol used to provide dial-in authentication.

remote journaling (RJ)   The transfer of live transactions to an off-site facility.

replay attack   An attempt to resubmit a recording of a deciphered authentication to gain entry into a secure source.

reverse proxy   A service that acts as a proxy for inbound connections.

risk assessment specialists   Individuals who understand financial risk assessment techniques, the value of organizational assets, and the security methods to be used.

rootkit   A collection of software tools and a recipe used to gain control of a system by bypassing its legitimate security controls.

routing table   A map used by routing devices which matches externally known IP addresses to internal, hidden IP addresses.

rule base   List of rules kept by a firewall which it uses to evaluate data packets.

S

sag   A momentary low voltage.

salt   A randomly generated value used by Linux when encrypting passwords in the /etc/passwd file.

SA table   Routing table kept by each VPN hardware or software terminator in a VPN network to verify approved relationships.

scaled   Capable of growing and maintaining effectiveness.

script kiddies   Hackers of limited skill who use expertly written software to attack a system.

search warrant   Authorization to investigate by collecting relevant evidence at a particular location or locations.

secret key   A private key used to both encipher and decipher a message.

Secure Electronic Transactions (SET)   Cryptosystem developed by MasterCard and VISA in 1997 to provide protection from electronic payment fraud, it works by encrypting the credit card transfers with DES for encryption and RSA for key exchange.

Secure Hypertext Transfer Protocol (SHTTP)   Encrypted solution to the unsecured version of HTTP. It can provide secure e-commerce transactions as well as encrypted Web pages for secure data transfer over the Web.

Secure Multipurpose Internet Mail Extensions (S/MIME)   Cryptosystem that builds on the Multipurpose Internet Mail Extensions (MIME) encoding format by adding encryption and authentication via digital signatures based on public key cryptosystems.

Secure Shell (SSH)   Popular extension to the TCP/IP protocol suite, sponsored by the IETF. It provides security for remote access connections over public networks by creating a secure and persistent connection.

Secure Sockets Layer (SSL)   Cryptosystem developed by Netscape in 1994 to provide security for online electronic commerce transactions.

security association (SA)   An approved relationship between two participants in a VPN.

security blueprint   The basis for the design, selection, and implementation of all security program elements, including policy implementation, ongoing policy management, risk management programs, education and training programs, technological controls, and maintenance of the security program.

security domain   An area of trust inside the security perimeter of the organization within which users can freely communicate.

security education, training, and awareness (SETA)   A control measure designed to reduce the incidences of accidental security breaches by employees.

security framework   An outline of the overall information security strategy and a roadmap for planned changes to the organization's information security environment.

security perimeter   Defines the boundary between the outer limit of an organization's security and the beginning of the outside world, protecting all internal systems from outside threats.

security policy   In general, a set of rules that protect an organization's assets.

security policy developers   Individuals who understand the organizational culture, existing policies, and requirements for developing and implementing successful policies.

security professionals   Dedicated, trained, and well-educated specialists in all aspects of information security, both technical and nontechnical.

selected-plaintext attack   Scheme in which an attacker sends the potential victim a specific text that they are sure the victim will forward on to others. When the victim does encrypt and forward the message, it can be used in the attack, if the attacker can acquire the outgoing encrypted version. At the very least, reverse engineering can usually lead the attacker to discover the cryptosystem that is being employed.

sequential roster   An alert roster activation scheme that requires that a contact person call each and every person on the roster.

servant model   An extension of the peer-to-peer network, this model occurs when a client shares part of its resources, serving as a pseudo-server—a device that provides services to others.

service agreements   The contractual documents guaranteeing certain minimum levels of service provided by vendors.

Service Level Agreement (SLA)   *See* "service agreement."

session authentication   Authentication method that requires authentication whenever a client system attempts to connect to a network resource and establish a session (a period when communications are exchanged).

session hijacks   Attacks involving a communication session that has already been established between a server and a client. The hacker inserts confusing or misleading commands into packets, thus disabling the server and enabling the hacker to gain control of the session.

session key   A symmetric key for limited-use, temporary communications.

shadow password system   A feature of the Linux operating system that enables the secure storage of passwords.

shoulder surfing   A technique used to gather information one is not authorized to have, by looking over another individual's shoulder or viewing the information from a distance, in a public or semipublic setting.

signature   Preconfigured, predetermined attack pattern.

signature-based IDPS   IDPS that examines network traffic in search of patterns that match known signatures.

site policy   The rules and configuration guidelines governing the implementation and operation of IDPSs within the organization.

site policy awareness   An IDPS's ability to dynamically modify its configuration in response to environmental activity.

site-to-site VPN   One of two different types of VPNs. This type links two or more networks.

six-tape rotation   Method of backup that uses a rotation of six sets of media and is perhaps the most simple and well known. It uses five media sets per week and offers roughly two weeks of recovery capability in a five-step process.

smart card   A plastic card with an embedded microchip that can store data about the owner.

sniffer   A program or device that can monitor data traveling over a network.

social engineering   The process of using social skills to convince people to reveal access credentials or other valuable information to an attacker.

SOCKS   A set of protocols that enable proxy server access to applications without an assigned proxy server.

software piracy   The unlawful use or duplication of software-based intellectual property.

source routing   Technique in which the originator of a packet can attempt to partially or completely control the path through the network to the destination.

spam   Unsolicited commercial e-mail.

specific sign-on   System type in which clients must authenticate each time they access a server or use a service on the protected network.

spike   A momentary increase in voltage levels.

split tunneling   Two connections over a VPN line.

spoofing   A technique used to gain unauthorized access to computers, wherein the intruder sends messages whose IP address indicates to the recipient that the messages are coming from a trusted host.

standards   A set of guidelines that, though they have the same compliance requirement as policies, are more detailed descriptions of what must be done to comply with policy.

standard sign-on   System type in which the client, after being successfully authenticated, is allowed to access whatever resources the user needs or perform any desired functions.

stateful packet filtering   A packet-filtering method that can do everything a stateless packet filter can, while additionally maintaining a record of the state of a connection.

stateful protocol analysis (SPA) A process of comparing predetermined profiles of generally accepted definitions of benign activity for each protocol state against observed events, to identify deviations.

stateless packet filtering The simplest packet-filtering method, also called static packet filtering, reviews packet header content and makes decisions on whether to allow or drop the packets based on whether a connection has actually been established between an external host and an internal one.

statistical-anomaly-based IDPS (stat IDPS) IDPS that observes normal traffic to establish a statistical baseline then periodically samples network activity, which it then compares to the baseline. When the measured activity is outside the baseline parameters, the IDPS sends an alert.

storage area network (SAN) Data storage technique that is similar in concept to, but differs in implementation from, Network-Attached Storage (NAS). NAS uses TCP/IP-based protocols and communications methods, but SANs use fibre-channel or iSCSI connections between the systems needing the additional storage and the storage devices themselves.

strategic planning Process of moving the organization towards its vision.

strong authentication An authentication method that utilizes two different forms of confirming the proposed identity.

subject of an attack A computer that is used as an active tool to conduct an attack.

substitution cipher Encryption algorithm in which one value is substituted for another value.

sunset clause A policy expiration date—particularly in policies that govern information use in short-term business associations or agencies that are involved with the organization.

supervisor password A higher-level password used to gain access to the BIOS setup program or to change the BIOS password.

surge A prolonged increase in voltage levels.

symmetric encryption *See* "private key encryption."

system integrity verifier System that benchmarks and monitors the status of key system files and detects when an intruder creates, modifies, or deletes monitored files. These systems are also known as host-based IDPSs.

systems, networks, and storage administrators Individuals with the primary responsibility for administering the systems, storage, and networks that house and provide access to the organization's information.

T

team leader A project manager, who may be a departmental line manager or staff unit manager, who understands project management, personnel management, and information security technical requirements.

technical specifications A type of systems-specific policy a systems administrator may need to create in order to implement managerial policy. These specifications translate managerial intent into an enforceable technical approach for each type of equipment.

Terminal Access Controller Access Control System Plus (TACACS+) Commonly called "tac-plus," this is the latest and strongest version of a set of authentication protocols developed by Cisco Systems. It replaces its less-secure predecessor protocols, TACACS and XTACACS.

terminator *See* "endpoint."

theft The illegal taking of another's property.

threat In the context of information security, an object, person, or other entity that represents a constant danger to an asset.

threat agent An object, person, or other entity that launches an attack in order to damage or steal an organization's information or physical asset.

Ticket-granting server (TGS) Part of a Kerberos system; a server which, upon receiving a ticket-granting ticket (TGT) from a client, grants a session ticket and forwards it to the server holding the requested file or service. The client is then granted access to that resource.

Ticket-granting ticket (TGT) A session key generated by a Kerberos system which the client presents to a ticket-granting server (TGS) as part of the process of gaining access to system resources.

timing attack An attack technique that works by measuring the time required to access a Web page and deducing that the user has visited the site before by the presence of the page in the browser's cache.

token Physical object such as a smart card or other kind of physical item used to offer a more stringent level of authentication in which users need to have something in order to gain access.

topology   The geometric association of components of a network in relation to each other, either physical or logical.

transport mode   One of two modes in which IPSec operates. In this mode, only the IP data is encrypted—not the IP headers themselves.

transposition cipher   Encryption algorithm in which the values within a block are rearranged to create the ciphertext. This can be done at the bit level or at the byte (character) level.

trap and trace   A combination of techniques used to detect an intrusion and then to trace it back to its source.

trap door   *See* "back door."

trespass   Real or virtual actions that enable information gatherers to enter premises or systems without authorization.

trigger   The circumstances that cause an IR team to be activated and an IR plan to be initiated.

Triple DES (3DES)   An improvement to DES that uses as many as three keys in succession, making it substantially more secure than DES.

Trojan horse   A software program that reveals its designed behavior only when activated. Trojan horses are frequently disguised as helpful, interesting, or necessary pieces of software.

true attack stimulus   An event that triggers alarms and causes an IDPS to react as if a real attack is in progress.

tuning   The process of adjusting an IDPS to maximize its efficiency in detecting true positives, while minimizing both false positives and false negatives.

tunnel   A channel or pathway over a packet network used by a VPN that runs through the Internet from one endpoint to another.

tunnel mode   One of two modes in which IPSec operates. In this mode, the entire IP packet is encrypted and inserted as the payload in another IP packet.

two-factor authentication   Method that requires two things from the user for authentication.

U

unskilled hackers   Those who use the software scripts and program exploits developed by an expert hacker. This group includes script kiddies and packet monkeys.

URI Filtering Protocol server   A server that filters and processes requests for URIs and that can work in conjunction with firewalls.

URL redirection   Direction of clients to a different Web server based on the host being requested.

user authentication   Act of confirming the identity of a potential user of a system before granting access to protected resources.

utility   The quality or state of information having value for some purpose or end. To have utility, information must be in a format meaningful to the end user.

V

virtual private network (VPN)   A private, secure network operated over a public and insecure network.

virus hoax   E-mail and other communications warning of dangerous viruses that are fictitious.

vision   A written statement of the organization's long-term goals.

VPN appliance   A hardware device specially designed to terminate VPNs and join multiple LANs.

vulnerability   An identified weakness in a controlled system, where controls are not present or are no longer effective.

W

white noise   Unwanted noise due to a signal coming across the medium at multiple frequencies. This can also be referred to as static noise.

wide area network (WAN)   A very large network that covers a vast geographic region like a state, a country, or even the planet. These networks can actually comprise a collection of LANs and MANs.

work factor   The amount of effort (usually expressed in units of time) required to perform cryptanalysis on an encoded message.

X

XOR cipher conversion   Encryption algorithm in which the bit stream is subjected to a Boolean XOR function against some other data stream, typically a key stream.

Z

zombies   Compromised machines that are directed during a distributed denial-of-service (usually by a transmitted command) to participate in the attack.

Index